# The Economics of European Integration

## Richard Baldwin & Charles Wyplosz

*The* **McGraw·Hill** *Companies*

| London | Boston | Burr Ridge, IL | Dubuque, IA | Madison, WI | New York |
|---|---|---|---|---|---|
| St. Louis | San Francisco | Bangkok | Bogotá | Caracas | Kuala Lumpur |
| Lisbon | Madrid | Mexico City | Milan | Montreal | New Delhi |
| Santiago | Seoul | Singapore | Sydney | Taipei | Toronto |

The Economics of European Integration
Richard Baldwin and Charles Wyplosz
ISBN 0-077-103947

 **Education**

Published by McGraw-Hill Education
Shoppenhangers Road
Maidenhead
Berkshire
SL6 2QL
Telephone: 44 (0) 1628 502 500
Fax: 44 (0) 1628 770 224
Website: www.mcgraw-hill.co.uk

**British Library Cataloguing in Publication Data**
A catalogue record for this book is available from the British Library

**Library of Congress Cataloguing in Publication Data**
The Library of Congress data for this book has been applied for from the Library of Congress

Acquisitions Editor: Julian Partridge
Development Editor: Caroline Howell
Senior Production Editor: Eleanor Hayes
Marketing Director: Petra Skytte

Text Design by Inperspective Ltd
Cover design by Ego Creative
Typeset by Mathematical Composition Setters Ltd
Printed and bound in the UK by Ashford Colour Press Ltd, Gosport

*The McGraw·Hill Companies*

# Dedication

For Sarah, Ted, Julia and Nick.

R.B.

In memory of my parents, whose sufferings inspired my yearning for a Europe at peace, and who taught me the pleasure of learning.

C.W.

The 1

# **Brief** Table of Contents

# Detailed Table of Contents

EC ✓
European Community

CFSP : Common Foreign and Security Policy

JHA : Justice and Home affairs

# Preface

European integration keeps amazing its supporters and critics alike. No other region has displayed similar willingness to jettison important components of sovereignty in pursuit of shared, yet thoroughly imprecise goals. And, in its own peculiar way, European integration keeps forging ahead at a pace that is too fast for some and too slow for others. No one would deny, though, that the transformation of the past half century is spectacular – a clean break with centuries of intra-European warfare. This integration is clearly important for the 500 or so million Europeans it directly affects, but since Europe accounts for a quarter of the world economy, half of world trade and a third of world capital markets, European integration also affects the lives of most non-Europeans.

A subtle interplay of strictly economic and much broader, high-minded goals has driven European integration forward along political, cultural and economic dimensions. The goal of this book is to provide an accessible presentation of the facts, theories and controversies that are necessary to understand this process. Our approach is rooted deeply in economic principles for the simple reason that economic integration has been the vanguard since the Organization for European Economic Co-operation was founded in 1948. Yet economics is not enough; historical, political and cultural factors are brought into the picture when necessary.

## What this book is

This is a textbook for courses on European economic integration. Its emphasis is on economics, covering both the microeconomics and macroeconomics of European integration. Understanding European economic integration, however, requires much more than economics, so the book also covers the essential aspects of European history, institutions, laws, politics and policies.

The book is written at a level that should be accessible to second- and third-year undergraduates in economics as well as advanced undergraduates and graduate students in business, international affairs, European studies, and political science. Some knowledge of economics is needed to absorb all the material with ease – a first-year course in the principles of economics should suffice – but the book is self-contained in that it reviews all essential economics behind the analysis. Diligent students should therefore be able to master the material without any formal economics background.

## What is in this book

The book is organized into six parts that can be grouped into three categories – essential background (Part I), the microeconomics of European integration (Parts II and III), and the macroeconomics of European integration (Parts IV, V and VI).

Part I presents the essential background for studying European integration.

- An overview of the post-Second World War historical development of European integration is presented in Chapter 1, which will probably be useful to all students. Even students who are familiar with the main events should profit from this chapter since it stresses, wherever possible, the economic and political economy logic behind the events.

- A concise presentation of the indispensable background information necessary for the study of European integration is presented in Chapter 2. This includes key facts concerning European economies and a brief review of the EU's legal system and principles. Chapter 2 also presents information on the vital EU institutions and the EU's legislative processes as well as the main features of the EU budget.

- Chapter 3 presents an economic framework for thinking about EU institutions. The first part explains how the 'theory of fiscal federalism' can be used to consider the appropriateness of the allocation of powers between EU institutions and EU member states. The second part explains how economic reasoning – game theory in particular – can be used to analysis EU decision-making procedures for their decision-making efficiency as well as their implications of the distribution of power among EU members. While these are not classic topics in the study of European integration, they are essential to understanding the current challenges facing the European Union such as the Constitutional Treaty and the 2004 enlargement.

Part II presents the critical microeconomics of European integration.

- An introduction to the fundamental methods of trade policy analysis is presented in Chapter 4. The chapter introduces basic supply and demand analysis in an open economy, the key economic welfare concepts of consumer and producer surplus, and uses these to study the simple economics of tariff protection.

- An in-depth analysis of European preferential trade liberalization is given in Chapter 5. The focus is on how formation of a customs union or free trade area affects people, companies and governments inside and outside the integrating nations.

- A thorough study of how the market-expanding aspects of European integration affects the efficiency of European firms is presented in Chapter 6. The main line of reasoning explains how integration in the presence of scale economies and imperfect competition can produce fewer, bigger, and more efficient firms facing more effective competition from each other. The chapter also covers the main elements of the EU's competition policy and state aids policy.

- Chapter 7 gives a detailed study of the growth effects of European integration. The emphasis is on the economic logic linking European integration to medium-run and long-run growth effects. Neoclassical and endogenous growth theory are covered, as are the basic facts and empirical evidence. The chapter also discusses the economics, facts and evidence on capital and labour market integration.

Part III covers the two main EU policies – the Common Agricultural Policy (CAP) and Regional Policy.

- Chapter 8 looks at the CAP, presenting the economics and facts that are essential for understanding its effects. The chapter takes particular care to examine the economic forces behind recent CAP reform in the light of international trade negotiations (the Doha round) and the 2004 enlargement.

- Chapter 9 presents the economics that link European integration to the location of economic activities. This includes a presentation of the main facts on how the location of economic activity has shifted both within nations and between nations. To organize thinking about these facts – and to understand how EU Regional Policy might affect it – the chapter presents the locations effects of integration in the light of neoclassical theories (Heckscher–Ohlin) as well as the so-called New Economic Geography. The chapter also presents the main features of the EU's Regional Policy and considers the implications of the 2004 enlargement.

Part IV is where macroeconomics starts. It lays the ground for the analysis of monetary integration.

■ Chapter 10 returns to Europe's history, this time from the monetary angle. It recalls ancient times when Europe was a *de facto* monetary union under the gold standard, whose adjustment mechanism is now back at work. The disastrous inter-war period encapsulates all the policy mistakes that today's policy makers are determined to avoid. The chapter closes by showing how the European Monetary System paved the way to the adoption of a single currency.

■ Chapter 11 takes a step sideways. It deals with a very general question, the choice of an exchange rate regime. It presents a short summary of the basic macroeconomic principles needed to grasp the significance of exchange rate regimes. It then explains how to assess the desirability of each of the main arrangements, including the two-corner strategy that underlies Europe's shift to the euro while explaining why others have chosen to stay out.

■ Chapter 12 deals with the European Monetary System, the now defunct first version and the new version designed to provide a transition for future monetary union members. It shows that the successes of the EMS have provided a powerful incentive to go further and create a single currency, while its shortcomings have made the adoption of the euro look like the least inacceptable of all solutions.

Part V provides a detailed analysis of the monetary union, and proceeds in two steps: theory and practice.

■ Chapter 13 presents the optimum currency area theory that helps to understand the main costs and benefits from sharing a common currency. The theory does not provide a black and white answer; rather it develops a set of economic, political and institutional criteria to evaluate the costs and the benefits of forming a monetary union. In addition, the costs and benefits may be endogenous. Europe fulfils some criteria, not others, which explains the unending debates on the merits of the European Monetary Union.

■ The main features of the European Monetary Union are laid out in Chapter 14. This includes a description and an analysis of the institutions created by the Maastricht Treaty. It explains the importance attached to price stability and the measures adopted to achieve this objective. The chapter also provides a review of the first few years of the euro, assessing the performance of the ECB, including the democratic accountability gap.

Part VI moves away from purely monetary questions, taking up three issues important for the macroeconomic functioning of the monetary union.

■ Fiscal policy is the last national macroeconomic instrument remaining once national monetary policy has been lost. Chapter 15 looks at the Stability and Growth Pact, designed to deliver enough budgetary discipline not to endanger the overriding price stability objective. The analysis reveals how uncomfortable it is to preserve the macroeconomic instrument and to enforce strict enough rules.

■ The financial services industry is likely to be transformed by the adoption of a single currency. Chapter 16 starts with a review of what makes this industry special. This makes it possible to interpret the changes that have taken place and those that have not yet materialized. Financial markets are also important for monetary policy effectiveness, raising delicate questions: Is the single monetary policy symmetrically affecting member countries? How are financial institutions regulated and supervised? The chapter also examines whether the euro is becoming a worldwide currency, alongside the US dollar.

■ The last chapter looks at economic integration and the labour markets. The high level of unemployment that prevails in several countries, especially the largest ones, may greatly complicate the working of the euro area. It is natural to ask whether the euro will help to cure the unemployment problem or aggravate the situation. This calls for an analysis of labour market institutions and the political economy of reform.

# **Guided** Tour

Each part opens with an **introduction** to the key ideas to be considered within the part.

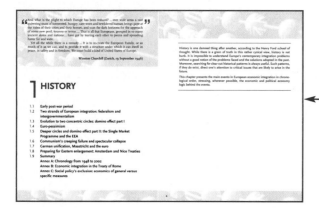

Each chapter commences with an **introduction** to the topic to be covered and indicates the ideas and concepts that will be presented on the following pages.

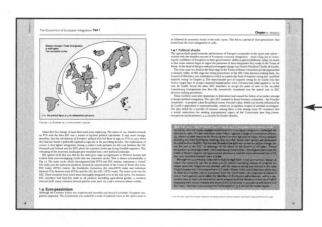

**Maps** and **diagrams** are provided throughout the text to show geographically the impact of changes in EU integration across the continent.

**Boxes** throughout the text provide further examples and explanations of key facts, events or economic ideas relating to the European Union.

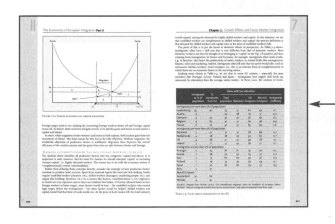

Clear presentation of **economic models** aids the interpretation of economic curves and graphs, with extra notes and explanations where appropriate.

**Tables** throughout the chapters provide relevant statistics and current data about the European Union and its member states.

**Summaries** at the end of each chapter recap the ideas introduced in the preceding pages and emphasize key findings.

**Self-assessment questions** test comprehension of the economic concepts and facts featured in the chapter.

**Essay questions** offer practice examples for exams or assessment, encouraging students to write full answers that explore ideas in more detail.

**Further reading**, **web links** and **references** provide direction for research around the topics covered in the chapter.

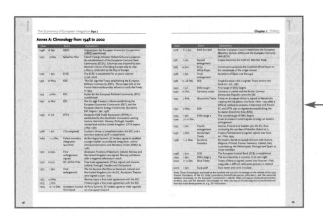

**Annex** sections offer further economic explanations, data or background information. The appendices enable further study to complement the chapter, covering more advanced concepts and providing greater detail.

# Teaching and Learning Resources

## Online Learning Centre

The history of European integration has flowed, like a great river, with long stretches of calm, slow-moving water interspersed with rapids and waterfalls. By this analogy, Europe today finds itself in the midst of raging white water. Integration initiatives are arriving at a tremendous pace as threats to continued integration multiply. Just before this book went to press in July 2003, an unprecedented Convention approved a draft Constitutional Treaty containing the most radical institutional reform the EU has ever seen. In the same month, a far-reaching reform of the Common Agriculture Policy was agreed. In mid-2004, the EU will experience its largest-ever enlargement with 10 new members joining the club. The shear number and diversity of the newcomers threatens to slow or reverse several aspects of economic integration and indeed may alter the very nature of progress. Also, since these newcomers are economically quite different to the EU15 incumbents, their entry will surely alter many existing policies, priorities and practices.

European integration can hardly be taught while pretending that these changes – and the many more that will undoubtedly occur in the next two or three years – did not occur. To keep our textbook as up-to-date as possible, the book has a website where we will periodically post essays that explain major developments and new challenges. These essays will refer to the specific sections of the textbook that are affected in order to facilitate integration of the essays and text in coursework. In addition to these regular updates, lecturers adopting the book will be able to access:

■ PowerPoint slides for use as lecture presentations and course handouts, with graphs, diagrams and data for manipulation and editing

■ Lecturer's manual with suggestions for further sources and reading

■ Further Tutorial and Essay questions for class and student assessments

■ Artwork from the book for use in class or lecture presentations.

Students will also be able to access the following supplementary resources:

■ Useful web links for EU studies and links to new articles, institutions and news

■ Updates of new information, articles, news and features about the EU to ensure the continued currency of the book for lecturers and students.

To explore the full range of supplements, visit the Online Learning Centre (OLC) at www.mcgraw-hill.co.uk/textbooks/baldwinandwyplosz.

# **Technology** to Enhance Learning and Teaching

## Visit www.mcgraw-hill.co.uk/textbooks/baldwinandwyplosz today

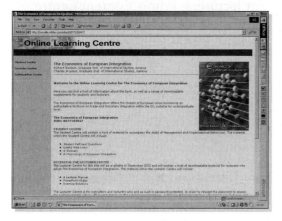

### Online Learning Centre (OLC)

After completing each chapter, log on to the supporting Online Learning Centre website. Take advantage of the study tools offered to reinforce the material you have read in the text, and to develop your knowledge further.

### Resources for students include:
- Useful web links for EU Economics
- Additional stories and up-to-date articles about EU integration

### Also available for lecturers:
- PowerPoint slides for lecture presentations
- Lecturer's Manual
- Tutorial and Essay questions
- Artwork and graphs from the book

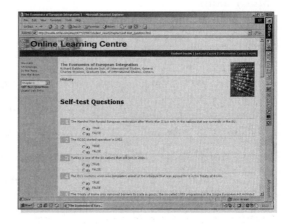

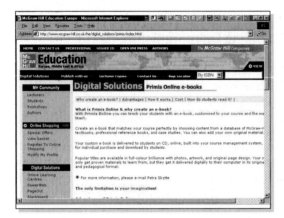

## For lecturers: Primis Content Centre

If you need to supplement your course with additional cases or content, create a personalized e-Book for your students.

Visit www.primiscontentcenter.com or e-mail primis_euro@mcgraw-hill.com for more information.

## Study Skills

Open University Press publishes guides to study, research and exam skills, to help undergraduate and postgraduate students through their university studies.

Visit www.openup.co.uk/sg/ to see the full selection.

## Computing Skills

If you'd like to brush up on your Computing skills, we have a range of titles covering MS Office applications such as Word, Excel, PowerPoint, Access and more.

Get a £2 discount off these titles by entering the promotional code app when ordering online at www.mcgraw-hill.co.uk/app

# Acknowledgements

Having matured this book over several years, we owe many debts to many people, and are glad to acknowledge them. First of all, to our students at the Graduate Institute of International Studies in Geneva, Bocconi and Catholic Universities in Milan, the Advance Studies Programme in Kiel, the World Trade Institute in Bern, and HEC in Lausanne; their reactions and comments on several drafts have helped us to better understand the students' needs.

Many colleagues have read parts of the books and have provided most valuable comments and suggestions. We have not always been able to fully use so much accumulated wisdom, but we wish to thank Samuel Bentolila, Giuseppe Bertola, Tito Boeri, Xavier Debrun, Philipp Hartmann, Wyn Grant and Henry Overman. In addition, our publisher arranged for repeated reviews of various drafts. We are enormously grateful to these anonymous referees whose comments and suggestions have profoundly affected the final shape and content of the text. We thank Laurent Corthay for doing an excellent job in checking the text, figures and problems in Parts I, II and III.

As the book deals with an ongoing and extremely lively real-life experiment, it draws heavily on current research and makes extensive use of newly produced evidence and data. Many colleagues have generously shared with us their work-in-progress and data. We now wish to express our gratitude to Tamim Bayoumi, Tito Boeri, Claudia Busch, Andrea Enria, Antonio Fatás, Daniel Gros, Philipp Hartmann, Patrick Honohan, Ryszard Kokoszczynski, Eduardo Levy-Yeyati, Simone Manganelli, and Marco Pagano.

## Publisher's acknowledgements

The publisher would like to thank the following reviewers for their comments at various stages in the text's development:

Thomas Alslev Christiansen, University of Copenhagen, Denmark
Simon Broome, National University of Ireland, Maynouth, Ireland
Steve Brown, University of Leicester
Niels Blomgren Hansen, Copenhagen Business School, Denmark
David Cleeton, Oberlin University, USA
Yannis Georgellis, Brunel University
Bernd Hayo, University of Georgetown, USA
Dr Kol, Erasmus University, The Netherlands
Charlotte Lythe, University of Dundee
Malcolm Macmillen, University of Exeter
Dermot McAleese, Trinity College Dublin, Ireland
Henry Overman, London School of Economics
Roxana Radulescu, University of Newcastle
Geoffrey Reed, University of Nottingham
Jim Rollo, University of Sussex
Hans Schenk, Utrecht University, The Netherlands
Thomas Verbeke, University of Ghent, Belgium
Roger Vickerman, University of Kent at Canterbury
Maurizio Zanardi, University of Tilburg, The Netherlands

# Acknowledgements

We would also like to thank the following organizations for permission to reproduce material in this book:

Audiovisual Library of the European Commission, p 5, 9, 11, 20, 48, 52, 54, 56.
*The Banker*, Financial Times Publications, p 406.
Herbert Bruecker, p 198.
Cambridge University Press, p 3, 7, 10, 176, 177, 178, 348.
*Economic Policy*, Blackwell Publishing, p 182, 247, 248, 270, 352, 421.
*European Economic Review*, Elsevier Science, p 342, 344.
Journal of Economic Integration, p 185, 187.
National Galleries of Scotland, p 277.
The Nobel Foundation, p 152.
*Oxford Review of Economic Policy*, Oxford University Press, p 411, 412.
Palgrave Macmillan, p 281.

Every effort has been made to trace and acknowledge copyright and to obtain permissions to reproduce material in the text. The publishers would be pleased to make arrangements to clear permission with any copyright holders it has not been possible to contact.

# PART **I** History, Facts and Institutions

The European Union is a truly unique endeavour. No where else in the world have a group of countries come to be so integrated by peaceful means. This uniqueness has implications that are important when thinking about the EU of today, so before turning to the microeconomics in Part II, Part I presents several important aspects of this uniqueness. The first concerns history.

Understanding the historical origins of the EU and the reactions it triggered throughout Europe are critical to a firm understanding of today's EU and European economic integration more generally. Accordingly, Chapter 1 provides a brief overview of the historical development of the EU from 1945 to the draft Constitutional Treaty in June 2003.

Chapter 2 presents a brief introduction to the EU's principal institutional features – EU law, EU institutions, EU legislative procedures, etc. – as well as some critical facts on the EU economies. Chapter 2 also presents information on the EU's budget – how it is spent, who pays for it and who gets the money.

The final chapter in Part I, Chapter 3, presents some economical reasoning on EU institutions and EU decision making. This is intended to help to organize thinking about the institutions and procedures studied in Chapter 2.

> "And what is the plight to which Europe has been reduced? ... over wide areas a vast quivering mass of tormented, hungry, care-worn and bewildered human beings gape at the ruins of their cities and their homes, and scan the dark horizons for the approach of some new peril, tyranny or terror. ... That is all that Europeans, grouped in so many ancient states and nations ... have got by tearing each other to pieces and spreading havoc far and wide.
>
> Yet all the while there is a remedy ... It is to re-create the European Family, or as much of it as we can, and to provide it with a structure under which it can dwell in peace, in safety and in freedom. We must build a kind of United States of Europe."
>
> Winston Churchill (Zurich, 19 September 1946)

# 1 HISTORY

History is one damned thing after another, according to the Henry Ford school of thought. While there is a grain of truth in this rather cynical view, history is not bunk. It is impossible to understand Europe's contemporary integration problems without a good notion of the problems faced and the solutions adopted in the past. Moreover, searching for clear-cut historical patterns is always useful. Such patterns, if they do exist, direct one's attention to critical issues that are likely to arise in the future.

This chapter presents the main events in European economic integration in chronological order, stressing, wherever possible, the economic and political economy logic behind the events.

## 1.1 Early post-war period

In 1945, a family standing almost anywhere in Europe found themselves in a nation which was, or had recently been: (a) ruled by a brutal fascist dictator, (b) occupied by a foreign army or (c) both. As a direct result of these governmental failures, tens of millions of Europeans were dead and Europe's economy lay in ruins. Worse yet, the Second World War was not an isolated historical event. If the parents were middle-aged, it would have been their second experience with colossal death and destruction; the Second World War started just two decades after the cataclysm of the First World War (1914–18). Indeed, the Second World War was the fourth time in 130 years that France and Germany had been at the core of increasingly horrifying wars.

In 1945, it was plain to all that something was desperately wrong with the way Europe governed itself. Minds were open to radical changes.

### 1.1.1 A climate for radical change

WAR TOLL

Table 1-1 shows some figures on the death and destruction in the Second World War. In Western Europe, the war killed about 8 million people, with Germans accounting for three-quarters of this total. In Central and Eastern Europe over 9 million perished, of which 6.3 million were Poles. The Soviet Union alone lost over 20 million. The war also caused enormous economic damage. Figures are difficult to find for Central and Eastern Europe, but the estimates for Western Europe are staggering, as the table shows. The war cost Germany and Italy four decades or more of growth and put Austrian and French GDPs back to nineteenth-century levels.

This fact is the key to understanding the post-1945 drive for European integration, but it may be difficult to imagine the mindset in 1945. To put it in perspective, note that the terrible attacks in the USA on 11 September 2001 resulted in about 3000 deaths. This event radically altered many peoples' and many governments' perception of the world. To approach the death toll during the

| Country | Death toll | The economic set-back: pre-war year when GDP equalled that of 1945 |
|---|---|---|
| Austria | 525 000 | 1886 |
| Belgium | 82 750 | 1924 |
| Denmark | 4 250 | 1936 |
| Finland | 79 000 | 1938 |
| France | 505 750 | 1891 |
| Germany | 6 363 000 | 1908 |
| Italy | 355 500 | 1909 |
| Netherlands | 250 000 | 1912 |
| Norway | 10 250 | 1937 |
| Sweden | 0 | 1939–45 [a] |
| Switzerland | 0 | 1939–45 [a] |
| UK | 325 000 | 1939–45 [a] |

(a) GDP grew during the Second World War.
SOURCE: GDP data from Crafts and Toniolo (1996, p. 4), death toll from http://encarta.msn.com.

TABLE 1-1: DEATH AND DESTRUCTION IN THE SECOND WORLD WAR

war in Western and Central Europe, it would have taken two '11 September' attacks on every single day between 1938 and 1945, and this excludes the 20-plus million people who perished in the Union of Soviet Socialist Republics (USSR).

## REFUGEES AND HUNGER

The economic and humanitarian situation in Europe was dire in the years 1945–47, especially in Germany. While the Western economies picked-up in 1946, much of Europe's infrastructure, industry and housing lay in ruins. Food production in 1946 was low and the 1946–47 winter was especially harsh. Hunger was widespread and food was rationed in most European nations up to the mid-1950s. At times, rations fell to just 900 calories per day in some parts of Germany (2000 calories per day is the standard today). Many Europeans in these years were dependent on humanitarian aid, much in the same way that people in war-torn African nations are today. The UN Relief and Rehabilitation Administration (UNRRA) spent nearly $4 billion on emergency food and medical aid, helped to return about 7 million displaced persons, and provided camps for about a million refugees who did not want to be repatriated.

As this level of disorganization, suffering and conflict in Europe may be difficult for twenty-first-century readers to imagine, the photos and videos on the Germany History Museum's website http://www.dhm.de/lemo/html/Nachkriegsjahre/DasEndeAlsAnfang/ may help. Also see Botting (1985) for an engaging account that includes such fascinating details as the plan to secretly ship 800 tonnes of cash to Germany as part of their monetary reform in 1948. A key excerpt can be found on http://mars.acnet.wnec.edu/~grempel/courses/germany/lectures/36airlift.html. The Truman Library website http://www.trumanlibrary.org/teacher/berlin.htm is a good source for background documents online.

## 1.1.2 The prime question and guiding ideologies

The shock and horror arising from this devastation pushed one question to the forefront in the mid-1940s: 'How can Europe avoid another war?' The solutions offered depended primarily on beliefs about the causes of the war, and three schools of thought were in evidence:

■ The first evoked the time-honoured response of blaming the war on the loser, Germany in this case. The clearest manifestation was contained in a plan, put forth by US Treasury Secretary Henry Morgenthau in 1944, which sought to avoid future European wars by stripping Germany of its industry and converting it into 'a country primarily agricultural and pastoral in character'. This reproduced the thinking that guided post-First World War arrangements in Europe. The war was blamed on Germany and the victors were rewarded with territorial gains and financial reparations. The result was yet another cycle of recovery and national rivalry that led to the Second World War.
■ The second school, Marxism–Leninism, blamed capitalism for most of the world's evils, including both world wars. This belief suggested that communism was the solution.
■ The third blamed destructive nationalism for the war, the solution being tighter integration of all European nations. While calls for a united Europe were heard after the 1914–18 war and during the 1939–45 war, the school's most famous post-war statement came in 1946 in a speech by Winston Churchill that called for a 'United States of Europe'.

As we shall see, the integration solution ultimately prevailed, but this outcome was far from clear in the late 1940s. Most European nations were either struggling to re-establish their governments and economies, or were under direct military occupation. Germany and Austria were divided into US, UK, French and Soviet zones, with Berlin also divided into four sectors. Soviet troops occupied all of Central and Eastern Europe. In Western Europe, 1945 and 1946 passed with hardly any progress towards the establishment of a post-war architecture. West European governments' limited governance capacity was simply overloaded by the dismal humanitarian situation.

Things moved more rapidly in the East. The Soviet Union – which believed that capitalism caused both world wars – had, during the war, already begun to implement its vision of a new Europe. Communism was imposed on the previously independent nations of Estonia, Latvia and Lithuania, and by 1948 communist parties had been pushed to power in every Soviet-occupied country. Communists took power in Albania and Yugoslavia, and were gaining strength in Greece. The communist point of view was also shared by many in Western Europe, where communist parties won substantial vote shares in Italy, France and other Western nations.

### BOX 1-1: KONRAD ADENAUER (1876–1967)

Born to a family of modest means, he rose to become Mayor of Cologne, a post he was stripped of by the Nazis in 1933. He was President of the 1948 Parliamentary Council that drew up Germany's constitution ('Basic Law') before becoming the first Chancellor (i.e. Prime Minister) of Germany – an office he held from 1949 to 1963. Under his leadership, Germany regained its sovereignty, joined the European Economic Community and NATO, and evolved into a cornerstone of Western European democracy and economic strength. Adenauer was a key promoter of close Franco-German co-operation and Germany's social welfare system.

KONRAD ADENAUER
Audiovisual Library of the
European Commission

## 1.1.3 Emergence of a divided Europe: the Cold War

As the USA and the UK were set against the Soviet's world vision, the wartime alliance with the USSR unravelled and the Cold War began. The USA and the UK had concluded by 1947 that an economically strong Germany would be essential to the defence of liberal democracy in Western Europe. They merged the UK and US zones into 'Bizonia' (September 1947), and France, which had originally favoured the Morgenthau Plan, added its zone in 1948. Germany drew up a constitution in 1948 under the leadership of Konrad Adenauer (see Box 1-1). In reaction to Western moves towards creating a West German government in their zones, the USSR escalated harassment of Western travel to Berlin. Ultimately, the Soviets imposed the famous Berlin blockade on 24 June 1948 and the Western powers countered with the equally famous 'Berlin air bridge' (see http://www.usafe.af.mil/berlin/facts.htm for facts, photos and videos). In May 1949, the Federal Republic of Germany was established. Konrad Adenauer, the Chancellor of the new government, agreed to make a military contribution to the Western defence effort.

In short, the Soviets' aggressive implementation of their solution triggered a reaction that narrowed the competing ideologies into two schools with an 'iron curtain' between them. East of the iron curtain, the post-war architecture was based on communism and one-party politics. To the west, it was built on multi-party democracy, the social market economics, and European integration.

The merger of the French, US and UK zones was a defining moment in Europe. Tentative, ideologically based support for European integration came to be strongly reinforced by nations pursuing their own interests. French leaders saw the Franco-German integration as a way of counter-balancing US–UK influence on the Continent while at the same time assuring that a reindustrialized Germany would become an economic partner rather than a military adversary. The UK and the USA supported European integration as the best way to counter the spread of communism in Europe. German leaders embraced European integration as the surest route to re-establishing Germany as a 'normal' nation (Germany was recognized as an independent nation only in 1955). Italian leaders also welcomed European integration, which provided them with an ideological counterbalance to communism and helped them to close the door on Italy's fascist past.

## 1.1.4 First steps: the OEEC and EPU

From the historical perspective, the most important result of the Western European effort to resist communism was the so-called Marshall Plan and the Organization for European Economic Co-operation (OEEC). In reaction to the dire economic conditions in Europe and the attendant threat that communists might come to power in Greece, Italy and France, US Secretary of State (i.e. Foreign Minister) George Marshall announced that the USA would give financial assistance to all European nations 'west of the Urals', if they could agree to a joint programme for economic reconstruction. Almost immediately, European nations gathered in Paris to study Marshall's proposal (the USSR and the Central and Eastern European countries eventually withdrew and never received Marshall Plan funds). The conference was intended to determine the amount of aid required and, at US insistence, to create a permanent organization in which Europeans would co-operate in their mutual economic recovery. A joint programme and organization were duly developed by the Europeans. The US Congress, which was initially reluctant, funded the Marshall Plan in April 1948 after the communist takeover in Czechoslovakia.

The new organization, the Organization for European Economic Co-operation (OEEC) was established in 1948 with an initial membership consisting of 13 of today's EU15 (Finland was under Soviet pressure to stay neutral and Spain was under Franco's dictatorship) plus Norway, Iceland, Switzerland, Turkey and the US–UK zone of the Free Territory of Trieste until it was merged with Italy. Germany was still under occupation, but representatives from the Western Zones participated. From 1948 to 1952, Marshall Plan aid amounted to $12 billion, with half of this going to the UK, France and West Germany. The Soviet bloc's counterpart to the OEEC, the Council of Mutual Economic Assistance (CMEA), was set up in 1949.

One of the OEEC's roles was to divide American aid among the Member States (see Box 1-2). A far more important role, as far as European history is concerned, was the OEEC's mandate to advance European economic integration. It did this by reducing intra-European trade barriers and improving the intra-European system of payments by establishing the European Payments Union (EPU), see Box 1-3. In 1949, the USA demanded that the OEEC make greater efforts to bring about direct European economic integration, especially intra-OEEC trade liberalization. Up to this point, Marshall Plan money was mainly used to finance European countries' dollar deficits in the EPU. In reaction to US pressure, the OEEC nations agreed to remove quantitative restrictions on private imports. While this had limited scope (at the time much of intra-European trade was conducted by government-controlled corporations), 60 per cent of private intra-European trade was freed thanks to OEEC action by 1950 with this figure rising to 89 per cent in 1959. The OEEC's trade liberalization was important in at least two ways.

■ The liberalization fostered a rapid expansion of trade and rapid income growth. As the figures in Table 1-2 show, the 1950s were marked by a remarkable increase in GDP and the export of manufactured goods, at least on the Continent.

■ The thinking of policy makers was profoundly affected by the fact that industrial output grew at historically unprecedented rates even as European trade was being liberalized. In the decades following the First World War, especially during the 1930s, economic growth had been viewed as a competition between nations – a competition in which trade barriers played the central role. In the 1940s and 1950s, by contrast, West European economic integration seemed to enhance the growth of all nations; intra-European imports and exports expanded even more rapidly than output. Europe's leaders came to view European integration as an idea that made as much sense economically as it did politically. Economists at the time explained the export-growth nexus by arguing that exports promoted savings and investment, thus allowing capacity and output to surge without raising inflation (Lamfalussy, 1963). As Milward (1992) put it: 'The proposals for trade liberalisation and customs unions that were made fell therefore on to a receptive soil.'

| Country | GDP growth % per annum | Manufacturing export growth % per annum |
|---|---|---|
| Germany (West) | 7.8 | 19.7 |
| Italy | 5.0 | 9.2 |
| Netherlands | 4.3 | 11.7 |
| UK | 2.0 | 1.8 |
| France | 4.4 | 3.8 |
| SOURCE: Milward (1992), Table 4.1. | | |

TABLE 1-2: WESTERN EUROPEAN TRADE AND OUTPUT GROWTH IN MANUFACTURES, 1950–58

**BOX 1-2: THE ORGANIZATION FOR EUROPEAN ECONOMIC CO-OPERATION (OEEC)**

The OEEC's members formed the Council of the Organization which ruled on the basis of unanimity. It was chaired by high-profile figures of the era (Paul-Henri Spaak, Paul van Zeeland, Dirk Strikker, Anthony Eden, Richard Heathcoat Amory). The OEEC's importance waned in 1952 as Marshall Plan aid ended and the focus of American spending shifted to more explicitly military ends in the form of the North Atlantic Treaty Organization (NATO). In 1961 the OEEC was transformed into the Organization for Economic Co-operation and Development (OECD).

*This box is based on the OECD's web site www.oecd.org*

**BOX 1-3: THE EUROPEAN PAYMENTS UNION (EPU), JULY 1950 TO DECEMBER 1958**

Most European nations were bankrupt after 1945, so trade was generally conducted on the basis of bilateral agreements, often involving barter. The EPU multi-lateralized these bilateral deals. Each month, EPU members added up the deficits and surpluses in their bilateral trade accounts with other EPU members. These were offset against each other so that each nation remained with an overall surplus or deficit with respect to the EPU as a whole. The great advantage of this was that nations no longer owed money to each other directly. This removed debt-based incentives for importing from or exporting to a particular partner. As a consequence, it was easy to loosen the web of bilateral trade restrictions that had been set up in the early post-war years. In its first year, the EPU removed all discriminatory trade measures among EPU members. EPU/OEEC membership also fostered overall trade liberalization via its 'Code of Liberalization'. This required members to lower trade barriers progressively by 25 per cent of their initial levels. During this time intra-European trade boomed, more than doubling in the EPU's lifetime (1950–58), while imports from North America grew by only 50 per cent. The trade surplus with the United States allowed European national central banks to accumulate substantial dollar reserves. This restored their financial stability while at the same time fostering trade liberalization (it undermined balance-of-payments justifications for import restrictions). By 1958, the financial position of EPU members was strong enough to allow them to restore the convertibility of their currencies (prior to this, the currencies were unconvertible, e.g. it was illegal for private citizens to exchange French francs for dollars or deutschmarks without government permission).

*This box is based largely on Eichengreen and de Macedo (2001).*

### 1.1.5 The need for deeper integration

While the OEEC succeeded in economic terms, some OEEC members found it too weak and too limited to bring about the deeper integration that they felt was necessary to avoid future wars and restore economic strength. The Cold War lent urgency to this drive. With East–West tensions rising steadily, Germany would not only have to be allowed to regain its industrial might, it would have to be allowed to rearm in order to counter the threat of Soviet territorial aggression. Since many Europeans, including many Germans, were still uncomfortable with the idea of a Germany that was both economically and militarily strong, integrating Germany into a supranational Europe seemed a natural way forward.

## 1.2 Two strands of European integration: federalism and intergovernmentalism

While it was clear that European integration would be the foundation of the post-war architecture in Western Europe, a serious schism immediately emerged over the role of nation-states. Even today, this schism defines the debate over European integration, so it is worth considering the origins of the two positions.

- Some Europeans felt that national sovereignty and the nation-state constituted a fragile system prone to warfare. Since time immemorial, European states had been engaged in intermittent struggles for dominance – struggles that typically involved the invasion of other European nations. As the efficiency of killing rose along with industrialization, the cost of these struggles was magnified to the point where there could be no winners. To these thinkers, even democracy was insufficient to prevent horrifying wars. Hitler, after all, gained his first hold on power through democratic means. To prevent another cycle of recovery and national rivalry that might lead to a third world war, nations should be embedded in a *federalist* structure – a supranational organization embodied with some of the powers that had traditionally been exercised exclusively by nations.
- Other Europeans continued to view nation-states as the most effective and most stable form of government. To them, European integration should take the form of closer co-operation – especially closer economic co-operation – conducted strictly on an *intergovernmental* basis, i.e. all power would remain in the hands of national officials and any co-operation would have to be agreed unanimously by all participants.

It is perhaps not surprising that the extent of governmental failure and national suffering in the Second World War lines up closely with the federalist–intergovernmentalist divide. People who lived in nations that had experienced land combat and extensive death and destructions were naturally open to radical changes in the way Europe was governed; they were suspicious of nationalism and fully independent nation-states. This group included Belgium, the Netherlands, Luxembourg, France, Austria, Germany and Italy.

People who lived in nations whose governments somehow managed to avoid foreign occupation and/or catastrophic loss of life tended to maintain their traditional faith in the nation-state. This included the UK, Denmark, Norway and Iceland as well as the neutrals, Ireland, Sweden and Switzerland. Spain and Portugal remained under facist dictators until the 1970s.

### 1.2.1 Two early extremes: Council of Europe and the ECSC

Intergovernmentalism initially dominated the post-war architecture. In part, this was simply a matter of timing. The only major European nation with a truly effective, democratic government from 1945 to 1947 was the UK and it clearly believed in the primacy of the nation-state. The first three organizations – the OEEC, the Council of Europe and the Court of Human Rights – followed the intergovernmental tradition. The OEEC was strictly intergovernmental (see Box 1-2), and the 1948 'Congress of Europe', chaired by Winston Churchill in the Hague, established two intergovernmental structures, the Council of Europe (1949) and the Court of Human Rights (1950).

---

**BOX 1-4: ROBERT SCHUMAN (1886–1963) AND JEAN MONNET (1888–1979)**

Born in Luxembourg, Schuman studied and worked in Germany until the end of the First World War. He became French when Alsace-Lorraine reverted to France in 1918. He held several position in the post-war French governments including Finance Minister, Premier and Foreign Minister. Schuman provided the political push for the European Coal and Steel Community, which most consider to be the wellspring for the European Union. He was also the first President (1958–60) of the European Parliament.

ROBERT SCHUMAN
Audiovisual Library of the European Commission

JEAN MONNET
Audiovisual Library of the
European Commission

Jean Monnet, born in Cognac in 1888, was a brilliant organizer and as such helped to organize Allied military supply operations in the First World War (1914–1918) and the second. Near the end of the Second World War he joined Charles de Gaulle's provisional Free French government, and was responsible for the 'Monnet Plan', which is credited with helping France's post-war industrialization. Monnet was a convinced Europeanist and led the European movement in the 1950s and 1960s. Monnet, who is sometimes called the 'father of European integration', was the intellect behind the idea of the ECSC and the first president of its 'High Authority' (precursor of the European Commission) from 1952 to 1955. He continued to push for the European Economic Community and the European Atomic Energy Community (Euratom). He died in 1979.

The big first federalist step came only in 1952 with the implementation of the Schuman Plan inspired by the 'father of European integration', Jean Monnet, but promoted by French Foreign Minister, Robert Schuman (see Box 1-4). Schuman proposed that France and Germany should place their coal and steel sectors under the control of a supranational authority. This was a radical federalist move, as coal and steel were viewed as the 'commanding heights' of an industrial economy at the time and crucial to a nation's military and industrial strength. Schuman explicitly justified his Plan as a means of rendering future Franco-German wars materially impossible. Other European nations were invited to join this European Coal and Steel Community (ECSC), and Belgium, Luxembourg, the Netherlands and Italy actually did. This created a group of nations known simply as 'the Six' – a group that has been the driving force behind European integration ever since.

The ECSC's structure submerged the role of nation-states to an extent that seems unimaginable from today's perspective. It still represents the 'high water mark' of European federalism. Crucial decisions concerning such issues as pricing, trade, and production in the then-critical coal and steel sectors were placed in the hand of the 'High Authority'. This body, the forerunner of today's European Commission, consisted of officials appointed by the six member states. The High Authority's decisions, some made by majority voting, were subject to limited control by a member state governments. See Spierenburg and Poidevin (1994) for details on the ECSC.

By the time the Schuman Plan had been implemented and the ECSC was running, Europe was a very different place than it had been in 1945. The year was 1952 and Cold War tensions were high and rising. Economically, things continued to get better. As Table 1-3 shows, the Six had managed to get their economies back on track, having experienced miraculous growth in the late 1940s.

| Country | Back-on-track year (year GDP attained highest pre-1939 level) | Reconstruction growth (growth rate during reconstruction years, 1945 to back-on-track year) |
|---|---|---|
| Austria | 1951 | 15.2% |
| Belgium | 1948 | 6.0% |
| Denmark | 1946 | 13.5% |
| Finland | 1945 | n.a. |
| France | 1949 | 19.0% |
| Germany | 1951 | 13.5% |
| Italy | 1950 | 11.2% |
| Netherlands | 1947 | 39.8% |
| Norway | 1946 | 9.7% |

SOURCE: Crafts and Toniolo (1996, p. 4).

TABLE 1-3: POST-WORLD WAR TWO RECONSTRUCTION

## 1.2.2 Federalist track: the Treaty of Rome

The ECSC was a success, not so much in that it solved the thorny problems of Europe's coal and steel sectors, but rather as a training scheme for European integration. It showed that the Six could co-operate in a federal structure. The Six as a whole, but especially Germany, continued to grow spectacularly, while East–West tensions continued to mount. This combination made German rearmament essential.

In 1955, Germany joined Western Europe's main defence organization, the North Atlantic Treaty Organization (NATO), and began to rearm in earnest. This triggered a reaction from the Soviet bloc – the USSR and the Central and Eastern European nations formed the Warsaw Pact to counter NATO. It also brought back the question of deeper European integration. By 1955, it had become clear that coal and steel were no longer the 'commanding heights' of Europe's economy in economic or military terms. The ECSC might not be enough to ensure that another Franco-German war remained unthinkable; European leaders turned their minds to broader economic integration. Having failed to move directly to political or military integration (see Box 1-5), the natural way forward was broader economic integration.

Jean Monnet formed a high-powered pressure group – bluntly called the Action Committee for the United States of Europe – whose membership included leading figures from all the main political parties in each of 'the Six'. The group's aim was nothing less than to merge European nation-states into a supranational organization along the lines of the ECSC but much broader in scope.

NOTE: *Left photo*: Conference of Messina – the Foreign Ministers of the Six (left to right: Johan Beyen, Gaetano Martino, Joseph Bech, Antoine Pinay, Walter Hallstein, Paul-Henri Spaak).
*Right photo*: Signing of the Treaties establishing the EEC and Euratom in Rome (left to right: Paul-Henri Spaak, Jean-Charles Snoy et d'Oppuers, Christian Pineau, Maurice Faure, Konrad Adenauer, Walter Hallstein, Antonio Segni, Gaetano Martino, Joseph Bech, Joseph Luns, Johannes Linthorst Homan)
SOURCE: **European Commission Audiovisual Library.**

FIGURE 1-1: MESSINA CONFERENCE AND SIGNING OF THE TREATY OF ROME

Foreign ministers of the Six met in Messina in June 1955 to start a process that soon led to the signing, on 25 March 1957, of two treaties in Rome: the first created the European Atomic Energy Community (Euratom); the second created the European Economic Community (EEC). Because the EEC eventually became much more important than Euratom, the term 'The Treaty of Rome' is used to refer to the EEC treaty. The Treaty of Rome was quickly ratified by the six national parliaments and the EEC came into existence in January 1958. (The institutions of the ECSC, the EEC and Euratom were merged into the 'European Communities', or EC, in 1965.)

The Treaty of Rome committed the Six to extraordinarily deep economic integration. In addition to forming a customs union (removing all tariffs on intra-EEC trade and adopting a common tariff on imports from non-member nations), it promised free labour mobility, capital market integration and a range of common policies, some of which were to be implemented by the supranational European Commission. The Treaty also set up a series of supranational institutions such as the European Parliamentary Assembly (which became the European Parliament) and the European Court of Justice (see Chapter 2 for further details on the institutions and the supranationality).

> ### Box 1-5: Failed integration, EDC and EPC
> Encouraged by the rapid acceptance of the ECSC, Jean Monnet pressed ahead with even more ambitious plans for European unity. In the first years of the 1950s, leaders from the Six worked out plans for a supranational organization concerning defence – the European Defence Community (EDC) – as well as for deep political integration – the European Political Community (EPC). This remarkable enthusiasm for supranationality ultimately failed when the French parliament rejected the EDC. The EPC plans were subsequently abandoned.
>
> It is worth stressing just how revolutionary the ECSC, EDC and EPC proposals are by today's standards. European governments nowadays balk at pooling their sovereignty over comparatively trivial issues such as air traffic control; the goal of political union among EU members seems quixotic. In most non-European nations, advocating such massive transfers of sovereignty to supranational bodies would be unthinkable; in the USA it might even be considered treasonous. In the shadow of the death and destruction during the Second World War, it was, by contrast, mainstream thinking.

### 1.2.3 Intergovernmental track: from OEEC to EFTA

Formation of the EEC introduced an important new element into European economic integration. Hereto trade liberalization in Europe had been orchestrated by the OEEC with nations liberalizing on a non-discriminatory basis. The EEC, however, promised to go much further, removing *all* trade barriers, but this on a discriminatory, i.e. preferential, basis. Imports from non-member nations would not benefit from the opening. Moreover the Six were committed to adopting a common tariff against all imports from non-member nations. The other 11 OEEC members – most of them small – were left on the sidelines. Fearing the discrimination and marginalization that might occur if they faced the EEC bilaterally, seven of these 'outsiders' reacted by forming their own bloc in 1960, the European Free Trade Association (EFTA). This co-ordinated response was greatly facilitated by the UK's leadership. It is instructive to follow the behaviour of the few OEEC members that joined neither the EEC nor EFTA. In 1961 Finland essentially joined EFTA by signing an Association Agreement. Iceland applied for EFTA membership in 1968, acceding in 1970. By the early 1970s, all Western European nations had forsaken bilateralism except Ireland, which conducted much of its trade with the UK. Greece and Turkey both applied for associate EEC membership almost as soon as the Treaty of Rome was signed, and Spain signed a preferential trade agreement with the EEC in 1970 and another with EFTA in 1979.

### 1.2.4 Two non-overlapping circles: Common Market and EFTA

The 1960s saw the trade liberalization promised by the Treaty of Rome and the Stockholm Convention (EFTA's founding document) come to fruition (see Fig. 1-2). By the late 1960s trade arrangements in Western Europe could be described as two non-overlapping circles. This is schematically depicted in Fig. 1-2.

The lowering of intra-EEC trade barriers had an immediate and dramatic impact on trade patterns. During the formation of the Customs Union (CU), the EEC's share in its own trade rose from about 30 per cent to almost 50 per cent. At the same time, the share of EEC imports coming from six other major European nations remained almost unchanged, falling from 8 per cent to 7 per cent.

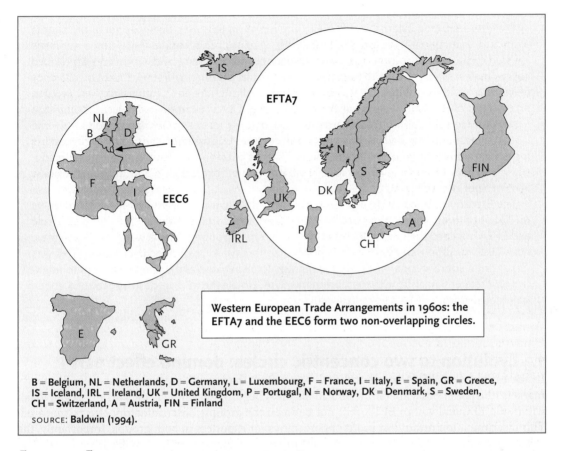

Western European Trade Arrangements in 1960s: the
EFTA7 and the EEC6 form two non-overlapping circles.

B = Belgium, NL = Netherlands, D = Germany, L = Luxembourg, F = France, I = Italy, E = Spain, GR = Greece,
IS = Iceland, IRL = Ireland, UK = United Kingdom, P = Portugal, N = Norway, DK = Denmark, S = Sweden,
CH = Switzerland, A = Austria, FIN = Finland
SOURCE: Baldwin (1994).

FIGURE 1-2: EUROPE OF 2 NON-OVERLAPPING CIRCLES

## BOX 1-6: FORMATION OF THE EEC CUSTOMS UNION AND EFTA
The nascent EEC spent much of its first year of life, 1958, setting up its administrative machinery in Brussels and developing an integration programme. It started with the most concrete part of the Treaty's ambitious integration scheme, namely the elimination of intra-EEC tariffs and quotas and the adoption of the common external tariff.

According to the Treaty, the elimination of intra-EEC tariffs was to take place in three stages of four years each: January 1958–December 1961, January 1962–December 1965 and January 1966–December 1969. The possibility of a three-year delay was foreseen, so the maximum liberalization period was 15 years. As it turned out, no extra time was needed. Intra-EEC import quotas were abolished ahead of schedule in 1961 and tariffs were liberalized faster than planned. Intra-EEC tariffs had come down 30 per cent by the end of 1960, down 60 per cent by July 1963, and down to zero by July 1968 – a year and a half ahead of schedule.

Why was the EEC able to achieve their ambitious Common Market 18 months early? The formation of the Customs Union coincided with a period of unprecedented economic prosperity and this largely offset the political and economic costs of liberalization-induced restructuring. Indeed, during this so-called 'golden age' of growth 1950–73, European unemployment averaged only 2.5 per cent and incomes either doubled, as in France, Belgium and the Netherlands, or tripled, as in Germany and Italy.

The new 'common external tariff' (CET) applied by all EEC members was set at the simple arithmetic average of the Six's pre-EEC tariffs. Typically this meant that France and Italy lowered their external tariffs, the Benelux nations raised theirs and Germany, which had approximately average tariffs to begin with, changed its external tariffs very little. Under Treaty of Rome rules, the tariff revenue was paid directly to the European Commission. This avoided discussions over a 'fair' division of the revenue (e.g. Dutch authorities collected the tariff in Rotterdam even though Rotterdam was the port of entry for many German imports from the USA). At least until the end of the 1970s, tariff revenue was an important source of financing for the Community. In the course of various GATT/WTO global trade talks, the EU has gradually lowered its CET to a fairly low level, so the revenue from the CET now accounts for only about 10 per cent of the EU's total budget.

The Stockholm Convention – EFTA's founding document – committed the EFTA nations (EFTAns) to removing tariffs on trade among themselves in tandem with the EEC's schedule and EFTA matched the EEC accelerated tariff-cutting. Importantly, EFTA was a free trade area, not a customs union, so external trade policy did not have to be decided in common. This was important if supranational decision making was to be avoided and it allowed the UK to maintain its preferential tariffs with the Commonwealth. Unlike the EEC, trade in agricultural goods was excluded from EFTA's liberalization.

## 1.3 Evolution to two concentric circles: domino effect part I

In the early 1960s, EFTA-based and EEC-based firms had roughly equal access to each others' markets (the preferential liberalization had only just begun). However, as the barriers began to fall within the EEC and within EFTA (but not between the groups), discriminatory effects appeared. This discrimination meant lost profit opportunities for exporters in both groups. Importantly, the relative economic weight and economic performance of the two circles was far from equal. The GDP of the six EEC nations was more than twice that of the seven EFTA nations and was growing faster. Thus the EEC club was far more attractive to exporters than the EFTA club. Accordingly, the progressive reduction of within-group barriers generated new political economy forces in favour of EEC enlargement, but how did discriminatory liberalization create these forces for inclusion?

Discriminatory liberalization is studied in depth in Chapter 5, but the idea behind these new political economy forces can be illustrated with an anecdote. Two campers in Yellowstone National Park, who have just settled down in their tent, hear the roar of a hungry Grizzly bear very close by. One camper sits up and starts putting on his running shoes. The other camper says: 'Are you crazy? You can't outrun a bear!' The first camper, who continues tying his laces, replies: 'Oh, I don't have to outrun the bear. I just have to outrun you.' When it comes to outrunning bears and succeeding in business, relative competitiveness is the key to success. A firm is harmed by anything that helps its rivals.

In the case at hand, closer EEC integration diminished the relative competitiveness of non-EEC firms in EEC markets, thereby harming their sales and profits. Of course, the same happened to EEC firms in EFTA, but given the EEC's much greater economic size, pressures on EFTA members (often referred to as EFTAns) to adjust were much greater than those on EEC nations. As history would have it, the British government was the first to react to the pressure.

### 1.3.1 First enlargement and EEC–EFTA FTAs

In 1961, Great Britain applied for EEC membership. If the EEC were enlarged to include Britain, the other EFTAns would face discrimination in an even larger market. What this meant was that the initial shock (UK applying) led other nations to change their attitude towards membership. In this case, Ireland, Denmark and Norway quickly followed Britain's unilateral move.[1] The other EFTAns did not apply for political reasons such as neutrality (Austria, Finland, Sweden and Switzerland), or lack of democracy (Portugal), or because they were not heavily dependent on the EEC market (Iceland).

In a renowned January 1963 press conference, French President Charles de Gaulle said 'non' to this first enlargement attempt, but the same four EFTAns reapplied in 1967 (see Box 1-7). De Gaulle issued another famous 'non', but after he retired, the applications were reactivated by invitation from the EEC.[2] After many delays, membership for the four was granted in 1973. At that time, Norway's population refused EEC membership in a referendum.

---

### Box 1-7: Charles de Gaulle (1890–1970)

Charles André Marie Joseph de Gaulle was born in Lille into a family that was comfortably well off (his father was a professor of literature and history). He was educated in the St Cyr Military Academy and thereafter began his army career. Twice wounded in the First World War, he was eventually captured by German forces and held as a prisoner of war despite his best efforts to escape (he made five attempts). He was a colonel when the war broke out, but was rapidly promoted to brigadier general (the youngest general in the French Army at age 49). De Gaulle was strongly opposed to the French surrender in June 1940 (after just two weeks of combat) and broadcast his renowned 'Appeal of June 18' from London: 'France has lost a battle, but France has not lost the war.' His appeal won over leaders in some of the French Overseas Territories and he created the Free French Movement which provided an alternative to the collaborationist Vichy Republic lead by Marshal Petain. After the war, he was elected to head the provisional government which organized elections and launched a plan to modernize and industrialize the French economy. He resigned in 1946, frustrated by the dominance of the legislature. He returned to power in 1958 in a crisis atmosphere.

De Gaulle, like Adenauer, was a strong proponent of Franco-German co-operation, but he was only a reluctant Europeanist. He had always objected to supranational organisations, including the ECSC, but France had already adopted the Treaty of Rome before he came back to power. In 1966, he orchestrated the 'empty chair' policy that essentially eviscerated much of the supranationality in the Treaty of Rome. The General dominated French political life until he resigned again in 1969. He died the following year.

This box is based largely on http://www.info-france-usa.org/atoz/bio/bio_degaulle.asp

---

The impending departure of four EFTAns to the EEC was anticipated well in advance and triggered a secondary domino effect. The 1973 EEC enlargement meant a swelling of the EEC markets and a shrinking of the EFTA markets. Firms based in the remaining EFTA states would suffer a disadvantage (compared to their EEC-based rivals) in more markets and enjoy an advantage (over their EEC-based rivals) in fewer markets. Accordingly, EFTA industries pushed their governments to redress this situation. The result was a set of bilateral free trade agreements (FTAs) between each remaining EFTAn and the EEC designed to take effect when the UK and company acceded to the EEC.

---

[1] For details on the domino theory, see Baldwin (1994, 1995).
[2] You can find the grandiloquent rejection on http://www.fordham.edu/halsall/mod/1967-degaulle-non-uk.html. See http://www.charles-de-gaulle.org/en/books_art/fiches_t/cdg_europe.htm for de Gaulle's motives.

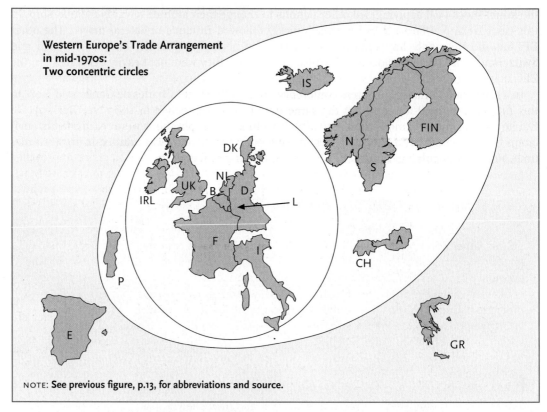

**Western Europe's Trade Arrangement in mid-1970s: Two concentric circles**

NOTE: **See previous figure, p.13, for abbreviations and source.**

FIGURE 1-3: EUROPE OF 2 CONCENTRIC CIRCLES

Notice that this change of heart does need some explaining. The stance of, say, Sweden towards an FTA with the then EEC was a matter of top-level political calculation. It may seem strange, therefore, that the calculations of Sweden's political élite led them to sign an FTA in 1972 when they had not found it politically optimal to sign one in the preceding decades. The explanation, of course, is that tighter integration among a nation's trade partners (in this case between the UK, Denmark and Ireland and the EEC) alters the economic landscape facing Swedish exporters. This reshaping of the economic landscape gets translated into a new political landscape.

The upshot of all this was that by the mid-1970s trade arrangements in Western Europe had evolved from non-overlapping circles into two concentric circles. This is shown schematically in Fig. 1-3. The outer circle, which encompassed both EFTA and EEC nations, represents a 'virtual' free trade area for industrial products, formed by concatenation of the Treaty of Rome (for intra-EEC trade), EFTA's charter, the Stockholm Convention (for intra-EFTA trade) and individual bilateral FTAs between each EFTAn and the EEC (for EEC–EFTA trade). The inner circle was the EEC. These countries were much more thoroughly integrated, even in the mid-1970s. For instance, EEC members had duty-free trade in all products (including agricultural goods), a common external tariff, many common sectoral policies (coal, steel, etc.) and a common labour market.

## 1.4 Euro-pessimism

Although the Customs Union was implemented smoothly and ahead of schedule, European integration stagnated. The Community was rocked by a series of political crises in the 1960s soon to be followed by economic shocks in the early 1970s. This led to a period of 'Euro-pessimism' that lasted from the first enlargement to 1985.

### 1.4.1 Political shocks

The spectacularly good economic performance of Europe's economies in the 1950s and 1960s – teamed with the manifest success of European economic integration – went a long way to restoring the confidence of Europeans in their governments' ability to govern (Milward, 1984). So much so that some nations began to regret the promises of deep integration they made in the Treaty of Rome. At the head of this pro-national sovereignty charge was French President Charles de Gaulle.

The issue came to a head as the final stage in the Treaty of Rome's transition period approached (1 January 1966). At this stage the voting procedures in the EEC's key decision making body, the Council of Ministers, was scheduled to switch to a particular kind of majority voting (see 'qualified majority voting' in Chapter 2). The objectionable part of majority voting for de Gaulle was that France might have to accept a majority-backed policy even if France had voted against it. In the end, de Gaulle forced the other EEC members to accept his point of view in the so-called Luxembourg Compromise (see Box 1-8); henceforth, unanimity was the typical rule in EEC decision making procedures.

These conflicts came after opposition to federalism had caused the failure of an earlier attempt at deeper political integration. The 1961 EEC summit in Bonn formed a committee – the Fouchet committee – to propose a plan for political union. Fouchet's plan, which was heavily influenced by de Gaulle's opposition to supranationality, rested on scrupulous respect of national sovereignty. The plan failed for a number of reasons, among them a fear among some EU members that it would undermine the existing supranational aspect of the Community (see http://www.europarl.eu.int/factsheets/1_1_2_en.htm for further details).

---

**BOX 1-8: THE 'EMPTY CHAIR' POLICY AND THE 'LUXEMBOURG COMPROMISE'**

De Gaulle, who had always opposed supranationality in European integration, challenged the principle in 1966. The test case came when France opposed a range of Commission proposals, which included measures for financing the Common Agricultural Policy. France stopped attending the main Community meetings (the so-called 'empty chair' policy) and threatened to withdraw from the EEC. This marked the end of the post-war climate for radical change, but not the end of the EEC.[3] In exchange for its return to the Council of Ministers, France demanded a political agreement – the Luxembourg Compromise – that *de facto* overturned the Treaty of Rome's majority voting provisions whenever a member state announced that it felt that 'very important interests' were at stake.

Although the Luxembourg Compromise had no legal force, it had an enormous impact. It meant that unanimity was the *de facto* rule for almost everything. Almost all progress on deeper economic integration was blocked until the majority voting was restored in the 1986 Single European Act. The compromise in full reads: 'Where, in the case of decisions which may be taken by a majority vote on a proposal from the Commission, very important interests of one or more partners are at stake, the Members of the Council will endeavour, within a reasonable time, to reach solutions which can be adopted by all the Members of the Council while respecting their mutual interests and those of the Community, in accordance with Article 2 of the Treaty.' See http://www.europarl.eu.int/factsheets/1_3_6_en.htm for further details.

---

[3] Some historians argue that European integration was always driven by national interests; see Milward (1984) and Moravcsik (1998).

### 1.4.2 **Failure of monetary integration**

In the late 1960s, the USA began to run an irresponsible monetary policy – essentially printing money to pay for the Vietnam War. Since all major currencies were linked to the dollar at the time (via the global fixed exchange rate system called Bretton Woods), US inflation was more or less automatically translated into rising inflation in Europe and elsewhere. The political pressures that arose led to the gradual breakdown, between 1971 and 1973, of the global fixed exchange rate system. (See Chapter 10 for further details.)

Exchange rate stability was widely viewed as a critical factor supporting the rapid post-war growth in trade and international investment and the rising prosperity these brought. The EEC searched for ways of restoring exchange rate stability among members. Drawing on studies undertaken in the 1960s, the Werner Committee laid out a step-by-step approach to monetary union. This was adopted in 1971, with the goal being nothing less than full monetary union by 1980. (See Chapter 10 for further details.)

The economic environment for this new European monetary arrangement could not have been worse. Months after it was launched, the Yom Kippur War in the Middle East triggered an Arab oil boycott of Western states. The resulting sharp rise in oil prices turned out to be a bonanza for all the oil-exporting nations. The economic impact on Western Europe, however, was ruinous. Just as inflationary tendencies were heating up from the actions of the USA, the oil shock severely dampened economic activity in Europe and all of its global trading partners. Most European nations adopted expansionary monetary and fiscal policies to compensate for the economic downturn and these further fuelled inflation. The resulting falling income levels and rising inflation rates came to be known as 'stagflation'. Just as the world was recovering from the 1973 oil shock, a second massive oil price hike came in 1979, aggravating stagflation. A debilitating series of exchange rate crises – which stemmed directly from these massive external shocks – condemned this first post-war attempt at European monetary integration to failure.

### 1.4.3 **Failure of deeper trade integration**

Even as tariff barriers were being phased out, Europeans began to erect new trade barriers among themselves. These new barriers consisted of detailed technical regulations and standards, which had the effect of fragmenting the European markets. While these policies, called 'technical barriers to trade' (TBTs), undoubtedly inhibited intra-European trade, their announced goal was to protect consumers. Indeed, EEC leaders recognized the trade-inhibiting effects of TBTs from its start in 1957. Article 100 of the EU's founding Treaty requires 'approximation' (Euro-speak for harmonization) of national regulations for the 'proper functioning of the common market'.

The EU first systematically took up the removal of technical barriers in 1969 with its 'General Programme'. This launched what came to be called the 'traditional' or 'old' approach to TBT liberalization. The approach adopted relied on detailed technical regulations for single products or groups of products implemented by unanimously agreed directives. Since unanimity was required, this approach failed. Harmonization proceeded much more slowly than the development of new national barriers. For example, 10 years were required to adopt a directive on gas containers made of unalloyed steel and nine and a half years was the average delay for the 15 directives adopted *en masse* in 1984. In the meantime, member states were implementing thousands of technical standards and regulations a year.

The combination of extremely poor macroeconomic performance (slow growth, high unemployment and high inflation) and failure of Europe's monetary and trade liberalization scheme created a sort of gloom over the 'European project'. Many inside and outside Europe suspected that the ideals that had driven European integration since the late 1940s were dying or dead.

### 1.4.4 Bright spots

There were some bright spots in European integration during this period. Spain, Portugal and Greece all adopted democratic governments, thus rendering them suitable for EEC membership. Greece joined in 1981 followed by the Iberian nations in 1986. The European Monetary System (EMS), which had good success in stabilizing intra-EEC exchange rates, started operation in 1978. Moreover, the EEC put its financing on a firm footing with two budget Treaties, one in 1970 and one 1975 (see Chapter 2 for further details). The institutions of the three communities (ESCS, Euratom and EEC) were rationalized by the Merger Treaty (1965) and the EU Parliament was directly elected for the first time in 1979 (previously, its members came from the members' national parliaments).

In the USA and Europe, central bankers decided to fight inflation (which had reached double digit figures in most industrial nations) the old-fashioned way – by inducing a long hard recession. Between 1981 and 1983 growth was negative or only slightly positive in most of Europe. While inflation rates did decline, this was at the cost of a significant increase in unemployment. Starting in 1984 economic growth recovered. Political attitudes also changed – in particular, a deepened belief in market economics began to spread throughout the industrialized world. US President Reagan, and British Prime Minister Thatcher are often cited as vanguards, but even the Socialist French President Mitterrand adopted a much more favourable attitude towards market-based solutions. While there are many causes for this philosophical shift, the fact that highly interventionist policies had failed to prevent 10 years of poor economic performance is surely one of the most important.

## 1.5 Deeper circles and domino effect part II: the Single Market Programme and the EEA

This favourable economic climate was matched with the arrival of a talented promoter of European integration, Jacques Delors (see Box 1-9). Delors, who was appointed to the Presidency of the European Commission in 1985, was devoted to the idea of kick-starting European integration (see Annex A for a chronology of post-1974 events). To this end, he pushed a programme that would complete the internal market. He dubbed this the 'Single Market Programme', although it was often referred to as 'Internal Market Programme', the 1992 Programme, or EC92 for short. It was framed by Lord Cockfield's 1985 White Paper which listed 300 measures necessary to transform the Common Market into the Single Market. By July 1987, all member states had adopted the Single European Act, which is the Community legislation that implemented the Single Market measures (along with many other changes).

### 1.5.1 The Single Market Programme: EC92

In 1985, EU firms enjoyed duty-free access to each other's markets, however they certainly did not enjoy free trade. Intra-EC trade was shackled by a long list of trade-inhibiting barriers such as differing technical standards and industrial regulations, capital controls, preferential public procurement, administrative and frontier formalities, VAT and excise tax rate differences and differing transport regulations, to mention just a few. Although the vast majority of these policies seem negligible individually, the confluence of their effects served to substantially restrict intra-Community trade.

Indeed, many of these barriers were introduced in the 1970s as European nations increasingly adopted standards and regulations that were aimed at protecting consumers and the environment. The free movement of goods was also restricted by practices of national and local governments such as biased purchasing patterns, exclusive production or service rights, and production subsidies to national champions. Likewise, the free movement of services was far from being a reality,

### Box 1-9: Jacques Delors (1925– )

Jacques Lucien Jean Delors, born in Paris, held a series of posts in banking and the French government. He was deeply engaged in the trade union movement and a devoted Catholic. After a stint in the European Parliament, he became Finance Minister under French President Mitterrand in the early 1980s. Always a committed European integrationist, he was chosen in 1985 to be President of the European Commission, a post he held for two four-year terms. This period was marked by the most important increase in European economic integration since the 1950s; most observers give much credit for this to the savvy and energy of Jacques Delors. The Single European Act, which reinstated majority voting on most economic integration issues, restored the Community's ability to act. This led to a sweeping economic integration effort known as the Single Market Programme, and while this formally ended in 1992, the programme continues to be extended and deepened.

Jacques Delors
Audiovisual Library of the
European Commission

Delors was also instrumental in adoption of the Economic and Monetary Union (EMU) which led to the creation of the euro in 1999. Delors' term as Commission President was extended to help the EU to deal with the Danish rejection of the Maastricht Treaty and exchange rate crises of the early 1990s. Among Delors' many other accomplishments, the two multi-year budget deals negotiated while he was President reformed EU financing and redirected EU spending away from agriculture and towards support for disadvantaged regions. His term as President ended in January 1995. Currently, he runs a European think-tank called 'Notre Europe' (www.notre-europe.asso.fr).

again largely due to national prudential and safety regulations. Service providers typically were required to possess local certification and the requirements for such certification often varied across nations. Moreover the certification process was often controlled or influenced by the national service providers who had an economic interest in excluding foreign competitors via this certification process.

The Single Market Programme, or SMP as it is often called, was set out in the celebrated Commission White Paper of June 1985 (Cockfield Report) and incorporated into the EU legal system by the 1986 Single European Act. The SMP included almost 300 individual measures necessary to complete the internal market. The intention was to create 'an area without internal frontiers in which the free movement of goods, persons, services and capital is ensured'. The key changes were:

### Goods trade liberalization
- Streamlining or elimination of border formalities
- Harmonization of VAT rates within wide bands
- Liberalization of government procurement
- Harmonization and mutual recognition of technical standards in production, packaging and marketing.

### Factor trade liberalization
- Removal of all capital controls
- Increase in capital market integration
- Liberalization of cross-border market-entry policies, including mutual recognition of approval by national regulatory agencies.

The Single European Act also implement important institutional changes. To clear the decision making log-jam that had held up similar integration initiatives in the 1970s, EC92 included a major change in the EU's decision making procedures. In particular, decisions concerning Single Market issues would be adopted on the basis of majority voting instead of on a basis of unanimity (see Chapter 2 for a discussion of EU decision making procedures). This change in voting procedures was part of the so-called 'new approach' to TBT liberalization. For further details, see http://europa.eu.int/comm/internal_market/en/index_ob.htm.

## FOCUS ON CAPITAL MOBILITY

Without a doubt the most novel aspect of the Single Market Programme was its focus on capital mobility; other features can be viewed as deepening or extending integration initiatives already agreed. Some EU members had unilaterally liberalized capital mobility prior to EC92, but substantial pan-EU liberalization came only in the second half of the 1980s with a series of EC92 directives. The opening was completed in 1988 by a directive that ruled out all remaining restrictions on capital movements among EU residents. (The definitive system was codified in the Maastricht Treaty's Article 56, which prohibits all restrictions on the movement of capital and payments with few exceptions relating to crime, national security and internal issues.)

## 1.5.2 The EEA and the fourth enlargement

Since the Single European Act promised much tighter economic integration among EU members, non-EU nations again found themselves threatened by the discriminatory effects of integration in the EU. Since EFTAns exported heavily to the EU, the discrimination posed significant problems for EFTA-based firms. As in the 1960s and early 1970s, EFTA firms again prompted their governments to offset the discrimination by seeking closer ties. Again, the EFTAns did so in a co-ordinated fashion. As we shall see, however, a new element emerged during this exercise.

In the late 1980s, EFTAn governments had decided that they must react to the Single Market. Several considered applying for EU membership (Austria actually did), while others considered bilateral negotiations. Jacques Delors forced the decision in January 1989 by proposing the EEA agreement (initially called the European Economic Space agreement). The final version of this agreement is highly complex, but, for our purposes, it can be thought of as extending the Single Market to EFTA economies, apart from agriculture and the common external tariff.

Given the political economy forces described above, it is easy to understand why the EFTAns would want to participate in the Single Market. There are, however, two aspects of the EEA that are truly extraordinary. First, the EEA seemed, from some perspectives, to be unbalanced in terms of the rights and obligations of EFTAns when it comes to future EEC legislation. In essence, it forces the EFTAns to accept future EEC legislation (the *Acquis Communautaire*) concerning the Single Market, without formal input into the formation of these new laws. Second, the EEA created a good deal of supranationality among the EFTAns, and forced the EFTAns to speak with one voice on many issues during the negotiations. This supranationality was extraordinary for two reasons. First, the EU imposed this supranationality on the EFTAns in order to simplify the task of keeping the Single Market homogeneous. Second, the EFTAns had resisted such supranational authority since the end of the war, so it is astounding that they now said they would accept it.

As it turned out, virtually none of the EFTAns were willing to live with the EEA as it was negotiated. By the end of negotiations on the EEA, Austria, Finland, Sweden, Norway and Switzerland had put in EU membership applications. For these countries, the EEA was viewed as a transitional arrangement. Swiss voters rejected that EEA in December 1992, effectively freezing their EU application. Accession talks with the four EFTAns were successful, so the EEA consisted of the

EU15 on one hand with Norway, Liechtenstein and Iceland on the other (Norway's voters rejected membership in a referendum).

Of course, the membership bids of Sweden, Switzerland, Finland and Austria would have been unthinkable in the old Cold War environment. From 1989, the East–West political division of Europe crumbled and then vanished. These profound political changes, which allowed Sweden, Finland and Austria to join the EU, had far more dramatic implications for the Central and Eastern European nations – the topic to which we turn next.

## 1.6 Communism's creeping failure and spectacular collapse

The division of Europe into communist and capitalist camps was cemented, quite literally, in 1961 by the construction of the Berlin Wall. While living standards were not too dissimilar to begin with, by the 1980s, Western European living standards were far higher than those in Eastern Europe and the USSR. Quite simply, the West's economic system (based on free markets and an extensive social welfare system) when teamed up with its political system (based on multi-party democracy and freedom of the press) provided far greater benefits to its citizens than did the East's system of planned economies and one-party rule.

This 'creeping failure' of communism was soon apparent to the Central and Eastern European Countries (CEECs). Soviet leaders, however, repeatedly thwarted reform efforts in the CEECs via constant economic pressure and occasional military intervention. By the 1980s, the inadequacy of the Soviet's economic system forced changes inside the USSR. Under Soviet President Gorbachev, the USSR adopted a policy of timid pro-market reforms (*perestroika*) and a policy of openness (*glasnost*), which involved a marked reduction in internal repression and diminished intervention in the affairs of the Soviet republics and Soviet-bloc nations.

As far as European integration was concerned, the Soviet foreign policy changes were critical. Pro-democracy forces in the CEECs, which had been repeatedly put down by military force hereto, found little resistance from Moscow in the late 1980s. The first breach came in June 1989 when the Polish labour movement 'Solidarity' forced the communist government to accept free parliamentary elections. The communists lost and the first democratic government in the Soviet bloc took power. Moscow rapidly established ties with the new Polish government.

Moscow's hands-off approach to the Polish election triggered a chain of events over the next two years that revolutionized European affairs. Pro-reform elements inside the Hungarian communist party pressed for democratic elections, and, more dramatically, Hungary opened its border with Austria. Thousands of East Germans reacted by moving to West Germany via Hungary and Austria. This set off mass protests against communist repression in East Germany, protests that culminated in the opening of the border between East and West Germany. On 9 November 1989, thousands of West and East Berlin citizens converged on the Berlin Wall with pickaxes and sledge hammers to dismantle that symbol of a divided Europe. By the end of 1989, democratic forces were in control in Poland, Hungary, Czechoslovakia and East Germany. In 1990, East and West Germany formed a unified Germany and three Soviet Republics – Estonia, Latvia and Lithuania – declared their independence from the USSR. By the end of 1991, the Soviet Union itself broke up, putting a definitive end to its interference in Central and Eastern Europe. The European Union reacted swiftly to this geopolitical earthquake by providing emergency aid and loans to the fledgling democracies.

### 1.6.1 First steps: Europe Agreements with the CEECs

Given that almost every other nation in the area had free trade access to the enormous EU market, free trade agreements were a commercial necessity for the newly free Central and Eastern European Countries (CEECs). There was no thought of forming their own free trade area, or of joining EFTA. The EU could also provide a degree of security that other arrangements could not. In the early days, CEEC leaders felt unsure that the new situation was permanent. If things went wrong and the iron curtain re-descended, each CEEC wanted to be sure that the curtain would, this time, come down east of their borders.

Thus for geopolitical and economic reasons, all CEECs soon expressed their firm intention of joining the European Union. The EU, by contrast, was initially reluctant. Instead of acknowledging the CEECs' interests in membership, the EU signed Association Agreements, commonly known as Europe Agreements, with Poland, Hungary and Czechoslovakia in 1991. Europe Agreements for other CEECs followed, and by 1994 the EU had such deals with Romania, Bulgaria, Albania, Estonia, Latvia and Lithuania. Throughout the early 1990s, EFTA followed a policy of 'parallelism' concerning East–West ties. That is, as soon as a CEEC had a Europe Agreement with the EU, EFTA quickly negotiated its own bilateral free trade agreement with that nation. Some CEECs also signed trade arrangements among themselves. The most important being the 1991 Central European Free Trade Agreement that initially promoted trade liberalization among Czechoslovakia, Hungary and Poland. It was subsequently extended to include both successor states to Czechoslovakia as well as Slovenia, Bulgaria and Romania.

Of these arrangements, the EU–CEEC Association Agreements were by far the most important economically and politically. These Agreements established bilateral free trade between the EU and each individual CEEC. They committed the EU to removing tariffs and quantitative restrictions on most industrial products by the end of 1994, with the CEECs being allowed a longer transition period. Importantly, substantial protection remained for a group of 'sensitive' industrial products including some textiles, some coal and steel products, and almost all agricultural trade. Beyond the liberalization of most industrial goods, a further goal was to make progress towards 'realizing between them the other economic freedoms on which the Community is based'. To this end, the Europe Agreements contain provisions governing the movement of services, capital and people. The Agreements progressively liberalize trade in services. They also provide for bilateral national treatment of firms. Finally, a very important element of the Europe Agreements is the commitment of the CEECs to adopt laws on economic and related issues that approximate the EU laws. This includes competition rules and limits on state aid to industries.

The modest nature of the Europe Agreements, i.e. bilateral free trade agreements instead of a deeper pluri-lateral arrangement such as the EEA, reflected the profound ambivalence that many in the West initially had towards EU membership for the CEECs. For instance, the entry into force of the Europe Agreements was substantially delayed by the slow action of the Parliaments of EU Member States. The Europe Agreements signed with Hungary and Poland in December 1991 entered into force only in February 1994. Among others factors, the lack of a grand vision for Europe and the lack of high-level political engagement in many EU Member States contributed to the long delay.

### 1.6.2 Copenhagen to Copenhagen: from 1993 accession criteria to EU membership

The EU officially ended its hesitancy concerning full East–West integration in June 1993. The European Council decided at its Copenhagen summit that 'the associated countries in Central and Eastern Europe that so desire shall become members of the European Union'. This was the first time the EU leaders explicitly sanctioned membership for the CEECs. The Council also defined what has come to be known as the Copenhagen Criteria for EU membership. Quoting the final document from the June 1993 summit (known as the Presidency Conclusions in EU jargon):

Membership requires that the candidate country has achieved stability of institutions guaranteeing democracy, the rule of law, human rights and respect for and, protection of minorities, the existence of a functioning market economy as well as the capacity to cope with competitive pressure and market forces within the Union. Membership presupposes the candidate's ability to take on the obligations of membership including adherence to the aims of political, economic and monetary union.

Nine years later, the European Council met again in Copenhagen to finish the enlargement process. As the Presidency Conclusions of the 12–13 December 2002 meeting state:

Today marks an unprecedented and historic milestone in completing this process with the conclusion of accession negotiations with Cyprus, the Czech Republic, Estonia, Hungary, Latvia, Lithuania, Malta, Poland, the Slovak Republic and Slovenia. The Union now looks forward to welcoming these States as members from 1 May 2004. This achievement testifies to the common determination of the peoples of Europe to come together in a Union that has become the driving force for peace, democracy, stability and prosperity on our continent.

## 1.7 German unification, Maastricht and the euro

The 1989 'political earthquake' also yielded substantial changes within the EU. With the Berlin Wall gone, unification of the Western and Eastern parts of Germany was the natural next step, but a unified Germany would be a behemoth. With 80 million citizens and 30 per cent of Europe's output, Germany would be much larger than France, the UK, or Italy. This raised many fears, ranging from a disturbed political balance in the EU to the unlikely, but still scary spectre, of German militarism. Many Europeans, both within, and outside Germany, felt that Germany would be best unified in conjunction with a big increase in the forces tying EU members together.

Riding on his success with the Single Market, Jacques Delors seized this moment to propose a radical increase in European economic integration – the formation of a monetary union. A step that many thought would eventually lead to political integration. The idea was quickly championed by French President François Mitterrand and German Chancellor Helmut Kohl. After extensive negotiations, the EU committed itself to a target of forming a monetary union by 1999 and adopting a single currency by 2002 (see Chapter 14 for details). This commitment was made in the Treaty of Maastricht. Monetary union, however, was not the only significant deepening of European integration found in the Maastricht Treaty, which is formally known as the Treaty on European Union.

The Treaty also established the EU's current 'three pillar' structure (see Chapter 2 for further details). The principal difference between the various pillars concerns the decision making procedures involved. All the economic integration issues, where federalist principles such as majority voting had long prevailed, were grouped in the first pillar. The second and third pillars consisted of policies in which co-operation was on an intergovernmental basis. Co-operation in the areas of national security and foreign policies were placed in the second pillar, while the third pillar grouped together domestic policies such as co-operation among the Member States' justice systems (courts, police, etc.), and immigration policy.

## 1.8 Preparing for Eastern enlargement: Amsterdam and Nice Treaties

Once the EU15 leaders had confirmed that the CEECs would eventually become EU members, it became clear that EU institutions and procedures would have to be reformed. Structures designed for six members were groaning under the weight of 15 members. Adding 5 to 10 newcomers would surely bring the structure down. Recognizing this need for reform, EU leaders launched the 1996–97 Intergovernmental Conference (IGC) that produced the Amsterdam Treaty.

### 1.8.1 Amsterdam Treaty: cleaning up the Maastricht Treaty

While the ambitions for the Amsterdam Treaty were high, the IGC failed to produce agreement on reform of the main institutions. The IGC did not end in failure, however, it produced a treaty that is best thought of as a tidying up of the Maastricht Treaty. The substantive additions included a more substantial role for the EU in social policy, which was not included in the Maastricht Treaty due to objections by the then Conservative UK government. The European Parliament powers were modestly boosted, and the notion of flexibility integration, so-called 'closer co-operation', was introduced (see Chapter 2 for further details).

The key enlargement-related reform issues were not settled (adjusting voting rules in the Council of Ministers, the number of EU Commissioners, composition of the EU Parliament, etc.). Rather, EU leaders agreed to a list of issues that had to be solved before the enlargement – the so-called Amsterdam leftovers – and then agreed to launch a new IGC in 2000. For more details, see http://europa.eu.int/scadplus/leg/en/s50000.htm.

### 1.8.2 Treaty of Nice

The 2000 IGC concluded with the EU leaders' summit in the French city of Nice in December. Agreement on a treaty was produced, but the Treaty of Nice was not a success. The key three issues left open by the Amsterdam Treaty were the size and composition of the Commission, extension of qualified-majority voting in the EU's Council of Ministers, and reform of Council voting rules. The Nice Treaty solved none of these. On Commission reform the Treaty adopted a temporary, makeshift reform – temporary since it applies from 2005 to the date when the 27th member has joined; and makeshift since the long-term solution was not set. On the extension of qualified voting issue, Nice was basically a house-cleaning exercise with little or no change in the areas to be subject to majority voting. On Council decision making reform, the Treaty of Nice actually made things worse. With little more than hurried, late-night staff work and their political instincts to guide them, EU leaders adopted a massively complex system, and the Nice Treaty voting reforms actually made it more difficult for the enlarged EU to act (see Chapter 3 for further details). The decision making efficiency in the EU27 would have been higher with no reform at all. The Treaty also shifted power to large nations in a major way.[4] The Treaty of Nice came into force in 2003, but its main institutional reforms are already being reconsidered in the draft Constitutional Treaty that was endorsed by the European Council at its June 2003 meeting in Greece.

### 1.8.3 The European Convention

Recognizing the failure of the Treaty of Amsterdam and the Treaty of Nice to readjust the EU's institutions to the reality of 25 members or more, the 2002–2003 European Convention produced a draft Constitutional Treaty that greatly alters the EU's institutions (and much more). Since the draft emerged just as this book went to press, we are unable to describe the implications of the draft Constitutional Treaty. Moreover, the actual text of the Treaty is being reconsidered by an Intergovernmental Conference (IGC) that should begin its work in October 2004. Chapter by chapter updates on the Constitutional Treaty's impact will be posted on the book's OLC website www.mcgraw-hill.co.uk/textbooks/baldwinandwyplos2.

---

[4] See the Commission's Treaty of Nice site, www.europa.eu.int/comm/nice_treaty/index_en.htm, for details and a copy of the Treaty.

## 1.9 **Summary**

It is impossible to summarize 50 years of European integration in a few paragraphs. But it is possible to highlight the main events and lessons as far as the economics of European integration are concerned.

■ European integration has always been driven by political factors, ranging from a desire to prevent another European war to a desire to share the fruit of integration with the newly democratic nations in Central and Eastern Europe. Yet while the goals were always political, the means were always economic.
■ There have been basically three big increases in European economic integration. Formation of the customs union from 1958 to 1968 eliminated tariffs and quotas on intra-EU trade. The Single Market Programme implemented between 1986 and 1992 (although elements are still being implemented today) eliminated many non-tariff barriers and liberalized capital flows within the EU. Finally, the Economic and Monetary Union melded together the currencies of most EU members.
■ Each of these steps towards deeper integration – but especially the Customs Union and the Single Market Programme – engendered discriminatory effects that triggered reactions in the non-member nations. Just as the knocking down of one domino triggers a chain reaction that leads to the fall of all dominos, the discriminatory effects of EU integration has created a powerful gravitational force that has progressively drawn all but the most reluctant Europeans into the EU. If there is a lesson to draw from this for the future, it is that the 2004 enlargement is likely to greatly magnify the pro-EU membership forces in the nations further east and south.

### SELF-ASSESSMENT QUESTIONS

**1.** Draw a diagram (or diagrams) that graphically shows the major steps in European economic integration along with dates and the names of the countries involved. Be sure to explicitly discuss the removal of various barriers to the movement of goods, labour and capital.
**2.** Draw a diagram like Fig. 1-3 that shows the current state of trade arrangements in Europe, including all European nations west of the Urals.
**3.** Make a list of all the EU treaties (with dates) and provide a 10-words-or-less explanation of each treaty's major contribution to European integration.
**4.** What were the main challenges posed by Eastern enlargement of the European Union and how was the Nice Treaty meant to address these challenges?
**5.** Some European integration experts subscribe to the so-called bicycle theory of integration, which asserts that European integration must continually move forward to prevent it from 'falling over', i.e. breaking down. List a sequence of events from 1958 to 1992 that lend support to the theory.
**6.** Explain how Cold War politics accelerated European integration in some ways but hindered it in others, such as geographic expansion of the EU.
**7.** Explain when and by which means the organization that is known as the European Union has changed names since its inception in 1958.

### ESSAY QUESTIONS

**1.** What role has the Council of Europe, which is a non-EU institution, played in pan-European integration?
**2.** How important was the USA's role in promoting European integration. Do you think Europe would have formed the EEC, or something like it, if the USA had not made the creation of the OEEC a condition for aid?
**3.** Describe the evolution of the various British governments' attitudes towards European integration in the 1945 to 1975 period. In the early years Labour opposed membership while Conservatives supported it, but recently the roles have reversed. Why do you think this is so?

**4.** Provide an explanation for why only six of the EU15 nations joined in 1957. You should list specific reasons for each non-member.

**5.** Write an essay on the work towards deeper European integration that was done in the context of the OEEC. Why did this fail?

**6.** Write an essay on whether Charles de Gaulle promoted or hindered European integration. Chapter 8 of Urwin (1995) is a good place to start.

**7.** Why did the EPC and EDC plans fail when the ECSC succeeded?

## FURTHER READING: THE AFICIONADOS CORNER

For a good, general description of the development of European integration see:
Urwin, D. (1995) *The Community of Europe*, Longman, London.

Two books that challenge the traditional view that federalist idealism was important in the development of Europe are:
Milward, A. (1992) *The European Rescue of the Nation-State*, Cambridge University Press, Cambridge.
Moravcsik, A. (1998) *The Choice for Europe: Social Purpose and State Power from Messina to Maastricht*, Cornell University Press, Ithaca.

A detailed description of post-war growth can be found in:
Crafts, N. and G. Toniolo (1996) *Economic Growth in Europe since 1945*, Cambridge University Press, Cambridge.

## USEFUL WEBSITES

The Truman Library website http://www.trumanlibrary.org/teacher/berlin.htm is a good source for early post-war background documents online.

The European Parliament's 'factsheets' provide an excellent, authoritative and succinct coverage of many historical institutions, policies and debates. For example, it has pages on the historical development of the Parliament's role, on historical enlargements, and on every Treaty. See http://www.europarl.eu.int/factsheets/default_en.htm.

## REFERENCES

Baldwin, R. (1994) *Towards an Integrated Europe*, CEPR, London. Freely downloadable from http://heiwww.unige. ch/~Baldwin/papers.htm.
Baldwin, R. (1995) 'A domino theory of regionalism' In R., Baldwin, P. Haaparanta and J. Kiander (eds) *Expanding European Regionalism: The EU's New Members*, Cambridge University Press, Cambridge.
Botting, D. (1985) *From the Ruins of the Reich: Germany 1945–1949*, New American Library, New York.
Eichengreen, B. and J.B. de Macedo (2001) 'The European Payments Union: history and implications for the evolution of the International Financial Architecture', in A. Lamfalussy, B. Snoy and J. Wilson (eds) *Fragility of the International Financial System*, P.I.E.-Peter Lang, Brussels.
Lamfalussy, A. (1963) *The UK and the Six: An Essay on Economic Growth in Western Europe*, Macmillan, London.
Jackson, J. (2003) *The Fall of France*, Oxford University Press, Oxford.
Milward, A. (1984) *The European Rescue of the Nation-State: 1945–51*, Routledge, London.
Milward, A. (1992) *The European Rescue of the Nation-State*, Cambridge University Press, Cambridge.
Moravcsik, A. (1998) *The Choice for Europe: Social Purpose and State Power from Messina to Maastricht*, Cornell University Press, Ithaca.
Spierenburg, D. and R. Poidevin (1994) *The History of the European Coal and Steel Community*, Weidenfeld & Nicolson, London.
Urwin, D. (1995) *The Community of Europe*, Longman, London.

# Annex A: Chronology from 1948 to 2002

| Date | | Event | Explanation |
|---|---|---|---|
| 1948 | 16 Apr | OEEC | Organization for European Economic Co-operation (OEEC) established |
| 1950 | 9 May | Schuman Plan | French Foreign Minister Robert Schuman proposes the establishment of the European Coal and Steel Community (ECSC). Schuman was inspired by Jean Monnet's vision of building Europe step by step. 9 May is celebrated as the Day of Europe |
| 1952 | 1 Jan. | ECSC | The ECSC is established for 50 years; expired 23 Jul. 2002 |
| 1952 | 27 May | EDC | 'The Six' sign the Treaty establishing the European Defence Community (EDC). The project fails as the French National Assembly refuses to ratify the Treaty in 1954 |
| 1953 | 9 Mar. | EPC | A plan for the European Political Community (EPC) is published |
| 1957 | 25 Mar. | EEC | The Six sign Treaties in Rome establishing the European Economic Community (EEC) and the European Atomic Energy Community (Euratom). EEC begins 1 Jan. 1958. |
| 1959 | 21 Jul. | EFTA | European Free Trade Association (EFTA) is established by the Stockholm Convention among Austria, Denmark, Norway, Portugal, Sweden, Switzerland and the United Kingdom. EFTA begins 3 May 1960 |
| 1968 | 1 Jul. | CU completed | Customs Union is completed within the EEC and a common external tariff is established |
| 1969 | 1–2 Dec. | Failed monetary integration launched | At the Hague Summit, EC leaders agree to establish a single market, to accelerate integration, and to introduce Economic and Monetary Union (EMU) by 1980 |
| 1972 | 22 Jan. | First enlargement, signed | Accession Treaties of Denmark, Ireland, Norway and the United Kingdom are signed. Norway withdraws after a negative referendum result |
| 1972 | 22 Jul. | EC–EFTA FTAs | Free trade agreements (FTAs) signed with Austria, Iceland, Portugal, Sweden and Switzerland |
| 1973 | 1 Jan. | First enlargement | The Six become the Nine as Denmark, Ireland and the United Kingdom join the EC. Accession Treaties were signed 22 Jan. 1972. |
| 1973 | 14 May | | Norway signs a free trade agreement with the EEC |
| 1973 | 5 Oct. | | Finland signs a free trade agreement with the EEC |
| 1974 | 9–10 Dec. | European Council formalized | At Paris Summit, EC leaders agree to meet regularly as a European Council |

| Date | | Event | Explanation |
|---|---|---|---|
| 1978 | 6–7 Jul. | EMS founded | Bremen European Council establishes the European Monetary System (EMS) and the European Currency Unit (ECU) |
| 1981 | 1 Jan. | Second enlargement | Greece becomes the tenth EC Member State |
| 1985 | 14 Jun. | EC92 White Paper | Commission presents the Cockfield White Paper on the completion of the single market |
| 1986 | 1 Jan. | Third enlargement | Accession of Spain and Portugal |
| 1986 | 17, 28 Feb. | SEA | Single European Act is signed. Treaty enters into force on 1 Jul. 1987. |
| 1990 | 1 Jul. | EMU stage 1 | First stage of EMU begins |
| 1990 | 10 Oct. | Germany unites | Germany is united and the former German Democratic Republic joins the EEC |
| 1992 | 7 Feb. | Maastricht Treaty | Treaty on European Union is signed in Maastricht, creating the EU; enters into force 1 Nov. 1993 after a difficult ratification process in Denmark and France |
| 1992 | 2 May | EEA | EC and EFTA sign an Agreement establishing the European Economic Area (EEA) |
| 1994 | 1 Jan. | EMU stage 2 | The second stage of EMU begins |
| 1994 | 9–10 Dec. | | Essen European Council agrees strategy on eastern enlargement |
| 1995 | 1 Jan. | Fourth enlargement | Austria, Finland and Sweden join the EU, thus increasing the number of Member States to 15 |
| 1997 | 2 Oct. | Amsterdam Treaty | Treaty of Amsterdam is signed; comes into force on 1 May 1999 |
| 1998 | 1–2 May | Euroland founders | EU leaders decide to launch the euro with Austria, Belgium, Finland, France, Germany, Ireland, Italy, Luxembourg, the Netherlands, Portugal and Spain as initial members |
| 1998 | 1 Jun. | ECB | The European Central Bank (ECB) is established |
| 1999 | 1 Jan. | EMU stage 3 | The euro becomes a currency in its own right |
| 2000 | 7–9 Dec. | Nice Treaty | Treaty of Nice is signed; comes into force on 1 Feb. 2003 after a difficult ratification process in Ireland |
| 2002 | 1 Jan. | Euro cash | Euro notes and coins circulate |

Note: These chronologies are based on the excellent and succinct chronology on the website of the 1999 Finnish Presidency of the EU (http://presidency.finland.fi/doc/eu/eu_5chro.htm), and the extremely detailed chronology on the European Commission's website (http://europa.eu.int/abc/history/index_en.htm); also see the thematic chronologies on http://europa.eu.int/abc/obj/chrono/en/themhome.htm that trace developments in, e.g., EU institutions.

# Annex B: Economic integration in the Treaty of Rome

The ends were political; the means were economic. The architects of the European Economic Community had radical goals in mind when they wrote the Treaty of Rome in 1957. As pointed out in the text, the Treaty's main architect, Jean Monnet, headed an influential pan-European group that was quite bluntly called the Action Committee for the United States of Europe. Economic integration was the announced means of achieving this lofty goal. The idea was to fuse the six national economies into a unified economic area – the Common Market – in which firms, consumers, capital owners and workers faced no discrimination on the basis of nationality.

Articles 2 and 3 of the Treaty (see Box B1-1) set out the main economic goals and integration initiatives among the Six. (Here we use the original numbering of articles since they roughly indicate relative importance, but many articles have been renumbered; interested readers can find a complete correspondence in the appendix of the freely downloadable 'The ABC of Community Law' http://europa.eu.int/eur-lex/en/about/abc/.)

## How to create a unified economic area

To understand the logic of economic integration in the Treaty of Rome, it is useful to group its provisions around the goal of creating a unified economic area. In a unified economic area, firms and consumers located anywhere in the area should have equal opportunities to sell or buy goods in all markets. Moreover, owners of productive factors such as labour and capital should be free to employ their resources in any economic activity anywhere in the area. The necessary steps are presented below.

### Free trade in goods

The most obvious requirement for this is the removal of all barriers to buying and selling across national borders. This is the first order of business in Article 3. Article 3a removes all tariffs and quantitative restrictions among members, thus establishing a free trade area for all goods. Tariffs and quotas, however, are not the only means of discriminating against foreign goods and services at the border. Throughout the ages, governments have proved wonderfully imaginative in developing tariff-like and quota-like barriers against foreign goods and services. To remove such 'non-tariff' barriers, and to prevent new non-tariff barriers from offsetting the tariff liberalization, the Treaty rules out all measures that act like tariffs or quotas (in Article 3a). As part of this, the Treaty, in Article 3e (and elaborated in Articles 74–84), explicitly calls for a common transportation policy to avoid discrimination. This may sound strange from a twenty-first-century perspective, and indeed very little has actually been done, but in the 1950s the rail networks were controlled by national monopolies and trains were the main means of moving traded goods at the time; it was thought that national transportation policies might be used in protectionist ways.

### Common external tariff

Trade can never be truly free among nations if they do not harmonize their tariffs towards non-members. If members had different external tariffs, trade among the Six would have had to have been closely controlled to prevent 'trade deflection', i.e. imports from non-members pouring in through the member with the lowest external tariff. To avoid such controls, Article 3b requires the Six to adopt identical external tariffs thereby turning the free trade area into a customs union. Note that a customs union automatically impels some political integration since it forced the Six to decide together on any change in external trade policy stemming from, for example, multilateral trade negotiations sponsored by the GATT/WTO, or imposition of anti-dumping duties.

## Ensuring undistorted competition

Even a customs union is not enough to create a unified economic area. Trade liberalization can be offset by other public and private measures that operate inside the borders of EU members. The Treaty therefore calls for the institution of a system ensuring that competition in the common market is undistorted (in Article 3f). This general principle is fleshed out in a series of articles that: (i) prohibit trade-distorting subsidies to national producers, (ii) create a common competition policy, (iii) harmonize national laws that affect the operation of the common market, and (iv) call for some harmonization of national taxes. Let us consider why each of these provisions is necessary to ensure undistorted competition.

- *State aids prohibited.* Perhaps the most obvious distortions to competition stem from production subsidies or other forms of government assistance granted to producers located in a particular nation. Such subsidies (called 'state aid' in Euro jargon) allow firms to sell their goods cheaper and/or allow uncompetitive firms to stay in business. Both effects put unsubsidized firms in other nations at a disadvantage and are thus inconsistent with the goal of achieving a unified economic area. Most forms of 'state aid' are prohibited by the Treaty (in Article 92) although a list of exceptions is specified.
- *Anti-competitive behaviour.* Discrimination from a private agreement operating within a Member State – e.g. a cartel or exclusive purchasing deal – can also distort competition. To prevent discrimination arising from such agreements, the Treaty prohibits any agreement that prevents, restricts or distorts competition in the common market. The focus is on two types of agreements, *restrictive business practices* (in Article 85) and *abuse of a dominant position* (in Article 86). Restrictive business practices include a host of unfair practices undertaken by private or state-owned firms. For example, the Treaty explicitly outlaws price-fixing agreements, controls on production, marketing, R&D or investment, and allocation of exclusive territories to firms in order to reduce competition. The Treaty also requires government monopolies of a commercial character to avoid discrimination based on the nationality of suppliers or customers.
- *Approximation of laws.* Another source of discrimination stems from product standards and regulations since differences in national laws, regulations, standards and practices can have a dramatic impact on competition by indirectly favouring products made by national firms. Moreover, since many product standards are highly technical, so national firms are typically involved in writing a nation's rules. The national firms, quite naturally, advise the government to adopt rules that discriminate in favour of their products. Preventing this form of distortion to competition is the subject of Article 100, which states that Member State laws shall be harmonized ('approximated' in Euro jargon) to allow the proper functioning of the common market.
- *Taxes.* Finally, taxes applied inside Member States can distort competition directly or indirectly by benefiting national firms. On countering this type of discrimination, the Treaty of Rome is weak, requiring only that the Commission consider how taxes can be harmonized in the interest of the common market. Of course, if a particular tax provision clearly benefits a well-identified firm or sector within one Member State, then it could be considered as a subsidy and thus directly forbidden.

## Unrestricted trade in services

This is also considered, as Article 3c establishes the principle of freedom of movement of services.

## Labour and capital market integration

If it works properly, a customs union with undistorted competition allows firms and consumers to buy and sell goods throughout the area without facing discrimination based on nationality. This is sufficient to create a unified economic area as far as the trade in goods is concerned. It is not, however, sufficient to fuse national economies into a unified economic area. Accomplishing this also requires integration of capital and labour markets. Article 3c extends integration to factor markets by instituting a common employment and investment area. It does this by abolishing barriers to the free movement of workers and capital.

■ The basic principles of labour and capital mobility are elaborated in subsequent articles. For instance, the freedom of movement for workers means the elimination of any form of discrimination based on nationality regarding hiring, firing, pay and work conditions (Articles 48–51). The Treaty also explicitly allows workers to travel freely in search of work.

■ As for capital mobility, the Treaty focuses on two types of freedom. The first is the right of any Community firm to set up in another Member State (Articles 52–58). These 'rights of establishment' are essential to integration in sectors with high 'natural' trade barriers, e.g. in sectors such as insurance and banking, where a physical presence in the local market is critical to doing business. The second type concerns financial capital and here the Treaty goes deep. It states (in Articles 67–73) that all restrictions on capital flows (e.g. cross-border investments in stocks and bonds, and direct investment in productive assets by multinationals) shall be abolished. It applies the same to current payments related to capital flows (e.g. the payment of interests and repatriation of profits). But, very little capital-market liberalization was undertaken until the 1980s since the Treaty provided an important loophole. It allowed capital market restrictions when capital movements create disturbances in the functioning of a Member State's capital market. Moreover, it did not set a timetable for this liberalization. As we shall see below, capital market liberalization did not really become a reality for 30 years.

## Exchange rate and macroeconomic co-ordination

Fixed exchanges rates were the norm in the post-war period, and throughout the late 1940s and 1950s nations occasionally found that the level of their fixed exchange rate induced their citizens to purchase a value of foreign products and assets that exceeded foreigners' purchases of domestic goods and assets. Such situations, known as balance-of-payments crises, historically led to many policies – such as tariffs, quotas and competitive devaluations – that would be disruptive in a unified economic area (see Chapter 11 for details). To avoid such disruptions, the Treaty calls for mechanisms for co-ordinating members' macroeconomic policies and for fixing balance of payments crises (in Article 3f). The actual proposals in the Treaty of Rome are quite unspecific, but the Treaty does indicate that national exchange rates are a matter of common concern. This axis of economic integration did not really come to fruition until the adoption of the euro in 1999.

## Common policy in agriculture

In the 1950s, Europe's farm sector was far more important economically than it is today. In most European nations, a fifth or more of all workers were employed in the sector. Moreover, European policies in the sector were far from *laissez-faire*. In reaction to the great economic and social turmoil of the 1920s and 1930s most European nations had adopted highly interventionist policies in agriculture, most of which involved price controls teamed with trade barriers (Milward, 1992). Moreover, in the 1950s, the competitiveness of the Six's farm sectors differed massively. French and Dutch farmers were far more competitive than German farmers. If the Six were to form a truly integrated economic area, trade in farm goods would have to be included. However, sharp differences among the Six prevented the Treaty of Rome writers from including more than the barest sketch of a common policy. They did manage to agree on the goals and general principles in Articles 38–47 and a two-year deadline for establishing the common policy.

## Omitted integration: social policies

The Treaty was enormously ambitious with respect to economic integration. It was, however, noticeably silent on the harmonization of social policies (the set of rules that directly affects labour costs such as wage policies, working hours and conditions, and social benefits). This section considers the economic and political logic behind this omission.

**Box B1-1: Principles of Economic Integration in the Treaty of Rome, Articles 2 and 3**

Article 1 of the Treaty simply announces the establishment of the European Economic Community. The core EEC principles are set out in Articles 2 and 3, quoted here verbatim.

ARTICLE 2. The Community shall have as its task, by establishing a common market and progressively approximating the economic policies of Member States, to promote throughout the Community a harmonious development of economic activities, a continuous and balanced expansion, an increase in stability, an accelerated raising of the standard of living and closer relations between the States belonging to it.

ARTICLE 3. For the purposes set out in Article 2, the activities of the Community shall include, as provided in this Treaty and in accordance with the timetable set out therein:

(a) the elimination, as between Member States, of customs duties and of quantitative restrictions on the import and export of goods, and of all other measures having equivalent effect;
(b) the establishment of a common customs tariff and of a common commercial policy towards third countries;
(c) the abolition, as between Member States, of obstacles to freedom of movement for persons, services and capital;
(d) the adoption of a common policy in the sphere of agriculture;
(e) the adoption of a common policy in the sphere of transport;
(f) the institution of a system ensuring that competition in the common market is not distorted;
(g) the application of procedures by which the economic policies of Members States can be co-ordinated and disequilibria in their balances of payments remedied;
(h) the approximation of the laws of Members States to the extent required for the proper functioning of the common market;
(i) the creation of a European Social Fund in order to improve employment opportunities for workers and to contribute to the raising of their standard of living;
(j) the establishment of a European Investment Bank to facilitate the economic expansion of the Community by opening up fresh resources;
(k) the association of the overseas countries and territories in order to increase trade and to promote jointly economic and social development.

*Note: You can download the original treaty from http://europa.eu.int/eur-lex/en/search/treaties_founding.html.*

## The difficult politics of social harmonization

Social harmonization is very difficult politically for at least two reasons. First, nations – even nations as similar as the Six – held very different opinions on what types of social policies should be dictated by the government, and since social policy very directly and very continuously touches the lives of most citizens, these opinions tend to be held strongly; much more strongly, than, for example opinions on the common external tariff or the elimination of intra-EEC quotas. The second reason concerns difficulty of viewing social harmonization as a give-and-take exercise.

With tariffs, all Six lower their tariffs against each other's goods. Although the tariffs might not have been identical to start with, there is, manifestly, a certain balance to the notion that we eliminate our tariffs and they eliminate theirs. With social policy, it is much more difficult to view harmonization as providing a similar balance. Harmonization will tend to be viewed as either upward harmonization (e.g. all adopt a 35-hour week) or downward harmonization (e.g. all have to allow stores to open on Sundays). Since the level of social policies in each nation is the outcome of a finely balanced political equilibrium, changes that are 'imposed' by the EU are easy to characterize as undue interference by foreigners, rather than two-way exchange. For instance, it would be hard to view as 'balanced' a demand that Germans allow Sunday shopping in the name of social policy harmonization. The same could be said if France were forbidden from imposing the 35-hour week in the name of European integration.

In addition to social harmonization being significantly more difficult politically, there are economic arguments suggesting that it is not necessary.

## THE ECONOMICS: TWO SCHOOLS OF THOUGHT

Does European economic integration demand harmonization of social policies? This question has been the subject of an intense debate for decades. It arose when the Benelux nations formed their customs union in 1947, when the OEEC was established in 1948, and when the European Coal and Steel Community was created in 1953. From the very beginning of this debate there have been two schools of thought.

One school of thought, the harmonize-before-liberalizing school, holds that international differences in wages and social conditions provide an 'unfair' advantage to countries with more *laissez-faire* social policies. In contrast, the no-need-to-harmonize school argues that wages and social policies are reflections of productivity differences and social preferences – differences that wage and exchange rate adjustments will counter. This school rejects calls for harmonization and notes that, in any case, social policies tend to converge as all nations get richer.

The harmonize-before-you-liberalize school is the easier to explain. To illustrate the point, consider the impact of altering social policies in only one nation when trade in goods is already free. Moreover, suppose that exchange rates between nations – France and Italy for example – were immutably fixed and, importantly, that both French and Italian wage rates were somehow fixed. Under these assumptions, the imposition of a 35-hour working week in France without a change in the weekly pay to French workers would have severe implications for French competitiveness, with these implications felt most heavily in labour-intensive sectors. Every French company would see its wage costs rise by 5/40, i.e. 12.5 per cent. This would force French firms to raise prices in the face of unchanged Italian prices. The result would be an important loss of sales by French firms and a corresponding reduction in French production and employment.

With this small example, it is easy to see the harmonize-first argument. If nations initially have very different social policies, then lowering trade barriers will give nations with low social standards an unbalanced advantage, assuming that exchange rates and wages do not adjust.

The other school of thought – i.e. whose ideas prevailed in the Treaty of Rome – points out that wages and/or exchange rates do adjust. In the case discussed above, either the Franc would depreciate, thereby lowering French wages *vis-à-vis* Italian wages in a coordinated fashion, or, if exchange rates were fixed, the resulting unemployment would lead to a reduction in French take-home wages to the point where French competitiveness was restored. This line of thinking involves reliance on the functioning of markets and so it is less easily grasped.

See Annex C for a more formal analysis of the comparison of the two schools of thought on social policy harmonization.

# Annex C: Social policy's exclusion: the economics of general versus specific measures

When policies that are applied to all sectors, they are called 'general' policies. Those that are applied to only some sectors are called 'specific' policies. As we shall see, 'general' policies will lead to wage adjustments that fully, or at least largely, offset the competitiveness effects. For this reason, the no-need-to-harmonize school felt that social policies did not have to be harmonized because social policies are typically general policies.

To get a handle on the basic issues, we make strong assumptions to radically simplify the range of issues at hand. Consider France as a small nation in the sense that the prices faced by French firms are fixed by international trade. Moreover, suppose there are just two industries, chemicals and textiles. The two industries' demands for labour are quite different with textiles using labour more intensively. A handy way to measure labour intensity is by the fraction of total production cost due to labour cost, i.e. wages and payroll taxes such as social security and retirement benefits. We suppose that for textiles, 75 per cent of the cost is due to labour, while for chemical the figure is just 25 per cent. Given this, the textile labour demand curve will be flatter since a given rise in wages will have a bigger impact on costs and prices and therefore will result in a bigger reduction in output and employment by the sector.

In Fig. C1-1, the solid lines show the labour demand curves for each industry in the two left curves and the aggregate French labour demand in the right curve. In the right curve, the labour supply curve is also shown with a solid line. It is vertical since we suppose, for simplicity, that the labour force is of a fixed size. If there were no labour unions or government regulations in operation, the wage would eventually adjust to ensure full employment. This equilibrium wage rate is marked $w_{lf}$ for 'laissez-faire'.

Now suppose the French government adopted a whole series of social policies, e.g. limits on working hours, obligatory retirement benefits, maternity leave, sick leave, six weeks of annual holidays, etc. Importantly, suppose that these policies apply to both sectors, i.e. they are 'general' policies. These policies would undoubtedly be good for most workers. Indeed, many of these are

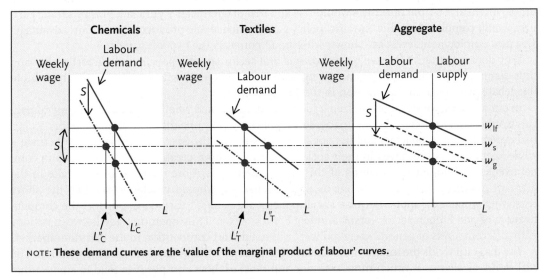

NOTE: **These demand curves are the 'value of the marginal product of labour' curves.**

FIGURE C1-1: SOCIAL POLICY AND DISTORTIONS: GENERAL VERSUS SPECIFIC POLICIES viewed as necessities in advanced industrial societies. However, such policies are expensive for firms. To be specific, suppose that they raise the cost of employing workers by $S$ euros per week. This shows up as a downward shift (by $S$) of the labour demand curves in both the chemical and textile industries and thus the aggregate demand curve as well. These new curves are shown with dashed lines.

The new equilibrium wage with the general policy will be $w_g$, which is exactly $S$ lower than the *laissez-faire* wage. Why does the weekly take-home pay fall when social policies are imposed? Competitive firms hire workers up to the point where the total labour cost equals the weekly productivity of workers. Firms cannot pay higher labour costs if they want to avoid losing money, and they cannot pay any lower costs, since we are assuming that the labour market is competitive. Without social policies, the total labour cost at full employment is $w_{lf}$, so we know that this is the highest labour cost that firms can support with full employment. Importantly, this level is fixed by the productivity of workers. Given this fixity, everything – including social policies – that raises non-wage labour costs must force down the take-home pay of workers. In a competitive market, workers are paid their marginal product; in essence, social policies are a way of 'forcing' workers to take part of their remuneration in the form of non-wage 'payment', e.g. six weeks of paid holiday, or generous sick leave.

Next, consider the impact of these social policies on the pattern of production in the French economy. As the left panels show, neither sector changes its level of employment. Consequently, the imposition of the social policies would have no impact on French production and therefore no impact on French trade. The point here is that the wages adjusted to ensure that the competitiveness of the French textile and chemical sectors were unchanged.

The analysis, however, would be quite different if the social policies were only imposed on, say, the chemical sector. In this case, textile's labour demand curve would correspond to the original solid line, but the chemical industry's demand would correspond to the dashed line. The aggregate labour demand would be the dotted line shown in the right panel, which is in between the solid and dashed lines. Here we see that the French take-home wage would fall somewhat, to $w_s$, with the sector-specific policy. As a result, the French textile sector would become more competitive (due to the lower wage and the absence of social policies) while French competitiveness in the chemical sector would suffer (the wage drop would not fully offset the extra non-wage costs, $S$). Employment and output of textiles would rise and that of chemicals would fall. France's trade partners would complain that this 'specific' policy gave French textile producers an 'unfair' advantage. The new employment levels are shown with the $L''$ points in the two left panels.

Why does it matter? What we have shown is that sector-specific policies will distort output and thus distort competition in the common market. General policies will not. How is this relevant to the debate over social harmonization in the Treaty of Rome?

In our analysis, we started from free trade in goods and asked whether specific and general policies would be distortionary. In the 1950s, social policies were quite different (France, in particular, had expensive social policies) and the question was whether the Six could implement free trade – while keeping big differences in their social policies – without creating large distortions in competitiveness. Although the analysis of this latter question is more difficult to undertake in the diagram (mainly since prices change as trade opens), you should be able to see that the above reasoning would still apply. Because social policies are general, they do not distort the competitiveness of one French sector versus another French sector. Thus opening trade between nations with different levels of general social policies will not distort competition in the common market.

The diagram yields the unambiguous result that general policies do not distort competition. The real world, as always, is much more complex and most of these complexities tend to suggest that even general policies can have some distortionary effect. For example, if the labour supply were upward sloped, we would have to modify our conclusion (interested readers may want to redraw the diagram to check this). With an upward-sloped labour supply curve, even general social policies will lead to a drop in the equilibrium take-home pay that would not fully offset the extra cost imposed by the social policies. Consequently, total labour cost would rise somewhat in France. This would have different effects on the two sectors. In particular, since textiles is labour-intensive relative to chemicals (as shown by the flatter demand curve), the higher labour costs would reduce French employment in textiles more than it would in chemicals.

In summary, in a more realistic model, the social policies do distort French competitiveness with the labour-intensive sectors suffering disproportionately, but the size of these distortions is likely to be small as long as the policies are 'general'.

In the end, the architects of Europe faced a trade-off. On one hand, harmonizing social policies would have been enormously difficult from a political point of view; this was the cost. On the other hand, such harmonization would have avoided some sort of distortion in the common market; this was the benefit. Since social policies are general rather than specific, the size of these distortions is not large, so the size of the economic benefit of harmonization would have been small. Confronted with large political costs and modest economic gains, Europe's architects decided to omit social policy harmonization (with only minor exceptions).

Indeed, even now at the turn of the century the EU has done very little to harmonize social policies. One important reason for this is that EU Member States have spontaneously adopted social policies that are not radically different and this has managed to keep a cap on pressures for social harmonization.

# 2 Facts, Law, Institutions and the Budget

This chapter covers four separate topics, each of which can be thought of as important background information for the study of the economics of European integration. The chapter starts by presenting some key facts concerning the EU national economies before proceeding to a brief review of the EU's main legal system and principles. EU institutions and legislative processes are the topics of the next two sections. The subsequent section presents the EU's budget, focusing on the questions of what the money is spent on, how it is raised, and who benefits the most financially. The final section presents a summary as usual.

The draft Constitutional Treaty, which was delivered to EU leaders just as this book went to press, proposes a massive reform of the EU's institutional system. At the time of writing, the draft Treaty had been endorsed by EU leaders at their June 2003 meeting and sent to an Intergovernmental Conference (IGC) for further refinement. The IGC is scheduled to start in the fall of 2003 and finish some time in 2004. Since the Constitution would change so much, but so little is decided yet, the Chapter presents only briefly the main institutional changes proposed in the draft Constitution. We will post periodic updates on the Online Learning Centre (OLC) website that refer to this chapter section by section.

## 2.1 Some important facts

The nations of the European Union (EU) and the 'candidate countries' (scheduled to join in 2004) vary enormously in their populations, as the lower panel Fig. 2-1 shows. It is useful to group them into three broad categories: big, small and tiny.

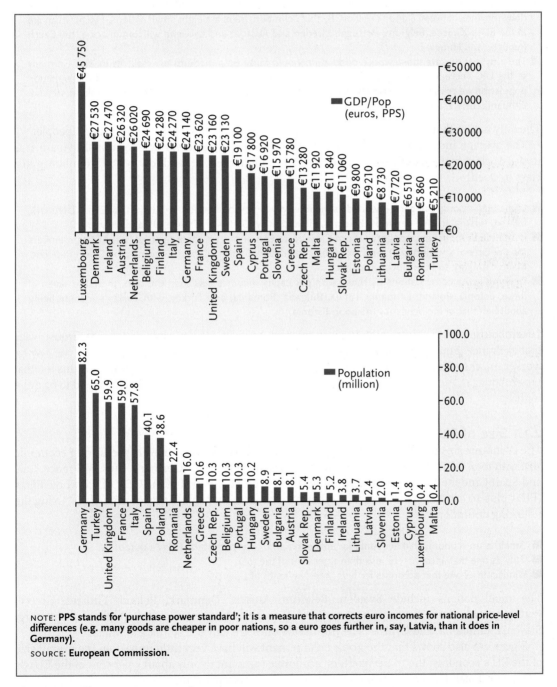

NOTE: **PPS stands for 'purchase power standard'; it is a measure that corrects euro incomes for national price-level differences (e.g. many goods are cheaper in poor nations, so a euro goes further in, say, Latvia, than it does in Germany).**

SOURCE: **European Commission.**

FIGURE 2-1: EUROPEAN NATIONS' POPULATION AND INCOME PER CAPITA, 2001

■ The 'big' nations have 35 million people or more, and there are six of these – the five big EU15 members (Germany, the UK, France, Italy and Spain) and Poland (Turkey also falls in this category, but its membership negotiations have not begun). Germany is substantially larger than the others, more than twice the size of the smallest in the group. The total population of the 'Big-5' accounts for about three-quarters of the 450 million living in the 25 nations consisting of the EU15 and the 10 newcomers.
■ The populations of the 'small' nations are like that of a big city, say London or Paris; to be concrete, we draw the lines between 8 and 11 million. By this definition, there are eight small nations, five of which are in the EU15 (Greece, Belgium, Portugal, Sweden and Austria) and two who will join in 2004, the Czech Republic and Hungary.
■ The 'tiny' nations are those whose population would make up a medium to small city in, say, Germany or the UK. There are 11 of these, but altogether they account for less than 5 per cent of the 25-nation population we consider. Specifically, the tiny nations are the Slovak Republic, Denmark, Finland, Ireland, Lithuania, Latvia, Slovenia, Estonia, Cyprus, Luxembourg and Malta.

The only nation that falls between these categories is the Netherlands, with 16 million people.

The average income level of the people in these nations also varies enormously. Again it is useful to classify the nations into three categories, high, medium and low, with Luxembourg in a class by itself.

■ In the high income category – defined as incomes over €20 000 in 2001 – we have 11 of EU15 (Denmark, Ireland, Austria, the Netherlands, Belgium, Finland, Italy, Germany, France, UK and Sweden).
■ In the medium income category – from €10 000 to €20 000 – are three relatively poor EU15 members (Spain, Greece and Portugal), and six of the candidate countries (Cyprus, Slovenia, the Czech Republic, Malta, Hungary and the Slovak Republic).
■ Defining low income nations as those with per capita incomes less than €10 000, there are seven of these, Estonia, Poland, Lithuania, Latvia, Bulgaria, Romania, and Turkey, with Turkey's income being about half that of the richest-of-the-poor, Estonia.

Luxembourg is in the super-high income category by itself. Its per capita income is almost twice that of France. Since only about 40 per cent of Luxembourgers work, this implies that the *average* worker in the Grand Duchy earns over €100 000 a year! One explanation for this is that Luxembourg is, economically speaking, a medium-sized city and incomes in cities tend to be quite high.

## 2.1.1 Size of EU economies

The economic size distribution of European economies is also very uneven, measuring economic size with total GDP. As Fig. 2-2 shows, just six nations, the 'Big-5' (Germany, the UK, France, Italy and Spain) and the Netherlands, account for more than 80 per cent of the GDP of the whole EU25 (EU15 plus 10 candidate nations). The other nations are either small, tiny or minuscule, using the following definitions:

■ 'Small' is an economy that accounts for between 1 and 3 per cent of the EU25's output
■ 'Tiny' is one that accounts for less than 1 per cent of the total
■ Minuscule as one that accounts for less than one-tenth of 1 per cent.

The small nations include Sweden, Belgium, Austria, Denmark, Poland, Finland, Greece, Portugal and Ireland. The tiny ones are Czech Republic, Hungary, Slovak Republic, Luxembourg, Slovenia, Lithuania, and Cyprus. The minuscule ones are Latvia, Estonia and Malta.

Figure 2-2 also shows that the 2004 enlargement will have very little impact on the overall size of the EU's economy; the 10 newcomers' economies amount to only about 5 per cent of the EU15's GDP, with Poland alone accounting for about half of this 5 per cent.

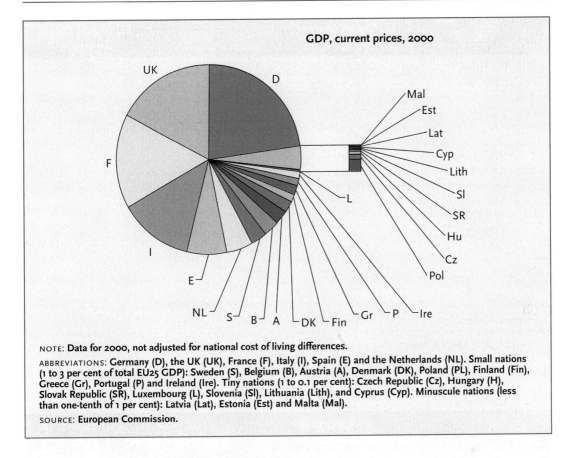

**GDP, current prices, 2000**

NOTE: **Data for 2000, not adjusted for national cost of living differences.**
ABBREVIATIONS: **Germany (D), the UK (UK), France (F), Italy (I), Spain (E) and the Netherlands (NL). Small nations (1 to 3 per cent of total EU25 GDP): Sweden (S), Belgium (B), Austria (A), Denmark (DK), Poland (PL), Finland (Fin), Greece (Gr), Portugal (P) and Ireland (Ire). Tiny nations (1 to 0.1 per cent): Czech Republic (Cz), Hungary (H), Slovak Republic (SR), Luxembourg (L), Slovenia (Sl), Lithuania (Lith), and Cyprus (Cyp). Minuscule nations (less than one-tenth of 1 per cent): Latvia (Lat), Estonia (Est) and Malta (Mal).**
SOURCE: **European Commission.**

FIGURE 2-2: SIZE DISTRIBUTION OF EU25 ECONOMIES

## 2.1.2 Trade

The EU trades mainly with Europe, especially with itself; about two-thirds of EU exports and imports are to or from other Western European nations, and if we add in Central and Eastern European nations and the Commonwealth of Independent States (CIS), the figure rises to about three-quarters. The EU's exports to North America amount to only 10 per cent of its exports, and Asia's share is only 8 per cent. As far as individual nations are concerned, the USA is the EU's biggest single partner followed by Switzerland on the export side and China on the import side.

About 80 per cent of EU exports consist of industrial goods both for intra-EU trade and external trade. Especially for the trade within the EU much of this involves two-way trade in similar goods – what is often called 'intraindustry' trade.

The members and soon-to-be members of the EU are all comparatively open economies when it comes to trade in goods. As Table 2-2 shows, the openness ratio (average of imports and exports over GDP) for the EU15 ranges from 17 per cent for Greece up to 75 per cent for the Belgium–Luxembourg economic union (these nations have been in a customs union and monetary union since just after the Second World War). The figures for the 10 newcomers are all higher than that for Greece. By way of comparison, note that the same figures for Japan and the USA are 10 per cent and 8 per cent respectively, so even the most closed of EU members is twice as reliant on exports as the USA.

| | EU Export shares by region | | | EU Import shares by region |
|---|---|---|---|---|
| Western Europe | 67% | Western Europe | | 66% |
| North America | 10% | Asia | | 12% |
| Asia | 8% | North America | | 8% |
| CEECs and CIS | 6% | CEECs and CIS | | 6% |
| Africa | 3% | Africa | | 3% |
| Middle East | 3% | Latin America | | 2% |
| Latin America | 2% | Middle East | | 2% |
| | Top 7 partners | | | |
| European Union (15) | 62% | European Union (15) | | 61% |
| United States | 9% | United States | | 7% |
| Switzerland | 3% | China | | 3% |
| Japan | 2% | Japan | | 3% |
| Poland | 1% | Switzerland | | 2% |
| China | 1% | Russian Federation | | 1% |
| Russian Federation | 1% | Poland | | 1% |

SOURCE: WTO's Annual Report, 2002.

TABLE 2-1: EU15's GLOBAL TRADE PATTERN, 2001

| | Openness ratio | Exports to EU15 as % total exports | | Openness ratio | Exports to EU15 as % total exports |
|---|---|---|---|---|---|
| Greece | 17% | 49% | Malta | 44% | 48% |
| Italy | 22% | 51% | Slovenia | 25% | 57% |
| Finland | 30% | 53% | Turkey | 62% | 58% |
| Sweden | 33% | 53% | Latvia | 69% | 59% |
| Germany | 29% | 53% | Bulgaria | 56% | 59% |
| United Kingdom | 21% | 54% | Slovak Rep. | 45% | 62% |
| Ireland | 61% | 57% | Lithuania | 38% | 66% |
| France | 22% | 58% | Cyprus | 62% | 67% |
| Austria | 36% | 59% | Romania | 26% | 68% |
| Denmark | 29% | 59% | Czech Rep. | 36% | 68% |
| Spain | 23% | 69% | Poland | 51% | 69% |
| BLEU | 75% | 75% | Hungary | 67% | 70% |
| Netherlands | 55% | 76% | Estonia | 25% | 70% |
| Portugal | 29% | 80% | | | |

SOURCE: Eurostat and IMF Direction of Trade Statistics, 2002.

TABLE 2-2: EU25 OPENNESS AND DEPENDENCE ON EU MARKET, 2001

The table also shows how important the EU15 market is for the nations listed. For the EU15 nations, the share of total exports going to the EU15 ranges between 50 and 80 per cent, with most of the shares around 60 per cent. The shares for the candidate countries are in a similar range.

## 2.2 EU law

One of the most important things to understand about the EU is its supranational legal system. By the standards of virtually every other international organization in the world, this system is extremely supranational – e.g. even the highest courts in EU Member States can be and have been overruled by the EU's Court of Justice, whose members are drawn from all Member States. While the topic of EU law is as intricate as it is fascinating, we only present the barest outlines here, focusing on the elements that are essential for understanding the decision making process in particular, and the economics of European integration more generally.

Note that this section is largely based on the freely downloadable book by Borchardt (1999), *The ABC of Community Law* (http://europa.eu.int/eur-lex/en/about/abc/) and www.riksdagen.se/english/eu/eufacts/index.asp, the excellent website of Sweden's Riksdag (parliament). Interested readers will want to consult these sources for further details.

### 2.2.1 'Sources' of EU law

The legal systems of most democratic nations are based on a constitution. At the time this book went to press, the EU did not have a constitution, although a draft had been endorsed at the June 2003 European Council summit in Thessaloniki, Greece. One may then wonder: 'Where did the EU's legal system come from?' As is true of so many things in the EU, a complete answer to this question would fill a book or two, but the short answer can be given in a few paragraphs. Again, history provides the best organizing principle for the answer. We start with the Treaty establishing the European Economic Community, also known as the Treaty of Rome, or TEEC for short. (Note on notation: in legal matters, it is important to distinguish between the European Community and the European Union, so in this section we use EU and EC to mean different things. Also, the old name for the EC was the European Economic Community, EEC, but we use EC throughout.)

The Treaty of Rome committed EC members to a series of general goals and a number of specific economic integration initiatives. It also established a set of decision making institutions and empowered these institutions to issue laws that would apply to all EC members. In short, the Treaty of Rome is the wellspring of EC law, but – and this is where the complexity comes in – the Treaty also created ways of making new laws and modifying old ones.

In the early days, the key institutions from the law-making point of view were: (i) the Commission, which was tasked with drawing up laws necessary to implement the Treaty, and (ii) the Council of Ministers, consisting of a representative from each Member State, which was tasked with accepting or rejecting Commission proposals (the European Parliament gained power later). Another key institution from the legal point of view was the Court of Justice. The Court was empowered to interpret the Treaty and subsequent EC laws. As we shall see below, the legislative process in today's EU is massively complex, but in those simpler times one could sum it up as follows: the Commission proposes, the Council disposes and the Court rules.

### 2.2.2 EC legal system: main principles

The Court, having been created by the TEEC, set about the task of creating the Community's legal system. In particular, two landmark cases in 1963 and 1964 established the key principles of the EC legal system. According to Borchardt (1999, p. 24), EC law (also known as 'Community Law') was established by the Court on the basis of:

- the EU institutions ensuring that actions by the EC take account of all members' interests, i.e. the Community's interest; and
- the transfer of national power to the Community, far exceeding the degree observed in other international organizations.

The key principles of the EC legal system are:

- *Autonomy*: The EC legal system is independent of the Member States' legal orders.
- *Direct Applicability*: Community law has the force of law in Member States so that Community law can be fully and uniformly applicable throughout the EU. As part of this, Community law gives both rights and obligations on EU members and their citizens. For example, an EU citizen can take his/her own government to the Court over matters of EC law.
- *Primacy of Community law*: This means that Community law has the final say. For example, say the highest court in France rules one way in a case on a matter pertaining to intra-EC imports. If the EU Court rules in a different way on the same case, the French court's decision is overruled and cannot be appealed. This principle ensures that Community law cannot be altered by national, regional or local laws in any Member State.

These principles, which are still the main principles of today's Community legal system, make it clear that EC law contains some powerfully supranational elements – supranational in the sense that a Member State may be forced to comply with a Court ruling even if it disagrees. This is one of the features that make the EU unique in the world.

### 2.2.3 Ever wider and deeper?

Over the years, the original Treaty was amended repeatedly, and the Council–Commission team produced a steady stream of new laws. Most of these laws and Treaty changes deepened the degree of economic integration among members in areas where integration had already begun. For example, they deepened the degree of trade integration by removing non-tariff barriers after all tariffs had been removed. However, some of the Treaty amendments and new laws had the effect of widening the areas in which integration occurred. Some of these laws and amendments involved the EU in, for instance, environmental policy, social policy, and exchange rate policy as well as the free movement of capital and the harmonization of VAT tax rates.

Up to the Maastricht Treaty, all this progressive widening and deepening of European integration was subject to the supranationality of Community Law and the supranational decision making procedures laid out in the Treaty of Rome. For example, the rules governing the detailed implementation of deeper economic integration (called 'completion of the internal market') were adopted by majority voting of EU members. This meant that all Member States had to comply with such rules, even those Member States that voted against them. Moreover, the Court was the ultimate authority over disputes involving all such rules.

This supranationality created two related problems when faced with the diversity of Member States' opinions on how deep and how broad EU integration should be.

On the one hand, some EU members – the 'vanguard' – wished to widen European integration to areas that were not covered in the original Treaties. On the other hand, another group of members – call them the 'doubters' – worried that the supranational decision making procedures were producing an irresistible increase in the depth and breadth of European integration. Particularly worrisome was the ability of the Court to interpret the Treaty of Rome and subsequent amendments. The Treaty of Rome says that the EC could make laws in areas not mentioned in the Treaty, if the Court rules that doing so was necessary to attain Treaty objectives. The problem for the doubters was that the objectives of the original Treaty of Rome were enormously ambitious (see Chapter 1 on this point). For example, its first line says that the members are 'determined to lay the foundations of an ever closer union among the peoples of Europe'. The conjunction of the Treaty's ambitious objectives and the Court's ability to sanction law making in areas not explicitly mentioned in the Treaties seemed to put almost no limit on how much national sovereignty might eventually be transferred to the EU level. (For more discussion of this point see www.europarl.eu.int/factsheets/1_2_2_en.htm.)

## MAASTRICHT AND THE DIFFERENCE BETWEEN EU LAW AND EC LAW

Both concerns were addressed when EU members adopted a second key Treaty – the Treaty on European Union (Maastricht Treaty) – which developed the 'pillars' approach. After the Maastricht Treaty a clear line was drawn between the types of policies that could be subject to supranational decision making (so-called first-pillar areas) and those where integration would require the consent of all integrating members (second- and third-pillar areas). This created the distinction between EC law, which is highly supranational, and EU law, which is considered much less supranational since it also includes the weaker parts pertaining to the second and third pillars.

The upshot of all this is simple. Today's European Union and its legal system are based on two main treaties – the Treaty establishing the European Community, or TEC (the post-1993 name for the TEEC) and the Treaty on European Union, or TEU. There is a raft of other treaties, but these either modify the two main treaties (Single European Act, Amsterdam Treaty, Nice Treaty, etc.), or are important only in very specific areas (Treaty establishing the European Coal and Steel Community, Treaty establishing the European Atomic Energy Community, etc.). As usual, the full picture is more complex. Interested readers will find Borchardt (1999) very helpful in filling in the details. Also the European Parliament's factsheets 1.1.1 to 1.1.3 provide a detailed but highly readable history of the Treaties' developments (www.europarl.eu.int/factsheets/default_en.htm).

The pillar structure is important for understanding the EU's institutions and decision making procedures, so we turn now to considering it in more detail.

## 2.2.4 The EU's 3-pillar structure

What is the difference between the European Community and the European Union? Many well-informed Europeans make it through life never knowing the answer to this question. Indeed throughout this book we use the term 'EU' to refer to both the EC and the EU, unless a distinction is critical to the point at hand. Since the distinction is important when it comes to institutions and laws, we provide the answer.

The first pillar, which encompasses the vast majority of EU activity, is called the European Community (formerly known as the European Economic Community, or European Communities). The second pillar concerns 'security' matters, and the third concerns 'justice' matters. The European Union is the 'roof' for the three pillars. As Fig. 2-3 shows, saying 'EU' logically implies that one is talking about all three pillars, but because 'European Union' sounds better, the term EU is used almost universally in the media and by politicians even when they are talking about purely first-pillar issues.

The distinguishing feature of the first pillar is the degree of supranationality involved in the decision making. First-pillar issues include all the Treaty-based integration that had taken place up to the Maastricht Treaty in 1993. For example, the Common Market, the Single Market Programme, Competition Policy, the Common Agricultural Policy, etc. It also includes the Economic and Monetary Union (EMU) and thus comprises the European Central Bank, the single money, and all the attendant rules and procedures.

The second pillar consists of the Common Foreign and Security Policy, and the third pillar of Justice and Home Affairs. Integration efforts in second- and third-pillar areas are intergovernmental in the sense that such efforts are undertaken by direct negotiation among Member States

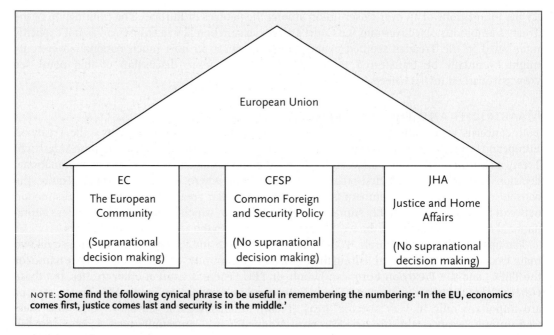

NOTE: **Some find the following cynical phrase to be useful in remembering the numbering: 'In the EU, economics comes first, justice comes last and security is in the middle.'**

FIGURE 2-3: THE 3-PILLAR STRUCTURE

and any agreement requires unanimity. As we shall see below, the Amsterdam and Nice treaties subtly modified the pillar structure by allowing 'clubs' of like-minded nations to pursue deeper integration, subject to some controls.

The draft Constitutional Treaty would remove the three pillars, making all EU decisions subject to the power of the EU Court. Since the three-pillar system was set up, in part, to ensure that only first-pillar issues were subject the Court's rulings, this aspect may be reformed. See the OLC website for an update on the current status of the Constitution.

## 2.2.5 Types of EU legislation and 'watchdogs'

EC law consists of rules that are usefully divided into primary legislation and secondary legislation. Primary legislation is made up of the treaties; secondary legislation consists of the collection of decisions made by EU institutions (see Box 2-1 for further details on the types of secondary legislation).

To ensure that EU law works properly in all parts of the EU, the Commission, the Court of Justice and national authorities in the Member States are responsible for surveillance and enforcement. Of these three, the Commission is the main 'watchdog'. It can fine a Member State for certain violations and can bring a case against a Member State in the Court of Justice.

As mentioned above, the vast majority of EU activities that get covered on TV, radio and in the newspapers are first-pillar activities. The integration in these areas heavily involves the five main EU institutions, so we shall now describe them in some detail.

BOX 2-1: SECONDARY LEGISLATION: 'ACTS OF COMMUNITY LAW'
There are five types of EU legislation other than the Treaties.
A *regulation* applies to all Member States, companies, authorities and citizens. Regulations

apply as they are written, i.e. they are not transposed into other laws or provisions. They apply immediately upon coming into force.

A *directive* may apply to any number of Member States. However, directives only set out the result to be achieved. The Member States decide for themselves, within a prescribed time frame, what needs to be done to comply with the conditions set out in the directive. For instance, one Member State may have to introduce new legislation, while another may not need to take any action at all if it already meets the requirements set out in the directive.

A *decision* is a legislative act that applies to a specific Member State, company or citizen.

*Recommendations* and *opinions* are two other types of legislative acts. They are not legally binding.

## 2.3 The 'Big-5' institutions

While there are many, many EU agencies, bodies and committees, one can achieve a very good understanding of how the EU works knowing only about the 'Big-5' institutions: the Council of the European Union (generally known by its old name, the Council of Ministers), the European Council, the European Commission, the European Parliament and the EU Court.

For information on the other institutions, see http://europa.eu.int/inst-en.htm. For further details on the 'Big-5', see the excellent websites maintained by the European Parliament and the Swedish Parliament (www.europarl.eu.int/factsheets and www.riksdagen.se/english/eu/index.asp); indeed much of the information in this section is based on those sites.[1]

As mentioned above, the 2003 draft of the Constitutional Treaty proposed many important changes in the institutions. You can find out what parts of this section are revised by the Constitution by visiting the OLC website.

### 2.3.1 Council of the European Union

The Council of the European Union – also known as the Council of Ministers or 'the Council' for short – is the EU's main decision making body. It is also the final legislative authority since almost every piece of legislation is subject to approval by the Council. The Council consists of one representative from each EU member. The national representatives must be authorized to commit their governments to Council decisions, so Council members are the government ministers responsible for the relevant area – the finance ministers on budget issues, agriculture ministers on farm issues, etc. Since all EU governments are elected (democracy is a criteria for membership) and the Council members represent their governments, the fact that the Council is the final legislative authority means that it is also the ultimate point of democratic control over the EU's actions and law making.

The main task of the Council is to adopt new EU laws (directive, regulations, rules, etc.). Most of these laws concern measures necessary to implement the Treaties, but they also include measures concerning the EU budget and international agreements involving the EU. The Council also is supposed to co-ordinate the general economic policies of the Member States in the context of the Economic and Monetary Union (EMU) – for example, the famous 3 per cent deficit rule is part of this co-ordination effort. On many issues, passing new laws also requires approval of the European Parliament, so on these issues, the Council's legislative power is shared with the Parliament.

In addition to these tasks that fall under the first pillar (the Community pillar), the Council takes the decisions pertaining to Common Foreign and Security Policies and measures pertaining to police and judicial co-operation in criminal matters.

[1] Interested readers may also want to consult the 400-page book by Peterson and Shackleton (2002).

The Economics of European Integration: **Part I**

SOURCE: **European Commission Audiovisual Library.**

FIGURE 2-4: HEADQUARTERS OF THE COUNCIL OF MINISTERS IN BRUSSELS

The Council has two main decision making rules. On the most important issues – such as Treaty changes, the accession of new members, and setting the multi-year budget plan – Council decisions are by unanimity. On most issues (about 80 per cent of all Council decisions), the Council decides on the basis of what is known as 'qualified majority voting', (QMV). Understanding the QMV rules takes some effort, but is essential for an understanding of the EU.

### QUALIFIED MAJORITY VOTING (QMV) AND 'SHADOW' VOTING

The QMV rules are in flux at the time this book went to print since at least two changes in the procedure are foreseen. To keep things simple, we start with the procedure that was in place in 2003 before turning to the changes.

The basic form of the QMV procedure has been unchanged from its origin in the 1958 Treaty of Rome right up to the year 2003. Each member's minister casts a certain number of votes, with the more populous members having more votes. Large members, however, have fewer votes than population-proportionality would suggest; for example, France with its 60 million citizens has 10 votes while Denmark with its 5 million citizens has 3. The total number of votes in the EU15 is 87. The threshold for a winning majority, what is called a 'qualified majority', is 62 votes. This means that a majority of about 71 per cent of all votes is required to adopt a proposal.

The implications of this system are complex. Since bigger members have more votes, 71 per cent of the votes does not mean 71 per cent of members. Three large members voting 'no' could block adoption even if the other 12 voted 'yes'. And since small nations get far more votes than strict population-proportionality would suggest, 71 per cent of the votes does not mean 71 per cent of the EU population. The 71 per cent threshold can theoretically be reached, for example, by a coalition of just eight members representing 58 per cent of the EU population. See Chapter 3 for details on how this voting affects the distribution of power among EU members and EU institutions.

Note that even though QMV is the basis of most Council decisions, the Council rarely votes – preferring instead to decide things by 'consensus'. This does not diminish the importance of QMV and voting weights. If nations know they would be outvoted, if a vote were to be held, they usually join the consensus to be collegial. Thus, even without formal voting, nations go through a mental process of 'shadow voting' before deciding to join the consensus – that is, they talk to other members to consider what the outcome would be if a vote were held.

## TREATY OF NICE AND ACCESSION TREATY REFORMS

As mentioned in Chapter 1, enlargement of the EU was widely seen as requiring a reform of the QMV rules. The basic problem is that most of the 10 newcomers are small or tiny. Because the vote share of small countries was far bigger than their population share under the vote allocation rules that were used in previous enlargements, most observers predicted that decision making would become extremely difficult in the enlarged EU (see Chapter 3 for more on this point). To redress this potential problem, EU15 leaders agreed to a change in the rules. The political agreement to change the QMV system was contained in the Treaty of Nice, but it is the Treaty of Accession for the newcomers that makes the new rules binding. The Accession Treaty reforms – which are scheduled to take effect in November 2004 – change qualified-majority voting in two main ways. [2]

First, it makes the system more complex. It keeps the basic shape of the current framework but adds two new criteria that a winning majority must meet. After the enlargement, a proposition passes the Council only when the coalition of yes-voters meets *three* criteria: votes, number of members, and population. Specifically, the triple criteria require that a winning coalition must have at least 72 per cent of the Council votes (232 votes of the 321 Council votes in the EU25). It must also represent at least 50 per cent of the EU Member States, and at least 62 per cent of the EU population.

Second, it reallocates the number of votes in a way that favours the larger nations, as Fig. 2-5 shows.

## ANOTHER REFORM? THE DRAFT CONSTITUTIONAL TREATY

Since the rules in the Nice and Accession treaties were widely viewed as failing to meet the goal of maintaining the Council's ability to act (see Chapter 3 for details), the European Convention proposed a radical reform of QMV procedures in the 2003 draft Constitutional Treaty. Namely, a qualified majority should consist of at least half the Member States representing at least 60 per cent of the EU population. However, as the draft Constitution also says that the new rules will not take effect until 2009, the Nice rules may be in place for several years. Note also that the draft Constitution will be re-worked by an Intergovernmental Conference in 2003 and 2004, and as the new voting rules are among the most controversial changes, the proposed reforms may never be implemented. For an update on the latest developments, see the OLC website for this textbook.

## EU PRESIDENCY AND CONFUSING TERMINOLOGY

In the EU15, one EU member holds the Presidency at any one time, with this office rotating among EU members every six months. The Council of Ministers is chaired by the presiding member and generally meets in Brussels (April, June and October meetings are held in Luxembourg). For more details see the Council's website, which was at ue.eu.int/en/summ.htm in 2003. Although the Council is a single institution, there is a somewhat confusing practice of using different names to describe the Council according to the matters being discussed. For example, when the Council

---

[2] You can download the Accession Treaty from http://www.europarl.eu.int/enlargement_new/treaty/default_en.htm. The full document is 30 Mb, but the key points are in the 'Act' which is only 240 kb.

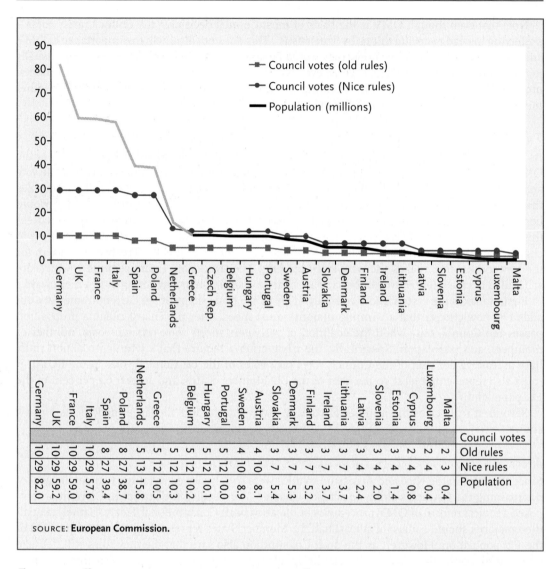

| | Germany | UK | France | Italy | Spain | Poland | Netherlands | Greece | Belgium | Hungary | Portugal | Sweden | Austria | Slovakia | Denmark | Finland | Ireland | Lithuania | Latvia | Slovenia | Estonia | Cyprus | Luxembourg | Malta | Council votes |
|---|---|---|---|---|---|---|---|---|---|---|---|---|---|---|---|---|---|---|---|---|---|---|---|---|---|
| Old rules | 10 | 10 | 10 | 10 | 8 | 8 | 5 | 5 | 5 | 5 | 5 | 5 | 4 | 4 | 3 | 3 | 3 | 3 | 3 | 3 | 3 | 3 | 2 | 2 | 2 |
| Nice rules | 29 | 29 | 29 | 29 | 27 | 27 | 13 | 12 | 12 | 12 | 12 | 12 | 10 | 10 | 7 | 7 | 7 | 7 | 7 | 4 | 4 | 4 | 4 | 4 | 3 |
| Population | 82.0 | 59.2 | 59.0 | 57.6 | 39.4 | 38.7 | 15.8 | 10.5 | 10.3 | 10.2 | 10.1 | 10.0 | 8.9 | 8.1 | 5.4 | 5.3 | 5.2 | 3.7 | 3.7 | 2.4 | 2.0 | 1.4 | 0.8 | 0.4 | 0.4 |

SOURCE: **European Commission.**

FIGURE 2-5: ENLARGEMENT AND THE REWEIGHING OF COUNCIL VOTES IN FAVOUR OF LARGE NATIONS

addresses EMU-linked matters, such as deciding whether a nation has violated the Maastricht budget restrictions, it is called the Economic and Financial Affairs Council, or 'ECOFIN' to insiders.

Note that under the proposed changes in the 2003 draft Constitutional Treaty, the Presidency would cease to rotate among nations, being assumed instead by a single person serving for a two-and-a-half-year term. The chair of the Council of Minister meetings, however, would rotate among EU members.

## 2.3.2 The European Council

The European Council consists of the leaders of each EU member plus the President of the European Commission. It is by far the most influential institution because its members are the leaders of their respective nations. The European Council provides broad guidelines for EU policy and thrashes out the final compromises necessary to conclude the most sensitive aspects of EU business, including reforms of the major EU policies, the EU's multi-year budget plan, Treaty changes, and the final terms of enlargements.

The European Council meets at least twice a year (June and December), but meets more frequently if the EU faces major political problems. The highest profile meetings are those held at the end of each six-month term of the EU Presidency. These meetings are important political and media events since the European Council's decisions determine all of the EU's major moves. For example, major steps in European integration are announced at these meeting. The most important decisions of each Presidency are contained in a document, known as the 'Conclusions of the Presidency', which is published at the end of the each European Council meeting. For example, the decision to accept the 10 new members in the 2004 enlargement was announced in the Presidency's Conclusions released after the December 2002 European Council in Copenhagen.

See http://ue.eu.int/en/Info/eurocouncil/index.htm for recent Conclusions.

One peculiarity of the EU is that the European Council has no formal role in EU law making even though it is the most influential body in the process (this is why we do not have a photograph of its headquarters – the European Council had no headquarters in 2003, its business was conducted in the EU nation who had the Presidency). The political decisions of the European Council have to be translated into law following the standard legislative procedures that we review below. These procedures involve the Commission, the Council of Ministers and, depending upon the area, the European Parliament.

Confusingly, the European Council and the Council of Ministers are often both called the Council. The Council of Ministers and the European Council should also not be confused with the Council of Europe (an international organization that is entirely unrelated to the EU – indeed, it was set up before the EU was created).

The 2003 draft Constitution proposes to make the European Council a formal part of the EU institutional structure and, as mentioned above, to create a President of the European Council that is selected by EU Member States.

## 2.3.3 Commission

The European Commission is at the heart of the EU's institutional structure and is a driving force behind deeper and wider European integration. This body, which is based in Brussels, has three main roles:

- ■ to propose legislation to the Council and Parliament
- ■ to administer and implement EU policies
- ■ to provide surveillance and enforcement of EU law in co-ordination with the EU Court.

As part of its third role, the Commission is considered to be the 'guardian of the Treaties', i.e. the body that is ultimately charged with ensuring that the Treaties are implemented and enforced.

The Commission also represents the EU at some international negotiations, such as those relating to trade and co-operation with non-member nations. The Commission's negotiating stances at such meetings are closely monitored by EU members.

### COMMISSIONERS AND THE COMMISSION'S COMPOSITION

Before the 2004 enlargement, the European Commission was always made up of one Commissioner from each EU member with an extra Commissioner from the Big-5 (Germany, UK, France, Italy and Spain in the EU15). This included the President (Romano Prodi up to 2005), two

Vice-Presidents and 17 other Commissioners. In the enlarged Union, each nation will have one Commissioner. The 2003 draft Constitution proposes to limit the number of 'European Commissioners' to 15 with the nationalities of these 15 rotating evenly among all members. This would be a big reform as it breaks the tradition of having at least one Commissioner from each member. To mitigate the problem of non-representation, the draft proposes the creation of a lesser post, called 'non-voting Commissioner', with one of these from each nation that did not have a European Commissioner. (See Chapter 3 for details and the OLC website for updates.)

In the EU15, Commissioners are chosen by their own national governments, but the choices are subject to political agreement by other members. The Commission as a whole, and the Commission President individually, must also be approved by the European Parliament. Note, however, that Commissioners are not supposed to act as national representatives. They should not accept or seek instruction from their country's government. In practice, Commissioners are generally quite independent of their home governments, but since they have typically held high political office in their home nations, they are naturally sensitive to issues that are of particular concern in their home nations. This ensures that all decisive national sensitivities are heard in Commission deliberations.

Commissioners, including the President of the Commission, are appointed all together and serve for five years. This is why people often refer to each Commission as being the 'Prodi Commission' or the 'Santer Commission'. The appointments are made just after European Parliamentary elections and take effect in the January of the following year. The current Commission's term ends in January 2005. Readers can find the Commissioner from their favourite EU member at http://europa.eu.int/comm/commissioners/index_en.htm (the URL may change when the next Commission takes power in 2005).

SOURCE: **European Commission Audiovisual Library.**

FIGURE 2-6: HEADQUARTERS OF THE EUROPEAN COMMISSION IN BRUSSELS

The Commission has a great deal of independence in practice and often takes views that differ substantially from Member States, the Council, and the Parliament. However, it is ultimately answerable to the European Parliament since the Parliament can dismiss the Commission as a whole by adopting a motion of censure. Although this has never happened, a censure motion was almost passed in 1999, triggering a sequence of events that ended in mass resignation of the Commission led by President Jacques Santer (the Prodi Commission's predecessor).

Each politically appointed Commissioner is in charge of a specific area of EU policy. In particular, each runs what can be thought of as the EU equivalent of a national ministry. These 'ministries', called Directorate-Generals or DGs in EU jargon, employ a relatively modest number of international civil servants (the Commission as a whole employs about 17 000, which is fewer than the number of people who work for the city of Vienna). Before the Prodi Commission, the DGs were labelled by number. (Many EU experts could recognize a handful of DGs – DG4 was competition, DG2 was Economic and Financial Affairs, etc. – but only true EU insiders could name them all.) Just as in national ministries, Commission officials tend to provide most of the expertise necessary to administer and analyse the EU's vastly complex network of policies since the Commissioners themselves are typically generalists.

## LEGISLATIVE POWERS

The Commission's main duty is to prepare proposals for new EU decisions. These range from a new directive on minimum elevator safety standards to reform of the Common Agricultural Policy (CAP). Neither the Council nor the Parliament can adopt legislation until the Commission presents its proposals. This monopoly on the 'right to initiate' makes the Commission the gatekeeper of EU integration. It also allows the Commission to occasionally become the driving force behind deeper or broader integration. This was especially true under the two Delors Commissions that served from 1985 to 1994.

Commission proposals are usually based on general guidelines established by the Council of Ministers, the European Council, the Parliament, or the Treaties. A proposal is prepared by the relevant Directorate-General in collaboration with other DGs concerned. In exercising this power of initiative, the Commission consults a very broad range of EU actors including national governments, the European Parliament, national administrations, professional groups, and trade union organizations. This complex consultation process is known in EU jargon as 'comitology'.

## EXECUTIVE POWERS

The Commission is the executive in all of the EU's endeavours, but its power is most obvious in competition policy. As Chapter 5 explains in more detail, the Commission has the power to block mergers, to fine corporations for unfair practices and to insist that EU members remove or modify subsidy to their firms. The Commission also has substantial latitude in administering the Common Agricultural Policy, including the right to impose fines on members that violate CAP rules.

One of the key responsibilities of the Commission is to manage the EU budget, subject to the supervision by a specialised institution called the EU Court of Auditors. For example, while the Council decided the programme-by-programme allocation of funds in the EU's current multi-year budget (Financial Perspective in EU jargon), it was the Commission that decided the year-by-year indicative allocation of Structural Funds across members.

## DECISION MAKING

The Commission decides, in principle, on the basis of a simple majority. The 'in principle' proviso is necessary because the Commission makes almost all of its decision on the basis of a consensus. The 'shadow voting' point from above does apply, but in the Commission's case, the consensus often reflects substantive positions of the Commissioners. The reason is that the Commission has direct power in very few areas apart from competition policy, state aids and the CAP. Almost all Commission decisions need to be ratified by the Council and Parliament, or at least they can be overturned by the Council or Parliament. Because of this, the Commission rarely decides anything that does not have approval of a very substantial majority of the Commissioners. Any proposal that failed to garner the support of most Commissioners would be very unlikely to get past the Council and Parliament.

The Commission will also be reformed according to the draft Constitution. The proposed changes, however, are so contentious that they are unlikely to survive in their current form. The OLC website provides an update on the state of play.

### 2.3.4 The European Parliament

The Parliament has two main tasks:

■ it oversees all EU institutions, but especially the Commission; and
■ it shares legislative powers, including budgetary power, with the Council and the Commission.

The Parliament, on its own initiative, has also begun to act as the 'conscience' of the EU, for example, condemning various nations for human rights violations via non-binding resolutions.

#### ORGANIZATION

Up to the 2004 enlargement, the European Parliament (EP) will have 626 members. After the enlargement, it will have 732. These Members of European Parliament (MEPs) are directly elected by EU citizens in special elections organized in each Member State. The number of MEPs per nation varies with population, but as with Council votes, the number of MEPs per million EU citizens is much higher for small nations than for large. For example, in the 1999–2004 Parliament, Luxembourg has 6 MEPs and Germany has 99, despite the fact that Germany's population is about 160 times that of Luxembourg.

SOURCE: **European Commission Audiovisual Library.**

FIGURE 2-7: HEADQUARTERS OF THE EUROPEAN PARLIAMENT IN STRASBOURG AND BRUSSELS

MEPs are supposed to represent their local constituencies, but the Parliament's organization has evolved along classic European political lines rather than along national lines (Noury and Roland, 2002). The EP election campaigns are generally run by each nation's main political parties and MEPs are generally associated with a particular national political party. Although this means that over a hundred parties are represented in the Parliament, fragmentation is avoided because many of these parties have formed political groups. As in most EU Member States, two main political groups – the centre-left and the centre-right – account for two-thirds of the seats and tend to dominate the Parliament's activity. The centre-left grouping in the EP is called the Party of European Socialists, the centre-right group is called the European People's Party.

As in most parliaments, the European Parliament's physical, left-to-right seating arrangement reflects the left-to-right ideology of the MEPs. In the 1999–2004 Parliament, the left flank is occupied by the radical left (communist, former communist, extreme left parties and the Nordic Green Left parties). Continuing left to right, the next is the Party of the European Socialists, the Greens and allies (e.g. regional parties from Spain), the European Liberal Democrat and Reformists group, and the European People's Party. On the far right flank are the Eurosceptic Gaullists and other rightist groups. Details on the size and national composition of the European Parliament can be found on www.europarl.eu.int. These party groups have their own internal structure, including Chairs, secretariats, staffs, and 'whips' who keep track of the attendance and voting behaviour. The political groups receive budgets from the Parliament.

Statistical analysis of MEPs' voting patterns shows that they vote more along party lines than they do along country lines. Indeed, cohesion within European political groupings is comparable to that in the US Congress, while cohesion of country delegations is significantly lower and is declining, as Noury and Roland (2002) show.

## LOCATION

The Parliament is not located in Brussels, the centre of EU decision making, but rather in Strasbourg due to France's dogged insistence that this EU institution remains in France (the Parliament's predecessor in the European Coal and Steel Community, the Common Assembly, was located there). Equally determined insistence by Luxembourg has kept the Parliament's secretariat in Luxembourg. Since Brussels is where most of the political action occurs, and is also the location of most of the institutions that the Parliament is supposed to supervise, the Parliament also has offices in Brussels (this is where the various Parliamentary committees meet). The staffs of the Parliament's political groups work in Brussels. It is not clear how much this geographic dispersion hinders the Parliament's effectiveness, but the time and money wasted on shipping documents and people among three locations occasionally produces negative media attention. This shifting location may also help to account for the fact that many MEPs do not attend all sessions. In the third Parliament, an average of 17.6 per cent of the MEPs were absent and 35.5 per cent were physically present but did not vote; this improved in the fourth where the respective figures were 16.8 per cent and 21.6 per cent (Noury and Roland, 2002).

## DEMOCRATIC CONTROL

The Parliament and the Council are the primary democratic controls over the EU's activities. The MEPs are directly elected by EU citizens, so European Parliamentary elections are – in principle – a way for Europeans to have their voices heard on European issues. In practice, however, European Parliamentary elections are often dominated by standard left-versus-right issues rather than by purely EU issues. Indeed, European Parliamentary elections are sometimes influenced by pure national concerns with the voters using the elections as a way of expressing disapproval or approval of the ruling national government's performance. Moreover, in many Member States, participation in European Parliamentary elections tends to be fairly modest, and MEP absenteeism is a problem. By contrast, the elections by which national governments are chosen have very high levels of popular participation. The national elections, however, involve many issues, so voters may find it difficult to influence their nation's stance on EU issues via national elections.

The 2003 draft Constitutional Treaty proposes few changes for the Parliament, although it does expand its power somewhat by giving the Parliament a voice in almost all legislative activities. As usual, see the OLC website for the latest information.

### 2.3.5 European Court of Justice

In the EU, as in every other organization in the world, laws and decisions are open to interpretation and this frequently leads to disputes that cannot be settled by negotiation. The role of the European Court of Justice (ECJ, or sometimes known as the 'EU Court') is to settle these disputes, especially disputes between Member States, between the EU and Member States, between EU institutions, and between individuals and the EU.

What is highly unusual about the EU Court is its supranational power. For example, the European Commission can ask the Court to rule on what they feel is an infringement of EU law. If the Court finds that the rules have been broken, the 'guilty' Member State must comply with the judgement – there is no way to appeal against the EU Court's decision. The EU Court is the highest authority on the application of EU law. (Of course, the EU has no enforcer, no police force, so the Court's decisions cannot be physically imposed; moral suasion and peer pressure are the enforcement devices.)

SOURCE: **European Commission Audiovisual Library.**

FIGURE 2-8: HEADQUARTERS OF THE EUROPEAN COURT OF JUSTICE IN LUXEMBOURG

The Court also interprets EU law for national courts. For example, national courts that are uncertain about how to apply EU law can get 'preliminary rulings' from the EU Court that provide guidance in legal interpretation. The Supreme Courts of the Member States are obliged to consult th EU Court when they suspect that a particular piece of legislation can be interpreted in different ways. The national court that receives these rulings must comply with the Court's interpretation.

#### INFLUENCE

As a result of this power, the Court has had a major impact on European integration. As mentioned above, a 1964 judgement established EC law as an independent legal system that takes precedence over national laws in EC matters, and a 1963 ruling established the principle that EC law was directly applicable in the courts of the members. Its ruling in the 1970s on non-tariff barriers triggered a sequence of events that eventually led to the Single European Act (see Chapter 4 for details). The Court has also been important in defining the relations between the Member States and the EU, and in the legal protection of individuals (EU citizens can take cases directly to the EU Court without going through their governments).

## Organization

The European Court of Justice, which is located in Luxembourg, consists of one judge from each Member State. Judges are appointed by common accord of the Member States' governments and serve for six years. The Court also has eight 'advocates-general' whose job is to help the judges by constructing 'reasoned submissions' that suggest what conclusions the judges might take. The Court reaches its decisions by majority voting. The Court of First Instance was set up in the late 1980s to help the EU Court with its ever-growing workload.

## 2.4 Legislative processes

As mentioned, the European Commission has a near monopoly on initiating the EU decision making process. It is in charge of writing proposed legislation, although it naturally consults widely when doing so. The next step is to present the proposal to the Council for approval. Most EU legislation also requires the European Parliament's approval, although the exact procedure depends upon the issue concerned. (The Treaties specify which procedure must be used in which areas.[3])

The main procedure, called the *codecision procedure*, gives the Parliament equal standing with the Council. This procedure is used for about 80 per cent of EU legislation, including those dealing with the free movement of workers, creation of the single market, research and technological development, the environment, consumer protection, education, culture and public health. Specifically, the codecision procedure requires the Commission's proposal to be adopted by the Parliament (deciding by simple majority) and Council (deciding by qualified majority) before it becomes law. If the Parliament and/or the Council disagree with the Commission's proposal, the latter is only be adopted if a Council–Parliament compromise can be reached. The compromise procedure involves back-and-forth interaction between the Council and the Parliament. Details of the procedure are provided in Box 2-2.

The *consultation procedure* is used for a few issues – e.g. the Common Agricultural Policy's periodic price fixing agreements – where the Member States wish to keep tight control over politically sensitive decisions. Under this procedure, the Parliament must give its opinion before the Council adopts a Commission proposal. Such opinions, when they have any influence, are intended to influence the Council, or the shape of the Commission's proposal. Another procedure in which the Parliament plays a subsidiary role is the *assent procedure*. For example, on decisions concerning enlargement, international agreements, sanctioning Member States and the co-ordination of the Structural Funds, the Parliament can veto, but cannot amend a proposal made by the Commission and adopted by the Council. The final procedure, the *co-operation procedure*, is a historical hangover from the Parliament's gradual increase in power. Specifically, before the codecision procedure was introduced in the Maastricht Treaty, the co-operation procedure was the one that granted the most power to the Parliament. It is best thought of as a codecision procedure, in which the Parliament's power to amend the proposal is less explicit. Also, the Council can overrule an EP rejection by voting unanimously.

---

[3] See Hix (1999) for a detailed analysis of the politics of the EU legislative process.

> **BOX 2-2: THE CODECISION PROCEDURE IN DETAIL**
>
> The procedure starts with a Commission proposal. The Parliament then gives its 'opinion', i.e. evaluates the proposal and suggests desired amendments, by simple majority. After seeing the Parliament's opinion, the Council adopts a 'common position' by a qualified majority, except in the fields of culture, freedom of movement, social security and co-ordination of the rules for carrying on a profession, which are subject to a unanimous vote. The Parliament then receives the Council's common position and has three months in which to take a decision. If the Parliament expressly approves it, or takes no action by the deadline, the act is adopted immediately. If an absolute majority of Parliament's Members rejects the common position, the process stops, and the act is not adopted. If a majority of MEPs adopts amendments to the common position, these are first put to the Commission for its opinion and then returned to the Council. The Council votes by a qualified majority on Parliament's amendments; although it takes a unanimous vote to accept amendments that have been given a negative opinion by the Commission. The act is adopted if the Council approves all Parliament's amendments no later than three months after receiving them. Otherwise the Conciliation Committee is convened within six weeks.
>
> The Conciliation Committee consists of an equal number of Council and Parliament representatives, assisted by the Commission. It considers the common position on the basis of Parliament's amendments and has six weeks to draft a joint text. The procedure stops and the act is not adopted unless the Committee approves the joint text by the deadline. If it does so, the joint text goes back to the Council and Parliament for approval. The Council and Parliament have six weeks to approve it. The Council acts by a qualified majority and the Parliament by an absolute majority of the votes cast. The act is adopted if Council and Parliament approve the joint text. If either of the institutions has not approved it by the deadline the procedure stops and the act is not adopted.

## 2.4.1 Enhanced co-operation

The tension between the 'vanguard' members, who wish to broaden the scope of EU activities, and the 'doubters', who do not, led to the introduction of a new type of integration process called 'closer co-operation' in the Amsterdam Treaty and 'enhanced co-operation' in the Nice Treaty. This allows subgroups of EU members to co-operate on specific areas while still keeping the co-operation under the general framework of the EU.

Subgroups of Member States have long engaged in closer intergovernmental co-operation. What the Amsterdam Treaty did by creating 'closer co-operation' was to allow such subgroups to proceed while at the same time keeping them under some form of EU discipline and co-ordination. However, the conditions for starting new closer co-operations were so strict that no new closer co-operation was established under the Amsterdam rules. The Nice Treaty made it easier to start such subgroups and relabelled them as 'enhanced co-operation' arrangements (ECAs). Although this form of integration has not yet been used, it may come to play a much more important role once the EU enlarges. The point is that the diversity of members' preferences for integration will become even more diverse, so subsets of members may well find that starting an ECA is the only way to get things done. See Baldwin et al. (2001) for an analysis of this possibility.

There are also some potentially serious risks involved in this sort of clubs-within-the-club integration. First, ECAs could lead to divisiveness: by allowing a separation of members into groups, it risks fragmenting the EU politically. Second, ECAs could result in an erosion of existing integration, and in so far as ECAs create diversity in integration, they might erode the consistency of

European economic and social integration. To guard against these twin risks, the Nice Treaty gives the Commission a central role in the decision to create and enlarge any enhanced co-operation. Specifically, the Commission can veto ECAs covering deeper economic integration (i.e. first-pillar areas) and it controls subsequent membership enlargements of these. In other areas, the Commission has a strong voice in the process of setting up and expanding ECAs, but less so in the Security and Foreign Policy area (second pillar) than in Justice and Home Affairs areas (third pillar). It can also be the administrator of such groups.

## 2.5 The budget

The EU budget is the source of a great deal of both solidarity and tension among EU members, so a full understanding of the EU requires some knowledge of the budget. This section looks at the following questions in order. What is the money spent on? Where does it come from? Who gets the most on net? What is the budget process?

### 2.5.1 Expenditure

Total EU spending is now about €100 billion. While this sounds like a lot to most people, it is really fairly small – only about 1 per cent of total EU15 GDP, or €270 per EU15 citizen. Our first priority is to look at the two main ways in which this money is spent: spending by area and by EU member. We look at each in turn, starting with spending by area.

### EXPENDITURE BY AREA, 2003

As with so many things in Europe, understanding EU spending in all its detail would take a lifetime, but understanding the basics takes just a few minutes. Starting at the broadest level, it is useful to think of the EU budget as being divided into three categories: (i) agriculture, (ii) poor regions and (iii) other things. Agriculture takes up half the budget, poor regions take a third, and the remainder is split among many different uses. Spending on agriculture and poor regions is so important that we have written separate chapters dealing with each, so we do not go into further detail here (see Chapter 8 on agriculture and Chapter 9 on poor regions). Figure 2-9 shows spending priorities graphically for the year 2003.

At a slightly finer level of analysis, we break the 'other things' category into four areas:

- *Other Internal Policies* (7 per cent of budget). Here 'other' means other than agriculture and poor regions. As the name suggests, this category is very diverse and includes spending on research and development (R&D), spending on trans-European transport, energy and telecommunications networks, spending on training and student mobility, the environment, culture, information and communication.
- *External Action* (5 per cent of budget). This money is spent mainly on humanitarian aid, food aid and development assistance in non-member countries throughout the world. Small amounts are also spent on the Middle East peace process, the reconstruction of Kosovo, the European initiative for democracy and human rights world wide, international fisheries agreements, and the Common Foreign and Security Policy.
- *Administration* (5 per cent of budget). This concerns the cost of running the European Commission, the European Court of Justice, and all other European institutions. Taken together, they employ surprisingly few people (about 30 000).
- *Pre-accession Aid* (3 per cent of budget). During the years prior to the 2004 enlargement, the EU spent money helping the Central and Eastern European countries to prepare for EU membership. This money goes to modernizing agriculture, establishing transport and environmental structures, and to improving government administrations.

For further details, see the very accessible publication 'The budget of the EU: How is your money spent?' on http://europa.eu.int/budget/.

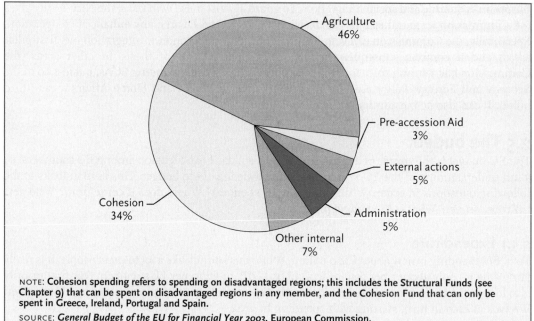

NOTE: **Cohesion spending refers to spending on disadvantaged regions; this includes the Structural Funds (see Chapter 9) that can be spent on disadvantaged regions in any member, and the Cohesion Fund that can only be spent in Greece, Ireland, Portugal and Spain.**

SOURCE: *General Budget of the EU for Financial Year 2003*, European Commission.

FIGURE 2-9: THE EU'S 2003 BUDGET: SPENDING

## HISTORICAL DEVELOPMENT OF EU SPENDING BY AREA

The EU's spending priorities and the level of spending has changed dramatically since its inception in 1958. This is shown graphically in Fig. 2-10.

As the top panel shows, the budget grew rapidly, but started at a very low level (just 8/100ths of 1 per cent of the EEC6's GDP). EU spending was negligible until the late 1960s, amounting to less that €10 per EU citizen. This changed as the cost of the Common Agricultural Policy (CAP) started to rise rapidly in the 1960s and Cohesion spending started to rise in the 1980s. From the early 1970s to the early 1990s, the budget grew steadily as a fraction of EU GDP, starting from about 8/10ths of 1 per cent and rising to 1.2 per cent in 1993. Since the 1994 enlargement, the budget as a share of GDP has remained quite stable at about 1 per cent. (The share of GDP, figures are not shown in the diagram.) According to the EU long-term spending plan – the so-called Financial Perspective – EU spending should peak in 2003 and then fall gradually until the end of the plan in 2006.

The bottom panel of Fig. 2-10 depicts the spending by area in shares to illustrate how the EU's budget priorities have changed over the last half century. Until 1965, the budget – tiny as it was – was spent mainly on administration (this was the period when all the European institutions were set up and the customs union was being implemented). CAP spending began in 1965 and soon dominated the budget. For almost a decade, farm spending regularly took 80 per cent or more of total expenditures; at its peak in 1970, it made up 92 per cent of the budget!

From the date of the first enlargement, 1973, Cohesion spending began to grow in importance, pushing down Agriculture's share in the process. Indeed, the sum of the shares of these two big-ticket items has remained remarkably steady from 1973 to 2000, ranging between 80 and 85 per cent of the budget. In a very real sense, we can think of Cohesion spending as steadily crowding out CAP spending over the past three decades.

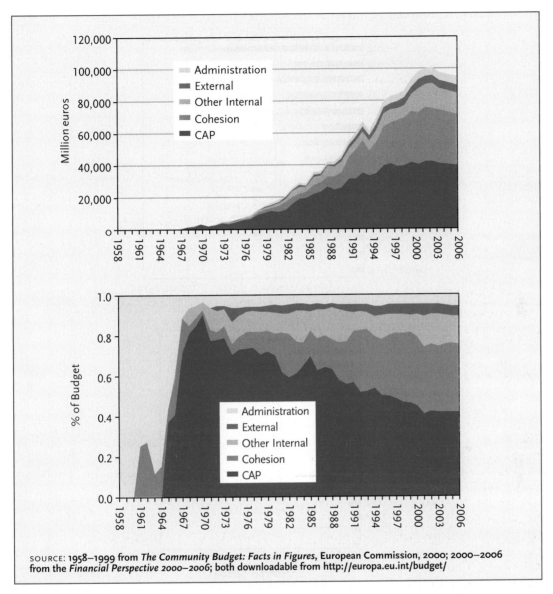

SOURCE: 1958–1999 from *The Community Budget: Facts in Figures*, European Commission, 2000; 2000–2006 from the *Financial Perspective 2000–2006*; both downloadable from http://europa.eu.int/budget/

FIGURE 2-10: THE EU BUDGET SPENDING, 1958–2006

## 2.5.2 Expenditure by member

By far the most important benefit from EU membership stems from the economic effects discussed in subsequent chapters. By comparison, the financial transfers involved in EU spending are minor. Remember the whole budget is only about 1 per cent of EU GDP. Be this as it may, it is interesting to see which members receive the largest shares of EU spending since a great deal of political difficulty arises from these imbalances, even though they are minor from an economy-wide perspective.

The amount of EU spending varies quite a lot across members, both in terms of the total amount and its nature. As the upper panel of Fig. 2-11 shows, France is the main recipient with

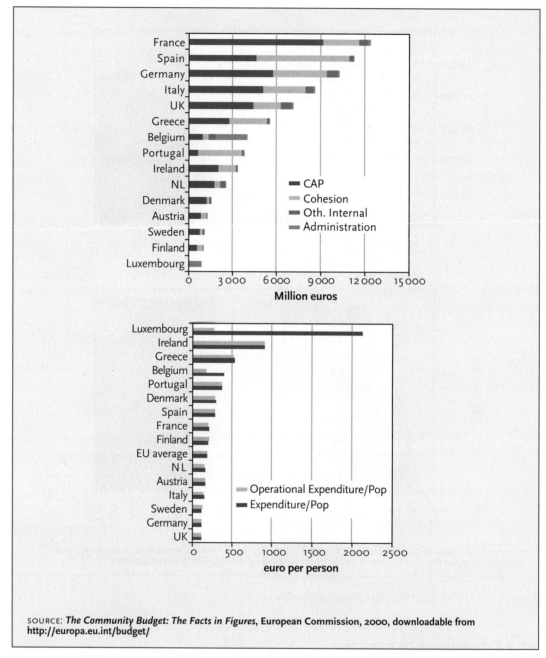

SOURCE: *The Community Budget: The Facts in Figures*, European Commission, 2000, downloadable from
http://europa.eu.int/budget/

FIGURE 2-II: THE EU SPENDING BY MEMBER, BY TYPE AND PER CAPITA, 1997

Spain and Germany close behind. Most of the French receipts come from the CAP, while
Cohesion spending is the most important source for Greece.

The figures, however, are entirely different when we look at receipts per capita (see the dark bars
in lower panel). By far the largest receiver per capita is Luxembourg (almost all of this is administrative spending on EU institutions located in the Grand Duchy). Ireland also has a very large per

capita receipt, almost €1000 per person. The EU average is about €200 per person, which means that Finland, France, Spain, Denmark, Portugal, Belgium, Greece, Ireland, and Luxembourg are all above-average recipients.

Because the per-capita numbers for Luxembourg are so high (and Luxembourg is the richest member by a long way), the European Commission prefers to calculate receipts excluding administrative expenditures. These figures – called 'operational allocated expenditures' – are shown by the light bars in the lower panel.

Readers may find the figures in the lower panel to be rather strange. Why should rich nations like Luxembourg, Belgium, Denmark, Finland and France be above-average recipients of EU spending? The answer, which lies in the nature of the EU's decision making process, is pursued in much greater depth in Chapter 3.

### 2.5.3 Revenue

The EU's budget must, by law, be balanced every year. All of the spending discussed above must be financed each year by revenues collected from EU members or carried over from previous years.

Up to 1970, the EEC's budget was financed by annual contributions from the members. A pair of Treaties in the 1970s and a handful of landmark decisions by the European Council established the system we have today in which there are four main sources of revenue. (See Box 2-3 for further details.) According to the EU Treaties, the Union is legally entitled to this revenue, so it is known as 'own resources' in EU jargon.

There are four main types of these own resource and Fig. 2-12 shows how their relative importance has varied over the years. Two of the four have long been used, and indeed in the early days of the Union they were sufficient to finance all payments. These so-called 'traditional own resources' are:

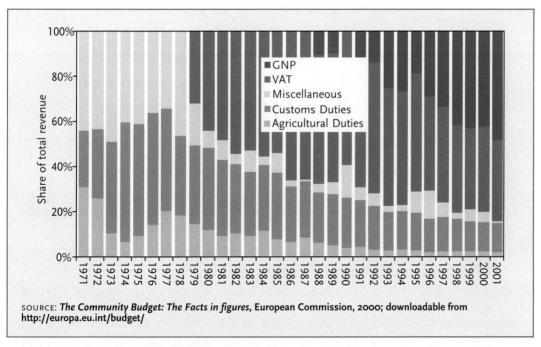

SOURCE: *The Community Budget: The Facts in figures,* European Commission, 2000; downloadable from http://europa.eu.int/budget/

FIGURE 2-12: SOURCES OF EU FUNDING, 1971–2001

■ Tariff revenue stemming from the Common External Tariff. Although trade within the EU is tariff-free, tariffs are imposed on imports from non-member nations. This money accrues to the EU rather than to any particular member.

■ 'Agricultural levies' are tariffs on agricultural goods that are imported from non-members. Conceptually, these are the same as the previous categories (they are both taxes on imports from third nations), but are viewed as distinct since the levies are not formally part of the Common External Tariff. Historically, the level of these tariffs have fluctuated widely according to market conditions (they were part of the CAP's price support mechanism; see Chapter 8 for more details).

The importance of these two revenue items has fallen over the years to the point where they are no longer major items (together they make up only one-seventh of the revenue needs). This reduced importance stems from the way that the level of the Common External Tariff has been steadily lowered in the course of World Trade Organization (WTO) rounds (e.g. the 1986–94 Uruguay Round). Moreover EU enlargement and the signing of free trade agreements with non-members means that a very large fraction of EU imports from non-members are duty free. The level of the agricultural levies has also been reduced in the context of CAP reform. The third and fourth types of 'own resources' provide most of the money. They are:

■ 'VAT resource'. As is often the case when it comes to tax matters, the reality is quite complex, but it is best thought of as a 1 per cent value added tax. The importance of this resource has declined and is set to decline further.
GNP based. This revenue is a tax based on the GNP of EU members. It is used to top up any revenue shortfall and thus ensures that the EU never runs a deficit.

The other revenue sources – labelled 'miscellaneous' in the diagram – have been relatively unimportant since 1977. Now, they include items such as taxes paid by employees of European institutions (they do not pay national taxes), fines, and surpluses carried over from previous years. Until the 1970s budget treaties came fully into effect, 'miscellaneous' revenue included direct member contributions, which, were a crucial source of funding in the early years.

---

**BOX 2-3: MILESTONES IN THE EU BUDGET PROCEDURE**

1958–70. The EU's budget was financed by contributions from its members.

April 1970. The Luxembourg European Council. The 'own resources' system is introduced. These included customs duties, agricultural levies (i.e. variable tariffs), and a share of VAT revenue collected by EU members. The Treaty of July 1975 refined and reinforced the system, establishing the European Court of Auditors to oversee the budget and giving the European Parliament the formal right of rejection over annual budgets.

1975–1987. This period was marked by sharp disputes over the budget contributions and ever-expanding CAP spending. The UK's Margaret Thatcher in particular complained repeatedly about the UK's position as the largest net contributor.

1984. The Fontainebleau European Council. The VAT-based revenue source was increased and the UK was awarded its famous 'rebate'.

1988. Delors I package. This reform established the basis of the current revenue and spending system. It introduced a fourth 'own resource' based on members' GNPs, established an overall ceiling on EU revenue as a percentage of the EU's GNP, and started reducing the role of VAT-based revenue. The package, decided at the Brussels European Council in June, also established the EU's multi-year budgeting process whereby a Financial Perspective sets out the evolution of EU spending by broad categories. Substantively, the financial perspective adopted provided for a major reorientation of EU spending from the CAP to Cohesion spending; Cohesion spending was doubled and CAP spending growth was capped.

1992. Delors II package. The Edinburgh agreement of December 1992 increased the revenue ceiling slightly to 1.27 per cent, further reduced the role of VAT-based revenue. It also adopted a new Financial Perspective for 1993–99 which amplified the shift of EU spending priorities away from the CAP and towards Cohesion.

1999. Agenda 2000 package. The Berlin European Council adopted the 2000–06 Financial Perspective. There were no major changes on the revenue side and the only major change on the spending side was creation of a new broad category, 'Pre-accession' expenditures meant to finance programmes in Central and Eastern European nations and provide a reserve to cover the cost of any enlargements in this period.

The material in this box was drawn from *The Community Budget: The facts in figures*, European Commission, 2000. Also see, *Financing the EU: Commission report on the operation of the Own Resource system*, 1998, especially Annex 1. Both from http://europa.eu.int/budget/

## BUDGET CONTRIBUTION BY MEMBER

On the contribution side, EU funding amounts to basically 1 per cent of each member's GDP. Some observers find this anomalous since taxation in most nations, especially in Europe, is progressive, i.e. the tax rate that an individual pays rises with his or her income level.

The precise figures are shown in Fig. 2-13. Here we see that the contributions as a share of GDP do not vary much from the median figure of 0.9 per cent. The highest figure in 1999 was 0.99 per cent (for Greece and Ireland). The lowest figure was the UK's 0.61 per cent due to the UK rebate; see Box 2-4 for details on the rebate. (Note that some budget items, such as reserves held over from previous years, cannot be allocated by member, so the total of contributions from members is less than the total budget.) The precise contribution rate varies from year to year by Member State due to the complexities of the system.

For comparison, the nations are ordered by increasing income (the line in the figure shows the national GDP per capita). The GDP figures here are not corrected for prices, so the per capita GDP figures are not measures of material standards of living. For example, the prices of many goods and especially services are systematically higher in, say, Denmark than they are in Portugal. Because of this, the figures overstate the purchasing power of Danes versus Portuguese. This is intentional. When nations set tax rates they do not adjust for price differences. For example, despite the fact that living in a city is systematically more expensive than living in the countryside, national income taxes ignore price differences; rates are based on income per capita, or income per family. What the line shows is that there is basically no correlation between national income levels and the national 'tax rates', i.e. the contribution as a share of GDP.

## 2.5.4 Net contribution by member

Putting together the receipts by member and the contributions by member allows us to show the net financial contributions in Fig. 2-14 Seven of the EU15 are net contributors (they pay more to the budget than they receive from it) with Germany being by far the largest. Indeed in 1999, Germany's net contribution was larger than that of all the other net contributors put together.

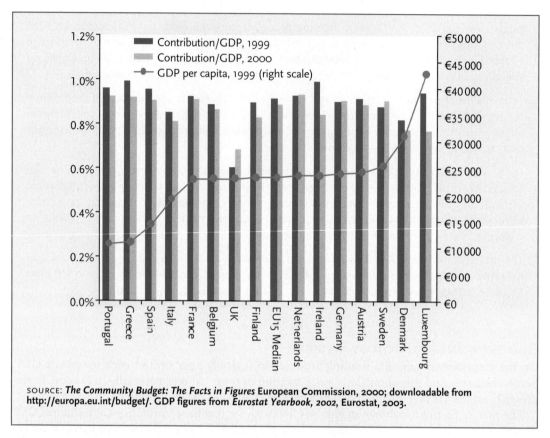

SOURCE: *The Community Budget: The Facts in Figures* European Commission, 2000; downloadable from http://europa.eu.int/budget/. GDP figures from *Eurostat Yearbook, 2002*, Eurostat, 2003.

FIGURE 2-13: CONTRIBUTION VERSUS GDP BY EU MEMBERS, 1999, 2000

Other net contributors are the UK, the Netherlands, Sweden, Austria, Italy (in 1999, but not in 2000) and Finland. The net recipients, those with negative net contributions, are led by Spain, Greece and Portugal, followed by Belgium, Luxembourg, France and Denmark.

Note that the net transfers are much smaller than the overall budget. In other words, most of the EU budget can be thought of as staying inside each nation. France paid €12.5 billion to the budget and received €13.1 billion from it in 1999, so we can think of the French government as spending €12.5 billion on EU programmes that directly benefit its own citizens with Brussels sending only €0.6 billion to Paris to add to this. Even for the biggest contributor, Germany, most of its payment can be thought of as being spent on Germans. Ten billion of €18.9 billion that the German government gave to Brussels was spent on Germans.

The ratio of net contributions (contribution minus receipts) to gross contribution (total contribution to the budget) are shown in the second column of Table 2-3.

Starting at the bottom we see that for the net payers, the ratio is modest; less than half their total contribution ends up being spent in other EU nations. The numbers for some of the net recipients, however, are quite different. For Luxembourg, Ireland, Greece, Portugal, Belgium and Spain, EU membership provides decisive financial advantages. For all of these nations, their net contributions are between one and four times the amount they pay to the EU, with Luxembourg taking the gold medal.

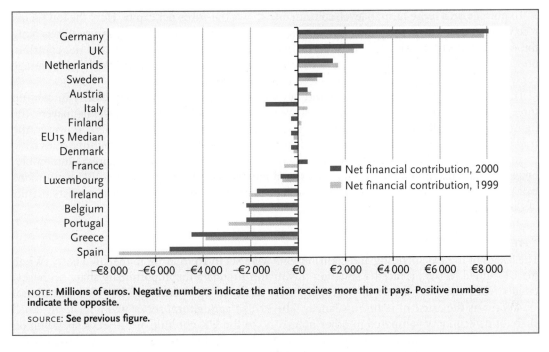

NOTE: **Millions of euros. Negative numbers indicate the nation receives more than it pays. Positive numbers indicate the opposite.**

SOURCE: **See previous figure.**

FIGURE 2-14: NET FINANCIAL CONTRIBUTION BY EU MEMBERS, 1999 AND 2000

|  | Euros Net/Pop | % Net/Gross | % Net/GDP | Million euros | |
|---|---|---|---|---|---|
|  |  |  |  | Receipts | Contribution |
| Luxembourg | −1 537 | 379 | −3.6 | 833 | 174 |
| Ireland | −541 | 229 | −2.3 | 2 910 | 885 |
| Greece | −367 | 333 | −3.3 | 5 027 | 1 161 |
| Portugal | −290 | 278 | −2.7 | 3 940 | 1 043 |
| Belgium | −204 | 100 | −0.9 | 4 180 | 2 093 |
| Spain | −192 | 140 | −1.3 | 12 965 | 5 413 |
| Denmark | −37 | 14 | −0.1 | 1 554 | 1 360 |
| France | −10 | 5 | 0.0 | 13 116 | 12 508 |
| Italy | 7 | 4 | 0.0 | 9 081 | 9 487 |
| Finland | 28 | 13 | 0.1 | 936 | 1 083 |
| UK | 40 | 29 | 0.2 | 5 919 | 8 305 |
| Austria | 70 | 31 | 0.3 | 1 242 | 1 809 |
| Sweden | 94 | 42 | 0.4 | 1 165 | 1 993 |
| Germany | 96 | 44 | 0.4 | 9 995 | 17 881 |
| Netherlands | 107 | 49 | 0.5 | 1 788 | 3 479 |

NOTE: GDP at current market prices. Receipts include all allocatable EU spending.
SOURCE: Authors' calculation based on European Commission and Eurostat data.

TABLE 2-3: NET AND GROSS CONTRIBUTIONS IN PERSPECTIVE, 1999

To put this on a more human level, column one shows the euros per capita. Here the top six net receivers get more than 190 euros per person on average, with Luxembourg, as usual, receiving the most about €1500, which is three times more than its closest rival in terms of net contributions. The per capita net contribution numbers also show that the Dutch are the largest average contributors to the EU budget, with the Germans and Swedes close behind.

The asymmetry between net payers and net recipients also comes through clearly in column three, which presents the net receipts as a share of the nation's GDP. For all of the net payers, the figure is fairly small, never more than half of 1 per cent. For the four big receivers, however, the numbers are 3 per cent or more of national income. To summarize, EU membership makes a big financial difference for four EU15 members – the richest one and the three poorest. Remember, however, that Luxembourg's receipts correspond almost entirely to spending on EU institutions that have been located there, while the spending in Ireland, Greece and Portugal consists mainly of Cohesion and CAP spending.

## THE UK REBATE

The basics of the EU spending and contributions were set in 1970, prior to the UK's entry. When the UK joined in 1973 it faced a situation in which it funded a disproportionate share of the EU budget while receiving a less than proportionate share of EU spending. The UK's agricultural situation was the cause of both imbalances. The British agricultural sector was a relatively small share of its economy compared to other members, so the UK got little of the EU's spending on agriculture (this accounted for three-quarters of the budget at the time). The UK also imported a larger share of its food from non-member nations. Since the import taxes charged on such imports are turned over to the EU budget, the UK faced a situation where it was a large net contributor to the budget.

According to some, the 1970 funding system was intentionally aimed at disfavouring the UK once it entered (the UK's application was first put in 1961 and renewed in 1967). For example Peet and Ussher (1999) state: 'To an extent the original Own Resources Decision, adopted before Britain joined, was deliberately skewed to Britain's disadvantage.' The budgetary imbalance worsened as CAP spending continued to rise and when a new source of EU funding was added in 1979 – the levy on value added tax (VAT) income.

After years of dispute and complaints from the UK over this imbalance, EU leaders decided at their June 1984 meeting in Fontainebleau to give the UK back part of its contribution. The basic principle was that the UK should be rebated something like two-thirds of its net contribution. The process that led up to this debate is cloaked in folklore and usually described in colourful terms; see Box 2-4.

---

### BOX 2-4: LADY THATCHER'S 'HAND BAGGING' AND THE UK REBATE

The British perspective on the budget is succinctly put by Peet and Ussher (1999): 'The European budgetary picture after 1973 was simple enough: the Germans and British would pay, but everybody else would benefit. Thanks partly to residual war-guilt, and also to their relative wealth, the Germans were prepared to live with this. But Britain, relatively low down Europe's prosperity league, was never likely to.'

The UK government that negotiated membership in 1971, and the one that renegotiated it in 1973, worried about Britain's position as EU paymaster but did little to redress it. For a while, the net contribution was limited by annual adjustments, but such an approach was unsatisfactory to the new government of Margaret Thatcher.

As Peet and Ussher describe it, 'Her performance at the Dublin summit in December 1979 has become legendary. The patrician Valéry Giscard d'Estaing and the haughty Helmut Schmidt were horrified by her vulgar insistence on getting "my money back". But as she continued to bang the table at subsequent summits, they and their successors were forced to offer a British rebate: first of all a series of cash sums, but by 1984 a permanent mechanism known as an abatement, which reimbursed 66 per cent of the difference between the British contribution to VAT-based revenue and the amount of EU expenditure in the UK.'

Newspapers described the event in more flamboyant terms, asserting that the rebate was won through Thatcher's handbag diplomacy. 'The former British prime minister, now Lady Thatcher, is remembered for slamming her handbag on the table and yelling at the other leaders, "I want my money!"' (*International Herald Tribune* article by Barry James, 8 October 1998).

The exact procedure for calculating the rebate is complex and results in a fairly wide fluctuation in the UK's net contribution. The mechanism also explicitly distributes the burden of paying for the UK rebate among the other members; a fact that creates contention each time the budget in reviewed. (For more information see 'Annex 4' on http://europa.eu.int/comm/budget/agenda2000/reports_en.htm.)

## 2.5.5 Budget process

The EU's annual budget is guided primarily by a medium-term agreement on spending priorities, called 'Financial Perspectives' as mentioned above. The current Financial Perspective sets out broad spending guidelines for the annual budgets from 2000 to 2006. Since the Financial Perspective is adopted by all the institutions involved in budgeting (the Commission, the European Parliament, and the Council), its existence reduces dispute over each annual budget.

The procedure for drawing up the budget (as laid down in the Treaties) calls for the Commission to prepare a preliminary draft budget. The Commission's draft is presented to the Council for amendments and adoption. Once it has passed the Council, the budget goes to the European Parliament which has some power to amend the budget. According to the Treaties, the Parliament cannot touch so-called 'compulsory' expenditures (basically agriculture spending), which accounts for about 40 per cent of the budget, but it can amend the rest. After two readings in the Council and the Parliament, it is the European Parliament which adopts the final budget, and its President who signs it. This formal procedure has been augmented by inter-institutional arrangements between the Parliament, the Council and the Commission that are meant to improve co-operation. For more information see 'The budget of the EU: How is your money spent?' on http://europa.eu.int/budget/.

## 2.6 Summary

This chapter covered four very different topics.

### Facts

A dominant feature of the EU members is their diversity in size and income levels. In the EU15, there are only five large nations (40 million or more). The rest, with the exception of the

Netherlands, are small or tiny, with national populations smaller than that of large cities like Paris or London. The 2004 enlargement will greatly increase this dispersion since out of the 10 new-comers, only Poland is large (almost 40 million citizens). The economies of Member States are also extremely disparate in size. Just four of the EU15 economies account for two-thirds of the EU15's GDP, i.e. the economies of the other 11 members add up to only one-third of the EU15's GDP. Again this dispersion will greatly widen with the 2004 enlargement. Taking all the 10 new-comers economies together will add only 5 per cent to the EU15's current GDP.

## Law

The EU is unique in that it has a supranational system of law. That is, on matters pertaining to the European Community, EU law and the EU Court take precedent over Member States' laws and Courts.

## Institutions and legislative procedures

While there are many EU institutions, only five really matter for most things. These are the European Council, the Council of Ministers, the Commission, the Parliament and the Court. These five institutions work in concert to govern the EU and to pursue deeper and wider European economic integration. Under the main legislative procedure, the 'Codecision procedure', the Commission proposes draft laws which have to be approved by the Council of Ministers and the European Parliament before taking effect. Most EU legislation has to be turned into national law by each Member State's parliament.

## Budget

The EU budget is rather small, representing only 1 per cent of the EU15's GDP. It is spent mainly on a set of agricultural programmes known as the Common Agricultural Policy (half the budget), and on Cohesion, resources destined for poor regions in the EU (a third of the budget). The budget is funded through four main mechanisms but, in the final analysis, each EU member pays roughly 1 per cent of its GDP. The distribution of net contributions (receipts minus contributions) by Member State is quite unequal. In the EU15, the biggest net recipients are Luxembourg (the richest member) and the three poorest members (Greece, Portugal and Spain).

### SELF-ASSESSMENT QUESTIONS

1. Draw a diagram that summarizes the connections between the Council of Ministers, the European Commission and the European Parliament when it comes to passing laws. Use the example of the Codecision Procedure.

2. Draw a diagram that shows the main steps (and dates) in the development of the Big-5 EU institutions. (*Hint*: You may have to turn to the websites referred to in the text to find the dates.)

3. Develop an easy way of remembering the names of all of the EU15 members (e.g. there are 4 big ones, 4 small ones, 4 poor ones and 3 new ones). Do the same for the 10 newcomers who will join in 2004.

4. Explain in 25 words or less the difference between EC law and EU law.

5. List the main sources of EU revenue and the main spending priorities. Explain how each of these has developed over time

6. Explain why it is important that the ECJ rulings cannot be appealed in Member States' courts.

## ESSAY QUESTIONS

**1.** The general term for the way in which the EU institutions interact is the 'Community Method'. Describe what this is and how it has evolved over time.

**2.** Describe the historical origins of the European Council and how its role has evolved over time. Be sure to cover the way it is addressed in the draft Constitutional Treaty.

**3.** The European Parliament has progressively gained strength since the EU's inception. Describe this process and explain the forces driving it forward.

**4.** Compare the powers of the European Parliament to that of the parliament in your nation.

**5.** If the EU Court decides on a matter, is there any way that EU leaders can overrule that decision?

**6.** Find where the key elements of EU law discussed in this chapter are transcribed into the draft Constitutional Treaty. Do you think it is a good idea to have these principles in the Constitution?

**7.** Download the publication *The Community Budget: The Facts in Figures*, European Commission, 2000, and illustrate the evolution of receipts and payments of your favorite EU member in recent years.

**8.** Ireland is the only EU member that is a large recipient of both CAP spending and Cohesion spending. Did Ireland gain or lose from the shift in EU spending priorities that have, since 1986, reduced the CAP's budget share at the expense of Cohesion's share?

## FURTHER READING: THE AFICIONADOS CORNER

For more economic statistics on Europe see the most recent issue of the *Eurostat Yearbook*. This is well organized and provides directly comparable figures for all EU members, but unfortunately cannot be downloaded for free from the web (Eurostat is the only EU institution that routinely charges for data). Much of the same information can be had for free in the Statistical Appendix of the Commission publication called *European Economy* see http://europa.eu.int/. The OECD also provides an excellent statistical overview in its 'OECD in figures'. You can download the latest issue for free from www.oecd.org.

On EU law an excellent source is *The ABC of Community Law* by Borchardt; this webbook can be freely downloaded from http://europa.eu.int/eur-lex/en/about/abc/.

Comprehensive information on EU institutions and legislative processes are provided by Peterson and Shackleton (2002), and Hix (1999).

Good sources for further information on the budget are Peet and Ussher (1999) as well as the Commission publication 'The budget of the EU: How is your money spent?', downloadable from http://europa.eu.int/budget/.

## USEFUL WEBSITES

The European Parliament's 'factsheets' provide excellent, authoritative and succinct coverage of EU law, institutions, decision making procedures and the budget process. These pages are especial useful in that they provide brief accounts of the historical development of various institutional aspects of the EU. See http://www.europarl.eu.int/factsheets/default_en.htm.

A similar source that is more to the point, easier to read but less comprehensive is the website of the Swedish parliament, see www.riksdagen.se/english/eu/eufacts/index.asp.

The most exhaustive source for information on EU law is the Commission's excellent website: http://europa.eu.int/scadplus/.

## REFERENCES

Baldwin, R., *et al.* (2001) *Nice Try: Should the Treaty of Nice be Ratified?*, CEPR, London.

Hix, S. (1999) *The Political System of the European Union*, Palgrave, London.

Noury, A. and G. Roland (2002) *European Parliament: Should it have more power?*, Economic Policy.

Peet J. and K. Ussher (1999) *The EU budget: An Agenda for Reform?*, CER Working Paper, February.

Peterson, J. and M. Shackleton (2002) *The Institutions of the European Union*, Oxford University Press.

" Nothing is more difficult, and therefore more precious, than to be able to decide. "

Napoleon Bonaparte

# 3 Decision Making

Chapter 2 described how EU institutions work and how they make their decisions. This chapter presents a framework for thinking about EU decision making at a more abstract and more analytical level. The discussion is organized around two major questions.

■ Who should be in charge of what? That is, which decisions should be taken at the EU level and which should be taken at the national or sub-national levels?
■ Is the EU-level decision making procedure efficient and legitimate?

In answering these questions we shall examine the EU's actual practice and develop a number of specific analytic tools. Moreover, we shall look at reforms of the system since the 2004 enlargement poses huge difficulties for the EU's decision making structure. Indeed, one can see the Amsterdam Treaty, the Nice Treaty and the draft Constitutional Treaty as attempts to solve enlargement-related challenges to EU decision making.

# 3.1 Task allocation and subsidiarity: EU practice and principles

Governments set policies in many areas, ranging from the speed limit on local roads to the nation's stance on nuclear weapons. These policies are made at different levels of government. The decision of which speed limit to apply to local roads is typically made by the local city or town government; the question of nuclear arms is usually settled at the national level. Most European nations have at least three levels of government: local, provincial and national. EU members have a fourth level of government in the form of the EU's supranational decision making structure.

Before turning to a framework for thinking about why various tasks should be allocated to various government levels, we discuss the EU's current practices and principles as well as potential reforms.

In EU jargon, task allocation is referred to as the question of 'competencies'. Some tasks and decisions are assigned to the EU level (i.e. areas where the EU has 'exclusive competence'; such tasks are known as 'Community competencies'), tasks where responsibility is shared between the EU and the national governments of its members ('shared competence'), and tasks where national or sub-national governments decide ('national competence').

There are some clear examples of national competencies, like secondary school curriculum; and there are clear examples of Community competencies, like competition policy where the European Commission has the final say on, for example, mergers that affect the European market. However, as is true of so many things in the European Union, the exact dividing lines are unclear. The European Parliament's factsheet on subsidiarity explains:

> The demarcation of the areas of exclusive Community competence continues to be a problem, particularly because it is laid down in the Treaties not by reference to specific fields but by means of a functional description.
>
> (http://www.europarl.eu.int/factsheets/1_2_2_en.htm)

The task allocation is further blurred by the fact that the Treaty says that the Community's areas of competence can be extended if necessary to attain Treaty objectives. As Chapter 1 pointed out, the objectives of the original Treaty of Rome were enormously ambitious, so this proviso puts a great many tasks in the grey area between Community competence and national competence. Often, the dividing line must be established by the EU Court. As the factsheet notes:

> In a number of decisions stemming from the Treaties, for example, the Court has defined and recognized certain competences (which are not explicitly regulated in the Treaties) as exclusive, but it has not laid down a definitive list of such competences.

## 3.1.1 Subsidiarity

To help to reduce the blurriness of the task allocation, the EU formally embraced the so-called subsidiarity principle in the Maastricht Treaty. The word 'subsidiarity' has a distinct meaning in the EU – even though it is not defined exactly (see Box 3-1). Subsidiarity basically means that *decisions should be made as close to the people as possible*, that the EU should not take action unless doing so is more effective than action taken at national, regional or local level.

BOX 3-1: DEFINING SUBSIDIARITY

The term 'subsidiarity' is often used in a broad sense even though its legal definition is quite narrow. The broad sense is that decisions should be taken at the lowest level possible. As the European Commission's website defines it:

'The subsidiarity principle is intended to ensure that decisions are taken as closely as possible to the citizen and that constant checks are made as to whether action at Community level is justified in the light of the possibilities available at national, regional or local level.'
(http://europa.eu.int/scadplus/leg/en/cig/g4000.htm).

Or, as the European Parliament's factsheet on subsidiarity puts it:

'The general aim of the principle of subsidiarity is to guarantee a degree of independence for a lower authority in relation to a higher body or for a local authority in respect of a central authority ... When applied in a Community context, the principle means that the Member States remain responsible for areas which they are capable of managing more effectively themselves, while the Community is given those powers which the Member States cannot discharge satisfactorily.'

The precise definition set out in the Treaties and various Court decisions is much narrower. The Parliament's factsheet states:

'The principle of subsidiarity applies only to areas shared between the Community and the Member States. It therefore does not apply to areas which fall within the exclusive competence of the Community or those which fall within exclusively national competence.'

The problem with this is that – as pointed out in the text – the dividing lines between EU, shared and national competencies are unclear and ever changing. Given this fundamental ambiguity, economists, political scientists, lawyers and others have struggled with this important concept for years. See, for example, Begg et al. (1993), Dewatripont et al. (1995) and Berglof et al. (2003) for book-length discussions.

### 3.1.2 3 Pillars

Another step towards clarity came with the '3 Pillar' structure of the EU set up by the Maastricht Treaty (see Chapter 2 for details). This explicitly delimited the range of Community competencies and shared competencies by defining areas (second and third pillars) where the EU would not normally be able to make policy, i.e. where co-operation would be of the more standard intergovernmental type where all the members have to agree unanimously on any common policy.

To summarize the discussion in Chapter 2, the first pillar (the EC pillar) includes policy issues relating to the single market, the free movement of persons, goods, services and capital among EU members, and co-operation in the areas of agricultural, environmental, competition and trade policies. It also encompasses Economic and Monetary Union (EMU). The second pillar consists of the Common Foreign and Security Policy (CFSP). The third pillar covers Justice and Home Affairs, i.e. police co-operation and criminal matters.

The first pillar is where EU members have allocated decision making to the EU level, in effect transferring parts of their national sovereignty by empowering EU institutions to draw up and interpret laws and regulations. Specifically, the Commission has a monopoly on the right to initiate proposals for new laws. The Council and (usually) the European Parliament decide whether to adopt them, often by majority voting. It is exactly this majority-voting element that tells us that Member States have transferred sovereignty to the EU level. An EU member can be outvoted on a particular law, but it still must accept the adopted policy. In many first-pillar areas, the laws are directly enforceable in member countries and the EU Court of Justice can overrule any national court on such matters.

Although the details are complex, the basic rule in second- and third-pillar areas is that members can pursue co-operation, but they do not transfer sovereignty to the EU level. That is, members will not be bound by decision with which they disagree. This does not mean that they do not co-operate. EU members and even non-members do co-operate in initiatives such as the Schengen Accord.

### 3.1.3 Reform

Ambiguities in the Treaties have led to a systematic 'competence creep', i.e. an ever-widening range of areas in which EU policy making is important. In fact that might well have been the intention of the EU founders since they were committed to an ever closer union. The objectives of the EC Treaty are hugely ambitious, and the Treaty allows for an expansion of competencies to attain these objectives. There are thus no hard limits as to what tasks the EU should be assigned (see Chapter 2 for more on this point). In recent years an increasingly wide range of Europeans have questioned whether the EU should continue to expand its list of competencies. Recognizing this line of thinking, EU leaders have said that one of the tasks that the 2002–03 European Convention was supposed to address is a clearer definition of the 'task allocation' between EU, national and sub-national governments.

At the time of writing, the draft Constitutional Treaty had just been accepted as a good starting point for the Intergovernmental Conference (IGC) that will draft the actual Constitution. The Constitution is supposed to better define the competencies, but this aspect may be altered by the IGC. See the OLC website for updates on this topic.

With this admittedly blurry notion of how the EU actually allocates tasks at hand, we turn to an analytic framework that helps us think about the pros and cons of allocating some tasks to the EU level and some to lower levels of government.

## 3.2 Fiscal federalism and task allocation among government levels

The main line of thinking here, the theory of fiscal federalism, considers how best to allocate areas of policy making among various levels of government. A complete consideration of this question, however, would take us into subjects (political science, sociology, national identity, etc.) that are too far a field for this book. Yet even though the theory of fiscal federalism provides only an incomplete approach to the question, it provides a very useful framework for thinking about the basic trade-off faced when deciding whether decisions in a particular policy area should be made at the EU level, or at the national or sub-national level.

### 3.2.1 The basic trade-offs

We focus on five important considerations when thinking about the proper allocation of policy making among the various levels of government. The first concerns local diversity.

DIVERSITY AND LOCAL INFORMATIONAL ADVANTAGES

When people in different nations have very different preferences for a particular type of public service, a centralized decision making process that results in the choice of a single, one-size-fits-all compromise is likely to produce an outcome that is inferior to the outcome one would observe if the decision making were decentralized. To illustrate this general idea more concretely we turn to the left panel of Fig. 3-1. (The figure employs supply and demand analysis and the notion of consumer surplus; see Chapter 4 if you are unfamiliar with this type of reasoning.)

The left panel shows demand curves for a particular public service. One is for an individual located in region 1 (marked as $D_1$) and the other for a person in region 2 (marked as $D_2$). We

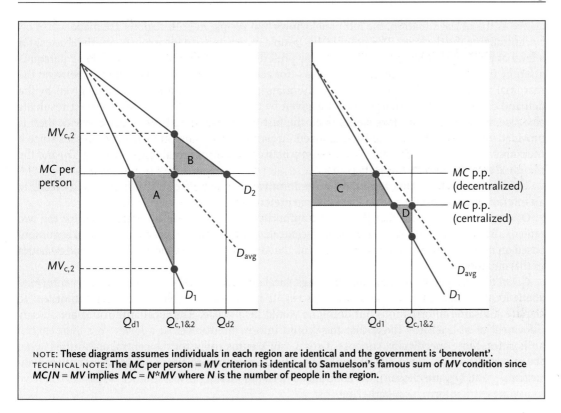

NOTE: **These diagrams assumes individuals in each region are identical and the government is 'benevolent'.**
TECHNICAL NOTE: **The MC per person = MV criterion is identical to Samuelson's famous sum of MV condition since MC/N = MV implies MC = N*MV where N is the number of people in the region.**

FIGURE 3-1: DIVERSITY AND SCALE ECONOMIES

assume that for some reason, people in the two regions have different preferences for public services. For example, if we are talking about the density of public bus service, then people in region 2 may have a stronger preference for bus services – maybe because they live in a city where commuting by car is difficult. People in region 1 have a lower preference for bus service. This can be seen from the fact that $D_1$ is below $D_2$; from the consumer surplus analysis in Chapter 4, this means that the marginal value of a slight increase in the density of bus service is lower for individuals in region 1 than it is in region 2 at any level of service (other than zero).

To start the analysis, we work out the level of bus service that would be provided if the levels were chosen separately by the region 1 and region 2 governments. This is compared to what would be chosen by a central government that covered the two regions.

The region 1 government would best serve its citizens by choosing the level where a typical region 1 person's marginal value of a denser bus service (i.e. more buses per day and/or more routes) was just equal to the per-person cost of providing the extra service. In the left panel, this optimal level is $Q_{d1}$ for region 1 (the 'd' stands for decentralized and '1' for region 1). Region 2's government would choose a higher level, namely $Q_{d2}$. (This assumes, for simplicity, that the marginal cost is constant at all levels of service and identical across regions.) Contrast this with the situation where the policy decision is centralized so that the same level is chosen for both regions. In this case, the central government would look at the *average* preference for bus services as reflected by the average demand curve marked as $D_{avg}$. Using the same reasoning as with local governments, the optimal average provision is shown by $Q_{c, 1\&2}$.

How do these two situations compare in terms of people's welfare? Taking the decentralized choice as the initial situation, the left panel shows that people in both regions are made worse off by centralizing the decision. The point is that people in region 1 are force to pay (via their taxes) for a level of bus service that is too high for their preferences. The loss to a typical region 1 person is given by the triangle 'A' since this measures – for each extra increase in $Q$ – the gap between the marginal value of the denser service and the marginal cost. The marginal value is given by the demand curve $D_1$ and the marginal cost is given by the 'MC per person' line. Region 2 residents also lose, but for them the loss stems from the fact that they would like a denser service than is provided when decision making is centralized. In particular, the area B shows their losses since it measures, for each unit reduction of $Q$, the gap between their marginal value (given by $D_2$) and the marginal cost (given by 'MC per person').

The conclusion from this analysis is quite intuitive. Choosing a one-size-fits-all policy leads to an inferior outcome when people have diverse preferences.

Of course, it is possible that the central authority could also choose separate $Q$'s for the two regions. But then there is no real reason to centralize the decision. Indeed, there is an argument based on *information costs* that leads us to think that decentralized decision making would be better in this situation.

Given the way people find out about things, local authorities are almost surely better informed about local conditions (costs and preferences). It might be possible for central authorities to acquire the same information, but doing so would be a waste. The local authorities are already informed, or at least it is likely that they could inform themselves at a lower cost than central authorities. More specifically, suppose it costs, say $X$ euros more for the central authorities to get the information than it would cost local authorities. Since the decision would be the same in both cases ($Q_{d1}$ and $Q_{d2}$ are chosen), the centralized decision making is worse since taxpayers will have to pay the extra information-gathering cost, $X$.

## SCALE ECONOMIES

The advantage of localized decision making in terms of information efficiency is really quite a robust result. Yet in many situations there are gains from operating at higher scales. For example, in the case of bus services, it seems reasonable to believe that the cost per kilometre of bus service tends to fall as the number of buses gets larger. A large bus company can more easily ensure that the right number of drivers is available, the fixed cost of a maintenance centre can spread over more buses, and the per-bus cost of administration may fall – at least up to a point – when the bus company is larger. Imagine an extreme situation where every bus in, say, Paris were owned and operated by separate companies versus the situation where all the buses were owned by a single company. Surely the latter would be more efficient in terms of costs.

The widespread presence of scale economies in the provision of public services – transport services, medical services, etc. – tends to favour centralisation. To see this point, we refer to the right panel of Fig. 3-1. The diagram focuses only on the impact of centralization on the typical region 1 individual. In the decentralized situation the marginal cost per person of a denser bus service is shown by the line marked 'MC p.p. (decentralized)'. In the case of centralized service, the marginal cost is lower, namely 'MC p.p. (centralized)' due to scale economies.

The right panel shows that there is a trade-off between having the level of service precisely adjusted to local preferences and having the service cost less due to scale economies. When the decision is local, the optimal provision is – as in the left panel – $Q_{d1}$. When it is centralized, the marginal cost is lower so the intersection of marginal value of the average citizen ($D_{avg}$) and marginal cost is at $Q_{c,1\&2}$. As before, the level that is optimal for the average citizen is not right for region 1 people, so there is an inefficiency; again this is measured by a triangle, marked D in the right panel. This inefficiency, however, is offset by the gain from scale economies. That is, the region 1 person faces a lower marginal cost; the benefit of this is shown by the four-sided area C. (The gain is just like a price reduction in standard consumer surplus analysis; see Chapter 4 for details.)

It appears, from Fig. 3.1, that the gain from scale economies outweighs the loss from one-size-fits-all decision making. But of course, if the scale economies were less important (i.e. the MC fell by less), or preferences were more diverse (i.e. the $D_{avg}$ curve was further from the $D_1$ curve) then decentralization would be the superior outcome. The analysis for region 2 is quite similar and so it is omitted for the sake of brevity.

To sum up, economies arising from joint decision making tend to favour centralization while diversity of preferences and location information advantages favour decentralization. We turn next to another key issue that arises when the decisions made in one region affect people in other regions. In economics jargon, these are called 'spillovers'.

## SPILLOVERS

Many public policy choices involve multi-region effects. National defence is one extreme. The presence of an army almost anywhere in the country deters foreign invasion for the country as a whole, so all the nation's citizens benefit from the army. It would be silly in this case to have taxpayers in each city decide separately on the army's size since, in making their decision, each set of taxpayers is likely to undervalue the nationwide benefit of a slightly bigger army. This is why the size of the army is a decision that is made at the national level in almost every nation. This is an example of what are called 'positive spillovers', i.e. where a slightly higher level of a particular policy or public service in one region benefits citizens in other regions.

A similar line of reasoning works when there are negative spillovers, i.e. when one region's policy has a negative effect on other regions. A good example of this is found in taxation. The value added tax (VAT) rate is set at the national level in all EU nations, but consider why this is so. If the VAT were chosen by each region, regions might be tempted to lower their VAT rate in an attempt to lure shoppers. For example, if the VAT in the centre of Frankfurt were 25 per cent, one of its suburbs might set its VAT at, say, 15 per cent in order to draw shoppers to its shops. In fact, if this tax undercutting were effective enough, the suburb would actually see its tax collection rise. (If the rate reduction was more than matched by an increase in local sales, the total VAT collected by the suburb would increase.) Of course, if the suburb's tax cutting worked, Frankfurt would probably have to respond by lowering its rate to 15 per cent. In the end, both Frankfurt and the suburb would charge VAT rates below what they would like, but neither would gain shoppers by doing so. This is a negative spillover since the tax undercutting in one region negatively affects tax revenue in other regions. Again, the solution that is adopted by most nations is to set the VAT rate at the national level, but this time it is done to avoid negative spillovers.

As it turns out, cross-border shopping is not much of a problem in most parts of the EU, so there is little incentive to completely harmonize VAT rates at the EU level. The EU does, however, require VAT rates to fall within a wide band so that the maximum difference between VAT rates cannot be massive.

In summary, the existence of important negative or positive spillovers suggests that decisions made locally may be suboptimal for the nation (or EU) as a whole. The very existence of spillovers, however, does not force centralization. First, it may be possible to take account of the spillovers via *co-operation* among lower-level governments. This does not work for all policies, however, since co-operation is very difficult to sustain when the policies are difficult to observe directly and the spillovers are difficult to quantify. Moreover, even if decentralized co-operation does not work well, one may still resist centralization when there are big differences in preferences. A very interesting case study in this sort of fiscal–federalism trade-off concerns the EU's different treatment of general VAT and extra sales taxes, or excise taxes on alcohol and tobacco. National preferences within the EU vary enormously when it comes to alcohol and tobacco, so although there is at least as much an argument for partly harmonizing these taxes as there is for partly harmonizing general VAT rates, the EU has never been able to do so. See Box 3-2 for details.

---

### Box 3-2: Beer, cigarettes and VAT harmonization

Since 1 January 1993, EU travellers have been allowed to buy unlimited quantities of alcohol and tobacco (for their own use) in any Member State, and, as long as they pay taxes due in the Member State where they bought the goods, no additional taxes are due when they return home. This has posed some problems for British fiscal authorities since Britain has some of the highest 'sin' taxes in Europe.

While there has been some progress towards the harmonization of excise duties across the EU (incorporated into EC directives adopted on 19 October 1992), this effort consists of establishing specific minimum rates that are quite low. As Commons (2002) notes: 'The sheer variation in duty rates between countries made any closer form of harmonization politically infeasible.' For example, in the UK beer duty is 34p per pint (5p in France, 3p in Germany and 7p in the Netherlands), duty on a 70-cl bottle of spirits is £5.48 (£2.51 in France and £1.19 in Spain), duty on a 75-cl bottle of wine is £1.16 in the UK (2p in France and 0p in Spain), and the total excise duty on a packet of 20 cigarettes is £2.80 in the UK (£1.22 in France, £1.00 in the Netherlands and 99p in Belgium).

Such differences could, of course, lead to massive tax fraud, if, for example, all British publicans stocked up in France, claiming that their truck load of beer was for personal use. To prevent this, Britain sets indicative levels for how much alcohol and tobacco constitutes 'for personal use'. These levels are rather generous: 10 litres of spirits, 20 litres of fortified wines, 90 litres of wine, 110 litres of beer, 200 cigars, 400 cigarillos, 800 cigarettes, and 1 kg of smoking tobacco. The problem has become so severe that the UK has begun to seize the vehicles used in this sort of fiscal smuggling – taking over 10 000 vehicles in 2000–01.

*Source*: This box is based on Commons (2002).

---

## DEMOCRACY AS A CONTROL MECHANISM

The analysis up to this point has assumed that governments are only interested in the well-being of their citizens. While there are such perfect public servants in this world, not all are totally selfless. Indeed, assuming that all politicians are interested in things other than the welfare of their electors is probably closer to reality than the other extreme of assuming they are all perfect public servants. For example, it is quite common for politicians to systematically favour politically powerful special interest groups – e.g. granting them tax breaks, subsidies and favourable laws – even when this is bad for the average citizen.

Because of this divergence of interests between voters and decision makers, all European nations have adopted arrangements that check the power of politicians and force governments to stay close to the interest of the people. Democracy is the most powerful of these mechanisms.

Since politicians must win approval of the citizens on a regular basis, they are reluctant to misuse their decision making power. From this perspective, democracy can be thought of as a control mechanism. The importance of this observation is that it helps to inform the allocation of policy making among levels of government. To understand this, however, we need to think more carefully about how elections discipline politicians.

Although democratic procedures vary across European nations, the following is meant as a stylized version. When a politician runs in an election, the politician or his/her party presents a package of promises to the voters. The voters choose between packages and hope that the winner will actually do what he/she promised (deviations without good reason can be punished in the next election). The fact that issues are packaged together and that voters face a limited range of packages gives politicians some leeway. That is to say, their package does not have to fully represent the best interest of the voters, it only has to be good enough to get elected. Due to this logic, parties and politicians have room to slip in policies that favour small but influential special interest groups. Because special interest groups tend to provide money and other support in election campaigns, skewing the package in favour of these groups tends to increase the likelihood of winning an election.

Given this logic, voters' control over their elected decision makers depends upon the breadth of the package of promises. If democracy consists only of electing national officials once every four or five years, the package of promises must include a vast range of things. This gives politicians and parties a great deal of room to undertake policies that are not in the interest of the general public. By contrast, if the election is for a town mayor, the package will be quite specific and this tends to reduce the room for special interest politics.

This logic is important. It underpins the basic presumption that decisions should be made at the lowest practical level of government. Or, to put it differently, decisions should be made as close to the voters as possible. As mentioned in the previous chapter, the EU's 'subsidiarity principle' does just this.

## JURISDICTIONAL COMPETITION

The final element to consider also favours decentralized decision making. It is called 'jurisdictional competition'. Voters can influence the sort of government they live under in two main ways, 'voice' and 'exit'. Voice is what we just discussed – the ability to control politicians and parties by speaking up, in particular by voicing one's opinion at the ballot box. The other way is to leave the jurisdiction that is imposing the policy. This is exit.

While exit is not a option for most voters at the national level, it usually is at the sub-national level. For example, if someone strongly objects to a lack of, say, parks and green areas in a particular town they can move to a different town. This is called jurisdictional competition since the fact that people *can* move forces decision makers to pay closer attention to the wishes of the people. By contrast, if all decisions are centralized, voters do not have the exit option. This reduces the pressure on local governments to be efficient in the provision of public services. To put this differently, even if voters rarely move, the fact that they could move if things got bad enough goes some way to ensuring that politicians keep things from going terribly wrong.

To recap, decentralization tends to improve government since it allows (or forces) regions to compete with each other in providing the best value for money in local services. In the marketplace, competition usually improves quality and reduces prices; in local government, competition provides the same sort of benefits.

## 3.2.2 From theory to practice

The five points discussed above provide principles rather than precise guidelines. The situation with respect to particular policies can be extremely complex, making it difficult or impossible to determine the 'correct' level of government for each task. Such debate inevitably turns on personal judgements and so takes us into an area where economists have no particular advantage. Be that as it may, it is interesting to speculate briefly on how our framework helps us to think about the EU's actual allocation of tasks between the EU-level and national level.

The one thing that is clear is that subsidiarity is probably a good idea. When in doubt, allocate the task to the lowest practicable level since higher level decisions are less subject to democratic control via voice and exit. Going further is trickier.

In the European Union, the main area of centralization has been economic policies (EC pillar), especially policies affecting the Single Market. As the discussion of the Treaty of Rome in Chapter 2 showed, virtually every policy that directly affects the competitiveness of particular industries is subject to control at the EU level. For example, import taxes, government subsidies (called state aid in EU jargon), exceptional tax benefits, and anticompetitive behaviour by firms are subject to EU-wide rules that are enforceable in the EU's Court. The thinking here is that such policies are marked by important and systematic *negative spillovers*. When one EU nation sub-sidizes its firms in a particular industry, firms in other EU nations suffer from the artificially intensified competition. As in the tax example above, a likely outcome is a Prisoners' Dilemma – all EU nations end up providing subsidies, but the subsidies cancel each other out. Likewise, each nation might be tempted to introduce idiosyncratic product regulation in an attempt to favour local firms, but the end result would be a highly fragmented European market with too many small firms (see Chapter 6 for an analysis of the economics of this).

The exceptions to centralization in economic policy can also be understood in the light of our five principles. The EU does not attempt to harmonize social policies or general labour market policies. Nor does it centralize decision making on general taxes, like income taxes and corporate taxes. As explained in Annex C of Chapter 1, general policies like these do not necessarily affect the competitiveness of particular firms and so are subject to a much lower level of negative spillovers. Moreover, national preferences for such policies are very diverse. In Spain, for example, the primary form of labour market protection for workers is Employment Protection Legislation, i.e. laws that make it difficult to fire workers. Germany relies much more on unemployment benefits. Given this divergence of nation preferences, the losses from a one-size-fits-all policy would be likely to outweigh any gains in efficiency or avoidance of negative spillovers. Of course one can argue with this and it is impossible to settle the argument scientifically. For example, German labour unions insisted that nationalized, one-size-fits-all wage bargaining should also apply to the Eastern Länder despite the great diversity of economic conditions, and they insisted on the same homogeneity of labour market laws.

Most non-economic policies are decided at the national level. For example, most foreign policy, defence policy, internal security and social policies are made at the national level. Of course, various nations co-operate on some of these policies – a good example is the recent agreement between France, Germany, Spain and the UK to produce a common military transport plane – but the decision making is allocated to the national level and co-operation is voluntary.

Roughly speaking, first-pillar policies are where there are important spillovers, where national preferences are not too great and common policies tend to benefit from scale economies. The theory of fiscal federalism thus helps us to organize our thinking about why such policies are centralized.

Second-pillar policies – Common Foreign and Security Policies – are marked by enormous scale economies. For example, unifying all of Europe's armies would result in a truly impressive force and allow Europe to develop world-class weapon systems. However, second-pillar policies are also marked by vast differences in national preferences. Some EU members – France and the UK, for example – have a long history of sending their young men to die in foreign lands for various causes. Other EU members – such as Sweden and Ireland – shun from almost any sort of armed conflicts outside their own borders. Given this diversity of preferences, the gains from scale economies would be more than offset by adopting a one-size-fits-all policy. Because of this, the only common EU policies in these areas are those arrived at by common consent, i.e. by co-operation rather than centralization.

Third-pillar policies lie somewhere between first- and second-pillar policies, both in terms of the gains from scale economies and in terms of the diversity of preferences.

### 3.2.3 Constitutional Treaty

At the time this book went to press, the EU's draft Constitutional Treaty was set to specify much more precisely a number of things discussed in this chapter. For instance, it proposes a more complete definition of subsidiarity as well as more precisely defining the areas of exclusive competencies, shared competence and Member State competence. Since this is a very contentious part of the Treaty – one that pits federalists against anti-federalists – the Intergovernmental Conference (IGC) set up in 2003 is very likely to change the details. See the OLC website for the latest developments.

# 3.3 Economical view of decision making

The previous sections looked at factors affecting the proper allocation of tasks between the EU and its Member States. This abstracted from the actual process by which EU-level decisions are made. In other words, we simplified away the question of how decisions were made at the EU level in order to study the issue of which decisions should be made at the EU level.

In this and subsequent sections we reverse this simplification, focusing on the question of *how* the EU makes decisions rather than the question of *which* decisions it should make. In particular, we shall concentrate on how the decision making mechanisms affect the EU's ability to act, how they affect the distribution of power among EU nations, and how they affect democratic 'legitimacy'.

Efficiency, power and legitimacy are inherently vague concepts. To make progress, we adopt the tactic of progressive complexity. That is, we start by taking what may seem to be a very shallow view of political actors and their motives. These simplifying assumptions allow us to develop some very precise measures of efficiency, legitimacy and national power in EU decision making. The benefit is that these precise measures permit us to comment on how efficiency and legitimacy have evolved in the EU and how it will evolve as the EU enlarges and applies the new decision making rules contained in the 2004 Accession Treaty.

We start with efficiency.

### 3.3.1 EU ability to act: decision making efficiency

In economics, 'efficiency' usually means an absence of waste. In the EU decision making context, the word has come to mean 'ability to act'.[1] While 'ability to act' is more specific than efficiency, it is still a long way from operational. For instance, on some issues the EU finds it very easy to make decisions, yet on other issues it finds it impossible to find a coalition of countries that would support a particular law. The perfect measure of efficiency would somehow predict all possible issues, decide how the members would line up into 'yes' and 'no' coalitions, and use this to develop an average measure of how easy it is to get things done in the EU. Such predictions, of course, are impossible given the uncertain and ever-changing nature of the challenges facing the EU.

An alternative approach, which we shall study here, sounds strange at first, but it is really the best way of thinking systematically about the issue. Rather than trying to predict details of decision making on particular topics, we adopt a 'veil of ignorance'. That is, we focus on a randomly selected issue – random in the sense that no EU member would know whether it would be for or against the proposition.

---

[1] See http://europa.eu.int/comm/archives/igc2000/index_en.htm or Baldwin et al. (2001).

## A QUANTITATIVE MEASURE OF EFFICIENCY: PASSAGE PROBABILITY

The specific measure we focus on is called the 'passage probability'. The passage probability measures how easy it is to find a majority given the specific voting rule. Specifically, it is the number of all possible winning coalitions divided by the number of all possible coalitions. If each conceivable coalition is equally likely, the measure tells us the likelihood of approving a randomly selected issue; that is why it is called the passage probability, and it works as follows.

First, we have to be very specific about decision making rules. As Chapter 2 pointed out, the EU has several different decision making procedures, however about 80 per cent of EU legislation is passed under what is called the 'Codecision' procedure. This requires the Council of Ministers to adopt the legislation by a 'qualified majority' and the European Parliament to adopt it by at least a simple majority, i.e. 50 per cent. (See Chapter 2 for further details on qualified majority voting.)

Second, we have to be very specific about voting behaviour. As part of our simplification, we assume that nations are the only players in the EU's decision making process. That is, we allow Germans and Italians to differ on a proposal, but we do not consider, for example, a coalition of German and Italian Green parties. A side effect of this simplification is that it makes the Parliament's role unimportant in efficiency calculations. Box 3-3 explains why.

### BOX 3-3: PARLIAMENT'S (NON)IMPACT ON EFFICIENCY

Although the Parliament's size and national composition has changed over time, this does not affect its passage probability because it uses the simple majority rule. When a body takes its decisions by simple majority, an increase in the number of voters increases the number of ways to win exactly in line with the increase in the number of ways to block. To see this, note that under the 50 per cent rule any coalition that could block by voting 'no', could win by voting 'yes'. (A bit of reflection reveals that the same does not hold for other thresholds, such as the Council's 71 per cent rule.) As a consequence, the passage probability is always 50 per cent. Of course, this fact reveals the simplicity of our efficiency measure.

Given these simplifications, calculation of the passage probability is straightforward. One uses a computer to calculate all possible coalitions among EU members. That is to say, it looks at every possible combination of 'yes' and 'no' voting by EU Member States. Since one can combine the 15 different players in many different ways, there are quite a few possible coalitions (in the EU15, for example, there are 32 768 possible coalitions). Next, the computer uses each member's number of votes and the 71 per cent majority threshold to determine how many of these are winning coalitions. Finally, we assume that for a randomly chosen proposal, all coalitions are equally likely.

The level of the passage probability is affected by the number of members, the distribution of votes and, above all, by the majority threshold. It is important to note, however, that the exact *level* of the passage probability is not very important. As Chapter 2 explained, most EU legislation is proposed by the European Commission and the Commission often refrains from introducing legislation that it unlikely to pass.

## HISTORICAL EFFICIENCY AND TREATY OF NICE REFORMS

It is interesting to see how the EU's efficiency has changed over time. Above all, it is interesting to see how the 2004 enlargement will affect the EU's decision making efficiency.

The five leftmost bars in Fig. 3-2 show the passage probability for qualified majority voting (QMV) in the current and historical EU. These indicate that although efficiency has been declining,

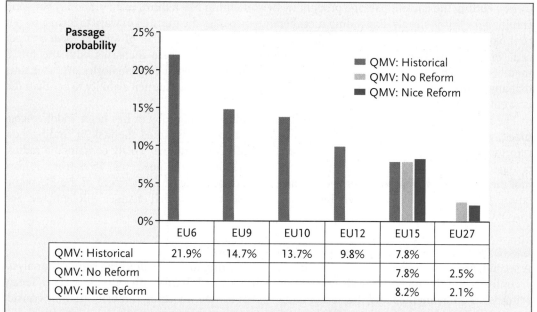

**Passage probability**

| | EU6 | EU9 | EU10 | EU12 | EU15 | EU27 |
|---|---|---|---|---|---|---|
| QMV: Historical | 21.9% | 14.7% | 13.7% | 9.8% | 7.8% | |
| QMV: No Reform | | | | | 7.8% | 2.5% |
| QMV: Nice Reform | | | | | 8.2% | 2.1% |

NOTE: The figures show the 'passage probability' which measures the likelihood that a randomly selected issue would pass in the Council of Ministers. Historical voting weights are used for the EU15 and earlier EUs. The enlargement evaluated is the EU27 (EU15 plus the 10 CEEC applicants, Cyprus and Malta) using the Treaty of Nice 'protocol on enlargement' voting weights. Looking further ahead, consider efficiency in an EU36. Given the 27 points of comparison in the Nice Treaty's protocol on enlargement, it is easy to guess the number of votes that would be allocated to Norway, Iceland, Albania, Bosnia-Herzegovina, Yugoslavia, Croatia, Macedonia, Switzerland, and Turkey. Using these the passage probability turns out to be just nine-tenths of 1% under Treaty of Nice rules.

SOURCE: Baldwin et al. (2001).

FIGURE 3-2: HISTORICAL VOTING EFFICIENCY

past enlargements have only moderately hindered decision making efficiency. The last enlargement lowered the probability only slightly, from 10 to 8 per cent, and the Iberian expansion lowered it from 14 to 10 per cent. The figures also hide the fact that the Single European Act, which took effect in 1987, greatly boosted efficiency by shifting many more decisions from unanimity to qualified majority voting.

The Accession Treaty for the 2004 enlargement changes EU decision making rules in an important way. In particular, the Accession Treaty implements the changes in QMV procedures that were adopted in the Treaty of Nice. Chapter 2 reviews the changes in details, but the essence is fairly simple. First, the Treaty reallocated votes among members, systematically shifting power from small members to large members. Second, it added two more thresholds for obtaining a qualified majority. In addition to the number of votes, a winning coalition would need at least half the members (number of members criterion) and must represent at least 62 per cent of the EU population (population criterion). Finally, the vote threshold was raised.

The idea behind these changes was to streamline the decision making process in order to ensure that the EU could continue to act even after the 2004 enlargement. However, the changes actually reduced efficiency, at least according to the passage probability. To see this, note that Fig. 3-2 shows what would have happened to efficiency if enlargement occurred *without any reform* of qualified majority voting rules. The results – illustrated by the middle bars in the two rightmost groups – show that accepting in 12 newcomers without reform would dramatically reduce efficiency, cutting the current passage probability by something like a third, from 7.8 to 2.5 per cent. Intuition for this is simple. Expanding membership increases the number of ways to form a 30 per cent blocking coalition much more rapidly than it increases the number of ways to form a 71 per cent winning coalition. Moreover, the gap between these numbers increases with the initial membership. This is a clear-cut implication of the mathematics of combinatorics and it means that any future enlargement will have a much larger effect on the Council's ability to act than did past enlargements.

The failure of the Nice Treaty voting reforms to address the problem has been widely recognized, which is why the 2002–03 European Convention was assigned the task of finding new reforms. At the time this book went to press, the draft Constitutional Treaty contained a radical change in the Council's majority rule – a winning coalition would need 'yes' votes from at least half the members which, together, would have to represent at least 60 per cent of the EU population. This reform is likely to be highly contentious, so it is likely that changes will be made. See the OLC website for updates.

## CRUDER EFFICIENCY MEASURES: BLOCKING COALITION ANALYSIS

A second, cruder but more transparent efficiency-measuring tool – i.e. blocking minority analysis – confirms the findings that decision making will get much harder after the Accession Treaty reforms are implemented and the new members start to vote. Blocking minority analysis consid-

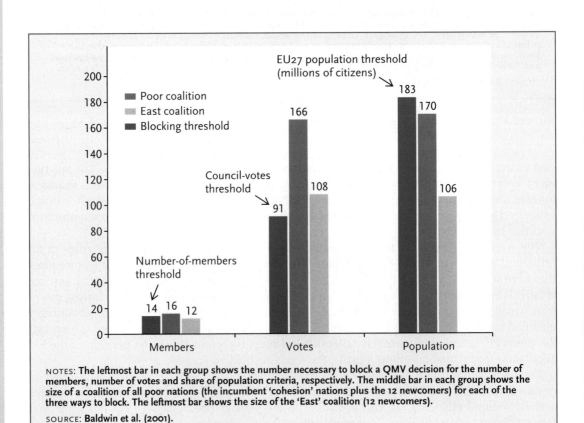

NOTES: The leftmost bar in each group shows the number necessary to block a QMV decision for the number of members, number of votes and share of population criteria, respectively. The middle bar in each group shows the size of a coalition of all poor nations (the incumbent 'cohesion' nations plus the 12 newcomers) for each of the three ways to block. The leftmost bar shows the size of the 'East' coalition (12 newcomers).

SOURCE: Baldwin et al. (2001).

FIGURE 3-3: BLOCKING POWER OF EAST AND POOR COALITIONS IN THE EU27

ers the ability of a handful of 'likely' coalitions to block decisions. Decisions that require unanimity can be blocked by any nation and this never changes regardless of the number of members. The analysis becomes more interesting when considering qualified majority voting in the Council.

The two coalitions we consider are an alliance of Easterners and an alliance of poor nations. How much blocking power would these two coalitions have under the Accession Treaty rules?

Figure 3-3 shows that a coalition of poor nations would easily be able to block any decision in the Council. On the 'number of members' criterion, they will have 2 more than the 14 needed to block, and on the votes criterion they will have 80 per cent more votes than they would need to block any proposal. On the population criterion, not even the poor-coalition could block, but this does not matter; a measure can be blocked on any of the three thresholds. Once again we conclude that legislating under the Accession Treaty rules (that were first agreed in the Nice Treaty) will be very difficult.

# 3.4 The distribution of power among EU members

The next aspect of EU decision making that we address is the distribution of power among EU members. As with efficiency, there is no perfect measure of power. The tactic we take is to rely on the Law of Large Numbers. That is, we look to see how likely it is that each member's vote is crucial on a randomly drawn issue. Before turning to the calculations, however, we lay out our specific definition of power.

For our purposes, power means influence, or, more precisely, the ability to influence EU decisions by being in a position to make or break a winning coalition in the Council of Ministers. Of course, no one has absolute power in the EU, so we focus on the likelihood that a Member State will be influential. On some things Germany's vote will be crucial, on others it will be irrelevant, and the same goes for all other members. What determines how likely it is that a particular nation will be influential?

The most direct and intuitive measure of political power is national voting shares in the Council of Ministers. Under current EU rules, each Member State has a fixed number of votes in the Council of Ministers. Up to the 2004 enlargement, 87 Council-of-Minister votes are divided among the 15 EU nations, with large nations receiving more votes than small ones (see Chapter 2 for details). It seems intuitively plausible that nations with more votes are more likely to be influential on average, so the first power measure to try is a nation's share of Council votes. But how can we tell if this power measure captures anything real?

## 3.4.1 Empirical evidence on power measures' relevance

One cannot measure a nation's power in EU decision making directly, but the exercise of power does leave some 'footprints' in the data. Budget allocations are one manifestation of power that is both observable and quantifiable. To check whether our power measure is useful we see if it can help to explain the budget allocation puzzles we discussed in Chapter 2.

To understand why our power measure should be related to outward signs of power like the budgetary spending allocation, we need to briefly review the budget process explained in detail in Chapter 2 and then discuss 'back scratching' and 'horse trading'.

The annual budget must be passed by both the Council of Ministers and the European Parliament (EP). These annual budgets, however, are constrained by medium-term budget plans called 'Financial Perspectives' (the current one covers 2000–06). The Financial Perspectives require unanimity in the Council, but the annual budgets are passed on the basis of qualified majority. For both the Financial Perspectives and the annual budgets, EP decision making is on the basis of a simple majority. As it turns out, the EP does not matter from a *national* power perspective. This notion is explained in detail in Box 3-4, but the basic notion is based on the different majority thresholds. That is, since the EP's majority threshold (50 per cent) is much lower than the Council's (71 per cent) and the allocation of MEP per nation in the EP is similar to the allocation of votes per nation in the Council, any coalition of nations that can pass a budget in the Council can also pass it in the Parliament. For this reason, we focus solely on vote shares in the Council of Ministers.

### BOX 3-4: WHY PARLIAMENT REFORM DOES NOT AFFECT NATIONAL POWER DISTRIBUTIONS

Most EU legislation these days must be approved by both the Council and the Parliament. As it turns out, the allocation of seats in the European Parliament does not affect national power, *per se*. The reason rests on three facts: (i) the national distribution of Council votes and MEP seats is quite similar, as Fig. 3-4 shows; (ii) to pass the Council, a proposal must garner at least 71 per cent of votes; and (iii) to pass the Parliament, a proposal needs to win only half the MEP votes.

To illustrate how these three facts affect the Parliament's power from a purely national perspective, we must cover a few preliminaries. First, we start with a simple assumption – that MEPs act as national representatives and indeed that their votes are controlled directly by national governments (obviously this is false, but going to this extreme helps to build intuition for more realistic cases). Second, recall that we define power as the ability to break a winning coalition, so the question is: 'Can a nation use the votes of its MEPs to block a coalition that it cannot otherwise block?' If the answer is 'no', then the votes of MEPs do not affect a nation's power, even under the extreme assumption that MEP votes are controlled by governments. And, of course, if national power is not affected by MEP votes when they are directly controlled, national power is certainly not affected when the MEPs vote by their own conscience. Finally, we assume that each nation's share of Council votes is *identical* to its share of MEP votes (rather than just similar). Under these assumptions, we can think of the actual procedure as a double majority system. To pass, a proposal needs to attract the votes of Member States that have at least 50 per cent of MEP votes, and 71 per cent of Council votes.

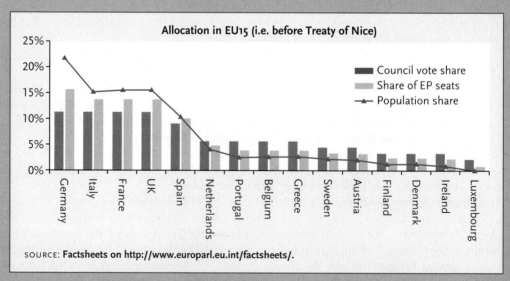

SOURCE: **Factsheets on http://www.europarl.eu.int/factsheets/.**

FIGURE 3-4: SHARE OF MEPS, COUNCIL VOTES AND POPULATION IN THE EU15

Now here is the main point. The first criterion is redundant since the Council vote threshold is higher than the MEP threshold. That is, since the distributions of Council and MEP votes is assumed to be identical, any coalition that has 71 per cent of Council votes will automatically have 71 per cent of MEP votes, which is plainly more than the 50 per cent necessary.

Some careful thought and a little mental gymnastics reveal the implications of this for national power; there are no instances when a nation's MEP votes increase its power to block. In every instance where it can block on the basis of MEP votes, it can also block on the basis of Council votes.

Even under a more realistic view of the process, the same conclusion holds. The fact that the distribution of MEP votes is similar to the distribution of Council votes teamed with the fact that the Council threshold is much higher than the Parliament's threshold, means that MEPs' votes could never increase a nation's ability to block, even if the MEPs voted on strictly national lines.

Interestingly, this suggests one indirect reason why the Parliament has tended to form cross-national coalitions. If they acted on purely national lines, MEPs would, on typical issues (i.e. where the national government accurately represents the national view), act as rubber stampers. If they form cross-national coalitions, they may bring something new to the process.

An important caveat to all this is the fact that EU nations are made up of diverse groups. Since some groups are less well represented in their nation's government than they are in the European Parliament (e.g. labour unions when a conservative government is in power), having more seats means that these special interest groups will have a larger say in EU decision making.

For a more detailed analysis, see Bindseil and Hantke (1997).

As pointed out in Chapter 2, about 80 per cent of Council decisions are made on the basis of qualified majority voting. Since the Council decides many issues each year, and members do not care dearly about all of them, countries tend to trade their votes on issues that they view as minor in exchange for support on an issue that they view as major, even if the two issues are totally unrelated. This sort of natural activity is referred to by the colourful names of 'back scratching' and 'horse trading'.

Now that we have discussed the background, we can turn to the main reasoning. Citizens in EU nations, or at least some citizens, benefit when EU money is spent in their district. Successful politicians, responding to the desires of their citizens, use their political clout to direct money homewards. For example, suppose that countries ask for a little 'gift' each time they find themselves in a position that is critical to a winning coalition. In the data, the 'gift' ends up as EU spending, but the actual mechanism could be subtle, say a more favourable treatment in the allocation of EU subsidies to hillside farmers, a more generous allocation of milk quotas, or inclusion of reindeer meat in the CAP's price support mechanism. In this light, it seems natural that a country's power measure would equal its expected fraction of all special gifts handed out. If one goes to the cynical extreme and views the whole EU budget as nothing more than a pile of 'gifts', then our power measures should meet the EU's budget allocation perfectly. If high-minded principles such as helping out disadvantaged regions also matter, then the power measure should only partially explain the spending pattern.

As it turns out Council vote shares go a long way towards solving the 'puzzle' of EU budget allocation discussed in Chapter 2. The horizontal axis in the top panel of Fig. 3-5 plots a measure of the 'bias' in each nation's power per person; specifically, it plots the ratio of each nation's share of Council votes to its share of EU15 population. To understand why this reflects the power bias,

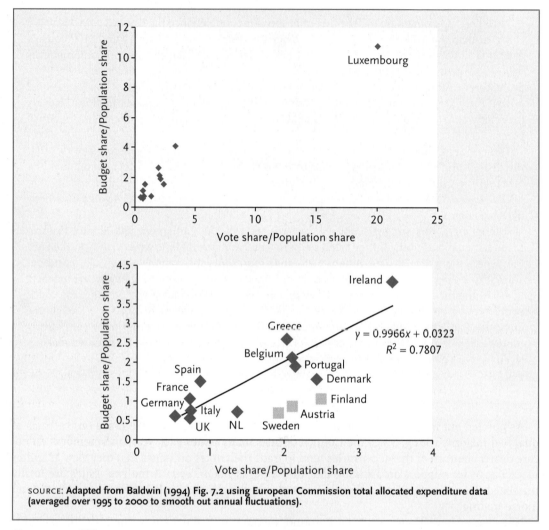

SOURCE: **Adapted from Baldwin (1994) Fig. 7.2 using European Commission total allocated expenditure data** (averaged over 1995 to 2000 to smooth out annual fluctuations).

FIGURE 3-5: EU15 PER CAPITA VOTE SHARES AND BUDGET SHARE (AVERAGE 1995–2000)

suppose a nation has a ratio of exactly 1.0. This would imply that the Council votes per citizen in that nation is exactly equal to the EU15 average. For example, Spain's vote share to population share ratio is 0.9. This means that Spaniards have slightly less than the average number of votes. Greece, on the other hand, has a ratio of 2.6, which means Greeks have 2.6 times more votes per person than the EU average.

The vertical axis plots a measure of the bias in each nation's receipt per capita. Again, to put everything on a common scale, the precise measure we use is the ratio between the nation's share of EU spending and its share of the EU's population. As with the per capita power measure on the horizontal axis, 1.0 on the vertical axis implies the average receipts per person, taking the EU15 as a whole.

Each point in the top panel indicates an EU15 member. There are two salient findings here. First, there is a distinct positive relationship between power per person and receipts per person. In other words, it seems as if politicians use their power in the Council of Ministers to direct EU spending towards their home countries. Second, Luxembourg is a real outlier. Luxembourger's have 20 times more votes per person than the EU average and they get almost 11 times more spending per person than the EU average. Because a huge outlier can make it difficult to see what is going on with the others, the bottom panel shows the same figure without Luxembourg.

The bottom panel confirms the positive relation between power and spending, but it also allows us to pick out a few more interesting features. Note that the newest EU members – Austria, Finland and Sweden – are far below the average relationship between power and spending. In other words, given their level of votes per person, the relationship between power and spending that one sees in the older members (the EU12) suggests that they should be getting more EU spending per person. Perhaps this reflects the fact that these newcomers have not yet learned how to work EU politics in their favour, or maybe they have not had time to do enough 'back scratching'. We can also see that the UK is the nation that receives the least per capita of all EU15 nations. It also has one of the lowest vote ratios, but not the lowest – Germany has that distinction.

Voting weights are a great rough-and-ready power measure that has the great merit of transparency. Unfortunately, voting weights can give a very misleading depiction of the power distribution.

### 3.4.2 Vote shares as a power measure: the shortcomings

To illustrate the potential pitfalls of vote weights as a power measure, consider a 'toy model' of the Council. Suppose there are only three countries in this toy model – imaginatively called A, B and C – and they have 40, 40 and 20 votes respectively. Decisions are based on a simple majority rule (+50 per cent to win). If we used voting weights as a measure of power, we would say that countries A and B, each with their 40 votes, were twice as powerful as C with its 20 votes. This is wrong.

With a bit of reflection you can convince yourself that all three nations are equally powerful in this toy Council. The point is that *any winning coalition requires two nations, but any two nations will do.* Likewise, any pair of nations can block anything. As a consequence, all three nations are equally powerful in the sense that they are equally likely to make or break a winning coalition.

The level of the majority threshold can also be important for power. For example, continuing with our toy model, raising the majority rule from 50 to 75 per cent would strip nation C of all power. The only winning coalition that C would belong to is the grand coalition A&B&C, but here C would not be able to turn it into a losing one by leaving the coalition. Therefore C's vote can have no influence on the outcome. Again, vote shares in this example would give a very incorrect view of power.

More generally, power – i.e. the ability to make or break a winning coalition – depends upon a complex interaction of the majority threshold and exact distribution of votes. Indeed, the useless-vote-situation in which nation C found itself in our second example actually occurred in the early days of the EU. See Box 3-5 for details.

---

**Box 3-5: Luxembourg's useless vote, 1958–73**

The 1958 Treaty of Rome laid down the rules for qualified majority voting in the EEC6. The big three – Germany, France and Italy – got 4 votes each, Belgium and the Netherlands got 2 each, and Luxembourg got 1. The minimum threshold for a qualified majority was set at 12 of the 17 total votes.

A little bit of thought shows that the Treaty writers did not think hard enough about this. As you can easily confirm, Luxembourg's 1 vote never matters. Any coalition (group of 'yes' voters) that has enough votes to win can always win with or without Luxembourg. According to formal power measures, this means that Luxembourg had little power over issues decided on a QMV basis. As Felsenthal and Machover (2001) write: 'This didn't matter all that much, because the Treaty of Rome stipulated that QMV would not be used until 1966; and even in 1966–72 it was only used on rare occasions. Still, it seems a bit of a blunder.' All changed from 1973 on when the weights were altered to allow for the accession of Britain, Denmark and Ireland. Indeed, since then Luxembourg's votes have turned out to be crucial in a surprisingly large number of coalitions. Maybe that is why Luxembourg has the highest receipt per capita in the EU despite being the richest nation by far.

*Source*: This box is based on the excellent web book, Felsenthal and Machover (2001), which provides a much better in-depth look at voting theory.

Simple counterexamples such as these led to the development of several more sophisticated power indices. We shall focus on the 'Normalized Banzhaf Index'.

### 3.4.3 Power to break a winning coalition: the Normalized Banzhaf Index

In plain English, the Normalized Banzhaf Index (NBI) gauges how likely it is that a nation finds itself in a position to 'break' a winning coalition on a randomly selected issue. By way of criticism, note that the setup behind the NBI provides only a shallow depiction of a real world voting process. For instance, the questions of who sets the voting agenda, how coalitions are formed and how intensively each country holds its various positions are not considered. In a sense, the equal probability of each coalition occurring and each country switching its vote is meant to deal with this shallowness. The idea is that all of these things would average out over a large number of votes on a broad range of issues. Thus, this measure of power is really a very long-term concept. Another way of looking at it is as a measure of power in the abstract. It tells us how powerful a country is likely to be on a randomly chosen issue. Of course on particular issues, various countries may be much more or much less powerful.

The calculation of NBI for all EU members is a topic that may fascinate some readers, but it is not essential to our study of EU decision making, so we relegate its discussion to Box 3-6.

### BOX 3-6: CALCULATING THE NORMALIZED BANZHAF INDEX (NBI)

The mechanical calculation of the NBI is easy to describe and requires nothing more than some patience and a PC with lots of horsepower. To work it out, we ask a computer to look at all possible coalitions (i.e. all conceivable line-ups of yes and no votes) and identify the winning coalitions. Note that listing all possible coalitions is easy to do by hand for low numbers of voters; in a group of 2 voters there are only 4, in a group of 3 there are 8. However, the general formula for the number of all possible coalitions for a group of $n$ voters is $2^n$, so determining which coalitions are winners by hand quickly becomes impractical; in the EU15, 32 768 coalitions have to be checked. In the EU27, the number is over 134 million. The computer's next task is to work out all the ways that each winning coalition could be turned into a loser by the defection of a single nation. Finally, the computer calculates the number of times each nation could be a 'deal breaker' as a fraction of the number of times that any country could be a deal breaker. The theory behind this is that the Council decides on a vast array of issues, so the NBI tells us how likely it is that a particular nation will be critical on a randomly selected issue.

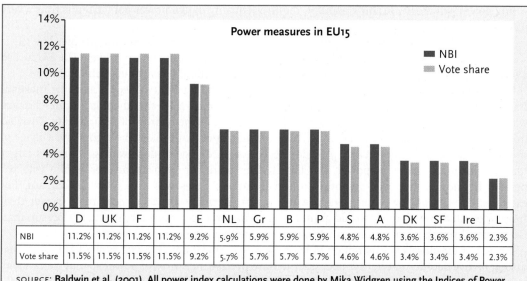

FIGURE 3-6: COMPARING EU15 POWER MEASURES: NBI AND VOTE SHARES

For the EU15, it turns out that the theoretically superior power measure (NBI) is not very different from the rough-and-ready national vote-share measure, as Fig. 3-6 shows. The measures also are quite similar for EU27. Readers who distrust sophisticated concepts should find their confidence in the Banzhaf measure bolstered by this similarity – and the same applies to readers who distrust rough-and-ready measures.

If you like this sort of reasoning, see the excellent website, http://powerslave.val.utu.fi, which is devoted to power indices of all types.

# 3.5 Legitimacy in EU decision making

The EU is a truly unique organization. Nowhere else in the world has so much national sovereignty been transferred to a supranational body. As Chapter 1 pointed out, the massive death and destruction of two world wars is what led the EU's founders to contemplate this transfer, but the continual willingness of the current generation of Europeans to accept it depends upon much more practical considerations. One consideration is the EU's ability to deliver results, but another important consideration is the democratic legitimacy of the EU's decision making process.

## 3.5.1 Thinking about democratic legitimacy

What makes a decision making system legitimate? This is a difficult question so it helps to start with an extreme and obviously illegitimate voting scheme and to think about why it seems illegitimate. Almost every European would view as illegitimate a system that allowed only land-owning males the right to vote. Why? Because those without votes would find it unjust. And if the land-owning men were forward looking, they would also find it illegitimate since they or their male offspring might one day lose their land.

In short, a good way to think about legitimacy is to apply the 'in the other person's shoes' rule. A system is legitimate if all individuals would be happy with any other individual's allocation of voting power, which, if you think about it, requires equality. Equal power per citizen is thus a very natural legitimacy principle.

But what constitutes a citizen? In the EU there are two answers: nations and people. The EU is a *union of states*, so each state is a citizen and should thus have equal voting power. The EU is also a *union of people*, so people are citizens and so each person should have equal voting power.

The problem is that the EU is both a union of states and a union of people and this makes it impossible to apply the equality principle in a simple manner. Note that there is a more classical way to phrase this same point. Democracy, it has been said, is the tyranny of the majority. To avoid this tyrannical aspect, democracies must have mechanisms that protect the rights and wishes of minorities. Indeed, many nations provide mechanisms for giving disadvantaged groups larger than proportional shares of power, but the starting point for such departures is one vote per person. In the EU, the over-weighting of small nations' votes was one such mechanism. For example, equality of power per person would grant Germany 2000 per cent more power than Ireland; equality per member would grant Luxembourgers 160 times more power per person than Germans. Given the dual-Union nature of the EU, neither extreme is legitimate.

To look more closely at this notion of legitimacy and how it has changed as the EU has evolved during its five decades of life, it is necessary to have precise measures of power so that we can look at how 'power per person' and 'power per nation' have changed.

### 3.5.2 Legitimacy by the numbers

Given the measures of power described above, it is a fairly easy matter to measure Union-of-People legitimacy and Union-of-States legitimacy. An EU that was 100 per cent Union-of-States legitimate would give equal power to all member nations. An EU that was 100 per cent Union-of-People legitimate would give equal power to all EU citizens. This point is illustrated for the EU15 with the two dashed lines in Fig. 3-7.

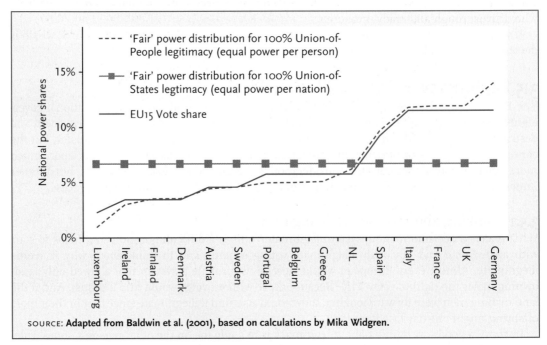

SOURCE: Adapted from Baldwin et al. (2001), based on calculations by Mika Widgren.

FIGURE 3-7: ILLUSTRATION OF 'FAIR' POWER DISTRIBUTIONS FOR TWO TYPES OF EU15

The 'fair' power distribution for the Union-of-States view is trivial; in the EU15, each member should get 1/15th of the power. For the Union-of-People view the calculation is more complex and involves some reckoning to which we now turn.

## FAIRNESS AND SQUARE-NESS

Strange as it may seem, ensuring Union-of-People fairness – that is to say, a Council in which each EU *citizen* has equal power – requires each Council member to have power in the Council that is proportional to the square root of her nation's population.

Why? The basic reason is that Council decision making is a two-step procedure: Citizens elect national governments, and those governments vote in the Council.

In his/her national election, a typical German citizen has less power than a typical Luxembourger. Each group of voters chooses one government but German voters are 160 times more numerous. Thus in national elections, a German voter has much less influence than a Luxembourger voter. To ensure that each EU citizen is equally powerful in Council decisions, the German Council representative must have more power than the Luxembourger representative. That much is easy to see, but how much more?

A first guess is that in a national election, a German voter is only 1/160th as influential as a Luxembourger voter in a national election. In this case, making EU citizens equipotent in the Council would require the German Minister to be 160 times more powerful in the Council than the Luxembourger Minister. That seems right: 1/160th as powerful in the national election and 160 times more powerful in the Council. But this is wrong since it misses a subtlety that requires some mental gymnastics to comprehend.

In national elections, two things change as the number of voters rise. First, the likelihood of being critical in a particular winning coalition decreases and – as intuition dictates – it declines linearly with the number of voters. Second, the number of winning coalitions increases.[2] Thus, the German has 1/160th the chance that a Luxembourger does of making or breaking a given winning coalition, but for the German this is applied to many more coalitions. Taking this into account, one can see that the German voter's power is less than that of a Luxembourger in his/her respective national elections, but the figure is not 1/160th as powerful, it is higher. As a consequence, the German Minister's power in the Council should not be proportional to the German population; it should be *less than proportional*. The precise answer is that for all EU citizens to be equally powerful in the Council, their Ministers should have power in the Council that is proportional to the *square root* of their national populations. This is called Penrose's rule. Admittedly, it is not the easiest concept to grasp, but it is correct and has a cherished position in the mathematics of voting system. (See Box 3-7 for an alternative explanation.)

---

### BOX 3-7: THE MATHEMATICS OF THE SQUARE ROOT RULE

If everything in the Council of Ministers were decided by an EU-wide referendum, proportional representation would clearly provide each EU citizen with equal power. But even ignoring the Commission, decision making in the EU is a two-step procedure – citizens elect national governments, which then vote in the Council – and this changes everything. In her national election, a typical Frenchwoman is less likely to be influential than a Dane since each chooses one government but French voters are more numerous. Thus small-nation citizens have a

---

[2] Try a simple example. With a 50 per cent majority rule and one-vote per citizen, there are 4 winning coalitions when there are 3 citizens (A&B, A&C, B&C, A&B&C). With 5 voters there are 11 winning coalitions (A&B&C, A&B&D, A&B&E, A&C&D, A&C&E, A&D&E, B&C&D, B&C&E, A&B&C&D, A&B&C&E, A&B&C&D&E).

power-edge going into the Council meeting and to even out the power, the votes of big-nation representatives should have more weight in the Council.

But how much more? The formal power measures discussed above yield a simple answer. National power in the Council should increase with the *square root* of national population. The reason is that power per citizen in national elections declines with the square root of the population, so national power in the Council should increase with square root in order to have a fair system, i.e. a system where each EU citizen is equally powerful in the Council of Ministers.

Where, you may ask, does the square root come from? The answer requires a bit of maths. Consider a randomly selected yes–no issue and suppose that member nations decide their stance on this issue by a referendum; define $P_N$ as the probability that a typical citizen's vote is critical in the referendum outcome. Then the member states vote in the Council and define $P_{MS}$ as the probability that the Member State is critical in the Council vote. A citizen's probability of being critical is thus $P_N$ times $P_{MS}$ and our fairness metric requires this to be equal for all Member States.

$P_{MS}$ has nothing to do with the number of voters (proxied by population), but $P_N$ falls at the square root of population. This sounds peculiar since most numerate people would think the probability of being critical in a national election decreases in a straight-line relationship with population. But this misses a subtlety. Two things change with the voter headcount. The probability of a typical voter being critical to a particular winning coalition decreases linearly with the headcount, but the number of distinct winning coalitions rises with the number of voters. The probability of being critical falls at a less than linearly pace. The mathematics of combinatorics gives us an exact formula assuming a voter's stance is randomly determined on a randomly selected issue. The equation is complex, but can be well approximated as the square root of $2/n\pi$, where $n$ is the number of voters (this is Stirling's formula). Hence the square root rule. For a more mathematical presentation of this, see the downloadable book, Felsenthal and Machover (2001).

### THE EU15's LEGITIMACY

The solid line in Fig. 3-7 shows the actual allocation of Council of Minister votes. This plainly shows that the EU's allocation is now quite close to what would be fair under the square root rule. Most of the deviations are towards the Union-of-States rule, so we can say that the EU15's allocation of power is indeed somewhere between the two perspectives, although it is far closer to the Union-of-People view.

### 3.5.3 Two-Union legitimacy: Nice reform vs historical outcomes

The correct blend of the two Unions is not possible to determine objectively, but we can easily compare the post-Nice system to historical blends, as Laruelle and Widgren (1998) showed. Here is the idea.

Actual power distributions can be thought of as a blend of two extreme power distributions: equipotent people and equipotent states. One way to determine the blend is to eyeball figures such as Fig. 3-7. A more objective procedure is to use simple statistical techniques (least squares) to find the blend that best fits the actual power distribution. The results of this are displayed in Fig. 3-8.

The diagram shows that the EU's voting rules have always favoured the Union-of-People interpretations (since populous nations get more votes). Since the UK, Denmark and Ireland joined in 1973, the mix has been approximately 80–20. For the EU12, for example, the actual distribution of

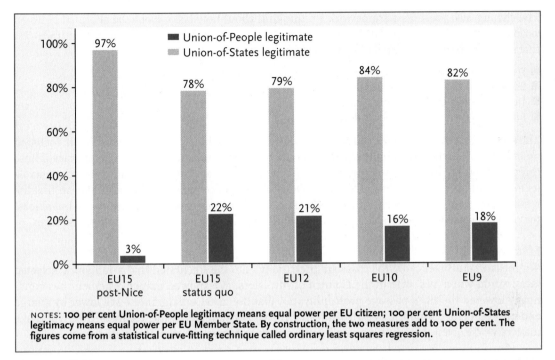

NOTES: **100 per cent Union-of-People legitimacy means equal power per EU citizen; 100 per cent Union-of-States legitimacy means equal power per EU Member State. By construction, the two measures add to 100 per cent. The figures come from a statistical curve-fitting technique called ordinary least squares regression.**

FIGURE 3-8: NICE VERSUS THE HISTORICAL TWO-UNION LEGITIMACY BLEND

power among members was a 79 : 21 per cent blend of an equal-power-per-member scheme and an equal-power-per-person scheme.

The Treaty of Nice changed the distribution of votes in the Council, favouring large nations at the expense of small nations. Our measure permits us to see how this changed the balance between Union-of-States and Union-of-People. The two leftmost pairs of bars, which show it with and without the Nice reforms, indicate that the Nice reforms heavily disfavour the Union-of-States legitimacy and shift the balance far from its historical blend.

## 3.6 Summary

Just to continue to operate, the EU must make a steady stream of decisions to adjust to the ever-changing economic and political landscape. This chapter looked at the EU decision making process from two perspectives. First, it considered the EU current allotment of 'competencies' between the EU level and national governments of its members. In terms of actual practices and principles, the key points were:

■ Policy making is categorized into areas where the EU has 'exclusive competence', i.e. where the decision is made only at the EU level; areas where competence is shared, and areas where the EU has no competence, i.e. where decisions are made only at the national or sub-national level.

■ The allocation of policy areas to these three categories is determined by the Treaties and decisions of the EU Court of Justice. This allocation, however, is blurred since the Treaties do not refer to specific fields; they refer only to areas by functional description. To clarify the allocation, the EU operates on the principle of subsidiarity, which says that unless there is a good reason for allocating a task to the EU level, all tasks should be allocated to national or sub-national governments. The 3-pillar structure of the European Union also helps to clarify the allocation. First-pillar (Community pillar) issues are under EU competence while second- and third-pillar issues are not.

The chapter also presents a framework for thinking about how tasks *should* be allocated between various levels of government (theory of fiscal federalism). This framework stresses four trade-offs that suggest whether a particular decision should be centralized or not:

- Diversity and information costs favour decentralized decision making.
- Scale economies favour centralization.
- Democracy-as-a-control-device favours decentralization.
- Jurisdictional competition favours decentralization.

The second part of the Chapter considers the EU decision making process in more detail, focusing on efficiency (i.e. the EU's ability to act), national power shares, and democratic legitimacy. These three concepts are inherently vague, but the chapter assumes a series of simplifications that enable us to present precise measures of all three. Of course the necessary simplifications mean that the resulting measures provide only shallow measures of efficiency, power and legitimacy, but at least the measures permit a concrete departure point for further discussion. These measures were:

## Efficiency

We measured efficiency by the 'passage probability', i.e. the likelihood that a randomly selected issue would win a 'yes' vote in the Council of Ministers. We showed that enlargement has continually lowered the EU's passage probability, but that the 2004 enlargement will lower by a large and unprecedented amount. We also saw that the voting reforms in the Treaty of Nice will make matters worse, even though they were intended to maintain decision making efficiency.

## National power distributions

We showed that the vote shares of small nations far exceed their population shares. Interpreting vote shares as a measure of power, this says that power in the EU is biased towards small nations. We also showed that this allocation of power goes a long way to explain why actual EU spending patterns may seem strange, i.e. that several rich nations receive above-average receipts per capita. This section also presents a more sophisticated measure of power called the Normalized Banzhaf Index; it measures the probability that a given nation will find itself in a position where it can break a winning coalition.

## Legitimacy

This is by far the vaguest of the three concepts. The approach we adopt is to check whether the allocation of votes in the EU's Council of Ministers lines up against two notions of legitimacy. If the EU is viewed as a Union-of-People, a natural yardstick is equal power per citizen. If the EU is viewed as a Union-of-States, the natural metric is equal power per Member State. Under the principle of equal power per EU citizen, the mathematics of voting tells us that this requires that the Council's votes per country rise with the square root of the country's population. The benchmark of equal power per EU Member State requires an equal number of votes per nation. What we find is that the EU has historically been an 80–20 blend of these two, with the Union-of-People perspective dominating. The reforms in the Treaty of Nice will shift the blend a long way away from the historic mix, favouring the Union-of-People view.

### SELF-ASSESSMENT QUESTIONS
**1.** List the main trade-offs stressed by the theory of fiscal federalism. Discuss how the tension between negative spillovers and diversity can explain the fact that the EU has adopted only very limited harmonization of social policies. (*Hint*: See Annex C of Chapter 1.)

**2.** In many European nations, the trend for the last couple of decades has been to decentralize decision making from the national level to the provincial or regional level. How could you explain this trend in terms of the theory of fiscal federalism?

**3.** Using the actual Council of Minister votes that will come into force after the 2004 enlargement, list five blocking coalitions that you might think of as 'likely'. Do this using the Nice Treaty definition of a qualified majority. Do the same using the qualified majority definition proposed in the draft Constitutional Treaty.

**4.** The formal power measure discussed in the chapter assumes that each voter has an equal probability of saying 'yes' or 'no' on a random issue, and that the votes of the various voters are uncorrelated. That is, the likelihood that voter A says 'yes' on a particular issue is unrelated to whether voter B says 'yes'. However in many situations, the votes of a group of voters will be correlated. For example, poor EU members are all likely to have similar views on issues concerning spending in poor regions. Work out how this correlation changes the distribution of power (defined as likelihood that a particular voter can break a winning coalition). To be concrete, assume that there are five voters (A, B, C, D and E), that each has 20 votes, that the majority rule is 51 per cent, and that A and B always vote the same way.

**5.** Using the definition of legitimacy proposed in the text (equal power per person), try to determine whether the US Congress is 'legitimate'. Note that the US Congress has two houses; the Senate and the House of Representatives. In the Senate, each of the 50 states has two Senators, while the number of Representatives per state is proportional to the state's population.

## ESSAY QUESTIONS

**1.** Obtain a copy of the proposed Constitutional Treaty produced by the European Convention in 2003. Use the theory of fiscal federalism to discuss the appropriateness of the allocation of competencies between the EU and Member States.

**2.** Using the QMV voting weights in the EEC6 (see Box 3-5), calculate all possible coalitions, i.e. combinations of yes and no votes among the Six. (*Hint*: There are $2^6 = 64$ of them.) Identify the winning coalitions and find the passage probability.

**3.** The 10 newcomers joining the EU in 2004 will greatly increase the diversity of preferences inside the EU. Use the theory of fiscal federalism to discuss how this change might suggest a different allocation of competencies between the EU and the Member States.

**4.** Discuss how 'enhanced co-operation' agreements (see Chapter 2 for details) fit into the theory of fiscal federalism. Do you think the increase in the diversity of preferences in the EU stemming from the 2004 enlargement will make these agreements more or less attractive to Member States?

**5.** The Constitutional Treaty produced by the European Convention was first released in draft form in May 2003. Download this draft and compare the Council of Minister's voting scheme to the scheme in the final version in terms of efficiency and legitimacy.

**6.** The Accession Treaty, which you can download from the European Parliament's website, contains the number of Council votes that each of the 10 new members will receive under the system that will operate from November 2004 until the Constitutional Treaty enters into force. Use a diagram like Fig. 3-7 to see how the enlargement changes the Union-of-People's versus Union-of-States' legitimacy.

## FURTHER READING: THE AFICIONADOS CORNER

More wide-ranging introduction to fiscal federalism applied to the European Union can be found in Dewatripont et al. (1995) and Berglof et al. (2003). The latter includes a general discussion that applies the theory to the Constitutional Treaty.

For an opinionated view of what decisions should be allocated to the EU, see Alesina and Wacziarg (1999), *Is Europe Going to Far?*, Carnegie-Rochester Conference on Public Policy. Although this contains several factual errors concerning EU law and policies, it contains a highly cogent application of the theory of fiscal federalism to decision making in the EU.

To learn more about formal measures of power and legitimacy, see Felsenthal and Machover (2001). For historical power distributions see Laruelle and Widgren (1998).

## USEFUL WEBSITES

Extensive explanation and use of formal voting measures can be found on http://powerslave.val.utu.fi.

## REFERENCES

Commons (2002) 'Crossborder shopping and smuggling', *House of Commons Library*, Research paper 02/40, London.

Baldwin, R. (1994) *Towards an Integrated Europe*, CEPR, London.

Baldwin, R., E. Berglof, F. Giavazzi and M. Widgren (2001) *Nice Try: Should the Treaty of Nice be Ratified?*, CEPR Monitoring European Integration 11, CEPR, London.

Begg, D. et al. (1993) *Making Sense of Subsidiarity: How Much Centralization for Europe?*, CEPR Monitoring European Integration 4, CEPR, London.

Berglof, E. et al. (2003) *Built to Last: A Political Architecture for Europe*, CEPR Monitoring European Integration 12, CEPR, London.

Dewatripont, M. et al. (1995) *Flexible Integration: Towards a More Effective and Democratic Europe*, CEPR Monitoring European Integration 6, CEPR, London.

Felsenthal, D. and M. Machover (2001) *Enlargement of the EU and Weighted Voting in the Council of Ministers*, LSE web book on www.lse.ac.uk.

Laruelle, A. and M. Widgren (1998) 'Is the allocation of voting power among EU Member States fair?', *Public Choice*, 94: 317–339.

Peet J. and K. Ussher (1999) *The EU budget: An Agenda for Reform?*, CER Working Paper, February.

Bindseil, U. and C. Hantke (1997) 'The power distribution in decision making among EU Member States', *European Journal of Political Economy*, 13: 171–185.

# PART II The Microeconomics of European Integration

Learning economics is a bit like learning a language. If you want to read Shakespeare, Zola or Goethe in the original, you start by memorizing simple, rather inane conversations in English, French or German. If you want to understand the full range of microeconomic effects of the European integration, you start by working through simple, rather unrealistic cases. Accordingly, the economics in this book are organized by increasing complexity.

We first study the economics of simple trade policy changes in settings that assume away much real-world complexity. Although the simplifying assumptions are frequently spectacularly unrealistic, they allow us to get straight to the core logic of the economic interaction under study. Having got a handle on the core logic, we progressively introduce more realism and more complications. Such an approach may seem circuitous, but it proves an excellent way of tackling difficult problems. The alternate approach – to admit from the start that everything affects everything – often results in muddled thinking.

We apply this progressive complexity approach to the three types of economic effects:

■ *Allocation effects*: Integration's impact on the sectoral allocation of economic resources and thus on the economy's efficiency; these are sometimes called 'static effects'.
■ *Accumulation effects*: Also known as 'growth effects', these encompass integration's impact on the accumulation of economic resources, especially capital.
■ *Location effects*: Integration's impact on the geographical location of economic activity; at the European perspective these are geographic reallocations of resources, but from the regional perspective they look like accumulation effects.

Allocation effects are addressed in Chapters 4 to 6. Chapter 4 introduces the tools used in Chapter 5 to study the essential economics of preferential trade liberalization. The key simplification in Chapters 4 and 5 are 'perfect competition' and 'constant returns to scale'. Chapter 6 looks at additional effects that arise once one allows for a more realistic framework in which imperfect competition and scale economies are important; the main focus is on how integrating Europe's many small markets can lead to lower price and more efficient firms. Chapter 7 expands the range of effects by considering accumulation, i.e. growth effects. Consideration of the economics of location effects is most naturally presented together with the EU's policies aimed at affecting the location of economic activity. For this reason, we postponed consideration of location effects to Chapter 9.

# 4 Essential Microeconomic Tools

This chapter presents the tools that we shall need when we begin our study of European economic integration in the next chapter. The tools are simple because we make a series of assumptions that greatly reduce the complexity of economic interactions. The primary simplification in this chapter concerns the behaviour of firms. In particular, all firms are assumed to be 'perfectly competitive', i.e. we assume that firms take as given the prices they observe in the market. Firms, in other words, believe that they have no impact on prices and that they could sell as much as they want at the market price. A good way of thinking about this assumption is to view each firm as so small that it believes that its choice of output has no impact on market prices. This is obviously a very rough approximation since even medium-sized firms – the Danish producer of Lego toys, or the Dutch brewer of Heineken, for example – realize that the amount they can sell is related to the price they charge. The second key simplification concerns technology, in particular increasing returns to scale, also known as scale economies. Scale economies refer to the way in which the average cost of producing a good tends to fall as the firm produces at higher scales of production. Although almost every industry is subject to some sort of falling average cost, consideration of increasing returns to scale greatly complicates the analysis. Here we assume away such complications, assuming instead that the marginal cost of producing goods rises with a firm's level of output.

## 4.1 Preliminaries I: supply and demand diagrams

To assess the economics of European integration it proves convenient to have a simple yet flexible diagram with which to determine the price and volume of imports, as well as the level of domestic consumption and production. The diagram we use – the 'import supply and import demand diagram' – is based on straightforward supply and demand analysis. But to begin from the beginning, we quickly review where demand and supply curves come from. Note that this section assumes that readers have had some exposure to supply and demand analysis; our treatment is intended as a review rather than an introduction. Readers who find it too brief should consult an introductory economics textbook such as Mankiw (2000).

Those readers with a good background in microeconomics may want to skip this section, moving straight on to the import demand and supply reasoning introduced in section 4.2.

### 4.1.1 Demand curves and marginal utility

A demand curve shows how much consumers would buy of a particular good at any particular price. Since we assume that consumers' behaviour is driven by a desire to spend their money in a way that maximizes their material well-being, it is clear that the demand curve is based on a kind of optimization exercise. To see this, the left panel of Fig. 4-1 plots the 'marginal utility' curve for a typical consumer, i.e. the 'happiness' (measured in euros) that a consumer gets from consuming one more unit of the good under study. If we are considering the demand for music CDs, the marginal utility curve shows how much extra joy a consumer gets from having one more CD. Typically the extra joy from an extra CD will depend upon how many CDs the consumer buys per year. For example, if the consumer buys very few CDs a year, say $c'$ in the diagram, the gain from buying an extra one is likely to be pretty high, for example, $mu'$ in the diagram. If, however, the consumer buys lots of CDs, the gain from one more is likely to be much lower, as shown by the pair, $c''$ and $mu''$.

This marginal utility curve allows us to work out how much the consumer would buy at any given price. Suppose the consumer could buy as many CDs as she likes at the price $p^*$. How many would she buy? If the consumer is wise, and we assume she is, she will buy CDs up to the point where the last one bought is just barely worth the price. In the diagram, this level of purchase is given by $c^*$ since the marginal benefit (utility) from buying an extra CD exceeds the cost of doing so (the price) for all levels of purchase up to $c^*$. At this point, the consumer finds that any further CD would not be worth the price. For example, the marginal utility from buying $c^*$ plus one CD would be below $p^*$. As usual, one gets the market demand for CDs by adding all consumers' individual marginal utility curves horizontally (e.g. if the price is $p^*$ and there are 12 000 identical consumers, market demand will be 12 000 times $c^*$).

A key point to retain from this is that the price consumers face reflects the marginal utility of consuming a little more.

### 4.1.2 Supply curves and marginal costs

Derivation of the supply curve follows a similar logic, but here the optimization is done by firms. The right panel of Fig. 4-1 shows the 'marginal cost' curve facing a typical firm (assume they are all identical for the sake of simplicity), i.e. the extra cost involved in making one more unit of the good. While the marginal cost of production in the real world often declines with the scale of production, allowing for this involves consideration of scale economies and these, in turn, introduce a whole range of complicating factors that would merely clutter the analysis at this stage. To keep it simple, we assume that firms are operating at a point where the marginal cost is upward sloped, i.e. that the cost of producing an extra unit rises as the total number of units produced rises. The

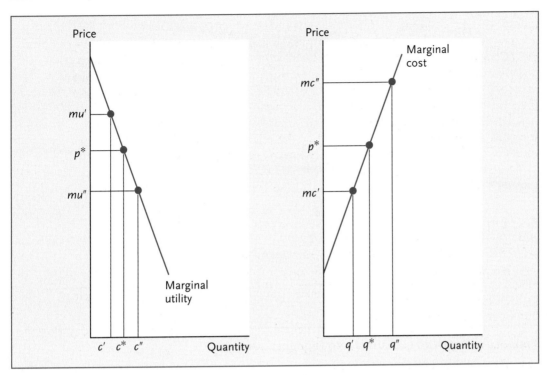

FIGURE 4-1: OPTIMIZATION AND DEMAND AND SUPPLY CURVES

curve in the diagram shows, for example, that it costs $mc'$ to produce one more unit when the production level (e.g. the number of CDs produced per year) is $q'$. This is less than the cost, $mc''$, of producing an extra unit when the firm is producing $q''$ units per year.

Using this curve we can determine the firm's supply behaviour. Presuming that the firm wants to maximize profit, the firm will supply the number of goods where the marginal cost just equals the price. For example, if the price is $p^*$, the firm will want to supply $q^*$ units. Why? If the firm offered one less than $q^*$ units, it would be missing out on some profit. After all, at that level of output, the price the firm would receive for the good, $p^*$, exceeds the marginal cost of producing it. Likewise, the firm would not want to supply any more than $q^*$ since for such a level of output, the marginal cost of producing an extra unit is more than the price. Again, we get the aggregate supply curve by adding all the firms' individual marginal cost curves horizontally.

A key point here is that under perfect competition, the price facing producers reflects the marginal production cost, i.e. the cost of producing one more unit than the firm produces in equilibrium.

## 4.1.3 Welfare analysis: consumer and producer surplus

Since the demand curve is based on consumers' evaluation of the happiness they get from consuming goods and the supply curve is based on firm's evaluation of the cost of producing it, the curves can be used to show how consumers and firms are affected by changes in the price. The tools we use, 'consumer surplus' and 'producer surplus', are described below.

Consumers buy up to the point where the marginal utility from the last unit bought just equals the price. For all the other units bought, the marginal utility exceeds the price, so the consumer

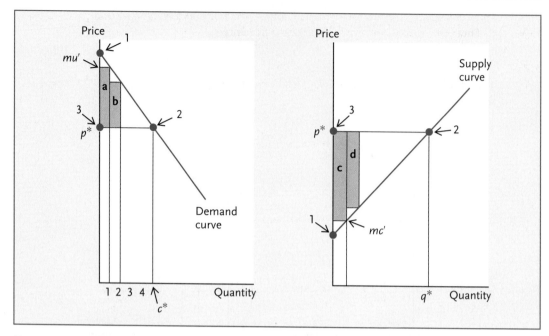

FIGURE 4-2: DERIVING CONSUMER AND PRODUCER SURPLUS

gets what is known as 'consumer surplus' from buying $c^*$ units at price $p^*$ (see Fig. 4-2). How much? For the first unit bought, the marginal unit was $mu'$ but the price paid was only $p^*$ so the surplus is the area shown by the rectangle **a**. For the second unit, the marginal utility was somewhat lower (not shown in the diagram), so the surplus is lower, specifically it is given by the area **b**. Doing the same for all units shows that buying $c^*$ units at $p^*$ yields a total consumer surplus equal to the sum of all the resulting rectangles. If we take the units to be very finely defined, the triangle defined by the points 1, 2, and 3, gives us the total consumer surplus.

An analogous line of reasoning shows us that the triangle 1, 2, 3 in the right panel gives us a measure of the gain firms get from being able to sell $q^*$ units at a price of $p^*$. Consider the first unit sold. The marginal cost of producing this unit was $mc'$ but this was sold for $p^*$ so the firm earns a surplus, what we call the 'producer surplus', equal to the rectangle **c** in the right panel. Doing the same exercise for each unit sold shows that the total producer surplus is equal to the triangle defined by the points 1, 2 and 3.

If the price changes, the size of the consumer surplus triangle and the producer surplus triangle will change. By drawing similar diagrams, you should be able to convince yourself that a price rise increases producer surplus and decreases consumer surplus.

## 4.2 Preliminaries II: introduction to open economy supply and demand analysis

This section introduces the 'workhorse' diagram in our study of the essential microeconomics of European economic integration – the open economy supply and demand analysis. Readers who have had a good course in international trade may consider skipping this section and moving straight on to the tariff analysis in section 4.3. The diagram, however, is used throughout this

chapter and the next, so even advanced students may wish to briefly review the diagram's foundations; if nothing else, such a review will help with the terminology.

## 4.2.1 The import demand curve

We first look at where the import demand curve comes from; Fig. 4-3 facilitates the analysis.

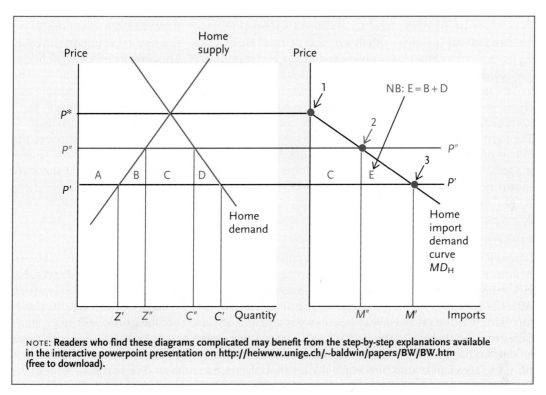

NOTE: **Readers who find these diagrams complicated may benefit from the step-by-step explanations available in the interactive powerpoint presentation on http://heiwww.unige.ch/~baldwin/papers/BW/BW.htm (free to download).**

FIGURE 4-3: DERIVING THE IMPORT DEMAND CURVE AND WELFARE CHANGES

The left panel of the diagram depicts a nation's supply and demand curves. If imports were banned for some reason, the nation would only be able to consume as much as it produced. The normal market interactions would result in a market price of $P^*$ since this is the price where the amount that consumers are willing to buy just matches the amount firms want to produce. Plainly, import demand is zero at $P^*$ (for simplicity, we assume that imported and domestic goods are perfect substitutes). This zero-import point is marked in the right panel as point 1.

How much would the nation import if the price were lower, say $P'$? The first thing to note is that the import price will fix the domestic price. Since consumers can always import the goods at $P'$, no consumer would pay more than $P'$ for the good. Likewise, there is no reason for domestic firms to charge anything less than $P'$, so $P'$ becomes the domestic price. At price $P'$, consumption demand would be $C'$ and domestic production would be $Z'$. Since consumers want to buy more of the good at $P'$ than domestic firms are willing to produce, the excess demand would be met by imports. That is to say, imports would be the difference between $C'$ and $Z'$ (in symbols, $M' = C' - Z'$).

What this tells us is that import demand at $P'$ is $M'$. This point is marked in the right panel of the diagram as point 3. Performing the same exercise for $P''$ yields point 2, and doing the same for every possible import prices, yields the import demand curve, i.e. the amount of imports that the nation wants at any given price of imports. The resulting curve is shown as $MD_H$ in the right panel. (For convenience, we often call the nation under study the 'Home' country to distinguish it from its trade partners, what we call the 'Foreign' nation.)

### WELFARE ANALYSIS: $MD$ CURVES AS THE MARGINAL BENEFIT OF IMPORTS

Welfare analysis is simple with this import demand curve. Consider a rise in the import price (i.e. the price faced by Home consumers and producers) from $P'$ to $P''$. The corresponding equilibrium level of imports drops to $M''$, since consumption drops to $C''$ and production rises to $Z''$. The welfare analysis employed in the left panel involves the notions of consumer and producer surpluses (see section 4.1 for a review of these concepts). Specifically, the price rise from $P'$ to $P''$ lowers consumer surplus by A + B + C + D. The same price rise increases producer surplus by A. The right panel shows how this appears in the import demand diagram. From the left panel, the import price rise means a net loss to the country of B + C + D, since the area A cancels out (area A is a gain to Home producers and loss to Home consumers). In the right panel, these changes are shown as area C and E, where E equals B + D.

### A POWERFUL PERSPECTIVE: TRADE VOLUME EFFECTS AND BORDER PRICE EFFECTS

It proves insightful to realize that the $MD_H$ curve shows the marginal benefit of imports to Home. Before explaining why this is true, we show that it is a useful insight. Direct reasoning showed that Home loses areas C and E from a border price rise from $P'$ to $P''$. Area C is easy to understand. After the price rise, Home pays more for the units it imported at the old price. Area C is the size of this gain. (Say the price rise was 1.2 euros per unit and $M''$ were 100; the gain would be 1.2 euros times 100; geometrically, this is the area C since a rectangle's area is its height times its base.) Understanding area E is where the insight comes in handy. Home reduces its imports at the new price and area E measures how much it loses from the drop in imports. The marginal value of the first lost unit of import is the height of the $MD_H$ curve at $M''$, but Home had to pay $P'$ for it, so the net loss is the *gap* between $P'$ and $MD_H$ curve. If we add up the gaps for all the extra units imported, we get the area E. The jargon terms for these areas are the 'border price effect' (area C), and the 'import volume effect' (area E).

To understand why $MD_H$ is the marginal benefit of imports we use three facts and one bit of logic: (i) the $MD_H$ curve is the difference between the domestic demand curve and the domestic supply curve; (ii) the domestic supply curve is the domestic marginal cost curve, and the domestic demand curve is the domestic marginal utility curve (see section 4.1 if these points are unfamiliar); and (iii) the difference between domestic marginal utility of consumption and domestic marginal cost of production is the net gain to the nation of producing and consuming one more unit. The logical point is that an extra unit of imports leads to some combination of higher consumption and lower domestic production, and this leads to some combination of higher utility and lower costs; the height of the $MD_H$ curve tells us what that combination is. Or, to put it differently, the nation imports up to the point where the marginal gain from doing so equals the marginal cost. Since the border price is the marginal cost, the border price is also an indication of the marginal benefit of imports.

To see these points in more detail, see the interactive powerpoint presentations available for free on http://heiwww.unige.ch/~baldwin/papers/BW/BW.htm.

## 4.2.2 The import supply curve

Fig. 4-4 uses an analogous line of reasoning to derive the import supply schedule. The first thing to keep in mind is that the supply of imports to Home is the supply of exports from foreigners. For simplicity's sake, suppose that there is only one foreign country (simply called 'Foreign' hereafter) and its supply and demand curves look like the left panel of the figure.

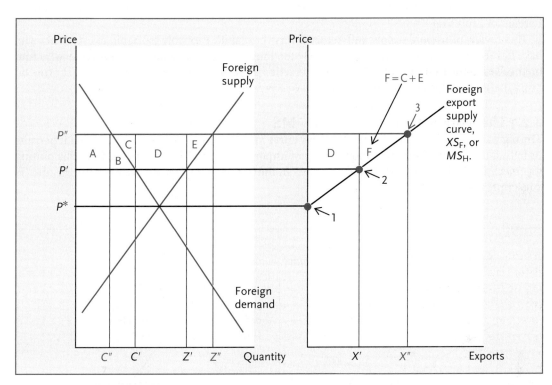

FIGURE 4-4: DERIVING THE EXPORT SUPPLY CURVE AND WELFARE CHANGES

As with the import demand curve, we start by asking how much Foreign would export for a particular price. For example, how much would it export, if the price of its exports was $P'$? At price $P'$, Foreign firms would produce $Z'$ and Foreign consumers would buy $C'$. The excess production, equal to $X' = Z' - C'$, would be exported. The fact that Foreign would like to export $X'$ when the export price is $P'$ is shown in the right panel at point 2. As the price for Foreign exports (i.e. the Home's import price) rose, Foreign would be willing to supply a higher level of exports for two reasons. The higher price would induce Foreign firms to produce more and Foreign consumers to buy less. (Note that as in the case of import demand, the export price sets the price in Foreign; Foreign firms have no reason to sell for less since they can always export, and competition among Foreign suppliers would prevent any of them from charging Foreign consumers a higher price). For example, the price $P''$ would bring forth an import supply equal to $X''$ (this equals $Z''$ minus $C''$); this is shown as point 3 in the right panel. At price $P^*$, exports are zero. Plotting all such combinations in the right panel produces the export supply curve $XS_F$. We stress again the simple but critical point that the Foreign export supply is the Home import supply, thus we also label $XS_F$ as $MS_H$.

### WELFARE

The left panel also shows how price changes translate into Foreign welfare changes. If the export price rises from $P'$ to $P''$, consumers in the exporting country lose by A + B (these letters are not related to those in the previous figure), but the Foreign firms gain producer surplus equal to A + B + C + D + E. The net gain is therefore C + D + E. Using the export supply curve $XS_F$, we can show the same net welfare change in the right panel as the area D plus F. Note that the insight from the $MD_H$ curve extends to the $XS_F$ curve, i.e. the $XS_F$ curve gives the marginal benefit to Foreign of exporting.

This review of import supply and demand was very rapid. Probably too rapid for students who have never used such diagrams and probably too long for students who have. For those who find themselves in the first category, there are interactive powerpoint presentations available for free on http://heiwww.unige.ch/~baldwin/papers/BW/BW.htm.

### 4.2.3 The workhorse diagram: MD–MS

The big payoff from having an import supply curve and an import demand curve is that it permits us to find the equilibrium price and quantity of imports. The equilibrium price is found by putting together import demand and supply as shown in the left panel of Fig. 4-5; we drop the 'H' and 'F' subscripts for convenience.

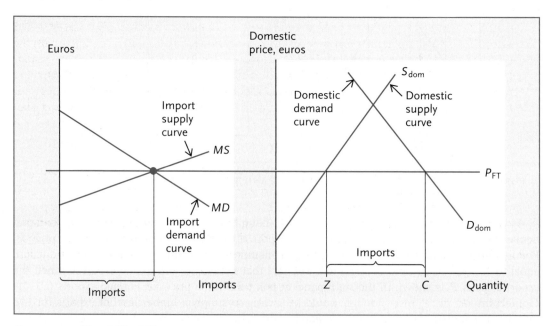

FIGURE 4-5: THE $MD$–$MS$ AND OPEN ECONOMY SUPPLY AND DEMAND DIAGRAMS

Assuming imports and domestic production are perfect substitutes, the domestic price is set at the point where the demand and supply of imports meet, namely $P_{FT}$ (FT stands for free trade). While the import supply and demand diagram, or $MD$–$MS$ diagram for short, is handy for determining the price and volume of imports, it does not permit us to see the impact of price changes on domestic consumers and firms separately. This is where the right panel becomes useful. In particular, we know that the market clears only when the price is $P_{FT}$, so we know that Home production equals $Z$ and Home consumption equals $C$. The equilibrium level of imports may be read off of either panel. In the left panel, it is shown directly; in the right one, it is the difference between domestic consumption and production. As usual, the equilibrium price is given by the intersection of the import demand and import supply curves, namely $P_{FT}$. The right panel of the figure shows that when the domestic equilibrium price is $P_{FT}$, domestic production and consumption are $Z$ and $C$.

## 4.3 MFN tariff analysis

The principle of progressive complexity directs us to take a detour in our drive towards the analysis of preferential trade liberalization in Europe. To introduce the basic method of analysis and gain experience in using the diagrams, we first study the impact of removing the simplest type of trade barrier – a tariff. Although discriminatory liberalization is what happened in Europe, we first look at the non-discriminatory case since it is less complex. For historical reasons, a non-discriminatory tariff is called a 'most favoured nation' tariff, which provides the handy abbreviation, MFN. We also note that all European nations have undertaken substantial MFN tariff liberalizations in the context of WTO trade negotiations, such as the Uruguay Round.

### 4.3.1 Price and quantity effects of a tariff

The first step is to determine how a tariff changes prices and quantities. To be concrete, suppose that the tariff imposed equals $T$ euros per unit.

The first step in finding the post-tariff price is to work out how the tariff changes the $MD$–$MS$ diagram and here Fig. 4-6 facilitates the analysis. (See section 4.2 if your are unfamiliar with the $MD$–$MS$ diagram.) The right panel of Fig. 4-6 shows the pre-tariff import demand and import supply curves, as $MD$ and $MS$ respectively. The left panel shows the foreign export supply curve as $XS$. Note that the vertical axis in this right-panel shows the domestic price, while the vertical axis in the left panel shows the border price – the difference between the two is simple, but critical (see the note to Fig. 4-6).

A TARIFF SHIFTS UP THE $MS$ CURVE

Imposition of a tariff has no effect on the $MD$ curve in the right panel since the $MD$ curve tells us how much Home would like to import at any given domestic price. By contrast, imposing a tariff on imports shifts up the $MS$ curve by $T$. The reason is uncomplicated. After the tariff is imposed, the domestic price must be higher by $T$ to get Foreign to offer the same quantity as they offered before the tariff. Consider an example. How much would Foreign supply *before the tariff*, if the Home domestic price before the were $P_a$? The answer, which is given by point 1 on the $MS$ curve, is $M_a$. After the tariff, we get a different answer. To get Foreign to offer $M_a$ after the tariff, the domestic price must be $P_a + T$ so that Foreign sees a border price of $P_a$.

So far we see that the tariff shifts up the $MS$ curve. Now we consider the impact on equilibrium prices and quantities.

THE NEW EQUILIBRIUM PRICES AND QUANTITIES

Even without a diagram, readers would surely realize that a tariff raises the domestic price and lowers imports. The diagram helps us be more specific about this intuition. After the tariff, the old import supply curve is no longer valid. The new import supply curve, labelled '$MS$ with $T$', is what matters and the equilibrium price is set at the point where the new import supply curve and the import demand curve cross. As intuition would have it, the new price – marked $P'$ in the diagram – is higher than the pre-tariff price $P_{FT}$ (as already noted, FT stands for free trade). Because of the

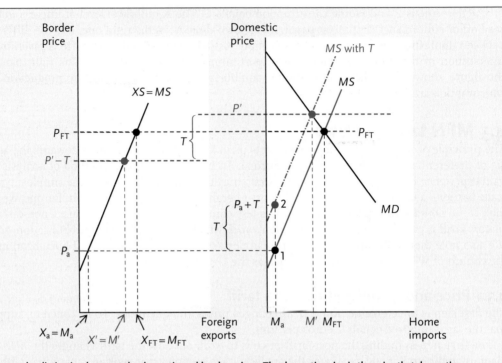

NOTE: the distinction between the domestic and border prices: The domestic price is the price that domestic consumers pay for the good. The border price is the price foreign producers receive when they sell the good to home. Why can they differ? Because of the tariff, which is nothing more than a tax on imports. When you buy a coffee at a café for, say, 1 euro, the café owner does not get the full 1 euro because the owner has to pay a tax, called the VAT, on your purchase. As a result, the price that the café owner receives is only 80 cents (the VAT is 20 per cent in this example) even though you pay 100 cents. In exactly the same way, foreigners receive a price (the border price) that equals the domestic price minus the tariff.

FIGURE 4-6: PRICE AND QUANTITY EFFECTS OF AN MFN TARIFF

higher domestic price, Home imports are reduced to $M'$ from $M_{FT}$. To summarize, there are five price and quantity effects of the tariff:

- The price facing Home firms and consumers (domestic price) rises to $P'$.
- The border price (i.e. the price Home pays for imports) falls to $P' - T$; this also means that the price received by Foreigners falls to $P' - T$.
- The Home import volume falls to $M'$.

The other two effects cannot be seen in the diagram, but are intuitively obvious and could be illustrated explicitly if we included another panel in Fig. 4-6 that resembled the right panel in Fig. 4-5:

- Home production rises since Home firms receive a higher price (they see the domestic price since they do not pay the tariffs).
- Home consumption falls in response to the higher domestic price.

## 4.3.2 Welfare effects of a tariff
With the price and quantity effects in hand, it is simple to calculate the welfare effects, i.e. who wins, who loses and by how much.

Recall that the *MD* curve comes from optimization by Home consumers and producers, while the *XS* = *MS* curve reflects optimization by Foreign consumers and producers. What this means is that we can evaluate the Home welfare effects of the price and quantity changes using only the *MD* curve, and the Foreign welfare effects using only the *XS* = *MS* curve, as shown by Fig. 4-7.

We start with the Foreign welfare impact since it is easier. At an intuitive level, we should expect the tariff to harm Foreigners since it means they get a lower price (the border price drops) and they export less. Using the diagram we can quantify these losses. The welfare impact of these two changes are shown by the areas B + D in the leftmost panel. The area B represents the direct loss from the lower price and D represents the loss from the lower level of sales.

The diagram also shows the impact of the price change on the welfare of Home residents. Intuitively, it should be clear that Home consumers will lose from the higher domestic price and Home firms will gain from the same, but that the losers will lose more than the gainers will gain since Home consumption exceeds Home production. The diagram allows us to be more precise about these intuitively obvious welfare effects.

As we showed in section 4.1, the loss in the 'private surplus' (i.e. the sum of the changes in consumer surplus and producer surplus) from the price rise from $P_{FT}$ to $P'$ is given by the area A + C in the middle panel. The last thing to consider is the impact of the tariff on Home government revenue. Since Home collects tariff revenue equal to the tariff times the number of units imported, this gain equals the area A + B in the middle panel of Fig. 4-7. Adding up the change in private

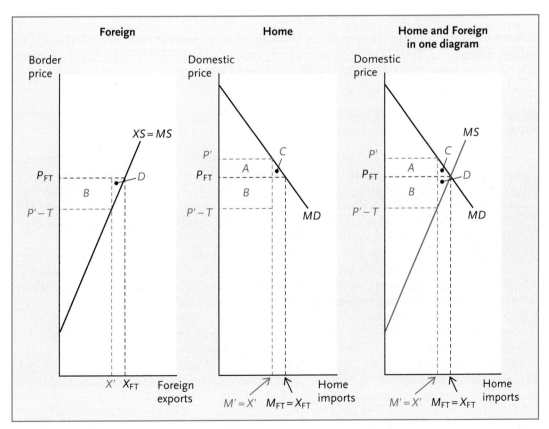

FIGURE 4-7: WELFARE EFFECTS OF AN MFN TARIFF

surplus (minus A and minus C) and the gain in revenue (plus A plus B), the net effect is the area C minus the area B, which we write at C − B for short.

## A USEFUL CONDENSATION

The first time one works through these welfare calculations, it is useful to separate the Home and Foreign effects using separate diagrams (the left and middle panels in Fig. 4-7). This separation emphasizes the fact that Foreign welfare effects can be derived from the price and quantity changes using only the *XS* curve, and, similarly, the Home welfare effect can be derived from the price and quantity effects using only the *MD* curve. Yet, once one is familiar with the under-pinnings of the areas A, B, C and D, it is convenient to condense the analysis into a single diagram, like the right panel in Fig. 4-7.

To summarize, using either the two-panel analysis or the condensed analysis, we find:

- The tariff reduces Foreign welfare since it means they sell less and receive a lower price. The loss in welfare, measured in euros, equals the area of B and D.
- The tariff creates private-sector winners and losers (Home firms gain, Home consumers lose), but the losers (consumers) lose more than gainers (firms) gain; the net impact is −A − C.
- Home collects tariff revenue equal to A + B.
- The overall Home welfare change, including both revenue and the net private loss, is B − C.
- The net effect, B − C, may be positive or negative; the relative sizes of B and C depend upon the slopes of the *MD* and *MS* curves and on the size of *T*.
- The global impact of the tariff, adding Home and Foreign welfare changes together, is definitely negative and equal to the area −C − D.

Before moving on, note that, as in section 4.1, we can trace through the distributional effects of the welfare changes, e.g. the loss to Home consumers and the gains to Home firms, using a diagram that resembles the right panel in Fig. 4-5. This is done in Box 4-1.

---

### BOX 4-1: HOME AND FOREIGN WELFARE EFFECTS: DISTRIBUTIONAL CONSEQUENCES

The analysis in Fig. 4-7 focused on the overall welfare impact on Home and Foreign. It did not allow us to see the distributional effects of the tariffs, i.e. the impact of the tariff on different groups within Home. Since the politics of an import tariff often depend heavily on the tariff's distributional impact, it is handy to have a diagram where we can see the distributional effects and the overall effects. Figure 4-8, which is based on the open-economic supply and demand diagram, is the diagram that serves this purpose.

In both panels of the diagram, the tariff-induced changes in prices and quantities are shown. As noted in the text, the overall private surplus change – that is, the loss to Home consumers minus the gain to Home producers – is minus the areas A and C in the left panel. The right panel allows us to see the producer and consumer surplus components separately. The loss to consumers from the price rise (from $P_{FT}$ to $P'$) is minus the areas $E + C_1 + C_2 + A$. The gain to Home producers is the area E. Note that the area C in the left panel equals the sum of the two triangles, $C_1 + C_2$, in the right panel. The gain in government revenue from the tax on imports is just equal to the areas A and B.

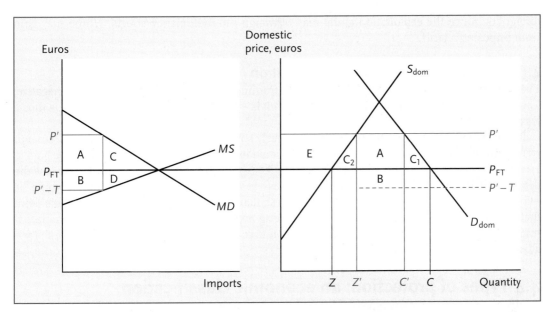

FIGURE 4-8: DISTRIBUTIONAL AND OVER WELFARE EFFECTS OF AN MFN TARIFF

## 4.3.3 Tariffs as a way of taxing foreigners

The result that a tariff might make the Home country better or worse off is worth looking at from a different angle. The two parts of Home's net welfare impact, namely B – C, represent very different kinds of changes.

■ The area B is the 'border price effect', i.e. the gain from paying less for imports. We can also think of it as the amount of the new tariff revenue that is borne by foreigners. This statement requires some explaining. In the real world, the importing firm pays the whole tariff, so one might think that the importing firm bears the full burden of the import tax. This would be wrong. Part of the burden is passed on to Home residents via higher prices. How much? Well pre-tariff, the domestic price was $P_{FT}$ and post-tariff it is $P'$, so the difference shows how much of the tariff is passed on to Home residents. Since this price hike applies to a level of imports equal to $M'$, we can say that the share of the tariff revenue paid by Home residents is area A. Using the same logic, we see that some of the tariff burden is also passed back to Foreign suppliers. The before-versus-after border price gap is $P_{FT}$ minus ($P' – T$) and this applies to $M'$ units of imports. So area B, which is the gap times imports, is a measure of how much of the tariff revenue came from foreigners.

■ Area C is the 'import volume effect', i.e. the impact of lowering imports. Here is the argument.
The $MD$ curve shows the marginal benefit to Home of importing each unit (see section 4.2 if this reasoning is unfamiliar to you). Given this, the gap between the $MD$ curve and $P_{FT}$ gives us a measure of how much Home loses for each unit it ceases to import. The area of the triangle C is just all the gaps summed from $M'$ to $M_{FT}$.

To put it differently, area B represents Home's gain from taxing foreigners while area C represents an efficiency loss from the tariff.

Given all this, we can say that *if T raises Home welfare, then it does so only because the tariff allows the Home government to indirectly tax foreigners enough to offset the tariff's inefficiency effects on the Home economy.* That is, T causes economic inefficiency at Home but T is also a way of exploiting foreigners. Since the exploitation gains may outweigh the inefficiency effects, Home may gain from imposing a tariff.

### 4.3.4 Global welfare effects and retaliation

The global welfare impact is simply a matter of summing up effects and it turns out to be negative. The net Home welfare effect is B – C. For foreign it is –B – D. The global welfare change is thus a loss, namely –C – D.

Put in this way, the gains from a tariff are clearly suspect. For example, if Home and Foreign were symmetric and both imposed tariffs, both would lose the efficiency triangle C and the gain to Home of B on imports would be lost to Home on its exports to Foreign. Home would also lose the deadweight triangle D on exports, so the net loss to each of the symmetric nations would be –C – D. In short, protection by all nations is worse than a zero-sum game. It is exactly this point that underpins the economics of WTO tariff-cutting negotiations. If only one nation liberalizes it might lose. If, however, the nation's liberalization is co-ordinated with its trading Partners' liberalization, the zero-sum aspect tends to disappear.

## 4.4 Types of protection: an economic classification

Tariffs are only one of many types of import barriers that European integration has removed. The first phase of EU integration, 1958–68, focused on tariff removal, but the Single Market Programme that was started in 1986 focused on a much wider range of 'non-tariff barriers'.

While there are several methods of categorizing such barriers, it proves useful to focus on how the barriers affect so-called trade rents. A tariff, for instance, drives a wedge between the Home price and the border price (i.e. the price paid to foreigners). This allows someone (in the tariff case it will be the Home government) to indirectly collect the 'profit' from selling at the high domestic price while buying at the low border price. For historical reasons, economists refer to such profits (area A + B in Fig. 4-9) as 'rents'. When it comes to welfare analysis, we must watch the trade rents closely. For some import barriers, Home residents get the rents, but for others no rents are created, or foreigners get the rents. This distinction is highlighted by distinguishing three categories of trade barriers: domestically captured rent (DCR) barriers; foreign captured rent (FCR) barriers; and 'frictional' barriers.

### DCR Barriers

Tariffs form the classic DCR barrier. Here the Home government gets the trade rents. From a Home nationwide welfare perspective, however, it does not really matter whether the government, Home firms or Home consumers earn these rents, as long as the rents are captured domestically. What sorts of barriers other than tariffs would lead to domestically captured rents? Some forms of quotas are DCR barriers. A quota is a quantitative limit on the number of goods that can be imported per year. To control the number of foreign goods entering the country, the government hands out a fixed number of import licences and 'collects' one licence per unit imported. The price and quantity effects of a quota that restricts imports to $M'$ in Fig. 4-9 are identical to the effects of a tariff equal to $T$. The point is that if imports are limited to $M'$, then the gap between domestic consumption and production can be no more than $M'$, implying that the domestic price must be driven up to $P'$. Another way to say this is that $T$ is the 'tariff equivalent' of the quota. Now consider the trade rents. With a quota, whoever has the licence can buy the goods at the border price $P' - T$ and resell them in the Home market for $P$. This earns the licence holders A + B. If the government gives the licences to Home residents, then the quota is a DCR barrier. If it gives them to foreigners, the quota is an FCR barrier.

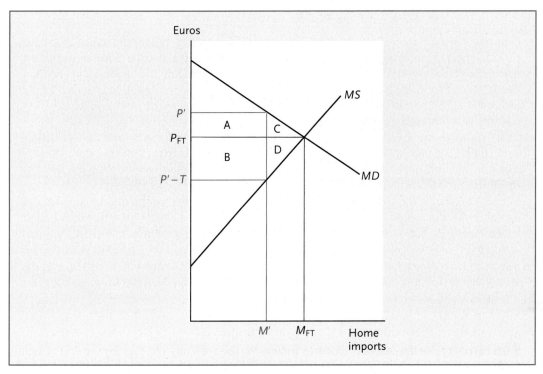

FIGURE 4-9: HOME WELFARE EFFECTS OF IMPORT PROTECTION

FIGURE 4-9: HOME WELFARE EFFECTS OF IMPORT PROTECTION

## FCR BARRIERS

A prime example of an FCR barrier is a 'price undertaking', a trade barrier commonly imposed against imports from Central and Eastern Europe, for example. This is where the EU strikes an agreement whereby foreign producers agree to sell their goods at a price no lower than an agreed level. For example, if the agreed level were $P'$ from Fig. 4-9, the price undertaking would have the same price and quantity effects as a tariff $T$. Importantly, however, the undertaking allows foreign producers, rather than the Home government, to garner the rents A + B. Throughout the indus-trialized world, and in the EU in particular, it is very common for trade barriers to be arranged so that foreigners earn the rents. One reason is that trade rents are used as a kind of gift to soothe foreign companies and governments that are likely to be angered by the imposition of a trade barrier.

Finally, note that an FCR barrier harms national welfare more than a DCR barrier. Specifically the welfare cost of an FCR is always negative, i.e. −A − C, instead of being ambiguous, i.e. B − C. Moreover, the foreign welfare impact is now A − D, so an FCR may end up helping foreigners!

## FRICTIONAL BARRIERS

The main type of trade barrier remaining inside the EU consists of what are sometimes called 'technical barriers to trade' (TBTs). Western European countries often restrict imports by subjecting them to a whole range of policies that increase the real cost of buying Foreign goods. Some examples are excessive bureaucratic 'red-tape' restrictions and industrial standards that discriminate against Foreign goods. One of the most famous examples is discussed in Box 4-2.

**Box 4-2: Cassis de Dijon: A history-making technical barrier to trade**
One very common type of frictional barrier concerns health and safety regulations that have the side effect of hindering trade. Perhaps the most famous of these was a German regulation that forbade the importation of certain low-alcohol spirits including the sweet French liqueur, Cassis – used in making the famous white wine drink, 'Kir'. This regulation was challenged before the EU's Court of Justice as a barrier to trade. When challenged on this regulation, the German government argued that the prohibition was necessary to protect public health (since weak spirits more easily promote alcohol-tolerance) and to protect consumers (since consumers might buy weak spirits, thinking they were strong). In 1979, the Court ruled that the measure was not necessary since widespread availability of low-alcohol drinks in Germany made the prohibition ineffective in furthering public health. It also found that putting the alcohol content on the label was sufficient to protect consumers, so the import ban was not necessary for the protection of consumers. This Court ruling resulted in the frictional barrier being removed. More importantly, it established the basic principle known as 'mutual recognition' whereby goods that are lawfully sold in one EU nation shall be presumed safe for sale in all EU nations. Exceptions to this principle require explicit motivation. By the way, the formal name for this Court case is 'Rewe-Zentral AG v. Bundesmonopolverwaltung für Branntwein'; no wonder it is called Cassis de Dijon.

Such barriers raise the cost of imports by increasing the difficulty and thereby the cost of selling to the Home market. Nobody gets the rents with such barriers since no rents are created. From the Home perspective, frictional and FCR barriers have identical effects; using the areas in Fig. 4-9, Home loses $A + C$. From the Foreign perspective, an FCR barrier is superior. Specifically, the Foreign welfare change is $A - D$ for FCR, but $-B - D$ for a frictional barrier.

Since frictional barriers are bad for a nation, one may ask why they are so prevalent. Box 4-3 provides one explanation.

**Box 4-3: Why do frictional barriers arise so often?**
Government agencies charged with formulating and enforcing standards are often 'captured' by special-interest groups from the regulated industries. Moreover, the Home firms that are to be subjected to the standards often play an important role in setting the standards. For example, when regulating a highly technical field such as elevators, the government (who probably does not employ many full-time elevator experts) naturally asks the opinions of domestic firms that produce elevators. With an eye to their foreign competitors, they quite naturally push for standards that raise the cost of imported goods more than the cost of locally produced goods.

An example can be found in the paper industry. Sweden and Finland produce paper mainly from new trees while French and German paper producers use a lot of recycled paper and rags. In the early 1990s, the EU was considering a regulation that would require all paper sold in the EU to contain a certain fraction of recycled paper. This sounds like a 'public interest' regulation. However it also would have had the effect of eliminating the resource-based advantage of Swedish and Finnish firms, much to the joy of French and German firms. In other words, it would have raised the real cost of imports (since the Nordic producers would have had to switch to less efficient techniques). As it turns out, it is not clear which production method is 'greener'. Recycling paper requires lots of chemicals that may be released into the environment while growing more trees is, well, green – a point that was not raised by French and German paper producers.

Since Finland and Sweden joined the EU, the regulation was not adopted, but this shows the subtle mixing of public interest and protectionism that inevitably arises when nations adopt regulations and standards.

Of course nations do need health, safety, environmental and industrial standards, so we cannot eliminate frictional barriers by just abolishing all regulation. This is one of the things tackled by the EU's 1992 programme.

One important class of frictional – i.e. cost-creating – barriers involves industrial and health standards that are chosen at least in part to restrict imports. For example, some countries refuse to accept safety tests that are performed in foreign countries, even in highly industrialized nations. This forces importers to retest their products in the local country. Beyond raising the real cost of imported goods, this sort of barrier delays the introduction of new products. While this clearly harms consumers, Home producers may benefit since it may give them time to introduce competing varieties. Another example involves imposing industrial, health, safety or environmental standards that differ from internationally recognized norms. It is often difficult to objectively know whether an unusual regulation or standard represents a valid 'public interest' concern or whether it is just a protectionist device. In fact, both motives are usually behind the adoption of such measures.

Regardless of why such policies are adopted, they have the effect of protecting Home producers or service providers. Home firms design their products with these standards in mind while foreign firms, for whom the Home market may be relatively unimportant, are unlikely to do so. Bringing imported products into conformity raises the real cost of imports.

For example, all cars sold in Sweden must have wipers for the headlights. While this policy may have some merit as a safety regulation (in the old days Sweden had lots of dusty rural roads), it also has the effect of raising the price of imported cars more than it raises the price of Swedish cars. From the drawing board onwards, all models of Volvos and Saabs – and their production facilities – are designed with these headlight wipers in mind. For other carmakers, take Renault as an example, the Swedish market is far too small to really matter. The design of Renaults and Renault's mass production facilities are not optimized for the installation of headlight wipers. Consequently, while it is expensive to put headlight wipers on both Swedish and French cars, it is much more so for French cars. This gives the Swedish carmakers an edge in Sweden. Similar sorts of barriers give the French an edge in their domestic market.

Such barriers are extremely common (Box 4-3 explores why). In fact, the EU initiated the 1992 Single Market Programme with the express intent of eliminating such barriers via the mutual recognition of product standards (with minimum harmonization).

With the MFN case as background, we are ready to turn to the following chapter, namely the analysis of discriminatory trade liberalization of the types undertaken in Europe.

## 4.5 Summary

This chapter presents the essential microeconomic tools for trade policy analysis in the simplified world where we assume there is no imperfect competition and no increasing returns. The two most important diagrams are the open-economy supply and demand diagram (right panel of Fig. 4-5), and the $MD$–$MS$ diagram (left panel of Fig. 4-5). The $MD$–$MS$ diagram provides a compact way of working out the impact of import protection on prices, quantities and overall

Home and Foreign welfare. The open-economy supply and demand diagram allowed us to consider the distributional impact of import protection, i.e. to separate the overall effect into its component effects on Home consumers, Home producers and Home revenue.

The chapter also discusses types of trade barriers in Europe. One useful way of classifying them is to focus on what happens to the trade 'rents'. Under the first type, DCR barriers, the rents go to domestic residents. For FCR barriers, the rents go to foreigners, and with frictional barriers the rents disappear. European integration consisted primarily of removing DCR barriers up until the mid-1970s. Subsequent goods–market liberalization has focused on frictional barriers.

### SELF-ASSESSMENT QUESTIONS

**1.** Using a diagram like Fig. 4-8, show the full Foreign welfare effects of imposing a Home tariff equal to $T$, i.e. show the impact on Foreign producers and Foreign consumers separately.

**2.** One way to think about the slope of the $MS$ curve is in terms of the 'size' of the home nation. The idea is that the demand from a very small nation has a very small impact on the world price. For example, Switzerland could probably increase its oil imports by 10 per cent without having any impact on the world oil price. Using a diagram like Fig. 4-7, show that the welfare costs of imposing an MFN tariff are larger for smaller nations, interpreting this in terms of the $MS$ curve's slope. Show that when the $MS$ curve is perfectly flat, the welfare effects are unambiguously negative.

**3.** Using a diagram like Fig. 4-7, show that a country facing an upward-sloped $MS$ curve can gain – starting from free trade – from imposing a sufficiently small tariff. (*Hint*: The rectangle gains and triangle losses both increase in size as the tariff gets bigger, but the rectangle gets bigger faster.) Show that any level of a frictional or FCR barriers lowers Home welfare.

**4.** Using the results from the previous exercise, consider the impact of Home imposing a tariff on Foreign exports and Foreign retaliating with a tariff on Home's exports. Assume that the $MS$ and $MD$ curves for both goods (Home exports to Foreign and Foreign export to Home) are identical. Starting from a situation where Home and Foreign both impose a tariff of $T$, show that both unambiguously gain if both remove their tariffs, but one nation might lose if it removed its tariff unilaterally. By the way, this exercise illustrates why nations that are willing to lower their tariffs in the context of a WTO multilateral trade negotiations are often not willing to remove their tariffs unilaterally.

**5.** Using a diagram like Fig. 4-5, show that an import tariff equal to $T$ has *exactly* the same impact on prices, quantities and welfare as a domestic consumption tax equal to $T$ and a domestic production subsidy equal to $T$. (*Hint*: A production subsidy lowers the effective marginal cost of domestic firms and so lowers the domestic supply curve by $T$.)

**6.** Using a diagram like Fig. 4-7, show the impact on quantities, prices and welfare when Home has no tariff, but Foreign charges an export tax equal to $T$.

**7.** Using a diagram like Fig. 4-5, show the impact on quantities, prices and welfare when Home has no tariff, but Foreign charges an export tax equal to $T$.

**8.** Using a diagram like Fig. 4-7, show that the welfare effects of a quota that restricts imports to $M'$ are exactly the same as a tariff equal to $T$; assume that each quota licence (i.e. the right to import one unit) is sold by the government to the highest bidder.

### ESSAY QUESTIONS

**1.** The concepts of consumer surplus, producer surplus and tariff revenue are meant to capture the key welfare effects of trade policy. Discuss two or three aspects of socio-economic well being that are not captured by these concepts.

**2.** The welfare analysis in this chapter assumes that governments weigh one euro of consumer surplus and producer surplus equally. Find an account in a newspaper of a real-world trade policy change and summarize the analysis in the article (the basic facts, the points of view report, etc.). Does the newspaper article make it seem like the government cares equally about consumers and producers?

**3.** Go on to the European Commission's website and find an example of a frictional barrier that the Commission is trying to remove. Explain what the barrier is, how it is justified by Member States and why it was not removed during the 1992 Single Market Programme. One URL to try is: europa.eu.int/comm/internal_market/en/index.htm

**4.** The EU imposed 'price undertakings' on several Central European steel makers in the 1990s. Describe the facts surrounding these FCR barriers and discuss the politics – both on the EU side and the Central European side – that lead to these barriers being imposed.

**5.** Write a brief historical overview of all the multilateral trade liberalizations in which the EU has participated. A good place to start your research is: europa.eu.int/comm/external_trade/.

## FURTHER READING: THE AFICIONADOS CORNER

Every undergraduate textbook on international economics has a chapter on tariff analysis that covers the same material as this chapter. One particular accessible treatment can be found in Krugman and Obstfeld (2000). For much more on the economics of trade protection see Vousden (1990).

## USEFUL WEBSITES

The World Bank's website provides extensive research on trade policy analysis. This includes many papers on non-discriminatory trade policy but also a very large section on preferential trade arrangements under the heading of 'regionalism'. See www.worldbank.org.

## REFERENCES

Krugman, P. and M. Obstfeld (2000) *International Economics*, Harper Collins, New York.
Mankiw, G. (2000) *Principles of Economics*, Thomson Learning, New York.
Vousden, N. (1990). *The Economics of Trade Protection*, Cambridge University Press, Cambridge.

> " ... the ideas of economists and political philosophers, both when they are right and when they are wrong, are more powerful than is commonly understood. Indeed the " world is ruled by little else. Practical men, who believe themselves to be exempt from any intellectual influences, are usually the slaves of some defunct economist.
>
> **John Maynard Keynes, 1935**

# 5 The Essential Economics of Preferential Liberalization

---

This chapter begins our progressive study of the microeconomics of European integration, focusing on the preferential, i.e. discriminatory, aspects. The discriminatory effects are important since they played a central role in the spread of European integration, as was discussed in Chapter 1. The main goal of this chapter is to provide a framework for analysing the essential economics of preferential liberalization.

---

# 5.1 Analysis of unilateral discriminatory liberalization

The non-discriminatory liberalization presented in the previous chapter assumed that Home imposed the same tariff against imports from all nations since all trading partners were lumped into one nation called 'Foreign'. While useful for pedagogical purposes, all European countries, and indeed most countries in the world, maintain different barriers against imports from different nations.

The organization of our study of the economic impact of discriminatory liberalization is directed by the principle of progressive complexity. In this section, we look at what happens when a nation removes its tariff on imports from only one of its trading partners. Of course, European integration has always involved two-way reductions in tariffs (e.g. France and Germany lowered their tariffs against each other's exports at the same time during the 1960s), but we postpone consideration of changes in partner tariffs until the next section for the sake of clarity.

Again, we continue with the last chapter's simplifying assumptions of no imperfect competition and no increasing returns (NICNIR). While these assumptions are both monumentally unrealistic, they are pedagogically convenient (see Box 5-1).

Before starting, we note that the theory of preferential liberalization is often taught using an additional simplifying factor called the 'small economy' assumption. While this simplifies the analysis from the perspective of the Home country, it also assumes away the critical impact that preferential liberalization has on excluded nations. Interested readers can find this case in Annex A at the end of the chapter.

---

## Box 5-1: Why use the NICNIR framework?

There are two good reasons for starting our study of the economics of European integration in the highly simplified NICNIR framework.

NICNIR is the simplest framework that allows us to understand the discriminatory effect of preferential liberalization – an effect that plays a central role in understanding the economic forces driving the spread of European integration. In the early 1960s, in the mid-1970s and again in the mid-1980s, EU members embarked on liberalizations that created discriminatory effects that induced non-members to react (see the Chapter 1 for details). In the 1960s, the UK reacted by forming a parallel free trade area, the European Free Trade Association (EFTA), and, in the following year, by putting in an application for EU membership. That application was received a curt '*non*' from French President Charles de Gaulle, but when it was renewed and eventually accepted in the early 1970s, the EFTA members that did not follow the UK into the EU reacted by signing FTAs with the enlarged EU. The NICNIR framework allows us to present the core logic behind these reactions in a setting that is as intellectually uncluttered as possible.

Because the NICNIR framework is so simple, it is a good tool for illustrating a variety of effects and studying a variety of policies that would be too complex to study in more realistic frameworks – at least too complex for the sort of diagrammatic analysis employed in this book.

---

## 5.1.1 The PTA diagram

Consideration of discriminatory liberalization requires at least three countries – at least two integrating nations and at least one excluded nation. Our first task is to extend our workhorse $MD$–$MS$ diagram to allow for two sources of imports. Figure 5-1 shows how.

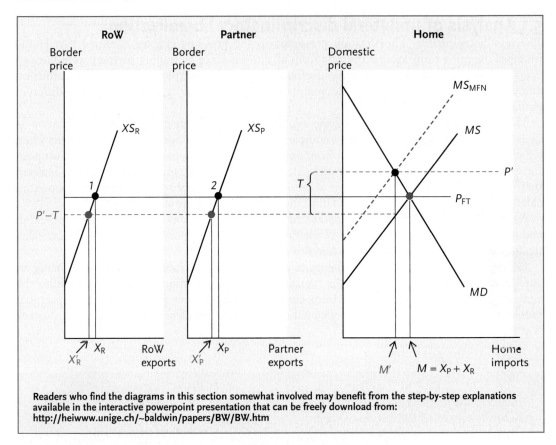

RoW        Partner        Home

Border price        Border price        Domestic price

> Readers who find the diagrams in this section somewhat involved may benefit from the step-by-step explanations available in the interactive powerpoint presentation that can be freely download from: http://heiwww.unige.ch/~baldwin/papers/BW/BW.htm

FIGURE 5-1: THE PTA (PREFERENTIAL TRADE ARRANGEMENT) DIAGRAM

## FREE TRADE EQUILIBRIUM

The two leftmost panels of Fig. 5-1 show the export supply curves for two individual countries, which we call Partner and Rest of World (RoW) for reasons that will become obvious. To minimize complications, we assume that Partner and RoW are identical; interested readers may want to work out how the diagram and analysis change when the foreign countries are asymmetric.

To find the free trade price in equilibrium, we need to find the intersection between the $MD$ curve and the $MS$ curve. But what is the $MS$ curve when there are two potential suppliers of imports? As in standard microeconomics, the total supply of imports to Home is the horizontal sum of the two export supply curves. This summed curve is shown as $MS$ in the right panel (it is flatter than $XS_P$ and $XS_R$ since a given price increase will raise supply from both Partner and RoW). The equilibrium price, when no tariff is imposed, is where $MS$ and $MD$ cross, namely $P_{FT}$. Total imports are $M$. To find the imports from both Partner and RoW, we use each supplier's $XS$ curve to see how much would be offered at the price $P_{FT}$. The answers are given by the points 1 and 2 in the diagram, namely Partner and RoW export $X_P$ and $X_R$, respectively.

## MFN TARIFF WITH TWO IMPORT SUPPLIERS

In order to investigate the impact of removing a tariff on a preferential basis, we need to establish the baseline where a tariff, equal to $T$, is applied to both nations. To this end, we first work out the effects of Home imposing a tariff of $T$ on both RoW and Partner. As always, the first task is to find how the tariff affects the $MS$ curve. As we saw in Chapter 4, an MFN tariff shifts the $MS$ curve up by $T$ since the domestic price would have to be $T$ higher to elicit the same quantity of imports after the tariff is imposed. The new $MS$ curve is shown in the diagram as the curve marked $MS_{MFN}$. As before, tariff protection does nothing to the $MD$ curve.

The intersection of $MS_{MFN}$ and $MD$ tells us that the post-tariff equilibrium domestic price for imports is $P'$ and the new import level is $M'$; with $P'$ as the new domestic price, the new border price is $P' - T$. At this border price, both import suppliers are willing to supply less, namely $X_R'$ and $X_P'$, as shown in the diagram.

### 5.1.2 Price and quantity effects of discriminatory liberalization

What happens when Home removes $T$ but only for imports from Partner, i.e. when Home unilaterally liberalizes on a preferential basis?

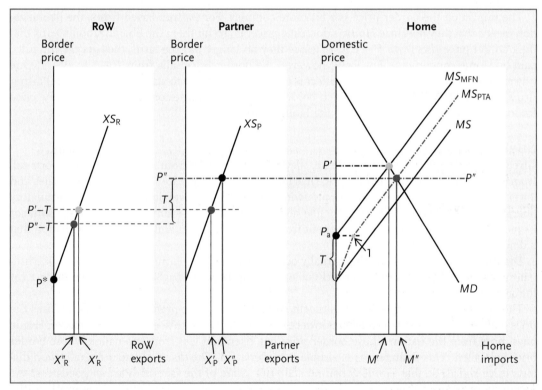

FIGURE 5-2: PRICE AND QUANTITY EFFECTS OF UNILATERAL, DISCRIMINATORY TARIFF LIBERALIZATION

The first step in answering this question is, as always, to see how the preferential liberalization alters the $MS$ curve. The new $MS$ curve, which we will call $MS_{PTA}$, where PTA stands for preferential trade arrangement, is shown in Fig. 5-2.

It seems intuitive that the preferential tariff liberalization, a liberalization that applies to only half of Home's import suppliers, will shift $MS_{MFN}$ downward to a point that is half-way between the import supply curve with no tariffs, namely $MS$, and the import supply curve with tariffs on all

imports, namely $MS_{MFN}$. This is the correct answer, with one small modification; considering this modification also helps us see how $MS_{PTA}$ is constructed.

The tariff prevents RoW firms from exporting until the domestic price in Home rises above the price marked $P_a$ in Fig. 5-2. The reason is that when Home's domestic price is below $P_a$, the border price faced by RoW exports is below their zero-supply price (marked as $p^*$ in the diagram). Yet even though RoW would not supply anything at below $P_a$ prices, Partner-based firms would do it since they face Home's domestic price instead of the domestic price minus the tariff. As a consequence, Partner firms – but only Partner firms – will supply imports at the domestic price $P_a$, i.e. up to the point marked 1 in the diagram. Thus the $MS_{PTA}$ curve is Partner's $XS$ curve up to point 1. After that, both foreigners supply imports, so the $MS_{PTA}$ resumes its normal slope.

## THE DOMESTIC PRICE CHANGE AND CONFLICTING BORDER PRICE CHANGES

The $MS_{PTA}$ and $MD$ curves intersect at $P''$, so this is the new, post-PTA domestic price. As expected, the new domestic price is lower than the old MFN tariff price since imports from Partner can now enter duty free.

The impact on the border price is a bit more complex. For Partner-based firms, the liberalization means that they now face Home's domestic price, $P''$, so for them the liberalization means that their border price *rises* from $P' - T$ to $P''$ (since they no longer pay the tariff, they get the full price paid by Home consumers). For RoW, however, the border price falls from $P' - T$ to $P'' - T$. One way to think of the RoW border price effect is to note that in order to stay competitive with Partner firms' exports, RoW firms must cut their border price so that Home consumers see the same price for imports from RoW and Partner in the Home market.

## SUPPLY SWITCHING

Given that Partner firms see a price rise, they increase exports from $X_P'$ to $X_P''$. RoW exports fall from $X_R'$ to $X_R''$ because their border price has fallen. This combination of higher Partner sales and lower RoW sales is known as the 'supply switching', or 'trade diversion' effect of discriminatory liberalization. That is, a discriminatory liberalization induces the Home nation to switch some of its purchases to the nation that can benefit from the liberalization and away from the nation that did not benefit from it.

Did this sort of supply switching actually occur when the EEC eliminated tariffs on a discriminatory basis during the formation of its customs union between 1958 and 1968? See Box 5-2 for the answer.

These price and quantity effects may seem strange at first. The preferential tariff cut raises the price that Partner exporters receive but lowers the price faced by RoW exporters. Moreover, Home buys more from the nation whose border price has risen and less from the nation whose border price has fallen. This strangeness is simple to understand. The discriminatory liberalization distorts price signals so that Home consumers are not aware of the fact that Partner goods cost the nation more than RoW goods. To the Home consumer, imports from the two sources cost the same, namely $P''$. To summarize, the price and quantity effects are:

- Home's domestic price falls from $P'$ to $P''$.
- The border price falls from $P' - T$ to $P'' - T$ for RoW imports.
- The border price rises from $P' - T$ to $P''$ for Partner imports.
- The RoW exports fall.
- The Partner exports rise.
- Total Home imports rise from $M'$ to $M''$.

Interested readers may want to add a fourth panel to the diagram by drawing a standard open economy supply and demand figure for Home to the right of the *MD–MS* panel. Doing so allows you to see that Home production falls and Home consumption rises due to the domestic price drop.

> **BOX 5.2: THE SUPPLY-SWITCHING EFFECTS OF THE FORMATION OF THE EEC CUSTOMS UNION**
>
> Figure 5-3 shows the trade volume effects that occurred when the EEC6 removed their internal tariffs between 1958 and 1968. In the left panel, the columns show the import shares broken down into intra-EEC6 imports, imports from six other European nations (the ones who joined in the EU's first three enlargements), and the rest of the world.
>
> Note that as the EEC6 share of exports to itself rose from about 30 per cent in 1958 to about 45 per cent in 1968, the share of EEC imports from other nations had to fall. Part of the displacement occurred with respect to imports from other non-EEC European nations. As the dark bars show, the import share from six other Western European nations (UK, Ireland, Portugal, Spain, Denmark and Greece) fell during this period by a small amount, from 8–9 per cent to 7 per cent. The main displacement came from the rest of the world, mainly imports from the USA. The right-panel, however, shows that imports from all sources were in fact growing rapidly. Thus we have to interpret the 'supply switching' as a relative thing. That is, if the customs union had not been formed, imports from non-EEC6 members would have risen even faster.

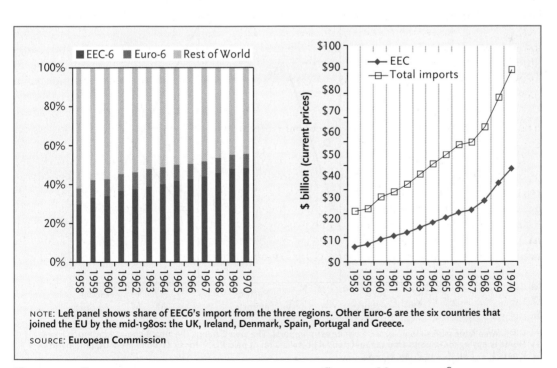

NOTE: Left panel shows share of EEC6's import from the three regions. Other Euro-6 are the six countries that joined the EU by the mid-1980s: the UK, Ireland, Denmark, Spain, Portugal and Greece.

SOURCE: **European Commission**

FIGURE 5-3: SUPPLY SWTICHING AND FORMATION OF THE COMMON MARKET, 1958-70

### 5.1.3 Welfare effects

Showing the welfare implications in the same figure as the price and quantity effects would complicate the diagram too much. Figure 5-4 reproduces the previous figure, omitting unnecessary lines to reduce its 'clutter factor'. All the welfare effects stem from the price and quantity changes, so these are all that we really need to keep track of.

The welfare effects on foreigners are straightforward. Partner gains D since it gets a higher price and sells more. In other words, Partner experiences a positive border price effect and a positive trade volume effect. RoW's losses are E for the reverse reasons; it gets a lower price and sells less (a negative border price effect and a negative trade volume effect).

Home's welfare effects are slightly more complex due to the two-fold impact on the border price. The direct way of gauging Home's net welfare effect is to use the concepts of 'trade volume effects' and 'border price effects' that were introduced in Chapter 4. This direct approach is also the easiest way to remember the Home welfare effects and it is the easiest way to understand them, so this is what we do in Fig. 5-4. Some readers, however, may benefit from working through the welfare impact using the indirect method of adding up the separate impact on consumer surplus, producer surplus and tariff revenue (see Box 5-3). The two methods lead to the same answer.

Returning to the direct analysis, we note that the preferential tariff liberalization has increased imports, and produced two conflicting border price effects. By the usual reasoning (see Chapter 4),

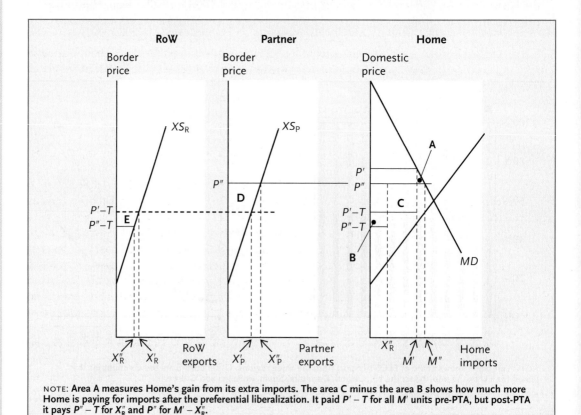

NOTE: Area A measures Home's gain from its extra imports. The area C minus the area B shows how much more Home is paying for imports after the preferential liberalization. It paid $P' - T$ for all $M'$ units pre-PTA, but post-PTA it pays $P'' - T$ for $X_R''$ and $P''$ for $M' - X_R''$.

FIGURE 5-4: WELFARE EFFECTS OF UNILATERAL DISCRIMINATORY LIBERALIZATION

the increase in imports raises Home welfare, with the exact measure being the gap between the $MD$ curve and $P''$ summed over all the extra units imported. This equals the area marked as A in Fig. 5-4.

The border price effect tells us how much more or less Home is paying for the goods it imported before the PTA. Home imports amounted to $M'$ before the PTA. After the PTA, an amount equal to $X''_R$ comes from RoW and the rest of $M'$, namely $M' - X''_R$, comes from Partner. The goods coming from RoW have fallen in price, so Home gains on these. The exact size of the gain is just the amount of imports affected times the price drop; in the figure this gain equals the area B. The goods coming from Partner have risen in price, so Home experiences a loss. The size of the loss is again the amount of imports affected (namely, $M' - X''_R$) times the price rise, namely the difference between $P' - T$ and $P''$. Graphically, this is the area C. What about the border price effect on the extra imports, $M'' - M'$? The border price effect does not apply to these units; since Home did not import them to begin with, it does not make sense to talk about how much more or less they cost post-liberalization.

Putting together the trade volume effect and the border price effects, Home's overall welfare change is equal to the areas marked as A, B minus the area C. A key point to remember and understand is that this welfare effect may be positive or negative. As drawn, the net welfare impact looks negative. Interested readers should be able to show that discriminatory liberalization will lead to a welfare gain if $T$ is large enough. Moreover, as usual with tax analysis, the slopes of the supply and demand curves also affect the size of the welfare effects.

We turn next to building intuition for the key point – the ambiguity of Home's welfare effect.

## 5.1.4 Intuition for Viner's ambiguity: trade creation and trade diversion

The fact that the Home country might gain or lose from a unilateral preferential liberalization is known as *Viner's ambiguity* since Jacob Viner was the first to crystallize economists' thinking about this ambiguity.

### INTUITION

The fact that a discriminatory tariff liberalization may help or harm a country is extremely easy to understand at an intuitive level – a point we can make by studying the two words in the term 'discriminatory liberalization'.

Start with the 'liberalization' part. In the NICNIR framework, we know that firms produce up to the point where their marginal cost equals the price they receive, so the price they receive tells us what their marginal cost is (see Chapter 4 if this point is not familiar). Tariffs keep domestic prices above foreign prices, so we know that Home consumers are buying some of their consumption from higher-marginal-cost domestic producers and some from lower-marginal-cost foreign producers. This is plainly inefficient. Home could get more for its money by shifting some purchases from domestic firms to foreign firms. Removing the tariff wedge between domestic firms and Partner-nation firms (this is the liberalization part of discriminatory liberalization) tends to improve Home's welfare by shifting some purchase from higher-cost Home firms to lower-cost Partner firms.

But because the liberalization is 'discriminatory', a new wedge appears between the prices faced by Partner-nation firms and Rest of World (RoW) firms. (Partner-based firms see Home's domestic price since they face no tariff, but RoW-based firms face Home's domestic price minus the tariff.) Just as the domestic-versus-foreign wedge led to an inefficient buying pattern to start with, the appearance of the Partner-versus-RoW wedge – a wedge that did not exist before the discriminatory liberalization – leads to a new source of inefficiency. Specifically, it leads Home to buy more from Partner firms (whose costs are now higher) and less from RoW firms (whose costs are now

> ### Box 5-3: Home welfare effects of discriminatory tariff cutting in detail
>
> Here we consider the 'gross' welfare implications of the price and quantity changes derived in Fig. 5-4. To see consumer and producer surplus separately, we put the rightmost panel from Fig. 5-4 in the left panel of Fig. 5-5 and add to it a right panel consisting of a standard open-economy supply and demand diagram. (As we are focusing on Home welfare, we shall drop the two foreign panels.) Turn first to the right panel. The drop in the domestic price from $P'$ to $P''$ raises consumer surplus by $D + A_2 + A_1 + A_3$, but lowers producer surplus by $D$ (see Chapter 4 if this reasoning is unfamiliar). The net change in the private surplus (i.e. producer and consumer surplus combined) is $A_2 + A_1 + A_3$. The change in tariff revenue is slightly more involved than usual. Originally, the tariff revenue was $A_1 + B_1 + C$ (i.e. $T$ times $M'$). After the PTA, the tariff revenue is $B_1 + B$ since $T$ is charged only on $X''_R$. Thus, the change in tariff-revenue is $B - A_1 - C$. Adding the private surplus change and the net revenue change, we find that the net impact on Home is: $A_2 + A_1 + A_3 + B - A_1 - C$. Cancelling, this becomes $A_2 + A_3 + B - C$. In Chapter 4 we showed that $A_2 + A_3$ equals $A$ in the left panel, so the net effect is just $A + B - C$ as in Fig. 5-4.

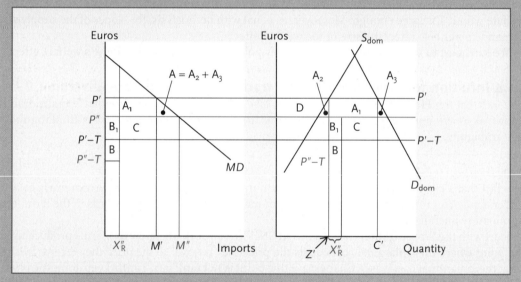

lower). In short, the 'liberalization' part removes one source of inefficiency, but the 'discrimination' part introduces a new one. No wonder then that discriminatory liberalization has ambiguous welfare effects.

These points are quite general and flow directly from the powerful set of NICNIR tools developed in the decades following the Second World War. For example, the basic points would apply to an analysis of any 'discriminatory' change in tax rates, say, a reduction in the VAT rate that was applied to some firms but not others. Unhappily, the first post-war economist to carefully illustrate the ambiguous welfare effects of a customs union, Jacob Viner, did not have the benefit of this powerful toolkit. Instead, he invented new terms to describe these two basic effects – *trade creation* and *trade diversion*. Since they do capture the basic intuition behind the ambiguity, these terms have become quite standard, so much so that one really cannot talk about preferential liberalization without mentioning them. This is somewhat unfortunate since they are slightly misleading (suggesting that trade volumes are the key even though they refer to cost/price changes). They also fail to cover all the effects (e.g. gains from increased imports). For more on the famous 'trade creation–trade diversion' phraseology, see Box 5-4.

---

**Box 5-4: Terminology in detail: trade creation, trade diversion**

If one were to sneak into the bedroom of almost any famous international economist, shake that famous economist awake and shout loudly: 'Free trade area – good or bad?', the first words out of the economist's mouth would surely include 'trade creation and trade diversion'. Indeed, these terms are so influential that one really must know them despite their shortcomings.

It should be clear to readers who have worked through the PTA diagram that this terminology fails to capture all welfare effects of discriminatory tariff liberalization, and, as we shall see in section 5.2.3, it is completely useless when it comes to the type of barriers European integration has addressed since the mid-1970s, i.e. non-tariff barriers. One economist who has studied the history of 'customs union theory' suggests that the terms persist since they are 'highly effective tools of focusing policy makers' attention on the ambiguous welfare effects of PTAs' (Panagariya, 1999).

Economists have dealt with the incompleteness of Viner's terms in two ways. Some stretch the original meaning of his terms to cover the full effects in the simplest case where the *MS* curves are flat (see Annex A at the end of this chapter). Others have introduced new jargon – adding terms like 'internal versus external trade creation', and 'trade expansion'. All this variance in literary interpretation is possible because Viner did not use diagrams in his book and certainly no maths, so there is some debate over exactly what he meant. The most convincing translation of Viner's words into modern economics was undertaken by Nobel Laureate James Meade in his famous 1955 book *The Theory of Customs Unions*. That book employed a general approach based on the powerful NICNIR toolkit developed, *inter alia*, by Paul Samuelson, Kenneth Arrow, James Mirrles, and Meade himself. Namely, he breaks down net welfare effects into what we have called trade volume effects and border price effects. To judge for yourself, read the core of Viner's original analysis (it is only a page) in this chapter's Web Appendix, which can be freely downloaded from http://heiwww.unige.ch/~baldwin/BW/BW.htm.

---

## 5.2 Analysis of a customs union

Until now we have considered only unilateral tariff cuts. European integration, however, involved a sequence of free trade agreements (FTAs), namely trade agreements where two or more nations agree to charge zero tariffs on the trade among themselves. One type of FTA – the type adopted by the EEC, where all members also charge the same tariff against imports from third nations – is called a 'customs union'. Given the symmetry of our three-nation setup, an FTA between Home and Partner is automatically a customs union; in the real world, things are more complicated (see section 5.3)

As it turns out, the study of a customs union is an easy stretch of the unilateral PTA analysis. The main extra insight we get from studying a customs union (CU) arises from the fact that a CU is systematically more favourable for participating countries than unilateral liberalization schemes since Home exporters gain from Partner tariff cuts.

To keep things simple, we shall look at the formation of a CU between Home and Partner, assuming that all three countries (Home, Partner and RoW) are symmetric initially in all aspects, including the MFN tariff they initially impose on all imports. To do this carefully, we must address the question of the three-nation trade pattern. Again to streamline the analysis, we adopt the simplest combination that permits us to study the issues. This leads us to assume that three goods are traded (goods 1, 2 and 3). Each country produces all three goods, but costs structures are such that it exports two of the three goods while importing the remaining one. The trade pattern, shown schematically in Fig. 5-6, entails Home importing good 1 from Partner and RoW, and Partner importing good 2 from Home and RoW.

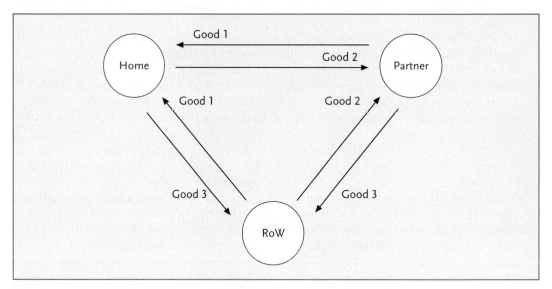

FIGURE 5-6: THREE-NATION TRADE PATTERN

### 5.2.1 Price and quantity effects

The formation of a CU between Home and Partner involves Home eliminating $T$ on imports of good 1 from Partner, and Partner eliminating $T$ on imports of good 2 from Home. The tariffs facing RoW exports are not changed, and since Home's and Partner's MFN tariffs were identical to start with, there is no need to harmonize their tariffs towards RoW; $T$ becomes the common external tarrift.

We first address the price and quantity effects. Plainly the impact of Home's discriminatory liberalization is exactly the same as the impact shown in Fig. 5-2, so there is no need to repeat it here. The impact of Partner's discriminatory liberalization of imports of good 2 from Home can also be seen using the same diagram. Here is the key point.

A moment's reflection reveals that, given the assumed symmetry of nations, what happens to Home's exports when Partner lowers its barriers is exactly what happened to Partner's exports when Home lowered its barriers. We can, therefore, rely on analysis with which we are already familiar. More specifically, the price of good 2 in Partner falls from $P'$ to $P''$, but the border price facing Home exporters when they sell good 2 to Partner rises; it rises from $P' - T$ to $P''$. Nothing happens to domestic prices in RoW (since they did not liberalize), but RoW exporters face a lower border price for its exports to Partner. The trade volume effects are similarly simple. Partner imports rise from $M'$ to $M''$ and Home exports to Partner rise; using the terminology from Fig. 5-2, Home exports to Partner rise from $X'_P$ to $X''_P$. RoW's exports to Partner fall as in Fig. 5-2.

## 5.2.2 Welfare effects

The welfare effects are also just a matter of adding up effects illustrated above. On Home's import side (i.e. in the market for good 1), Home gains the usual $A + B - C$ in the right panel of Fig. 5-7. On Home's export market (good 2), Home's situation is shown in the left panel, so it gains area D. The welfare effects on Partner are identical to this due to the assumed symmetry of goods and nations.

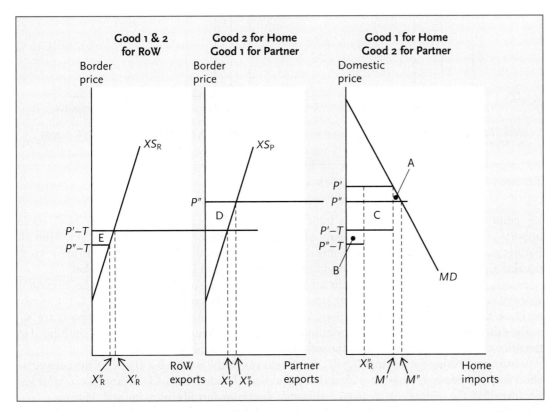

FIGURE 5-7: WELFARE EFFECTS OF A CUSTOMS UNION

It is useful to study the welfare effects a bit closer, using Fig. 5-8. This diagram only shows the two liberalizing nations, Home and Partner. To be concrete, suppose this is the market for good 1, which Home imports and Partner exports. The diagram is based on the two rightmost panels of Fig. 5-7 but we have added further detail to the areas. In particular, the trade price loss associated with area C is here split into two parts, $C_1$ and $C_2$, for a good reason.

Recall that Home loses $C_1 + C_2$ because the tariff cut raised the price it paid for imports from Partner (from $P' - T$ to $P''$). The first area, $C_1$, identifies how much it pays for the units it continues to import from Partner ($M' - X'_P$). Home's loss of $C_1$, however, is exactly matched by a gain to Partner of the same size; the higher price for the $X'_P$ units transfers $C_1$ from Home to Partner. The

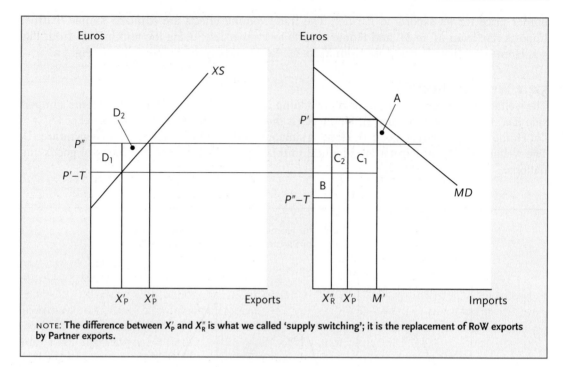

NOTE: The difference between $X'_P$ and $X''_R$ is what we called 'supply switching'; it is the replacement of RoW exports by Partner exports.

FIGURE 5-8: WELFARE EFFECTS OF A CU IN DETAIL

key point is that because $C_1$ is just a transfer between CU members, Home's loss of $C_1$ on its imports of good 1 will be offset by a gain of $D_1 = C_1$ on its exports of good 2 to Partner. After all, Partner also lowers its tariff against Home exports, so we know that Home will gain an area exactly equal to $C_1$ in its exports of good 2. In addition, Home will gain $D_2$ in its export market.

Area $C_2$ is quite different. It identifies the direct cost of the supply switching (trade diversion), so there is no offset gain on the export side. More specifically, recall that from pre-CU symmetry, we know that RoW exports to Home pre-CU were equal to $X''_P$. After the CU, RoW exports are $X''_R$, so the difference, $X''_P - X''_R$, measure the amount of supply switching. This quantity is multiplied by the price change ($P' - T$ to $P''$) to get the welfare cost of the supply switching.

In summary, using the fact that $D_1 = C_1$, the net gain to Home is $+A + B + D_2 - C_2$. This net welfare effect may still be negative, but it is clear that the welfare change from a CU is more positive (or less negative) than the welfare change from a unilateral discriminatory liberalization with Partner.

The losses to RoW from the CU are twice the size of their losses shown in Fig. 5-4, since they lose E both on the exports of good 1 to Home and on their exports of good 2 to Partner. Readers who find this reasoning a bit complex may benefit from the step-by-step explanation in the interactive Power-point presentation for Fig. 5-8 that can be freely downloaded from http://heiwww.unige/ch/~baldwin/BW/BW.htm.

## SECOND-ORDER TERMS OF TRADE CHANGES
Lastly, we must consider the indirect or second-round implications of the CU.

RoW experiences a reduction in the value of its exports, yet has not reduced the value of its imports from Home and Partner. While this sort of trade deficit may be sustainable in the short run, eventually RoW must turn the situation around. In the real world, this is usually accomplished by a real depreciation of its currency (or a terms of trade worsening if it is in a monetary union). This makes all RoW exports to Home and Partner cheaper and simultaneously makes imports from those two countries more expensive. Both changes have positive welfare implications for the Home and Partner countries; they earn more on their exports to RoW and pay less for their imports from RoW. This is a further negative trade price effect for RoW stemming from general equilibrium effects of the CU between its trading Partners. Such effects, however, are likely to be small.

## 5.2.3 Frictional barriers: the 1992 Programme

Having dealt with tariff liberalization, which was an important aspect of European integration up to the mid-1970s (see Chapter 1 for details), our next task is to study the economics of frictional-barrier liberalization, the type of liberalization that has dominated European economic integration over the past three decades. Fortunately, the tools we developed while looking at tariff liberalization make this a simple task.

### PRICE AND QUANTITY EFFECTS

Removing of frictional barriers (see Chapter 4 if this terminology is not familiar) was a critical element of the EU's programme to complete the Single Market by 1992. Although several important aspects of the Single Market Programme (EC92 for short) cannot be understood in the uncomplicated framework used in this chapter, the most basic points can. To keep things simple, suppose that initially all three nations, Home, Partner and RoW, impose a frictional barrier whose tariff equivalent is $T$ (i.e. it drives a wedge equal to $T$ between the border price and the Home price). The specific policy change to be studied is a lowering of $T$ to zero on all trade between Home and Partner with no change in the barriers on RoW–Home or Partner–RoW trade.

The price and quantity effects of the preferential liberalization are very similar to those discussed in Fig. 5-2. The only change concerns the border price. With frictional barriers the domestic price is the border price for the importing nation, so the liberalization lowers Home's border price. At the same time, the exporter that benefits from the liberalization receives a higher price for its exports, so the exporter's border price rises.[1] For example, the price and quantity effects in the good-1 market are: (i) Home imports of good 1 rise, (ii) the domestic price of good 1 in Home falls from $P'$ to $P''$, (iii) the border price of good 1 for Partner exporters rises from $P' - T$ to $P''$, (iv) the border price of good 1 for RoW exporters falls from $P' - T$ to $P'' - T$, and (v) as usual, we get supply switching since Partner exports rise and RoW exports fall.

### WELFARE EFFECTS

The welfare effects on Home are simple. As with tariffs, the change in Home private surplus equals areas F + A in Fig. 5-9. This is not offset by a loss in tariff revenues, as was the case in Fig. 5-4. Removing frictional barriers, even on a preferential basis, always lowers the price that the nation pays for its imports. Although both Partner and RoW exporters see changes in the prices they receive for exports to Home, and this leads to supply switching, this 'trade diversion' has no welfare consequences for Home.

In the good-2 market, where Home is an exporter to Partner, the welfare effect is also positive. Home exporters get a higher price and sell more, so they gain the area D. The overall welfare effect of the FTA is thus +D + F + A.

---

[1] As discussed in Chapter 4, the importer's and exporter's border prices are different with a frictional barrier; the importer's border price is $T$ higher than that of the exporter.

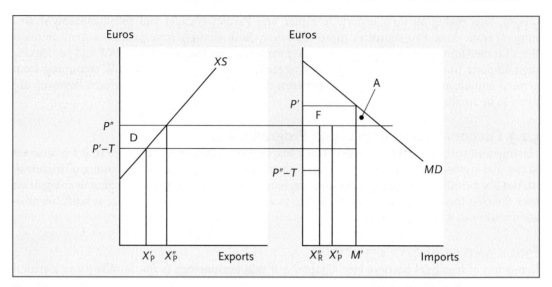

FIGURE 5-9: WELFARE EFFECTS OF PREFERENTIAL FRICTIONAL BARRIER LIBERALIZATION

### NON-APPLICABILITY OF TRADE CREATION AND TRADE DIVERSION CONCEPTS

Notice that Viner's ambiguity has disappeared. With frictional barriers, any kind of liberalization will lead to positive border price effects and positive trade volume effects since the border price equals the domestic price with frictional barriers. In a sense, it is a shame that half a century ago Viner used a name, trade diversion, that suggests that import volumes are important, when what he was really talking about was costs. It is, nonetheless, understandable. If the only barriers being liberalized are tariffs, then supply switching only occurs when a negative border price effect also occurs. Viner was writing in the 1940s when tariffs were a dominant form of protection in Europe and elsewhere.

## 5.3 Customs unions versus free trade agreements

The 1957 Treaty of Rome committed the six original EU members to eliminating all tariffs and quotas on trade among themselves, i.e. to form an FTA, but it also committed them to completely harmonizing their tariffs on imports from non-member nations. This type of trade arrangement – zero tariffs on trade among members combined with complete harmonization of all members' tariffs on imports from non-members – is known as a 'customs union', and the harmonized non-member tariff is known as the 'common external tariff' (CET). In reaction to this customs union, other Western European nations formed another trade bloc – known as the European Free Trade Association (EFTA) – in 1960. This was not a customs union, however, it was a free trade area since while trade among EFTA members was duty free, EFTA members did not adopt a common external tariff.

What are the key differences between a customs union and a free trade area? Why did the EEC go for a customs union while EFTA went for an FTA? We address these questions in order, starting with the main economic differences.

### 5.3.1 Stopping tariff cheats: 'trade deflection' and 'rules of origin'

When tariffs between two nations are zero, yet they charge two different tariffs on imports from third nations, an incentive to cheat arises. Take our three-nation example. If all Home–Partner trade is duty free, yet Home charges a 10 per cent tariff on imports from RoW while Partner charges only a 5 per cent tariff on goods coming from RoW, Home-based buyers of RoW goods would be tempted to import the goods first into Partner (thus paying only a 5 per cent tariff) and then to import them duty free from Partner to Home. To thwart this practice – known as trade deflection – Home and Partner have two choices. They can eliminate the temptation by harmonizing their external tariffs (thus turning their FTA into a customs union), or they can stay with the FTA but restrict duty free treatment to goods that are actually *made* in Home or Foreign. The set of rules that enforce the latter option are called 'rules of origin'.

One problem with rules of origin, and thus with FTAs, is that it can be difficult to know where a product is made in today's highly globalized markets. Personal computers made in, say, Switzerland will contain components from all over the world. The Swiss company may be doing little more than customized assembly of parts from the USA and Asia. In the extreme, it may be doing nothing more than opening the box of a US-made computer and putting in an instruction manual translated into Norwegian. Should the full value of this computer be given duty free treatment when it is exported to Norway? (Switzerland and Norway are both EFTA members.)

## THE COSTS OF RULES OF ORIGIN

For manufactured goods, the basic rule of origin is that a good has to have changed its 'tariff classification' to qualify for duty free treatment. If the component comes into Switzerland under 'TV and computer monitors', for example, but the good to be exported to Norway is classed as 'Office equipment', then the good is considered Swiss and thus granted duty free access to Germany. But for many products, the rules can be much more complex and much more expensive to comply with. Another popular rule requires that some fixed percentage of the product's value-added be done in the exporting nation. Due to the high cost of compliance with these rules, many non-EU firms who could in principle qualify for duty-free treatment (e.g. Swiss firms) decide instead to pay the EU's CET.

An additional problem with rules of origin is that they can end up as hidden protection. Since rules of origin are specified at the product level, they can be difficult for non-experts to evaluate – just as is the case with technical barriers to trade. As a consequence, rules of origin are usually written in consultation with domestic firms who have an incentive to shape the rules into protectionist devices.

One great advantage of a customs union like the EU is that firms do not have to demonstrate the origin of a product before it is allowed to cross an intra-EU border duty free. Any good that is physically in Germany was either made in Germany or paid the common external duty when it entered. In either case, the good deserves duty free passage into France, or any other EU member without any documentation at all.

## 5.3.2 Political integration and customs unions

With the important exception of the EU, most preferential trade arrangements in the world are free trade agreements rather than customs unions. Indeed customs unions are quite rare world wide. The reason is simple – political integration. Getting a group of nations to agree on a common external tariff at the launch of a customs union is difficult, but the real problems begin as time passes. For instance, if one member nation believes its industry is being undercut by some non-member nation who is exporting its goods at a price that is below cost (so-called dumping), it may want to impose anti-dumping duties (i.e. a tariff that offsets the below-cost pricing). In a customs union, however, all nations must agree on every dumping duty since external tariffs must always remain constant. This can lead to political difficulties since one member may like the low price (say, its companies use the good as an input) while another member may dislike it due to the negative impact on its firms competing with the cheap import. Likewise, nations typically reduce their tariffs in the context of GATT/WTO negotiations. For a customs union, this requires all members to agree on a common negotiating position on every single product.

In practice, keeping the common external tariff common requires some integration of decision making. In the EU, the Commission formally has the power to set tariffs on goods (even though it naturally consults with Member States before doing so), but very few groups of countries are willing to transfer that amount of national sovereignty. As a result, most trade blocs, such as EFTA and NAFTA, are free trade areas rather than customs unions.

Another way to 'solve' the decision making problem is for the members to let one nation – the large dominant nation – decide everything. This is the case in all the successful, non-EU customs unions. For example, South Africa is the dominant nation in the Southern African Customs Union (see http://www.dfa.gov.za/for-relations/multilateral/sacu.htm).

## 5.4 WTO rules

The world trading system is governed by a set of rules, known as the General Agreement on Tariffs and Trade (GATT), and an organization, known as the World Trade Organization (WTO). The most important guiding principle of the WTO/GATT is non-discrimination in trade policy, i.e. the so-called most favoured nation principle, or MFN for short.[2] This says that nations should, in principle, impose tariffs on a non-discriminatory basis. Of course, all of the preferential liberalization discussed above contradicts this principle, so why is it allowed? As it turns out, the GATT created an explicit loophole for FTAs and customs unions.

The basic economic idea was that if two nations removed *all* trade barriers between them and adopted a common external tariff, they would – from the perspective of other trading nations – look like one big nation instead of two small nations. Thus at a high level of abstraction, the formation of a customs union (CU) is very much like one nation growing in size. Since it is difficult to object to countries getting bigger, one cannot object to CUs on principle. The force of this logic is not quite so clear for FTAs where each trading Partner continues to maintain its own tariffs against third nations.

Recognizing this economic point – and the political desire of some of the original GATT members to maintain existing preferential arrangements (especially Great Britain's Commonwealth Preferences) – the GATT's Article 24 specifically allows preferential liberalization, subject to a few restrictions. The most important of which are:

- ■ Free trade agreements and customs unions must completely eliminate tariffs on 'substantially all the trade' among members.
- ■ The phase-out of tariffs must take place within a reasonable period. Although there are no hard definitions, 'substantially all trade' is usually taken to mean at least 80 per cent of all goods and a 'reasonable period' is taken to be 10 years or less.
- ■ For a customs union, there is the additional requirement that the common external tariff (CET) 'shall not on the whole be higher or more restrictive' than before the customs union. That is, when forming the customs union, the members cannot harmonize the CET to the highest level of any member. In the case of the EEC's customs union formation, external tariff harmonization generally involved a reduction in French and Italian tariffs, a rise in Benelux tariffs and little change in the German tariffs.

## 5.5 Empirical studies

Modern empirical analyses of European integration goes far beyond the NICNIR framework we employed in this chapter to include effects that we shall study in subsequent chapters. Indeed, no major study of EU economic integration has relied solely on the NICNIR framework since the

---

[2] For more on the WTO see the interactive e-booklet *Trading into the Future* on http://www.wto.org/.

mid-1980s. There are, however, many examples of empirical studies based on NICNIR reasoning from the 1970s.

For example, the UK's entry into the EU elicited a large volume of empirical work in the early 1970s. While economists at the time knew of scale effects and growth effects, they did not have the theoretical tools necessary to handle them. Moreover, few economists had access to computers (PCs became widespread only in the mid-1980s), so much of the empirical work in the NICNIR framework consisted of what we would today call rough calculations, or 'back of the envelope' methods. The most popular method was to loosely associate the positive effects of CU formation with an increase in imports and the negative effects loosely with diverted imports. Since most studies at the time found little or no evidence that the EEC's formation was trade diverting (Balassa, 1975), the general conclusion was that the EEC must have been good for the EEC and not bad for the rest of the world. The main challenge in these studies was to determine what the trade pattern would have been without the EEC – a problem that is more difficult to resolve than one might think since imports from all sources were growing rapidly (see Fig. 5-3).

Since these NICNIR studies are now 20 years out of date, we do not review their findings here (see Artis and Lee, 2001, for a summary). One thing that is worth discussing is the fact that all empirical studies using the NICNIR framework found that the EEC had a negligible impact on national welfare.

Balassa (1975), for example, concluded that the EU's customs union added only 0.5 per cent to the Six's GDP. This struck most observers as far too low, but such low estimates are inevitable in the NICNIR framework for the following reason. To make things simple, suppose that Home is a small country and removes all tariffs on an MFN basis. As the Annex A shows, the welfare impact of this on Home will be *larger* than the welfare impact of any possible free trade area, so we know that the number we shall arrive at will be an overestimate of the true gain. The welfare impact of this is 0.5 times the change in imports times the level of the tariff. In symbols, this is $\Delta W = (\Delta M)(\Delta T)/2$, where $\Delta$ means 'the change in' and $W$ stands for welfare, $M$ for imports and $T$ for the tariff. The change in imports is related to the responsiveness of imports to price changes, i.e. Home's import demand elasticity, $\varepsilon$, defined as $(\Delta M/M)/(\Delta P/P)$. In symbols, $\Delta M = \varepsilon(\Delta T)(M/P)$, so the welfare gain as a share of GDP is $\Delta W/\text{GDP} = \varepsilon(M \times P/\text{GDP})(\Delta T/P)^2/2$. Now, as a typical import demand elasticity is something like 2.0, a typical EEC nation had an import to GDP ratio, i.e. $(M \times P/\text{GDP})$, equal to about 0.2 in the 1960s, and the level of tariffs averaged less than 25 per cent of the price. Taking all this together means that the gains would be 2(0.2)(0.625)/2 which equals just 0.0125 or 1.25 per cent of GDP – and that is an overestimate of the NICNIR effects.

The general point to learn from this back-of-the-envelope calculation is that NICNIR welfare gains just cannot be big. They inevitably involve the multiplication of several fractions and this inevitably produces small numbers. If trade liberalization is to have a welfare effect that is big enough to matter, it will be due to the scale effects, growth effects and location effects, which we discuss in Chapters 6 and 7.

## 5.6 Summary

This chapter introduced the graphical methods necessary to study preferential trade liberalization in a NICNIR setting. After going over the preliminaries, we studied the price and quantity and welfare effects of the formation of a customs union. The main technical points are:

■ Formation of a preferential trade arrangement like the EEC's customs union, or EFTA's free trade area, tend to lower domestic prices and raise imports overall, but the discriminatory aspects of these liberalizations also produce supply-switching, that is to say, a switch from non-member supplier to member-based suppliers.

■ The welfare effects of any trade liberalization, including PTA liberalization, can be captured by standard public-finance concepts, which we here call trade volume effects and border price (or trade price) effects.
■ The welfare impact of preferential tarriff liberalization is ambiguous for the liberalizing nations; this is called Viner's ambiguity. The deep fundamental reason is that PTAs are discriminatory liberalizations; the liberalization part – what Viner called trade creation – tends to boost economic efficiency, while the discrimination part – what Viner called trade diversion – tends to lower it. The impact on excluded nations is always negative.
■ Estimates of the welfare impact of trade liberalization in the NICNIR setting are inevitably very small. This suggests to most observers that one has to look to more complicated frameworks if one is to understand why trade liberalization in general, and European integration in particular, matter.

The bigger lessons from the chapter concern the way in which the economic analysis helps us to understand the big-think trends in European integration.

■ The NICNIR framework helped us to study the impact of discriminatory liberalization on outsiders in an intellectually uncluttered setting. This helps us to understand why outsiders always reacted to the deepening and widening of EU integration. As we showed, preferential liberalization definitely harms excluded nations since it leads them to face lower prices for their exports to the customs union and lower export sales. It seems natural, therefore, that the outsiders would react either by forming their own preferential arrangements (as happened in the 1960s with EFTA), or by deepening the integration between the outsiders and the EU (as outsiders did in the 1970s and again in the 1990s), or by joining the EU (as nine formerly outsider Western European nations had done by 1994).

### SELF-ASSESSMENT QUESTIONS

The NICNIR was the backbone of 'customs union theory' for years, so quite a number of extensions and provisos were put forth in the NICNIR setting. Some of them are still insightful and the following exercises illustrate the basic points.

**1.** (Kemp–Wan theorem.) Starting from a situation like that shown in Fig. 5-1, where the three nations are symmetric in everything including the initial MFN tariff $T$, suppose that Home and Partner form a customs union *and* lower their common tariff against RoW to the point where the new, post-liberalization border price facing RoW exporters is the same as it was before the liberalization, i.e. $P' - T$. Show that this 'Kemp–Wan' adjustment ensures that Home and Partner gain while RoW does not lose from this CU-with-CET-reduction scheme.

**2.** (Cooper–Massell extended.) We can think of a preferential unilateral liberalization in the following roundabout manner. Home lowers its tariffs to zero on an MFN basis, but then raises it back to $T$ on imports only from RoW. Now suppose that Home faces a flat $MS$ curve for imports from both Partner and RoW (this is the 'small country' case). Moreover, suppose that Partner's $MS$ is somewhat above that of RoW. First work out the welfare effects on Home. (*Hint*: This is covered in Annex A.) Second, show that Home would gain more from a unilateral MFN liberalization than it would from a unilateral preferential liberalization. (*Historical note*: Taking their NICNIR analysis as definitive, this result led Cooper and Massell to suggest that small countries must join customs unions for political reasons only. You can see that this is only a partial analysis by realizing that a customs union also lowers tariffs facing Home-based exporters.) Try to figure out how Home gains from Partner's removal on Home-to-Partner exports. After doing this, see if you can say definitely whether Home gains more from unilateral free trade, or from joining the customs union. You should also be able to show that the optimal policy for a small nation is to have unilateral free trade AND join every FTA that it can.

**3.** (Large Partner rule of thumb.) Redo the FTA formation exercise from the text assuming that RoW is initially a much smaller trading partner of Home and Partner in the sense that most of Home's imports are from Partner and most of Partner's imports are from Home when all three nations impose the initial MFN tariff, $T$. Show that the 'net border price effect' (area $B - C_1 - C_2$ in Fig. 5-8) is smaller when RoW is initially a less important trade partner of Home and Partner nations. (*Hint*: Focus on the Home country and start with a diagram like Fig. 5-1. Keep the vertical intersections of $XS_P$ and $XS_R$ at the same height, but make the $XS_R$ steeper and the $XS_P$ flatter in a way that does not change $P''$; our thanks to Jonathan Gage for help with this problem.)

**4.** (Growth effects and RoW impact.) Suppose that signing an FTA between Home and Partner produces a growth effect that raises their income level and thus shifts their $MD$ curves upwards. Use a diagram like Fig. 5-4 to show how big the upward shift would have to be to ensure that RoW did not lose from the Home—Partner FTA. (In the 1970s, this was the informal explanation for why the EEC6 formation did not lead to trade diversion.) Can you show the welfare impact of this growth on Home?

**5.** (Hub and spoke bilateralism.) Using PTA diagrams, show what the price, quantity and welfare effects would be of a hub-and-spoke arrangement among three nations. (Hub-and-spoke means that country 1 signs FTAs with countries 2 and 3, but 2 and 3 do not liberalize trade between them.) Assume that there are ONLY frictional barriers in this world, that initially all import barriers have a tariff equivalent of $T$, and that the FTAs concern only frictional barrier liberalization. Be sure to look at the price, quantity and welfare impact on (i) a typical spoke economy (2 or 3) and (ii) the hub economy.

**6.** (Sapir 1992.) Consider a situation where Home and Partner have formed a customs union but have not eliminated frictional barriers between them. Specifically assume that all trade flows among Home, Partner and RoW are subject to frictional trade barriers equal to $T'$ and additionally the tariff on trade between the CU and RoW is equal to $T''$. Show that eliminating frictional barriers inside the CU might harm welfare since it leads to a reduction in the amount of tariff revenue collected on imports from RoW.

**7.** Suppose Home has no trade barriers, except anti-dumping measures. These anti-dumping measures take the form of price undertakings, i.e. instead of Home imposing a tariff on RoW and Partner imports, Home requires Partner and RoW firms to charge a high price for their sales to Home. Show the price, quantity and welfare effects of imposing this import price floor (look at all three nations). Next, show the price, quantity and welfare effects of removing the price undertaking (i.e. allowing free trade) only for imports from Partner. Be sure to illustrate the impact on all three nations. (*Hint*: The price undertaking is a price floor, so it does not act just like a tariff; be very careful in constructing the $MS_{PTA}$ for this situation.)

## Essay questions

**1.** Using the analysis of a customs union in this chapter, explain how the domino theory of integration could explain the fact that virtually all nations in and around Western Europe now have or want to have preferential trade arrangements with the European Union.

**2.** Using the economic analysis in this chapter, together with the political economy logic of special interest groups (well-organized groups often have political weight that is far in excess of their economic weight), explain why the WTO restrictions on customs unions and free trade areas might be a good idea.

**3.** Using the economic analysis in this chapter and political economy logic, explain why most trade liberalizations are reciprocal rather than unilateral.

**4.** Some international trade experts believe that formation of the EU's customs union lead to pressures from the USA and Japan for a multilateral tariff-cutting round called the Kennedy Round. Use the economic analysis in this chapter, together with the political economy logic of special interest groups, to explain why this view might make sense. (*Hint*: USA and Japanese exporters are a very powerful special interest group.)

**5.** When Bismarck led the drive to unify the many small regions and nation-states of Germany, he used a customs union (*Zollverien*) as both a carrot and a stick to encourage unification. Use the economic analysis in this chapter (especially the impact on RoW) to make sense of this strategy.

## FURTHER READING

### *The aficionados corner*

The modern study of European economic integration began life under the name of 'customs union theory' with Viner (1950). Viner's seminal text triggered a flood of work. At the time, tariffs were the key trade barriers and theorists had few tools for dealing with imperfect competition, so the early literature focused on tariff removals in the NICNIR setting. For a highly readable survey of this literature, see Pomfret (1986). O'Brien (1975) provides a review of pre-Vinerian literature.

Following Viner's theory, which associated welfare effects with changes in trade flows, early empirical studies focused on trade creation and diversion. Surveys of this literature include Srinivasan, Whalley and Wooton (1993), Mayes (1978), and Winters (1987).

A more extensively graphic presentation of pre- and post-1958 trade flows in Europe can be found in Neal and Berbezat (1998).

## USEFUL WEBSITES

While the EU's customs union has been completed for over three decades, some policy issues occasional arise. See the Commission's website
http://europa.eu.int/comm/taxation_customs/.
The history of EFTA's free trade area can be found on http://www.efta.int/.

Further information on WTO rules concerning preferential trade arrangements can be found on www.wto.org.

## REFERENCES

Artis, M. and F. Nixson (2001) *The Economics of the European Union*. Oxford University Press.
Balassa, B. (1975) 'Trade creation and trade diversion to the European Common Market' in B. Balassa (ed.) *European Economic Integration*, North-Holland, Amsterdam.
Baldwin, R.E. and A. Venables (1995) 'Regional economic integration.' In G. Grossman and K. Rogoff (eds) *Handbook of International Economics: Volume III*, North-Holland, Amsterdam.
Cooper, C. and D. Massell (1965) 'Towards a general theory of customs unions in developing countries,' *Journal of Political Economy*, 73, 256–83.
Kemp, M. and H. Wan (1976) 'An elementary proposition concerning the formation of customs unions', *Economic Journal*, 6, 95–7.
Mankiw, G. (2000) *Principles of Economics*, Thomson Learning, New York.
Mayes, D. (1978) 'The effects of economic integration on trade,' *Journal of Common Market Studies*, XVII, Sept, 1–25.
Meade, J. (1955) *The Theory of Customs Unions*, Oxford.
Neal, L. and D. Berbezat (1998) *The Economics of the European Union and the Economics of Europe*, Oxford University Press, London.
O'Brien, D.P. (1976) 'Classical Monetary Theory.' *The Classical Economists*, Oxford: Clarendon Press, 1975, 140–69.
Panagariya, A. (1999) 'Preferential trade liberalisation: The traditional theory and new developments', University of Maryland mimeo. (Download from www.bsos.umd.edu/econ/panagariya/song/surveypt.pdf)
Pomfret, R. (1986) 'The Theory of Preferential Trading Arrangements.' *Weltwirtschaftliches Archiv*, 122, 439–64.
Sapir, A. (1992) 'Regional integration in Europe', *Economic Journal*, 102 (415), 1491–1506.

Srinivasan, T.N., J. Whalley, and I. Wooton (1993) 'Measuring the Effects of Regionalism on Trade and Welfare'. in K. Anderson and R. Blackhurst (eds) *Regional Integration and the Global Trading System*, London: Harvester Wheatsheaf for the GATT Secretariat, 52–79.

Viner, J. (1950) *The Customs Union Issue*, Carnegie Endowment for International Peace, New York.

Winters, L. A. (1978) 'Britain in Europe: A Survey of Quantitative Trade Studies'. *Journal of Common Market Studies*, 25, 315–35.

## Annex A: Discriminatory liberalization, small country case

This background appendix presents the classic analysis of unilateral preferential tariff liberalization for the 'small country' case. The so-called small country case means that we make the simplifying assumption that the volume of a nation's imports is unrelated to the price of those imports. In this case, we do not need the import supply and demand diagram discussed above. Rather, we can work directly with a simpler open-economy supply and demand diagram.

Fig. A5-1, which allows for two potential sources of imports (countries A and B), helps to organize the reasoning. To set the stage, suppose that Home initially imposes a tariff of $T$ on imports from A and B. (Goods produced in the countries A, B and Home are all perfect substitutes.) The Home nation is assumed to face a flat import supply curve from both countries. The idea behind this simplification is that Home is so small that it can buy as much or as little as it wants without affecting the price. Specifically, the import supply curves from A and B are the flat curves at the levels $P_A$ and $P_B$. We can see that country A producers are more efficient since they can offer the goods at a lower price. That is, importing from A costs Home consumers $P_A + T$, while importing from B costs $P_B + T$. Plainly, all imports initially come from the cheaper supplier, namely A.

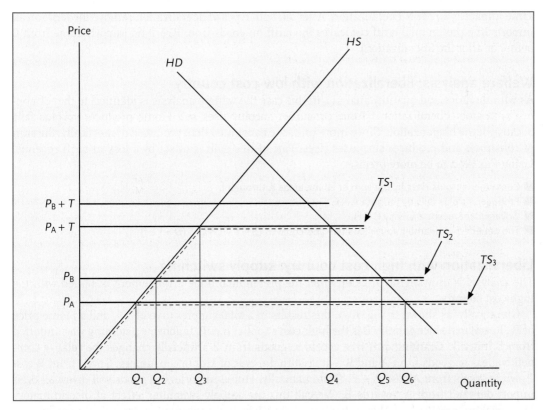

FIGURE A5-1: PRICE AND QUANTITY EFFECTS OF DISCRIMINATORY LIBERALIZATION (SMALL NATION)

Adding together the three sources of supply (Home, A and B), we find the pre-liberalization total supply curve to be $TS_1$. Because it is the horizontal sum of the Home supply curve and the two import supply curves, it follows the Home supply curve up to $P_A + T$ and beyond that, it follows A's import supply curve. The equilibrium Home price (i.e. the price facing Home consumers and producers) is $P_A + T$ since this is where total supply meets demand. The border price, namely the price that Home as a country pays for imports, $P_A$.

Next we ask, what would happen if the tariff were removed on a discriminatory basis? That is to say, if it were removed on imports from only A or only B. Both cases must be considered. We turn now to the price, quantity and welfare effects of the two cases.

## Price and quantity analysis, liberalization with low-cost country

In the first case, the liberalization is applied to Home's current trading partner, namely A. The total supply curve becomes $TS_3$, so the Home price falls to $P_A$. Home consumption rises, Home production falls, imports rise and nothing happens to the border price of imports. To summarize:

- The price in the Home market of both imports and Home import-competing goods falls to $P_A$.
- Home production falls from $Q_3$ to $Q_1$.
- Home consumption rises from $Q_4$ to $Q_6$.
- The import volume rises from the difference between $Q_3$ and $Q_4$ to the difference between $Q_1$ and $Q_6$.
- The border price (i.e. the price of imported good before the imposition of the tax) remains unchanged at $P_A$.

With some thought, it is clear that discriminatory liberalization with the low-cost country has the same impact as an MFN liberalization. After all, both types of liberalization remove the tariff on all imports (the preferential tariff cut leaves the tariff on goods from B, but no imports come from B before or after the liberalization).

## Welfare analysis: liberalization with low-cost country

As with the price and quantity analysis, in this case the welfare analysis is identical to that of non-discriminatory liberalization. Home consumer surplus rises and Home producer surplus falls because of the liberalization. Since more units are consumed than produced domestically, the sum of consumer and producer surpluses rises. Part of this gain is offset by a loss in tariff revenue. Using Fig. A5-2 to be more precise:

- Consumer surplus rises by the sum of all the areas A through J.
- Producer surplus falls by the area A + E.
- Government revenue falls by C + H.
- The net effect is unambiguously positive and equal to (B + F + G) and (D + I + J).

## Liberalization with high-cost country: supply switching

The analysis is only slightly trickier when the preferential trade arrangement is signed with the high-cost country.

Graphically, as shown in Fig. A5-1, this results in a total supply curve of $TS_2$ and a Home price of $P_B$. Recall that since country B is the high-cost supplier (i.e. $P_B$ is above $P_A$) nothing was imported from B initially. Granting duty-free access to goods from B artificially changes the relative competitiveness of goods from A and B – at least in the eyes of Home consumers. Goods from B cost $P_B$ while goods from A cost $P_A + T$. Quite naturally, Home importers of goods will divert all their import demand from A towards B. We call this the 'supply-switching' effect of discriminatory liberalization; it is the first of two elements that arise with discriminatory liberalization but do not

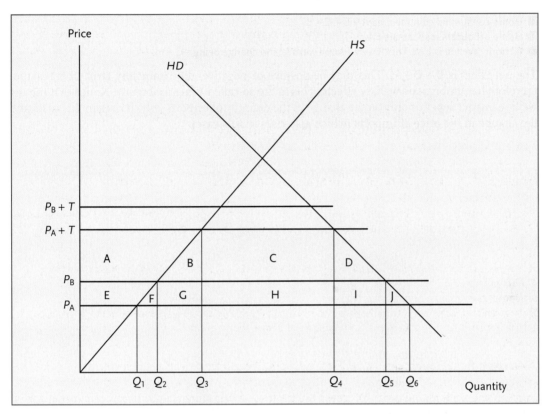

FIGURE A5-2: SMALL COUNTRY WELFARE ANALYSIS

arise with non-discriminatory liberalization. Note, however, that discriminatory liberalization does not always lead to supply-switching. It can only do so when it is done with the high-cost country. The second novel aspect of discriminatory liberalization is the border price impact. That is, as consumers switch from the low-cost source to the high-cost source (country B), the Home border price rises. We call this the 'border price' effect, or the import-price rising effect. The importance of this price change should be clear – such liberalization will raise the cost of imports to the country as a whole.

To summarize, there are six price and quantity effects:

- The preferential liberalization increases competition from imports and thereby forces down the Home price of locally made and imported goods to $P_B$.
- Consumption rises to $Q_5$.
- Some high-cost Home production is replaced by lower cost imports. This amount is equal to $Q_3 - Q_2$.
- The new Home production level is $Q_2$.
- Imports from A are entirely replaced by imports from B and the level of imports rises.
- The border price rises. That is to say, Home now pays more for its imports (namely, $P_B$) than it did before (namely, $P_A$).

## Welfare analysis: liberalization with high-cost country

When the tariffs come down only on imports from the country that initially sells nothing to Home, the welfare effects turn out to be ambiguous. To summarize using Fig. 5-A2, there are three welfare effects of a discriminatory liberalization of a tariff (or any DCR barrier):

- Home consumers gain the area A + B + C + D.
- Home producers lose the area A.
- All tariff revenue is lost. This lowers Home welfare; the change being −C − H.

The net effect is B + D − H. This may be positive or negative, discriminatory tariff liberalisation therefore has ambiguous welfare effects. This is the so-called Viner ambiguity. Notice that the net welfare impact depends only on the change in the quantity of imports (which rises in this case) and the change in the price of imports (which also rises in this case).

“ The countries of Europe are too small to give their peoples the prosperity that is now ”
attainable and therefore necessary. They need wider markets.

**Jean Monnet, 1943**

“ By its size – the biggest in the world – the single market without frontiers is an invalu- ”
able asset to revitalise our businesses and make them more competitive. It is one of the
main engines of the European Union.’

**Jacques Delors, July 1987**

# 6 Market Size and Scale Effects

---

Market size matters. From its very inception in the 1950s, an important premise behind European economic integration was the belief that unification of European economies would – by allowing European firms access to a bigger market – make European firms more efficient and this, in turn, would allow them to lower prices, raise quality and gain competitiveness in external markets.

This chapter explores the economic logic of how European integration can lead to fewer, larger firms operating at a more efficient scale and facing more effective competition. The chapter also considers policy responses to these changes, notably the enforcement of rules that prohibit unfair subsidization of firms and rules restricting anti-competitive behaviour. In the EU, such policies are called, respectively, ‘state aids’ policy and ‘competition policy’.

---

## 6.1 Liberalization, defragmentation and industrial restructuring: logic and facts

We start the chapter by verbally explaining the logic that links European integration to industrial restructuring before presenting some facts on mergers and acquisitions (M&As) and the effects on competition.

Europe's national markets are separated by a whole host of barriers. These included tariffs and quotas until the Common Market was completed in 1968 and tariffs between the EEC and EFTA until the EEC–EFTA free trade agreements were signed in 1974. Yet, even though intra-EU trade has been duty free for over three decades, intra-European trade is not as free as trade within European nations. Many technical, physical and fiscal barriers still make it easier for companies to sell in their local market than in other EU markets. While most of these barriers seem trivial or even silly when considered in isolation, the confluence of thousands of seemingly small barriers serves to substantially restrict intra-EU trade. As a result, EU firms can often be dominant in their home market while being marginal players in other EU markets (think of the European car market). This situation, known as market fragmentation, reduces competition and this, in turn, raises prices and keeps too many firms in business. Keeping firms in business is not, of course, a bad thing in itself. The problem is that this results in an industrial structure marked by too many, inefficient, small firms that can get away with charging high prices to cover the cost of their inefficiency. Due to the absence of competition, poor and/or low-quality services and goods may also accompany the high prices (think of the European telephone service before liberalization).

Tearing down these intra-EU barriers defragments the markets and produces extra competition. This 'pro-competitive effect', in turn, puts pressure on profits and the market's response is 'merger mania'. That is, the pro-competitive effect squeezes the least efficient firms, prompting an industrial restructuring where Europe's weaker firms merge or get bought up. In the end, Europe is left with a more efficient industrial structure, with fewer, bigger, more efficient firms competing more effectively with each other. All this means improved material well-being for Europeans as prices fall and output rises. In some industries, restructuring may be accompanied by a sizeable re-allocation of employment, as firms cut back on redundant workers and close inefficient plants and offices (a painful process for workers who have to change jobs). In other industries, however, liberalization can unleash a virtuous circle of more competition, lower prices, higher sales and higher employment.

In the remainder of the chapter we work through the logic of what was just presented informally. Schematically, the steps can be summarized as: liberalization $\rightarrow$ defragmentation $\rightarrow$ pro-competitive effect $\rightarrow$ industrial restructuring. The result is fewer, bigger, more efficient firms facing more effective competition from each other.

### 6.1.1 Some facts

As shown in the left panel of Fig. 6-1, the number of mergers and acquisitions (M&As) in the EU15 remained at a high steady level of about 10 000 operations per year until 1997 when the number started climbing steadily to a record total of 12 557 operations in 2000. In terms of the total value of deals, however, the EU figure climbed steadily and rapidly from 1991 to 2000, from about 100 billion euros to 2400 billion euros. The number and value were lower in 2001, reflecting the slowdown in economic activity, but at over 10 000 operations, it was still a considerable number.

It is interesting to note that much of this M&A activity consists of the mergers of firms within the same Member State, e.g. German firms buying other German firms. Indeed, at the end of the period, about 55 per cent of all operations were of this 'domestic' type. The remaining 45 per cent of the deals involved a non-domestic firm. This 45 per cent is split between operations where one

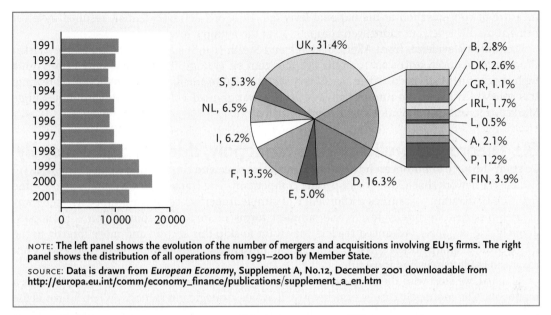

NOTE: **The left panel shows the evolution of the number of mergers and acquisitions involving EU15 firms. The right panel shows the distribution of all operations from 1991–2001 by Member State.**

SOURCE: **Data is drawn from** *European Economy*, **Supplement A, No.12, December 2001 downloadable from http://europa.eu.int/comm/economy_finance/publications/supplement_a_en.htm**

FIGURE 6-1: MERGERS AND ACQUISITIONS (M&As) INVOLVING EU15 FIRMS, 1991–2001

firm was a non-EU firm (24 per cent), where one firm was located in another EU nation (15 per cent) and operations where the counterparty's nationality was not identified (6 per cent).

The right panel of Fig. 6-1 shows the breakdown of firms by Member State. Two points are worth stressing. First, the distribution of M&A operations is quite varied. The big four economies (France, Italy, Germany and the UK) have the most operations, however, except for the UK, these nations' share of M&As activity is much lower than their share of the European economy. Italy, France and Germany together account for only 36 per cent of the M&As even though their economies account for 59 per cent of the EU15 economy. By contrast, many of the small EU15 members seem to have a share of M&A activity that is systematically higher than their share of the EU15's GDP. This link between domestic market size and the impact of integration on restructuring fits in with the basic logic described above. Stylizing the facts to make the point, we can say that the problem of a too-small market was most severe in the smaller EU members; integration produced the largest changes (large in proportion to their economy) in the smallest members. The second point comes from the exceptions to this rule. The EU has yet to harmonize rules on takeovers. Despite many years of trying, some members still have very restrictive takeover practices that make M&As very difficult while others, like the UK, have very liberal rules. The implication of this lack of harmonization is that the restructuring effects of integration have been felt very differently in the various Member States.

The sectoral composition of M&A activity (not shown in the figure) is also noteworthy. About two-thirds of all the activity in this period took place in service sectors, especially in banking. However, during the early years of the Single Market Programme (1986–92), the M&A activity was centred on manufacturing, with mergers often occurring in anticipation of liberalization that was scheduled (Commission, 1996). Interested readers can find a wealth of details on the nature of this activity in European Economy (2001).

This restructuring increased the level of concentration at the EU level. From 1987 to 1993, the share of the four largest firms in the EU's total market rose from 20.5 to 22.8 per cent, while this measure of concentration at the national level fell. In short, defragmentation resulted in fewer firms at the EU level, but more even competition at the national level.

Econometric evidence from Allen, Gasiorek and Smith (1998) suggests that the Single Market Programme reduced price-cost margins by 4 per cent on average. This impact varied from quite high, e.g. −15 per cent in the office machinery sector, to quite small, e.g. −0.1 per cent in brewing. It is noteworthy that in the auto sector – a sector that was granted a bloc exemption from the Single Market Programme – the price-cost margin actually rose.

## 6.2 Theoretical preliminaries: monopoly, duopoly and oligopoly

To study the logic of European integration's impact on scale and competition we need a simple yet flexible framework that allows for imperfect competition. The framework we employ below – the *BE–COMP* diagram – assumes a knowledge of simple imperfect competition models, so by way of preliminaries, we briefly review the simplest forms of imperfect competition – monopoly, duopoly and oligopoly. Advanced readers may want to skip this section and move directly to the *BE–COMP* diagram in section 6.3, but since it introduces notation and basic concepts, even advanced readers may find it useful.

As usual, we start with the simplest problem – namely, the decision faced by a firm that has a monopoly. The monopoly case is easy because it avoids strategic interactions. When a firm is the only seller of a product, it can choose how much to sell and what price to charge without considering the reaction of other suppliers. The only restraint a monopolist faces is the demand curve. A downward-sloping demand curve is a constraint because it forces the monopolist to confront a trade-off between price and sales; higher prices mean lower sales. When considering the impact of European integration on imperfectly competitive firms, we need to determine how various policy changes will alter prices and sales. The first step in this direction is to see what determines a monopolist's price and sales in a closed economy. The natural question then is: 'What is the profit-maximizing level of sales for the monopolist?'

An excellent way to proceed is to make a guess at the optimal level, say, $Q'$ in the left panel of Fig. 6-2. Almost surely this initial guess will be wrong, but what we want to know is whether $Q'$ is too low or too high. To this end, we calculate the profit earned when $Q'$ units are sold at the highest obtainable price, namely $P'$. The answer is A + B, since the total value of sales is price times quantity (area A + B + C) minus cost (area C).

Would profits rise or fall if the firm sold an extra unit? Of course, to sell the extra unit, the firm will have to let its price fall a bit to $P''$. The change in profit equals the change in revenue minus the change in cost. Consider first the change in revenue. This has two parts. Selling the extra unit brings in extra revenue (represented by areas D + E), but it also depresses the price received for all units sold initially (lowering revenue by an amount equal to area A). The net change in revenue – called 'marginal revenue' for short – is given by the areas D + E minus the area A. The change in cost – called marginal cost for short – is area E. Plainly, profit only increases if the extra revenue D − A exceeds the extra cost E. As it is drawn, D − A + E appears to be negative, so marginal revenue is less than marginal cost at $Q' + 1$. This means that raising output from $Q'$ would lower profits, so the initial guess of $Q'$ turned out to be too high.

To find the profit-maximizing level using this trial-and-error method, we would consider a lower guess, say $Q'$ minus 4 units, and repeat the procedure applied above. At the profit-maximizing level, marginal revenue just equals marginal cost. This level must be optimal since any increase *or* decrease in sales will lower profit. Increasing sales beyond this point will increase cost more than revenue, while decreasing sales would lower revenue more than cost. Both would reduce profit.

The right panel of Fig. 6-2 shows an easier way to find the point where marginal revenue equals marginal cost. The diagram includes a new curve, called the marginal revenue curve. This shows

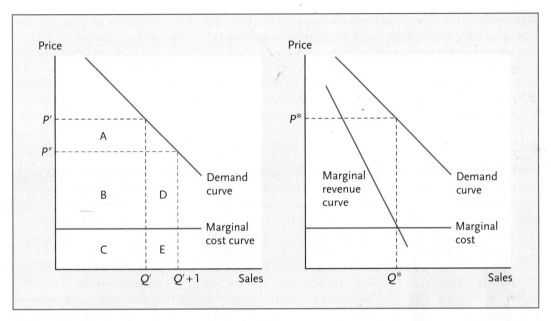

FIGURE 6-2: MONOPOLY PROFIT MAXIMIZATION GRAPHICALLY

how the marginal revenue (measured in euros) declines as the level of sales rises. (It declines since area A from the left panel gets very small for low levels of sales.) At the sales level marked $Q^*$, marginal revenue just equals marginal cost. The firm charges the most it can at this level of sales, and this is $P^*$. These are the profit-maximizing levels of sales and price.

## LESSONS
Several deep aspects of imperfect competition come through even in the monopoly case. First, in setting up the problem, we had to assume things about the firm's beliefs concerning the behaviour of other economic agents. In this case, the monopolist is assumed to believe that consumers are price-takers and that the trade-off between prices and sales depended only on the demand curve (rather than, for example, on the reaction of firms in other markets). Second, the critical difference between perfect and imperfect competition comes out clearly. As part of the definition, perfectly competitive firms are assumed to take the price of their output as given (a classic example is a wheat farmer who cannot set his own price; he just sells at the current market price). This means that such firms are assumed to be ignorant of the fact that selling more will depress the market price. In terms of the diagram, perfectly competitive firms ignore the area A, so they maximize profits by selling an amount where price equals marginal cost. Of course, any increase in sales would have some negative impact on price, so it is best to think of perfect competition as a simplifying assumption that is close to true when all firms have market shares that are close to zero. By stepping away from this simplification, imperfect competition allows firms to explicitly consider the price-depressing effect – area A – when deciding how much to sell.

## 6.2.1 Duopolist as monopolist on residual demand curve
The monopoly case is instructive, but not very realistic – most European firms face some competition. Taking account of this, however, brings us up against the strategic considerations

discussed above. The convention we adopt to sort out this interaction is the so-called Cournot–Nash equilibrium that won John Nash a Nobel prize (see Box 6-1). That is, we assume that each firm acts as if the other firms' outputs are fixed. The equilibrium we are interested in is where each firm's expectations of the other firms' outputs turn out to be correct, i.e. no one is fooled. This no-one-fooled notion proves to be somewhat difficult to comprehend in the abstract but, as we shall see below, it is easy in specific applications.

### The residual demand curve shortcut

Since firms take as given the sales of other firms, the only constraint facing a typical firm is the demand curve shifted to the left by the amount of sales of all other firms. In other words, each firm believes it is a monopolist on the shifted demand curve (we called the shifted demand curve the 'residual demand curve'). This realization is handy since it means that we can directly apply the solution technique from the monopolist's problem; the only change is that we calculate the marginal revenue curve based on the residual demand curve instead of the demand curve.

This trick is shown in Fig. 6-3 for a competition between two firms producing the same good – a situation that economists call 'duopoly'. For simplicity, we assume that the firms have the same marginal cost curves. Taking firm 2's sales as given at $Q_2$, firm 1 has a monopoly on the residual demand curve labelled $RD_1$. Firm 1's optimal output in this case is $x_1'$ (since at point $A_1$, the residual marginal revenue curve, $RMR_1$, crosses the marginal cost curve $MC$). The right panel shows the same sort of analysis for firm 2. Taking firm 1's output as fixed at $Q_1$, firm 2's optimal output is $x_2'$.

Note that the situation in Fig. 6-3 is not an equilibrium. To highlight the importance of the difference between expected and actual outcomes, the diagram shows the solutions of the two firms when there expectation about the other firm's output *do not match the reality*. The consistent-expectations outcome, i.e. the Nash equilibrium, is shown in Fig. 6-4, but we first consider why Fig. 6-3 is not an equilibrium.

As drawn, $x_1'$ and $x_2'$ are not a Cournot–Nash equilibrium since the firms' actual output levels do not match expectations; firm 1 produces $x_1'$, which is greater than what firm 2 expected (namely, $Q_1$), and likewise, firm 2 produces $x_2'$, which is greater than what firm 1 expected (namely, $Q_2$). We can also see the problem by observing that the implied prices are not equal. If $x_1'$ and $x_2'$ were actually produced by the firms, then firms would not be able to charge the prices they expected to charge. In other words, this is not an equilibrium because the outcome is not consistent with expectations.

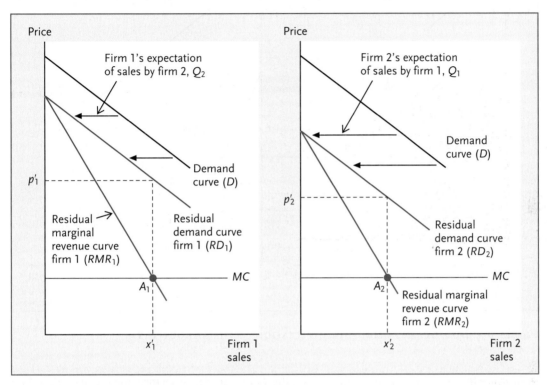

FIGURE 6-3: DUOPOLIST AS MONOPOLIST ON RESIDUAL DEMAND: EXAMPLE OF A NON-EQUILIBRIUM

### FINDING THE EXPECTATIONS CONSISTENT EQUILIBRIUM

How do we find the expectation-consistent set of outputs? The easiest way is to use the assumed symmetry of firms. In the symmetric equilibrium, each firm will sell the same amount. With this fact in mind, a bit of thought reveals that the residual demand curve facing each firm must be half of the overall demand curve. This situation is shown in the left panel of Fig. 6-4 for a duopoly. Some facts to note are that: (i) the optimal output for a typical firm is $x^*$, given by the intersection of $RMR$ and $MC$; (ii) the total sales to the market are $2x^*$ and at this level of sales the overall market price (given by the demand curve, $D$) is consistent with the price each firm expects to receive given the residual demand curve, $RD$; and (iii) the output of the identical firms are equal in equilibrium.

## 6.2.2 Oligopoly: Cournot–Nash for an arbitrary number of firms

While allowing for two firms was more realistic than just allowing for only one firm, studying the impact of European integration on mergers and acquisitions requires us to allow for an arbitrary number of firms. In economists' jargon, this situation is called an oligopoly. As it turns out, this situation is straightforward to deal with when firms are symmetric. The right panel of Fig. 6-4 shows the argument for the case of three firms.

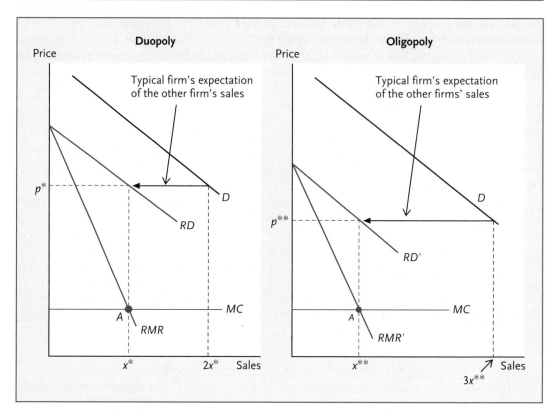

FIGURE 6-4: DUOPOLY AND OLIGOPOLY: EXPECTATION-CONSISTENT OUTPUTS

As more firms are competing in the market (here we consider three instead of two), the residual demand curve facing each one shifts inwards, so the residual marginal revenue curve also shifts inwards; the new curves are shown in the right panel as $RD'$ and $RMR'$. The implications of this shift for prices is clear. The new $RMR = MC$ point occurs at a lower level of per-firm output and this implies a lower price. In equilibrium (i.e. where outcomes match expectations), each of the three firms produces an identical amount, identified as $x^{**}$ in the diagram, and charges an identical price, $p^{**}$.

Given that we have worked through the 1, 2 and 3 firm cases, readers should be able to see what would happen as the number of firms continues to rise. Each increase in the number of competitors will shift in the $RD$ facing each one of them. This will inevitably lead to lower prices and lower output per firm.

Of course, this analysis is just formalizing what most readers would expect. If one adds more competitors to a market, prices will fall along with the market share of each firm. As is so often the case, the brilliant concepts are simple.

## 6.3 The *BE–COMP* diagram in a closed economy

To study the impact of European integration on firm size and efficiency, the number of firms, prices, output and the like, it is useful to have a diagram in which all of these things are determined. The presentation of this diagram, which actually consists of three subdiagrams, is the first order of business. To keep things simple, we begin with the case of a closed economy. Advanced readers may find the mathematical appendix to this chapter helpful in understanding the diagrams (freely downloadable from http://heiwww.unige.ch/~Baldwin/BW/BW.htm).

The heart of the *BE–COMP* diagram is the subdiagram in which the number of firms and the profit-maximizing price-cost margin are determined. As usual, the equilibrium will be the intersection of two curves, the *BE* curve and the *COMP* curve. We start by presenting the *COMP* curve.

### 6.3.1 The *COMP* curve

It is easy to understand that imperfectly competitive firms charge a price that exceeds their marginal cost; they do so in order to maximize profit. But how wide is the gap between price and marginal cost, and how does it vary with the number of competitors? These questions are answered by the *COMP* curve.

If there is only one firm, the price-cost gap – what we call the 'mark-up' of price over marginal cost – will equal the mark-up that a monopolist would charge. If there are more firms competing in the market, competition will force each firm to charge a lower mark-up. We summarize this 'competition-side' relationship between the mark-up and the number of firms as the '*COMP* curve' shown in Fig. 6-5. It is downward sloped since competition drives the mark-up down as the number of competitors rises as explained above. We denote the mark-up with the Greek letter μ, pronounced mu, since 'mu' is an abbreviation for **mark-up**. We call it the *COMP* curve since the size of the mark-up is an indicator of how competitive the market is.

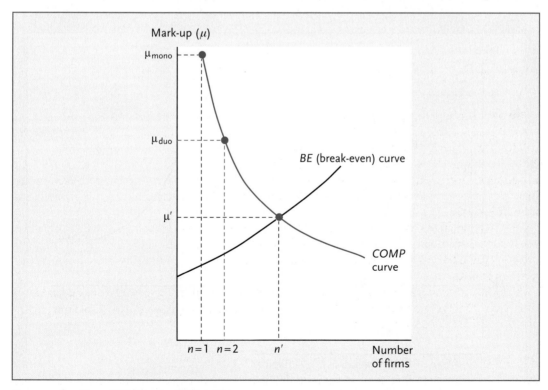

FIGURE 6-5: THE *COMP* AND *BE* CURVES

The Economics of European Integration: **Part II**

While this intuitive connection between price and marginal cost may suffice for some readers, extra insight is gained by considering the derivation of the *COMP* curve in more detail. This is done in Box 6-2.

---

### Box 6-2: *COMP* CURVE IN DETAIL

Consider how the profit maximizing mark-up changes when the number of firms increases. To keep the reasoning concrete, consider an increase from 1 firm (the monopoly case) to 2 firms (the duopoly case).

The solid lines in the left panel of Fig. 6-6 show the usual problem for a monopolist, with the demand curve marked as *D* and the marginal revenue curve marked as *MR*. (See section 6.2, if you are not familiar with the monopolist case.) The profit-maximizing output, $x_{mono}$, is indicated by the point *A*, i.e. the intersection of marginal cost (marked as *MC* in the diagram) and marginal revenue (marked as *MR* in the diagram). The firm charges the most it can for the level of sales $x_{mono}$, i.e. $p'$. The price-marginal-cost mark-up (called the mark-up for short) equals $p' - MC$ as shown. We can also see the size of operating profit (i.e. profit without considering fixed cost) in the diagram since it is, by definition, just the monopolist mark-up times the monopoly level of sales $x_{mono}$. In the diagram this is shown by the area of the box marked by the points $p'$, $A'$, $A$ and *MC*.

When a second firm competes in this market, we have a duopoly rather than a monopoly. To solve this, we adopt the standard 'Cournot–Nash' approach of assuming that each firm

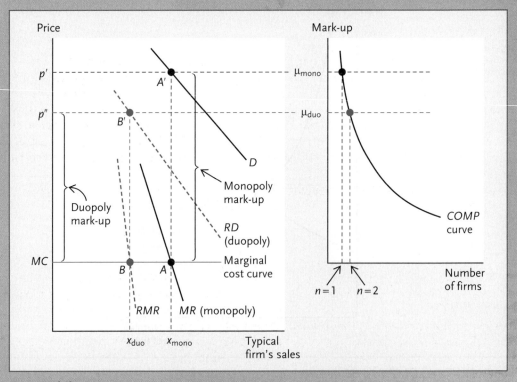

FIGURE 6-6: IMPACT OF MORE FIRMS ON PRICES AND PRICE-COST MARK-UPS

takes as given the output of the other firm(s). Practically speaking, this means that each firm acts as if it were a monopolist on the 'residual demand curve', i.e. the demand curve shifted to the left by the amount of other firms' sales (marked as $RD$ in the diagram). The exact equilibrium price and output are found by identifying the intersection of the residual marginal revenue curve ($RMR$) and the marginal cost curve; again, firms charge the highest possible price for this level of sales, namely $p''$. In drawing the diagram, we have supposed that the two firms have identical marginal cost curves (for simplicity), so the outcome of the competition will be that each firm sells an equal amount. You can verify, that $p''$ is the price that the full demand curve, $D$, says would result if two times $x_{duo}$ were sold.

The net result of adding an additional firm is that the price drops from $p'$ to $p''$ and thus lowers the equilibrium mark-up. We also note that more competition lowers the level of sales per firm, although the sum of sales of the two competing firms exceeds the sales of a monopolist. Finally, note that adding in more firms lowers each firm's operating profit since it reduces the mark-up and sales per firm. The duopoly operating profit is the duopoly mark-up times $x_{duo}$; this is shown by the area $p''$, $B'$, $B$, $MC$ in the diagram.

Here we have looked only at the switch from one to two firms, but it should be clear that continuing to add in more firms would produce a similar result. As the number of firms rose, the residual demand curve facing each firm would shift inwards, resulting in a lower price, lower level of output per firm and, most importantly, in a lower price-cost margin, i.e. a lower mark-up. In the extreme, an infinite number of firms would push the price down to marginal cost, eliminating the price-cost margin and all operating profits; each firm would be infinitely small (this is why perfectly competitive firms are sometimes called atomistic).

## 6.3.2 The break-even ($BE$) curve

The mark-up and number of firms are related in another way, summarized by the $BE$ curve.

When a sector is marked by increasing returns to scale, there is only room for a certain number of firms in a market of a given size. Intuitively, more firms will be able to survive if the price is far above marginal cost, i.e. if the mark-up is high. The curve that captures this relationship is called the 'break-even curve', or zero-profit curve ($BE$ curve, for short) in Fig. 6-5. It has a positive slope since more firms can break even when the mark-up is high. That is to say, taking the mark-up as given, the $BE$ curve shows the number of firms that can earn enough to cover their fixed cost, say, the cost of setting up a factory.

Again, this intuitive presentation of the $BE$ curve will suffice for many readers, but might well raise questions in the minds of more advanced readers. These questions are addressed in Box 6-3.

### Box 6-3: Derivation of the $BE$ curve

While the positive link between mark-up and the break-even number of firms is quite intuitive, it is useful to study the relationship more closely. To keep the reasoning as easy as possible we consider the simplest form of increasing returns to scale, namely a situation where the typical firm faces a flat marginal cost curve *and* a fixed cost of operating. The fixed cost could represent, for example, the cost of building a factory, establishing a brand name, training workers, etc. This combination of fixed cost and flat marginal cost implies increasing returns since the typical firm's average cost falls as its scale of production rises, as is shown in the left panel of Fig. 6–7.

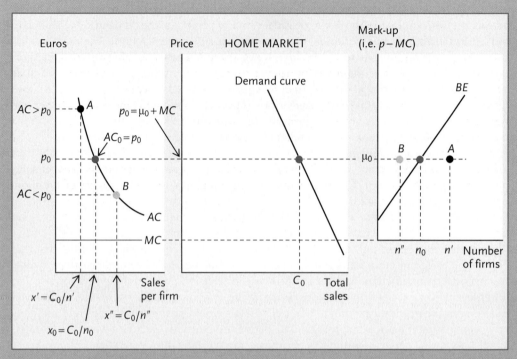

FIGURE 6-7: THE $BE$ CURVE IN DETAIL

If a firm is to survive in this situation, it must earn enough on its sales to cover its fixed cost. The amount it earns on sales is called its 'operating profit', and this is simply the mark-up times the level of sales. For example, if the mark-up (i.e. price minus marginal cost) is 200 euros and each firm sells 20 000 units, the operating profit per firm will be 4 million euros. As we shall see, this simple connection between the mark-up, sales and operating profit makes it quite easy to figure out the number of firms that can break even at any given mark-up.

Since all firms are identical in this example, a given mark-up implies that the price will also be given, specifically it will equal the mark-up plus marginal cost. For example, if the mark-up is $\mu_o$ as in the Fig. 6-7, then the price will be $p_o = \mu_o + MC$. At this price, the demand curve tells us that the level of total sales will be $C_o$. Finally, we again use the symmetry of firms to work out the level of sales per firm; this will be total sales divided by the number of firms, which, in symbols, is $C_o/n$. To see how many firms can break even when the mark-up is $\mu_o$, we turn to the left panel in the diagram. With a little thought, you should be able to see that a firm will make zero total profit (i.e. operating profit plus the fixed cost) when its average cost exactly equals the price. Using the average cost curve, marked as $AC$ in the left panel, we see that the typical firm's average cost equals price when the sales of the typical firm equals $x_o$. Because we know that sales per firm will be $C_o/n$, we can work out the number of firms where the sales per firm just equals $x_o$. In symbols, the break-even number of firms, call this $n_o$, is where $C_o/n_o$ equals $x_o$.

It is instructive to consider what would happen if the mark-up were $\mu_o$, but there were more than $n_o$ firms, say $n'$ firms, in the market. In this case, the sales per firm would be lower than $x_o$, namely $x' = C_o/n'$, so the typical firm's average cost would be higher and this means that the average cost of a typical firm would exceed the price. Plainly, such a situation is not sustainable since all the firms would be losing money (earning operating profits that were too low to allow them to cover their fixed cost). This case is shown by the point A in the left panel of the diagram. The same point A can be shown in the right panel as the combination of the mark-up $\mu_o$ and $n'$; we know that at this point, firms are not covering their fixed cost, so there would be a tendency for some firms to exit the industry. In the real world this sort of 'exit' takes the form of mergers or bankruptcies. The opposite case of too few firms is shown in the right and left panels as point B; here firms' average cost is below the price and so all are making pure profits (i.e. their operating profit exceed the fixed cost). Such a situation would encourage more firms to enter the market.

To work out all the points on the *BE* curve, we would go through a similar analysis for every given level of the mark-up. The logic presented above, however, makes it clear that the result would be an upward-sloped *BE* curve.

### 6.3.3 Equilibrium prices, output and firm size

It is important to note that firms are not always on the *BE* curve since they can earn above-normal or below-normal profits for a while. In the long run, however, firms can enter or exit the market, so the number of firms rises or falls until the typical firm earns just enough to cover its fixed cost. By contrast, firms are always on the *COMP* curve since firms can change prices quickly in response to any change in the number of firms.

With this in mind, we are ready to work out the equilibrium mark-up, number of firms, price and firm-size in a closed economy using Fig. 6-8. The right panel combines the *BE* curve with the *COMP* curve. The intersection of the two defines the equilibrium mark-up and long-run number

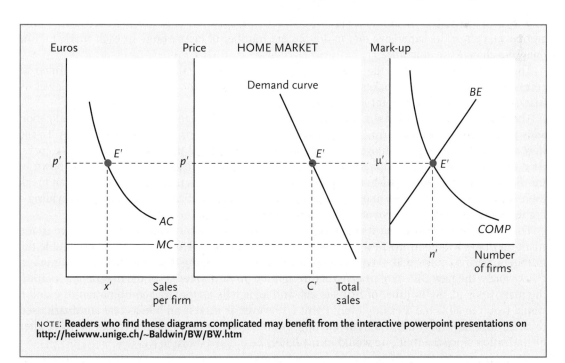

NOTE: **Readers who find these diagrams complicated may benefit from the interactive powerpoint presentations on http://heiwww.unige.ch/~Baldwin/BW/BW.htm**

FIGURE 6-8: PRICES, OUTPUT AND EQUILIBRIUM FIRM SIZE IN A CLOSED ECONOMY

of firms. More specifically, the *COMP* curve tells us that firms would charge a mark-up of $\mu'$ when there are $n'$ firms in the market, and the *BE* curve tells us that $n'$ firms could break even when the mark-up is $\mu'$. The equilibrium price is – by definition of the mark-up – just the equilibrium mark-up plus the marginal cost, *MC*. Using the *MC* curve from the left panel, we see that the equilibrium price is $p'$ (this equals $\mu'$ plus *MC*). The middle panel shows the demand curve and this allows us to see that the total level of consumption implied by the equilibrium price is $C'$.

The left panel helps us to find the equilibrium firm size, i.e. sales per firm, which we denote as $x$. This subdiagram shows the average and marginal cost curves of a typical firm. As a little bit of reflection reveals, a typical firm's total profit is zero when price equals average cost (when price equals average cost, total revenue equals total cost). Since we know that total profits are zero at the equilibrium and we know the price is $p'$, it must be that the equilibrium firm size is $x'$ since this is where the firm's size implies an average cost equal to $p'$.

In summary, Fig. 6-8 lets us determine the equilibrium number of firms, mark-up, price, total consumption and firm size all in one diagram. With this in hand, we are now ready to study how European integration has sparked a wave of industrial restructuring.

## 6.4 The impact of European liberalization

European integration has involved a gradual reduction of trade barriers. The basic economic effects of this gradual reduction can, however, be illustrated more simply by considering a much more drastic liberalization – taking a completely closed economy and making it a completely open economy. To keep things simple, we suppose that there are only two nations, Home and Partner, and that these nations are identical. Since they are identical, we could trace through the effects looking at either market, but we focus on Home's market for convenience.

### 6.4.1 No-trade-to-free-trade liberalization

The immediate impact of the no-trade-to-free-trade liberalization is to provide each firm with a second market of the same size *and* to double the number of competitors in each market. How does this change the outcome?

The competition aspect of the liberalization is simple to trace out. The increased number of competitors in each market makes competition tougher. In reaction, the typical firm will lower its mark-up in each market to point *A* in Fig. 6-9.

The doubling of the market size facing each firm also has an important effect. The liberalization adds a new market for each firm, so it makes sense that more firms will be able to survive. To see how many more firms can survive, we work out the impact of the liberalization on the *BE* curve. As it turns out, the liberalization shifts the *BE* curve to the right, specifically to $BE_{FT}$ as shown in the diagram. Why? Shifting *BE* to the right means that at any given mark-up more firms can break even. This is true since as the market size increases the sales per firm increases, thus providing a higher operating profit per firm at any given level of the mark-up.

The size of the rightward shift is determined without difficulty. If there were no change in the mark-up (there will be in the new equilibrium, but ignore this for the moment), then double the number of firms could break even since each firm would be selling the same number of units. In other words, the new BE curve must pass through the point marked '1' in the diagram; at point 1, the mark-up is $\mu'$, the number of firms is $2n'$, and logic tells us that this combination of $\mu$ and $n$ would result in all firms breaking even. Point 1, however, is merely an intellectual landmark used to determine how far out the *BE* curve shifts. It is not where the economy would be right after liberalization since the mark-up would immediately be pushed down to $\mu_A$.

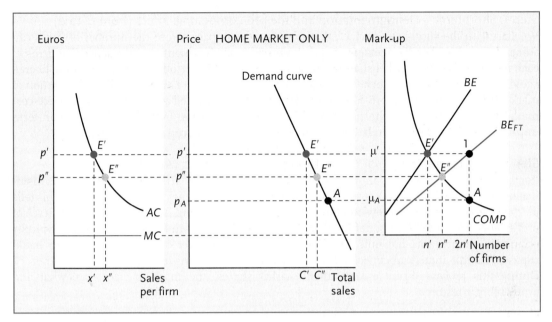

FIGURE 6-9: PRICES, OUTPUT AND EQUILIBRIUM FIRM SIZE WITH INTEGRATION

Because the increase in competition would immediately push down the mark-up to $\mu_A$, the two newly integrated markets will initially be at a point that is below the BE curve. We know that all firms will be losing money at point $A$ since the actual mark-up ($\mu_A$) is less than what would be needed to have all $2n'$ firms break even. Now, this loss of profit is not a problem in the short run since firms only need to break even in the long run. Indeed, the profit losses are what would trigger the process of industrial restructuring that will eventually reduce the number of firms.

The corresponding effect on prices is shown in the middle diagram as the move from $E'$ to $A$ and then to $E''$. Before explaining this, observe that the middle panel shows the demand curve for Home only, so the no-trade-to-free-trade liberalization does not shift the demand curve. The Foreign market has an identical demand, but since exactly the same thing goes on in Foreign, we omit the Foreign demand curve to reduce the diagram's complexity.

As mentioned above, the initial impact of the extra competition ($2n'$ firms selling to the Home market instead of $n'$) pushes the equilibrium mark-up down to $\mu_A$, so the price falls to $p_A$. Thus during this industrial restructuring phase, price would rise to $p''$ (from $p_A$), but this rise does not take the price all the way back to its pre-liberalization level of $p'$.

The impact of this combination of extra competition and industrial restructuring on a typical firm is shown in the left panel. As prices are falling, firms that remain in the market increase their efficiency – i.e. lower their average costs – by spreading their fixed cost over a larger number of sales. Indeed, since price equalled average cost before the liberalization and in the long run after liberalization, we know that the price drop is exactly equal to the efficiency gain. In the left panel, this is shown as a move from $E'$ to $E''$. Increasing returns to scale are the root of this efficiency gain. As the equilibrium scale of a typical firm rises from $x'$ to $x''$, average costs fall.

To summarize, the no-trade-to-free-trade liberalization results in fewer, larger firms. The resulting scale economies lower average cost and thus make these firms more efficient. The extra competition ensures that these savings are passed on to lower prices. It is useful to think of the integration as leading to two steps.

### Step 1: Short term – Defragmentation and the pro-competitive Effect (from E' to A)

We start with the short-term impact, that is to say, the impact before the number of firms can adjust. Before the liberalization, each market was extremely fragmented in the sense that firms in each nation had a local market share of $1/n'$ and a zero share in the other market. After the liberalization, the market share of each firm is the same in each market, namely $\frac{1}{2}n'$. This elimination of market fragmentation has a pro-competitive effect, which is defined as a decrease in the price-cost mark-up. This is shown in the right panel of Fig. 6-9 as a move from $E'$ to $A$. The short-term impact on prices and sales can be seen in the middle panel as a drop from $p'$ to $p_A$.

### Step 2: Long term – Industrial restructuring and scale effects (A to E'')

Point $A$ is not a long-term equilibrium since the operating profit earned by a typical firm is insufficient to cover the fixed cost. We see this by noting that point $A$ is below the $BE$ curve and this tells us that the mark-up is too low to allow $2n'$ firms to break even. To restore a normal level of profitability, the overall number of firms has to fall from $2n'$ to $n''$. In Europe, this process typically occurs via mergers and buy-outs, but in some cases the number of firms is reduced by bankruptcies. As this industrial consolidation occurs, the economy moves from point $A$ to point $E''$. During this process, firms enlarge their market shares, the mark-up rises somewhat and profitability is restored.

#### WELFARE EFFECTS

The welfare effects of this liberalization are quite straightforward. The 4-sided area marked by $p'$, $p''$, $E'$, and $E''$ in the middle panel of Fig. 6-9 corresponds to the gain in Home consumer surplus. As usual, this gain can be broken down into the gain to consumers of paying a lower price for the units they bought prior to the liberalization, and the gains from buying more ($C''$ versus $C'$). Note that the exact same gain occurs in the Foreign market (not shown in the diagram).

As it turns out, this 4-sided area is Home's long-term welfare gain because there is no offsetting loss to producers and there was no tariff revenue to begin with. Firms made zero profits before liberalization and they earn zero profits after liberalization. Note, however, that this long-term calculation ignores the medium-term adjustment costs. These costs, which stem from the industrial restructuring, can be politically very important. Indeed, many governments attempt to thwart the restructuring by adopting a variety of policies such as industrial subsidies and various anti-merger and acquisition policies (discussed further below). We should also note that the welfare gains shown can be rather substantial. Roughly speaking, the percentage gain in real GDP equals the share of the economy affected (industry in the EU, for instance, accounts for about 30 per cent of output) times the percentage drop in price.

## 6.4.2 Slow and fast adjustments

The discussion above has shown that the integration initially leads to big price reduction and large profit losses. These profit losses are eliminated as the number of firms falls and profits are restored to normal levels. During this industrial restructuring process, prices rise slightly. This sequence of steps – sometimes called industry 'consolidation' or an industry 'shake-out' – is relevant to some industries, for example, air travel. Here Europe's liberalization has resulted in large profit losses for many European airlines and big price reductions for consumers. At first, airlines were reluctant to merge – largely because most airlines were government-owned and their governments were willing to use taxpayer euros to cover the losses. More recently, however, European airlines are rationalizing their costs by forming co-operative alliances. While the actual number of firms has not yet fallen, the number of planes flying a particular route is reduced. For example, before the two firms went bankrupt, co-operation between Swiss Air and Sabena meant that instead of having two planes flying the Geneva–Brussels route (one Swiss Air and one Sabena), only one plane flew. Nevertheless, Swiss Air called it a Swiss Air flight and Sabena called it a Sabena flight. Such 'code-sharing' arrangements are a way of achieving scale economies without actually eliminating a national carrier. Interestingly, both airlines eventually went bankrupt but the Swiss and Belgian governments stepped in to create replacement airlines, Swiss and SN Brussels Airlines.

In other industries, firms anticipate the increased competition and undertake the mergers and acquisitions quickly enough to avoid big losses. European banking is an example. The introduction of the euro and continuing liberalization of the banking sector means that European banks will have to become fewer and bigger in order to break even. However, instead of waiting for profit losses to become intolerable, banks have launched a record-breaking series of mergers and acquisitions. In terms of Fig. 6-9, this would look like a move from $E'$ directly to $E''$.

## 6.4.3 Empirical evidence
There is ample empirical evidence that European industry is marked by fewer, bigger, more efficient firms since the Single Market Programme. For example, the 1996 Single Market Review by the European Commission presents several studies illustrating these trends (see Commission, 1996, for a brief review of this multi-volume study). Unfortunately, there is little direct evidence in Europe that it was caused by market integration, although this is what most economists believe is the obvious explanation. More direct evidence linking market size with efficiency and competition can be found in Campbell and Hopenhayn (2002). The authors study the impact of market size on the size distribution of firms in retail-trade industries across 225 US cities. In every industry examined, establishments were larger in larger cities. The authors conclude that their results support the notion that competition is tougher in larger markets and this accounts for the link between firm-size and market-size.

# 6.5 State aid
The reasoning laid out above immediately brings two questions to mind. First, as the number of firms falls, is there a tendency for the remaining firms to collude in order to keep prices high? Second, since industrial restructuring can be politically painful, is there a danger that governments will try to keep money-losing firms in business via subsidies and other policies? The answer to both questions is 'Yes'. There is a danger of collusion and there is a danger of governments thwarting the restructuring. In fact, both problems have arisen in an important way since the 1992 Single Market Programme. Fortunately, both problems were foreseen in the earliest discussions on European integration, so the 1957 Treaty of Rome adopted several measures to solve these problems.

In this section we address the problem of subsidies and the EU's solutions. The issue of competition policy is postponed to the next section.

## 6.5.1 Subsidies to prevent restructuring
The logic linking integration and industrial restructuring presumed that profit-losing firms would eventually leave the industry – that they would either be bought out by another firm, merged with other firms or, in rare cases, go bankrupt. All three of these exit strategies may involve important job losses, or at the very least an important reorganization that may require workers to change jobs or locations. Since job losses and relocations are painful, governments frequently seek to prevent them. For example, if the firm is government owned, trade unions may force the government to continue to shore up the money-losing enterprise. If it is privately owned, the government may provide subsidies through direct grants, or through long-term loans that may not be repaid.

What we want to do here is to look at the economics of such subsidies – called 'state aid' in EU jargon – under two distinct scenarios. The first is where all governments provide such support. The second is where only one does.

### EU-WIDE SUBSIDIES: THWARTING THE MAIN SOURCE OF GAINS

Start by supposing that both governments provide subsidies that prevent restructuring. To be concrete, we make the additional, more specific assumption that governments make annual payments to all firms *exactly* equal to their losses. Under this policy, all $2n'$ firms in the Fig. 6-9 analysis will stay in business, but, since no firms are making extraordinary profits, no new firms will enter. The economy, in short, remains at point $A$ due to the anti-restructuring subsidies.

An insightful way to think about this subsidy policy is as a swap, in who pays for the inefficiently small firms. Before integration, prices were high, so consumers paid for the inefficiency. After liberalization, competition drives down the price but this comes at the cost of extra pay-outs from the national treasuries, so now the taxpayers bear the burden of the industry's inefficiency. The integration-plus-subsidies scheme shifts the burden of supporting inefficiently small firms from consumers to taxpayers.

Moreover, since all the firms stay in business, integration is prevented from curing the main problem, i.e. the too-many-too-small firms problem. Firms continue to be inefficient since they continue to operate at too small a scale. As a consequence, the subsidies prevent the overall improvement in industry efficiency that was the source of most of the gains discussed in the previous section.

Do nations gain from this liberalize-and-subsidize scheme? As it turns out both nations do gain overall, even counting the cost of the subsidies. We shall show this with a diagram, but before turning to the detailed reasoning, it is instructive to explain the deep reason for this result.

Imperfect competition is inefficient since it leads prices to exceed marginal costs. Recalling from Chapter 4 that the consumer price is a measure of marginal utility, the fact that price exceeds marginal cost implies that the gain to consumers from an extra unit would exceed the resource cost of providing the unit. In short, society tends to gain from an expansion of output when price exceeds marginal cost. Because of this, policies that increase output tend to improve welfare. In the jargon of public economics, the subsidy is a 'second-best' policy since it reduces the market-power distortion.

Note, however, that this reasoning is very partial. This sort of 'reactive' subsidies turns out to be a very bad idea in the long run. The subsidies are paid to prevent firms from adapting to changed circumstances. While the government may occasionally improve things by preventing change, a culture of reactive interventionism typically results in a stagnant economy. Staying competitive requires industries to change – to adapt to new technologies, to new competitors and to new opportunities. When firms get used to the idea that their governments will keep them in business no matter what, the incentive to innovate and adapt is greatly weakened. Firms with this sort of mindset will soon find themselves far behind their competitors.

### WELFARE EFFECTS OF THE LIBERALIZE-AND-SUBSIDIZE POLICY

To explain the welfare effects of the liberalize-and-subsidize policy, we refer to Fig. 6-10. The policy we consider freezes the economy at point $A$ in the right and middle panels (this point A corresponds exactly to the point $A$ in Fig. 6-9). We know that the price falls from $p'$ to $p_A$ and consumption rises from $C'$ to $C_A$. Since the number of firms has not changed but total sales in each market (which must equal total consumption in each market) has increased, we know that the sales of each firm have increased somewhat, as shown in the left panel from $x'$ to $x_A$. At this point, firms are losing money, but the government offsets this with a subsidy.

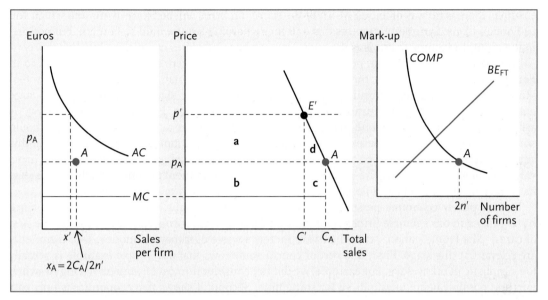

FIGURE 6-10: WELFARE ANALYSIS OF A LIBERALIZE-AND-SUBSIDIZE POLICY

How big will the subsidy be? The easiest way to make this comparison is to adopt a roundabout approach. First, consider the total size of operating profit that the whole Home industry needs to cover all fixed cost before the liberalization. The answer is already in the middle panel. Before the liberalization, the industry broke even by selling a total of $C'$ units at the price $p'$. The operating profit on this was the area **a + b** in the middle panel of the diagram, i.e. the gap between price and marginal cost times the units sold. After the liberalization, the industry's operating profit is area **b + c** (the new price-cost gap, $p_A - MC$, times the new sales, $C_A$). The drop in operating profit is thus area **c** minus area **a**. The subsidy we are considering would have to exactly offset the loss, so the subsidy would equal area **a − c**. With these facts established, we turn to the welfare calculation.

The consumer part of the welfare calculation is simple. Consumers see a lower price so consumer surplus rises by the area +**a + d**. To see the overall welfare effect, we subtract the subsidy, which equals **a − c**. The net welfare effect is **a + d − (a − c)** which equals **d + c**. We know this is right since this area is the gap between price and marginal cost summed over all the extra units consumed.

## 6.5.2 Only some subsidize: unfair competition

EU members' governments differ over how much they can or want to subsidize loss-making firms. Yet, when only some governments subsidize their firms, the outcome of the restructuring may be 'unfair' in the sense that it gets forced upon the firms in nations that do not subsidize, or stop subsidizing before the others. The real problem with this is that it may create the impression that European economic integration gives an unfair advantage to some nations' firms.

To examine this problem more closely while keeping the reasoning as tangible and simple as possible, we continue with the Fig. 6-9 example of two nations engaged in an extreme no-trade-to-free-trade integration. The integration moves each identical economy from the point $E'$ to $A$. At $A$, all firms in both nations are losing money. Now suppose that restructuring takes, say, five years in the sense that after that time the number of firms has adjusted from $2n'$ to $n''$. In our simple example, there is no way of telling which of the surviving firms will be Home firms and which will be Foreign firms. Symmetry suggests that half the remaining firms would be Foreign, but nothing in the example ensures that this is the case. This is where subsidies can make a big difference.

To be concrete, suppose that prior to the liberalization there were 10 firms in Home and 10 in Foreign, and that after restructuring there will be 12 firms in total. Furthermore, suppose that Home provides a five-year subsidy to all of its 10 firms, with the size of the subsidy being large enough to offset the liberalization-induced losses. The Foreign government, by contrast, is assumed to pursue a *laissez-faire* policy, i.e. it allows the market to decide which firms should survive – either because it believes in the market, or because it cannot afford the subsidies. In this situation, it is clear that 8 of the 10 Foreign firms will go out of business, while all 10 Home firms will survive. At the end of the five-year period, the Home government no longer needs to subsidize its firms since the exit of eight Foreign firms restores the industry to profitability.

From a purely economic perspective, the Foreign nation might have been the winner since having firms in our example brings nothing to national welfare (firms earn zero profit in the best of cases). The Home nation's subsidies were merely a waste of taxpayers' money. Two comments are relevant at this stage. First, this sort of conclusion shows that our simple example is actually too simplistic in many ways. For example, we did not consider the cost of workers having to switch jobs and possibly being unemployed for some time. Second, it shows that economics is only part of the picture.

From a political perspective, this sort of unfair competition would be intolerable. Indeed, if trade unions and business groups in Foreign anticipated that this would be the outcome, they might very well block the whole integration exercise. To avoid this sort of resistance to liberalization, the EU establishes very strict rules forbidding such unfair competition.

## 6.5.3 EU policies on 'state aids' 87/88/89

The EU's founders realized that the entire European project would be endangered if EU members felt that other members were taking unfair advantage of the economic integration (see Box 6-4 for an example of unfair competition in the EU energy market). To prevent this, the 1957 Treaty of Rome bans state aid that provides firms with an unfair advantage and thus distorts competition. Importantly, the EU founders considered this prohibition to be so important that they actually empowered the supranational European Commission to be in charge of enforcing the prohibition. Indeed, the Commission has the power to force the repayment of illegal state aid, even though the Commission normally has no say over members' individual tax and spending policies. For more information on EU state aid policy, see Box 6-5.

---

### Box 6-4: Subsidies and unfair competition in the energy market

The market for electricity was one of the few markets left largely untouched by the sweeping liberalization of the EU's Single Market Programme between 1986 and 1992. Until the 1990s, the sector was dominated by government-owned or controlled firms, but as part of the general trend towards market-oriented policies, many EU members privatized their state-owned energy monopolies and opened their markets to foreign competition. These moves, however, were not part of a co-ordinated EU strategy. The resulting difficulties provide an excellent illustration of how important the EU's anti-state aid policy is to keeping European economic integration on track.

As with much of European industry, the energy sector was and still is marked by too many firms which are too small to be truly competitive. As in many other sectors, a process of consolidation and industrial restructuring has begun. Unlike other EU sectors, however, liberalization varies greatly across Member States. France is one of the most closed markets in two senses. It is difficult for foreign firms to supply French customers and the French energy monopoly Electricité de France (EdF) is tightly controlled by the government so it cannot be bought. Moreover, EdF receives various subsidies that give it an advantage in the market.

Other EU members feared that France had embarked on a cynical campaign of ensuring that EdF would be one of the survivors of the industrial restructuring that would inevitably come when energy was eventually liberalized. For example, France consistently opposed full liberalization of energy markets, and when the EU adopted a partial opening measure in which members were bound to open up their energy markets to third-party competition, France delayed passing the necessary laws. The real trouble began when EdF launched an aggressive campaign of expanding rapidly into the power markets of neighbouring Member States (Britain, Germany, Italy and Spain) while remaining a state-owned monopoly in its home market.

Such expansion would be unremarkable in other sectors, but the perception that EdF's moves were 'unfair' led other EU members to postpone or restrict their own liberalization efforts. For example, in 2001, German economy Minister Werner Mueller threatened to prevent the French state-owned power giant EdF from importing electricity into Germany as long as France did not open up its power market to foreign companies. Italy had a similar reaction after EdF began to take over the Italian company Montedison. As Italy's treasury Minister Vincenzo Visco explained, it was 'unacceptable to let a player with a rigged hand of cards join the game'. The Italian government quickly introduced measures designed to block further takeovers.

To prevent this action–reaction chain from ruining prospects for liberalization, the Commission launched a investigation in 2002 into EdF's state aid. In particular, it is looking into potentially anti-competitive state aid given to London Electricity (which EdF owns) in the form of low interest rates on loans backed by the French government. It is also looking into a five-year-old accounting arrangement under which EdF qualifies for unusually generous tax relief. Separate action is being taken against Gaz de France for failing to comply with EU liberalization rules.

*This box is based mainly on BBC news stories dated 12 June 2001 and 16 October 2002 (see www.bbc.co.uk).*

## Box 6-5: EU state aid policy

The Treaty of Rome, formally called the Treaty Establishing the European Community, prohibits state aid that distorts competition in the EU. The Treaty defines state aid in very broad terms. It can, for instance, take the form of grants, interest relief, tax relief, state guarantee or holding, or the provision by the state of goods and services on preferential terms.

The reason for this prohibition is simple. As the Competition Directorate-General (the responsible department of the European Commission) writes in its excellent website:

> By giving certain firms or products favoured treatment to the detriment of other firms or products, state aid seriously disrupts normal competitive forces. Neither the beneficiaries of state aid nor their competitors prosper in the long term. Very often, all public subsidies achieve is to delay inevitable restructuring operations without helping the recipient return to competitiveness. Unsubsidized firms who must compete with those receiving public support may ultimately run into difficulties, causing loss of competitive-

ness and endangering the jobs of their employees. Ultimately, then, the entire market will suffer from state aid, and the general competitiveness of the European economy is imperilled.

(http://europa.eu.int/comm/competition/citizen/citizen_stateaid.html).

Some state aid, however, is allowed according to the Treaty since subsidies, when used correctly, are an essential instrument in the toolkit of good governance. The permitted exceptions include social policy aid, natural disaster aid and economic development aid to underdeveloped areas. More generally, state aid that is in the general interest of the EU is permitted. For example, the Commission has also adopted a number of bloc-exemption rules that explain which sorts of state aid are indisputable. These include aid to small and medium-sized enterprises, aid for training and aid for employment.

The Treaty charges the Commission with monitoring state aid and, indeed, the Commission has exclusive authority for evaluating state aid schemes of EU governments. As part of this, the Commission can require that aid that has already been granted by an EU member be repaid by receiving firms.

More information can be found in the fourth section of DG Competition's highly accessible document called '*Competition Policy in Europe and the Citizen*'. This can be downloaded from http://europa.eu.int/comm/competition/publications/.

### A CONTENTIOUS EXAMPLE: AIRLINES IN TROUBLE

The Commission department (Directorate-General, or DG, in EU jargon) in charge of enforcing anti-competitive state aid, DG Competition, is frequently in the headlines.[1] Its decisions often produce loud protests from firms and/or workers who benefited from any state aid that the DG Competition judges to be illegal. Many recent examples can be found on DG Competition's website http://europa.eu.int/comm/competition/index_en.html, but an excellent example concerns the airline industry – an industry where there are clearly too many firms in existence and the tendency to subsidize is strong. Many European airlines are the national 'flag carrier' and as such are often considered a symbol of nation pride.

Consolidation of the European airline industry has been in the cards for years, but the problem was exacerbated by the terrorist attacks of 11 September 2001. The ensuing reduction in air travel caused great damage to airlines all around the world and led to calls for massive state aid. To prevent these subsidies from being used as an excuse to put off restructuring, the Commission restricted subsidies to cover only the 'exceptional losses' incurred when transatlantic routes were shut down immediately after 11 September. To date, the Commission has managed to resist the desire of several Member State governments to support their national airlines to the same extent that the US government has supported US airlines.

It is easy to see the logic of the Commission's stance. Low-cost airlines, such as Ryanair and EasyJet, have done well without subsidies. Moreover, artificial support for inefficient national carriers hinders the expansion of low-cost airlines. As Bannerman (2002) puts it:

No-one will benefit from a return to spiralling subsidies, which damage the industry by encouraging inefficiency. Both consumers and taxpayers would suffer as a result. As for the national carriers, they would probably benefit from some market consolidation, creating fewer, leaner, pan-European airlines – although this process would need monitoring for its

---

[1] This section is based on Bannerman (2002), which should be seen for further details.

competitive effects on key routes. If the airline industry can use the crisis to create more efficient carriers, it will probably be the better for it. But this long-term view cuts little ice with workers who stand to lose their jobs, or with some politicians, for whom a flag carrier is a symbol of national pride. Unfortunately, the benefits of controlling state-aids occur mainly in lower fares and taxes, and are therefore widely diffused among the population. The costs, on the other hand, take the form of job losses, which hurt a small but vocal constituency.

We now turn to addressing the next question raised by the analysis in section 6.4: 'As the number of firms fall, is there a tendency for the remaining firms to collude in order to keep prices high?'

# 6.6 Competition policy and anti-competitive behaviour

Collusion is a real concern in Europe and there are good reasons for thinking that the dangers of collusion rise as the number of firms falls. We therefore turn now to considering the impact of collusion. Because simplicity led us to explicitly assume away the possibility of collusion in section 6.4, our first job is to expand the *BE–COMP* framework to allow for the possibility.

## 6.6.1 Allowing collusion in the *BE–COMP* framework

The analysis surrounding Fig. 6-9 assumed that firms did not collude. Both before and after the integration, we assumed that firms engaged in 'normal' competition; the *COMP* curve was constructed on the assumption that each firm decided on how much to sell, taking as given other firms' sales. In other words, each firm decided its output individually; they did not collude on output. This assumption of 'normal' competition is quite reasonable for many industries, but it is not the behaviour that is most profitable for firms in the industry. If firms were allowed to collude, they could raise profits by reducing the amount they sell and raising prices. There are many, many forms of collusion in the world. The first form of collusion we consider is the simplest form to study. Instead of assuming no collusion on output, we consider the extreme opposite of perfect collusion on output.

### PERFECT COLLUSION

If all firms could perfectly co-ordinate their sales, i.e. if they could act as if they were a single firm, they would limit total sales to the monopoly level. This would allow them to charge the monopoly price and to earn the greatest possible profit from the market. After all, the monopoly price–sales combination is – by definition – the combination that extracts the greatest profit from the market.

The hard part of collusion is finding a way to divide up the monopoly level of sales among the colluding firms. The problem is that because the price is so much higher than marginal cost, each firm would like to sell a little more than its share. To keep things simple, we assume that the firms manage the collusion by allocating an equal share to all firms. This type of behaviour can be illustrated in the *BE–COMP* diagram with the 'perfect collusion' line shown in Fig. 6-11. This line extends horizontally since it assumes that the mark-up always equals $\mu_{\text{mono}}$ regardless of the number of firms. Note that the monopoly mark-up is given by the point on the COMP curve where $n = 1$. The equilibrium number of firms under perfect collusion is given by the point $A$.

### PARTIAL COLLUSION

Perfect collusion, however, is difficult to maintain since the gains from 'cheating' on other colluders is quite high. To reduce the incentive to cheat, the actual degree of collusion may be milder than perfect collusion; this partial collusion restricts sales of all firms but not all the way back to the monopoly level, so the mark-up is lower than the monopoly mark-up but higher than the *COMP* mark-up. This makes it easier to sustain the collusion since the benefits from cheating are

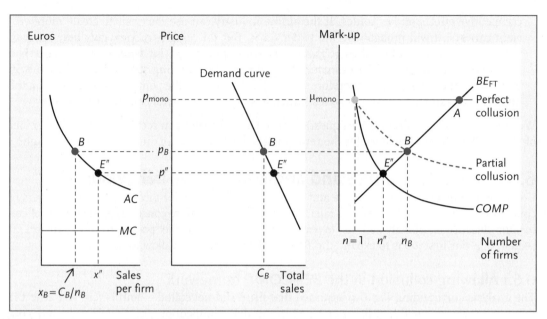

FIGURE 6-11: COLLUSION AND INDUSTRIAL RESTRUCTURING

not quite as large. But how much lower would the mark-up be under partial collusion? As it turns out, an understanding of advanced economics is needed to formalize this notion of 'partial collusion', so we do not address it here explicitly (see Mas-Colell, Whinston and Green, 1995, for an advanced treatment). Fortunately, the basic idea can be easily depicted in the diagram.

The curve labelled 'partial collusion' shows a level of collusion where the mark-up is somewhere between the monopoly mark-up and the no-collusion mark-up shown by the $COMP$ curve. We do not specify exactly where it lies between the two, but this turns out to be unimportant for the qualitative analysis that we turn to next.

Now consider the implications of the partial collusion supposing that the collusion emerges at the same time as the no-trade-to-free-trade liberalization. If firms do manage to collude in this partial manner, the market will be able to support more firms. In particular, the equilibrium mark-up and number of firms would be identified by the point $B$. What are the economic implications of such collusion?

The first point is that collusion will not in the end raise firms' profits to above-normal levels. Even with partial collusion, the initial number of firms after liberalization, namely $2n'$, is too high for all of them to break even. Industrial consolidation proceeds as usual, but instead of the zero-profit level being reached when the number of firms has dropped to $n''$, the process halts at $n_B$, where the $BE$ curve and the partial-collusion curve meet. Importantly, and quite naturally, prices are higher with collusion than they would be without collusion (i.e. $p_B$ exceeds $p''$). This also means that total sales are lower with collusion, since demand diminishes as the price rises. These two facts, that total sales are lower and that there are more firms, tells us that firms will be smaller under collusion than they would be without collusion ($x_B$ as opposed to $x''$). As the left panel of Fig. 6-11 shows, smaller firms mean higher average cost, i.e. less efficiency. The welfare cost of the collusion is measured by the four-sided area marked by $p_B$, $p''$, $E''$ and $B$.

To summarize, collusion prevents the full benefits of restructuring from occurring. By keeping too many firms in the market, anti-competitive behaviour thwarts part of the industry's adjustment that is the key to the gains from integration.

## 6.6.2 EU policies on anti-competitive behaviour

As with state aid, the EU's founders were fully aware that integrating Europe's market might heighten the dangers of collusive behaviour. To prevent such problems, the Treaty of Rome prohibited any action that prevents, restricts or distorts competition in the common market and put the Commission in charge of enforcing these strictures.

Collusion in diagram 6-11 was a simple matter of keeping the mark-up artificially high, but the real world of collusion is radically more complex. Reflecting this complexity, the Commission's actions focus on two main axes:

- *Anti-trust and cartels.* The Commission works to eliminate behaviours that restrict competition (e.g. price-fixing arrangements and cartels) as well as to eliminate abusive behaviour by firms that have a dominant position in their market.

The two main types of prohibited behaviour are: restrictive business practices (prohibited by Article 81 of the EC Treaty) and abuse of a dominant position (prohibited by Article 82 of the EC Treaty). Restrictive business practices include a wide range of unfair practices by firms. For example, the Treaty explicitly outlaws: agreements that fix prices; agreements that allocate 'exclusive territories' to firms in order to reduce competition; and agreements that control production, marketing, R&D or investment. The Treaty also requires government monopolies of a commercial character to avoid discrimination based on the nationality of suppliers or customers.

- *Merger control.* The Commission seeks to block mergers that would create firms that would dominate the market.

We stressed that the EU founders considered the control of such behaviour to be so important that they placed the power to enforce these rules in the hands of a supranational body, namely the European Commission. Even today, Commission decisions on matters of 'competition policy' are not subject to revision by the European Council or the European Parliament. This is an area where Member States truly did pool their sovereignty.

### INVESTIGATION AND FINES

The Commission has extensive powers to investigate suspected abuses of competition law. These get into the news when, for example, Commission officials 'raid' the headquarters of an EU company suspected of anti-competitive behaviour. Such investigations are started by the Commission, either on its own initiative or in reaction to complaints of anti-competitive practices from companies, consumer organizations or individual consumers. Any individual can lodge a complaint; see http://europa.eu.int/comm/competition/citizen/citizen_complaints.html.

To give 'teeth' to the Commission's decisions, the Treaty empowers the Commission to prohibit anti-competitive behaviour, to issue injunctions against firms, and to impose fines on firms. These fines vary according to the size of the violation, ranging from nothing to millions of euros.

## 6.7 Summary

Three main points have been made in this chapter.

- One very obvious impact of European integration has been to face individual European firms with a bigger 'home' market. This produces a chain reaction that leads to fewer, bigger, more efficient firms that face more effective competition from each other. Understanding the economic logic driving this chain reaction is the main goal of this chapter. This logic can be summarized as follows. Integration defragments Europe's markets in the sense that it removes the privileged position of national firms in their national markets. As a result, all firms face more competition from other firms in their national market, but at the same time they have better access to the other EU markets. This general increase in competition puts downward pressure on price-cost mark-ups, prices and profits. The profit-squeeze results in industrial restructuring, a process by which the total number of firms in Europe falls. The lower price and lower number of firms means that the average firm gets larger and this, in turn, allows firms to better exploit economies of scale. This efficiency increase, in turn, permits the firms to break even despite the lower prices.

■ The industrial restructuring is often politically painful since it often results in layoffs and the closure of inefficient plants. Governments very often attempt to offset this political pain by providing 'state aid' to their national firms. Such state aid can be viewed as unfair and the perception of unfairness threatens to undermine EU members' interest in integration. To avoid these problems, the founders of the EU established rules that prohibited state aid that distorts competition. The Commission is charged with enforcing these rules.

■ Industrial restructuring raises another problem that led the EU's founders to set out another set of rules. As integration proceeds and the number of firms falls, the temptation for firms to collude may increase. To avoid this, the EU has strict rules on anti-competitive practices. It also screens mergers to ensure that mergers will enhance efficiency. Again, the Commission is charged with enforcing these rules.

## SELF-ASSESSMENT QUESTIONS

**1.** Suppose that liberalization occurs as in section 6.4 and the result is a pro-competitive effect, but instead of merging or restructuring, all firms are bought by their national governments to allow the firms to continue operating. What will be the impact of this on prices and government revenues? Now that the governments are the owners, will they have an incentive to continue with liberalization? Can you imagine why this might favour firms located in nations with big, rich governments?

**2.** Use a 3-panel diagram, like Fig. 6-8, to show how the number of firms, mark-up and firm size would change in a *closed* economy if the demand for the particular good rose, i.e. the demand curve shifted out.

**3.** Using your findings from exercise 2, you should be able to consider the impact of a no-trade-to-free-trade integration between a large and a small nation, where size is defined by the position of the demand curve (the demand curve in the large nation will be further out than the demand curve for the small nation). To do this, you will need two of the 3-panelled diagrams of the Fig. 6-8 type to show the pre-integration situation. Then use a 3-panelled diagram of the Fig. 6-9 type to show what happens to prices, firm size and the number of firms in the integrated economy. Note that you will want to show both demand curves in the middle panel. As usual, assume that all firms have the same marginal cost. What does this analysis tell you about how integration affects firms in small nations versus large nations?

**4.** Consider a sequence of EU 'enlargements' where each enlargement involves a no-trade-to-free-trade addition of one more members. Specifically, suppose there are three initially identical economies, each of which looks like the one described in section 6.3. Initially, all nations are closed to trade. Now, consider a no-trade-to-free-trade integration between two of the nations (just as in section 6.4). Then consider a no-trade-to-free-trade integration of a third nation. (*Hint*: The second step will be very much like the integration between unequal-sized economies explored in exercise 3.) Calculate how much the third nation gains from joining and compare it to how much the existing 2-nation bloc gains from the third nation's membership. Who gains more in proportion to size: the 'incumbents' or the 'entrant'?

## ESSAY QUESTIONS

**1.** When the Single Market Programme was launched in the mid-1980s, European leaders asserted that it would improve the competitiveness of European firms *vis-à-vis* US firms. Explain how one can make sense of this assertion by extending the reasoning in this chapter.

**2.** While the case for strengthening European-wide competition policy in tandem with the Single Market Programme is clear, is it obvious that this task should be allocated to the EU level instead of being left in the hands of Member States?

**3.** Some EU members allow their companies to engage in 'anti-takeover' practices. Discuss how differences in EU members' laws concerning these practices might be viewed as unfair when EU industry is being transformed by a wave of mergers and acquisitions.

**4.** Look on the web for information on the debate over harmonization of EU takeover rules. Try to use the logic presented in this chapter to explain why some nations resist harmonization.

## FURTHER READING: THE AFICIONADOS CORNER

Consideration of imperfect competition and scale effects was made possible in the 1980s with development of the so-called new trade theory (Helpman and Krugman, 1985, 1989). The new theory was naturally applied to analysis of the Single Market Programme when it was first discussed in the mid-1980s. Many of the classic studies are contained in Winters (1992). Baldwin and Venables (1995) provides a synthetic, graduate-level survey of this literature.

An alternative presentation of the theory and a thorough empirical evaluation is provided by Allen, Gasiorek and Smith (1998b).

For a very accessible introduction to EU competition policy, see Neven, Seabright and Nutall (1996).

## USEFUL WEBSITES

A large number of evaluations of the Single Market, most of which employ ICIR frameworks, can be found on http://europa.eu.int/comm/economy_finance/publications/, the document *The Internal Market: 10 Years without Frontiers* is especially useful. This site also posts the annual *State Aids Report* which provides the latest data on subsidies.

The website of DG Competition has several highly accessible accounts of EU competition policy and information on recent cases, see http://europa.eu.int/comm/competition/.

## REFERENCES

Allen, C., M. Gasiorek and M.A.M. Smith (1998a) 'The competition effects of the Single Market', *Economic Policy*, London. Download from www.economicpolicy.org.

Allen, C., M. Gasiorek and A. Smith (1998b) 'European Single Market: How the programme has fostered competition', *Economic Policy*, 441–486.

Bannerman, E. (2002) *The Future of EU Competition Policy*, Centre for European Reform, London. Downloadable from http://www.cer.org.uk/publications/index.html.

Commission (1996) *The 1996 Single Market Review: Background Information for the Report to the Council and European Parliament*, Commission Staff Working Paper, Brussels. Download from http://europa.eu.int/comm/internal_market/en/update/impact/index.htm.

*European Economy* (2001) Supplement A, No.12, December. This contains many facts on the M&A wave. Download it from http://europa.eu.int/comm/economy_finance/publications/supplement_a_en.htm.

Mas-Colell, A., M. Whinston and J.R. Green (1995) *Microeconomic Theory*, Oxford University Press, New York.

Campbell, J. and H. Hopenhayn (2002) *Market Size Matters*, NBER Working Paper 9113, Cambridge, MA.

Winters, L.A. (1992) *Trade Flows and Trade Policies after '1992'*, Cambridge University Press, Cambridge.

Helpman, E. and P. Krugman (1985) *Market Structure and Foreign Trade: Increasing Returns, Imperfect Competition and the International Economy*, MIT Press, Cambridge MA.

Helpman, E. and P. Krugman (1989) *Trade Policy and Market Structure*, MIT Press, Cambridge MA.

Baldwin, R. and A. Venables (1995) 'Regional Economic Integration,' in G. Grossman and K. Rogoff (eds) *Handbook of International Economics*, North-Holland, New York.

Neven, D., P. Seabright and M. Nutall (1996) *Fishing for Minnows*, CEPR, London.

> " The Union has today set itself a new strategic goal for the next decade: to become the most competitive and dynamic knowledge-based economy in the world capable of " sustainable economic growth with more and better jobs and greater social cohesion.
>
> Presidency Conclusions, Lisbon European Council, March 2000

# 7 Growth Effects and Factor Market Integration

7.1     **The logic of growth and the facts**

7.2     **Medium-term growth effects: induced capital formation with Solow's analysis**

7.3     **Long-term growth effects: faster knowledge creation and absorption**

7.4     **Microeconomics of capital market integration**

7.5     **Microeconomics of labour market integration**

7.6     **Summary**

---

The two previous chapters looked at 'allocation effects' of European integration, i.e. the impact on the efficiency with which economic resources within nations are allocated across economic activities. Allocation effects are 'one-off' in the sense that a single policy change leads to a single reallocation of resources. European leaders, however, have long emphasized a different type of economic effect – the growth effect. Growth effects operate in a way that is fundamentally different from allocation effects; they operate by changing the rate at which new factors of production – mainly capital – are accumulated, hence the name 'accumulation effects'.

Factor market integration is another channel by which European integration can change the supply of productive factors within EU members. Under EU rules, citizens of any EU nation may work in any other EU nation. Similar rules guarantee the free movement of capital, so this aspect of European integration can – in principle – alter the amount of productive factors employed in any given EU member. Or, to put it differently, capital and labour movements can look like an allocation-of-resources effect from the EU perspective, but like an accumulation effect from the national perspective. This chapter therefore also studies the economics of factor market integration.

---

# 7.1 The logic of growth and the facts

The link between European integration and growth rests on the logic of growth. The logic of growth is simple, but widely misunderstood, so before looking at the facts, we briefly present the logic of growth in words.

## 7.1.1 The logic of growth: medium-run and long-run effects

Economic growth means producing more and more every year. Per capita growth means an annual rise in the output per person. In most Western European nations, output per capita rises at between 1 and 3 per cent per year in normal times. How does this happen?

If a nation's labour force is to produce more goods and services year after year, the economy must provide workers with more 'tools' year after year. Here 'tools' is meant in the broadest possible sense – what economists call capital – and three categories of capital must be distinguished: physical capital (machines, etc.), human capital (skills, training, experience, etc.) and knowledge capital (technology). Given this necessity, the rate of output growth is hitched straight to the rate of physical, human and knowledge capital accumulation. Most capital accumulation is intentional and is called investment. Accordingly, we can say that European integration affects growth mainly via its effect on investment in human capital, physical capital and knowledge capital. The qualification 'mainly' is necessary since integration may unintentionally affect accumulation, for instance, by speeding the international dissemination of technological progress (this is especially important in Central European nations).

Growth effects fall naturally into two categories: medium term and long term. An instance of medium-term effects is 'induced physical capital formation'. For all the reasons documented in the previous chapters, European integration improves the efficiency with which productive factors are combined to produce output. As a side effect, this heightened efficiency typically makes Europe a better place to invest, so more investment occurs. The result is that the initial efficiency gains from integration are boosted by induced capital formation. While the above-normal capital formation is occurring, the economies experience a medium-term growth effect. This growth effect is only medium term, since it will eventually peter out; as the amount of capital per worker rises, the gain from investing in each further unit of capital diminishes. Eventually the gain from investing in an extra unit reaches the cost of doing so and the above-normal capital formation stops. A good example of this is the investment boom that Spain experienced around the time of its accession to the EU.

Long-term growth effects involve a permanent change in the rate of accumulation, and thereby a permanent change in the rate of growth. Since the accumulation of physical capital faces diminishing returns, long-run growth effects typically refer to the rate of accumulation of knowledge capital, i.e. technological progress.

To summarize the logic of growth effects schematically: European integration (or any other policy) → allocation effect → improved efficiency → better investment climate → more investment in machines, skills and/or technology → higher output per person. Under medium-run growth effects, the rise in output per person eventually stops at a new, higher level. Under long-run growth effects, the rate of growth is forever higher.

## 7.1.2 Post-war European growth: the evidence

Any informed discussion of European integration and economic growth must begin with a fistful of overarching facts. We first cover these facts before setting out a prima facie case that European integration has, broadly speaking, been favourable to growth in the post-war period.

## PHASES OF EUROPEAN GROWTH

By historical standards, continuous economic growth is a relatively recent phenomenon. Before the Industrial Revolution, which started in Great Britain in the late 1700s, European incomes had stagnated for a millennium and a half. It has been estimated that the real earnings of a typical British factory worker in 1850 were no higher than those of a typical free Roman artisan in the first century (Cameron and Neal, 2003). Between the glory years of the Roman Empire and the Industrial Revolution, periods of prosperity were offset by famines, plagues and warfare that brought the average person back to the brink of starvation.

With industrialization, which had spread to most of continental Europe by 1870, incomes began to rise at a respectable rate of something like 2 per cent per year. Growth rates, however, were hardly constant from this date – four growth phases are traditionally defined, as Table 7-1 shows. During the 1890–1913 period (often called the *Belle Époque*) real GDP grew at 2.6 per cent. This is considered to be a very good growth rate, and is enough to double GDP every 27 years. Since population was also growing rapidly in this period, real GDP per person rose at only 1.7 per cent per annum. These rates were approximately halved during the 1913–50 period (i.e. from the First World War until the end of the post-Second World War reconstruction period). Despite this, the GDP per hour worked accelerated slightly to 1.9 per cent since the average hours worked per year fell with the introduction and spread of labour unions and social legislation.

| Period | Real GDP | Real GDP per capita | Real GDP per hour |
|---|---|---|---|
| 1890–1913 | 2.6 | 1.7 | 1.6 |
| 1913–50 | 1.4 | 1.0 | 1.9 |
| 1950–73 | 4.6 | 3.8 | 4.7 |
| 1973–92 | 2.0 | 1.7 | 2.7 |
| **Whole period 1890–1992** | **2.5** | **1.9** | **2.6** |

NOTES: Figures are annual averages for 12 nations (Austria, Belgium, Denmark, Finland, France, Germany, Italy, Netherlands, Norway, Sweden, Switzerland, United Kingdom all adjusted for boundary changes).
Note that the 1950–73 period is the aberration. Both before and after this period, growth rates were just under 2 per cent per annum (excluding the unusual 1913–50 period). The Golden Age was also the most intensive period of European integration and it was this correlation that first started economists thinking about the growth effects of European integration.
SOURCE: Crafts and Toniolo (1996, p. 2).

TABLE 7-1: EUROPEAN GROWTH PHASES, 1890–1992

The period from 1950 to 1973 is called the Golden Age of growth; throughout the world, but especially in Europe, growth rates jumped. Real GDP growth rates more than tripled and per capita GDP growth almost quadrupled. At this pace, per capita incomes would double every 18.6 years, implying that the material standard of living would quadruple in an average lifetime. Unfortunately, the Golden Age ended after only 23 years for reasons that are still not entirely understood. Since 1973, the date of the first oil shock, per capita incomes have progressed at only 1.9 per cent per year. However, as the working week has been further shortened during this period, GDP-per-hour-worked continued to progress at a respectable 2.7 per cent per annum.

Growth performance during the 1913–50 period was far from homogeneous. This phase, which Crafts and Toniolo (1996) aptly call the 'second Thirty Years War', contains the two World Wars and the Great Depression, each of which was responsible for massive income drops. It also, however, contains the most spectacular growth phase that Europe has ever seen, namely the years of reconstruction, 1945–50. Table 7-2 shows various aspects of this 'reconstruction period' for 12 European nations. The first point (a point we also made in Chapter 1) is that the Second World War caused enormous economic damage. It cost Germany and Italy four decades or more of growth and put Austrian and French GDPs back to nineteenth-century levels. Despite this, recovery was remarkably rapid. By 1951, every European nation was back on the pre-war growth path. This resurgence was due to a short period of truly astonishing growth. All the growth rates were double-digit (except Belgium's); France, for instance, grew at almost 20 per cent a year for four consecutive years and the Netherlands grew at almost twice that pace for two years. To a large extent, however, this rapid growth is a bit of an illusion. It consisted of merely setting back up, or repairing production facilities created in earlier years. This also indicates that much of the Second World War drop in GDP was due to the temporary disorganization of Europe's economy rather than permanent destruction.

| | The set-back pre-war year when GDP equalled that of 1945 | Back-on-track year when GDP attained highest 1945–50 level | Reconstruction growth rate during reconstruction years (1945 to column 2 year) |
|---|---|---|---|
| Austria | 1886 | 1951 | 15.2% |
| Belgium | 1924 | 1948 | 6.0% |
| Denmark | 1936 | 1946 | 13.5% |
| Finland | 1938 | 1945 | n.a. |
| France | 1891 | 1949 | 19.0% |
| Germany | 1908 | 1951 | 13.5% |
| Italy | 1909 | 1950 | 11.2% |
| Netherlands | 1912 | 1947 | 39.8% |
| Norway | 1937 | 1946 | 9.7% |
| Sweden | | | |
| Switzerland | These countries actually grew during the Second World War | | |
| UK | | | |

SOURCE: Crafts and Toniolo (1996, p. 4).

TABLE 7-2: GROWTH IN THE 1945–50 RECONSTRUCTION PHASE

## ARE GROWTH AND EUROPEAN INTEGRATION RELATED?

### THE PRIMA FACIE CASE

The Brothers Grimm's tale of the rooster who believes that he makes the sun rise each day (see, it works every morning!) should alert us to the dangers of confusing correlation and causality. There is, nonetheless, some general evidence – what might be called prima facie evidence in a court of law – that supports the integration-fosters-growth hypothesis.

The first element of the prima facie case concerns a country-by-country analysis of growth during the 1950–73 period. Recall from Chapter 1 that this period saw rapid integration among European nations. From 1950 to 1958, integration proceeded on a continent-wide basis under the

The Economics of European Integration: **Part II**

aegis of the Organization for European Economic Co-operation (OEEC) and the European Payments Union (EPU). From 1950 to 1958, the OEEC–EPU combination reduced trade and capital barriers in an important way. For example, in 1950, 43 per cent of intra-OEEC trade was subject to quotas or other forms of quantitative restrictions; by mid-1957, the figure was only 17 per cent. The year 1957 witnessed the signing of the Treaty of Rome and 1960 saw the signing of the Stockholm Convention, which, respectively established the European Economic Community (EEC) and the European Free Trade Association (EFTA). From 1958 to 1968 the Common Market was formed among the Six (Germany, France, Italy and the Benelux nations, Belgium, Luxembourg and the Netherlands). From 1960 to 1968 EFTA formed a free trade area in industrial goods among the UK, Sweden, Switzerland, Finland, Norway, Austria, Portugal and Iceland.

Table 7-3 shows the growth performance of various OEEC members during this period. Focusing, first, on the third column, we note that the EEC6 (data for Luxembourg was not

| | 1950 **GDP** (1990 $) | European rank 1950 | Change in rank 1950–73 | GDP growth rate 1950–73 |
|---|---|---|---|---|
| **EEC average** | **4825** | **8.0** | **+1.2** | **4.2** |
| Netherlands | 5850 | 5 | −1 | 3.4 |
| Belgium | 5346 | 6 | −2 | 3.5 |
| France | 5221 | 7 | +2 | 4.0 |
| Germany | 4281 | 9 | +5 | 5.0 |
| Italy | 3425 | 13 | +2 | 4.9 |
| | | | | |
| **EFTA average** | **6835** | **3.6** | **−1.4** | **3.0** |
| Switzerland | 8939 | 1 | 0 | 3.1 |
| UK | 6847 | 2 | −5 | 2.4 |
| Sweden | 6738 | 3 | +1 | 3.1 |
| Denmark | 6683 | 4 | +1 | 3.1 |
| Norway | 4969 | 8 | −4 | 3.2 |
| Finland | 4131 | 10 | 0 | 4.2 |
| Austria | 3731 | 11 | +2 | 4.9 |
| | | | | |
| **Others average** | **2401** | **14.3** | **−0.3** | **5.2** |
| Ireland | 3518 | 12 | −3 | 3.1 |
| Spain | 2397 | 14 | +1 | 5.8 |
| Portugal | 2132 | 15 | +1 | 5.6 |
| Greece | 1558 | 16 | 0 | 6.2 |
| | | | | |
| **For Comparison** | | | | |
| USA | 9573 | | | 2.4 |
| Japan | 1873 | | | 8.0 |

SOURCE: Crafts and Toniolo (1996, p. 3).

TABLE 7-3: GDP PER CAPITA AND RANKINGS, 1950 AND 1973 (1990 INTERNATIONAL DOLLARS)

available) rose in the GDP per capita rankings. Germany jumped five places, Italy jumped two while the Netherlands and Belgium slipped slightly. By contrast, the EFTAns lost ground, with the UK and Norway dropping five and four places respectively, with Sweden and Denmark gaining one, and with Austria gaining two. The non-EEC, non-EFTA nations also lost, especially Ireland, which was tightly linked to EFTA by a bilateral free trade agreement with the UK. Note also that the average growth performance of the EEC members was almost 50 per cent better than that of the EFTAns, although much of this may be explained by a 'catching-up' phenomenon (EEC nations were poorer than EFTAns in 1950 and poorer nations tend to grow more quickly than rich nations).

What is particularly striking is the performance of the 'big four' nations, France, Germany, Italy and the UK. The first three were members of the EEC and grew between 1.7 and 2.1 times faster than the UK. Again catch-up played some role in this, but by 1973 both France and Germany were richer than the UK, so the catch-up roles were reversed by the end of the period. This suggests a correlation between integration and growth since the economic integration in the EEC was much tighter than that of the EFTA during this period.

Of course not much should be read into such simple correlation, but at the time the UK's laggard growth performance in the face of the Continental growth booms played an important role in shaping British attitudes towards EEC membership.

The second line of suggestive evidence is more indirect. One of the few things that growth economists agree upon is the role of international trade in fostering growth. Quite simply nations that embrace international trade seem to grow faster, especially during periods of increasing openness. As we saw earlier in the chapter, the formation of the EEC and, to a lesser extent, the formation of EFTA, promoted a very rapid expansion of European trade. Intra-European trade grew much more rapidly than Europe's trade with the rest of the world exactly because of tighter economic integration on the Old Continent. Since trade fosters growth and European integration greatly fostered trade, it seems likely that European integration was pro-growth – a claim that is backed up by some statistical evidence.[1]

In a court of law, the above 'evidence' would hardly serve to accept the notion that European integration was pro-growth, but surely, it would be enough to prevent the case from being dismissed out of hand. We turn now to a more careful consideration of *how* integration might affect growth. Establishing such an analytical framework is useful to understanding the growth–integration link, but more importantly, it allows us to make more pointed predictions that can be confronted with the data.

## 7.2 Medium-term growth effects: induced capital formation with Solow's analysis

Spain's accession to the EU in the mid-1980s was accompanied by an investment boom that raised Spain's GDP growth by several percentage points for a few years. In this section, we consider ways of understanding how EU membership could yield such a medium-term growth bonus.

The key to the medium-term growth bonus is 'induced capital formation'. That is to say, integration induces firms to raise the level of capital per worker employed. For the moment, we focus exclusively on the machine per worker (i.e. physical-capital to labour) ratio, so the first step is to identify a means of determining the equilibrium capital/labour ratio. The approach we adopt was discovered by Nobel Laureate Robert Solow in the 1950s. It assumes that people save and then invest a fixed share of their income.

[1] See Henrekson, Torstensson and Torstensson (1997), Coe and Moghadam (1993), and Italianer (1994).

### 7.2.1 Solow diagram

To keep things easy, we start by viewing the whole EU as a single, closed economy with fully integrated capital and labour markets and the same technology everywhere. (Consideration of imperfect capital and labour market integration is postponed until sections 7.4 and 7.5.)

We begin with the connection between GDP-per-worker and capital-per-worker. When a firm provides its workers with more and better equipment, output per worker rises. However, output per worker does not increase in proportion with equipment per worker. To see this, consider the example of the efficiency of your studying and your personal capital/labour ratio. The most primitive method of studying would be to just go to lectures and listen. Buying some paper and pencils would allow you to take notes and this would enormously boost your productivity in terms of both time and quality. Going further, you could buy the book and again this would boost your productivity (i.e. the effectiveness per hour of studying) but not as much as the pencils and paper. It would also be nice to have, a calculator, a laptop, high-speed connection to the internet at home, and a laser printer of your own.

Each subsequent increase in your 'capital' would boost your effectiveness, but each euro of capital investment would provide progressively lower increases in productivity. As it turns out, this sort of 'diminishing returns' to investment also marks the economy as a whole. Raising the capital/labour ratio in the economy increases output per hour worked, but the rate of increase diminishes as the level of the capital/labour ratio rises.

This sort of less-than-proportional increase in efficiency is portrayed in Fig. 7-1 by the GDP/$L$ curve. This shows that raising the capital/labour ratio ($K/L$, which is plotted on the horizontal axis) increases output per worker, but a 10 per cent hike in $K/L$ raises GDP/$L$ by less than 10 per cent.

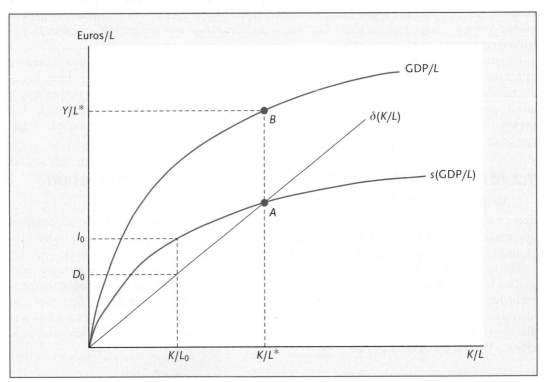

FIGURE 7-1: THE SOLOW DIAGRAM: DETERMINING THE EQUILIBRIUM CAPITAL/LABOUR RATIO

This is why the curve is bowed downwards. (Alternatively, think of the curve as rising less rapidly than a straight line.)

The GDP/$L$ curve shows us what output per worker would be for any given $K/L$, but what will the $K/L$ be? The equilibrium $K/L$ ratio depends upon the inflow and outflow of new capital per worker. The inflow is investment – firms building new factories, buying new trucks, installing new machines, etc. The outflow is depreciation – factories, trucks, machinery, etc., break down with use and must be repaired or replaced. The equilibrium $K/L$ is where the inflow of new investment just balances depreciation of capital. The reason is simple. If the flow of savings exceeds the depreciation of capital, then $K/L$ rises. If depreciation outstrips investment, $K/L$ falls. The next step is to find the inflow and outflow of capital.

Solow simply assumed that people save and invest a constant fraction of their income each year, so the inflow of capital is just a fraction of GDP/$L$; in the diagram, this constant savings and investment fraction is denoted as $s$, so the inflow-of-capital curve is marked as $s$(GDP/$L$). (In European nations, $s$ is somewhere between 20 and 35 per cent.) The investment-per-worker curve has a shape that is similar to that of the GDP/$L$ curve but it is rotated clockwise since the savings are a fraction of GDP/$L$. As for depreciation, Solow made an equally simple assumption. He assumed that a constant fraction of capital stock depreciates each year. In the figure, the constant fraction of the capital stock that depreciates each year is denoted with the Greek letter 'delta', $\delta$. (In Europe, something like 12 per cent of the capital stock depreciates each year.) The depreciation per worker line is shown as $\delta(K/L)$. It is a straight line since the amount of depreciation per worker increases in proportion with the amount of capital per worker.

The important point in Fig. 7-1 is point $A$, the crossing of the $s$(GDP/$L$) curve and the $\delta(K/L)$ line. This occurs at $K/L^*$. At this capital/labour ratio, the inflow of new investment just balances the outflow. For a ratio below $K/L^*$ the capital/labour ratio would rise since investment outstrips depreciation. For example, if $K/L$ were $K/L_o$, then the inflow would be $I_o$ and the outflow would be $D_o$. Since $I_o$ is higher than $D_o$, the amount of new capital per worker installed would be greater than the amount of capital per worker lost to depreciation. Naturally, the capital/labour ratio would rise. With more capital being installed for a ratio higher than this, depreciation surpasses investment, so $K/L$ would fall. The last thing to work out is the output per worker implied by the equilibrium $K/L$. The answer, which is given by the GDP/$L$ curve at point $B$, tells us that that output per worker in this equilibrium will be $Y/L^*$.

Although it is not essential to our main line of analysis, we finish our discussion of the Solow diagram with a consideration of long-run growth. The main point that Solow made with his diagram was that the accumulation of capital is not a source of long-run growth. Capital rises up to the point where the $K/L$ ratio reaches its equilibrium value and then stops, unless something changes. To explain the year after year growth we see in the modern world – about 2 per cent per year on average – Solow relied on technological progress. He assumed that technological advances would rotate the GDP/$L$ curve upwards year after year, pulling the $s$(GDP/$L$) curve up with it. As can be easily verified in the Solow diagram, such progress will lead to an ever-rising output per worker and an ever-rising capital/labour ratio. When we look at the growth effects of European integration we shall be referring to growth that is higher than the growth that would have otherwise occurred due to technological progress.

We next use the Solow diagram to study how European integration might boost growth.

### 7.2.2 Liberalization, allocation effects and the medium-run growth bonus

The verbal logic of growth effects is straightforward. Integration improves the efficiency of the European economy by encouraging a more efficient allocation of European resources. Not surprisingly, this improved efficiency also makes Europe a better place to invest and thus boosts investment beyond what it otherwise would have been. The extra investment means more tools per worker, and this raises the output per worker. As workers get more tools than they would have without integration, output per worker rises faster than it would have done otherwise. To put this differently, integration produces extra growth as the capital/labour ratio approaches its new equilibrium output. This is the medium-run growth bonus introduced by Baldwin (1989). It is medium term since the higher growth disappears once the new equilibrium capital/labour ratio is reached.

## MEDIUM-RUN GROWTH BONUS IN DETAIL

Figure 7-2 allows us to portray the logic in more detail. The first step is to realize how 'allocation effects' of European integration alter the diagram. For all the reasons presented in Chapters 4 to 6, European integration has improved the effectiveness with which capital, labour and technology are combined to produce output. To take one concrete example, we saw that integration can lead to fewer, more efficient firms. From the firm-level perspective, this improved efficiency means lower average cost. At the economy-wide perspective, the improved efficiency means that the same amount of capital and labour can produce more output. How can we show this in the Solow diagram?

The positive allocation effect shifts the GDP/$L$ curve to the dashed line marked GDP/$L'$. The new GDP/$L$ curve is the old one rotated up counter-clockwise since the improved efficiency means

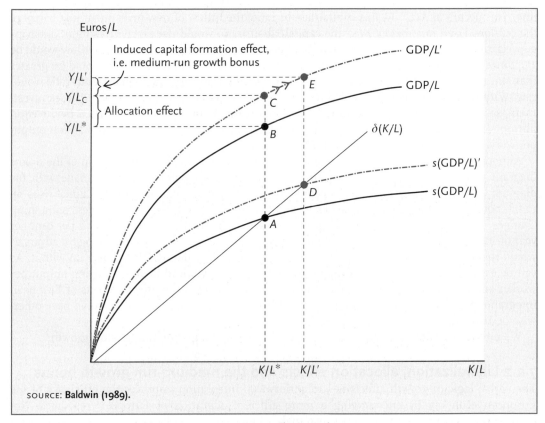

SOURCE: **Baldwin (1989).**

FIGURE 7-2: MEDIUM-RUN GROWTH BONUS FROM EUROPEAN INTEGRATION

that the economy is able to produce more output, say, 2 per cent more, for any given capital/labour ratio. This is the first step. The impact of the higher efficiency on output is shown by point $C$. That is, holding the capital/labour ratio constant at $K/L^*$, output would rise from $Y/L^*$ to $Y/L_C$. This is not the end of the story, however, since $K/L^*$ is no longer the equilibrium capital/labour ratio. This brings us to the second step.

The shift up in the GDP/$L$ curve to GDP/$L'$ also shifts up the investment curve to $s$(GDP/$L$)$'$. After all, the fixed investment rate now applies to higher output and so generates a higher inflow of investment for any given capital/labour ratio. This is shown in the diagram by the dashed curve $s$(GDP/$L$)$'$. Since the inflow has risen, $K/L^*$ is no longer the equilibrium. At $K/L^*$, the inflow exceeds the outflow, so the economy's capital/labour ratio begins to rise. The new equilibrium is at the new intersection of the inflow and outflow curves, namely point $D$, so the new equilibrium capital/labour ratio is $K/L'$. The rise from $K/L^*$ to $K/L'$ is called 'induced capital formation' and reflects the fact that improved efficiency will tend to stimulate investment.

What are the growth implications? As the capital/labour ratio rises from $K/L^*$ to $K/L'$, output per worker rises from $Y/L_C$ to $Y/L'$. This is shown in the diagram as the movement from point $C$ to point $E$. Since the capital stock builds up only slowly, the movement between $C$ and $E$ can take years. The key to the second step is to realize that the rise in output per worker between $C$ and $E$ would show up as faster than normal growth until the economy reaches point $E$. At that time, the growth rate would return to normal.

## SUMMARY IN WORDS

In words, the integration-causes-growth mechanism is: integration → improved efficiency → higher GDP/$L$ → higher investment-per-worker → economy's capital/labour ratio starts to rise towards new, higher equilibrium value → faster growth of output per worker during the transition from the old to the new capital/labour ratio. This is the so-called 'medium-term growth bonus' from European integration.

When it comes to welfare, however, it is important to note that higher output is not a pure welfare gain. In order to invest more, citizens must save more and this means forgoing consumption today. Consequently, the higher levels of consumption made possible tomorrow by the higher $K/L$ ratio are partly offset by the forgone consumption of today.

## 7.2.3 Other medium-run growth effects: changes in the investment rate

The Solow diagram relied on an extremely convenient simplifying assumption – a constant investment rate. Unfortunately, taking the investment rate as given severely limits the range of growth effects that we can study. As the introduction pointed out, the basic logic of growth rests on the decision to invest in new physical capital (machines), new human capital (skills), and/or new knowledge capital (innovations). Many growth effects operate by altering the costs and/or benefits of investing and thus by altering the investment *rate*, what we called $s$ in the diagram. For instance, many people claim that the euro will make it easier, cheaper and safer to invest in Europe. If this turns out to be true, the extra investment would boost growth at least in the medium term, but how would we get this into the Solow framework?

If European integration raises the investment rate from, say, $s$ to $s'$, the inflow of capital curve, namely $s$(GDP/$L$) will rotate upwards, as shown in Fig. 7-3. This change would in turn alter the equilibrium capital/labour ratio. Following the logic we considered above, the inflow of capital at the old capital/labour ratio $K/L^*$ would exceed the outflow, so the capital stock per worker would rise to the new equilibrium shown by point $C$ in the diagram. As before, the rising $K/L$ would raise output per worker from $Y/L^*$ to $Y/L'$ (these $Y/L^*$ and $Y/L'$ are unrelated to those in previous figures). During this process, growth would be somewhat higher than it would have otherwise been.

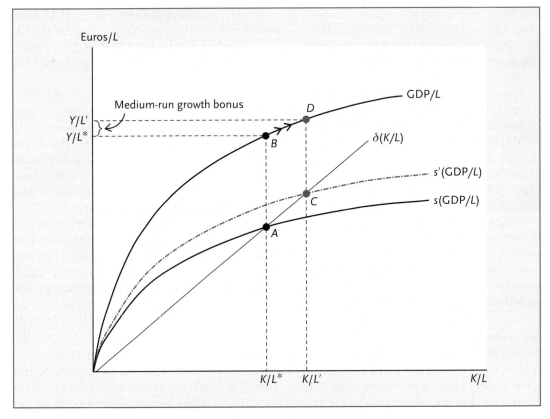

FIGURE 7-3: EUROPEAN INTEGRATION AND THE INVESTMENT RATE

This shows that it is straightforward to illustrate this second type of growth effect in the Solow diagram. We postpone our discussion of how various aspects of European integration might raise the investment rate to section 7.4, where we consider EU capital market integration.

### 7.2.4 Evidence from the 'poor four'

Western Europe grew rapidly in the post-war period and experienced rapid integration. The problem, however, is that it is very difficult to separate the effects of European integration from the many other factors affecting growth. One natural experiment is to look at what happened to nations that joined the EU. These nations experienced a rather sudden and well-defined increase in economic integration when they joined. Moreover, we shall study the impact that EU member-ship had on the four relatively poor entrants that joined the EU between 1960 and 1995: Ireland (in 1973), Greece (in 1981) and Portugal and Spain (in 1986).

The logic sketched out above explains how integration may raise a nation's steady-state capital stock. What sort of 'footprints' would this leave in the data? First, heightened efficiency makes investment more worth while, i.e. it tends to raise the real return to capital. Moreover, this will normally be associated with an increase in the profitability of existing capital and this, in turn, should show up in the average behaviour of the stock market (as long as the stock market reflects a broad sample of firms). An important caveat comes from the fact that liberalization usually harms some firms and sectors even when it is beneficial for the nation as a whole. If the stock market is dominated by, say, state-controlled 'white elephants' that will face increased pressure in a more liberal economy, a drop in the stock market index may accompany the enlargement. Second, the Solow diagram is too simple to distinguish between domestic and foreign investors, but we presume that an improvement in the national investment climate should attract more investment from both sources. These two effects are likely to leave four kinds of 'footprints' in the data:

- Stock market prices should increase
- The aggregate investment to GDP ratio should rise
- The net direct investment figures should improve
- The current account should deteriorate as more foreign capital flows in.

## PORTUGAL AND SPAIN

The case that EU membership induced investment-led growth is the strongest for the Iberians. Following restoration of democracy in the mid-1970s, Portugal and Spain applied to the EU in 1977, with membership talks beginning in 1978. The talks proved difficult, so accession occurred only in 1986. Growth in Portugal picked up rapidly and stayed high both during the negotiations and after accession; and between 1977 and 1992, Portugal expanded 13 per cent more than France (the country we have chosen as a 'control'). In Spain, however, growth was worse than that of France until accession. From 1986, it picked up significantly and between 1986 and 1992 Spain's cumulative growth edge over France amounted to 7.5 per cent, about the same as Portugal's.

As the bottom-left panel of Fig. 7-4 shows, much of this rapid growth was due to a higher rate of physical capital formation. Portugal's investment rate responded strongly and quickly to the

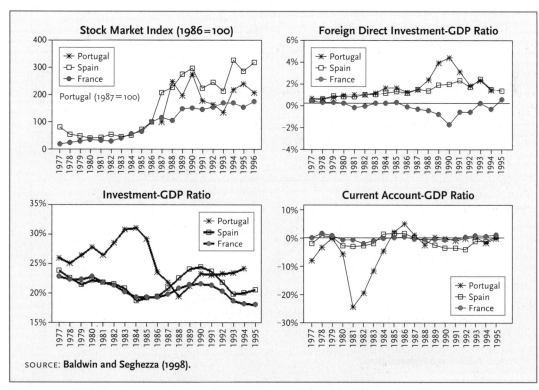

SOURCE: **Baldwin and Seghezza (1998).**

FIGURE 7-4: INTEGRATION-INDUCED INVESTMENT IN SPAIN AND PORTUGAL

combination of democracy and the prospects of EU membership. The importance of membership probably stems from some mixture of reduced uncertainty concerning the nation's stability and the prospects of improved market access. Note, however, that as a member of EFTA, Portugal already had duty-free access to the EU market for industrial goods. The pattern of the Spanish investment rate, in contrast, did not differ significantly from that of our 'control' country until accession actually occurred. At that point, however, the Spanish investment-rate pattern does follow the predictions of integration-induced investment-led growth.

The top-left panel of the figure shows the same pattern for the stock market price indices. Spain's index tracked that of France until accession but thereafter showed signs of a significant improvement in the investment climate. Portuguese data are available only from 1987, but clearly show a better-than-average performance in subsequent years. The other two panels display the evidence for net foreign direct investment and the current account. Here the prospect of membership and domestic market-oriented reforms boosted the attractiveness of Spain and Portugal as industrial locations. Note that the boom in Portuguese foreign direct investment came only after accession. Finally the current account shows that a good portion of high rates of investment in the Iberian peninsula was effectively financed by foreign capital inflows, although foreign capital played a more important role for Portugal prior to accession and for Spain after accession.

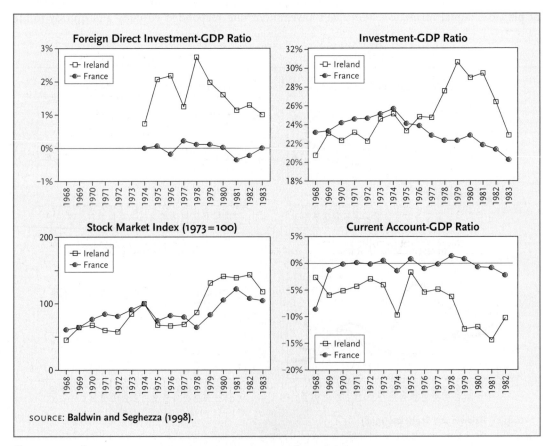

SOURCE: **Baldwin and Seghezza (1998).**

FIGURE 7-5: INTEGRATION-INDUCED INVESTMENT IN IRELAND

## IRELAND

Ireland's long trek to EU membership shadowed that of the UK. Namely, its first application in 1961 was rejected in 1963; its second application, which came in 1967, was accepted in 1972.

Ireland was the first poor country to join the EU and is a fairly clear case of integration-induced investment-led growth. Between its accession and 1983, Ireland experienced a cumulative growth differential of 12 percentage points over France (by 1995 the cumulative difference was almost 50 per cent). Figure 7-5 shows data on our four indicators of investment-led growth for the five years prior to, and 10 years after, the Irish accession. As the top-right panel of the figure shows, Ireland's investment rate picked up faster than that of France, once the first oil shock recession ended. The bottom-right panel (current account to GDP ratio) shows that much of the above-normal investment ratio was coming from foreign capital. As far as foreign direct investment is concerned, the top-left panel shows that Ireland's inflow was similar in magnitude and pattern to that of Spain, fluctuating between 1 and 3 per cent of GDP.

Irish stock prices, however, did respond directly to the accession. Part of this may be explained by the composition effect involved in Ireland's growth. Since its accession, Ireland's 'traditional' manufacturing sectors such as textiles, clothing and footwear have experienced a secular decline, while foreign-owned firms have expanded rapidly. To the extent that the Irish stock market was dominated by the declining traditional sectors – at least in the short run – it is not surprising that the Irish stock prices did not diverge significantly from those of the control nation.

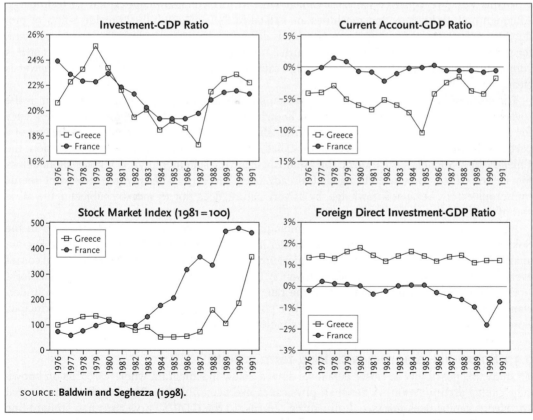

SOURCE: **Baldwin and Seghezza (1998).**

FIGURE 7-6: INTEGRATION-INDUCED INVESTMENT IN GREECE

### GREECE

As in the case of Portugal and Spain, the Greek accession (1981) came just after a period of unde-mocratic governments. However, unlike the Iberians, Greece continued its pervasive state controls of the economy. These controls prevented the Greek economy from reacting flexibly to any shock, and EU membership turned out to be one such example. Moreover, the poor macroeconomic management of the Greek economy further harmed the investment climate. The high and unstable inflation rate provides an example. While most European nations brought inflation down during the 1981–91 period, the Greek inflation rate hardly moved (from 25 per cent in 1981 to 20 per cent in 1991). Moreover, during this period inflation fluctuated greatly, jumping up or down by more than 3 percentage points in a single year in five out of the 10 years.

Given this background, it is not surprising that we find no evidence of investment-led growth in Greece. Figure 7-6 shows the Greek numbers for the five years prior to, and 10 years subsequent to, accession. None of the figures suggests that EU membership had any impact on our four indicators.

The sharp contrast between the Greek case and the other three tells an important lesson. While integration may improve the investment climate in a nation, this can certainly be offset by other factors.

## 7.3 Long-term growth effects: faster knowledge creation and absorption

Up to this point, we focused on physical capital. Here we focus on knowledge capital, i.e. technology. Although both technology and machines are capital in the sense that they provide a flow of pro-ductive services over time, there is an enormous difference between the two. The most important, for our purposes, concerns diminishing returns. It is easy to see that raising the physical capital is subject to diminishing returns. Is knowledge capital subject to the same effects? The answer is clearly no.

The stock of knowledge per worker has risen steadily at least since the Enlightenment in the seventeenth century. Moreover, even as the knowledge stock rises, there seems to be no tendency for the usefulness of more knowledge to diminish. In the late nineteenth century, at the end of a particularly impressive burst of innovation called, by some, the second industrial revolution, the Chief of the US Patent Office made the famously incorrect statement that Congress should close the Patent Office since everything had already been invented. This myopic viewpoint seems humorous exactly because knowledge, by its very nature, does not seem to be subject to the same sort of limits as physical capital.

As we pointed out in section 7.2.1, technological progress shifts the GDP/$L$ curve up in the Solow diagram and this raises output per worker in exactly the same way as we saw in the Fig. 7-2 analysis. In short, we can think of technological progress as an allocative efficiency gain that comes every year, but instead of the gain being driven by European integration, it is driven by technology.

From this perspective, it is clear that the rate of technological progress is the key to under-standing the long-term growth rate. The key point from our perspective is that, in principle, European integration can alter the rate of technological progress.

### 7.3.1 Solow-like diagram with long-term growth

To study this possibility in closer detail, we draw a Solow-like diagram where we focus on knowl-edge capital accumulation, rather than physical capital accumulation. The key difference is that knowledge capital does not face diminishing returns, so the GDP/$L$ curve rises in a straight-line fashion with respect to the knowledge-per-worker ratio, referred to as $K/L$ in Fig. 7-7 (note that the

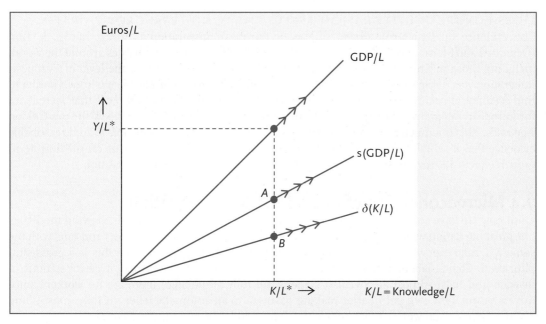

FIGURE 7-7: A SOLOW-LIKE DIAGRAM WITH LONG-TERM GROWTH

$K/L$ here is not the same as $K/L$ in the previous figures; here it is knowledge capital per worker instead of physical capital per worker).

To keep things simple, we continue to assume that each nation invests a constant fraction of its national income in the accumulation of knowledge capital – this rate, referred to as $s$ in the diagram, could be measured by the fraction of a nation's income invested in R&D, i.e. typically something like 3 to 5 per cent in European nations. To see how the total investment in new knowledge changes with the knowledge/labour ratio ($K/L$), we plot $s(GDP/L)$ as before. However, now it is a straight line since the $GDP/L$ curve is a straight line.

We also continue to assume that depreciation is constant in the sense that a given fraction of the national knowledge capital stock 'depreciates' each year. When it comes to knowledge, we usually say the knowledge capital has become obsolete rather than saying it has depreciated, but the wording does not change the logic. In both cases, a certain fraction of the capital becomes worthless every year.

As drawn in Fig. 7-7, the investment rate exceeds the depreciation rate at all levels of $K/L$. For example, at a moment in time when the $K/L$ ratio equals $K/L^*$, the amount of new knowledge capital per worker that is created is given by point $A$, while the amount of knowledge per worker that becomes obsolete is $B$. Since the inflow of new knowledge exceeds the outflow, the knowledge capital stock rises. This is shown by the arrow on the horizontal axis that suggests that $K/L$ will continually rise.

As $K/L$ rises forever, the output per worker will rise forever, along with the amount of new knowledge created and the amount of new knowledge that depreciates. These points are shown by the arrows on the $GDP/L$ line, the $s(GDP/L)$ line and the $\delta(K/L)$ line.

The diagram does not let us directly see how fast output per worker is rising, but it is easy to work this out. The further $s(GDP/L)$ is above $\delta(K/L)$ the larger is the annual net addition to $K/L$. Thus as $s$ rises, the nation will accumulate knowledge capital faster, and thus its income will rise faster.

DOES EUROPEAN INTEGRATION AFFECT THE LONG-TERM GROWTH RATE?
The evidence on long-term growth effects of European integration is much harder to find (Deardorff and Stern, 2002). The overarching fact is that long-term growth rates around the world, including those in Europe, returned to their pre-Golden Age levels. Since the level of European integration was rising more or less steadily during the whole post-war period, it is much harder to find evidence of positive long-term growth effects. What we would have to show is that, were it not for European integration, Europe's long-term growth rate would have fallen below the pre-Golden Age rates. This is a much more difficult task and economists have not been able to find reasonable evidence that it actually happened. For this reason, it is probably best to focus on medium-term growth effects, i.e. investment booms that are associated with European integration.

## 7.4 Microeconomics of capital market integration

Until now we have considered the impact of European integration on growth, viewing the EU as one great big nation with fully integrated capital, labour and technology markets and thus with the same $K/L$ ratio everywhere. Anyone who has travelled in Europe knows that this is a gross simplification. Capital/labour ratios do differ across Europe. Take the example of petrol stations in Sweden and Italy. Almost all Swedish stations are fully automated; there are no workers since drivers pump their own petrol after making payment to an automatic teller. In Italy, most filling stations have several workers that help with filling, window washing, and payment.

This section presents EU policies that foster capital market integration and the economic implications of such integration.[2]

### 7.4.1 EU policy on capital market integration

Until the 1986 Single European Act, EU capital markets were not very integrated. Although the free movement of capital is in the Treaty of Rome, the Treaty provided several large loopholes that EU members eagerly exploited. The basic problem was that, until recently, EU nations just did not believe that unrestricted capital mobility was a good idea – and Box 7-1 explains why.

The main goal of EU capital market liberalization prior to the 1980s was to facilitate real business activities. For example, national policies should not hinder a company based in one Member State from setting up business in another Member State. This so-called 'right of establishment' covered international transfers of capital that may be necessary to set up business. Likewise, national policies were not supposed to hinder the repatriation of profits or wages among Member States to the extent that such hindrances act as restrictions on the free movement of goods and workers.

As discussed in Chapter 1, the Single European Act instituted the principle that all forms of capital mobility should be allowed inside the EU. The actual liberalization was implemented by a series of directives which ended with the 1988 directive that ruled out all remaining restrictions on capital movements among EU residents. The resulting integration was raised to the level of a Treaty commitment by Article 56 of the Maastricht Treaty. This banned all national restrictions on the movement of capital except those required for law enforcement and national security reasons. (You can find all the details on current EU policy and its evolution on http://www.europarl. eu.int/factsheets/3_2_4_en.htm, which is one of the European Parliament's excellent internet 'factsheets'.)

As Box 7-1 suggests, the downside of international capital mobility is primary macroeconomic in nature. We therefore postpone detailed consideration of the costs until Chapters 12 and 13. The benefits of allowing capital to move across national boundaries fall into two categories: allocation efficiency and diversification, which we consider in turn.

---

[2] See http://europa.eu.int/scadplus/leg/en/lvb/l25001.htm for further details on EU policy and laws.

> ## Box 7-1: Fear of capital mobility
>
> Throughout the first half of the twentieth century, but especially in the 'teens', 1920s and 1930s, international capital flows were widely held responsible for repeated balance-of-payments crises and banking crises. In light of that experience, policy makers, including the founders of that bastion of global capitalism, the IMF, were reluctant to promote the free movement of capital. When its rules were founded in 1945, the IMF allowed members to control capital flows in whatever way they saw fit. Indeed, economists at the time, including John Maynard Keynes, argued forcefully against liberalizing international capital movements.
>
> Given the intellectual climate in the 1950s, it is thus not surprising that the Treaty of Rome imposed no formal requirements concerning capital market liberalization. The only stricture was a general one against capital restrictions that inhibited the proper functioning of the Common Market. The European Commission advanced capital-flow liberalization only modestly with directives in 1960 and 1962. These promoted partial liberalization but included numerous opt-out and safeguard clauses which were in fact extensively used by EU members.

## 7.4.2 Economics of capital mobility: allocation efficiency

The normal functioning of a market economy requires capital to be invested in the activities that yield the highest rewards. To the extent that capital market barriers inhibit this efficient allocation, capital controls lower the allocative efficiency of the European economy. To understand this point, we start with the simplest analytic framework that allows us to organize our thinking about the economic consequences of capital market integration. Specifically, we suppose that there are only two nations (Home and Foreign) and that, initially, capital flows are not allowed between them. We also assume that these nations initially have different returns to capital. To keep things simple, we suppose that there is only one good and it is produced by both nations using capital and labour.

The framework can be depicted with the diagram shown in Fig. 7-8. This will eventually allow us to look at the international distribution of capital and impact of capital flows, but to get started we focus on the outcome in Home, ignoring capital mobility. The $MPK$ curve in the diagram shows how the 'marginal product of capital' (the amount of output produced by an extra unit of capital) declines as the total amount of capital employed increases. The marginal product of capital is declining in this diagram for exactly the same reason that the $GDP/L$ curve was convex in Fig. 7-1. Holding constant the amount of labour employed in Home, the addition of more capital increases the overall output, but each additional unit of capital adds less output than the previous one.

If the capital stock in Home is given by $K_o$, then the equilibrium marginal product of capital in Home will be $r_o$, assuming that the capital market is competitive. The idea is that firms competing for Home's capital supply force the 'price' of capital, $r$, up to the point where the price they pay for capital just equals its marginal product. By the usual logic of competition, the outcome is that competitive firms pay $r_o$ and all capital is employed.

Next consider the situation in the other nation, Foreign. To keep everything in one diagram, we add the Foreign capital stock to that of Home's to get the total two-nation supply of capital. This is shown as $K_o + K_o^*$ on the horizontal axis. We also draw the marginal product curve for foreign capital, but we reverse it since we measure the amount of capital employed in Foreign from right-to-left (Home employment of capital is measured from left-to-right). Following the same competitive logic as for Home, we see that the foreign return to capital will be $r_o^*$ since this is the $MPK^*$ where all of the capital is employed in Foreign. (This way of depicting the Home plus Foreign

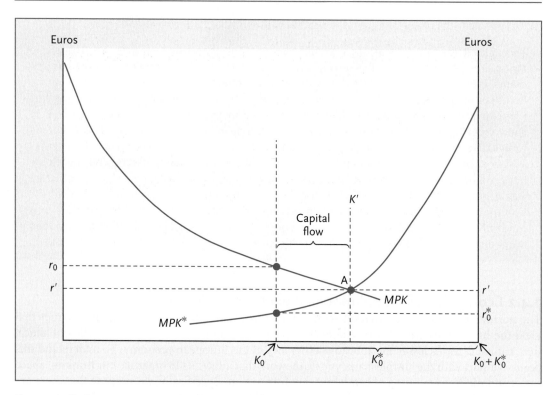

FIGURE 7-8: SIMPLE ECONOMICS OF CAPITAL MARKET INTEGRATION

capital stock makes it easy to study partitions of the total between the two nations; each point on the horizontal axis between zero and $K_o + K_o^*$ shows a different partition).

## ANALYSIS OF CAPITAL MARKET INTEGRATION

It is clear from the diagram that capital earns a higher return in Home than it does in Foreign. If we now allow international capital flows and, for the sake of simplicity, assume that such flows are costless, it is clear that capital will leave Foreign and move to Home in search of a higher reward. Such capital flows raise the level of capital employed in Home and lower it in Foreign, thus narrowing the gap between $r_o$ and $r_o^*$. Indeed, under our assumption that capital flows are costless, capital moves from Foreign to Home until the return is equalized. This occurs at the point where the two $MPK$ curves intersect, namely point $A$ in the diagram. The resulting capital flow and the common reward, $r'$, are illustrated in the diagram. Notice that the capital movement has raised $r$ in the sending nation and lowered it in the receiving nation.

## WINNERS, LOSERS AND NET WELFARE EFFECTS

Who wins and loses from this capital movement? What are the overall effects on native workers and capital owners?

To answer these questions, we need to show how one determines the impact of capital movements on the earnings of labour (we have already seen the impact on the reward to capital) and here Fig. 7-9 helps. First, we note that the area under the $MPK$ curve gives total Home output. The reason follows directly from the definition of the marginal product of capital. The first unit of capital employed produces output equal to the height of the $MPK$ curve at the point where $K = 1$. The amount produced by the second unit of capital is given by the level of $MPK$ at the point where $K = 2$, and so on. Adding up all the heights of the $MPK$ curve at each point yields the area under the curve.

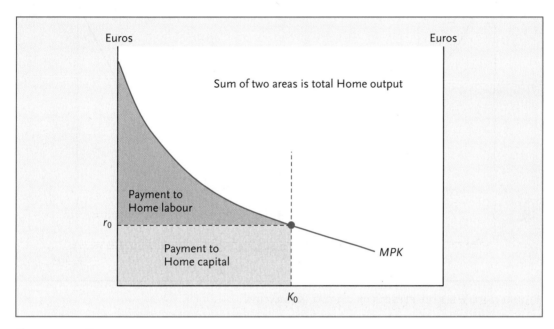

FIGURE 7-9: DIVISION OF OUTPUT BETWEEN CAPITAL AND LABOUR

The total earnings of Home capital is just the equilibrium reward, $r_o$, times the amount of capital, $K_o$. And, since we are assuming that capital and labour are the only two factors of production in this simple world, labour receives all the output that is not paid to capital. Graphically this means that capital's income is the rectangle shown in the diagram, while labour's income is the area between the $MPK$ curve and the $r_o$ line. With this in hand, we turn now to the welfare effects of capital flows.

In our simple, no-capital-mobility-to-free-capital-mobility policy experiment, the 'native' capital owners in Home lose since their reward has fallen from $r_o$ to $r'$ (see Fig. 7-8). The amount of the loss is measured by the rectangle marked 'A' in Fig. 7-10 (the 'A' in this diagram is unrelated to the A in Fig. 7-8). Home labour increases its earnings by area A plus the triangle B. Thus the total economic impact on Home citizens is positive and equal to the triangle B. Another way of seeing that Home gains from capital mobility is to note that the extra capital that flows in raises total output in Home by the areas $B + C + D + E$, but the payments to the new capital only equals the areas $C + D + E$ (i.e. $r'$ times the capital flow).

Correspondingly, Foreign output drops by $D + E$, while the capital remaining in Foreign sees its reward rise from $r_o^*$ to $r'$. The size of this gain is shown by rectangle F, which is the change in $r$ times the amount of capital left in Foreign after the integration (this is illustrated by point A). Foreign labour sees its earnings drop by $D + F$. Combining all these losses and gains, the Foreign factors of production that remain in Foreign lose overall by an amount measured by triangle D. However, if we count the welfare of Foreign factor owners, including the capital that is now

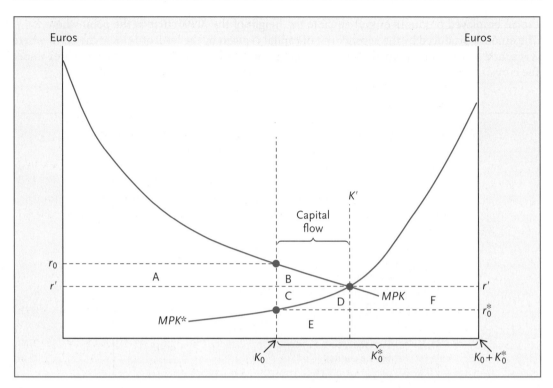

FIGURE 7-10: WELFARE EFFECTS OF CAPITAL 'MIGRATION'

working in Home, the conclusion is reversed. Total gains to Foreign capital are C + D + F, while the loss to Foreign labour is D + F. Foreign gains from the capital outflow by an amount equal to the triangle C.

In short, while capital flows create winners and losers in both nations, both nations gain from the movement of capital. The deep reason for this has to do with efficiency. Without capital mobility, the allocation of productive factors was inefficient. For example, on the margin, Foreign capital was producing $r_o^*$, while it could have been producing $r_o$ in Home. The capital flow thus improves the overall efficiency of the EU economy and the gains from this are split between Home and Foreign. Foreign gets area C; Home gets area B.

### 7.4.3 Foreign direct investment: win–win capital mobility
The analysis above represents the classic analysis of allocation inefficiency – in this case, the allocation of capital across nations was initially inefficient and efficiency was restored by allowing capital to move. This analysis, however, takes the level of technology in both nations as given. A very important aspect of international capital mobility is technology transfer. Considering this technology transfer aspect changes the analysis in many ways.

One of the most important types of capital mobility is known as foreign direct investment, or FDI. This is where a company from one nation builds or buys a factory or office in another nation. Take the example of a German industrial chemicals company that builds a factory in France. Since the company doing the FDI (the German company in our example) very often has superior technology compared to the companies in the receiving nation (French industrial chemicals companies in the example), FDI tends to bring new technologies that raise the productivity of the whole sector in the receiving nation (France). The importance of this is that such technology transfers can create a win–win situation. The better technology will typically mean that the same capital and labour can produce more output, with the extra output being split between capital and labour. In short, the better technology can raise the reward to French capital *and* labour in the industrial chemicals sector. Moreover, FDI very often involves little movement of capital across the border. For example, the German company may borrow most of the money to build the new factory from a French bank. Most of the capital being employed is French, but it is controlled by a German company who has superior technology. In this example it is easy to see that both French capital owners and French workers may gain from the FDI-with-technology-transfer.

In the EU, FDI is very often two-way. To explain this in the context of the example, two-way FDI would consist of a German industrial chemicals company investing in a French factory, while a French agrichemical company invests in a factory in Germany. With this type of two-way flow, we can see that everyone in the chemicals industry may be better off from allowing FDI. What are the deep fundamental sources of this win–win outcome?

Technology, unlike capital and labour, can be reproduced at a fairly low cost. Thus the two-way FDI is really 'creating' more technology rather than taking it away from one nation and putting it in another. The Germany-to-France FDI provides French workers and capital access to a superior technology in the industrial chemicals sector without reducing the level of technology in Germany. And, the France-to-Germany FDI raises the German technology level without lowering that of France.

Another way to think of this outcome is a micro-matching of technology to capital and labour. From this perspective, the important aspect of capital mobility is not the total volume of capital that flows from capital-rich nations to capital-poor nations; it is the fact that capital mobility allows technology owners to employ their technology in more nations.

The connection between this two-way FDI and European integration can readily be seen in the following fact: in the years in which the Single Market Programme was being implemented, intra-EU FDI flows increased four times faster than intra-EU trade flows (Commission, 1996).

We shall now turn to a very different kind of effect.

## 7.4.4 Economics of capital mobility: the diversification effect

An important aspect of European integration that we have not so far addressed concerns the integration of Europe's financial markets. Financial markets facilitate investment so it is natural that financial market integration may change the equilibrium rate of investment. Chapter 16 addresses the macroeconomic aspects of financial market integration, but here we shall address the microeconomic aspects. In particular we shall look at how capital market integration can increase the risk-adjusted rate of return to investment in Europe.

We shall start with some background on how financial markets help to solve two critical aspects of investment.

### MATCHING SAVERS AND INVESTORS

In the Solow diagram analysis (see Fig. 7-1) and the Fig. 7-8 analysis, we did not distinguish between saving and investing. We implicitly assumed that saving was translated directly into new capital. In the real world, however, things are not so easy. The people who do most of the saving – individual citizens as well as insurance companies and pension funds – cannot possibly be on top of all the investment opportunities in the economy. At the same time, those who know about good investment opportunities – typically companies – are generally not saving enough themselves to finance all the good investment opportunities they discover. The first role of financial markets is to bring savers and investors together; this is often called the 'intermediation' role.

When people save by, for example, putting money in the bank, it is the financial markets that 'put this money to work' in the sense of guiding the money into productive investments. There are many channels through which this can happen. One way is for banks to lend the money directly to corporations. For example, a company may borrow money in order to build an office building that it will then rent to businesses. Another way is for corporations to raise money on the financial markets directly. They can, for example, sell bonds or other forms of debt; these are essentially a promise to repay the borrowed money plus interest at a specific date in the future. Corporations also issue 'stocks' which are essentially promises to pay the stockholder a small share of the corporation's profit.

### DIVERSIFYING RISK

The second role of financial markets is to moderate the risk facing savers. Savers dislike uncertainty, yet uncertainty is an unavoidable aspect of business.

Consider the return to investing in a particular project, say a new factory. When the investment is made, there is usually no way of knowing for certain whether the project will yield profits tomorrow. And even if the venture proves profitable, the future profit level is uncertain. Tastes, exchange rates, prices, and the level of competition can all change unexpectedly, thereby altering profits. Of course, one can make a reasonable 'best guess' as to what the profit will be, i.e. calculate what the profit should be, on average. But in deciding whether to invest, the best-guess average is not enough. The owner of the investment must also consider uncertainty. If two projects have the same average return (i.e. expected value), but the profit flow is more variable (i.e. riskier) for one than the other, then savers should judge the riskier project to be worth less. 'One in the hand is worth two in the bush', is the colloquial way of expressing the common-sense principle that people tend to discount the expected value of a risky project more than that of a sure-thing project. The self-descriptive term for this concept is the *risk-adjusted rate of return*.

But what has this to do with financial markets? As it turns out, financial markets can raise the risk-adjusted rate of return on most investments by allowing savers to diversify. Because financial markets help investors to diversify risk, capital market integration in general, and financial market integration in particular, can raise the risk-adjusted reward to investors. Following the usual logic of economics, a rise in the risk-adjusted reward to investing tends to raise the investment rate triggering Fig. 7-3-like growth effects. To see this clearly, we first need to cover some background on risk-adjusted rates of return.

### RISK-ADJUSTED RATE OF RETURN: A SIMPLE EXAMPLE

The basic issues involved in calculating a risk-adjusted rate of return can be illustrated by an example. Ask yourself, 'How risky is it to bet on red at the roulette table?' You might answer that you win almost half the time since on a roulette wheel all numbers, except o and oo, are either red or black. This is the correct answer if you consider the bet-on-red 'project' in isolation. But there is a more complete answer. For instance, suppose you add a bet-on-black 'project' to your 'portfolio' of projects. That is, in addition to betting on red with each roll of the ball, you also bet on black with each roll. Now the effective risk of this betting venture is much reduced. You always win and always lose, except for when the ball lands on o or oo, in which case you lose both bets to the house.

The point to note here is that the average loss from either 'portfolio' – the only-on-red portfolio and the both-red-and-black portfolio – is the same. In both cases, you lose on average 2 out of every 38 rolls of the ball (there are 38 numbers on the wheel – 18 red numbers, 18 black numbers and the two zeros). However, the more 'diversified' portfolio (the both-red-and-black portfolio) provides less variation because one element of the portfolio does well when the other does badly. Clearly, the both-red-and-black betting strategy would take all the fun out of betting, but when we apply the same reasoning to a more serious investment – say a worker's pension fund – then the reduced volatility would be highly valued.

The lesson to be learned from this example is that the risk of a particular project must be evaluated from the perspective of the investor's total portfolio of projects. Typically, some projects will do well when others do badly, so the average return to the portfolio is less risky than any individual project. Or, to put it in terms of the 'risk-adjusted rate of return' phraseology, the risk-adjusted return on a diversified portfolio is higher than that on an undiversified portfolio of investment projects.

## MICROECONOMICS OF EXCHANGE RATE STABILITY AND FINANCIAL MARKET INTEGRATION

With this point in hand, it is straightforward to see how European capital market integration and the exchange rate stability that comes with the euro could raise the risk-adjusted reward to European savers. Both factors make it easier and cheaper for European investors to better diversify their risks. This, in turn, raises the risk-adjusted rate of return for European investors, making Europe a better place to invest. In this way, financial market integration can raise the investment rate and lead to the effects in Fig. 7-3.

Since European integration is rather gradual and many, many things affect the risk-adjusted rate of return, it can be difficult to figure out exactly how financial market integration affects the investment climate in Europe as a whole. The same logic, however, applies to individual nations joining the EU. Since the financial markets in some nations – for example, a small nation like Estonia – are relatively undeveloped, getting access to the European financial markets by joining may have a big impact on their risk-adjusted rate of return and thus a big impact on their investment rate.

Although there is little empirical evidence of such effects, one recent paper, Voth (2001), found that capital market liberalization in Europe lowered the cost of capital.

The chapter has so far focused mainly on capital, but another important aspect of European integration concerns labour mobility.

## 7.5 Microeconomics of labour market integration

The free movement of workers is one of the cornerstones of the EU's Single Market.[3] The goal of this integration is both economic and political. Allowing workers to move freely within the Community benefits economic efficiency by allowing workers to find the jobs that best suit their skills and experience while simultaneously allowing firms to hire the most appropriate workers. On a political level, the architects of the EU hoped that this sort of mobility would foster mutual understanding among the peoples of Europe. As many readers will know from first-hand experience, the fact that many young Europeans spend some time living, studying or working in other EU nations has had a big impact on the way Europeans view each other.

When viewed from this cool-headed economic and political perspective, it is difficult to understand why labour mobility – otherwise known as migration – creates such intense debates in EU nations. To understand this, we first turn to some facts.

### 7.5.1 Immigration facts

The spectacular growth performance of the EEC economies during the 1940s and 1950s brought about conditions of full employment. After this was achieved, Northern European governments and firms sought out foreign labour, and substantial south-to-north migration flows were the result. The turnaround in Northern Europe's economic fortunes, starting with the 1973 recession,

---

[3] See http://www.europarl.eu.int/factsheets/default_en.htm for further details on EU policy and laws.

produced a significant drop in migration, as Fig. 7-11 shows. (In the diagram, negative numbers indicate an outflow of workers; positive numbers an inflow.)

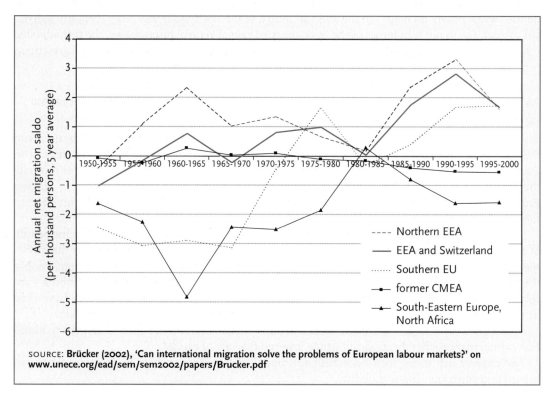

SOURCE: **Brücker (2002), 'Can international migration solve the problems of European labour markets?' on www.unece.org/ead/sem/sem2002/papers/Brucker.pdf**

FIGURE 7-11: EUROPEAN MIGRATION FLOWS 1950–2000

What we see is that Southern Europe (Italy, Spain, Portugal and Greece) and Southeastern Europe (mainly Turkey) were the prime sending nations up to the growth slowdown in 1973. The Northern European nations (the EEC6 less Italy plus the Nordics and alpine economies) were big receiving nations during the same phase. Migration rates overall were quite modest until the economic recovery began in the early to mid-1980s. At that point, Northern Europe regained its appetite for foreign workers, but, and most importantly, the Southern European nations, which had been net providers of workers pre-1973, became net importers. Some of this migration involves the return of Spanish, Italian and Portuguese workers, who had emigrated in the pre-1973 period, but it also reflects an increasing inflow of non-European workers from places such as northern Africa. Turkey, by contrast, resumed its role as a provider of migrants. In this role, Turkey was joined by Central and Eastern European nations who had, by the end of the 1980s, dropped general restrictions on emigration.

As far as European integration is concerned, it is also important to remember that immigration in Europe is not mainly related to the Common Market. Seven out of 10 foreign workers in EU Member States are from non-EU countries, and the policies that govern labour flows from non-member nations are entirely national – the EU does not try to impose what might be called a common external migration policy. To put it differently, being part of the EU's common labour market does not seem to matter very much, at least as far as the raw number of workers is concerned.

As Fig. 7-11 shows, the importance of migrants in the various nations' populations varies quite a lot, both within the EU and between EU and non-EU nations. Moreover, being part of a common labour market does not seem to be the key to determining the origin of migrants. Despite the fact that they do not have an automatic right to work in Switzerland and Norway, migrants from EU nations make up a much higher percentage of migrants in the Swiss and Norwegian labour markets than they do in the German and French labour markets. This shows that the discriminatory liberalization implied by the free mobility of workers within the EU (i.e. workers from one EU nation are free to work in any other EU nation, but they need special permission to work in non-EU nations such as Switzerland and Norway) is not a dominant factor in determining migration patterns. This contrasts sharply with discriminatory liberalization of goods. As we saw above, the composition of imports was strongly influenced by implementation of the customs union.

What this means is that being a member of the Common Market was not very important in boosting international labour movements. There is really no mystery here. In the 1950s and 1960s, nations across Northwestern Europe were experiencing such rapid growth that industry found itself short of workers. Individual nations responded by facilitating inward migration from many different nations. Not surprisingly, nations that wanted to 'import' workers found it easiest to induce migration from nations with low wages and relatively high unemployment. The fact that Spain, Portugal and Greece were not at the time members of the EU did little to hinder the flow of workers into EU members such as Germany. Indeed, German immigration policy in the 1960s was at least as welcoming to Turks and Spaniards as it was to southern Italians. Moreover, nations such as Sweden and the UK, whose industry also experienced labour shortages, managed to attract migrants – including some migrants from EU nations such as Italy – even without being part of the Common Market. In short, the Western European policies that fostered the big migration flows in the 1960s were basically unrelated to the policies of the Common Market.

### 7.5.2 Economic analysis

Labour migration is probably the most contentious aspect of economic integration in Europe. In most Western European nations, popular opinion holds immigrants responsible for high unemployment, abuse of social welfare programmes, street crime, and deterioration of neighbourhoods. As a result, a number of explicitly anti-immigration political parties have faired well in elections. We turn now to economic analysis of labour migration, focusing on the question of how immigration affects the sending and receiving nations, and who gains and loses from it.

#### SIMPLEST FRAMEWORK

We start with the simplest analytical framework that allows us to organize our thinking about the economic consequences of labour migration. As it turns out, this framework is just like Fig. 7-8, the diagram we used above to study capital mobility. We suppose that immigration is not allowed between two nations (Home and Foreign) who initially have different wages. Again we suppose that there is only one good and it is produced by both nations. Fortunately, we have already dealt with this in the previous section on capital mobility, and by reversing the roles of capital and labour, the Fig. 7-8 analysis can again be used to study the allocative efficiency effects and distribution effects of labour mobility.

Figure 7-12 shows the position with the roles of capital and labour reversed. Workers initially earn better wages in Home than in Foreign, and migration will tend to flow from Foreign to Home. This will push down wages in Home and thus harm the Home workers, while benefiting Home capital owners. The opposite happens in Foreign. As some Foreign labour moves to Home,

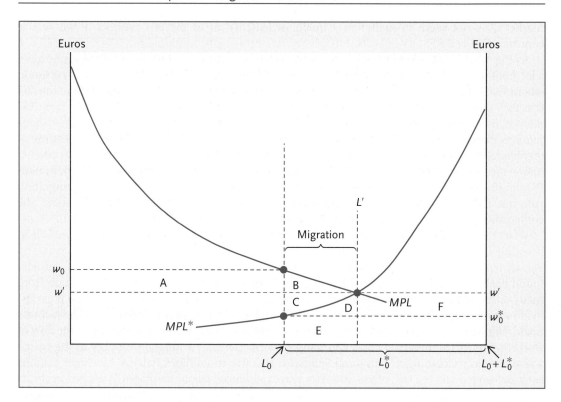

FIGURE 7-12: SIMPLE ECONOMICS OF LABOUR MIGRATION

Foreign wages tend to rise, making the remaining Foreign workers better off and Foreign capital worse off. As before, both countries will gain overall, if we add the gains and losses to each nation's capital and labour.

In short, while migration creates winners and losers in both nations, both nations gain from the movement of labour. The deep reason for this has to do with efficiency. Without migration, the worldwide allocation of productive factors is inefficient. Migration thus improves the overall efficiency of the world economy and the gains from this are split between Home and Foreign.

### BROADER INTERPRETATION OF THE RESULTS AND EMPIRICAL EVIDENCE

The analysis above classifies all productive factors into two categories: capital and labour. It is important to note, however, that for most EU nations we should interpret 'capital' as including 'human capital', i.e. highly educated workers. The reason has to do with the economic notion of 'complementarity' versus 'substitutability'.

Rather than defining these concepts directly, consider the example of how productive factors combine to produce hotel services. Apart from material inputs like food and bed clothing, hotels require unskilled workers (cleaners, etc.), skilled workers (managers, marketing people, etc.), and capital (the building, furniture, etc.). In a country like Norway, unskilled labour is very expensive so hotels are very expensive and so there are relatively few hotels. If Norway allowed hotels to hire foreign workers at lower wages, some factors would be hurt – the unskilled workers who earned high wages before the immigration – but other factors would be helped. Skilled workers and capital would find that their rewards would rise. As the price of hotel rooms fell, the hotel industry would expand, raising the demand for highly skilled workers and capital. In this situation, we say that unskilled workers are complements to skilled workers and capital; the precise definition is that demand for skilled workers and capital rises as the price of unskilled workers falls.

The point of this is to put the losses to domestic labour in perspective. As Table 7-4 shows, immigrants often have a skill mix that is very different from that of domestic workers. Most domestic workers can thus be thought of as belonging to 'capital' in the Fig. 7-8 analysis and thus winning from immigration. In France and Germany, for example, immigrants often work at jobs, e.g. in factories, that boost the productivity of native workers in related fields like management, finance, sales and marketing. Indeed, immigrants often fill jobs that no native would take, such as restaurant–kitchen workers, street sweepers, etc.; this is an extreme form of complementarity in which there are no economic losers in the receiving nation.

Looking more closely at Table 7-4, we see that in some EU nations – especially the poor members like Portugal, Greece, Ireland and Spain – immigrants have higher skill levels (as measured by education) than the average native worker. In these cases, the analysis of immi-

| | Immigrants as % of population | % immigrants from EU | Share with low education | | | | |
|---|---|---|---|---|---|---|---|
| | | | Total population | Nationals | EU foreigners | Non-EU foreigners | Immigrants (millions) |
| Immigrants are more than 5% of population | | | | | | | |
| Luxembourg | 33 | 90 | 55 | 51 | 62 | 42 | 0.1 |
| Austria | 9 | | 29 | 28 | 16 | 51 | 0.7 |
| Germany | 9 | 25 | 30 | 30 | 36 | 56 | 7.3 |
| Belgium | 9 | 63 | 41 | 41 | na | 48 | 0.9 |
| France | 6 | 37 | 41 | 31 | 65 | 69 | 3.6 |
| Immigrants are more than 3% of population | | | | | | | |
| Denmark | 5 | 21 | 31 | 31 | 28 | 66 | 0.2 |
| Netherlands | 4 | 28 | 28 | 27 | 32 | 60 | 0.7 |
| UK | 4 | 38 | 41 | 41 | 49 | 28 | 2.1 |
| Ireland | 3 | 71 | 51 | 52 | 38 | 21 | 0.1 |
| Immigrants are less than 2% of population | | | | | | | |
| Portugal | 2 | 25 | 81 | 81 | 23 | 50 | 0.2 |
| Greece | 2 | 28 | 50 | 50 | 25 | 37 | 0.2 |
| Italy | 2 | 15 | 60 | 60 | 30 | 36 | 0.9 |
| Finland | 1 | 19 | 33 | 33 | 23 | 24 | 0.1 |
| Spain | 1 | 47 | 62 | 62 | 29 | 37 | 0.5 |
| EU15 | 5 | 31 | | | | | |
| Non-EU nations | | | | | | | |
| Switzerland | 19 | 60 | | | | | |
| Norway | 4 | 41 | | | | | |

SOURCE: Adapted from Brücker (2002) 'Can International Migration Solve the Problems of European Labour Markets?'; Data on immigrant numbers and source countries from 1998; data on education levels from 1996.

TABLE 7-4: FACTS ABOUT IMMIGRANTS IN THE EU

gration is somewhat different. Instead of shifting $L$ from Foreign to Home, migration shifts 'capital'. Graphically this raises the $MPL$ curve in Fig. 7-12 for Home and lowers it for Foreign. The reason is that the presence of more skilled workers tends to raise the productivity of unskilled workers. If you want a mental picture of this process, think of American entrepreneurs coming into Ireland and starting businesses that hire Irish workers away from the farm sector. Again, we see that immigration can be a win–win situation for the receiving nation.

Another insight that comes from the notion of complementarity is that of micro-level matching. Some immigration into the EU consists of workers who have very specific skills – computer programming in English, for example – that are lacking in the receiving nation. Since these workers do not compete with native workers, or compete with very few native workers, such immigration is usually less contentious since it creates few losers. This level of matching among countries can proceed to an even lower level. For example, even within a single company, the experiences of workers vary, and free mobility of labour may make it easier to move workers into jobs that best fit their experience. Again, it is entirely possible that everyone gains from such matching.

More generally, immigrants who have skills that are complementary to the skill mix in the receiving nation are typically less likely to create losers in the receiving nation. Close inspection of the numbers in Table 7-4 reveals that, in many EU nations, the skill mix of immigrants from other EU nations tends to be more complementary to that of immigrants from non-EU nations. This may help explain why immigrants from other EU nations tend to generate less controversy than immigrants from outside the EU.

### EMPIRICAL EVIDENCE

So much for the theory. What does the evidence tell us?

Given the importance of immigration in the various national debates in Europe, economists have done a great deal of work estimating the impact of migration on the wages of domestic workers. Generally, these studies find that a 1 per cent rise in the supply of workers via migration changes the wages of native workers by anywhere between +1 per cent and −1 per cent, with most studies putting the figure in the even narrower range of ± 0.3 per cent. There are two key points to take away from these findings. First, it is not obvious that immigration always lowers wages. Since nations tend to let in workers who have skills that are complementary to those of domestic workers, the impact is often positive. Second, whether it is slightly positive or slightly negative, the impact is quite small. Again this outcome is due in part to the fact that countries tend to restrict the types of labour inflow that would have large negative effects on wages.

## 7.5.3 Unemployment

One common belief is that immigrants cause unemployment. To understand the logic of how this might be true we need an analytical framework in which unemployment arises naturally. Chapter 17 looks at unemployment in detail, but here we just mention the bare essentials that are necessary to understand the evidence.

We start by noting that the simple framework discussed above will not do since it implicitly assumes that all workers get jobs, or more exactly that the market wage rises or falls until firms want to hire all the workers that want jobs. A worker is defined as an unemployed person when he/she has looked for work but was unable to find it, thus unemployment is nothing more than a mismatch between supply and demand in the labour market. If wages were perfectly flexible, the wage rate paid for each hour of work would adjust to match the amount of labour workers were willing to supply to the amount that firms were willing to buy.

Of course wages in Europe are not flexible. For many reasons, some good and some bad, European societies chose not to let the 'price' of labour (i.e. wages and salaries) jump around like the price of crude oil; the whim of the market is disciplined. In some countries, wages are set at the national and/or industry level as the outcome of bargaining between unions and firms (sometimes the government also participates). In almost all European nations, workers sign, or implicitly agree to contracts that lock in the price of labour for one or two years, or perhaps for just a month. Via these mechanisms and many more, the price of labour gets fixed in a way that depends upon many things in addition to the supply and demand for labour. It is therefore no wonder that the market typically finds the supply and demand for labour mismatched. But why is the outcome almost always excess supply (unemployment) rather than excess demand (labour shortage)?

National labour market institutions in Europe – call them trade unions for the sake of simplicity (although the real story is much more complex) – are typically biased in favour of workers who already have jobs. These insiders naturally like to have high wages and since they have some control over this price, they – like any smart monopolist – tend to restrict supply in order to jack up the price. The result is unemployment, mainly among workers who were out of a job to start with. We illustrate this with a slightly modified version of the textbook model of European unemployment by Burda and Wyplosz (2001).

We start with no immigrants, so the left panel of Fig. 7-13 shows the situation. The curve marked $S$ shows the number of hours that people would like to work for any given wage. $S_c$ shows the labour supply that a monopolistic union would offer to firms at any given wage ('c' stands for collective). The union, of course, holds back a bit of supply to push up the price and this shows up in the fact that the $S_c$ curve is to the left of the $S$ curve. When the union and firms negotiate they settle on a wage rate (adjusted for the price level of goods) such that $S_c$ and the labour demand curve, $D$, meet; this is marked as $w_o$ in the diagram. Unemployment is the natural outcome of this. The union's effort to boost the well-being of those that have a job pushes up the price of labour, but this means that not everyone who wants to work at the going wage will find a willing employer. The essence of monopoly power is, of course, the restriction of supply of goods on the market.

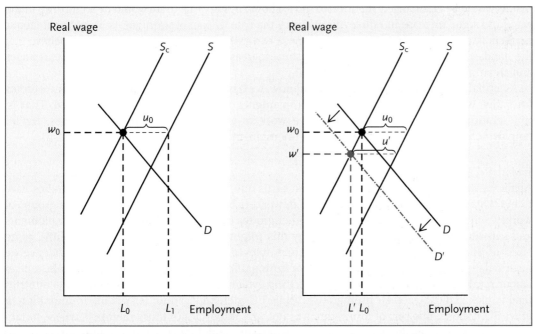

FIGURE 7-13: A SIMPLE MODEL OF UNEMPLOYMENT

Specifically, the level of unemployment is the difference between the labour that people would like to supply at the going wage (this is $L_1$) and the number of workers actually hired (this is $L_0$); this is marked as $u_0$ in the left panel of the diagram.

Next we suppose that some immigrants enter the country. The impact of immigrants is not obvious since we do not know whether immigrants will operate in the labour market in the same way as native workers. To be concrete, consider one extreme, namely the immigrants are willing and able to get jobs at a wage that is below the union-set wage. In this extreme case, the impact of migration is to shift the demand curve for native workers to the left, as shown in the right panel of the diagram. The idea here is that firms first hire cheap immigrants and then turn to the native market to fulfil any remaining demands. The result is that the union-set wage and native employment fall somewhat. Two points, however, are worth stressing. First, even in this extreme case – where firms are able to hire immigrants at below market wages – the drop in native employment is less than the number of immigrants. As a consequence, total employment of natives and immigrants rises. That is, the horizontal shift of the demand curve from $D$ to $D'$, the size of which exactly equals the number of jobs taken by immigrants, is less than the change in equilibrium employment, namely $L_0$ to $L'$. This dampening is due to the resulting drop in native wages.

Second, there may be no change in unemployment. Because unemployment is a result of the labour market's structure, immigration will affect unemployment only to the extent that it affects the structure of the labour market. In the example shown in the diagram, there is no change in the number of unemployed natives since the drop in wages from $w°$ to $w'$ decreases the number of native workers who say they want to work at the going wage by as much as the drop in native employment. If we had drawn the two labour supply curves as converging or diverging instead of parallel, we would have got a different answer. The main point, however, is that if immigration is to affect unemployment, it must do so by altering labour market structure.

Another way to capture the impact of immigration would be to make the other polar assumption that immigrants participate in the labour market in exactly the same way as native workers do. In this case (not shown in the diagram), both the $S$ and $S_c$ curves would shift to the right. The results would be qualitatively identical to those shown in Fig. 7-13; there would be some drop in the wage and some increase in employment. Since the true impact of immigrants on national labour markets is probably somewhere between these two extremes, it seems reasonable to believe that the standard impact of immigration will be some increase in employment, some decrease in wages and an ambiguous effect on unemployment.

As a final analytic note, observe that, until now, we have been viewing immigrants as substitutes for native workers. If, instead, they are complements, the Fig. 7-13 analysis is reversed. That is, immigration raises the demand for native workers and this results in higher wages, higher employment and an ambiguous impact on unemployment.

### EMPIRICAL EVIDENCE

Again we turn from theory to evidence. As it turns out, the evidence is mixed. Some studies have found that immigrants increase the chance of workers becoming unemployed for some groups of workers while it has the opposite effect on other groups of workers. (Think about the complements and substitutes analysis to understand why this might be true.) Other authors find little or no effect of immigration on the risk of being unemployed. In summary, the empirical evidence we have to date does not support the notion that immigration has large, negative effects on European labour markets. As usual, this lack of convincing evidence is due in part to the fact that countries tend to pick and choose their immigrants. While EU members cannot restrict the immigration of other EU nations, this sort of immigration is not very important in those members where certain types of immigration are really important (Germany and France alone account for 11 of the

18 million migrants currently located in the EU). EU members can and do control labour flows from non-EU nations, especially when they would otherwise have large negative effects on employment and/or unemployment.

## 7.6 Summary

The logic of accumulation effects of European integration is based on the fundamental logic of economic growth. A nation's per capita income can rise on a sustained basis only if its workers are provided with a steadily rising stock of physical, human and/or knowledge capital. Consequently, European integration will affect the growth rate only to the extent that it affects the rate of accumulation of physical, human and knowledge capital.

The chapter focused on two basic mechanisms through which European integration affects capital accumulation.

- Insofar as European integration makes the European economy more efficient, i.e. leads to a positive allocation effect, it raises output and this – assuming a constant investment rate – leads to more investment. The end result of this higher level of investment is a higher long-term equilibrium capital stock and thus a higher equilibrium income per person.
- European integration may also raise the investment rate by making investment less risky. As with the previous effect, the end result is a higher capital stock and a higher output per worker.

Examples of this integration-induced, investment-led growth are fairly common.

Long-term growth effects were also studied. The underlying mechanism is the same as for medium-term growth effects, but because knowledge capital does not face diminishing returns, an increase in investment in knowledge (R&D) can lead to a permanent increase in the growth rate. There is little empirical evidence that European integration has had a major impact on long-term growth rates in Europe.

The chapter also studied the impact of capital and labour mobility. We showed that such mobility typically leads to overall gains for both the sending and receiving nations, but the flows have important distributional effects within each nation.

When it comes to labour migration, the chapter emphasized the fact that different types of labour can be complements to each other, so immigration may actually raise wages in the receiving nation.

### SELF-ASSESSMENT QUESTIONS

**1.** When the German reunification took place, Germany's labour force rose much more than its capital stock (since much of East Germany's capital stock was useless in the market economy). Use Fig. 7-1 to analyse what the medium-term growth effects should have been. Go on the internet to find what actually happened to German growth after reunification.

**2.** It is often said that the prospect of EU membership made Central European nations a better, safer place to invest. Using the Solow diagram, show how this would affect medium-term growth in these nations. What sort of 'footprints' would this leave in the data?

**3.** Use a diagram like Fig. 7-2 to analyse the medium-term growth effects of the following situation. Assume: (1) Serbia's $K/L$ was pushed below its long-term equilibrium by war damage to its capital stock, and (2) the EU signs a free trade agreement with Serbia that has two effects: (2a) it increases the efficiency of the Serbian economy (allocation effect), and (2b) it raises the Serbian investment rate ($s$) but only temporarily, for, say, 10 years. (i) Show what (1), (2a) and (2b) would look like; (ii) show where the Serbia economy would end up in the long run (i.e. after $s$ returned to its normal rate), and (iii) show how the integration would affect Serbia's growth path.

**4.** European governments as well as European companies borrow by issuing debt on the capital markets. As a consequence, governments and private firms are in some sense competitors for Europe's pool of savings. How can the Solow diagram be used to study the growth effects of a rise in government borrowing? (*Hint*: Assume that the investment rate is constant and assume that the government borrowing is used to finance consumption rather than investment.)

## ESSAY QUESTIONS

**1.** In most analyses, growth in per capita GDP is taken to be a good thing. Write an essay that critiques GDP as a measure of economic welfare. Be sure to consider issues of income distribution and leisure time.

**2.** The analysis of migration in the chapter stressed economic considerations. Write an essay that argues that the ability of EU citizens to work or retire in any other EU nation has an impact on attitudes towards European integration. Draw on your personal experience, if appropriate.

**3.** Write an essay that puts the attitude towards capital market integration of the founders of the EU into historical perspective. Focus on the period after 1914.

**4.** Write an essay that discusses and analyses the post-1989 growth experience of one Central European nation. Be sure to use the concepts introduced in this chapter.

**5.** When Spain and Portugal were admitted to the EU in 1986, Portuguese and Spanish workers were not allowed to work freely in other EU Member States for five years. Write an essay that explains the political economy reasoning behind such a restriction.

## FURTHER READING: THE AFICIONADOS CORNER

An extensive description and analysis of growth in Europe can be found in Crafts and Toniolo (1996).

An alternative presentation of the Solow model, one that allows for several extensions such as population growth and continuous technological progress, can be found in Mankiw (2000).

An advanced treatment of neoclassical and endogenous growth can be found in Barro, R. and X. Sala-I-Martin (1995) *Economic Growth*, McGraw-Hill, New York.

For a recent and comprehensive review of capital market integration and its economic effects, see 'Quantification of the macro-economic impact of integration of EU financial markets', *London Economics*, November 2002, which can be downloaded from http://europa.eu.int/comm/economy_finance/publications/.

For an analysis of the migration impact of the 2004 enlargement, see Boeri et al. (2002) *Who's Afraid of the Big Enlargement? Economic and Social Implications of the European Union's Prospective Eastern Expansion*, CEPR Policy Paper No. 7 (www.cepr.org).

## USEFUL WEBSITES

For the latest data on European growth and forecasts, see the website of DG Economy and Finance: http://europa.eu.int/comm/economy_finance/.

See http://www.europarl.eu.int/factsheets/default_en.htm for further details on EU policy and laws concerning labour mobility, and http://europa.eu.int/scadplus/leg/en/lvb/l25001.htm for details on EU policy and laws concerning capital mobility.

A wealth of information and analysis concerning labour mobility can be found on the excellent website entitled 'History of International Migration Site'. The URL is http://www.let.leidenuniv.nl/history/migration/contents.html

## REFERENCES

Baldwin, R. and E. Seghezza (1998) 'Regional integration and growth in developing nations', *Journal of Economic Integration*, **13** (3), 367–99.
Baldwin, R. (1989) 'The growth effects of 1992', *Economic Policy*, **9**, 247–82.

Baldwin, R. and R. Forslid (2001) 'Trade liberalization and endogenous growth: A *q*-theory approach', *Journal of International Economics*, **50**, 497–517.

Burda, M. and C. Wyplosz (2001) *Macroeconomics*, Oxford University Press, Oxford.

Cameron, R. and L. Neal (2003) *A Concise Economic History of the World*, Oxford University Press, Oxford.

Coe, D. and R. Moghadam (1993) 'Capital and trade as engines of growth in France', *IMF Staff Papers*, **40**, 542–66.

Commission (1996) *The 1996 Single Market Review: Background Information for the Report to the Council and European Parliament*, Commission of the European Communities, SEC (96) 2378, Brussels. http://europa.eu.int/comm/internal_market/en/update/impact/bgrounen.pdf.

Crafts, N. and G. Toniolo (1996) *Economic Growth in Europe since 1945*, Cambridge University Press, Cambridge.

Deardorff, A. and R. Stern (2002) *EU Expansion and EU Growth*, Ford School of Public Policy, Working Paper 487.

Henrekson, M., J. Torstensson and R. Torstensson (1997) 'Growth effects of European integration', *European Economic Review*, **41** (8), 1537–57.

Italianer, A. (1994) 'Whither the gains from European economic integration?', *Revue Economique*, No. 3 (May), 689–702.

Mankiw, G. (2000) *Principles of Economics*, Thomson Learning, New York.

Voth, H. (2001) *Convertibility, Currency Controls and the Cost of Capital in Western Europe, 1950–1999*, Economics Working Paper 552, Universitat Pompeu Fabra, Barcelona.

# PART III EU Policies

The European Union has hundreds of policies, and it would take a lifetime to study them all. However, as is true of so much of the EU, less is more when it comes to policy. Studying the main policies in detail provides a much better understanding of the EU than a superficial coverage of all the policies. The major policies in the EU are its Common Agricultural Policy (CAP) and its 'cohesion' policy (also called regional policy). These two polices, which are actually collections of related programmes and practices, account for 80 per cent of the EU budget. They will also continue to 'be in the headlines' since they will be a source of continual friction between the incumbent members of the EU15 and the 10 new members that will join in 2004. For all these reasons, we cover the CAP in Chapter 8 and the Regional Policy in Chapter 9.

What don't we cover? A standard list of the other main EU policies would include: Competition, Economic and Financial Affairs, Education and Culture, Employment and Social Affairs, Energy and Transport, Enterprise,

Environment, Fisheries, Health and Consumer Protection, Information Society, Internal Market, Research, Justice and Home Affairs, Research, Taxation and Customs Union, and Development Assistance, External Trade Policy. None of these is very important in terms of spending, or in terms of understanding the essence of the European Union. Nevertheless, some of them are very important in particular areas (e.g. the fishery policy is critical in northern Spain), or in very specific sectors (e.g. the transport policy is important to the trucking sector), or in specific instances (e.g. the competition policy is pivotal in certain merger cases). Apart from considerations of space, there is one other very important reason for not covering these.

Just a few years ago, succinct information on EU policies was difficult to find, so EU textbooks had to cover at least five or six policies. Today, the web-friendly Prodi Commission has posted extremely well-written accounts of all the policies (often in a dozen languages). The following are URLs for the most important policies we do not cover:

- Competition Policy: http://europa.eu.int/comm/competition/publications/
- Development: http://europa.eu.int/comm/development/index_en.cfm
- Environment: http://europa.eu.int/comm/dgs/environment/index_ en.htm
- External Relations: http://europa.eu.int/comm/dgs/external_relations/ general/mission_en.htm
- External Trade: http://europa.eu.int/comm/trade/whatwedo/index_en.htm
- Fisheries: http://europa.eu.int/comm/fisheries/doc_et_publ/pub_en.htm
- Industrial Policy: http://europa.eu.int/comm/enterprise/enterprise_ policy/ industry/index.htm
- Research: http://europa.eu.int/comm/research/index_en.cfm
- Social Policy: http://europa.eu.int/comm/employment_social/index_en.htm
- Tax and Customs Union: http://europa.eu.int/comm/taxation_ customs/

These can be complemented by the European Parliament's excellent 'factsheets' found on www.europarl.eu.int/factsheets/default_en.htm.

> " A common agricultural policy that encourages surpluses which then have to be disposed of – again at considerable costs – is no longer acceptable or sustainable. Public expenditure must yield something in return – whether it is the food quality, the preservation of the environment and animal welfare, landscapes, cultural heritage, or enhancing social balance and equity. "
>
> **European Commissioner Franz Fischler, 2002**

# 8 The Common Agricultural Policy

---

The Common Agricultural Policy (CAP) is a set of policies aimed at raising the farm incomes in the EU. The CAP is problematic. It accounts for about half the EU budget but farmers continue to leave the land. It accounts for many of the quarrels among EU members and between the EU and third nations, yet it is extremely difficult to reform. Given all these problems and its dominant role in the budget, a good understanding of the CAP is essential to the study of European integration. This chapter presents the essential elements and economics of the CAP.

A major CAP reform was announced just as this book went to press. See the OLC for an update on the June 2003 reform package and its implications.

---

## 8.1 Early days: domestic price supports

Today's CAP is a massively complex matrix of policies, but it was not always that way. The CAP started life in 1962 as a rather straightforward policy of keeping agricultural prices high and stable. The policy led to a series of problems that triggered a series of reforms. While these reforms addressed some of the CAP's main defects, most of the original problems remain. These facts suggest a natural organization for this chapter. First we study the CAP in its simple form. Then we present the problems that this created and the reforms they triggered. Before closing the chapter with some discussion of the future challenges facing the CAP, we consider the problems that still plague today's CAP.

Most nations treat farming differently. Rich nations tend to support their farmers with subsidies and high prices; poor countries tend to tax their farmers, especially those producing export crops. In Europe, the special treatment of farming began in the 1920s and 1930s (Millward, 1992, ch. 5). By the 1950s, all six of the original EU members intervened in agricultural markets in an effort to stabilize prices, the main difference being the height at which prices were stabilized.

As Zobbe (2001) says, 'it is easy to see how a CAP based on price support as the main instrument must have looked extremely simple to the decision makers in the early 1960s'. Moreover, there was no question of leaving agriculture out of the EU's design. As Chapter 1 showed, the EU's founders had grand plans for an 'ever closer union among the peoples of Europe' and agriculture accounted for a good fraction of those peoples in the 1950s – about one in five Europeans lived on farms when the Treaty of Rome was written (Zobbe, 2001).

### 8.1.1 Basic price-floor diagram for a net importer

Standard economic terminology for a 'domestic price support' is a 'price floor', so this is the term we shall employ. Note, however, that the phraseology of the CAP is far more involved since it must capture aspects of reality that we ignore for the sake of clarity (see Box 8-1).

---

**BOX 8-1: CAP PRICE SUPPORT JARGON**

For historical reasons, the terms used for the price floor vary according to the product (intervention price, guaranteed price, basic price or norm price), as does the exact procedure for setting them. The wheat jargon and procedures, however, serve as a fairly representative model.

Around April of every year, EU farm ministers meet in the Council of Ministers to fix prices for the coming crop year. The first price to set is a theoretical price – the 'target price' – as a guideline for the practical prices. Strange as it may seem, the target price refers to the wholesale price of wheat in Duisburg, a city right in the middle of the Ruhr (since this was the locality of shortest supply, see Nevin 1990). The main operational price – the 'intervention price' – is set lower than the target price, typically 12 to 20 per cent lower. As its name suggests, authorities are committed to 'intervene', i.e. buy unlimited quantities of wheat at the 'intervention price' in any EU member's market. This ensures that no EU market prices fall below the intervention price, so the intervention price is the price floor. Each EU member has its own authority, often a semi-official producers' organization; these 'buyers of last resort' are responsible for storing or otherwise disposing of goods they buy to support the price floor. The funding for this is drawn from the Guarantee section of the EU's European Agricultural Guidance and Guarantee Fund (EAGGF, or FEOGA in French). The second practical price, the 'threshold price' is the minimum price at which wheat can be imported into the EU from third nations. This is set at the target price minus the transport and handling costs for imported wheat arriving at Europe's largest port, Rotterdam, and sold in Duisburg. The threshold price is

---

always above the intervention price so that intervention authorities will not have to spend EU money buying imported wheat at the intervention price. In normal years, the threshold price is far above the world price so the import tariff – the 'variable import levy' – is set so that wheat is never imported below the threshold price. The simplification in Fig. 8-1 assumes that the intervention price and threshold price are the same.

A taste of the CAP's complexity can be had by considering the impact of higher wheat prices. Various grains – wheat, maize, etc. – are somewhat substitutable, especially when they are used to feed farm animals. Because of this, avoiding excessive substitution requires that a high target price for wheat be accompanied by a high price for other grains. Moreover, since feed grain is an important input in milk and meat production, high grain prices would squeeze EU milk and meat producers unless their prices were also raised. Likewise, much of the EU's beef comes from dairy cows that are too old to produce milk efficiently, so higher milk production means more cows and this means a higher supply of beef.

*Source*: This box is based mainly on Chapter 14 of Nevin (1990).

The EU set (and still sets) price floors for all the major farm products including grains, dairy products, beef, veal and sugar. For most of the CAP's existence, these prices were between 50 and 100 per cent higher than world prices (Molle, 1997, Table 11.4). These price floors were enforced by guaranteed, unlimited purchase by CAP authorities at the price floor, but only as a last resort. In the early days of the CAP, the EU was a net importer of most farm products, so it could ensure that supply and demand matched at high prices by manipulating the amount of foreign food that entered the EU market. The manipulation was done with import tariffs, so the best way to understand the early CAP is with a standard open-economy supply and demand diagram of the type we considered in Chapter 4.

The economics of the tariffs used to raise EU food prices above the price floor are quite similar to the standard tariff analysis presented in Chapter 4. For convenience, we briefly repeat the analysis here, pointing out the minor differences (the presentation in Chapter 4 provides much more detail and explanation). The goal of these tariffs – called 'variable levies' in the parlance of the CAP – is to ensure that the imported food does not push EU prices below the price floor.

The left panel of Fig. 8-1 helps us to analyse the impact of such a price floor in cases where it is set above the world price ($P_w$) but below the level where the EU would import no food (in agricultural economics, this level is called the point of 'self sufficiency', so we mark the level as $p_{ss}$ in the diagram). As we saw in Chapter 4, the domestic price ends up as the world price plus the tariff. The reason is that potential competition from imports (priced at $P_w$ plus the tariff, $T$) means that no one would pay more than $P_w + T$. And the inability of domestic producers to make enough food to satisfy the demand at $P_w + T$ means that farmers would never accept a price lower than $P_w + T$. At $P_w + T$, domestic production is $Z_f$ while domestic consumption is $C_f$; the difference between consumption and production equals the level of imports. The subscript 'f' indicates 'floor'.

Price instability is a key feature of food markets, so we need to consider what happens when the world price changes to, say, $P'_w$. In this case, maintaining its price floor requires the EU to apply a lower tariff. Specifically, it cuts its tariff to $T'$ so that $P'_w + T'$ equals the price floor. Until the practice was abandoned in 1995, variable levies richly deserved their name; they were adjusted *daily* to reflect changes in world market prices (ERS, 1999, p. 12). Because of these tariffs, EU agricultural product prices were typically between 50 and 100 per cent above world prices. Note that from 1995, the EU was forbidden from varying its agricultural tariffs under a WTO agreement called the Uruguay Round.

What is the economic impact of a price floor? The higher price induces EU farmers to produce more. An unintended side effect of the higher price is to discourage food consumption. Since imports exactly equal the gap between EU consumption and production, a tariff-induced reduction in consumption and increase in production reduces imports, i.e. it moves the EU towards self-sufficiency in food with domestic production rising and consumption falling. Self-sufficiency is usually measured as the ratio of domestic production to domestic consumption, so the self-sufficiency ratio rises from $Z/C$ to $Z_f/C_f$ (this ratio cannot be seen directly in the diagram). Finally, note that the EU receives tariff revenue equal to the area B in the right-panel (i.e. the level of imports times $T$).

### THE FOOD TAX INTERPRETATION

An excellent way of thinking about a price floor supported by a tariff is to view it as an all-in-one package made up of simpler policy measures. The all-in-one package consists of (i) free trade in the presence of (ii) a consumption tax equal to $T$ and (iii) a production subsidy equal to $T$. Under this thought-experiment package, the consumption tax means that consumers pay the world price plus $T$ (this is exactly equal to the price floor in the left panel of Fig. 8-1) so they consume $C_f$. EU producers sell at the world price but they also receive the production subsidy $T$ (i.e. they sell all output at the world price but they also get a payment from the government equal to $T$ for each unit of output they sell), so the amount they actually get per unit sold is the price floor, $P_w + T$; given this, they produce $Z_f$. The consumption tax revenue from this scheme is consumption $C_f \times T$, and

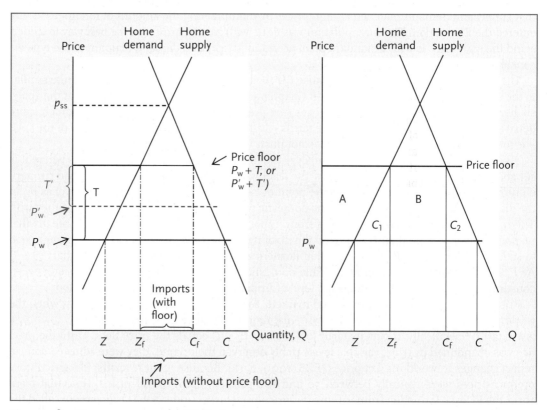

FIGURE 8-1: ECONOMICS OF THE CAP'S 'VARIABLE LEVIES'

the production subsidy payment to farmers is production $Z_f \times T$, so the government's receipt net of its payments is equal to $(C_f - Z_f) \times T$. This is exactly equal to the tariff revenue B.

This way of looking at the price floor is insightful since it makes it quite plain that consumers are the ones who pay for a price floor enforced with a variable levy. Part of what they pay goes to domestic farmers (area A), part of it goes to the EU budget (area B) and part is wasted (areas $C_1$ and $C_2$). This interpretation also applies to the analysis of a tariff, and becomes important when we think about the distributional impact of price floors in more detail.

## 8.1.2 Effects on taxpayers, farmers and consumers

OVERALL WELFARE EFFECTS

The overall welfare effects of the tariff should be familiar from Chapter 4; for convenience they are briefly reviewed in the right panel of Fig. 8-1. The higher price ($P_w + T$ instead of $P_w$) means that consumer surplus falls by $A + C_1 + B + C_2$. The first part of this, $A + C_1 + B$, reflects the higher cost consumers pay for the food they continue to consume. The second part, $C_2$, is what they lose from the tariff-induced drop in consumption. For producers, the gain in producer surplus is equal to area A. As with consumers, we can think of this as consisting of the impact of getting a higher price for the amount they would have produced without the tariff (i.e. Z) plus the gain in producer surplus from the higher sales. Since the EU would be a large importer of food under free trade, the tariffs tend to lower the world price. This effect, not shown in Fig. 8-1 for the sake of simplicity, counts as a welfare improvement for the EU.

This overall welfare analysis lumped all EU farms together, and while this is useful to get started, it hides a very important effect of price floors – the distribution of benefits among farms.

## 8.1.3 Farm size, efficiency and distribution of farmer benefits

Anyone who has done much travelling in Europe realizes that a 'farm' means very different things in different places. Consider the specific example of a farm in the Parisian basin and one in the Greek islands. On the Parisian plain, farms tend to be very large and very, very high tech. They use expensive, high-yield, disease-resistant seeds to boost their 'yield' (food produced per hectare), they apply large quantities of pesticides to control bugs, large quantities of chemical fertilizers to maintain the soil's fertility, and they use massive, labour-saving machines to plant, tend and harvest. In the Greek islands, farming is a lot more traditional. Farms tend to be smaller and agricultural equipment much simpler. As a result, the big French farms are substantially more efficient and much, much larger. Moreover, the French farm is likely to be run by a corporation while the Greek island farm is likely to be a family farm. As it turns out, these differences have important implications for the distribution of gains from price floors.

The logic is best illustrated with the help of Fig. 8-2. To keep things simple, suppose there are only two farms in the EU, one large commercial farm and one small family farm (Box 8-2 presents some facts on the farm-size distribution). The supply curve of the family farm is shown in the left panel, the supply curve of the commercial farm in the middle panel, and the total supply curve in the right panel. Note that the small (family) farm's supply curve is above the large (commercial) farm's supply curve, reflecting the fact that large farms are typically more efficient. (Remember from Chapter 4 that the supply curve shows marginal cost, so a higher supply curve means that the small farm has higher marginal cost at any level of output.)

The world price is marked as $P_w$. Note that at this price only the commercial farm would produce anything. The small farm would stop farming, since with free trade the EU price would fall to the world price, which is lower than the small farm's marginal cost of producing. However, with the

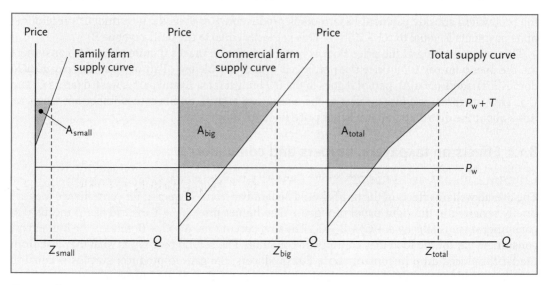

FIGURE 8-2: DISTRIBUTION OF GAINS, BIG AND SMALL FARMS

## BOX 8-2: BIG AND SMALL FARMS: UNEQUAL DISTRIBUTION OF LAND OWNERSHIP IN THE EU12

To look at the size distribution of farms more closely, consider the figures for 1987 in Table 8-1. Here the size classes range from 1 to 5 hectares at the bottom to over 50 hectares at the top. This leaves off micro farms (less than a hectare) and provides no detail at the high end. Just for comparison, note that the *average* US farm at the time had over a 100 hectares, and the average UK farm in the 30 + class had 171 hectares.

The figures show how remarkably skewed the ownership of farmland was in the EU12 (this got worse with the EU15 and will become much, much worse after the 2004 enlargement, as we shall see below). Key points:

■ At the big-farm end of the scale, about half the EU12 farmland was own by just 7 per cent of the farmers.
■ At the small-farm end, about 7 per cent of the EU12's farm land was split among 50 per cent of the farmers.

price floor at $P_w + T$, both farms do produce. Specifically the family farm produces $Z_{small}$ and the large farm produces $Z_{big}$. Total output is just the sum of the two.

From the diagram we see that the producer surplus generated by the price floor is quite unevenly distributed. The small, low-technology, high-cost family farm earns only $A_{small}$, while the large, modern industrial farm earns $A_{big}$. This should be intuitively obvious. Since a price floor helps producers in proportion to their production, big producers will benefit more from the policy.

How is this connected with income levels? The benefit from owning a farm is the producer surplus it yields, so the income generated by the small farm is $A_{small}$ and the income for owners of the large farm is $A_{big} + B$, since B measures the producer surplus that the large farm would have without the price floor. Plainly, the owners of big farms tend to be richer than the owners of small farms. This is the main point. Price floors help all farmers but most of the gains go to large farmers who tend to be richer; after all they own larger farms.

| Farm size class (hectares) | Number of farms (millions) | Share of EU12 | | Average farm size (hectares) |
|---|---|---|---|---|
| | | Number of farms as share of total | Farm land in size class | |
| 1 to 5 | 3.411 | 49.2% | 7.1% | 2.4 |
| 5 to 10 | 1.163 | 16.8% | 7.1% | 7.0 |
| 10 to 20 | 0.936 | 13.5% | 11.5% | 14.1 |
| 20 to 50 | 0.946 | 13.7% | 25.7% | 31.2 |
| over 50 | 0.473 | 6.8% | 48.6% | 117.6 |
| **Total** | **6.929** | **100%** | **115 (mill.ha)** | **16.5** |

SOURCE: Table 3.5.4.1, *The Agricultural Situation in the Community*, 1993, European Commission.

TABLE 8-1: DISTRIBUTION OF FARMLAND BY FARM SIZE, EU12, 1987

## HOW INEQUITABLE WERE CAP BENEFITS?

According to one widely cited estimate by the European Commission concerning the pre-reform CAP, 20 per cent of the farmers got 80 per cent of the benefits of the CAP (European Commission, 1994, p. 27). The basic reason is that about 80 per cent of the farm output comes from the big, efficient farms and a price floor rewards output regardless of farm size.

A little maths reveals the grave implications of this. In 1987, the EU12 had 6.9 million farms and spent €23 billion on the CAP (65 per cent of the EU budget). The 20–80 estimate meant that €18.4 billion was spent on 1.38 million farms, which works out to €13 333 per farm. The remaining 20 per cent of the CAP spending, €4.6 billion, was spread over 5.52 million farms, implying an average of €833 per farm. For 80 per cent of the farms, the CAP's spending was peanuts; little wonder most farmers said the CAP was inadequate and protested vehemently against any cuts in CAP spending. The same numbers also show that the 1.38 million big-farm owners received 52 per cent of the whole EU budget! We do not know exactly how many owners there are per farm, but let us estimate it as one owner per farm. If this estimate is roughly right, over half the budget went to help just 0.4 per cent of the EU population. Worse yet, these owners overwhelmingly tended to be the richer ones (European Commission, 1994, p. 27).

This inequity of the CAP support is worth exploring more carefully. As we saw in Fig. 8-1, CAP spending is not a good indication of how much farms benefit from the CAP. Indeed, in Fig. 8-1 the CAP actually costs nothing to the EU budget while the benefit to farmers was measured by the area A. Fortunately we have more specific statistics that permit us to refine our view.

Table 8-2 shows the figures. The first column lists the income classes. The range of classes starts with quite small farms (the average income in EU12 at the time was more than twice €5000) and ends with the open-ended category of farms whose incomes are over €30 000. Note that this high-end category hides a huge variation in farm size; in Germany, the average farm in this category had about 50 hectares while the average UK farm in the same category had 200. The second and third columns show how many farms were in each class and the class's number of farms as a share of the total. The important point here is that 45 per cent of the farms are small. The crucial column is the fourth one: 'Average annual farm income per farmer.' This shows that the income generated by small farms is tiny, just €900 per year, or less than €3 per day. That would be considered a low income even in India and China; farming for these farm-owners must have been a part-time occupation, with their family's income supplemented by off-farm work or by social welfare payments. At the other extreme, large-scale farming is rather lucrative, providing an average annual income of over €50 000.

| Income generated by the farm, by income class (euros per year) | Number of holdings (millions) | Number of holdings as share of all holdings | Average annual farm-income per farmer[1] | Average size (hectares) | Farm net value-added per hectare |
|---|---|---|---|---|---|
| 0–5 000 | 2.0 | 45% | €900 | 15.0 | €287 |
| 5 000–10 000 | 1.0 | 22% | €7 300 | 18.4 | €668 |
| 10 000–20 000 | 0.9 | 20% | €14 100 | 27.8 | €813 |
| 20 000–30 000 | 0.3 | 7% | €24 300 | 37.4 | €1 061 |
| over 30 000 | 0.3 | 6% | €51 800 | 55.4 | €1 527 |
| **All holding** | **4.4** | **100%** | **€9 300** | **22.3** | **€762** |

[1] Specifically, per unit of full time equivalent of unpaid labour. Hectares refer to Utilized Agricultural Area (UAA). Sample includes only 'commercial farms'; see text. Here 'euros' means ECU, the euro's predecessor which was used in EU accounting.

SOURCE: Table 3.2.4, *The agricultural situation in the Community*, 1993, European Commission.

TABLE 8-2: FARMER INCOME BY FARM SIZE, EU12, 1991/92

The situation, however, was even more inequitable than Table 8-2 suggests. The figures on which Table 8-2 are based included only farms that exceeded a certain minimum size. This cut-off excluded a few million very small farms. The key point comes from comparing the average farm sizes in Table 8-2 and Table 8-1. The average size of farms in the small class in Table 8-2 was 15 hectares. It is interesting to note that Table 8-1 shows that most EU12 farms were smaller than this. Summing over the first two rows, we see that two-thirds of EU12 farms have less than 10 hectares. Given the link between farm size and farm output and between farm output and CAP support, this suggests that €900 per year was more than most EU12 farmers earned. In this light, it is fairly easy to understand why so many Europeans have abandoned farming. It also shows just how inequitable a farm policy based on output tends to be.

This uneven-distribution point is critical – the key to many of the CAP's paradoxes – so it is worth presenting it from another angle. Few readers will be familiar with modern farming, but everyone has been to a food store. Box 8-3 presents an analogy by considering what would happen if a CAP-like policy were used to support food stores.

BOX 8-3: AN ANALOGY WITH HYPOTHETICAL SUPPORT FOR FOOD STORES

In most European nations, there are many, many food stores, but food sales are dominated by huge supermarket chains. Simplifying to make the point, we can think of there being two types of stores: small, family-run stores and hypermarkets. The small stores are much more numerous, but since many people do their main food shopping at hypermarkets, the total sales of the many small stores is only a fraction of the hypermarkets' sales. To be concrete, suppose that the hypermarkets account for only 20 per cent of the total number of stores, but account for 80 per cent of the sales. Now suppose that small, family-owned stores experienced severe problems and that the EU decided to support them. However, instead of subsidizing only the small stores, the EU decides to subsidize the sales of *all* food stores. Plainly, 80 per cent of the subsidies would go to the hypermarkets that did not need them. Once the hypermarkets got used to the billions, you can bet that they would engage in some pretty fierce politicking to hold on to the money. Moreover, the public might support the policy in the belief that the funds are helping the millions of small, family-owned stores.

## 8.1.4 Income inequality effects on consumers and 'regressive taxation'

For convenience, the Fig. 8-1 analysis lumps all consumers together, but this aggregation hides an important factor. As it turns out, high food prices hit poor consumers harder than they hit rich consumers. The point is very simple and is best illustrated by thinking of the price floor in terms of the all-in-one policy package described above. In particular, we focus on the food consumption tax part of the package.

Being a necessity, food tends to come first in people's weekly budget. People tend to spend on other items only when they have at least enough to eat. Clearly, rich people have incomes that allow them to buy much more than just food. Poor people, at least in Europe, also tend to buy much more than the 'bare necessities', but the *fraction* of poor people's incomes that is spent on food is higher than that of rich people. This means that the food tax as a fraction of poor people's incomes is higher than it is for rich people.

For example, about 18 per cent of an average French family's total spending is on food and drink, but this average hides a wide dispersion among families (for figures on expenditure shares by nation see www.ers.usda.gov/briefing/EuropeanUnion/). The figure could be doubled for a poor family and halved for a rich family. To be concrete, suppose the poor family spends 30 per cent of its income on food, while the rich family spends 9 per cent. Now consider the impact of raising the price-floor 'tax', by one-third, for example. Since prices would be one-third higher, we can say that the average French family would have to spend more on food, roughly 6 per cent more of their total expenditure (one-third of 18 per cent). But for poor families, spending one-third more means raising food's share in the income from 30 to 40 per cent. This would be equivalent to a 10 per cent income tax on the poor family with no price change. For rich families, the one-third higher prices would increase food's share in their budget from 9 to 12 per cent. This would be equivalent to a 3 per cent income tax on the rich family. In this sense, the price floor can be thought of as being paid for by a 'regressive' tax, that is to say, a tax whose rate is higher for poor families than it is for rich families.

In summary, the distributional consequences of using price floors to support the EU farm sector are quite regressive.

■ The benefits of price supports go mainly to the largest EU farms because large farms produce a lot (and the support is tied to the level of production) and because large farms tend to be more efficient (so their costs are lower). Since the owners of large farms tend to be rich, the benefits of a price floor are systematically biased in favour of large, rich farmers.

■ Since price floors are paid for by consumers (they are the ones that have to pay the higher price), and food tends to be more important in the budget of poor families than it is in the budget of rich families, price floors are in essence paid for by a regressive consumption tax. In short, a price floor has a tendency to redistribute spending power from relatively poor consumer families to relatively rich farmers.

## 8.2 CAP problems

In its first few years of life, the CAP was a politician's dream. By setting the price floors above the world price, the CAP provided higher prices to farmers, so they were happy. This boost to farm incomes also suited the EU's goal of fostering 'social cohesion' between rural and urban Europe. The higher prices substantially raised food production and this, at the time, was viewed as a good thing. The extra production furthered Europe's goal of reducing its dependence on imported food. Best of all, since the EU continued to import food, the tariffs that supported the price floors generated an important amount of revenue.

The only ones who might have objected were European consumers, since they paid for the policy via higher prices. As it turned out, consumers were also happy about the CAP for three reasons:

- Average incomes in the 1950s and 1960s rose rapidly – much faster than food prices – so the share of people's income spent on food actually fell, although not as fast as it would have without the CAP.
- During the Second World War and its aftermath, food was in short supply and rationed in most European nations. The memory of this – and the hunger that came with it – was still fresh in people's minds in the early 1960s. More food and lower dependence on food imports seemed like good ideas to most Europeans.
- Consumers had a great deal of empathy with farmers. As is still the case today, most Europeans viewed agriculture as a form of economic activity unlike others. As former CAP administer Rolf Moehler points out:

   At the Stresa Conference in 1958, which laid the basis for the development of the CAP, Ministers of the six original member states stressed the importance of the farming population for social stability ... Rural life and thus the farmer had a symbolic value for all those who felt uncomfortable with or hostile to modernisation of society triggered by industrialisation and urbanisation.

   There was a belief that 'as the farmer is ensuring the livelihood of society, society has to ensure the farmer's livelihood. In addition he was still representing the good old times, when European countries were basically rural societies' (Moehler, 1997).

The CAP's 'honeymoon', however, was soon to end.

### 8.2.1 The supply problem

The post-war period saw revolutionary advances in the application of science to agricultural production. This technology allowed farmers to substantially boost their productivity. The new technology involved the development of superior strains of wheat and other main crops, the development of effective pesticides to control insect damage, and herbicides to control weeds. Also part of this was the development of highly efficient chemical fertilizers and the development of effective and affordable farm machines that radically reduced the labour needed to plant, tend and harvest. Strange as it may seem today, this chemical and machine intensive technology was known as the 'green revolution'.

Since the CAP rewarded output, farmers switched to these new, more intensive farming methods. The result was impressive. As the left panel of Fig. 8-3 shows, EU wheat production rose rapidly in the CAP's first 10 years – not because the area planted rose, but because the yield jumped 50 per cent between 1961 and 1971. Similar productivity advances were seen in all the farm products supported by the CAP. As the right panel of Fig. 8-3 shows, the EU swung from an importer to an exporter in most farm products between the 1960s and the 1990s.

In most goods, this sort of rapid productivity growth would be a cause for celebration. And the first objective listed in Article 39 of the Treaty of Rome was 'to increase agricultural productivity by promoting technical progress'. But one should be careful about what one wishes; as Benjamin

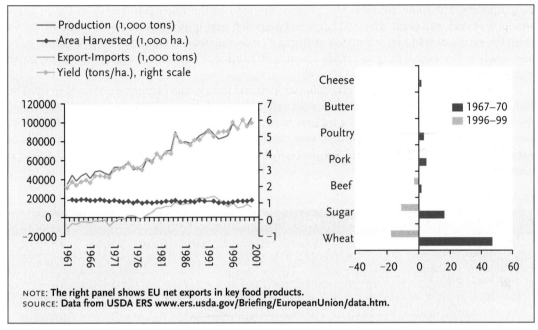

FIGURE 8-3: EU WHEAT PRODUCTION, 1961–2000 AND TRADE BALANCE IN OTHER PRODUCTS

Franklin put it, 'If a man could have half his wishes he would double his troubles.' Rising productivity has been an unrelenting source of problems for the CAP.

The foundation of the problem is the unresponsiveness of food demand to food prices (how much would the price of bread have to fall to get you to double your consumption?). This unresponsiveness means that productivity gains normally result in steeply falling prices. World prices for food, for example, have been falling at about 2 per cent per year for decades (European Commission, 1994). Yet EU political leaders did not want EU farmers to see the price of their output fall, so they set EU food prices above the world price. Not surprisingly, supply continued to rise. Indeed, supply rose so much faster than consumption that the EU switched from being a net importer of most agricultural goods to a net exporter of most agricultural goods. For example, the left panel of Fig. 8-3 shows that 1977 was the last year the EU was a net importer of wheat (i.e. had negative exports). The story for other crops is similar as the right panel of Fig. 8-3 shows. This is where the problems began for the CAP's price floor.

## EU BECOMES A MAJOR FOOD BUYER

When the EU stopped being an importer, it could no longer enforce the price floor using only a tariff to manipulate the amount of foreign food reaching the EU. Even when tariffs shut off all imports, EU supply exceeded EU demand. In this situation, the EU had to manipulate demand to ensure that supply and demand met at the price floor. In other words, the EU had to act as the 'buyer of last resort' and this meant that the EU became a major buyer of food. This posed two immediate problems, disposal and finance.

## 8.2.2 Grain, beef and butter mountains: the disposal problem

The EU had no particular use for the food it bought, so it faced the question of what to do with its newly purchased wheat, butter, etc. When the food 'surpluses' first appeared, the EU viewed them as temporary. The main solution was to store the food in the hope that supply in future years would shift back to a point where EU demand exceeded supply at the price floor, so the EU could meet the excess demand by selling out of storage. Unfortunately, the high prices, guaranteed sales and steady technological progress made investment in agriculture very attractive. The supply curve continued to shift out.

The EU continued to buy large quantities of food and the storage facilities continued to fill. The EU found itself the owner of what the media called 'wheat, beef and butter mountains'. As Table 8-3 shows, in 1985 the EU had 18.5 million tonnes of cereals stored. To put the size of this into perspective, this worked out to about 70 kilos per EU9 citizen. The result was a serious amount of spoilage, and a major public relations problem (it looks bad to pay high prices for food that is allowed to rot).

|  | 1983 | 1984 | 1985 | 1986 | 1987 | 1988 | 1989 | 1990 |
|---|---|---|---|---|---|---|---|---|
| All cereals | 4 335 | 13 927 | 18 502 | 14 271 | 11 748 | 9 146 | 11 795 | 18 729 |
| Butter |  |  | 1 122 | 1 188 | 640 | 64 | 820 | 324 |
| Skimmed milk powder |  |  | 646 | 765 | 240 | 7 | 21 | 354 |

SOURCE: European Commission (1994), *EC Agricultural Policy for the 21st Century* European Economy, Reports and Studies, No.4. Table 19.

TABLE 8-3: EU FOOD STORAGE (INTERVENTION STOCKS, 1000 TONNES), 1983–90

## 8.2.3 Dumping and international objections

Exporting was one alternative to storing the surplus food. Because EU prices were above world prices, exporters found themselves buying at a high price and selling at a lower price. To convince traders to do this, the EU had to pay them 'restitution' or 'export refunds' equal to the difference between EU and world prices. 'Dumping' is the standard name given to the practice of exporting goods at a price that is below cost. Under WTO rules for non-food items, this is normally not permitted, especially when the practice is driven by government subsidies. Until the Uruguay Round agreement (see below), however, the WTO placed few restrictions on the dumping of agricultural goods.

The problem with dumping is that it depressed the world price of food and thereby infuriated food exporters based outside the EU. The biggest losers from the CAP's dumping were the largest food-exporting nations. In terms of overall volume, this is the so-called Cairns group (Argentina, Australia, Bolivia, Brazil, Chile, Colombia, Costa Rica, Guatemala, New Zealand, Paraguay, the Philippines, South Africa, Thailand and Uruguay) as well as the USA and Canada. As we shall see below, the objections of these nations to the CAP played a major role in its 1992 reform – and they will surely continue to play a role in the future – so it is worth looking at the economics of this more carefully.

### ECONOMICS OF THE CAP'S IMPACT ON WORLD FOOD MARKETS

Even in the early days, the CAP's price floor policy harmed other nations. By shutting off EU markets to the exports of non-members, the CAP reduced the world price of food as well as reducing the volume of non-members' exports. As the EU's food surplus grew, and the EU started to subsidize its exports, non-members were further harmed.

The economics of this can be seen in Fig. 8-4. The solid lines marked '*MD* (no CAP)' and '*MS* (no dumping)' show the world import demand (i.e. *MD*) and import supply (i.e. *MS*) without the CAP's tariffs and without the CAP's dumping. The price would be $p_{w,o}$ and total food exports would be $X_o$. In the first stage, the CAP harmed the market by reducing the demand for world imports. That is, the EU was and still is one of the largest importers of food in the world, so the tariff-induced reduction in its demand for imported food shifted the world import demand inwards to *MD* (CAP). This resulted in lower export prices for non-EU members (the price falls to $p'_w$) and lower exports (the quantity drops to $X'$). When the CAP led the EU to become a net exporter, the market was further harmed since these subsidized exporters shifted out the world *MS* curve to *MS* (with dumping). Note that the EU pays whatever it takes to sell its surplus on the world market, so the size of the horizontal shift between *MS* (no dumping) and *MS* (with dumping) is exactly equal to the amount of food dumped by the EU. This practice further erodes prices (to $p''_w$) and further reduces non-member exports to $X''$.

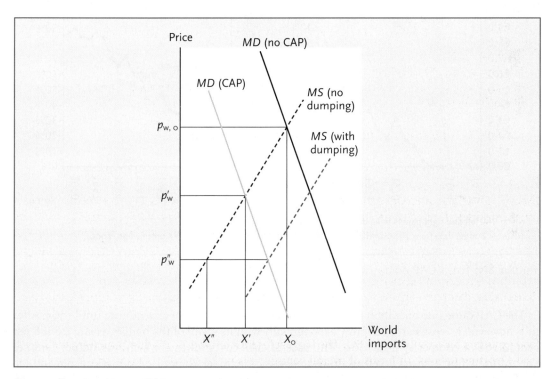

<small>FIGURE 8-4: IMPACT OF CAP PROTECTION AND DUMPING ON WORLD MARKETS</small>

Most countries practise some form of import protection on food, so while the CAP's tariffs were harmful to the world market, they were not viewed as particularly out of line with the rest of the world's practice. The subsidized exports of food, however, was more unusual. Additionally, the USA and the EU were, at the time, the only major subsidizers and often engaged in subsidy wars. (We shall study the world-market effects of the current CAP in more detail below.)

## 8.2.4 Budget troubles

The second immediate difficulty posed by the supply problem was budgetary. Instead of earning money by imposing tariffs, the EU had to dole out large sums from its budget to buy the 'excess' food. As discussed above, the EU sold the food at subsidized prices to get back some of the money spent buying food and to alleviate the storage problem. Some of this subsidized food was sold to non-standard consumers within the EU. For example, a sixth of the wheat crop in 1969 was rendered unfit for human consumption and sold as animal feed at a subsidized price. However, the major destination for the subsidized sales were foreign markets. This practice of buying high and selling low was not cheap, as Fig. 8-5 shows.

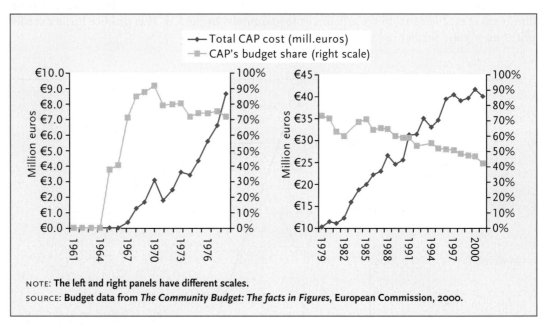

NOTE: **The left and right panels have different scales.**

SOURCE: **Budget data from *The Community Budget: The facts in Figures*, European Commission, 2000.**

FIGURE 8-5: TOTAL CAP COSTS AND BUDGET SHARE, 1961–2000

The CAP came into operation in 1962 and did not incur a positive expenditure until 1965. After this, however, its cost started to grow exponentially with its share of the budget, rising from 8 per cent in 1965 to 80 per cent in 1969. The pace of CAP-cost growth – which was 90 per cent per annum in its first 15 years – settled down to something under 10 per cent per year; from 1974 to 1990, the budgetary outlays rose at an average of 7.6 per cent per year in real terms (European Commission, 1994).

The link between the EU farm sector's rapidly rising productivity and the EU budget is explored in greater depth in Box 8-4.

BOX 8-4: THE ECONOMICS LINKING THE SUPPLY PROBLEM AND BUDGET EFFECTS

The logic of the supply-budget link underpins all of the CAP reforms that have been adopted and it is likely to rule all future CAP reforms, so we examine it more carefully with the help of Fig. 8-6.

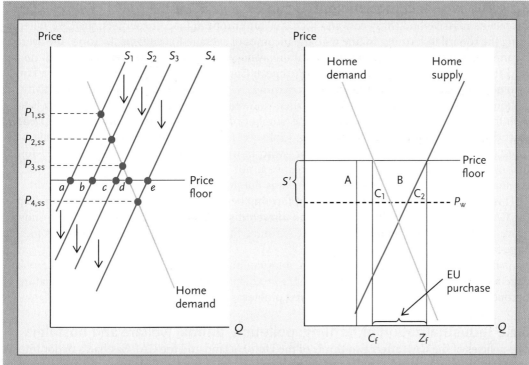

FIGURE 8-6: THE SUPPLY PROBLEM AND BUDGET TROUBLES

The left panel of the diagram shows how technological improvement in the farming market shifts the supply curve down (recall that the supply curve is marginal cost, so cost-lowering technology shifts the whole curve downwards). If the supply curve is as the one labelled $S_1$, then the EU will be an importer of food. Why? The price floor is below the self-sufficiency price $p_{1,ss}$, so demand exceeds supply at the price floor. Imports are the difference between consumption at point $d$ and production at point $a$. Since the price floor did not fall (in fact it rose somewhat relative to the world price but we ignore this for the sake of simplicity), a technological improvement that shifts the supply curve to $S_2$ reduces the level of EU food imports (from point **d** minus point **a** to point **d** minus point **b**). At this point, the EU is still an importer since the new self-sufficiency point $p_{2,ss}$ is above the price floor. Continual technological innovation – spurred in part by the guarantee that all output can be sold at the high price floor – shifted the supply out to $S_3$ and then to $S_4$. Importantly, at $S_4$ the price floor is above the corresponding self-sufficiency price $p_{4,ss}$, so the EU ceases to import. With $S_4$ the EU produces more food than it consumes. To support the price floor, the EU must buy a quantity of food equal to the horizontal difference between the point $e$ and the point $d$. We show this in the right panel as $Z_f - C_f$. If the food is destroyed or stored until it spoils, the cost will be the price floor times the volume purchased. If it is exported, the EU will have to pay a subsidy equal to the difference between the price floor and the world price $P_w$. The cost of this will be $B + C_1 + C_2$.

Next we look at one of the most puzzling problems the CAP had at the time, the farm income problem.

### 8.2.5 The farm income problem

Despite its massive budgetary cost and high 'tax' on European food consumers, the CAP failed to bring the reward to farming in line with the incomes of average EU citizens. In 1990, the average income from farming per worker in agriculture averaged less than 40 per cent of the income per worker in the EU12 economy as a whole (European Commission, 1994). While most farm family income was augmented by some non-farm earnings, farming was not a very attractive activity. In addition to occasional demonstrations, farmers showed their discontent with the CAP by 'voting with their feet', i.e. quitting the sector. The number of farms and farmers has declined steadily since the CAP's inception (see Nevin, 1990, Table 15.1, for data stretching back to 1958). This is the truest indication that the average EU farmer – who, as we saw above, had a very small farm – found that even with CAP support, farm incomes were not keeping up with those in the rest of the economy. In short, farmers felt that the CAP was not providing them with sufficient support.

This would seem to be a puzzle: how can farming be unattractive to the average farmer despite the CAP's billions? The solution lies in the uneven distribution of CAP benefits. As we showed above, most EU farms get little from the CAP since the lion's share of the support goes to help large farms.

As if disposal problems, budget troubles, international problems and the farm income problem were not enough, technology's and the CAP's productivity effects transformed the very nature of European agriculture. This created three new problems.

### 8.2.6 Industrialization of farming: pollution, animal welfare and nostalgia

The policies of the CAP affect two-thirds of the Union's land and the CAP has had a major impact on how the land is used. The resulting change, that might be called 'the industrialization of farming', has occurred throughout the developed world, but its appearance in Europe was fostered and guided by CAP spending. The problem is that industrial farming led to more intensive use of some land and, as the Commission put it: 'This had a negative impact on, amongst other things, the environment, the countryside and the quality of certain products offered to the consumer' (European Commission, 1999).

As the public's interest in environmental concerns reawakened in the 1980s and 1990s, these harmful effects of the CAP eroded public support for the CAP. We consider the environmental effects first.

#### NEGATIVE ENVIRONMENTAL IMPACT

The EU Court of Auditors produced a highly critical evaluation of the CAP's environmental impact in 2000. It stated:

> Agriculture has become increasingly polarised in recent years, with the intensification of practices in certain regions and abandonment of farming in other areas. This development has created environmental problems: nitrates and other pollution of rivers, lakes and groundwater, including sources of drinking water; erosion, pollution and impoverishment of soil; reduction of wildlife; damage to the atmosphere and to the rural landscape; and abandonment of environmentally beneficent extensive farming in poorer regions.

The basic problem was that the CAP's price support mechanism encouraged farmers to produce more than they otherwise would and the best way to produce more on a farm was to use more chemicals. Box 8-5 provides more detail on the CAP's environmental impact.

## BOX 8-5: THE CAP'S ENVIRONMENTAL IMPACT

According to a 2002 report to the British agricultural ministry (JNCC, 2002), the CAP has changed agricultural land use in four ways: specialization, intensification, marginalization, and abandonment. To quote the report, these are:

*Intensification*   Encouraged by the CAP, many farmers have sought to raise yields through increased use of fertilizers and pesticides and higher stocking densities. The associated changes in the way land is managed have led to a decline in the area of semi-natural habitats, populations of associated wildlife species, and the diversity of landscape features. The amount of available land has been increased through the removal of hedges, walls, farm ponds etc. These changes have allowed easier access for larger machinery which in turn has reduced farm labour requirements and has led to damaging effects on soil structure and functionality.

*Specialisation*   The CAP has encouraged specialization of particular crops (e.g. cereals, oilseeds and peas/beans) and livestock enterprises (e.g. dairy) as a result of market inter-vention, particularly high levels of subsidy and quota systems. Such changes have encouraged monocultures with the loss of mixed farming enterprises, and have had impacts on land use, landscape character and biodiversity in these areas.

*Marginalization*   In areas where land is of poor agricultural quality, traditionally under mixed and low-productivity livestock systems, the low returns from these enterprises have required farmers to seek alternative sources of income or to intensify production methods. These changes have led to the social and economic marginalization of farming.

*Abandonment*   Parts of Europe with poor infrastructure provision, low economic vitality, declining populations and low agricultural productivity have seen the abandonment of farmed land. These areas are concentrated in southern Member States and France, although in parts of the UK land abandonment has played a part in the switch from farming to forestry (JNCC, 2002 p. 3).

Deteriorating water quality due to the application of chemical fertilizers is a problem. Chemical fertilizers, which are necessary to replace the soil's fertility when it is intensively farmed, are a main culprit in the nitrate and phosphate pollution of EU water supplies. Nitrates and phos-phates tend to soak through the soil into the groundwater or get into streams and rivers via runoff from fertilized farmland. High levels of these chemicals tend to 'kill' lakes (eutrophica-tion) by over-stimulating water plants; this reduces aquatic biodiversity. In extreme cases, nitro-gen can be a threat to human health. In some areas where pork and beef production are particularly intensive, animal manure is even more of a problem than agrichemicals.

A second clear-cut problem stems from pesticide use. The CAP encourages its use in the same way it encourages fertilizer usage. That is, farmers find it profitable to use them in reducing weeds and insect damage in order to increase output. The problem, as the JNCC report says, is that 'high levels of pesticides reduce the biodiversity of on-farm ecosystems, e.g. arable weed communities and farmland birds'. And, pesticides may get into streams through runoff and may drift into adjacent semi-natural habitats, thus damaging plant and animal communities.[1]

---

[1] Also see European Commission, 1999, for an extensive review of the CAP's environmental impact; it is carefully worded to avoid making the CAP look bad, but most of the facts necessary to make the environment case against the CAP are included.

## ANIMAL WELFARE AND 'FACTORY FARMING'

Just as science improved the yields of crops, science has also been applied to boost the efficiency with which animal products – meat, eggs, milk, etc. – are produced.

Efficiency in this sense typically means producing the most meat at the least costs. Doing so has involved studying the most efficient density of animals, the use of antibiotics to control disease and promote growth, the scientific design of animal feed, and the breeding of higher yielding, disease-resistant animals. While raising farm productivity, these practices have moved modern farming a very long way from the pastoral scenes still in the minds of many Europeans. As the non-governmental organization, Compassion in World Farming, puts it:

> CAP has encouraged the industrialization of agriculture, giving rise to factory farming practices and widespread animal suffering. Through the CAP, animals have been taken off the land and put into overcrowded buildings, straw-based housing has been replaced with bare concrete or slatted floors and live animals have been transported over much greater distances. The CAP also pays very generous subsidies to dealers who export live cattle from Europe to the Middle East. The long journeys often inflict tremendous suffering on the animals and end in slaughter in far away abattoirs where all too often the conditions can only be described as appalling.
>
> (http://www.ciwf.co.uk/Pubs/Briefings/BR5600.htm).

Some aspects of industrial farming became known to the wider public as the result of two animal diseases:

- ■ 'Mad Cow' disease, which was spread by the practice of processing the carcasses of dead cows (some of which had the disease) into feed that was then given to healthy cows; and
- ■ 'foot and mouth' disease in which large numbers of animals were destroyed to mitigate the economic consequences; the disease does not kill the animals but renders them uneconomical; the alternative to 'culling' (killing massive numbers of animals) was vaccination, but this would have made the export of healthy animals very difficult.

Some Europeans reacted strongly against this 'factory farming' as inhumane treatment of animals. While there are some extremists, the concern has become quite mainstream. For instance, a million people from all Member States signed a 1991 petition to the European Parliament calling for animals to be given a new status in the Treaty of Rome as sentient beings. In 1994, the Parliament endorsed the petition, and in 1995 it called for the Treaty to be strengthened to make concern for animal welfare one of the fundamental principles of the EU. Indeed, the Maastricht Treaty includes a 'Declaration on the Protection of Animals' and the Amsterdam Treaty includes a protocol stating that the EU should 'pay full regard to the welfare requirements of animals'. This legal recognition is included in the draft Constitutional Treaty endorsed by EU leaders in June 2003. See Halverson (1987) for further details on factory farming.

## THE VANISHING FAMILY FARM

The industrialization of European farming has also changed its fundamental character. At the CAP's inception, most European farms were family-run affairs (Zobbe, 2001). As mentioned before, this fact, teamed with the view that rural Europe – family farming in particular – was a key element in the fabric of European societies, was important to the CAP's support among the wider public. Europeans by and large felt that family farmers deserved special treatment on cultural, historic and nostalgic grounds. Many of these family farms, however, were too small to operate efficient farming techniques; consequently, there has been steady reduction in the total number of farms, which has changed the nature of EU farming.

As Fig. 8-7 shows, the number of large farms has risen greatly by the end of the 1980s, while the number of small farms had shrunk. Interestingly, the drop in small farms was less marked for really small farms, i.e. farms that are less than 5 hectares. Since such farms are unlikely to yield a full-time living, this suggested that a dual structure was emerging in European farming. On one hand, the majority of farms provided only a part-time occupation for the millions of farmers who work on them. On the other hand, a very few large farms provided most of Europe's food and a handsome living for a few hundred thousand farmers. The intermediate-sized farm, whose owners were trying to make a living at farming, found themselves continually on the edge of bankruptcy (European Commission, 1994, p. 53).

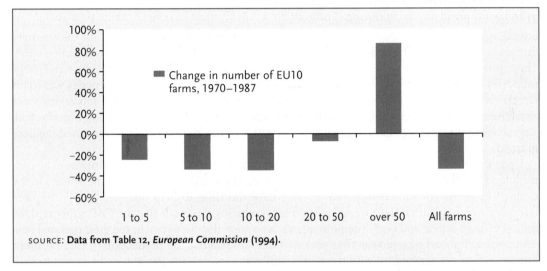

SOURCE: **Data from Table 12, *European Commission* (1994).**

FIGURE 8-7: CHANGE IN SHARES OF BIG AND VERY SMALL FARMS, 1970 TO 1987

The disappearance of the family-farm can also be seen in the most recent figures on farmland ownership. According to OECD (2003), less than 60 per cent of EU farmland is owned by the farmer. The same source shows that total farm household income is increasingly coming from off-farm sources. The figures range from two-thirds and three-quarters in the UK and Sweden, to about 20 per cent in Germany.

## 8.3 Reforms

As the analysis above shows, all the CAP's biggest problems stemmed from the EU's determination to keep EU domestic prices far above world prices. The most obvious reform solution would have been to reduce these prices. This, however, was not politically feasible.

Although the number of farmers was small – less than 5 per cent of the population – their political power was, and still is, enormous. Large commercial farmers have become used to the extra billions that the high prices brought them. Moreover, they have invested in restructuring their farms and reorienting their operations to focus on the farm goods most heavily supported by the CAP. Small farmers earned much less from the CAP but without the higher prices, many would be driven out of farming altogether. Part of the farmers' disproportionate power stemmed from the fact that average Europeans continued to approve of the CAP's support for farmers.

It is important to note that the EU's special treatment of farmers was not unusual. In the early 1990s, the EU's generosity was only in the middle of the OECD pack. OECD (1994) reports that the subsidy equivalent per EU farmer was $13 000, less than half the amount for EFTA members (Sweden, Switzerland, Norway, Finland and Austria) and about equal with that of the USA and Japan.

This political roadblock posed a reform dilemma; lowering prices was out, but buying all the excess food was too expensive. The EU's first reaction was to try to work around the problem, dealing with the surplus situation without fundamentally changing the price-floor system. As European Commission (1994) puts it, the 1983 to 1991 period were 'years of experimentation'.

### 8.3.1 Supply control attempts

Throughout the 1980s, the EU experimented with an ad hoc and extremely complex set of controls on EU agricultural production. We can point out two notable policies. Production quotas were introduced in 1986 for dairy farmers; they had been in place for sugar-beet growers since 1968. These production quotas were relatively easy to administer since sugar has to pass through large refineries and milk has to be pasteurized in centralized facilities. Another type of policy was to tax farmers when they exceeded specified output limits. These so-called 'co-responsibility levies' were attractive since they directly helped with the budget problem and tended to discourage production. One problem was that they created great administrative difficulties, which in turn opened the door to fraud.

Up to the mid-1980s, the primary way of dealing with higher CAP costs was to increase the contribution from the members. However, when Spain and Portugal joined in 1986, the politics in the Council of Ministers shifted importantly. The CAP did little to help Spanish and Portuguese farmers since their climates prevented them from producing the goods that the CAP supported the most, i.e. dairy, wheat and beef. The newcomers, who were thus reluctant to see their national contributions to the budget rise year after year in order to subsidise the production of rich northern European farmers, teamed up with the two incumbent poor nations (Ireland and Greece) to shift EU spending priorities towards 'structural spending' in poor nations (see Chapter 3 for further details). This forced the first really general programme aimed at limiting the cost of the CAP in 1988 into being.

The reforms of 1988 (this coincided with the Delors II multi-year budget plan) were complex, but the basic thrust was to institute 'maximum guaranteed quantities' for all major farm products except beef. Price support for quantities beyond these maximums was automatically reduced. In essence, the EU stopped acting as the buyer of last resort for all and any food produced by EU farmers. There was also a solid commitment to ensure that total CAP spending expanded at less than three-quarters of the EU's GDP growth. While this capped the CAP's share of the budget, it did nothing to solve the fundamental problems of over-supply. The wheat and butter mountains continued to grow along with subsidized exports, budget expenditures continued to rise, and, despite this, average farm incomes continued to fall relative to the EU-wide average.

The ultimate trigger for deep CAP reform came from outside the EU.

### 8.3.2 MacSharry reforms

In 1986, the world embarked on a set of trade talks (called the Uruguay Round) that were supposed to end in four years. One of the explicit goals was to reduce protectionist farm policies such as those of the USA, the EU and Japan. While earlier world trade talks had repeatedly failed to tackle the issue, the situation in the 1980s was quite different. In particular, instead of opposing agricultural liberalization as it had done in the past, the USA backed liberalization in the Uruguay Round. Moreover, a group of food-exporting countries – called the Cairns Group – steadfastly refused any agreement that did not include important farm trade liberalization. Throughout the talks, the EU declined to agree to any substantial liberalization. When the 'final' meeting came in December 1990, the EU's refusal to liberalize led to a walk-out by the Cairns Group.

This crisis threatened the whole future of the world trading system – an outcome that most EU exporters could not accept (over 80 per cent of EU exports involve industrial goods). EU governments began to face very serious pressure from their own industrialists and export-oriented service sectors. In the end, this pressure was sufficient to force a reform of the CAP that was substantial enough to allow a Uruguay Round agreement that was acceptable to the Cairns Group. The reform package, which was called the MacSharry reforms after the EU Farm Commissioner responsible for it, was adopted in mid-1992. The Uruguay Round deal was struck 18 months later.

### DECOUPLING, DIRECT PAYMENTS, SET-ASIDES AND PRICE CUTS

The foundation of the MacSharry reforms was a substantial cut in EU farm product prices that brought EU prices for arable crops near to world market levels. To make these price cuts politically acceptable to farmers, the EU started to pay farmers directly. These payments, sometimes called 'compensatory payments' since they were viewed as a compensation for the price cuts, went a long way to 'decoupling' production from farm support.

The economics of this decoupling is simple. In contrast to guaranteed purchases at the price floor, direct payments did not reward farmers for every extra unit of output; the payment was linked to the number of hectares farmed. While this helped to keep EU farmland in production, it did not encourage production as intensively as the high price floors did. The 'supply problem' was further addressed by the MacSharry reform's 'set-aside' provisions. That is, receipt of the direct payments was linked to a new form of supply control called 'set-asides'. To get the direct payment, farmers had to agree to reduce the area they planted by 15 per cent. Schemes of a similar nature were also implemented for animal products and the package contained a number of pro-environmental and animal-welfare measures. For example, farmers received a premium per animal for keeping the number of cattle per hectare below specified limits. Importantly, the milk and sugar sectors were not reformed.

## 8.3.3 Uruguay Round Agricultural Agreement

The 1994 Uruguay Round agreement also had important effects on EU farm policies, of which three liberalizing elements stand out. First, variable levies and quantitative import restrictions had to be converted into standard, non-fluctuating tariffs. In the end, the EU subverted the liberalizing intent of this by setting their fixed tariffs at extremely high levels, typically between 40 and 150 per cent. The Uruguay Round, however, insisted that nations allow imports of most products equal to at least 5 per cent of domestic consumption, so some import liberalization did occur. The second element was a reduction of domestic support, however, the EU's compensatory payments were not covered. The final element was a commitment to gradually reduce the subsidization of exports by between one-fifth and one-third.

## 8.3.4 Agenda 2000 CAP reforms

At their March 1999 meeting in Berlin, the EU leaders agreed to a further reform of the CAP in the context of the medium-term budget plans for 2000–06. The reforms are basically an amplification of the MacSharry reforms. That is, they further reduce the price floors and compensate farmers for part of the loss by increasing direct payments. Importantly, the Agenda 2000 reform commits the EU to fixing total CAP spending in real terms. This is new since the MacSharry reforms made no overall budget commitments and, indeed, CAP spending continued to rise during the 1990s.

## 8.4 Evaluation of the today's CAP

The reform of the CAP – in particular the lowering of the EU price floor towards world prices – solved some of the CAP's problems detailed above. One thing it did not remedy was the rising budget cost even though it did change the nature of CAP spending. The overall level of CAP spending continued to rise, but the EU now spends most of the money on direct payments to farmers instead of on buying mountains of food (see the left panel of Fig. 8-8).

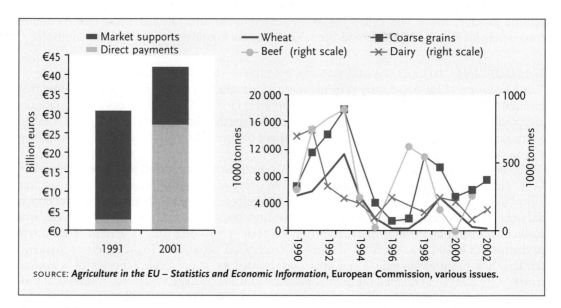

SOURCE: *Agriculture in the EU – Statistics and Economic Information*, European Commission, various issues.

FIGURE 8-8: CAP SPENDING 1991 VS 2001 AND EVOLUTION OF FOOD 'MOUNTAINS' 1990–2002

### 8.4.1 Supply problem and food mountains

Lower prices reduced the artificial incentive to produce, while at the same time stimulated EU demand. This allowed the EU to sustain the price floors without having to buy and store massive quantities of food. Indeed, for various unanticipated reasons, the world wheat price rose sharply in the late 1990s, pushing the world price above the EU price floor. The result was an impressive drop in the size of the wheat, butter and beef mountains, as the right panel of Fig. 8-8 shows. As the 1992 reforms were instituted, the EU food stocks fell sharply. While there is some evidence that they are starting to pile up again, the overall stock levels are less than half of what they were before the 1992 reform.[2]

### 8.4.2 Dumping food on world markets

Restrictions imposed by the Uruguay Round agreement on agriculture obliged the EU to reduce its dumping of food on world markets. By bringing EU supply quantities and demand quantities closer together, the price-lowering aspects of the MacSharry and Agenda 2000 reforms allowed the EU to meet this commitment while at the same time taming the lowering its food stocks.

---

[2] Readers can find the most recent figures on the European Commission's website (in very convenient, downloadable Excel files). As of mid-2003, the site was http://europa.eu.int/comm/agriculture/publi/index_en.htm, but this could change when the new Commission takes over after the 2004 enlargement.

Reduced dumping by rich nations, especially the EU and the USA, did have positive effects on world market prices. EU food dumping, however, continues. In fact, the EU members are now the only rich nations that continue to subsidize food exporters in a major way. Figure 8-9 shows that the EU has been responsible for over 90 per cent of worldwide food dumping in recent years.

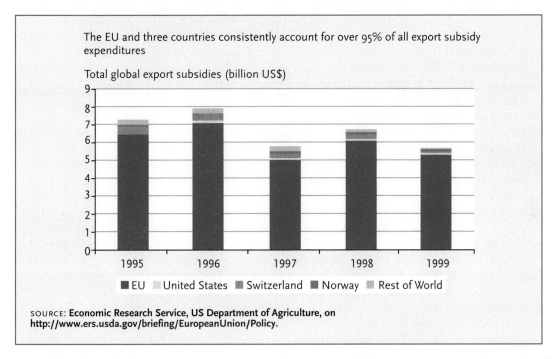

The EU and three countries consistently account for over 95% of all export subsidy expenditures

Total global export subsidies (billion US$)

■ EU  ■ United States  ■ Switzerland  ■ Norway  ■ Rest of World

SOURCE: **Economic Research Service, US Department of Agriculture, on http://www.ers.usda.gov/briefing/EuropeanUnion/Policy.**

FIGURE 8-9: WORLD AGRICULTURAL EXPORT SUBSIDIES, 1995–99

The EU dumping practice is most strongly opposed by the world's major food exporters, but its saddest impact is what it does to some of the world's poorest countries. EU sugar exports have been singled out as especially harmful.

Sugar produced from sugar cane is one of the few products in which really poor tropical nations have a comparative advantage, and sugar is most definitely not one of the EU's comparative advantages. Given that sugar cane cannot grow in most EU nations, sugar in Europe is produced from sugar beet – a crop that can be grown in northern Europe. Although the CAP limits sugar beet production via production quotas, its high sugar prices induce EU farmers to produce far more sugar than they would in a free market. This artificial production, which is protected by high EU tariffs and export subsidies, increases the world supply and thus harms sugar producers in the world's poorest nations, as the Fig. 8-4 analysis showed. See Box 8-6 for more details on the damage caused by EU sugar exports.

---

**BOX 8-6: EU SUGAR POLICY AND MOZAMBIQUE**

The CAP's sugar policy is one of the oldest and most complex EU policies. EU sugar prices are maintained at about three times the world price, but not for all production. At the high price, many EU farmers would find it profitable to switch to growing sugar beet. EU leaders recognized this impending 'supply problem' from the beginning, so the amount of sugar for which farmers receive the high price is capped. Since the EU produces more sugar than it consumes at the high prices, the EU has to subsidize the export of the excess, but again, not for all production. The EU sets a quota for the maximum amount of exports it will subsidize; anything beyond this must be sold at world prices. One more strange thing about EU sugar policy is that it actually *taxes EU farmers* in order to raise the money for the export subsidies. High EU tariffs shut off almost all imports, but again with an exception. The EU allows entry for some imported sugar from its former colonies, the so-called ACP nations (ACP stands for African, Caribbean and Pacific), but the EU must re-export this, with subsidies, since it already produces more sugar than it consumes. Note that more than half the EU's sugar is grown in Germany and France.

All this manipulation has made the EU the world's largest exporter of white sugar (it accounts for about two-fifths of world white-sugar exports). EU subsidies depress the world price and its tariffs deny other nations the opportunity to sell in the EU market. Taken together, the CAP's sugar policy has a powerfully negative impact on poor countries, especially on poor-nation farmers – a group that tends to be the poorest people in poor countries.

By way of illustration, the non-governmental organization Oxfam has highlighted the impact of EU sugar policies on Mozambique (Oxfam, 2002, http://www.oxfam.org.uk/policy/papers/32trade/32trade.html). This points out that per capita income in Mozambique is under €250 per year and two-thirds of the population lives below the poverty line. The 80 per cent of the population that lives in rural areas rely mainly on agriculture for their living, with sugar production being the single largest source of jobs in the country. Oxfam estimates that Mozambique is one of the lowest-cost producers of sugar in the world, with a production cost under €300 per tonne. Removal of EU sugar tariffs would help Mozambique directly, but even a cessation of export subsidies would be welcome. For example, the EU exports almost a million tonnes of sugar to Algeria and Nigeria, nations that would otherwise be natural markets for Mozambique's sugar.

### 8.4.3 Farm income and the inequity of CAP support

Income from farming activities did rise sharply just after the MacSharry reforms, but have risen little ever since. Moreover, the gross inequity of the CAP's farm support has also continued, so we still see farmers leaving the sector despite the spending. One unintentional merit of the reformed CAP, however, is that it forced Member States to gather extremely detailed information on all their farms (to enforce, for example, the set-aside measures). These new data allow analysts to more accurately gauge how the CAP's support system works. Recent analysis has pointed out two important problems that help us to solve the 'farm income puzzle' discussed above. First, the figures show quite clearly that most of the CAP's support goes to a narrow minority of farmers whose incomes are far above the average in the farm sector; indeed, many of them are rich by any standard. Second, we can see that only a modest fraction of the CAP's support actually makes it through to EU farmers. We address these points in turn.

#### REFORMED CAP SUPPORT GOES MOSTLY TO BIG, RICH FARMERS

Figures released by the OECD make the point that big well-off farmers get the most out of the CAP. Specifically, 25 per cent of the farms get 70 per cent of the support (OECD, 2003). The basic economics of this is easy to understand using the analogy we introduced above in Box 8-3 – where we thought about applying a CAP-like policy to helping food store owners. Continuing with the analogy, the switch from price support to direct payments based on hectares would be like switching from a subsidy to stores based on sales, to a subsidy based on floor space. Obviously, the hypermarkets would continue to gather up the lion's share of such support. In the case of the CAP, the continued inequity is even more obvious. The size of the direct payments were calculated in such a way as to offset the loss of the price cuts. Since the big rich farmers got most of the gains from high prices in the unreformed CAP, it is natural that the compensatory direct payments are at least as inequitable.

Since direct payments are much easier to track than support that takes place through price floors, it is now possible to more clearly identify the beneficiaries of CAP support. Only 65 per cent of the CAP spending goes in the form of direct payments, so the figures do not capture everything, but what they do show is an eye-opener. See Box 8-7 for the numbers.

## FARMERS ONLY GET ABOUT HALF OF THE CAP'S SUPPORT

The 2003 OECD study also examined the actual beneficiaries of the reformed CAP. In particular it estimated how much of CAP support actually ends up in the pockets of farmers. It may seem strange that CAP payments would go to someone other than farmers, but there two major sources of 'leakage'. First, getting the payments requires the farmers to do things that cost money. In other words, the net benefit to the farmer is lower than the gross benefit. The second leakage involves payments that go to other groups such as input suppliers like non-farming landowners and agrichemical firms.

When it comes to direct payments based on hectares, one euro of payment ends up having a minimal impact on the earning of farm household labour. Since the payments are tied to the land, it is the land price that soaks up most of the subsidy. This is not a problem for farmers who owned their land before the area payments were instituted, but about 40 per cent of EU farmland is not owned by the people who farm it. The OECD calculates that about 45 cents of every euro of direct payment benefits non-farming landowners instead of farmers. The other major CAP policy – market price support – does even worse. Farmers get only 48 cents on the euro with 38 cents going to real resource costs and input supplies.

> ## BOX 8-7: MOST RECENT FIGURES ON THE UNEVEN DISTRIBUTION OF CAP SPENDING
>
> Table 8-4 shows the distribution of direct payments to farmers according to the size of the farm. The most startling number is the payment per farm for really big farms.
>
> There are 610 farms in the EU15 that earn more than €750 000 a year from direct payments. These are the most efficient farms and there is little doubt that their owners are quite affluent, or at least the corporations that own the farms find farming very profitable. The numbers at the other end of the size scale are also astounding. Over half of EU farms are in the smallest category, but taken altogether, they receive only 4.3 per cent of all payments made in the EU; this works out at an average of €405 each. To put it differently, the group of the 2.4 million farms in the smallest class get about the same amount as the group of 1880 farms in the largest class – about 4 per cent of the budget for each group. The inequity of the distribution varies somewhat across EU Member States. Readers can check the situation in their favourite EU nation by downloading the original data from europa.eu.int/comm/agriculture/agrista/2002/table_en/full2002.zip.

| Size class | Payment per farm | % of EU15 farms in size class | Number of farms in size class | % of EU15 payments to size class | Cumulative % of budget (from largest to smallest) | Cumulative % of farms (from largest to smallest) |
|---|---|---|---|---|---|---|
| 0–1.25 | €405 | 53.76% | 2 397 630 | 4.3% | 100.0% | 99.97% |
| 1.25–2 | €1 593 | 8.54% | 380 800 | 2.7% | 95.7% | 46.21% |
| 2–5 | €3 296 | 16.30% | 726 730 | 10.7% | 93.0% | 37.67% |
| 5–10 | €7 128 | 9.17% | 409 080 | 13.0% | 82.2% | 21.37% |
| 10–20 | €13 989 | 6.81% | 303 500 | 19.0% | 69.2% | 12.20% |
| 20–50 | €30 098 | 4.13% | 184 100 | 24.8% | 50.2% | 5.39% |
| 50–100 | €67 095 | 0.94% | 41 700 | 12.5% | 25.4% | 1.27% |
| 100–200 | €133 689 | 0.24% | 10 720 | 6.4% | 12.9% | 0.33% |
| 200–300 | €241 157 | 0.05% | 2 130 | 2.3% | 6.5% | 0.09% |
| 300–500 | €376 534 | 0.03% | 1 270 | 2.1% | 4.2% | 0.04% |
| Over 500 | €768 333 | 0.01% | 610 | 2.1% | 2.1% | 0.01% |
| **Average, all farms** | **€5 015** | | | | | |

SOURCE: Table 3.6.1.10 in *Agriculture in the EU – Statistics and Economic Information*, 2002, European Commission.

TABLE 8-4: INEQUITY OF DIRECT PAYMENTS, RECEIPTS PER FARM BY FARM SIZE, 2000

### 8.4.4 Environmental impact, animal welfare and family farms

The reformed CAP has started to take account of farming's environmental impact. In particular, the lower prices have reduced the artificial incentives to farm intensively. Moreover, the EU has started to directly address the issue of animal welfare with a series of rules forbidding the worst practices. This progress, however, is probably only the beginning of incorporating 'green' concerns into the CAP. Environmental groups and political parties continue to criticize the reformed CAP for its negative impact on EU landscape, water quality and bio-diversity.

Since the reformed CAP continues to provide most of its support to very large EU farms, family-farming has continued to decline. Indeed, the farm-size distribution has continued to develop in the 'twin peaks' direction presented in Fig. 8-7. One peak consists of small farms run by part-time farmers, i.e. by farm families whose income depends mainly on non-farm sources. The other peak consists of large and very large farms. The intermediate-sized farms that used to provide a living for a full-time farming family are increasingly being squeezed out of the sector.

## 8.5 Future challenges

While CAP reforms have helped to address some of the CAP's problems, EU agriculture is facing two new important challenges: Eastern enlargement and the new Round of WTO talks known as the Doha Development Agenda.

The June 2003 reform of the CAP goes some way to meeting these challenges. The reforms, however, were extremely complex, so we do not yet know what their real impact will be. The OLC website for this book will post periodic updates as the relevant research emerges. The actual reform adopted and some analysis can be found on the European Commission's website, http://europa.eu.int/comm/agriculture/mtr/index_en.htm.

## 8.5.1 Eastern enlargement

The 2004 enlargement will have important effects on EU farm markets and EU farm policy. The basic point is simple. The new members are blessed with an abundant quantity of farmland that is well suited to producing the products that the CAP supports most heavily – dairy, beef, wheat and sugar beets. Moreover, a much larger fraction of the newcomers' populations works on the land. Basic facts are shown in Table 8-5.

| | Farmland (million hectares) | Number of farms (millions) | Average farm size (hectares) | Agricultural employment (millions) | Ag. share of employment (%) | Ag. share of GDP (%) |
|---|---|---|---|---|---|---|
| Czech Rep. | 4.3 | 3.9 | 1.1 | 0.23 | 4.9 | 1.7 |
| Estonia | 0.9 | 0.6 | 1.6 | 0.04 | 7.1 | 3.2 |
| Cyprus | 0.1 | 0.2 | 0.7 | 0.01 | 4.9 | 3.9 |
| Latvia | 2.5 | 1.0 | 2.6 | 0.15 | 15.1 | 3.0 |
| Lithuania | 3.5 | n.a. | n.a. | 0.25 | 16.5 | 3.1 |
| Hungry | 5.9 | 3.7 | 1.6 | 0.24 | 6.1 | 3.8 |
| Malta | 0.0 | n.a. | n.a. | 0.00 | 2.1 | 2.2 |
| Poland | 18.2 | 12.3 | 1.5 | 2.74 | 19.2 | 3.1 |
| Slovenia | 0.5 | 0.7 | 0.7 | 0.09 | 9.9 | 2.0 |
| Slovak Rep. | 2.4 | 1.6 | 1.5 | 0.13 | 6.3 | 1.9 |
| Newcomer total | 38.3 | 23.9 | 1.6 | 3.9 | 13.2 | 3.1 |
| EU15 | 128.3 | 6.8 | 18.7 | 6.7 | 4.2 | 1.7 |

SOURCE: Table 2.0.1.2 in *Agriculture in the EU – Statistics and Economic Information*, 2002, European Commission.

TABLE 8-5: BASIC AGRICULTURAL FACTS FOR 2004 ENTRANTS, 2001

We see that the 2004 enlargement will bring in almost 24 million new farms – a staggering 350 per cent increase. The number of farmers will rise by less – 'only' 60 per cent – since the average farm in the newcomers is much, much smaller: 1.6 hectares as opposed to the current EU15 average of 18.7. All three of these facts suggest that the enlargement will have a massive impact on the CAP.

Budget matters are one point of contention that is likely to arise after the newcomers have their votes in the EU's decision making bodies. The terms of accession that were finalized by EU leaders at their 2002 Copenhagen summit provided very limited budget resources for the newcomers' farmers. The agreement stipulated that CAP spending on the 10 new member nations can be no more than €3.7 billion in their first full year of membership, 2005, rising to €4.1 billion in 2006. Many experts believe that the newcomers' farms are not ready to meet the quality standards that the CAP now imposes as a condition for payments (Swinnen, 2002), so these low figures may well be realistic. This, however, could change.

CAP spending is decided by politicians in the Council of Ministers. Once the newcomers get their voting power in the Council, their farmers are very likely to push hard for a fairer treatment under the CAP. Under the 2002 Copenhagen deal – which was decided without the newcomers – the CAP spending per newcomer farm is just €172 apiece. This is so far below the EU15 average of €5000 that political difficulties are inevitable. After all, why should a relatively poor nation like Poland contribute to a budget of which a large part is paid to rich farmers in the rich EU nations? While it might be difficult to alter the CAP in the very near term, the current multi-year budget plan ends in 2006. What comes next is completely undecided.

### 8.5.2 Doha Round

The Doha Round is supposed to finish in 2004. One of the key issues on the table is agriculture, just as in the Uruguay Round. The Cairns Group is again at the forefront of the pro-liberalization forces, but many developing nations are also calling for reform. And just as in the Uruguay Round, agriculture is likely to be one of the stickiest issues. At the time this book went to press, the negotiations had made no progress on farm issues. As mentioned above, however, the 2004 enlargement will totally reorient the balance of political power in the EU's Council of Ministers and this may open the door to substantial CAP revisions before 2006.

#### MULTI-FUNCTIONALITY

One new element introduced by the EU and other European nations such as Switzerland and Norway is the notion of 'multi-functionality'. This asserts that farming is much more than an economic activity. Farmers are 'custodians of the countryside' and guardians of rural cultural and social traditions. A good example of this is the reform package proposed by EU Agriculture Commissioner Franz Fishler, a modified version of which was adopted by the EU in June 2003. To recognize agriculture's unique role, the EU wants to be able to subsidize its farmers to an extent that would not be allowed under WTO rules if farming were treated like other products. Cynics view multi-functionality as a gimmick for maintaining huge payments to the big EU farms. After all, if the EU is paying farmers to take care of the land, it is natural that the largest farms should get most of the money.

## 8.6 Summary

The CAP started in the 1960s as a way of guaranteeing EU farmers high and stable prices. Because agricultural technology advanced rapidly, and because the high prices encouraged farm investment, EU food production rose rapidly, much faster than EU food demand. As a consequence, the EU switched from being an importer of food to being an exporter of food. This change meant that supporting prices required much more than keeping cheaper foreign food out with high tariffs. Supporting the above-market prices required the EU to purchase massive amounts of food – an operation that became very expensive, consuming over 80 per cent of the EU's budget in the 1970s. Since the EU had no use for the food it bought, it disposed of the surplus by storing it or dumping it on the world market. The former was expensive and wasteful; the latter had serious international repercussions since it tended to ruin world markets for non-EU producers.

A combination of budget constraints and pressure from EU trade partners forced a major reform of the CAP in the 1990s, the so-called MacSharry reform. This reform lowered the guaranteed prices, and thus reduced the amount of food the EU had to buy, but it compensated farmers for the price-cut by providing them with direct payments. This type of price-cut-and-compensate reform was carried further by the so-called Agenda 2000 reforms and the June 2003 reforms.

The economic impact of the CAP is quite unusual at first glance. Despite high prices and massive subsidies, the EU farming population continues to decline because CAP support is distributed in an extraordinarily unequal way. The largest farms, which account for just 5 per cent of all EU15 farms, receive half the money, while the small farms, which account for over 50 per cent of the EU15 farms, receive just 4 per cent of the money. In short, CAP payments to most EU farms are too small to prevent many farmers from quitting. Yet despite the small size of most payments, the total cost of the CAP is huge since payments to big farms are big. The MacSharry and Agenda 2000 reforms did little to change this since the direct payments are related to farm size.

The CAP is headed for very serious reforms in the near future. Despite the reforms to date, the CAP continues to consume half the EU's budget, continues to tax food imports heavily, and continues to subsidize the export of some foods. All this means that the EU continues to face serious international pressure to produce further reforms. Indeed, even if the June 2003 reforms are sufficient to allow the ongoing WTO talks to succeed, reform pressure will not cease. The 2004 enlargement may redouble this reform pressure since the newcomers' economies are much more reliant on agriculture. Yet, despite the importance of agriculture, the newcomers' farmers are scheduled to get very little CAP support since their farms are quite small on average. The political agreement that fixed the enlargement at the 2002 Copenhagen summit also fixed the CAP payments for the newcomers. According to that plan, the average newcomer farm will get just €170 on average – a far cry from the €5000 or so received by the average farm in the EU15. Given that the newcomer farmers are quite poor, and that the EU15 farmers who get most of the money are quite rich, reform is virtually certain once the newcomers begin to vote in the EU's decision making bodies.

## SELF-ASSESSMENT QUESTIONS

**1.** In 2003, the world wheat price is above the CAP's target price so the price floor has become a price ceiling. (i) Using a diagram like Fig. 8-1, show how the EU could implement the price ceiling with an export tax. (ii) What are the positive and normative effects of this in the EU and in the rest of the world?

**2.** Some developing nations accuse the EU of using technical standards for food (pesticide content, etc.) as a barrier to trade. Suppose they are correct. Use diagrams to show how you would analyse the impact of such protection on EU and RoW welfare. (*Hint:* See Chapter 4's analysis of 'frictional' barriers.)

**3.** Before the UK adopted the CAP, it supported its farmers with a system of 'deficiency payments', which is the agro-jargon for production subsidies. Using a diagram like Fig. 8–1, analyse this policy assuming that the import of food was duty free, but the government directly paid farmers the difference between the market price and a target price for each unit of food they produced. Be sure to consider the implications for world prices, UK production, UK imports as well as the welfare implications for UK farmers, consumers and taxpayers.

**4.** Suppose that the EU allowed free trade in food and subsidized EU farm production, but only for small farms. Analyse the price, quantity and welfare implications of this policy using a diagram like Fig. 8-2.

**5.** The text mentions (in section 8.4.3) that since direct payments are tied to the land, it is the land price that soaks up most of the subsidy. Use a classic supply and demand diagram to demonstrate this result. (*Hint:* This is a standard exercise in what is known as the 'incidence of a tax' since a subsidy is just a negative tax.)

**6.** The European Commission has proposed putting an upper limit on the total direct payment per farm of approximately €300 000. What would be the impact of this on prices, output, and the distribution of farm incomes?

### ESSAY QUESTIONS

**1.** Compare the EU's agricultural policy to that of the USA. The EU's policy is based on price support plus direct payments. Does the USA have the same system? Which policy provides a higher level of support to farmers? (*Hint*: The US Department of Agriculture has an excellent website, and the OECD annually publishes a comparison of farm policies.)

**2.** What sort of CAP reforms are proposed by environmental groups in Europe? Choose one group's policy recommendations and discuss its implications for the overall level of support to the farm sector, its distribution among farmers, and its implications for world food markets.

**3.** Select a particular European nation and investigate the political influence of its farmers. In particular, identify the main farm lobby group(s) and show how they put pressure on politicians to continue the high level of support.

**4.** What is the overall impact of the EU's CAP on farmers in developing nations. (*Hint*: The IMF published a study on this issue in its September 2002 *World Economic Outlook*.)

**5.** Using the theory of fiscal federalism presented in Chapter 2, can you argue that agricultural policy should be set at the EU level?

### FURTHER READING: THE AFICIONADOS CORNER

A wide-ranging and accessible consideration of the CAP can be found in K. Hathaway and D. Hathaway (eds), *Searching for Common Ground. European Union Enlargement and Agricultural Policy*, FAO, Rome.

### USEFUL WEBSITES

For a non-institutional view of the CAP, and a series of readable and informative essays, see http://members.tripod.com/~WynGrant/WynGrantCAPpage.html.

The Commission's web site http://europa.eu.int/comm/agriculture/ provides a wealth of data and analysis, although much of it is politically constrained to be fairly pro-CAP. The US government's Agricultural Department provides even more analysis and tends to be more openly critical of the CAP; the pages of the Economic Research Service are especially informative. See http://www.ers.usda.gov/briefing/EuropeanUnion/PolicyCommon.htm.

Every year, the OECD publishes an excellent report on agricultural policy of all OECD members (this includes the CAP). For the latest figures and exhaustive analysis, see www.oecd.org.

### REFERENCES

ERS (1999) *The EU's CAP: Pressures for Change*, US Department of Agriculture Economic Research Service, International Agriculture and Trade Reports, WRS-99–2.
www.ers.usda.gov/publications/wrs992/wrs992.pdf

EU Court of Auditors (2000) '*Greening the CAP*, Special Report No. 14/2000.
http://www.eca.eu.int/EN/rs/sommaire_00.htm

European Commission (1994) (1994a) (1994b), 'EC Agricultural Policy for the 21st Century, European Economy, Reports and Studies, No. 4.

European Commission (1999) *Agriculture, Environment, Rural Development: Facts and Figures – A Challenge for Agriculture*, DG Agriculture.
http://europa.eu.int/comm/agriculture/envir/report/en/

Halverson, D. (1987) *Factory Farming: The Experiment That Failed*, Animal Welfare Institute, London.

IMF (2002) *World Economic Outlook*, September. http://www.imf.org

JNCC (2002) *Environmental Effects of the Common Agricultural Policy and Possible* Mitigation Measures, Report Prepared for the Department for Environment, Food and Rural Affairs by the Joint Nature Conservation Committee. http://www.jncc.gov.uk/

Milward, A. (1992) *The European Rescue of the Nation-State*, University of California Press, Berkeley.

Moehler, R. (1997) 'The role of agriculture in the economy and society', in K. Hathaway and D. Hathaway (eds) *Searching for Common Ground. European Union Enlargement and Agricultural Policy*, FAO, Rome (www.fao.org/docrep/W7440E/w7440e00.htm).

Molle, W. (1997) *The Economics of European Integration*, Ashgate, London.

Nevin, E. (1990) *The Economics of Europe*, Macmillian, London.

OECD (2003) *Farm Household Income: Issues and Policy Responses*, Paris.

Swinnen, J. (2002) *Towards a Sustainable European Agricultural Policy for the 21st Century*, CEPS Task Force Report No. 42, Brussels.

Zobbe, H. (2001) *The Economic and Historical Foundation of the Common Agricultural Policy in Europe*, Working paper, The Royal Veterinary and Agricultural University, Copenhagen.
www.flec.kvl.dk/kok/ore-seminar/zobbe.pdf

> " ... the Community shall aim at reducing disparities between the levels of development of the various regions and the backwardness of the least favoured regions or islands, " including rural areas
>
> **Treaty Establishing the European Community, 1958**

# 9 Location Effects, Economic Geography and Regional Policy

When deeper European economic integration took off in the 1950s, rural Europe was really poor. Electricity and telephones were far from standard in rural households and many were without indoor plumbing. The rapid economic growth that Europe experienced at the time seemed mainly to benefit cities and a few industrial regions. Recognizing this, the founders of the European Union made a concern for rural Europe one of the key goals of European integration as the quote above makes clear.

The problems of poor regions, however, are not just historical. Even today, there are enormous gaps among EU15 regions in terms of average incomes. And these differences are set to increase massively with the 2004 enlargement since the per capita incomes in the Central and Eastern European nations are far below the EU15 average.

This chapter looks at the facts, theory and policy connecting European integration to the location of economic activity in Europe.

# 9.1 Europe's economic geography: the facts

Europe is a highly centralized continent as far as economic activity is concerned. The area made up of western Germany, the Benelux nations, northeastern France and southeastern England, for example, contains only one-seventh of the EU's land but a third of its population and half its economic activity, as Fig 9-1 and Table 9-1 show. This area, which we call the 'EU core' or 'Core regions', is the economic centre of Europe. Although distance is continuous, it proves convenient to group other European regions into two groups: 'intermediate' regions and 'peripheral' regions (section 9.2 explains the criteria used to separate the regions into the three categories). The peripheral regions have 65 per cent of the land and 40 per cent of the population but only 20 per cent of the economic activity.

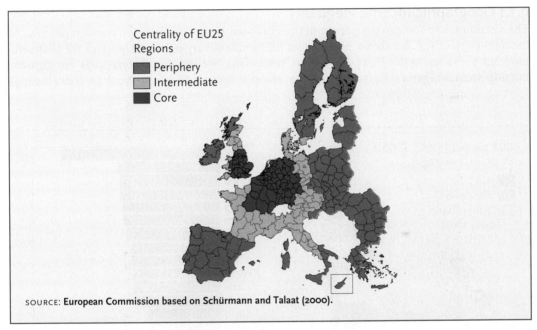

Centrality of EU25 Regions
- Periphery
- Intermediate
- Core

SOURCE: **European Commission based on Schürmann and Talaat (2000).**

FIGURE 9-1: CORE AND PERIPHERAL REGIONS, EU27

| Regions | Land share | Population share | GDP share | Unemployment rate (EU27 = 100) | Youth unemployment rate (EU27 = 100) | Share of population with income above EU27 average |
|---|---|---|---|---|---|---|
| Core | 14.0 | 33.2 | 47.2 | 74.0 | 60.5 | 88.8 |
| Intermediate | 21.1 | 25.5 | 31.7 | 101.0 | 95.3 | 70.3 |
| Peripheral | 64.9 | 41.3 | 21.1 | 120.8 | 134.2 | 18.1 |

NOTE: EU27 includes the EU15 and the 10 nations that will join in 2004, plus Bulgaria and Romania. Regions are defined at the NUTS2 level of aggregation; see http://europa.eu.int/comm/regional_policy/ for definitions.

SOURCE: '*Second Report on Economic and Social Cohesion*', European Commission (2001).

TABLE 9-1: ECONOMIC ACTIVITY IN THE EUROPEAN CORE AND PERIPHERY, EU27, 1998

Why should anyone care about the location of economic activity? There are, after all, very few people in northern Finland. Why is it a problem that there is also very little economic activity there?

The last three columns in Table 9-1 go a long way to answering this question. As it turns out, the peripheral regions score low on measures of economic performance that directly affect people's well-being. The periphery's unemployment rate is much higher than it is in the core, especially among young workers, and only 20 per cent of the people located in the periphery have above-average incomes while the figure for core-based people is almost 90 per cent. Much more detail on the state of the EU's economic and social cohesion can be found in the Cohesion reports and annual updates ('Progress Reports') that are posted on http://europa.eu.int/comm/regional_policy/.

### 9.1.1 Geographic income inequality

The distribution of income per person in the European Union is very uneven geographically. As the right panel of Fig. 9-2 shows, incomes for EU members vary enormously across the continent. Limiting ourselves to the EU15 and the 10 newcomers, we see that income gaps are gigantic, ranging from Bulgaria's €4750 per person (26 per cent of EU26 average) to Luxembourg's

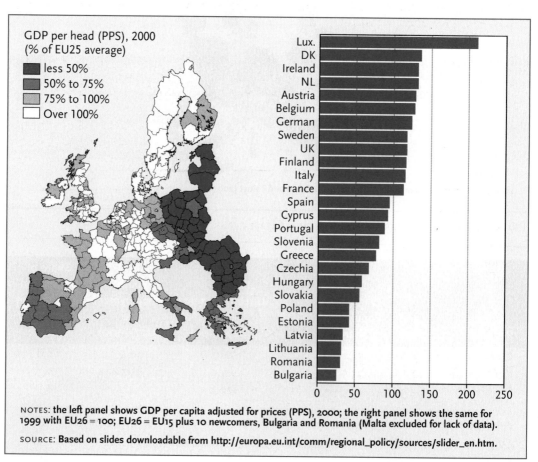

NOTES: the left panel shows GDP per capita adjusted for prices (PPS), 2000; the right panel shows the same for 1999 with EU26 = 100; EU26 = EU15 plus 10 newcomers, Bulgaria and Romania (Malta excluded for lack of data).

SOURCE: Based on slides downloadable from http://europa.eu.int/comm/regional_policy/sources/slider_en.htm.

FIGURE 9-2: INCOME DISPARITY IN THE EU27, 1999 AND 2000, REAL GDP PER CAPITA (PPS)

€38 800 (212 per cent of EU26 average). Even within the EU15, income differences are huge; the average Dane, for example, earns about twice what Greeks do.

The disparity is even greater when looking at subnational regions. As the left panel of Fig. 9–2 shows, distribution of per capita income is quite wide even within nations. The richest UK region, Inner London, has a per capita income that is 166 per cent higher than the EU25 average while incomes in the poorest British region, Merseyside, are 30 per cent below the average. One sees a similar situation in most other EU nations. In Spain, Madrid's income is 21 per cent over the EU25 average while Extremadura's income is 47 per cent below; incomes in the Italian northern region Trentino-Alto Adige is 50 per cent over the average while Campania's is 28 per cent below it. The narrowest gap is found in Sweden, and even there, average incomes in the richest region are 60 per cent higher than those in the poorest Swedish region.

## EVOLUTION OVER TIME: NARROWER NATIONAL DIFFERENCES, WIDER REGIONAL DIFFERENCES

While the dispersion of income levels across nations is still very high, the gaps among EU members have been steadily narrowing. The first part of Table 9-2 displays some figures on this, showing that a common measure of income dispersion across EU members (standard deviation of national incomes per capita) fell by 4.4 points from 1983 to 1993. In the remainder of the table the same measure shows that income inequality among nations continues to fall, with smaller drops from 1990 to 1994 and from 1995 to 2000.

| | Change in standard deviation across EU nations | | |
| | 1983–93 | 1990–94 | 1995–2000 |
|---|---|---|---|
| EU15 | −4.4 | −2.7 | −1.1 |
| | **Change in standard deviation across regions in each nation** | | |
| | **1983–93** | **1990–94** | **1995–2000** |
| Belgium | 2.6 | 0.8 | −1.4 |
| Germany | | 9.5 | 0.6 |
| excl. New Länder | 3.8 | 1.6 | 2.0 |
| Greece | 1.0 | 1.5 | −0.8 |
| Spain | 2.6 | 1.0 | 1.3 |
| France | 0.9 | 1.9 | 0.1 |
| Ireland | | 0.0 | 5.1 |
| Italy | 1.2 | 0.7 | −1.3 |
| NL | −15.9 | 0.2 | 2.0 |
| Austria | | 0.6 | −1.5 |
| Portugal | 5.2 | 0.3 | 1.4 |
| Finland | | −0.8 | 5.5 |
| Sweden | | 0.2 | 8.9 |
| UK | 0.6 | −1.9 | 2.7 |

NOTE: Important statistical redefinition occurred in 1995. Luxembourg and Denmark report no regional level data.

SOURCE: 1983 and 1993 data from European Commission (1996); 1990–2000 data from European Commission (2003).

TABLE 9-2: REGIONAL INCOME-PER-CAPITA DISPARITY BY EU MEMBER, 1983–2000

The catch-up has been particularly important in the 'cohesion four', Greece, Ireland, Spain and Portugal, with Ireland's growth being downright brilliant. Between 1988 and 2000, the Irish went from an income level that was just 64 per cent of the EU15 average to a level that is 15 per cent *above* average, and Spanish income jumped from 73 per cent of the average in 1988 to 82 per cent in 2000. The figures for Portugal were 59 versus 68 per cent, and for Greece 58 versus 70 per cent.

The convergence across nations, however, hides an important trend. Income inequality across regions *within* EU nations has been rising steadily. The other rows show how a measure of within-nation regional income inequality has changed since 1983. From 1983 to 1993, regional inequality rose in every member with one exception, the Netherlands. The same can be said about the early 1990s, with Finland being the exception. The picture in the end of the 1990s is a little less bleak, since regional income disparities rose in only 10 of the 13 nations on which we have data, but it is still clear that in most Member States, the regional distribution of per capita income is getting worse.

The 2004 enlargement of the Union will greatly increase regional income disparity. To see this, consider average incomes in two groups of regions, the 'rich regions', which consist of all the regions at the top of the income scale and the 'poor regions', which is made up of regions at the bottom of the scale. To be concrete, we take 10 per cent of the EU population as the cut-off, so the rich group and the poor group each contain 10 per cent of the EU population. In the EU15, the rich regions have an average income that is 180 per cent higher than that of the poor regions. With the 10 new members, the figure will be 340 per cent.

## 9.1.2 Integration and production specialization

The evidence presented up to this point suggests that European economic integration has had only a modest impact on the location of industry as a whole, with the many changes occurring within nations rather than across nations. Lumping all economic activity (i.e. measuring activity by total GDP), however, may hide changes in the *composition* of economic activity within each nation or region. European integration may have encouraged a clustering of manufacturing by sector rather than by region. To explore this possibility we look at region's and nation's industrial structures and their evolution. We focus on industry since it is difficult to get comparable data on services.

### FIGURES FOR EUROPEAN NATIONS

Using a particular measure of specialization – called the Krugman specialization index – we look at how different the industrial structures are in various European nations and how they have evolved. The Krugman index tells us what fraction of manufacturing activity would have to change sector in order to make the particular nation's sector-shares line up with the sector-shares of the average of all other EU15 nations (see Annex B for details).

The indices for the EU15 are shown in Fig. 9-3. The dark bars show the level of Krugman index for each nation in 1970–73. The light bars show how the index changed from 1970 to 1997. Since almost all the changes are positive, we conclude that the industrial structures of most nations are diverging from the average EU industrial structure. In other words, taking the EU average as our standard, most European nation's experienced an increase in the extent to which they specialized in the various manufacturing sectors. The only major exception is that of Spain, whose industrial structure became substantially more similar to the EU average over this period.

How important is this increase in specialization? To take one example, Ireland's index in 1970–73 was 70 per cent, which means that 35 per cent of total production would have to change sector to bring it into line with the rest of the EU. Ireland's index had increased by 8 per cent by 1997, so by 1997, 38 per cent of Ireland's manufacturing would have to change sector to get in line

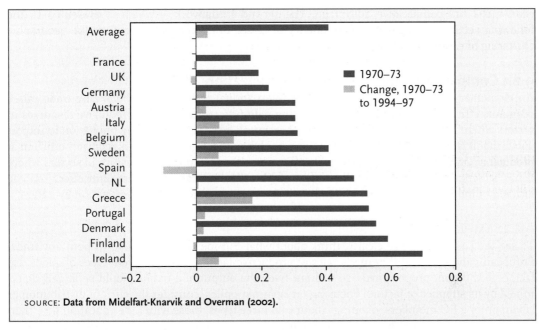

SOURCE: **Data from Midelfart-Knarvik and Overman (2002).**

FIGURE 9-3: SPECIALIZATION OF EUROPEAN INDUSTRIAL STRUCTURE, 1970–73 AND CHANGE 1970–97

with the EU average. For most EU nations, the change has been fairly mild, on the order of 5 or 10 per cent.

### 9.1.3 Summary of facts
To summarize, the facts are:

- Europe's economic activity is highly concentrated geographically at the national level as well as within nations.
- People located in the core enjoy higher incomes and lower unemployment rates.
- While the income equality across nations has narrowed steadily with European integration, the geographical distribution of economic activity within Member States has become more concentrated (taking income per capita as a measure of economic activity per capita).
- As far as specialization is concerned, European integration has been accompanied by only modest relocation of industry among nations, at least when one lumps all forms of manufacturing together.
- The little movement that there has been tends to lean in the direction of manufacturing activities having become *more* geographically dispersed across nations, not less.
- Most European nations have become more specialized on a sector-by-sector basis.
- At the subnational level, we see that industry has become more concentrated spatially (details on this are in Annex A).

## 9.2 Theory part 1: comparative advantage
We now turn to the economic logic that connects European integration and the location of economic activity, focusing on two aspects in particular: specialization at the international level and agglomeration at the intranational level.

To keep things simple, we consider each effect in isolation, using a separate framework for each. The first framework focuses on natural differences among European nations – what economists call comparative advantage. The second framework – which is presented in the following section – focuses on the tendency of closer integration to encourage the geographic clustering of economic activity.

### 9.2.1 Comparative advantage and specialization

An elementary proposition in the theory of international trade is that liberalizing trade raises economic efficiency by allowing the liberalizing nation to concentrate its productive resources in sectors where it is relatively more efficient. It accomplishes this by allowing the nation to import goods that it is relatively inefficient at making in exchange for goods that it is relatively efficient at producing. Or, to use the jargon, trade liberalization allows a nation to specialize in sectors where it has a comparative advantage. This effect of liberalization can have important effects on the location of industry. In particular, it tends to encourage sectoral specialization nation-by-nation.

AN EXAMPLE

To see the basic idea more clearly, think about what Europe would look like without any trade. European nations have different supplies of productive factors – and different types of goods use factors in different proportions – so without trade the output of a nation would be largely determined by its supplies of factors. Focusing on labour supplies, consider the current distribution of labour among EU members, dividing labour into three types: those with little education (less than secondary), those with at least secondary education, and highly educated workers (researchers). To make the numbers comparable, we compute each nation's supply of low-education workers relative to its total supply of workers and compare this to the same ratio calculated for the EU as a whole (EU's supply of low-educated labour to overall labour) – and we do the same for the other two labour types.

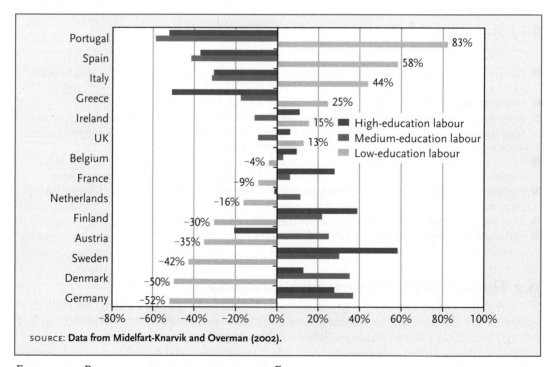

SOURCE: **Data from Midelfart-Knarvik and Overman (2002).**

FIGURE 9-4: RELATIVE LABOUR ENDOWMENTS IN EUROPE

The numbers are shown in Fig. 9-4. For example, we see that Portugal's supply of low-education workers (divided by Portugal total supply of workers) is 83 per cent above the EU average. Germany's is 52 per cent below the EU average. Now consider what this means for the price of a good that uses low-education labour intensively, such as clothing. Without any trade, Germany and Portugal would have to make all their own clothes. Since the factor that is used intensively in clothes production is relatively abundant in Portugal and relatively scarce in Germany, we should expect clothing to be more expensive in Germany than in Portugal, if there were no trade.

Now think about what would happen if trade between Germany and Portugal opened up. Since clothes are relatively cheap in Portugal, we would see Portugal exporting clothing to Germany. But what would Germany export to Portugal in exchange? As Fig. 9-4 shows, Germany is relatively abundant in high-education labour. Using the same logic that told us clothing would be relatively cheap in Portugal without trade, we know that goods that are intensive in their use of high-education labour – for example, pharmaceuticals – would be relatively cheap in Germany. In this highly simplified world with trade only between Portugal and Germany, we would see Portugal exporting clothing (and other goods that are intensive in the use of low-education labour) in exchange for pharmaceuticals (and other goods that are intensive in the use of high-education labour) from Germany.

Germans would get their clothes for less and Portuguese would get the pharmaceuticals for less, so this exchange would be good for both nations (although individual workers might be hurt by the attendant structural adjustment). The key to this 'gain from trade' is the way in which trade allows for a more efficient allocation of production across countries. Instead of each nation having to make everything it consumes, trade allows production to locate in its 'natural' place. In this case, some production of low-education-intensive goods shifts to the nation that is relatively abundant in this type of labour.

Before turning to the main point – the implication of this trade liberalization for the spatial allocation of manufacturing – it is worth stressing the logical necessity of each nation having a comparative advantage in something. The way we defined our measure of relative factor abundance, each nation's labour supplies must either be exactly in line with the EU average (Belgium's is very close to this), or it must be abundant in some types of labour and scarce in other types of labour. Thus without trade, each nation would have some goods that were relatively expensive and some goods that were relatively cheap. This type of comparative advantage, based on relative factor endowments, is known to economists as 'Heckscher–Ohlin' comparative advantage.

## THE SPATIAL IMPLICATIONS OF HECKSCHER–OHLIN COMPARATIVE ADVANTAGE

How does trade change the geographical pattern of production in this framework? In the example, trade induces an expansion in Portuguese sectors that are intensive in the use of low-education labour. Since the resources needed to expand output in these sectors must come from somewhere, trade also induces a contraction of other Portuguese sectors, in particular, the sectors that had relatively high prices without trade, e.g. pharmaceuticals and other goods that are intensive in the use of high-education labour. In the simple example, the mirror-image shift would occur in Germany's industrial structure. If we view this from the international level, the resulting structural changes would look like a shift of clothing production from Germany to Portugal and a shift of the production of pharmaceuticals in the opposite direction. As a result, the industrial structures of both Portugal and Germany would become more specialized.

More generally, post-war trade liberalization has involved all European nations as well as other nations from around the world. It is thus not possible to characterize the resulting shift in resources as simply as we did in the example, but the overall impact will be quite similar. Trade liberalization of any type – including European economic integration – tends to lead nations to specialize in goods whose production is intensive in the use of those factors with which the nation is relatively well endowed. Economic resources get shifted between sectors within each nation and, as a result, it seems as if production is being reallocated sector-by-sector across nations.

From the point of view of economic geography, this shows up as an increase in national specialization sector-by-sector. While this is not the only possible explanation for the increased specialization we saw in Fig. 9-3 (more on this below), it provides a very natural way of understanding why European integration was so systematically associated with an increase in specialization by nation.

We turn now to the logic behind the increased concentration of economic activity within European nations.

## 9.3 Theory part 2: agglomeration and the new economic geography

The comparative advantage mechanism just discussed works without any mobility of productive factors across nations. Indeed, it is very insightful to think of this sort of trade as a substitute for international labour mobility. The ultimate cause of the trade was the existence of national differences in relative labour supplies. With a little mental gymnastics, one can see that if labour were perfectly mobile but goods were not, international movements of labour would be necessary to smooth out relative labour scarcities – and thus prices – across nations. What trade does is to allow the price differences to be smoothed out by an international shift of production internationally rather than an international shift of labour.

As we shall see in this section, the story can be quite different when productive factors can move across borders and trade is not costless. In particular, a combination of scale economies and trade costs generates forces that encourage geographic clustering of economic activity. This clustering can take two distinct forms.

- ‘Overall clustering’ that results in some areas with lots of economic activity and some areas with almost none.
- ‘Sectoral clustering’ where each sector clusters together in a region, but different sectors cluster in different regions, so all regions end up having some industry.

The economic logic connecting European integration to these clustering outcomes is based on ‘agglomeration’ forces. It is worth discussing these informally before turning to some diagrams that permit a more thorough analysis of the logic.

### 9.3.1 Agglomeration and dispersion forces: the logic in words

To put it simply, an agglomeration force exists when the spatial concentration of economic activity creates forces that encourage further spatial concentration. While this may seem more circular than the straight-line chain of causes-and-effects usually presented in economics, this circularity is the heart of the subject.

There are many agglomeration forces, but some of them only operate on a very local scale. These explain, for instance, why banks tend to group together in one part of London while dance clubs cluster in another part of the city. While the study of such agglomerations – urban economics – is fascinating, it is not the level of agglomeration that interests us. European policy is concerned with the impact of European integration on agglomeration at the level of regions and nations. As it turns out, the two most important agglomeration forces that operate across great geographical spaces are called demand linkages and cost linkages (also known as backward and forward linkages, respectively).

## BACKWARD AND FORWARD LINKAGES

To illustrate the logic simply, we make a couple of bold assumptions. First, we assume that firms will choose one location (see Box 9-1 for the economics behind this assumption). Second, we assume that there are only two possible locations, a region called 'north' and a region called 'south'.

---

### BOX 9-1: HOW SCALE ECONOMIES FORCE MANUFACTURING FIRMS TO CHOOSE A LOCATION

By definition, a firm that is subject to scale economies is one whose average cost – i.e. the per unit cost – of producing a good falls as the scale of production rises. This means that firms whose production is subject to scale economies will benefit from concentrating production in a single location – think of it as a single factory, rather than setting up a factory near every market. For example, contrast the production of car engines, which is marked by huge scale economies, with the production of cheese, which is economical even at fairly low levels of output (there are thousands of these around Europe). Due to scale economies, most European car companies make all engines of a particular type in a single factory located somewhere in Europe. The reason is that the per-engine cost of production is much lower in big factories. When it comes to cheese, however, the cost reduction from having a single massive cheese factory would not lower per-kilo production costs by much. For this reason, companies tend to put cheese factories near the milk production rather than ship massive quantities of milk to a massive cheese factory.

---

The demand linkage rests on market size issues. Firms want to locate where they will have good access to a large market in order to reduce trade costs. This is where demand linkages start. Firms want to be in the big market but in moving to the big market they tend to make the big market bigger. For example, the firms directly affect market size since firms buy goods from each other (these are called 'intermediate inputs'). Firms also affect the market size indirectly because workers tend to go where the firms and jobs are located. Since workers tend to spend their salaries locally, they also make the big market bigger. For example, when a firm leaves Dijon to set up in Paris, it makes the Dijon market smaller and the Paris market larger. This is an agglomeration force since spatial concentration (the Dijon-to-Paris move) of economic activity creates forces (the change in market sizes) that encourage further spatial concentration.

The cost linkage works in a similar fashion but involves the cost of production. Most firms buy plenty of inputs, raw materials, machinery and equipment as well as specialized services such as marketing and financial services. Due to trade costs (and other costs such as information costs that are related to distance), these inputs tend to be cheaper in locations where there are lots of firms making these inputs. Thus the cost linkage works by encouraging firms to locate near their suppliers, but since firms also supply other firms, moving to a low-cost location for intermediates tends to lower the cost of intermediates in that location even further. We call this an agglomeration force since again spatial clustering of economic activity creates forces that encourage further clustering.

## DISPERSION FORCES

There are, of course, many forces opposing concentration, and these are called 'dispersion' forces (they favour geographic dispersion of economic activity). For example, land prices and the cost of some forms of labour (mainly unskilled) tend to be higher in built-up areas. This counteracts the agglomeration forces by increasing the attractiveness of less-developed regions. While these congestion-based dispersion forces are important in the real world, we will ignore them to begin with. The sole dispersion force we consider is the so-called local competition force. That is, given trade costs and imperfect competition, firms are naturally attracted to markets where they would face few locally based competitors. In seeking to avoid local competition, firms spread themselves evenly across markets, which is why we call this a dispersion force.

Of course, the pro-concentration (agglomeration) forces and anti-concentration (dispersion) forces operate simultaneously, and the equilibrium outcome is a geographic distribution of economic activity. The main axis of our investigation will be to see how European integration affects the equilibrium location of industry.

### 9.3.2 The *EE–KK* diagram

The logic of agglomeration and dispersion forces can be illustrated more deeply with a diagram that relates relative market size to the relative number of firms. To make this diagram no more complicated than needed to illustrate the logic, it is helpful to make some simplifying assumptions.

We continue to work with only two regions, north and south, which have the same technology and factor supplies (this rules out comparative advantage effects). There will also be only two types of productive factors: labour, which is assumed to be immobile across regions (migration flows are quite small in Europe), and capital, which is assumed to be very mobile across regions. In particular, capital flows to the region with the highest rate of return, so in equilibrium the rate of return is equalized across regions (or else all capital is in the high-return region). There are two sectors, services and industry. Labour can work either in the service sector or in industry and we assume that industry is more capital intensive than services. Indeed, to minimize uninteresting complexity, we assume that each industrial firm requires some capital and some workers to produce its goods, while services are produced using labour alone. To make counting easy, we say that each industrial firm needs one unit of capital. This means that a region's share of total capital is identical to the region's share of industrial firms. Furthermore, to start with, we suppose that north and south have half of the total supply of the immobile factor, labour. Finally, we rule out cost linkages by assuming that neither sector buys intermediate inputs.

With all these simplifying assumptions spelled out, we turn to a diagrammatic analysis.

### THE *EE* CURVE

We start with the demand linkage, i.e. the relationship between the share of industry in the north and the north's share of expenditure. Suppose industry – and thus capital – were evenly split between north and south. In this case, the two regions would have the same size markets. Why? Market size depends upon the purchasing power of local consumers. Since there is the same amount of labour in the two regions and the same amount of capital, the regional income levels must be the same and thus the expenditure in each market must be the same. This case can be illustrated in Fig. 9-5 by point $A$, which is located at the $(\frac{1}{2}, \frac{1}{2})$ point. The diagram has $s_E$ (short for 'share of expenditure') on the horizontal axis and this measures the relative market size of north. That is, if $s_E$ is bigger than $\frac{1}{2}$ then north is the bigger market. On the vertical axis is $s_K$ which shows the share of industry that is in the north (share of industry and share of capital, $K$, are identical as mentioned above).

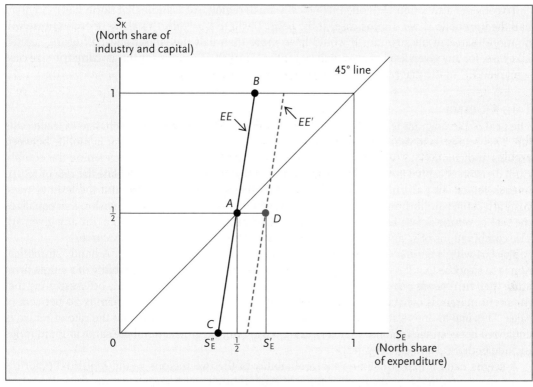

FIGURE 9-5: DEMAND LINKAGES: THE *EE* SCHEDULE

Consider what the north's share of expenditure would be if *all* industry and thus all capital were in the north. Clearly, $s_E$ would be greater than $\frac{1}{2}$ since north would have half the labour income and all the capital income. But $s_E$ would be less than 1, since south still has all the income of its immobile workers (who would be working only in the service sector). This is shown as point *B* in the diagram. In a similar fashion, point *C* shows the north's expenditure share when all the industry is in the south.

There are three main points to retain.

- *EE* is upward sloped since, as north gets a larger share of industry, its market becomes larger relative to that of the south.
- *EE* is steeper than the 45° line since the mobile factor makes up only part of total expenditure.[1]
- As far as the *EE* line is concerned, the impact of $s_K$ on $s_E$ has nothing to do with trade costs. What matters is how much labour and how much capital is in each region.

The last point to make with this diagram is to consider what happens when south is fundamentally smaller than north, i.e. when, in the initial situation, north has more than half the immobile factor. It is important to consider this case. Much of the real-world politics of EU regional policy is driven by the fears of small regions and countries.

[1] To put this differently, raising north's share of capital from, say 50 per cent to 75 per cent, raises north's share of income by less since capital is only, say, one-quarter of total income. (A numerical example may help. Suppose the $(\frac{1}{2}, \frac{1}{2})$ point means that capital income in the north is 50 and labour income is 50, with the incomes being exactly the same in the south. If half of south's capital moves north, the incomes will now be 75 plus 50 in the north and 25 plus 50 in the south. Thus the shifting of half of south's capital to the north raises north's income share to 125/200 = 5/8, from 100/200 = 1/2.)

To consider a situation with one intrinsically small region, we assume that north has more than half the immobile factor. In this case, at the point $D$ where $s_K = \frac{1}{2}$, north's share of expenditure will be more than half because north would have more than half the labour and half of the capital. Likewise, for any given level of $s_K$, $s_E$ will be higher. Thus the $EE$ curve for the asymmetric size case – marked $EE'$ in the diagram – is to the right of the original $EE$ curve.

## THE $KK$ LINE

The goal of the diagram is to determine both $s_E$ and $s_K$ and to see how these change as trade costs fall. This brings us to the second relationship between the two shares. Capital is mobile between regions and it moves to search out the highest rate of return possible. To determine the equilibrium division of capital (and thus industry) between regions, we need to calculate the rate of return in each region. In particular, we are interested in seeing how market size and the level of trade costs affect the equilibrium division of industry, where this is defined as the division that equalizes the rate of return across regions for any given distribution of market sizes (i.e. for any given $s_E$). The combinations of $s_K$ and $s_E$ that do equalize rates of return is called the $KK$ curve.

To start with, we must discuss the determinants of capital's rate of return. A handy simplification is to suppose that the reward to a unit of capital (which equals the profitability of a single firm, since each firm needs one unit of capital) is proportional to sales. How can this be? Assuming that the profit margin is constant, at, say, 20 per cent, the total profitability of a firm is 20 per cent of sales. This one-to-one relationship between sales and profitability means that the rate of return is equalized between the regions when a typical firm in either region can sell the same amount (sales include both local and export sales).

It seems natural that equalizing the profitability of the two regions would require the north's share of industry to rise as the north's share of expenditure rose. As argued above, firms that must choose one location will tend to prefer location in the big market, since this would allow them to economize on trade costs. But as more firms move into the big market, competition gets fiercer in the big market and gets weaker in the small market. Consequently, not all firms will move to the big market. The division of industry, i.e. $s_K$, adjusts to balance the agglomeration forces and dispersion forces.

To get a better handle on this interaction, consider how the $KK$ line would look if there were no trade between the regions, i.e. trade costs were prohibitive (although this situation is not very realistic, it provides a useful intellectual landmark). In particular, what would be the equilibrium division of industry for $s_E = \frac{1}{2}$? Remember that equalizing the rates of return requires equal sales per firm in the two regions. Since there is no trade in this simple case, equal sales means an equal number of firms in each region, i.e. that $s_K = \frac{1}{2}$. This is plotted as point $A$ in Fig. 9-6. The same sort of equalize-sales-per-firm reasoning shows that if north has 100 per cent of expenditure then it must also have 100 per cent of firms, and if it has 0 per cent of expenditure then the equilibrium $s_K = 0$. These points are plotted as $B$ and $C$, respectively. Repeating the reasoning for any $s_E$ reveals that the equilibrium division without trade would always equal the given $s_E$. In short, the no-trade $KK$ line coincides with the 45° line between $B$ and $C$.

But what does $KK$ look like in the more reasonable case when trade is possible but somewhat costly? To find the answer, it is useful to consider in depth why the no-trade $KK$ line had a slope of 1. Start at point $A$ in Fig. 9-6 and increase north's expenditure share by 10 per cent. This automatically reduces south's expenditure share by 10 per cent. If $s_K$ stayed at $\frac{1}{2}$ when $s_E$ was above $\frac{1}{2}$ then the firms in the north would sell more than those in the south and thus earn more. To restore equal profitability, the degree of competition in the north would have to rise by 10 per cent and the degree of competition in the south would have to fall by 10 per cent. Since there is no trade (i.e. total sales consist only of local sales), the 10 per cent increase in competition requires a 10 per cent

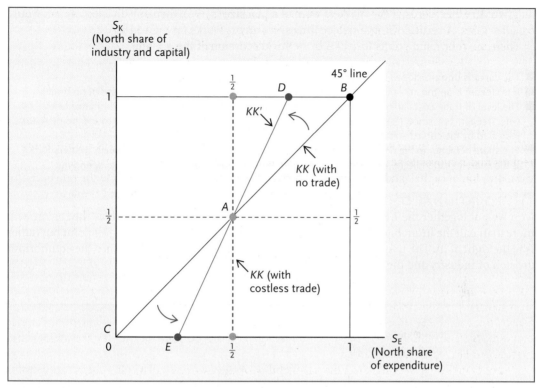

FIGURE 9-6: EQUALIZED RATES OF RETURN FOR CAPITAL: THE $KK$ SCHEDULE

increase in the number of firms in the north and a 10 per cent reduction in the number of firms in the south.

This reasoning was simple because there were no exports, i.e. competition was entirely local. Shifting firms from south to north has a more complex impact on the degree of competition when there is trade because each shift in firms changes the degree of competition in both markets. Specifically, if the number of northern firms rises by 10 per cent (by shifting firms from south to north), the degree of competition in the north will not rise by 10 per cent. Why not? The reason is that northern firms now face lower competition in their export market – the southern market – since there are fewer locally based firms in the south. What this means is that restoring equal sales when there is trade will require the number of north-based firms to rise *more than* 10 per cent. This piece of logic is known as the 'home market effect'.

Graphically, the fact that $s_K$ must increase by more than $s_E$ shows up as the $KK$ (with trade) line being steeper than the 45° line. In the diagram this is drawn as $KK'$ which reaches from point $E$ to point $D$. Of course it passes through point $A$ since equalization of sales-per-firm with $s_E = \frac{1}{2}$ requires that $s_K = \frac{1}{2}$.

How does European integration affect the $KK$ line? As it turns out, lower trade costs make $KK$ steeper. The easiest way to see this is to contrast two extremes – the no-trade extreme, in which case the slope of the $KK$ line is 45° as discussed above, and the costless trade case. When trade is costless, the division of firms between north and south is entirely irrelevant – any division would result in equal earnings per firm since each identical firm would sell the same amount in each region. Graphically, this is the vertical dashed line that extends from $\frac{1}{2}$ to $\frac{1}{2}$, as shown in the diagram. In other words, if the markets were of equal size ($s_E = \frac{1}{2}$), then any division of firm would equalize sales. A vertical *KK* line reflects this since any $s_K$ works for a given $s_E$.

There are four main points to retain from this discussion of the *KK* line:

- ■ The curve is upward sloped.
- ■ It is steeper than the 45° line due to the home market effect (except in the extreme case of no trade).
- ■ The level of trade costs affects the *KK* curve. In particular, as trade costs fall from prohibitive levels, *KK* gets steeper, but since $(\frac{1}{2}, \frac{1}{2})$ is always a point on the *KK* line, the curve rotates around point *A* (as indicated by the curved arrows in Fig. 9-6).
- ■ The share of labour in the two regions has no impact on *KK*. That is because all that really matters for *KK* is the share of expenditure, not whether this expenditure comes from labour or capital spending.

### The locational equilibrium

Next we put together the *EE* and *KK* curves in Fig. 9-7. The diagram has north as the region with more than half the immobile labour (this is why *EE* does not pass through the $(\frac{1}{2}, \frac{1}{2})$ point but rather is to the right of it). The intersection of the *EE* and *KK* curves, point *B*, determines the equilibrium division of industry and the relative market sizes. Why?

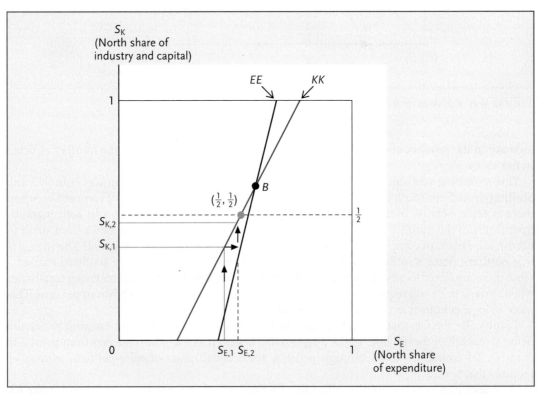

Figure 9-7: The locational equilibrium

*EE* tells us what $s_E$ will be for any given $s_K$ and *KK* tells us what $s_K$ will be for any given $s_E$. At the intersection of the two lines, the rewards to capital are equalized between regions (so there is no pressure for $s_K$ to change) and given this equilibrium $s_K$, the relative market sizes are given by *EE*.

It is easy to see that point $B$ is a stable outcome. For instance, suppose that for some reason, we started with $s_E$ equal to $s_{E,1}$. Given this level of $s_E$, the $KK$ lines tells us that firms would move until $s_K$ were equal to $s_{K,1}$. But, if $s_K$ were equal to $s_{K,1}$, then $EE$ tell us that $s_E$ would equal $s_{E,2}$. The iterations would continue, with $s_K$ and $s_E$ rising until $B$ is reached.

### 9.3.3 The impact of economic integration

Finally, we are ready to consider the impact of deeper European integration on the location of industry with the help of Fig. 9-8. As trade costs fall, $KK$ rotates counter-clockwise to $KK'$ and the new equilibrium is $B'$. That is, tighter integration favours concentration of industry in the market that was initially bigger. Indeed, in this very simple model – where competition is the only anti-concentration force – continued lowering of trade costs leads to the 'core–periphery' outcome. That is, a situation where all industry is in the big region (the core) and none is in the small region (the periphery).

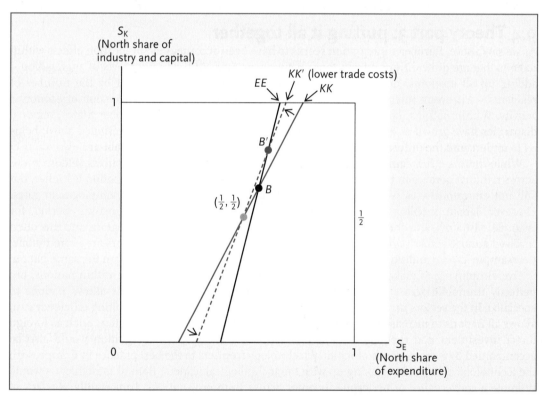

FIGURE 9-8: INTEGRATION ENCOURAGES GEOGRAPHIC CONCENTRATION

OVERALL VERSUS SECTORAL CLUSTERING

The logic that freer trade encourages agglomeration of industry in a particular region is quite robust. The outcome of this logic, however, can be very different depending upon how we interpret the resulting clustering. As mentioned above, clustering takes two very different forms. Overall clustering leads to polarization, i.e. big regional disparities in the levels of economic activity. But, the exact same logic can lead to sectoral clustering. That is, a circumstance where each region gets the 'core' of one specific industry and becomes the 'periphery' of other industries.

The importance of this comment is that it suggests that increased specialization by nation can be encouraged by agglomeration forces – not just comparative advantage forces. This is important in interpreting the results in Fig. 9-3.

### 9.3.4 Adding back some elements of reality

In the *EE–KK* diagram, local competition is the only dispersion force so the model quite easily produces full agglomeration of capital/industry. In the real world, many things, especially land prices, tend to discourage full clustering. That is, as economic activity tends to cluster in, say, Paris, Parisian land prices rise and provincial land prices fall. This geographic change in the relative price of productive factors tends to prevent all activities from moving to the biggest market.

There are many other dispersion forces. For example, some types of industries are intensive in the use of natural resources that are immobile. Steel production, for example, tends to locate near iron ore mines. Aluminium production, which requires huge inputs of electricity, tends locate near cheap sources of electricity, like hydroelectric dams and atomic energy plants.

## 9.4 Theory part 3: putting it all together

As we saw above, European integration seems to have been accompanied by location effects within nations that are quite different from those between nations. At the highest level of aggregation – adding up all economic activity within each Member State and dividing it by the number of residents – European integration seems to be associated with a greater dispersion of economic activity. Within nations, however, the opposite has happened. In most Member States, regional disparities have grown as European integration has deepened. The theory presented above helps us to understand the difference. The key factor is the mobility of capital and labour.

While there are few remaining restrictions on intra-EU labour flows, labourers seldom move across national borders in the EU. Labour mobility between regions within a nation is higher, but still not enormous – as we can see with the huge variation in regional unemployment rates. However, labour mobility has not always been low within nations. The post-war period, for example, saw a massive shift of the population from rural regions to urban regions and this often involved a move across regional boundaries. Moreover, other productive factors are more mobile; for example, capital and skilled workers are quite mobile between regions within the same nation.

Oversimplifying to make the point, think of all factors as perfectly mobile within nations, but perfectly immobile across nations. In this case, removing barriers to trade allows nations to specialize in the sectors in which they have a comparative advantage. The resulting efficiency gain allows all nations to increase their output. Moreover, deeper aspects of integration, such as foreign direct investment and mobility of students, suggest that European integration would also be accompanied by a convergence of national technology frontiers to the best practice in Europe, with the technological laggards catching up with the technological leaders. Both of these factors would promote a convergence of per capita incomes across European nations. Importantly, the lack of factor mobility across nations means that agglomeration forces are not dominant at the national level. That is to say, the cycles of circular causality that might lead all economic activity to leave a region have no chance of starting. This conclusion must be modified to allow for sector-specific clusters. Even if productive factors do not move across national boundaries, agglomeration forces operating at the sectoral level could result in nations specializing in particular industries. For example, deeper integration could foster greater geographic clustering of, say, the chemicals industry and the car industry, but in the end each nation ends up with some industry.

By contrast, the much greater mobility of factors within nations permits backward and forward linkages to operate. As one region grows, it becomes attractive to firms for demand reasons and cost reasons, so more firms and more factors move to the region thereby fuelling further growth.

## 9.4.1 Regional unemployment

The analysis so far has assumed that wages are flexible enough to ensure full employment of all labour. Since regional unemployment is a serious problem in Europe, we turn to the economic logic connecting delocation and unemployment. As usual, we follow the principle of progressive complexity by starting simple.

If wages were adjusted instantaneously across time and space, we would have no unemployment. The wage rate paid for each hour of work would adjust so that the amount of labour that workers would like to supply at that price just matched to the amount that firms would like to 'buy' (hire). In this hypothetical world, the wages would instantaneously jump to the market-clearing level, i.e. the level where labour supply matches labour demand. Things are not that simple, however.

For many reasons, most European nations have decide to prevent the wage – the 'price' of labour – from jumping around like the price of crude oil or government bonds. (See Chapter 7 for a more formal treatment of unemployment.) All sorts of labour market institutions, ranging from trade unions and unemployment benefits to minimum wages and employment protection legislation mean that the price of labour is systematically stabilized at a level that exceeds the market-clearing wage level. The direct logical consequence is that workers systematically want to offer more labour at the going wage than firms are willing to hire; this is the definition of unemployment. As in any market, if the price is fixed too high, the amount offered for sale will exceed the amount that is bought.

In most European nations, there is a strong spatial element to this price-fixing of labour. Take Germany for example. For many reasons, labour productivity in the eastern Länder is lower than it is in the western Länder. Thus, firms would only be willing to employ all the eastern labour offered, if wages were lower in the east. However, German labour unions have methodically prevented eastern wages from falling to their market-clearing level, either in an attempt to avoid downward pressure on their own wages, or, more charitably, in the spirit of solidarity with the eastern workers who actually do get employed. Whatever the source of regional wage inflexibility, its logical consequence is regional unemployment. Moreover, since firms can leave a region much more easily than workers, a continual within-nation clustering of economic activity will tend to be associated with high levels of unemployment in the contracting regions and low levels in the expanding regions.

Finally, it should be clear that this sort of mismatch of migration speeds (firms move faster than workers) – teamed with a lack of regional wage flexibility – has the effect of creating an agglomeration force. A little shift of industry raises unemployment in the contracting region and lowers it in the expanding region. Since unemployment is an important factor in workers' migration decisions, the initial shift makes workers more likely to migrate to the expanding region. Such migration, however, changes the relative market sizes in a way that tends to encourage more firms to leave the contracting region. (For a detailed account of geographical clustering of unemployment in Europe, see Overman and Puga, 2001).

## 9.4.2 Peripherality and real geography

Our theoretical discussion has intentionally simplified physical geography considerations by working with only two nations, both of which are thought of as points in space. Real-world geography, of course, is much more interesting and this matters for the location of economic activity. We can use the basic logic of demand-linked agglomeration forces to consider how one can put real geography back into the picture.

As discussed above, firms that want to concentrate production in a single location tend, other things being equal, to locate in a place that minimizes transportation costs. With only two markets, this means locating in the bigger market, but when the economic activity is spread out over real geography, the answer can be less obvious. However, the fact that economic activity is highly concentrated in Europe makes the problem easier. As the map in Fig. 9-1 and numbers in Table 9-1 show, locating somewhere in the core is likely to be the transport-cost minimizing solution.

Indeed, thinking about how the regions in the Fig. 9-1 map were allocated to the three categories (core, intermediate and peripheral) helps to sharpen our thinking about how one applies the agglomeration logic to Europe. The map is actually based on the 'accessibility measure' for each region, where accessibility means being close to other regions that have a lot of economic activity. For example, to calculate the accessibility of the region that contains Paris, the Ile de France, one calculates how long it would take to get from the centre of Paris to the main urban centre of every other region in the EU (the calculation varies somewhat according to the form of transport used, which the map assumes to be lorries). Finally, one weights each of these transport times by the destination region's share of the EU's total economic activity. Adding up these weighted times gives us an idea of how close Paris is to the bulk of EU economic activity. Doing the same for every other region gives us an index of accessibility by region. The regions that have accessibility indices more than 40 per cent above the EU average are considered to be core regions. Those with indices that are more than 75 per cent below the average are considered to be peripheral and those in between are considered to be intermediate.

## 9.5 EU regional policy

As mentioned in the introduction, a concern for Europe's disadvantaged regions has always been a headline goal of the European Union. For the first three and a half decades of the EU's existence, however, the task of helping less-favoured regions was left firmly in the hands of national governments. All European nations, both inside and outside the EU, spent huge sums on rural infrastructure. During the 1950s, 1960s and 1970s, national governments extended their electricity and telephone grids to every city, town, village and farmhouse. They built roads, rails and provincial universities in an effort to develop their less-favoured regions. In many cases, modern banking was extended to the rural community via the state-owned PTTs (Post, Telephone and Telegraph).

The EEC, as it was known at the time, did have some programmes for rural regions, but despite real poverty in some members' regions – like Italy's Mezzogiorno – the level of EU funding was negligible. Structural spending was only 3 per cent of the budget in 1970, rising to only 11 per cent by 1980. To the extent that the EEC was involved in helping rural communities at all, it did so by artificially raising the price of agricultural goods via the Common Agricultural Policy (CAP), as pointed out in Chapter 8. In the Union's first decade, the EU's budget consisted of little more than the CAP and administrative expenses.

Major EU funding for less-favoured regions would have to wait for a change in Community politics. When the first 'poor' member, Ireland, joined in 1973, a new fund – the European Regional Development Fund (ERDF) – was set up to redistribute money to the poorest regions, but its budget was minor. The situation changed in the 1980s when the EU admitted three new members, Greece, Spain and Portugal. These nations were substantially poorer than the incumbent members, and, importantly, their farmers did not produce the goods that the CAP supported most heavily (mainly wheat, sugar, dairy and beef). If these nations were to benefit financially from the EU's budget, EU spending priorities would have to be changed.

As it turned out, the voting power of Spain and Portugal, teamed with the votes of Ireland and Greece, was sufficient to produce a major realignment of EU spending priorities (see Chapter 2 for an analysis of how power politics shapes the EU budget). During the Iberian accession talks, the EU promised to substantially increase spending on poor regions. The official rationale for this increase was the assertion that economic integration implied by the 1986 Single European Act favoured Europe's industrial core. As the Commission's website puts it, the policy was 'designed to offset the burden of the single market for southern countries and other less-favoured regions'. Whether the real motive for the big increase in regional spending was power politics, a newfound concern for less-favoured regions, or a combination of the two, the fact is that EU spending on poor regions rose sharply in the mid- to late-1980s, as Fig. 9-9 shows.

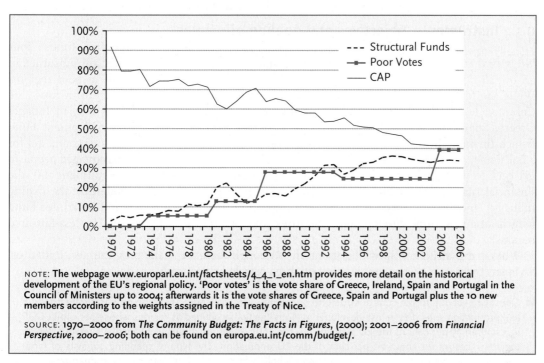

NOTE: The webpage www.europarl.eu.int/factsheets/4_4_1_en.htm provides more detail on the historical development of the EU's regional policy. 'Poor votes' is the vote share of Greece, Ireland, Spain and Portugal in the Council of Ministers up to 2004; afterwards it is the vote shares of Greece, Spain and Portugal plus the 10 new members according to the weights assigned in the Treaty of Nice.

SOURCE: **1970–2000** from *The Community Budget: The Facts in Figures*, **(2000)**; 2001–2006 from *Financial Perspective, 2000–2006*; both can be found on europa.eu.int/comm/budget/.

FIGURE 9-9: EU BUDGETARY EXPENDITURES, 1965–2006, CAP VS STRUCTURAL FUNDS

When the issue of monetary union was raised in talks leading up to the Maastricht Treaty, the 'poor-4' again managed to obtain a significant increase in regional spending via the creation of a new fund (the Cohesion Fund) that could be spent only in Greece, Ireland, Spain and Portugal. Again, the justification was that tighter economic integration would mostly favour Europe's industrial core, so peripheral regions should be compensated by a big increase in EU money for poor regions, what is known as 'structural spending' in EU jargon. The practical outcome was that structural spending doubled its share of the EU budget between 1986 and 1993.

This link between the political power of poor countries and the budget is clear to see in Fig. 9-9. The share of the EU budget going to poor regions rises in tandem with the share of poor countries' votes in the Council of Ministers. Up to the most recent enlargement, when Austria, Finland and Sweden joined, the correlation was remarkably good. Since 1994, however, the connection between poor nations and structural spending has been greatly diluted. Large parts of Finland and Sweden were designated as eligible, and even some Austrian regions, together with all of the former East Germany, were deemed as poor. The figure also projects the power of 'poor nations' after the 10 new members have joined, and compares this vote share to the budget projections in the EU's long-term budget plan. As we see, power and spending seem set to continue their co-movement.

### 9.5.1 Politics and the allocation of EU regional spending

The EU now spends about a third of its budget on less-favoured regions (about €200 billion over the seven-year budget planning period, 2000–06). How is this money allocated? As mentioned above, politics plays a role, but the EU does have a set of guidelines, objectives and principles that help to channel the spending to where it will do the most good. Here we just touch upon the main points (see http://europa.eu.int/comm/regional_policy/ for further details).

### 9.5.2 Instruments, objectives and guiding principles

For historical reasons, most EU regional spending is channelled through five 'funds': four 'Structural Funds' and the 'Cohesion Fund'. Although there are five funds, they are subsumed in an overall strategy aimed at fighting unemployment and stimulating growth in poor regions. While the four Structural Funds can be spent in any qualified EU region, the fifth fund, the Cohesion Fund, directly funds individual environment and transport projects only in Ireland, Greece, Spain and Portugal. The four funds are: the European Regional Development Fund (which finances infrastructure, job-creating investments, local development projects and aid for small firms), the European Social Fund (which helps the unemployed and disadvantaged people to get back to work, mainly by financing training measures and systems of recruitment aid), the Financial Instrument for Fisheries Guidance (which helps to adapt and modernize the fishing industry), and the Guidance Section of the European Agricultural Guidance and Guarantee Fund (which finances rural development measures and aid for farmers, mainly in less-favoured regions).

What is this structural spending spent on? Although there are many programmes, initiatives, and objectives, over 90 per cent is spent on three priority 'objectives'.

- *Objective 1* (about 70 per cent of structural spending). This concerns spending on basic infrastructure and production subsidies in less-developed regions (generally defined as regions whose per capita GDP is less than 75 per cent of the EU average). In the EU15, there are about 50 Objective 1 regions, which together account for about 20 per cent of the EU population. The type of spending consists of infrastructures (30 per cent), of which approximately half is for transport infrastructures, human resources (30 per cent), with priority given to employment policies and education and training systems, and aid for the production sectors (42 per cent).
- *Objective 2* (about 10 per cent of structural spending). This concerns projects in regions whose economies are specialized in declining sectors such as coal mining, fishing and steel production. The spending is supposed to support economic and social 'conversion', i.e. shifting employment and investment to more promising activities; about 18 per cent of the Union's population lives in 'Objective 2' regions. According to the rules, two-thirds of the population covered by this should come from industrial or urban areas; rural or fisheries-dependent regions account for the remaining third.
- *Objective 3* (about 10 per cent of the funding). This concerns measures aimed at modernizing national systems of training and employment promotion. It covers all EU regions, excluding Objective 1 regions. Eligible measures are broadly defined, e.g. active labour market policies to fight unemployment, the promotion of social inclusion and equal opportunities for men and women, and employability via lifelong education systems.

Which regions are eligible? As it turns out, most of EU15 is considered a less-favoured region in the sense of being eligible for structural spending under either Objective 1 or Objective 2.

#### GUIDING PRINCIPLES

The Structural Funds are not spent on projects chosen at the European level. The choice of projects and their management are solely the responsibility of the national and regional authorities. The projects, however, are co-financed from both national and Community funds. As a matter of principle, the so-called additionality principle, Community funding should not be used to economize on national funds. This principle is naturally difficult to verify; national budgetary priorities change frequently, so it is hard to know how much the members would have spent if the Community funding were not available.

Besides additionality, the structural spending is characterized by five other basic rules.

- *Concentration*: The spending should be geographically concentrated.
- *Programme planning*: Spending should be in the context of broad development programmes that are drawn up by EU members and approved by the Commission.
- *Partnership*: The Commission, the Member State concerned, the regional and local authorities, industry, and labour unions should co-operate in the spending.
- *Monitoring and evaluation*: The spending should be monitored and evaluated.
- *Consistency and complementarity*: The spending should be consistent with the provisions of the Treaties and other Community policies such as the Single Market, the CAP and the Common Fisheries Policy.

### 9.5.3 Political allocation

As part of its responsibilities within the framework of Structural Funds management, the European Commission takes decisions on the concrete implementation of the regulations. This includes allocating the money by Objective and by EU member. The outcome of the most recent deal is shown in Table 9-3. Note that this is set years in advance.

| | Objective 1 | Objective 2 | Total | Share |
|---|---|---|---|---|
| Spain | 37 744 | 2 553 | 43 087 | 23% |
| Italy | 21 935 | 2 145 | 28 484 | 16% |
| Germany | 19 229 | 2 984 | 28 156 | 15% |
| Greece | 20 961 | 0 | 20 961 | 11% |
| Portugal | 16 124 | 0 | 19 029 | 10% |
| UK | 5 085 | 2 989 | 15 635 | 9% |
| France | 3 254 | 5 437 | 14 620 | 8% |
| Ireland | 1 315 | 0 | 3 088 | 2% |
| NL | 0 | 676 | 2 635 | 1% |
| Sweden | 722 | 354 | 1 908 | 1% |
| Finland | 913 | 459 | 1 836 | 1% |
| Belgium | 0 | 368 | 1 829 | 1% |
| Austria | 261 | 578 | 1 473 | 1% |
| Denmark | 0 | 156 | 745 | 0% |
| Luxembourg | 0 | 34 | 78 | 0% |
| **EU15** | **127 543** | **18 733** | **183 564** | **100%** |

SOURCE: Commission Decision fixing an indicative allocation by Member State of the commitment appropriations for Objective 1 of the Structural Funds for the period 2000 to 2006. Downloadable from europa.eu.int/comm/regional_policy/sources/slides/Zir_en.ppt

TABLE 9-3: COUNTRY ALLOCATIONS IN THE FINANCIAL PERSPECTIVE, 2000–06

### 9.5.4 The great debate: the impact of Eastern enlargement

If all goes according to plan, 10 new members will be in the EU in 2004. With the exception of two tiny nations (Cyprus and Slovenia), all the new entrants have national per capita incomes that are below that of Greece, the poorest of the incumbent 15. In principle, this would make another 75 million people eligible for Objective 1 spending. Moreover, if the EU stays with the 75 per cent rule for Objective 1 eligibility, the entry of the newcomers will push out many of the current Objective 1 regions. Quite simply, Eastern enlargement will make many regions in the incumbent 15 look rich, since the newcomers will drag down the average EU income substantially.

It seems clear that the 2004 enlargement will reorient EU spending priorities, just as the entry of Spain and Portugal did. A quick look at what the EU15 leaders decided to allocate to the 10 new members reveals the magnitude of the potential problems. At the Copenhagen European Council meeting in 2002, EU leaders set down indicative amounts of aid for each of the 10 newcomers. As Fig. 9-10 shows, the average annual allocation for the CC10 (10 candidate countries that will join in 2004) are not low compared to the EU15 as a whole, but they are substantially lower than what is allocated to the poor EU members. And much lower than might be expected if the newcomers were treated in the same way as incumbents. How much lower?

The line in the figure shows how cohesion-cash-per-person and per capita income are related in the EU15 (as usual, Luxembourg's extraordinarily high income makes it an outlier, so we exclude it when fitting the cash–income line). This 'trend line' has a negative slope as expected, since in the EU15, cohesion-cash-per-person rises as a nation's income falls. The line shows the average relationship. Observe that the promised treatment of every single newcomer is below this line (each entrant is represented by a circle). That is, given how poor they are, the income-cohesion-cash link in the EU15 suggests that they should get much more than the poor nations in the EU15. To illustrate this point, the diagram plots the 'equal treatment' cohesion-cash-per-person that is

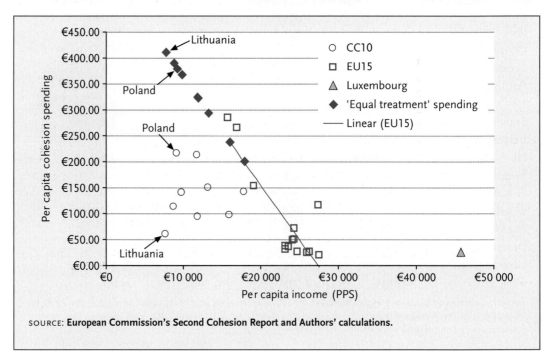

SOURCE: **European Commission's Second Cohesion Report and Authors' calculations.**

FIGURE 9-10: COHESION SPENDING AND INCOME LEVELS, EU15 VS CC10

predicted by the trend line; the predictions are shown with dark diamonds. Just to illustrate the point, Lithuania (the poorest of the newcomers) and Poland (the biggest of the newcomers) are identified explicitly. What this projection suggests is that Poland would have received €380 per person under 'equal treatment' instead of just €214. Lithuania would had received €411 instead of the €69 it was actually allocated.

The situation could change, of course. Once the 10 newcomers have voting rights in the Council of Ministers, in the Parliament, and in the Commission, pressure is likely to mount for a change in the allocation of structural spending.

## 9.6 Empirical evidence

The chapter has stressed three main determinants of the location of economic activity: regional policy and two purely economic determinants (comparative advantage and agglomeration). We now consider the importance of these three forces.

To evaluate the determinants of industrial location in the EU, researchers try to explain how regional and national shares of various types of manufacturing vary with regional and national characteristics, where it is useful to divide the national characteristics into three broad groups: relative labour supplies, economic geography features, and policies affecting industrial location.

For instance, the theory section explained why we should expect nations that have a relatively high share of the EU's skilled labour to also have a relatively high share of EU's manufacturing sectors that are relatively intensive in their use of skilled labour. The same link should be expected for relative endowments of other types of labour – low-skilled and medium-skilled workers – and sectors that use these types of labour intensively as well as regional endowments of agricultural land and industries that use agricultural inputs intensively.

The theory section also explained that the spatial allocation of demand affects the location of industry since sectors where firms tend to concentrate production in a single location (i.e. those marked by important economies of scale) will tend to favour locations that are near large markets. This so-called demand linkage (firms want to be near the demands for their goods) is complemented by so-called supply linkages – that is, firms in sectors that use lots of intermediate inputs will tend to favour locations with concentrations of their suppliers.

Finally, policy can directly encourage the location of particular types of sectors in particular locations and this effect can either amplify or dampen the impact of factor endowments and economic geography factors on the location of industry.

Although the research in this area is limited – mainly due to a lack of data on the location of manufacturing and regional labour endowments – the results so far suggest that all three factors matter. Interestingly, it seems that labour endowments have become more important in determining location as European economic integration has become tighter. One of the two agglomeration forces – namely, supply linkages – seems to be getting stronger, while the demand linkage is getting weaker. (See Redding, Overman and Venables, 2001, for a survey of empirical results. This can be downloaded from http://econ.lse.ac.uk/staff/ajv/research_material.html.)

Given that EU regional policy has been operating at a significant level only since the mid-1980s, results on the impact of policy are even more tenuous. The best study in this area, Midelfart-Knarvik and Overman (2002), finds that EU policy has significantly affected the geographical location of industry. In particular, these authors find that EU structural spending did affect the location of high-skilled intensive industries. For an integrated survey of the empirical evidence, see Combes and Overman (2003).

## 9.7 **Summary**

Europe's economic activity is highly concentrated geographically at the national level as well as within nations. This is a problem for social cohesion since people located in the 'core' enjoy higher incomes and lower unemployment rates. European integration seems to have led to a narrowing of income equality across nations, but an increase in inequality within nations. Nevertheless, European integration has been accompanied by only modest relocation of industry among nations, but the little movement we have seen has been in the direction of manufacturing activities having become *more* geographically dispersed, not less, while most European nations have become more specialized on a sector-by-sector basis.

The chapter presents two main theories that could account for these facts. The first – the comparative advantage framework – explains why nations have become more specialized while at the same time income differences have narrowed. The second – based on the so-called new economic geography – focuses on agglomeration forces that account for the way in which tighter economic integration can foster the clustering of economic activities within nations.

The chapter also presents the main outlines of the EU's regional policy. The goal of this policy is to help to disperse economic activity to less-favoured regions. Most of the money is spent on so-called 'Objective 1' regions that typically have per capita incomes that are less than 75 per cent of the EU average. The EU spends about a third of its budget on these policies. The 2004 enlargement will engender enormous changes for the EU's regional policies. All but two of the 10 newcomers are poorer than the poorest EU15 member. This will make the poor regions in the incumbent nations look relatively rich, as well as increasing the cost of the EU's regional policies.

### SELF-ASSESSMENT QUESTIONS

**1.** Show how the slope of the *KK*-line in Fig. 9-7 would change if agglomeration forces got stronger.

**2.** Show how a regional policy that subsidized firms in the small region would change the Fig. 9-7 diagram.

**3.** The educational level in all EU nations is rising. How would this affect the spatial allocation of production in the Heckscher–Ohlin framework?

### ESSAY QUESTIONS

**1.** EU regional policy was reformed in the context of 'Agenda 2000'. What were the major reform themes and how successfully were they implemented?

**2.** When the 10 newcomers join, some Objective 1 regions will become 'statistically' rich. That is, the lowering of the EU average will push their incomes above the 75 per cent threshold for Objective 1 status. Referring to the two theoretical frameworks discussed in the chapter, do you think it is correct for the EU to remove their Objective 1 status?

**3.** Many of the 10 newcomer members are both very agrarian and very poor. Some of them have agricultural land that is well suited to the production of the products that the CAP supports most. How do you think these nations will vote when the new long-term budget plan is drawn up for the post-2006 period? (*Hint*: Think about special interest group politics and the position of farmers in the political life of the newcomer countries.)

**4.** Using the theory of fiscal federalism presented in Chapter 2, can you argue that regional policy should be set at the EU level?

## FURTHER READING: THE AFICIONADOS CORNER

For a more extensive discussion of the facts concerning changes in the location of economic activity in the EU, see Brülhart and Traeger (2003).

Each year, the Commission produces a report on 'cohesion' in the EU. This contains a large number of maps showing things like unemployment, declining population, share of the economy in agriculture, industry and services. It also presents a large number of indicators of social cohesions such as youth unemployment and income distribution.

For an advanced treatment of the new economic geography, see part I of *Economic Geography and Public Policy* by Baldwin et al. (2003), freely downloadable from http://heiwww.unige.ch/~baldwin/.

## USEFUL WEBSITES

The webpage www.europarl.eu.int/factsheets/4_4_1_en.htm provides a wealth of information on EU regional policy.

The Commission department devoted to regional policy has an extensive website that provides masses of data and several highly readable explanations of EU policy in the area. See http://europa.eu.int/comm/regional/.

## REFERENCES

Brülhart, M. and R. Traeger (2003) *An Account of Geographic Concentration Patterns in Europe*, Cahiers de Recherches Economiques du Département d'Econométrie et d'Economie Politique (DEEP), Université de Lausanne. http://www.hec.unil.ch/deep/publications-english/e-cahiers.htm.

Combes, P. and H. Overman (2003) 'The spatial distribution of economic activity in the EU', in J. Thisse and V. Henderson (eds), *Handbook in Urban and Regional Economics* (volume 4).

European Commission (1996) *European Cohesion Report*, so-called first cohesion report; see http://europa.eu.int/comm/regional_policy/sources/docoffic/official/repor_en.htm.

European Commission (2001) 'Second Report on Economic and Social Cohesion.'

European Commission (2003) *Communication from the Commission: Second Progress Report on Economic and Social Cohesion*, COM (2003) 34 final. http://europa.eu.int/scadplus/leg/en/lvb/g24004.htm.

Midelfart-Knarvik, K.-H. and H. Overman (2002) 'Delocation and European integration: Is structural spending justified?', *Economic Policy*.

Overman, H. and D. Puga (2001) 'Regional unemployment clusters: nearness matters within and across Europe's national borders', *Economic Policy*.

Redding, S., H. Overman and A. Venables (2001) *The Economic Geography of Trade, Production and Income: A Survey of Empirics*, CEPR Discussion Paper, London.

Schürmann, C. and A. Talaat (2000) *Towards a European Peripherality Index*, Final Report, Institut für Raumplanung Fakultät Raumplanung, Universität Dortmund.

# Annex A: Dispersion of European industry: nations and regions

## National level

How unevenly is European manufacturing distributed across nations? There are two natural ways of approaching this question. The left panel of Fig. A9-1 shows each nation's share of EU15 industry for periods ranging from 1970 to 1997. The overall distribution of industry is quite uneven with just four nations – the UK, France, Germany and Italy – accounting for about three-quarters of the manufacturing. The left panel also shows that this distribution has been quite stable. The biggest gainer, Italy, increased its share by less than 2 percentage points and the biggest loser, the UK, saw its share fall by only 3 percentage points. All the other nations experienced gains or losses of less than 1 percentage point of total EU manufacturing output.

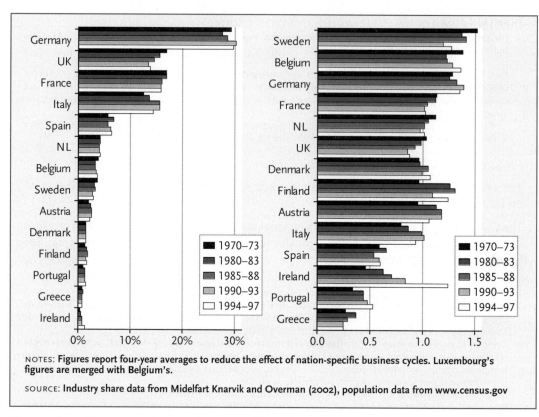

FIGURE A9-1: MANUFACTURING LOCATION IN EUROPE, 1970–97

NOTES: **Figures report four-year averages to reduce the effect of nation-specific business cycles. Luxembourg's figures are merged with Belgium's.**

SOURCE: **Industry share data from Midelfart Knarvik and Overman (2002), population data from www.census.gov**

The distribution of gains and losses, however, is not random. In the left panel, nations are listed in descending order of their 1970–73 share. We see that all of the nations that lost shares were among the eight biggest locations for industry at the beginning of the period. Indeed five of the eight largest locations lost shares, while all of the six smallest locations gained shares. At least at the aggregate level, i.e. when one lumps all types of manufacturing sectors into one, there is no evidence that European integration is accompanied by a shift of industry from Europe's 'periphery' to Europe's 'core'. On the contrary, it seems that manufacturing is becoming more evenly distributed at the national level.

The fact that the big-four Western European nations account for the lion's share of manufacturing is not very surprising; they also account for the lion's share of the EU15 population. The right panel in Fig. A9-1 shows the ratio between each nation's share of EU15 manufacturing and its share of EU15 population. The ratios, which provide a measure of manufacturing per person, show that manufacturing is much less unevenly distributed once one controls for population. The figures also confirm the notion that industry became more geographically dispersed as Europe integrated. Six nations had above-average manufacturing population ratios in 1970–73 and all but one of them saw their ratios fall by 1994–97, Germany being the exception. All nations that had below-average ratios to start with (i.e. ratios below 1.0 in 1970–73) saw their ratios rise, with the sole exception of Greece.

## Regional level

The preceding analysis looks at averages over whole nations. While this is useful for many purposes, it potentially hides changes in the geographic allocation of activity *within* nations. To see how the dispersion of manufacturing is changing among regions within European nations, we calculate each region's share of European manufacturing and then see how this share changes over time, i.e. as European economic integration has deepened. Since there is data on over 100 subnational regions even in the EU15, we cannot display as much detail as we did for nations. What we do instead is plot a region's initial share in the 1980–83 period on the horizontal axis and the average growth rate of the region's share over the 1980–95 period on the vertical axis. The result is shown in the left panel of Fig. A9-2.

The figure shows that there seems to have been something of a bifurcation in growth rates. Many growth rates are positive, between 2 and 4 per cent, and many growth rates are negative, between 0 and –3 per cent. There are relatively few regions, however, that grew at a rate lying between 0 and 2 per cent. Which regions took off and which stagnated? The figure shows that there is no simple answer. For example, it is not obvious that regions that were initially big gained, while the small lost (if this were the case, most of the points would lie around an upward sloped line since small initial shares would have been associated with negative growth rates).

To study the dispersion of European manufacturing and its evolution more precisely, we turn to a measure of 'unevenness' of shares. The idea behind this measure is to gauge how similar shares of manufacturing are among a group of regions or nations. If all of the regions have identical shares then the measure is zero. As the distribution of shares across regions becomes more uneven, the measure rises. The right panel of Fig. A9-2 shows this measure of regional unevenness for all the countries for which there are data. The nations are ranked in order of increasing concentration. What we see is that four of the eight experienced an increase in concentration (Portugal, Spain, Netherlands and Belgium), Germany saw no change and three saw a decrease in concentration.

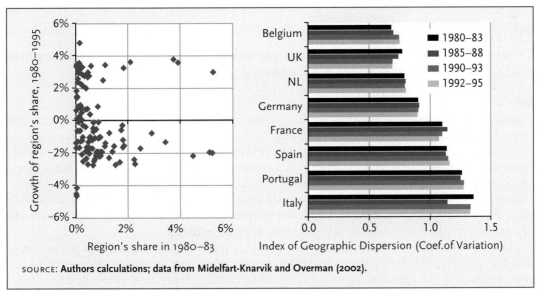

SOURCE: **Authors calculations; data from Midelfart-Knarvik and Overman (2002).**

FIGURE A9-2: REGIONAL MANUFACTURING SHARES IN 1980–83 VS SHARE GROWTH 1980–95

|  | 1980–83 | 1985–88 | 1990–93 | 1992–95 |
|---|---|---|---|---|
| Index of concentration among 119 EU regions | 1.3 | 1.3 | 1.5 | 1.5 |
| Index of concentration among 15 EU nations | 1.1 | 1.2 | 1.2 | 1.2 |

SOURCE: Midelfart-Knarvik and Overman (2002).

TABLE A9-1: CONCENTRATION OF EUROPEAN MANUFACTURING AND ITS EVOLUTION, 1980–95

Alternatively, we can look at this concentration index taking all the regions of Europe together. Table A9-1 shows the numbers. Note first that when we consider geographic units consisting of European regions versus European nations, we see that manufacturing is more concentrated, i.e. more unevenly distributed, at the regional level. Since the regions make up the nations, this tells us that, on average, the distribution of manufacturing is more uneven within nations than it is between nations. Second, while manufacturing dispersion has remained fairly constant over time when measured at the national level, it has become more concentrated when measured at the regional level. Again, since the regions make up the nations, this tells us that the unevenness of manufacturing's geographic location within European nations has increased over the 1980–95 period – a period marked by a very substantial increase in European economic integration.

The tendency for European integration to increase the internal concentration in EU members has been confirmed by recent statistical evidence; see Brülhart and Traeger (2003).

## Annex B: How to measure specialization and detailed results for EU regions

There are several ways to measure the extent of specialization in a region's or nation's production structure. One of the most common and most easily interpreted is the so-called Krugman index. This annex explains how the index is constructed. For information on alternative indices see Combes and Overman (2003).

### The Krugman specialization index

To consider the idea that nations and regions may be becoming more specialized, we want to be able to compare industrial structures in a compact way. To do this, we first must define a complete set of sectors and classify the economic activity of a particular region as falling into one of the sectors.

For example, one common classification divides all manufacturing into nine sectors (see column one of Table B9-1). This classification is far from perfect. Most importantly, it misses out all services because data on services are not very well developed in many EU nations. Since about two-thirds of all economic activity in most EU regions consists of services, this is not a minor problem. Nevertheless, the numbers are still useful since many of the services are really tied to industry, or to the spending of people who work in industry. (For example, if a big automobile plant closes in a region, the newly unemployed workers tend to reduce their spending on all sort of services, ranging from banking, to restaurants, to retail services.)

Since there is really no solution to this data problem, we do the best we can with the industrial data that are available. The first column of Table 9-B1 shows how important each sector's gross value added is in the Abruzzo region's total manufacturing output; these shares add to 100 per cent. The second column shows the same figures for Italy as a whole.

Having calculated these sector shares, the natural question is: How different is Abruzzo's

| | Percentage shares in manufacturing – gross value added | | |
| --- | --- | --- | --- |
| | Abruzzo | Italy | EU |
| Ferrous and non-ferrous ores and metals, other than radioactive | 2 | 5 | 5 |
| Non-metallic minerals and mineral products | 16 | 8 | 6 |
| Chemical products | 5 | 7 | 8 |
| Metal products, machinery, equipment and electrical goods | 22 | 31 | 31 |
| Transport equipment | 8 | 8 | 10 |
| Food, beverages, tobacco | 12 | 9 | 14 |
| Textiles and clothing, leather and footwear | 18 | 17 | 9 |
| Paper and printing products | 7 | 5 | 8 |
| Products of various industries | 9 | 11 | 9 |
| Krugman specialization index (Abruzzo vs. Italy) = 29.8% | | | |
| Krugman specialization index (Abruzzo vs. EU) = 38.6% | | | |

NOTES: The Krugman index ranges from zero (identical structures) to 200 per cent (since each column adds to 100 per cent any deviation enters twice, e.g. if Abruzzo's transport equipment share is 10 per cent higher than Italy's then its share in some other sector, or collection of sectors must be 10 per cent lower; thus the maximum difference is 200 per cent).

SOURCE: Author's calculations with data from Midelfart-Knarvik and Overman (2002).

TABLE B9-1: SPECIALIZATION INDEX EXAMPLE: ABRUZZO'S AND ITALY'S INDUSTRIAL STRUCTURE, 1980

industrial structure from Italy's? One answer is given by the so-called Krugman specialization index. This takes the absolute difference (i.e. the difference ignoring whether it is positive or negative) between Abruzzo's shares and Italy's shares, sector by sector, and adds up these differences. The Krugman specialization index for Abruzzo (compared to Italy) is 29.8 per cent. Note that if the two columns of shares were identical, the index would have been zero; if there were no overlap between sector shares in the two regions, the index would attain its maximum of 200 per cent.

What does Abruzzo's 29.8 per cent mean? If one wanted to bring Abruzzo's industrial structure exactly into line with the Italian average, then 14.9 per cent (i.e. 29.8/2) of Abruzzo's manufacturing activity would have to change sector. The table also shows that Abruzzo's structure differs more from the EU's than it does from Italy's (38.6 per cent is greater than 29.8 per cent).

# PART IV Monetary Integration: History and Principles

This part lays the ground for the analysis of monetary integration. Chapter 10 reviews Europe's monetary history, showing how the adoption of a single currency follows from previous experiments, some successful, some major failures. It pays particular attention to the Gold Standard mechanism, which can be applied to the internal functioning of the monetary union, to the disastrous inter-war period which still haunts policy makers, and to the natural evolution from the European Monetary System to the adoption of a single currency. Chapter 11 takes up the general question of the choice of an exchange rate regime. It presents a short summary of the basic macroeconomic principles needed to grasp the significance of exchange rate regimes. It describes the various regimes that have been tried, emphasizing their implications for inflation and economic growth. It then explains how to go about assessing the desirability of each of the main arrangements. Chapter 12 uses these insights to understand and interpret the European Monetary System (EMS). The EMS is partly of historical interest as it has provided some of the structures and incentives needed to eventually adopt the single currency. It is also important for the future of monetary integration since it continues to exist in a new version – EMS2 – that all future members of the Euro area will have to adopt as an entry pass.

# 10 A Monetary History of Europe

This chapter provides an overview of the role and uses of money in Europe (and the world) up to the creation of the monetary union. We start far back in the past, when hundreds of currencies existed in Europe. We next study the Gold Standard that prevailed until the First World War and was followed by a traumatic inter-war period. The chapter ends with a quick survey of the last half-century, thus providing an introduction to the issues studied in greater detail in the following chapters. The working of the Gold Standard is not just of historic interest, it also helps understand the internal functioning of the monetary union.

# 10.1 Metallic money

### 10.1.1 The world as a monetary union

From times immemorial until the end of the nineteenth century, money was metallic (mainly gold and silver) and a bewildering variety of currencies were circulating side by side. Each currency was defined by its content of precious metal and each local lord endeavoured to control the minting of currency in his fiefdom, chiefly because seigniorage was a key source of revenue. When public finances were under pressure, money was frequently debased, i.e. the metallic content was reduced through 'shaving' (rubbing off scraps of metal) or reminting coins. Exchange rates were relative values of different coins, and many coins were circulating in every political jurisdiction, creating confusion along the way:

> The multiplicity and diversity of 'sous' and 'deniers' is such that it would be nearly impossible to assess their precise values, and to sort out these various coins. It would lead to deep confusion which would increase work, trouble and other inconveniences of daily traffic.
>
> Nicolaus Copernicus, *Monetae Cudendae Ratio* (written in 1556, first published in 1816, quoted by Guggenheim (1973); our translation from French)

The identification of a state with its currency only came about during the nineteenth century as part of the process of building up nation states.[1] Currency denominations were largely symbolic and the metallic standards operated as a quasi-monetary union. All currencies based on gold or silver were really subdivisions of a single currency. The modern monetary union in Europe recreates an old mechanism, which is why the study of the Gold Standard in section 10.2 is useful.

### 10.1.2 The two first European monetary unions

By the early nineteenth century, most countries were operating a bimetallic standard: gold and silver coins circulated side by side. The exchange rate between gold and silver fluctuated depending on discoveries. Fundamentally, there were two currencies, gold and silver, and therefore two currency unions, which did not match national borders. Great Britain was the first large country to drop silver and adopt the Gold Standard. On the continent, bimetallism survived much longer, France being the key guarantor. Some countries (Germany, the Netherlands, the Scandinavian countries) favoured silver, until gold discoveries in the 1850s resulted in the disappearance of silver money on much of the continent.[2]

To preserve bimetallism, Belgium, France, Italy and Switzerland formed the Latin European Monetary Union in 1865 – a distant ancestor of today's monetary union. Greece joined in 1868. That effort foundered following the Franco-German war of 1870–71, when the newly established German empire shifted from silver to gold and weakened French finances by imposing war reparations to be paid in gold. Then, silver discoveries in Nevada pushed the price of silver down, with the result that the Latin European Monetary Union was abandoned in 1878 and gold became the monetary standard.

A second monetary union involved Denmark, Norway and Sweden. The Scandinavian

---

[1] Germany and Italy achieved political unification late and many different currencies still circulated in the 1850s. It took Italy two decades after its political unification in 1861 to achieve monetary unification and, when the German Reich was created in 1871, different monetary standards survived until the Bank of Prussia ultimately unified German monies.

[2] This is an illustration of Gresham's law, which states that 'bad money drives out good'. If two monies circulate alongside each other (e.g. gold and silver), and one of the currencies becomes overvalued, it is hoarded, and the other, depreciated, currency is the only one that circulates.

Monetary Union was created in 1873. These countries' currencies circulated widely in each other's territory, which was quite cumbersome. Additionally, at a time when nationalism was on the rise in Europe, 'Scandinavianism' favoured the symbol of a common krona. At the outbreak of the First World War, the Scandinavian Monetary Union ceased to exist, and was pronounced dead in 1924.

These historical precedents were really built on metal and they essentially harmonized coinage. They were not associated with any trade agreement and, more importantly, there was no common central bank and very little co-ordination among the national monetary authorities. When external conditions became difficult (the fall of the price of silver in the case of the Latin European Monetary Union, and the dislocations of war in the case of the Scandinavian Monetary Union), each country reacted in its own way to protect its own interests.

## 10.2 The Gold Standard

### 10.2.1 The link between money and the balance of payments: trade flows

The classic Gold Standard years are conventionally set as the period 1880–1914, with inter-war attempts to rebuild the system largely unsuccessful, as explained in section 10.3. A popular mystique attributes great merits to the Gold Standard – a taste of good old times when things were better and simpler. The truth is less rosy, with frequent financial crises, armed conflicts, uneven growth and occasional depressions accompanied by high unemployment and waves of bankruptcies.[3] Nor were exchange rates very stable. The Gold Standard operated as a de facto monetary union, but the many countries that remained outside the system faced substantial exchange rate fluctuations.

The working of the Gold Standard is described by Hume's (Box 10-1) price-specie mechanism. This mechanism is well worth a visit, as it also applies to the working of the EMU. It is based on two familiar macroeconomic principles: the long-run neutrality of money and the effect of money on interest rates.[4]

The neutrality of money states that the rate of inflation is driven by the rate of growth of money, at least in the long run. This is represented in the upper left panel of Fig. 10-1 by the upward-

---

DAVID HUME (1711–76)

Born in 1711 to a well-to-do family in Berwickshire, Scotland, Hume has mostly written on philosophy, including the *Principles of Morals* (1751) which fouded, inter alia, the theory of utility. His works were highly influential even though they were denounced at the time as sceptical and atheistic. His economic thinking, mainly contained in *Political Discourses* (1752) had a large impact on Adam Smith and Thomas Malthus .

Source: National Galleries of Scotland

---

[3] For a comparison of economic performance during and after the Gold Standard, see Burda and Wyplosz (2001), ch. 19.
[4] Both principles are presented in Chapter 10.

sloping schedule: more money eventually results in higher domestic prices. Next, in the same panel, we add international competition: if the price of domestic goods $P$ exceeds the price $P^*$ of foreign goods, exports decline, imports rise, and the current account worsens.[5] The horizontal line corresponds to the price level $P_I$ for which exports equal imports and the current account is in equilibrium. Moving upwards, the price level rises and the current account swings into deficit. The area below the horizontal line corresponds to lower prices and current account surpluses. External equilibrium is achieved when the money stock is $M_I$.

Under the pure Gold Standard, the stock of money is the quantity of gold held in the country. Where is the gold coming from? Some of it may be dug out from the ground, but Europe has been notoriously poor in that respect and we may as well ignore this source. The rest has to be imported. Some gold may be imported for use in jewellery or production; this is gold-commodity and it is part of the current account. Gold money is different: ignoring for the time being financial flows, it is earned through exports and spent on imports. Thus a current account surplus results in an inflow of gold money, the modern-day equivalent of the accumulation of foreign exchange reserves, the counterpart to a balance of payments surplus.

The downward-sloping schedule in the right panel of Fig. 10-1 shows that the higher the stock of money, the more the balance of payment deteriorates. Consider point $B$ where a high stock of money means high prices and an external deficit: gold is flowing out and the stock of gold money contracts. We move to a point like $B'$ where prices are lower and the deficit is reduced. At $B'$ the deficit is not yet fully eliminated, gold is still flowing out and the money stock keeps contracting, so we continue moving up and to the left until point $A$ is reached. At point $A$, the balance of payments is in equilibrium and the money stock is stabilized. Obviously, starting from a surplus, such as point $C$, will trigger an inflow of money (specie) and an increase in prices, bringing the economy gradually to point $A$. This link between money and external balance is Hume's price-specie mechanism.

### 10.2.2 The link between money and the balance of payments: financial flows

The link from the balance of payments to the money stock is instantaneous. The link from the money supply to the price level is slow, and operates via protracted booms and recessions. In the shorter run, most of the action takes place elsewhere, including the financial account which has been overlooked so far.

The downward supply schedule in the lower part of the left panel of Fig. 10-1 represents the money market: an increase in the stock of money results in a lower interest rate. When the domestic interest rate is below the rate $i^*$ prevailing abroad, it pays to borrow gold at home where interest is low and to ship it abroad for lending at the higher interest rate. The financial account is in equilibrium when the domestic interest rate is the same as abroad. Above this line, the financial account is in surplus; below it, it is in deficit. The financial account is balanced when the stock of gold money is $M_2$. If the stock of gold exceeds $M_2$, the interest rate is lower than $i^*$, capital flows out, gold is shipped abroad and the money supply contracts, giving the negative slope.

Changes in the money supply affect both components of the balance of payments – the current and the financial accounts – in the same direction: a large stock of money means an external deficit and an outflow of gold. The capital flow route is very fast while the trade route is slower, but both work in the same direction. The right-panel of Fig. 10-1 consolidates both accounts.

[5] It is the trade balance that changes. It is assumed that the other components of the current account remain unaffected.

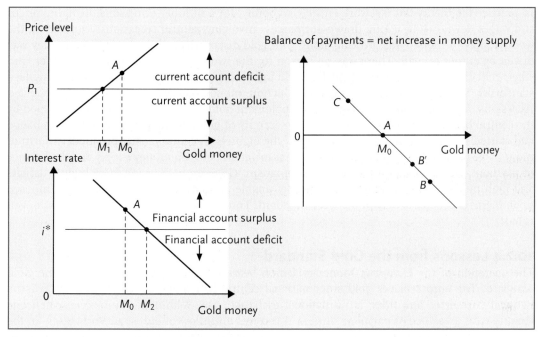

FIGURE 10-1: HUME'S PRICE-SPECIE MECHANISM

## 10.2.3 Automaticity: theory and practice

The right hand panel of Fig. 10-1 shows why balance of payment imbalances are automatically corrected. To the right of point $A$, money is in excess of $M_0$, external deficits automatically translate into outflows of gold, which eventually drive the stock of money back to $M_0$. To the left of point $A$, the balance of payment is in surplus and gold inflows raise the stock of money. Note that point $A$ may correspond to imbalances in both the current and capital accounts. For example, as drawn, point $A$ corresponds to a position between $M_1$ and $M_2$, where a deficit in the current account exactly matches a capital account surplus.

The automatic return to external balance is the main advantage of the Gold Standard. A country in deficit, for example, loses gold. As the money supply declines, in the shorter run, the interest rate rises, which attracts capital and partly helps to finance the current account deficit. Over time, money supply stringency creates slack in the domestic demand, growth declines and unemployment rises. This means that there is downward pressure on both prices and wages. All markets (financial, goods and labour) work towards eliminating the external imbalance and there is no need for the government to intervene. Note also that there is no monetary policy since the stock of gold money is determined endogenously.

This automaticity depends on the adherence to three principles, known as the 'rules of the game':

■ Full gold convertibility at fixed price of banknotes issued by central banks, so that paper money is merely a convenient surrogate to gold.
■ Full backing. The central bank holds at least as much gold as has been issued in banknotes. In the presence of gold inflows the central bank prints money, with gold outflows it retires previously created paper money.
■ Complete freedom in trade and capital movements, so as not to interfere with the two elements of the adjustment mechanism.

In practice the theory did not work entirely smoothly, for a number of reasons. Bringing prices and wages down can be a long drawn-out process involving painful recessions. In addition, the world supply of money was growing along with gold discoveries, while demand for money was driven by output growth. There was no reason for the two to grow harmoniously together, and when gold discoveries accelerated, so did world inflation (yet it always remained mild by modern standards). When growth outpaced gold production, money was scarce, which led to protracted recessions, and it then became natural to supplement gold money with paper money issued by the central banks. In fact, to make up for the scarcity of gold, privately-issued bills of exchange had started to circulate as early as the end of the eighteenth century. That pre-modern form of money acted as a buffer, but it relaxed the key association between money supply and the balance of payment, and therefore the system's automatism. Governments facing large budget deficits and high public debts, or otherwise politically unable to abide by the tight discipline imposed upon them, chose not to stay in the Gold Standard. Thus the system was not universal, nor even robust.

### 10.2.4 Lessons from the Gold Standard

The operation of the European Monetary Union bears more than a resemblance to the Gold Standard. The euro replaces gold since national central banks are no longer allowed to issue national currencies and there is no national exchange rate. Within the Euro-zone, when one country runs a balance of payment surplus, it receives an inflow of euros, and conversely in the case of a deficit. Thus, the Hume mechanism is at work inside Euroland. In particular, a deficit country can no longer use the exchange rate to re-establish its competitiveness, and adjustment will have to work through prices and wages, which have to increase more slowly than in the rest of the Euro area, possibly even to decline.[6] The comparison also means that the 'rules of the game' must be strictly adhered to if national imbalances are to be automatically corrected . Put differently, tinkering with the rules would destabilize the whole monetary union and the rules are therefore part and parcel of Euro area membership.

## 10.3 The unhappy inter-war period

The Gold Standard was suspended in 1914 when gold shipping became too dangerous, and the subsequent inter-war period left a bitter taste in Europe that still haunts the continent. Belligerent countries had emerged exhausted from the First World War, facing huge debts, and over the next 30 years they would never quite fully recover. After the Great Depression, the world monetary leadership shifted to the USA. In many respects, the post-war European economic and political integration represents an effort to rule out any repeat of the inter-war disaster.

### 10.3.1 The First World War inheritance: from public debts to inflation

Wars are expensive and strain budgets, especially as governments are loath to raise taxes. The two alternatives are either to issue debt or to run the printing press, both of which were used during the First World War. During the war, prices were kept artificially stable through rationing schemes; when prices were freed, the accumulated inflationary pressure burst into the open. Some of the most famous hyperinflations erupted during this period, with Germany, Hungary and Greece facing *monthly* inflation rates of 1000 per cent or more in the early 1920s.

---

[6] This observation is at the heart of the Optimum Currency Area principle presented in Chapter 12.

## 10.3.2 Returning to gold: three case studies

Post-war policy makers were committed to return to the Gold Standard as soon as practical, but at which exchange rate? Different European countries adopted different strategies, which ended up tearing them apart, economically and politically. We look at three prominent cases: the UK, France and Germany.[7]

### THE UK

Britain, hoping to retain its traditional leadership in international monetary matters, decided to return sterling to the Gold Standard at its pre-war parity, 'to look the dollar in the face'. The forced appreciation of the pound is shown in Fig. 10-2.[8] This decision has become a landmark policy mistake. Since 1914, prices had increased much more in Britain than in the USA, and returning sterling to its pre-war value resulted in overvaluation. The only solution was to bring prices back down, a lengthy and painful process. The result was poor growth, a weak current account, and the erosion of trust in sterling, once considered 'as good as gold'. The City of London lost ground to New York's Wall Street.

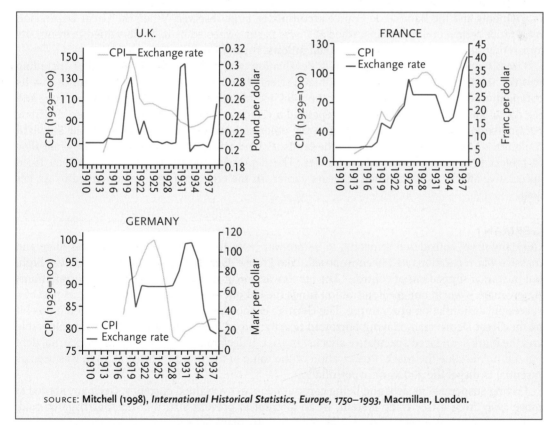

SOURCE: **Mitchell (1998),** *International Historical Statistics, Europe, 1750–1993,* Macmillan, London.

FIGURE 10-2: PRICES AND EXCHANGE RATES: FRANCE, GERMANY AND THE UK (1910–39)

---

[7] The reasoning implicitly uses the purchasing power parity principle, which is presented in Chapter 11.
[8] The exchange rate is expressed as the number of pounds needed to buy one dollar. A decrease means an appreciation, since less pounds are needed to buy one dollar.

Both industry and finance were weak so, when the Great Depression followed the crash on Wall Street in 1929, Britain was in no position to deal with yet more hardship. The exchange markets sensed the vulnerability and repeatedly launched speculative attacks on sterling. When, at long last, the Bank of England withdrew from the Gold Standard in 1931, sterling promptly lost 30 per cent of its value *vis-à-vis* gold and the dollar. An ambition was gone, and the price was high: a decade of miserable growth.

### FRANCE

France, too, initially expected to return to the Gold Standard at its pre-war parity, but it soon lost control of inflation for several years. The French debt had grown much more than Britain's, and continued to rise at a brisk pace after the war on the premise that Germany's huge war reparations would eventually pick up the bill. When, by 1924, it became clear that Germany would not pay, inflation soared to an annual rate of close to 50 per cent, the franc was attacked and sunk. When inflation was finally stopped in 1926, the franc was stabilized at one-fifth of its pre-war parity.

France officially returned to the Gold Standard in 1928 but, in contrast to the pound, its exchange rate was now undervalued. Over the next few years, France ran surpluses in its balance of payments and the Banque de France accumulated large reserves. When the Great Depression hit, France escaped relatively unscathed as it was partly protected by its undervalued currency. Its apparently superior health triggered capital inflows, further swelling its gold stock.

Trouble started when sterling's 1931 devaluation was followed by many others including Austria, the Scandinavian countries, Finland, Ireland and Portugal. As a result France lost its competitiveness. When, under duress, the USA too abandoned the Gold Standard in 1933 and the dollar was sharply devalued to be repegged a year later at a rate 40 per cent lower, the franc became seriously overvalued. France and the other countries remaining on the Gold Standard (Belgium– Luxembourg, Italy, the Netherlands, Poland and Switzerland) formed the Gold Bloc to protect their now overvalued currencies. The depression belatedly hit France, which faced speculative attacks as Britain had 10 years earlier. In the end, the franc was devalued by 42 per cent.

### GERMANY

Germany never considered returning to its pre-war level. Its domestic public debt was huge and massive war reparations had been imposed. Like France, Germany's post-war inflation was high, but in 1922 it slipped out of control.[9] The result was one of history's most violent hyperinflations. A new mark – worth one million million times the old one – was established in 1924 as part of a successful anti-inflation programme. The German economy started to pick up just when it was hit by the Great Depression. Having borrowed heavily abroad, Germany was particularly vulnerable and the mark soon faced speculative attacks. In 1931, it declared a moratorium on its external debt but did not devalue the mark. Preservation of the value of the mark restored in 1924 was seen as essential to dispel the ghosts of hyperinflation.

Having suspended its debt and being committed to an overvalued currency, Germany started to move away from a free trade system. In an attempt to prevent a further haemorrhage of gold, exchange controls were established. Like the franc, the mark became even more overvalued when more and more countries devalued their own currencies. As the depression deepened, the Nazis came to power. To pull the economy out of depression, they combined public spending with wage and price increases. This further dented external competitiveness and deepened the trade deficit.

---

[9] This is why pre-hyperinflation prices and exchange rates are not shown in Fig. 10-2.

The Nazi regime's response was to stop the conversion of marks into gold and foreign currencies and to develop a 'managed trade' system through ever-widening state controls on imports and exports. Bilateral barter agreements were worked out with one country after another, in effect allowing Germany to bypass completely the foreign exchange market. Step by step, the Nazis brought all international arrangements (trade and financial) under government control, with a view to protecting its industry and building up a war economy.

### 10.3.3 Lessons for exchange rate arrangements

A number of lessons can be learned from this unhappy period:

- Exchange rate misalignments breed trade barriers. Countries with overvalued currencies suffer from trade deficits and low growth. They soon view surpluses and good growth performance in countries with undervalued currencies as unfair. The next step is protectionism.
- Rigid adherence to fixed parities hurt. All three countries met deep economic hardship for clinging for too long to an overvalued parity.
- Piecemeal approaches to exchange rate arrangements do not work. Each country struggled independently, some left the Gold Standard when others joined, and there were no mutually accepted rules of the game. In that sort of environment, financial markets are highly unstable, which hurts trade.
- Domestic policy misbehaviour saps fixed exchange rates. France and Germany could not join the Gold Standard until after they had eliminated budget imbalances and rapid inflation. Britain could not stay on gold because this required excessively tight macroeconomic policies.
- Fragile systems eventually collapse. The Great Depression was a unique event, but other, milder shocks would have destroyed the inter-war version of the Gold Standard devoid of accepted rules of the game. The weakness of the inter-war Gold Standard may well have contributed to the spreading and deepening of the depression.
- Exchange rate arrangements need a conductor. The pre-war Gold Standard was managed by the Bank of England and supported by London's financial centre. In the inter-war period, the City could no longer assume that responsibility and Wall Street was not yet ready for it. It is sometimes felt that the world monetary system needs a 'hegemon', a country that dominates the system and sets its rules.

## 10.4 The post-war years: fear of the past

### 10.4.1 Jump-starting Europe after the war

Another lesson from the inter-war period was that peace cannot be long-lasting in the midst of economic turmoil. After the Second World War, there would be no sanctions or war reparations.[10] A new superpower, the USA, was in place and ready to make sure that the world economy, and Europe in particular, would soon resume 'normal' conditions.

Prompted by the emerging cold war, the Marshall plan, set up in 1948, provided funds (mostly grants, not loans) to pay for imports from the USA, focusing on goods deemed essential for the recovery from wartime destruction. This aid permitted to lessen the pressure on exchange rates and avoided the kind of destructive misalignments that had wrecked the recovery from the First World War. Importantly, war winners and losers alike were part of the programme, avoiding continuing divisions in Western Europe.

### 10.4.2 Bretton Woods as an antidote to the inter-war débâcle

When the USA and Britain started to plan the Bretton Woods conference towards the end of the

---

[10] Not completely, however: German factories were removed to be rebuilt and German patents were confiscated.

Second World War, they were determined to draw on the inter-war lessons. There would be no return to gold, there would be a collective construction with active management of the international monetary system, and exchange rates would be neither set free nor rigidly fixed.

The Bretton Woods system[11] retained gold as the ultimate source of value, but the only currency directly tied to gold was the dollar (at the pre-war parity of $35 per ounce of gold). All the other currencies were defined in terms of the dollar. Exchange rates were 'fixed but adjustable' to avoid both unreasonable adherence to an outdated parity (over- or undervaluation) and an inter-war-type free-for-all.

The system was a collective undertaking with a clear line of command. The International Monetary Fund would wield a carrot and a stick: a carrot in the form of loans, and a stick as enforcer of both discipline and flexibility. It would be formally asked to give its blessing to exchange rate realignments when needed and would provide loans to sustain embattled parities in the face of unjustified speculative attacks. By providing the system's central currency and hosting the IMF in Washington, the USA would be the ultimate political hegemon and guarantor of the system.

Fig. 10-3 shows the adequate evolution of the exchange rate between sterling and the Deutschemark (DM) between 1950 and 1998 (when the DM ceased to exist), using a logarithmic scale. The downward trend reflects the long-run tendency of sterling to decline *vis-à-vis* the DM. It closely follows the relative inflation rate in the two countries: the lighter line shows the ratio of German to British consumer price indices.[12]

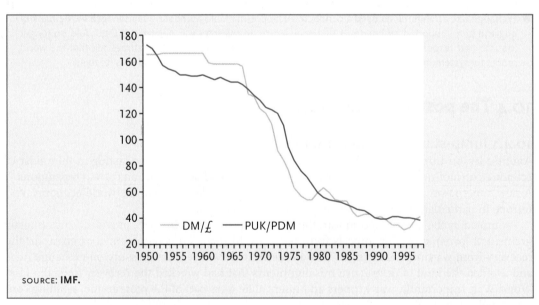

SOURCE: **IMF.**

FIGURE 10-3: STERLING VS THE DEUTSCHEMARK (1950–98)

---

[11] The Bretton Woods system is not presented here. For a detailed treatment, see e.g. Burda and Wyplosz (2001).
[12] The figure illustrates the purchasing power parity (PPP) principle presented in Chapter 11.

# 10.5 After Bretton Woods: Europe on its own

## 10.5.1 The collapse of Bretton Woods, the great inflation scare, and the Snake

Europe's golden years lasted until the late 1960s when inflation started to rise in a number of countries, partly because of local conditions, partly as the result of the Vietnam War. Staging an increasingly unpopular war, the US authorities allowed for a sizeable budget deficit, partly financed by money, which fuelled inflation and resulted in external deficits, an other manifestation of Hume's mechanism. Inflation eroded the value of the dollar as a safe standard and external deficits, paid for with dollars, fuelled doubts that the US stock of gold was large enough to back the dollar. Resting now on a wobbly anchor, the Bretton Woods system came under strain when the USA could no longer guarantee the gold value of the dollar. The demise came in two steps.

First, in 1971, the USA 'suspended' the dollar's gold convertibility and devalued by 10 per cent. The move was soon followed by a wave of exchange rate realignments designed to restore order in the system. But its credibility was undermined and the currency markets remained jittery, which led to the second decision. In 1973, the 'fixed but adjustable' principle was officially abandoned; each country would now be free to choose its exchange rate regime, effectively ending the Bretton Woods era.

Europe's early reaction in effect charted the way that would lead to a monetary union three decades later. France and the UK, two high-inflation currencies, had already undergone devaluations in the late 1960s and speculation soon started to tear European currencies apart from each other, as Fig. 10-4 shows. Concerned with the inter-war spectre of over- and undervaluation, the continental countries of Europe promptly resolved to limit exchange rate movements among themselves.

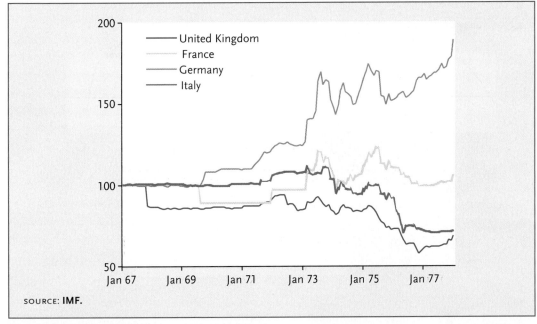

SOURCE: **IMF.**

FIGURE 10-4: DOLLAR EXCHANGE RATES (JANUARY 1967–DECEMBER 1977)

The first response was to set up the 'European Snake', a regional stepped-down version of the Bretton Woods system designed to limit intra-European exchange rate fluctuations, presented in Box 10-2. But the Snake was not equipped to survive the hectic conditions of the 1970s. Partly as a result of the first oil shock of 1973–74, inflation had become, again, a central preoccupation. However, the determination to combat inflation varied greatly in Europe. Table 10-1 shows that some countries (Germany, the Netherlands and Belgium) succeeded in keeping inflation in check, while others (e.g. Italy and the UK) did not. Maintaining exchange rate fixity under such conditions was hopeless and, indeed, several countries had to leave the Snake arrangement. More needed to be done, and the European Monetary System (EMS) was the response.

---

### Box 10-2: The Snake in the Tunnel

In 1971, in a last-ditch effort to save the Bretton Woods system, it was decided to widen the margins of fluctuations *vis-à-vis* the dollar from ±1 per cent to ±2.25 per cent. Non-dollar currencies, like the DM and the franc, would now fluctuate by as much as 9 per cent *vis-à-vis* each other, as is shown in the upper part of Fig. 10-5, which shows the evolution of the exchange rates of the French franc and the DM *vis-à-vis* the dollar. When both currencies are at their opposite extremes *vis-à-vis* the dollar (represented by both points A), the DM is 2.25 per cent above the dollar, and the franc 2.25 per cent below it. As a result, the DM is 4.5 per cent above the franc. At the opposite extremes (points B), the DM is 4.5 per cent below the franc, with a total amplitude of 9 per cent. A number of European countries (the EC members as well as Denmark, Ireland, Norway, the UK and Sweden) felt that this was too wide a margin and decided to maintain their bilateral rates within a common ±2.25 per cent band of fluctuation. This was called the 'snake in the tunnel' – a colourful representation of joint movement shown in the lower part of the figure. Although several countries were forced to leave the Snake under speculative pressure, when the Bretton Woods system was finally ended in 1973 and the links to the dollar were severed, the EC countries resolved to keep the Snake, even if the tunnel was gone, but realized that the arrangement would have to be stronger. This led to the EMS.

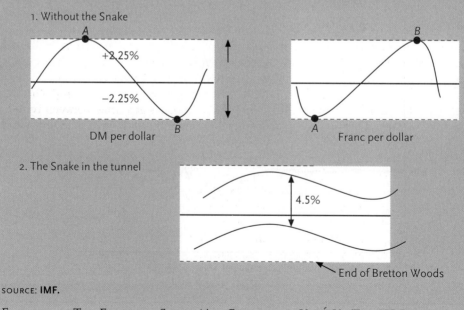

SOURCE: **IMF.**

FIGURE 10-5: THE EUROPEAN SNAKE (ALL CURRENCIES VIS-Á-VIS THE US DOLLAR)

| | 1960 | 1965 | 1970 | 1975 | 1980 | 1985 | 1990 | 1995 | 2000 |
|---|---|---|---|---|---|---|---|---|---|
| Austria | 1.9 | 4.9 | 4.4 | 8.4 | 6.3 | 3.2 | 3.3 | 2.3 | 2.4 |
| Belgium | 0.3 | 4.1 | 3.9 | 12.8 | 6.7 | 4.9 | 3.5 | 1.5 | 2.5 |
| Denmark | 1.3 | 5.5 | 6.5 | 9.6 | 12.3 | 4.7 | 2.7 | 2.1 | 2.9 |
| Finland | 3.2 | 4.8 | 2.7 | 17.8 | 11.6 | 5.9 | 6.1 | 1.0 | 3.4 |
| France | 4.1 | 2.7 | 5.8 | 11.7 | 13.5 | 5.8 | 3.4 | 1.8 | 1.7 |
| Germany | 1.5 | 3.2 | 3.4 | 5.9 | 5.4 | 2.2 | 2.7 | 1.7 | 1.9 |
| Greece | 1.6 | 3.1 | 2.9 | 13.4 | 24.9 | 19.3 | 20.4 | 8.9 | 3.2 |
| Ireland | 0.5 | 5.0 | 8.2 | 20.9 | 18.2 | 5.4 | 3.3 | 2.5 | 5.6 |
| Italy | 1.4 | 4.4 | 4.8 | 16.9 | 21.3 | 9.2 | 6.5 | 5.2 | 2.5 |
| Netherlands | 2.3 | 5.8 | 3.7 | 10.2 | 6.5 | 2.2 | 2.5 | 1.9 | 2.5 |
| Portugal | 3.0 | 3.5 | 4.5 | 20.4 | 16.6 | 19.3 | 13.4 | 4.1 | 2.9 |
| Spain | 1.2 | 13.2 | 5.8 | 16.9 | 15.5 | 8.8 | 6.7 | 4.7 | 3.4 |
| Sweden | 4.1 | 5.0 | 7.0 | 9.8 | 13.7 | 7.4 | 10.5 | 2.5 | 0.9 |
| UK | 1.0 | 4.8 | 6.4 | 24.2 | 18.0 | 6.1 | 9.5 | 3.4 | 2.9 |

SOURCE: IMF.

TABLE 10-1: INFLATION RATES

## 10.5.2 The European Monetary System (EMS)

The EMS is studied in detail in Chapter 13; here we just look at its historic role. At the heart of the EMS lay the Exchange Rate Mechanism (ERM): a system of jointly managed fixed and adjustable exchange rates backed to mutual support. Formally, all countries that were part of the European Community joined the EMS in 1979, although the UK decided to stay out of the ERM until October 1990. As new countries joined the European Community (later the European Union), EMS membership widened even though some countries delayed participation to the ERM, see Table 10-2.

During the first 10 years of the EMS, inflation rates diverged markedly in Europe (Table 10-1). With fixed nominal exchange rates, the result was chronic misalignments. For example, the inflation differential between Germany and Italy averaged more than 10 per cent per year between 1974 and 1982; a fixed parity between the DM and the lira would have undercut Italy's competitiveness on average by 10 per cent each year, clearly an untenable proposition. Unsurprisingly therefore, realignments were frequent and usually involved several currencies at a time. Between 1979 and 1987, this occurred no less than 12 times, once every eight months on average. The implicit rule was to observe inflation rates since the previous realignments and change the parities accordingly.

This process was a bit too transparent, allowing the exchange markets to easily foresee the next realignment and speculate accordingly. Most parity adjustments occurred in the midst of serious market turmoil, calling into question the sustainability of the ERM, and the obvious answer was to reduce the inflation differentials. Germany, the largest country with the lowest rate of inflation, naturally became the example to follow. As the other countries undertook to emulate its monetary policy the Bundesbank gradually emerged as the centre of the system. After 1986, each country was trying to anchor its currency to the DM and realignments became very rare.

However, inflation did not always decline to German levels and misalignments kept growing. The attempt to hold exchange rates unchanged eventually failed in 1992–93 when a succession of speculative attacks nearly destroyed the EMS. Italy and Britain were forced to leave the ERM, and

| | Joined | Left | Rejoined |
|---|---|---|---|
| Austria | 1995 | | |
| Belgium | 1979 | | |
| Denmark | 1979 | | |
| Finland | 1996 | | |
| France | 1979 | | |
| Germany | 1979 | | |
| Greece | 1998 | | |
| Ireland | 1979 | | |
| Italy | 1979 | 1992 | 1996 |
| Netherlands | 1979 | | |
| Portugal | 1992 | | |
| Spain | 1989 | | |
| Sweden | | | |
| UK | 1990 | 1992 | |

NOTE: Italy, Portugal and Spain initially operated a wider (±6%) band of fluctuation around the central parity than the normal (±2.25%) band.

TABLE 10-2: ERM MEMBERSHIP

such countries as Ireland, Portugal and Spain had to devalue their currencies repeatedly. France, which had adopted its 'franc fort' policy of shadowing the DM, adamantly refused to devalue. In order to save the system from further unravelling, the margins of fluctuations were widened to ±15 per cent in 1993.[13] The new ERM had very little of a fixed exchange rate regime left, but the principle of fixed exchange rates remained, keeping alive the prospects of a monetary union.

### 10.5.3 The road to and from Maastricht

Monetary union had been in the back of the minds of the signatories of the 1957 Treaty of Rome which established the European Community (the Common Market). Chapter 1 describes the first attempt to do so (the Werner Report that failed), and the second, successful one, the Delors Report.

Why was agreement promptly reached on a monetary union in the late 1980s? As the capital controls that had been in place in most countries since 1945 were dismantled by 1990, unfettered speculative flows could easily overwhelm the central banks. The old EMS was doomed. Convergence to the Bundesbank standard meant that, except for Germany, all countries had in effect lost monetary independence. Surely, replacing the Bundesbank with a common central bank would allow them to recover some influence over monetary policy. Initially, and understandably reluctantly, the German government decided to back the project, mostly on political grounds.

The Delors Report was formally adopted in July 1989 at the Madrid Summit. Two intergovernmental conferences were convened to study the creation of an economic and monetary union and of a political union. Both conferences reported in time for the Council meeting held in Maastricht at the end of 1991. The Maastricht Council decided the replacement of the European Community

[13] Germany and the Netherlands independently agreed to keep their bilateral parity within the old ±2.25 per cent margins. Belgium decided on its own to follow the same rule.

by an economic and political union, the European Union, and included a precise schedule to establish the monetary union.

On 4 January 1999, the exchange rates of 11 countries[14] were 'irrevocably' frozen. The old currencies formally became (odd) fractions of the euro, and the power to conduct monetary policy was transferred from each member country to the European System of Central Banks (ESCB), headquartered in Frankfurt. Average citizens had to wait another three years, until January 2002, to see and touch euro banknotes and coins, but an undertaking that long seemed beyond reach, or even wholly unrealistic, was complete. Europe is the first instance when politically independent countries merge their existing currencies, reviving among themselves the price-specie mechanics of the Gold Standard.

# 10.6 Lessons from history

History never repeats itself, it is said, but the study of historical systems can lead to a number of lessons on how to organize international monetary arrangements. Five of them are summarized in Table 10-3.

- Misalignments create deep problems, both in the country affected and in its trading partners. They often generate calls for protectionism, and inevitably lead to serious crises. Any good monetary system must have procedures that promptly eliminate misalignments. It was automatic in the Gold Standard system, and explicit procedures were in place in the Bretton Woods system and the EMS.
- Piecemeal system building does not work; there is a need for overall coherence. Hume's price-specie mechanism and the associated rules of the game provided for coherence in the Gold Standard system, while the Bretton Woods system and the EMS were carefully constructed.
- No system can survive if policy misbehaviour is tolerated. No system, until EMU, was able to impose policy discipline.
- Every monetary system must be ready to cope with a large variety of shocks, ranging from political disturbances to occasional misalignments and policy mistakes. The EMS provided for mutual support, as explained in Chapter 13, and yet failed. The EMU is, so far, untested. It rests on Hume's mechanism, whose automaticity imparts a strong discipline to policy.
- Someone has to assume responsibility for the smooth working of the system. Britain looked after the Gold Standard system, and the USA looked after the Bretton Woods system. The EMS and the EMU rely on institutions.

| | Gold Standard | Inter-war | Bretton Woods | EMS | EMU |
|---|:---:|:---:|:---:|:---:|:---:|
| Long-lasting misalignments must be avoided | ✓ | | ✓ | ✓ | |
| Systems need to be built coherently | ✓ | | ✓ | ✓ | ✓ |
| Policy misbehaviour must be ruled out | | | | | ✓ |
| Systems must be robust | | | | ✓ | ✓ |
| Any monetary system needs a conductor | ✓ | | ✓ | ✓ | ✓ |

TABLE 10-3: LESSONS FROM HISTORY

[14] Austria, Belgium, Finland, France, Germany, Ireland, Italy, Luxembourg, the Netherlands, Portugal and Spain.

## 10.7 **Summary**

■ For centuries, money was mostly metallic. There was no link between nations and currency, but rather a bewildering and cumbersome variety of currencies that circulated alongside each other.

■ Under the Gold Standard much of the world was in effect operating under a system close to a monetary union. The system was meant to provide for the automatic elimination of payment imbalances through the working of the price-specie mechanism.

■ Under the price-specie mechanism, a country running a balance of payments surplus accumulates gold money. The interest rate declines, prompting capital outflows; simultaneously prices rise, hurting competitiveness and the current account. Both channels work towards eliminating the surplus, and the opposite mechanism works in the case of a payments deficit.

■ The inter-war period is when paper money definitely replaced metallic money. Botched attempts to resurrect the Gold Standard failed, resulting in exchange rate instability. Competitive devaluations were followed by rising protectionism and the disintegration of Europe, economically and politically.

■ The Bretton Woods system was designed to avoid the disastrous inter-war experience. It had clear rules, and fixed and adjustable exchange rates. It relied on a new institution, the IMF, which was both providing financial support and overseeing national policies. It was built around the dollar, the new world monetary standard. When the USA failed to live up to its responsibilities, the system collapsed.

■ Continental Europe's reaction to the demise of the Bretton Woods system was to sever its dependence on the dollar and build up regional exchange rate stability. Lacking a clear rule and coherence, the first attempt (the Snake) failed.

■ The EMS, the second attempt, succeeded despite a chequered history. It gradually led the Member States to latch their currency to the DM. From there it was a short step to monetary union.

### Self-assessment questions

1. Using Fig. 10-1, work out graphically what happens following an initial balance of payments surplus. Why is the capital outflow, prompted by lower interest rates, only partially offsetting financing the current account surplus? Why is there automatic monetary relaxation despite capital outflows?

2. How can the Hume mechanism be applied to the flows of euros within the Euro area?

3. Why did fiscal and monetary indiscipline in the USA lead to the collapse of the Bretton Woods system?

4. Why did growing inflation differentials create a problem for exchange rate stability in Europe?

5. Why has the EMS been called a 'greater Deutschemark area'?

6. During the inter-war era, misalignments led to competitive devaluations, which then prompter a tariff war. Explain the links from one step to the next.

### Essay questions

1. The inter-war decline of Britain is sometimes imputed to the 1924 return to the Gold Standard at the overvalued pre-war parity. Explain how and why lasting overvaluation hurts.

2. Proposals to return the world to the Gold Standard are regularly put forward. Evaluate the pros and the cons of this idea.

3. Drawing lessons from history, determine the European Monetary System's strengths and weaknesses.

4. 'The creation of the European Snake was a sign of US decline in monetary matters.' Comment.

5. Is the EMU robust? Write the cases for and against.

6. Europe's monetary history is sometimes seen as a blueprint for other regions like South-East Asia or Latin America. Evaluate what can be replicated and what cannot. In doing so, keep in mind both the political aspects of monetary integration and the evolution of the international financial markets.

## FURTHER READING: THE AFICIONADOS CORNER

On the Gold Standard, recent studies include:

Obstfeld, M. and A. Taylor (2003) *Sovereign Risk, Credibility and the Gold Standard: 1870–1913 versus 1925–31*, Unpublished, University of California at Berkeley. The authors compare the 1914 Gold Standard with its post-1918 legacy and show that the earlier was more successful and resulted in lower foreign borrowing costs, a sign that risk was received lower. http://repositories.cdlib.org/iber/cider/

Bordo, M. (1999) *The Gold Standard and Related Regimes*, Cambridge University Press. This book offers a comprehensive and modern analysis of the Gold Standard and its relevance to today's discussions.

On early efforts at monetary unification:

Bergman, M., S. Gerlach and L. Jonung (1993) 'The rise and fall of the Scandinavian currency union 1873–1920', *European Economic Review*, **37**, 507–17.

Guggenheim, T. (1973) 'Some early views on monetary integration', in H.G. Johnson and A.K. Swoboda (eds), *The Economics of Common Currencies*, Harvard University Press, Cambridge, Mass.

Holtfrerich, C.L. (1993) 'Did monetary unification precede or follow political unification of Germany in the 19th century?', *European Economic Review*, **37**, 518–24.

On the need for an hegemon acting as leader of the international monetary system:

Eichengreen, B. (1989) 'Hegemonic Stability Theories of the International Monetary System', in R. Cooper, B. Eichengreen, R. Henning, G. Holtham and R. Putnam (eds) *Can Nations Agree? Issues in International Cooperation*, Brookings Institution, Washington, p. 255–98.

Duncan Snidal (1985) 'The limits of hegemonic stability theory' *International Organization*, Autumn.

On the evolution of Europe to the monetary union:

Kenen, P.B. (1995) *Economic and Monetary Union in Europe*, Cambridge University Press, Cambridge.

## USEFUL WEBSITES

The European Parliament's factsheet on monetary integration:

http://www.europarl.eu.int/factsheets/5_1_0_en.htm

General resources on monetary history:

http://www.ex.ac.uk/~RDavies/arian/other.html
http://www.micheloud.com/FXM/MH/Glossary.htm

## REFERENCES

Burda, M. and C. Wyplosz (2001) *Macroeconomics, A European Text*, Third Edition, Oxford University Press, Oxford.

Yeager, L. (1966) *International Monetary Relations*, Harper & Row.

# 11 The Choice of an Exchange Rate Regime

Why is it better to adopt a particular exchange rate regime? To deal with this old but recurring question, this chapter starts by clarifying the link between exchange rate and monetary policies. Two key principles – monetary neutrality and purchasing power parity – bring up the importance of separating out the long term from the short term. The different type of exchange rate regimes are next presented, and their pros and cons examined. The main conclusions are that money and the exchange rate are just two sides of the same coin, and that there is no universally better exchange rate regime, it is all a matter of trade-off. This chapter – a review of principles often developed in macroeconomics – lays the background for the analyses that follow, and can be skipped by well-trained readers.

## 11.1 **The exchange rate and monetary policy**

This section reviews the relationship between money and the exchange rate.[1] How money and the exchange rate interact depends on how far in the future we care to look. The long term, a period long enough for the real and monetary spheres to be separated, is easiest. It is characterized by two important results: the neutrality of money and purchasing power parity. In the short term, real and monetary matters interfere, which opens the door to the use of money and the exchange rate to deal with undesirable cyclical fluctuations. Yet, the choice of the exchange rate regime affects the way policies operate. Fundamentally, money and the exchange rate are just two sides of the same coin.

### 11.1.1 **The long term (1): Neutrality of money**

A key principle of macroeconomics is that, in the long term, money is *neutral*. Neutrality describes the situation where changes in nominal variables (e.g. the money supply or nominal interest rates) do not affect real variables such as growth, unemployment, wealth, productivity or competitiveness. Formally, this occurs because an increase in the money supply is eventually absorbed by proportional increases in prices.

This principle is illustrated in Fig. 11-1 which shows the differences in money growth and inflation between France and Switzerland. The principle implies that differences in inflation rates between these two countries should reflect differences in money growth rates, and France's exchange rate should depreciate *vis-à-vis* the Swiss franc at an equivalent rate. For the moment, we ignore the exchange rate. It is hard to detect any link in the first panel, which shows year-to-year changes. Clearly, there is a lot of 'noise' in the short term: money growth is quite volatile while inflation moves more smoothly. The second panel goes some way towards eliminating this noise by plotting five-year moving averages. A pattern starts to emerge, but the association remains loose. The last panel takes a really long-term view by displaying 10-year moving averages. The association is now unmistakable: the French money growth rate usually exceeds the Swiss rate, and this is accompanied by an almost equally high inflation in France.

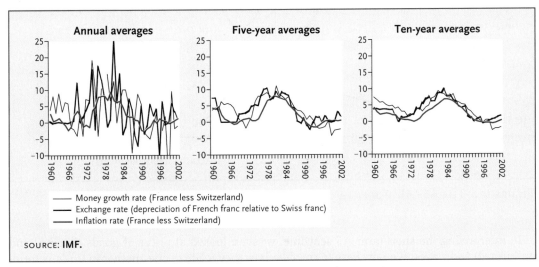

FIGURE 11-1: NEUTRALITY PRINCIPLE: FRANCE AND SWITZERLAND (1960–2002)

---

[1] This section summarizes much of the theory of open economy macroeconomics. Readers familiar with these principles can skim the section. Those who have never studied the theory ought first to understand it. For a complete exposition, see, e.g., Burda and Wyplosz (2001), chs 8–13.

Since the neutrality principle carries important implications for European monetary integration, a brief review of the underlying theory may be helpful. Figure 11-2 depicts the standard aggregate demand (*AD*) and aggregate supply (*AS*) schedules.[2] Each schedule explains a fundamental link between the rate of inflation on the vertical axis, and cyclical movements of output around its trend level, conventionally measured by the GDP (Gross Domestic Product) gap on the horizontal axis.

The downward-sloping *AD* schedule represents the fact that inflation erodes the purchasing power of money (and other nominal assets) and therefore discourages consumption by households and investment by firms. The upward-sloping short-term aggregate supply schedule corresponds to a very different mechanism: the setting of prices. Producers of goods and services keep an eye on their competition and costs, including wages. In recession times the market shrinks and firms attempt to retain their market shares by limiting cost and price increases, while workers, fearful of rising unemployment, accept wage moderation. In the opposite situation, in boom periods, demand is strong so profits can be made by jacking up prices and, as unemployment declines, workers push for better wage settlements. This explains why the *AS* schedule is upward sloping.

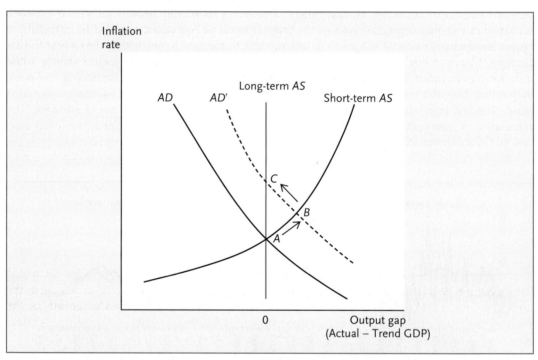

FIGURE 11-2: THE *AS–AD* MODEL

In interpreting the short-term *AS* schedule, we have looked at prices of goods (finished and unfinished) and wages. We now have to consider how they relate to one another in the long term. If good prices (represented by the price index *P*) rise faster than wages (represented by the average

[2] Note that it is the inflation rate that is shown on the vertical axis. The framework is sometimes presented with the price level instead, but the substance of the analysis is not affected.

wage $W$), the purchasing power of wages (measured as the ratio $W/P$) declines. Sooner or later, workers will want to catch up and will bargain for wage increases. Likewise, if wages rise faster than prices, firms face rising costs and sooner or later will have to raise prices. The long term is precisely the time that it takes for this cat and mouse game to end in a draw – that is, when real wages settle down.[3]

## 11.1.2 The long term (2): Purchasing power parity

The neutrality principle also extends to the exchange rate, and this aspect is known as the principle of purchasing power parity (PPP). Figure 11-1, which shows some supportive evidence, also plots the rate of change of the exchange rate between the French franc (FRF) and the Swiss franc (CHF). This exchange rate is expressed as the number of FRF needed to buy one CHF: when the CHF appreciates *vis-à-vis* the FRF, the exchange rate increases.

As before, over the short term, there is no visible link between the volatile exchange rate and money growth and inflation. As the horizon extends to the very long term, things fall nicely into place. The rate of appreciation of the CHF – or, equivalently, the rate of depreciation of the FRF – follows a pattern very similar to those of the money growth and inflation differentials. In brief, why is the CHF typically appreciating *vis-à-vis* the FRF? Because money growth, and therefore inflation, is higher in France than in Switzerland. Table 11-1 confirms that over the period 1958–2002 (when the FRF ceased to exist) the average annual rate of appreciation of the CHF *vis-à-vis* the FRF is approximately equal to the average difference between inflation in France and in Switzerland. This is PPP. It does not hold everywhere and at all times, but it is a good point to start thinking about the exchange rate. Box 11-1 develops this question further.

| | |
|---|---|
| Money growth: France less Switzerland | 2.5% |
| Inflation: France less Switzerland | 2.4% |
| Appreciation CHF vs FRF | 3.3% |
| SOURCE: IMF. | |

TABLE 11-1: FRANCE VS SWITZERLAND, 1958–2002

The PPP principle may be made more precise and formal. It rests on a crucial distinction between the nominal and the real exchange rates. The nominal exchange rate ($E$) is defined as the foreign price of the domestic currency. Denote by $E$ the nominal euro–dollar exchange rate, i.e. the number of dollars needed to buy 1 euro – for example, 1.1 dollars for 1 euro: $E = 1.1$. If $P$ represents the domestic currency price of a basket of domestic goods (e.g. €100), in dollar terms the same basket will cost $EP$ (e.g. $110). A depreciation of the euro – a decline in $E$ – makes domestic goods less expensive relative to foreign goods, and Europe's competitiveness improves. The way to measure Europe's competitiveness *vis-à-vis* the USA is to compare the dollar price of this basket of goods made in Europe to the dollar price $P^*$ of the same basket of goods made in the USA. This measure is called *the real exchange rate*. It is defined as the ratio of domestic to foreign good prices expressed in the same currency: $\lambda = EP/P^*$.[4]

---

[3] Real wages rise secularly as productivity allows increases in standards of living. For the sake of simplicity of exposition, we ignore this trend.
[4] It does not matter which currency is used to evaluate the prices. In the text, we use the foreign currency (the dollar). If we use the euro instead, the domestic currency of foreign goods is $P^*/E$ (e.g. if the foreign currency price of foreign goods is $550, the domestic currency price is €500), and the real exchange rate is $P/(P^*/E) = EP/P^*$, exactly the same as before!

> ### Box 11-1: Purchasing power parity in practice
>
> The PPP principle is simple and intuitive, but suffers from many exceptions and is very slow to assert itself. It fails badly when comparing countries with sharply different income levels. Travellers know that the cost of living is typically low in the poorer countries, but they also know that this is because of cheap service prices while internationally traded goods (e.g. cars, TVs, etc.) are not good buys, and are often much more expensive.
>
> PPP is best interpreted as saying that the real exchange rate returns to its equilibrium level, not necessarily that the equilibrium real exchange rate is constant. It has approximately been the case between sterling and the DM, but this is not always the case.[5] For example, the real exchange rate of the yen has considerably increased over 1950–90 because, during this period, Japan has transformed itself from a poor, war-torn and relatively backward country to one of the wealthiest and best-performing economies in the world. As it climbed the technology ladder, Japan became intrinsically more competitive, producing increasingly more sophisticated products that it could sell at higher prices, and its real exchange rate permanently appreciated. Table 11-2 shows that PPP does not apply well to this case. This phenomenon, called the Balassa–Samuelson effect, is quite general and currently operates, in the rapidly catching-up countries of Central and Eastern Europe, which will complicate matters once they join the Euro area, as discussed in Chapter 12.
>
> | | |
> |---|---|
> | Inflation: USA less Japan | 0.2% |
> | Appreciation yen vs US$ | 1.7% |
> | SOURCE: IMF. | |
>
> Table 11-2: Japan vs the USA, 1953–2002
>
> How fast does the real exchange rate return to its equilibrium level? Recent studies tend to conclude that the process is very slow. It is generally found that it takes two to four years for the difference between the actual and equilibrium real exchange rate to be halved.

When prices $P$ and $P^*$ remain unchanged, the nominal and real exchange rates move together. For instance, a nominal depreciation ($E$ declines) translates into an equiproportional real depreciation (a decline in $\lambda$). If prices in Europe rise while the nominal exchange rate remains unchanged, Europe's competitiveness declines and the real exchange rate appreciates – it increases. If the nominal exchange rate depreciates in the same proportion as domestic prices increase – e.g. both 10 per cent – the dollar price of European goods $EP$ is unaffected, as is Europe's competitiveness $\lambda$.

In the short term, Fig. 11-1 shows that the nominal exchange rate is quite volatile while prices are much more stable. Fluctuations of the nominal exchange rates are mirrored in fluctuations of the real exchange rate, which suggests that prices move little. This is how exchange rates affect competitiveness and the trade balance. Over the longer term, the nominal exchange rate, prices

---

[5] Formally, $\lambda = EP/P^*$ means that, approximately, $\Delta\lambda/\lambda = \Delta E/E + \Delta P/P - \Delta P^*/P^*$. If the real exchange rate $\lambda$ is constant $\Delta\lambda/\lambda = 0$ and $\Delta E/E = \Delta P^*/P^* - \Delta P/P$. This is PPP. If the real exchange rate changes, then $\Delta E/E = \Delta P^*/P^* - \Delta P/P + \Delta\lambda/\lambda$. As long as the change in the real exchange rate is small, PPP is an acceptable rule of thumb.

and wages all adjust to each other to re-establish competitiveness and restore external equilibrium. Put differently, PPP asserts that over the long term the real exchange rate returns to its equilibrium level. The behaviour of the nominal and real exchange rates between sterling and the DM, displayed in Fig. 11-3, conforms to this description: year-to-year movements in the nominal exchange rate are mirrored in a subdued way in movements in the real exchange rate (which still varies by some 25 per cent around its average). In the long term, the five-fold nominal depreciation of the pound since 1950 fails to leave the slightest impression on the real rate.

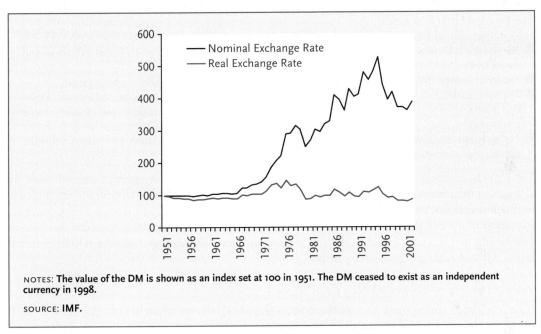

NOTES: The value of the DM is shown as an index set at 100 in 1951. The DM ceased to exist as an independent currency in 1998.

SOURCE: IMF.

FIGURE 11-3: NOMINAL AND REAL EXCHANGE RATES (GERMANY VS UK, 1951–2002)

The long-term tendency of the real exchange to return to its equilibrium rate is one aspect of the general principle that, in the long run, real variables are unaffected by nominal variables. Whatever happens to the latter (money growth, nominal depreciation or appreciation, inflation, nominal wages), all real variables tend to return to their trends, and this includes output (real GDP), real wages and real exchange rates. In Fig. 11-2, the neutrality principle is captured by the vertical long-term aggregate supply schedule. For example, an increase in money growth raises the AD schedule to AD': starting from point A, in the short term the economy moves to point B, and will reach point C eventually.

## 11.1.3 The short term

### THE INTEREST AND EXCHANGE RATE CONNECTION

We know that money does not have any real long-term effect, but what happens in the short term? An increase in the money supply, for instance, makes credit more abundant. This encourages a decline in interest rates with two main consequences. First, households take advantage of lower interest rates to borrow and spend. Similarly, firms step up investment in productive capacities because bank borrowing is cheaper and because stock prices typically rise when interest rates decline,[6] which makes it more desirable to issue new shares and expand. The result is higher aggregate spending, more GDP growth and a probable decline in unemployment.[7]

Second, investors will move some of their assets out of the country where yields become less appealing. This capital outflow results in a depreciating nominal exchange rate, when it is not pegged. The associated real depreciation represents a gain in competitiveness, exporters sell more and domestically produced goods tend to replace foreign imported goods.

All in all, the effect is expansionary as world (domestic and foreign) demand addressed to domestic goods increases. This is how, in the short term, money is not neutral. The main channels that we have identified are:

- *The interest rate channel.* More money means lower interest rates, which is an incentive to borrow and spend more.
- *The credit channel.* More liquidity encourages banks to compete more forcefully in offering loans.
- *The stock market channel.* Declining interest rates are typically accompanied by higher stock prices. Firms find it interesting to issue shares and invest the proceeds. Households feel wealthier and consume more abundantly.
- *The exchange rate channel.* The nominal depreciation is also a real depreciation and makes domestic goods more competitive.

The expansion fuels inflation. Indeed, in Fig. 11-1 changes in money growth are followed by changes in inflation with a lag of two years or more. Since prices ($P$) move slowly, a given increase in the nominal stock of money ($M$) is entirely translated initially into an increase in the purchasing power of money, the real money stock ($M/P$). Over time, inflation gradually erodes this gain in purchasing power, and eventually, the real money and the real exchange rate return to their initial levels, with no lasting expansionary impact.

## The case of a fixed exchange rate

If the exchange rate is fixed (as was the case in the EMS), the situation is radically altered. With gradually rising costs and prices, the real exchange rate appreciates, competitiveness declines and a trade deficit develops.[8] Lower interest rates exacerbate the financial account. Committed to a fixed exchange rate, the central bank must intervene on the exchange market, selling part of its foreign exchange reserves and buying back its own currency. In doing so, the central bank re-absorbs the money it has created, and the money supply shrinks. In fact, to avoid a speculative attack, the money stock will have to return promptly to restore the interest rate to its previous level and bring capital outflows to an end.

The striking implication is that efforts by the central bank to expand its money supply are frustrated by the need to conduct offsetting foreign exchange market operations in defence of the exchange rate. Monetary policy simply does not work. More precisely, monetary policy independence is lost, being wholly dedicated to the defence of the exchange rate commitment. Put differently, a central bank can control the money stock or the exchange rate, not both. This is quite obvious when one realizes that the exchange rate is the external price of money.[9]

---

[6] Stock prices are a claim of future firm profits, discounted back to the present at the going interest rate. When interest rates are lower, future earnings are less heavily discounted, and stock prices rise.

[7] The curious reader will observe that more investment leads to more growth – more precisely, to a higher potential GDP – and wonder whether this is a cause of non-neutrality. It could be, although the evidence on this effect is inconclusive. Yet, it is, in reverse, the question asked about the UK in the 1920s in the exercise section of Chapter 10.

[8] With $E$ fixed and $P$ rising, the real exchange rate $\lambda = EP/P^*$ rises and domestic goods become more expensive.

[9] This important result is sometimes described as the 'impossible trinity', which is presented in Chapter 13.

In practice, exchange rates are rarely rigidly fixed, and are usually allowed to move within bands. If the band is narrow (e.g. the 4.5 per cent width in the pre-1993 ERM, see Chapter 13), the room for monetary policy independence is very limited. As the band widens, of course, monetary policy can increasingly be used, but there is then little substantive difference between a fixed exchange rate with wide bands (like the post-1993 ERM, with 30 per cent wide bands) and a floating exchange rate.

## AN *IS–LM* INTERPRETATION

The short-term non-neutrality of money can be described with the *IS–LM* graphical apparatus.[10] The *IS* schedule in Fig. 11-4 describes the goods market equilibrium condition. It is downward sloping because a decline in the interest rate results in more demand and a higher output. The *LM* schedule describes equilibrium in the money market for a given real money supply ($M/P$). An increase in output generates more demand for money and for credit to which banks respond by raising interest rates, hence the upward slope of the schedule.

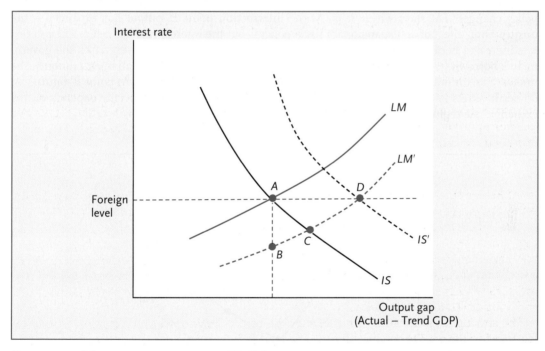

FIGURE 11-4: MONETARY POLICY IN THE *IS–LM* MODEL

An increase in the money supply is captured by a rightward shift of the *LM* schedule. At the initial level of money supply, interest rates are lower (point *B*). Spending gradually expands (as explained in section 1.2.1) and the economy moves from point *B* to point *C* while interest rates start rising, reflecting a stepped-up demand for money and credit.

As long as the interest rate remains low, as at point *C*, capital is likely to flow out – a situation that cannot last very long. What happens next depends on the exchange rate regime. If the

[10] This section can be skipped by readers familiar with this theory which describes the short term as the period during which prices and wages fail to respond to changing economic conditions. A complete exposition is available, e.g., in Burda and Wyplosz (2001), ch. 10.

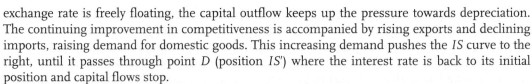

exchange rate is freely floating, the capital outflow keeps up the pressure towards depreciation. The continuing improvement in competitiveness is accompanied by rising exports and declining imports, raising demand for domestic goods. This increasing demand pushes the *IS* curve to the right, until it passes through point *D* (position *IS'*) where the interest rate is back to its initial position and capital flows stop.

If the exchange rate is fixed (as in the ERM), the central bank is bound to intervene on the exchange market. As it does, the money supply shrinks and the *LM* curve starts to move back to the left. This process must continue until the *LM* schedule is back in its original position and the economy is back at point *A*. This establishes the loss of monetary policy independence under a fixed exchange rate regime.

### 11.1.4 The role of the exchange rate regime on the effects of fiscal policy

The other macroeconomic policy tool is fiscal policy. The *IS–LM* framework can also explain how fiscal policy operates in a small open economy. By changing public spending or taxes, the government affects total spending: raising public expenditures or cutting taxes leads to more demand, which is captured by a rightward shift of the *IS* curve in Fig. 11-5. Unless monetary policy changes, *LM* stays where it is. At the intersection point *B*, output has expanded – the unsurprising effect of an expansionary fiscal policy – but the interest rate has risen. The interest rate increases because the budget deficit has risen and needs financing: exercises the government's borrowing increases upward pressure on the interest rate. In a small open economy, the interest rate cannot really diverge greatly from the worldwide interest rate. At point *B*, returns on domestic assets is attractive, capital flows in, and what happens next crucially depends on the exchange rate regime.

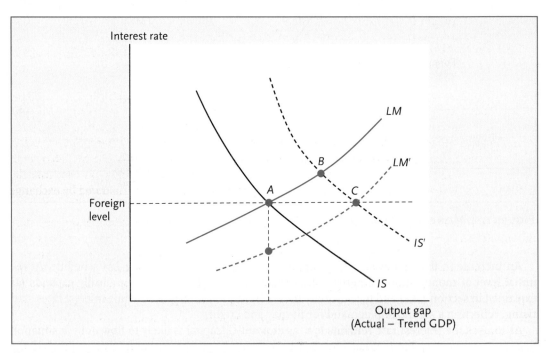

FIGURE 11-5: FISCAL POLICY IN THE *IS–LM* MODEL

If the exchange rate is fixed, the central bank finds that the capital inflows create pressure towards appreciation and must therefore intervene on the foreign exchange market, selling the domestic currency to counteract the pressure exerted by capital inflows. The money supply then rises, the *LM* schedule shifts to the right and we move down the new *IS'* curve. As long as the interest rate is higher than at point *A*, capital keeps flowing in, and the process will stop only when the *LM* schedule has moved all the way to *LM'* and the economy has reached point *C*.

If the exchange rate is freely floating, the central bank does not intervene on the foreign exchange rate market, it does not change the money supply, and the *LM* schedule does not move. Yet at point *B*, something must give in the face of capital inflows and an appreciating exchange rate. With sticky prices, the nominal appreciation results in a real appreciation, a loss of external competitiveness and a deterioration of the current account. Demand for domestic goods declines and the *IS* schedule starts shifting to the left. This will continue until the *IS* schedule has returned to its initial position and the economy is back at point *A*. Fiscal policy, therefore, does not work! Its expansionary effect is entirely offset by the contractionary effect of the exchange rate appreciation.

## 11.1.5 Wrap-up and implications for monetary integration

We have now seen that, under a fixed exchange rate regime, monetary policy is lost as an independent instrument, but fiscal policy works. Under a flexible exchange rate regime, the opposite occurs: monetary policy is fully available but fiscal policy ceases to be effective. These results, which apply to a small open economy (too small to affect the world interest rate) are summarized in Table 11-3.

|  | Monetary policy | Fiscal policy |
|---|---|---|
| Fixed exchange rate | Ineffective | Effective |
| Flexible exchange rate | Effective | Ineffective |

TABLE 11-3: POLICY EFFECTIVENESS AND THE EXCHANGE RATE REGIME

The underlying logic behind these results is both simple and central to the European integration process. Exchange rate policy, i.e. the choice of an exchange rate regime, is simply the same thing as monetary policy. Choosing one fully determines the other. Furthermore, the effect of fiscal policy depends on what the monetary authorities will do. If they are committed to an exchange rate target, they must passively validate the impact of fiscal policy on the financial markets, and if they concentrate on monetary policy alone, fiscal policy is frustrated by exchange rate movements.

These results are crucial to an understanding of what a country gives up by forming a monetary union with other countries. It should be clear by now that the answer 'monetary policy is lost' can be misleading. At most, the loss only matters in the short term since monetary policy is neutral in the long term. The real long-term implication of the loss of the monetary instrument is that the inflation rate is no longer established by domestic authorities. This may be highly desirable for inflation-prone countries like Italy, but worrisome for countries like Germany that have traditionally been able to contain inflation. This observation explains many features of the EMU, as is shown in Chapter 14.

These results also indicate that the choice of joining a monetary union cannot be evaluated without considering the alternatives. If the alternative is to let the exchange rate float freely, then there is a serious loss of monetary independence. If the alternative is a fixed exchange rate like the narrow-band ERM, the loss is very limited as the country imports the monetary policy of the country and currency to which it pegs its exchange rate – a point made clear in Chapter 13. Historically, as noted in Chapter 10, most European countries have demonstrated a great reluctance to let their exchange rate float freely. An exception is the UK, which has unsurprisingly displayed little enthusiasm towards EMU.

## 11.2 The range of exchange rate regimes

The debate regarding the choice of an exchange rate regime is very old, yet it remains as controversial as ever. Fashions come and go, and leave their imprint on history, but, in the end, there is no overwhelming case for any particular regime. The decision involves numerous trade-offs, with the pros and cons playing differently according to circumstances, countries and periods. This section looks at the rainbow of options and reviews some of the evidence; the following section recalls the debate, focusing on the issues that are most relevant to Europe.

### 11.2.1 When does the exchange rate regime matter?

It is important to first note that the choice of an exchange rate regime only matters if the exchange rate has real effects. If monetary policy were fully neutral, even in the short term, it would have no effect other than determining the rate of inflation. The real exchange rate would then never depart from its equilibrium level and the behaviour of the nominal exchange rate would be irrelevant for any practical purpose. Thus we care about the exchange rate regime only to the extent that money is not neutral in the 'short term' which, as Fig. 11-1 suggests, extends over a period of a few years.

Money is not neutral, and because prices and wages move slowly we say that they are 'sticky'. But are prices and wages really sticky? This is essentially the empirical question that has divided the economics profession at least since 1936 when Keynes launched his famous attack on the 'classics' who were, in his view, ignoring price and wage stickiness. The debate has not yet settled and is unlikely to do so for the foreseeable future. Figure 11-3 gives an idea why, showing clearly that movements in the real exchange rate reflect movements in the nominal exchange rate, thus rejecting neutrality. The link is, however, tenuous and short-lived, so neutrality may be an acceptable simplification. Put differently, are the non-neutral effects found in Fig. 11-3 large enough for us to care about them? If they are not, there is little reason to agonize over the exchange rate regime. For the sake of the argument at least – and also for realism – we assume that prices and wages are sticky enough, and last long enough, for the exchange rate regime to matter.

### 11.2.2 What's on the menu?

There are two conventional exchange rate regimes: fixed and flexible. In practice, however, exchange rate regimes come in all sorts of shapes and forms, with many hybrids and a few extremes. Except for a floating exchange rate, all other regimes require a foreign currency to be chosen as an anchor. The main anchors have traditionally been the US dollar and the Deutschemark, now replaced by the euro. An alternative is to adopt a basket of several currencies.

#### FREELY FLOATING

The simplest regime is when the monetary authorities decline any responsibility for the exchange rate. The rate is then freely determined by the markets and can fluctuate by any amount at any moment. Currently the US dollar, the euro and the British pound are among the freely floating currencies. The USA and the Euro area are large economies, so permitting the exchange rate to float freely does not fully eliminate the effectiveness of fiscal policy while allowing their central banks to operate freely.[11] The deal may be less sweet for the UK.

## MANAGED FLOATING

The monetary authorities may be concerned that a free float results in excessive exchange rate volatility and feel the need to intervene on the exchange markets from time to time, as they see fit. They buy their own currency when they consider it too weak, and sell it when they see it too strong, but they refrain from pursuing any particular target. This also allows them to use fiscal policy if they so wish, and they can do so as long as they accept the implied effect on the exchange rate. Japan is one country that is known to be frequently present on the foreign exchange markets.

## TARGET ZONES

Target zones imply the choice of a wide range within which the exchange rate is allowed to move *vis-à-vis* its chosen anchor. This leaves some room for manoeuvre for both monetary and fiscal policy. The central bank must intervene – and lose policy independence – when the exchange rate moves towards the edges of the zone, but it can also intervene more frequently to keep the exchange rate close to the mid-point. The authorities can either announce the range, or a mid-point with a tolerance for fluctuations around it, or refrain from stating any precise target and simply be active and enforce its implicit target range, which can be fuzzy. The current ERM (presented in Chapter 12), with a zone of ±15 per cent around the central parity, is an example of a target zone.

## CRAWLING PEGS

A crawling peg is characterized by the fact that the authorities allow the central parity, and the associated maximum and lower levels, to slide regularly. The rate of crawl is sometimes pre-announced. The difference between a crawling peg and a target zone is not clear cut, since both involve an acceptable range: margins considered narrow enough to be qualified as a pegged arrangement are typically less than ±5 per cent around the official parity. Many Latin American countries operated crawling pegs in the 1980s, as did Poland and Russia in the mid-1990s. Figure 11-6 shows the case of Poland; note that the rate of crawl has been gradually reduced while the width of the band has been progressively widened until the currency was allowed to float.

## FIXED AND ADJUSTABLE

Fixed exchange rate regimes are characterized by a central parity *vis-à-vis* an anchor currency and a narrow band of fluctuation. They are adjustable to allow the authorities to modify the parity without changing the regime itself. From 1945 to 1973, fixed and adjustable exchange rates were the rule world wide under the Bretton Woods agreement. The margins were initially set at ±1 per cent until 1971, and then widened to ±2.25 per cent. Between 1979 and 1993, the ERM also operated as a system of fixed and adjustable exchange rates, with a normal ±2.25 per cent band, which was enlarged to ±15 per cent after 1993.

This regime preserves the role of fiscal policy but it restricts the effectiveness of monetary policy. The adjustment option is mainly useful to deal with an inflation trend that exceeds that of the anchor currency and therefore calls for realignments when the real exchange rate has appreciated too far and external competitiveness is eroded.[12] This provides for a limited degree of

---

[11] For large, relatively closed economies, the standard close economy *IS–LM* model offers a good description of the situation.

[12] When the nominal exchange rate $E$ is constant and the domestic price level $P$ rises faster than the foreign one $P^*$, the real exchange $\lambda = EP/P^*$ rises. A devaluation – a reduction in $E$ – becomes the only way to lower it back to equilibrium.

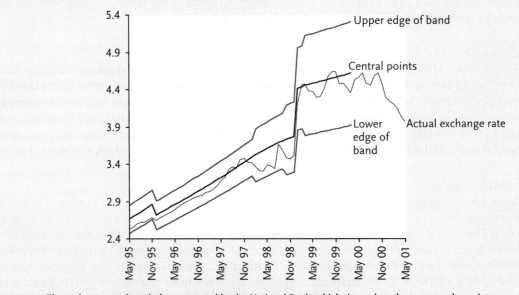

NOTES: The exchange rate is an index computed by the National Bank, which rises when the currency depreciates. The crawling band was introduced in March 1995 and lasted until April 2000 when the zloty was allowed to float, and soon appreciated. The anchor was a basket index whose composition was occasionally changed (in 1999, it included the euro, with a 55 per cent weight, and the US dollar, with a 45 per cent weight).

SOURCE: **National Bank of Poland.**

FIGURE 11-6: POLAND'S POLISH CRAWLING BAND (MAY 1995–MARCH 2000)

monetary policy independence – mainly the ability for the inflation rate to differ from that in the anchor currency country.

## CURRENCY BOARDS

A tighter version of pegged exchange rates is a currency board. The principle underpinning currency boards is based on the previous observation that, under a pegged regime, monetary policy has to be wholly dedicated to the exchange rate target. Adjustable pegs and target zones recognize that this can be too constraining for the everyday operation of monetary policy, hence the flexibility afforded by wide margins to occasionally realign the central parity. Currency boards reverse the logic: they put the declared exchange rate parity at centre stage and ensure that monetary policy is entirely consistent with the declared parity. This is done by imposing a very strict rule inspired from the Gold Standard (see Chapter 10): the central bank may only issue domestic money when it acquires foreign exchange reserves. If the exchange rate weakens, the central bank must spend its foreign exchange reserves to buy back its own currency, which is then retired from circulation, and the money supply shrinks – Hume's mechanism at work. If the exchange rate strengthens, the central bank must sell its own currency and accumulate foreign exchange reserves, and in this way it increases the money supply. Monetary policy is entirely passive and the money supply changes automatically as the balance of payments is in surplus or deficit. Fiscal policy, on the other hand, is effective.

Currency boards used to exist in the British Empire. They were adopted by a number of Caribbean Islands as they became independent, were revived by Hong Kong in 1983, and later by

Argentina, Estonia, Lithuania, Bosnia and Bulgaria. Argentina's system collapsed in 2002, illustrating the dangers of an unflexible arrangement.

## DOLLARIZATION/EUROIZATION AND CURRENCY UNIONS

A yet stricter way of pegging a currency is to irrevocably fix the exchange rate. This means that the anchor currency becomes the domestic currency. One approach is for a number of countries to adopt the same currency: the monetary union solution. Another approach is to adopt a foreign currency, hence the term *dollarization* (as in Ecuador, El Salvador, Panama, Liberia) or *euroization* (as in Bosnia, Kosovo, Montenegro). Box 11-2 presents existing arrangements. Fiscal policy is effective, although the sharing of a common currency may call for some restrictions – an issue discussed in detail in Chapter 15.

---

### BOX 11-2: MONETARY UNIONS

The CFA zone was created when the former French colonies reached independence in the 1960s. It includes two unions: the West African Economic and Monetary Union (Benin, Burkina-Faso, Côte d'Ivoire, Guinea Bissau, Mali, Niger, Senegal, Togo) and the Central African Economic and Monetary Union (Cameroon, Central African Republic, Chad, Republic of Congo, Equatorial Guinea, Gabon). These countries never established their own currencies (Mali and Equatorial Guinea did, until they joined the CFA zone in 1985). The two monetary unions were formally independent from each other and each had its own central bank, yet both pegged their currency to the French franc at the same rate, devalued together by 50 per cent in 1994, and have been pegged to the euro since 1999. The arrangement is special, a legacy of colonial times and based on a guarantee by France, but it is a true, modern monetary union.

The East Caribbean Common Market (Antigua and Barbuda, Dominica, Grenada, St Kitts and Nevis, St Lucia and St Vincent & The Grenadines) form a monetary union. These are small islands that can hardly be compared to the European Monetary Union.

Brunei and Singapore also form a currency union.

Other countries have unilaterally adopted a foreign currency and therefore do not actively participate in the running of the central bank. This is the case of Kiribati, Nauru and Tuvalu, which use the Australian dollar; Lesotho, Namibia and Swaziland, which use the South African rand; and Bahamas, Liberia, Marshall Islands, Micronesia, Palau and Panama, which have adopted the US dollar. More recently, Ecuador and San Salvador have also adopted the dollar since 2001. In Europe, Monaco uses the French franc (now the euro), Liechtenstein the Swiss franc, and San Marino the Italian lira (now the euro). These are not true monetary unions, however, since the centre country is not committed to take into account the interests and viewpoints of its 'satellites', and actually never does.

---

# 11.3 Choices

## 11.3.1 What drives the choice of an exchange rate regime?

It should be clear by now that the choice of an exchange rate regime is largely a choice concerning the use of policy instrument. Freely floating exchange rates allow the monetary authorities complete freedom but restrict the use of a fiscal policy. As the degree of fixity rises, i.e. moving down the list above, monetary policy autonomy is increasingly relinquished, but fiscal policy is recovered. There is no monetary autonomy left under currency boards and no domestic money under dollarization/euroization. The choice of the exchange regime also affects the way foreign disturbances are transmitted domestically, as explained in Box 11-3.

> ### Box 11-3: The insulation properties of exchange rate regimes
>
> The *IS–LM* framework can be used to think about the domestic impact of foreign distur- bances. A few cases are briefly presented here.
>
> An increase in worldwide interest rates is shown in panel (a) of Fig. 11-7. The immediate effect is an outflow of capital and a tendency for the exchange rate to depreciate. Under a flex- ible regime, the central bank does not intervene, and the *LM* schedule does not move. Depreciation improves the current account, which raises demand and moves the *IS* schedule up until it reaches point *C*. Under a fixed exchange rate, the central bank must intervene and buy back its own currency – drawing on its stock of foreign exchange reserves – which moves the *LM* schedule to the left until it reaches point *B*.
>
>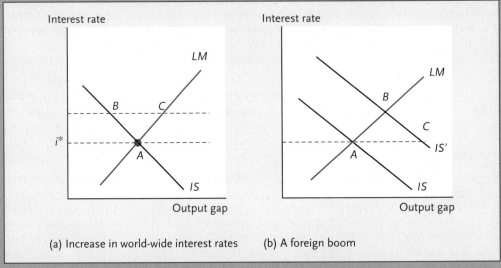
>
> (a) Increase in world-wide interest rates    (b) A foreign boom

FIGURE 11-7: FOREIGN DISTURBANCES

> An increase in world demand – because of a boom, for example – is shown in panel (b) as a rightward shift of the *IS* schedule to *IS'*. At point *B*, capital inflows tend to push the exchange rate upward. Under fixed rates, the central bank intervenes, sells money and the *LM* schedule moves rightward until point *C*. Under flexible rates, the appreciation pushes the *IS* schedule back to the left until we are back at point *A*.
>
> In the end, we see that foreign financial disturbances – a change in the worldwide interest rate – cannot be insulated against, but that the regime deeply affects the outcome in terms of output. Flexible exchange rate insulates the economy from foreign demand disturbances.

## MONETARY POLICY

Monetary policy can be a useful instrument, and may be used to cushion disturbances that affect the economy, whether of domestic or foreign origin. For example, facing a recession, a monetary policy relaxation can help to speed up the resumption of growth. Like all instruments, however, monetary policy can also be misused. Using the printing press to accommodate budget deficits is a temptation that regularly proves to be too hard to resist. This is the discipline argument, and is one[13] reason why some countries decide to tie their own hands and adopt some form of fixity. The existence, or the adoption, of good central banking practice enhances the appeal of exchange rate flexibility.

## FISCAL POLICY

Fiscal policy can also be a useful instrument, but it differs from monetary policy in important respects. It involves considerable politicization as the government must agree with the parliament. It is also slow to implement, partly because of the need for political negotiations and partly because spending and taxes cannot be phased in overnight. These limitations make flexible rates – which preserve the effectiveness of monetary policy – more appealing than fixed rates, which preserve the effectiveness of fiscal policy. The discipline argument also applies to fiscal policy, as governments tend to suffer from a 'budget deficit bias'. In this case, the discipline argument favours flexible rates where the incentive to overuse fiscal policy is lessened by its ineffectiveness.

## EXCHANGE RATE STABILITY

One lesson from Fig. 11-8 is that flexible exchange rates tend to fluctuate considerably, affecting the real exchange rate. These continuous changes in external competitiveness can be disruptive for international trade. For this reason, small, highly integrated economies tend to value some degree of exchange rate fixity.

This has long been the case of many European countries as they aimed at developing intra-European trade. Once the ERM was in place, many countries started to attach greater importance to the discipline argument (this evolution is documented in Chapter 13). Once EMU was established, with a highly determined central bank at its helm in charge of inflation within the Euro area, the policy of freedom argument became dominant, which explains why the euro is freely floating.

## 11.3.2 Fix or float?

Behind the variety of exchange rate arrangements, a central distinction is whether the monetary authorities are making a commitment to a parity or a range. Broadly speaking, arrangements from pegs to dollarization belong to the fixed exchange rate category, in contrast to freely or managed floats, with target zones in the middle grey zone.

The case for flexible exchange rates rests on three main considerations.

■ First, real life is full of surprises and disturbances. When shocks occur – national or worldwide recessions, oil shocks, technological change, etc. – prices must be adjusted to avoid the kind of disequilibria that develop into deepening cyclical fluctuations, unemployment and external imbalances. When prices and wages are sticky, the required adjustments may take far too long and misalignments occur. Flexible exchange rates provide an important, fast, adjustment way to adjust the relative position of domestic and foreign costs and prices.

---

[13] Other reasons are presented at length in the next chapter.

■ Second, exchange rate changes are unavoidably enmeshed with politics. An appreciation or a deprecia-tion affects income distribution and is seen as a judgement on the government's economic know-how. For example, a depreciation improves profits in the export and import competing sectors while hurting consumers who face more expensive imported goods. Politics do not always mix harmoniously with eco-nomics, so removing the exchange rate from the realm of politics may be helpful.

■ Third, the decision to constrain monetary policy is a commitment that is difficult to uphold in each and every circumstance. Failure to abide by the required discipline results in exchange market pressure, which not infrequently leads to bruising currency crises. More worrisome is the fact that the exchange markets themselves occasionally tend to over-react and to display apparently irrational behaviour, provoking unjustified crises.

In the opposite camp, the case for fixed exchange rates emphasizes the tendency of exchange markets to misbehave as well as cases where exchange rate policy is useful.

■ As just noted, destabilizing speculation occurs from time to time. The exchange markets are driven by a short-term financial logic, where information about the future is essential but highly imperfect, giving rise to fads, rumours and herd behaviour which occasionally provokes panic.

■ Even if the exchange market gyrations do not result in panic, they provoke large fluctuations. For inter-national traders and investors, these fluctuations are a source of uncertainty which can hurt trade and foreign direct investment. Box 11-4 provides an example.

■ Harnessing monetary policy to an exchange rate target introduces discipline since foreign exchange markets are likely to immediately sanction inflationary policies by launching speculative attacks.

■ Finally, in case of serious shocks, parity realignments are possible when the exchange rate is explicitly fixed but adjustable. In the Bretton Woods system, this was seen as an insurance against unexpected events, even though it has often been used as a way of escaping the discipline that a fixed exchange rate regime imposes on monetary policy and especially on inflation.

> ### Box 11-4: What difference can the exchange rate regime make: France vs the UK
>
> Except for a brief period of ERM membership in 1991–92, Britain has kept its exchange rate floating (at times with some management) since the collapse of the Bretton Woods system. France, on the contrary, has been an enthusiastic – if not always successful – supporter of pegging, especially with the other European countries. Figure 11-8 contrasts the experience of France and Britain between 1975 and 2002. It plots these countries' real exchange rates, measured as their unit labour costs relative to the average in their main trading partners, so that an increase in the index represents a real appreciation, i.e. a loss of competitiveness.[14] The contrast is sharp between the wide fluctuations of the British real exchange rate and the reasonably smooth evolution of the French rate. The dramatic real appreciation of sterling in the late 1970s corresponds to the discovery of oil in the North Sea, but the other movements are difficult to interpret. These movements mean rapidly changing conditions for British producers who, indeed, often complain about exchange rate instability. There is mounting evidence that large exchange rate volatility hurts trade. Note that being a 'petro-currency' is one reason advanced by British authorities to explain why they do not want to tie sterling.

[14] Following on footnote 4, these so-called effective real exchange rates are defined as $EW/W^*$, where $W$ is the unit cost of labour (the cost of producing one unit of GDP) at home and $W^*$ is the average of these costs in a number of countries selected by the IMF's statistical office.

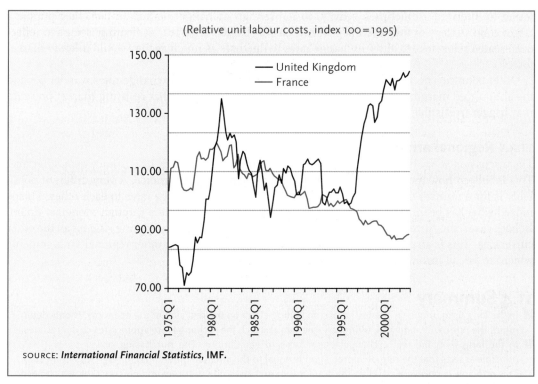

(Relative unit labour costs, index 100 = 1995)

FIGURE 11-8: REAL EXCHANGE RATES OF FRANCE AND THE UK (1975Q1–2002Q4)

### 11.3.3 The two corners

During the 1990s, many currency crises have occurred first in Europe, next in Latin America, then in South-East Asia and in Russia. In all cases, they have hit countries operating one form of a peg or another, but very hard peg countries like Hong Kong and Argentina, both with a currency board, escaped the apparently contagious wave. This has made popular the 'two-corner' view according to which the only safe regimes are the extremes ones, free floating or hard pegs like currency boards, monetary unions or dollarization. Hard pegs are seen as impregnable because the central banks have no opportunity to give in to market pressure, even if they wish to do so. Freely floating rates are presumed not to lead to speculative attacks, because there is no peg top attack; like soft pillows, they absorb any blow.

This view is yet another implication of the principles developed in section 11.1.3: either monetary policy is completely free or it is entirely committed to uphold the chosen peg. All the intermediate regimes, which attempt to combine irreconcilable objectives, are predestined to eventually fail, possibly badly. This has encouraged a number of countries to leave the middle ground over the 1990s. The two-corner view suffered a serious blow when the Argentine currency board collapsed in early 2002 and when, a few months later, Brazil faced furious attacks even though its currency was freely floating.

### 11.3.4 Fear of floating and fear of fixing

The fashion of the two corners is also challenged from a different angle. Most countries announce publicly their chosen exchange regime. However, a close inspection of their actual behaviour tells a different story. Some countries declare that their exchange rate is freely floating, yet they are found to intervene, sometimes heavily, in the foreign exchange market. In fact, they pursue a target zone strategy or they even peg within narrow bands. This 'fear of floating' seems to reflect deep-seated reluctance to allow exchange rates to fluctuate as much as they would if left to market forces.

Other countries declare pegs, with bands, but actually let their exchange rates wander beyond the announced margins. 'Fear of fixing' seems to reflect concerns that resisting market pressure may trigger irresistible speculative attacks.

### 11.3.5 Regional arrangements

The discussion so far has considered whether a country should attach its currency to another one. This is indeed how most countries consider the exchange regime choice. A very different possibility is for a number of countries to undertake to peg their exchange rates to each other. This is indeed what has been done in Europe, first through the EMS and then through monetary union. In both cases, the currencies are pegged *vis-à-vis* each other and freely floating *vis-à-vis* all the other currencies. This is an example of a regional arrangement. There are other regional arrangements which, so far, all involve monetary unions, as described in Box 11-2.

## 11.4 Summary

- In the long term, money is neutral. It has no lasting effect on the real side of the economy. It only determines the rate of inflation and, ultimately, the rate at which the exchange rate appreciates or depreciates.
- In the long term the real exchange rate returns to equilibrium. The purchasing power parity (PPP) principle asserts that the rate of appreciation is equal to the inflation differential (foreign less domestic). This principle is only verified when the equilibrium exchange rate is approximately constant, which need not always be the case.
- In the short term, monetary policy and nominal exchange rate changes affect the real economy. This is the case because prices and wages are sticky and they move slowly to achieve neutrality.
- If the exchange rate is fixed, it becomes impossible to use monetary policy effectively. In practice, monetary policy must be fully committed to upholding the exchange rate; it is not available to pursue domestic targets.
- Non-neutrality explains why the exchange rate regime matters. The exchange rate affects the country's competitiveness, which can be used to deal with disturbances.
- The choice of the exchange rate regime involves trading-off the ability to use monetary policy (sometimes to misuse it) against the tendency towards excessive exchange rate volatility. Announced pegs impose some discipline on monetary policy but at the risk of inviting speculative attacks.
- The exchange rate regime also affects the effectiveness of fiscal policy. In particular, under fully freely floating rates, fiscal policy is ineffective in a small open economy.
- There is a whole range of possible exchange rate regimes, ranging from full flexibility to complete fixity.
- The choice of an exchange rate regime involves various trade-offs: the ability and desirability to use monetary and fiscal policies, the importance of some degree of stability for trade purposes, the quality of domestic institutions in delivering policy discipline (inflation, budget deficits).

#### SELF-ASSESSMENT QUESTIONS

**1.** Section 11.1.3 explains that, when the exchange rate is fixed, a monetary expansion must be completely reversed through exchange market interventions. Why must the real money stock return *exactly* to its initial level?

**2.** Describe carefully how, following an increase in the supply of money, output initially rises but then returns to its initial level as the price level rises.

**3.** If the nominal exchange rate appreciates by less than the excess of foreign over domestic inflation, is the real exchange rate appreciating or depreciating?

**4.** Why are fixed exchange rates believed to impose discipline on monetary policy?

**5.** Why would the exchange rate regime be irrelevant if money were also neutral in the short term? What would make money neutral in the short term?

**6.** Re-do the analysis of section 11.1.4 assuming that the central bank has a policy of keeping the interest rate unchanged.

**7.** Why is it asserted that there cannot be speculative attacks against freely floating exchange rates?

**8.** Using the *IS–LM* framework, study the effect of a sudden increase in the foreign price level. Distinguish between a fixed and a floating exchange rate regime.

**9.** Why do small open economies tend to favour some degree of exchange rate fixity?

## Essay questions

**1.** The real, not the nominal, exchange rate is what matters for the real side of the economy. Why don't central banks attempt to control the real rather the nominal exchange rate?

**2.** Why does a fixed exchange rate allow a country to adopt an inflation rate that differs from that in the anchor currency country?

**3.** Why do many countries display fear of floating? Why don't they correctly report what they do?

**4.** Dollarization is a good regime only for countries that display a chronic lack of fiscal discipline. Explain and comment.

**5.** It is often believed that a peg encourages residents (households, firms, banks) to borrow in a foreign currency. Then, if the exchange rate is devalued, many residents face the risk of bankruptcy. Explain and comment.

**6.** Find out about the behaviour of the exchange rate of Switzerland, a country that is officially floating, *vis-à-vis* the DM and then the euro. Is this a case of fear of floating? Why?

**7.** Comment on the following assertion: 'Fixed exchange rate regimes are temporary arrangements.' What is the implication for Europe?

## Further reading: the aficionados corner

The following presents the debate about the choice of exchange rate regimes:

Eichengreen, B. (1999) *Toward a New International Financial Architecture: A Practical Post-Asia Agenda*, Institute for International Economics, Washington, DC.

For a good presentation and a defence of currency boards:

Gosh, A., A.-M. Gulde and H. Wolf (2000) 'Currency boards: More than a quick fix?', *Economic Policy*, **31**, 269–336.

Two studies show the difference between the officially declared regime and what countries actually do:

Levy-Yeyati, E. and F. Sturzenegger (2002) *Classifying Exchange Rate Regimes: Deeds vs. Words*, Universidad Torcuato Di Tella.

Reinhart, C. and K. Rogoff (2002) *The Modern History of Exchange Rate Arrangements: A Reinterpretation*, IMF Working Paper No. 8963.

A review of the evidence on purchasing power parity is:

Rogoff, K. (1996) 'The purchasing power parity puzzle', *Journal of Economic Literature*, **34** (2), 647–68.

## Useful websites

The IMF presents up-to-date evaluations of exchange rate policies:
http://www.imf.org

To find out about the exchange rate regime of a particular country, visit its central bank's website. The list of all central bank websites is at:
http://www.bis.org/cbanks.htm

Crises and regimes are debated on Professor Roubini's website:
http://www.stern.nyu.edu/globalmacro/

## REFERENCES

Burda, M. and C. Wyplosz (2001) *Macroeconomics, A European Text*, Third Edition, Oxford University Press, Oxford.
Frankel, J. (1999) *No Single Currency Regime is Right for all Countries at all Times*, NBER Working Paper 7338.

# 12 The European Monetary System

---

The European Monetary System (EMS) is the bridge between the dollar-centred Bretton Woods system and the monetary union but it is also the entry point for the next waves of countries accessing the EU. As can be guessed from the previous chapter, the quest for exchange rate stability within Europe required that monetary policies be restricted somehow. Failure to recognize this requirement, or perhaps the inability to agree on this technicality, resulted in an agitated history. Paradoxically, the EMS's shortcomings made the adoption of a single currency seen as a natural and desirable step. This in itself justifies a detailed study. In addition, the EMS did not cease to exist with the launch of the euro. The chapter first presents the rules that govern the EMS. Next, it describes the evolution of the system from a fully symmetric arrangement to what has been called the 'greater Deutschemark area'. The last section presents the changes that followed the speculative crises of 1993 and led to the currently existing EMS.

---

## 12.1 **The EMS agreements**

The decision to create the EMS was taken in 1978 by German Chancellor Helmut Schmidt and French President Valéry Giscard d'Estaing. They were alarmed by the monetary disorders that had followed the end of the Bretton Woods system and by the inability to sustain the Snake arrangement, described in Chapter 10. In line with a view long held in Europe, they saw large exchange rate movements as a direct threat to the Common Market. They wanted a stronger, more resilient arrangement.

Political sensitivities were important, however. Germany would never take the risk of weakening its star currency, the DM, while France could not be seen as playing second fiddle to Germany. Additionally, the smaller countries had to be brought along. Furthermore, the UK was staunchly opposed to a fixed exchange rate regime. The solution came close to squaring the circle. The chosen arrangement was explicitly symmetric, without any central currency, and it established a subtle distinction between the European Monetary System (EMS), to which all European Community countries were *de facto* members, and the Exchange Rate Mechanism (ERM), an optional scheme. The ERM was the only meaningful part of the EMS. It rested on four main elements: a grid of agreed-upon bilateral exchange rates, mutual support, a commitment to joint decision of realignments and the European Currency Unit (ECU).

### 12.1.1 **The ERM's parity grid**

All ERM currencies were fixed to each other, with a band of fluctuation of ±2.25 per cent around the central parity (Italy was initially allowed a margin of fluctuation of ±6 per cent, in recognition of its higher rate of inflation and internal political difficulties). The arrangement was represented by the parity grid, a matrix-like table collecting all pairwise central parities and their associated margins of fluctuations.

The arrangement carried a number of interesting features. First, the system was entirely European, with no reference to the dollar or to gold. Never before had European countries built an exchange rate system standing on its own. Second, the system was fully symmetric: no currency played any special role, in contrast to the dollar in the Bretton Woods system. Third, the responsibility for maintaining each bilateral exchange rate within its margin was explicitly shared by both countries,[1] thus removing the stigma of one weak and one strong currency.

### 12.1.2 **Mutual support**

The Snake had failed because the weak currencies had to fend for themselves. In contrast, the ERM included an agreement to automatically provide mutual support. By construction, exchange market pressure would simultaneously hit two countries. For example, the Danish krone–Dutch guilder bilateral exchange could be pressed against one of its margins where, say, the krone was weak and the guilder strong. The ERM agreement stipulated that in this case the Danish and Dutch central banks were obliged to intervene on the foreign exchange market. The Dutch would sell guilders to make them more abundant and therefore cheaper, and the Danish central bank would buy krone to raise its value. These interventions could be carried with any currency: for example, the Dutch central bank would sell guilders against US dollars, DMs, etc., including the krone.

Crucially, in principle, this commitment was *unlimited*. A central bank could not stop intervening as long as its parity *vis-à-vis* any other member currency was pressed against its limit. But what if it ran out of ammunition? In the above example, the Dutch central bank could never be in

---

[1] Since all arrangements were bilateral, it would always be the case that the threat to break through a band of fluctuation would simultaneously affect two currencies, a strong one and a weak one.

that position since it would be accumulating foreign exchange reserves while selling its own currency, which it could produce in unlimited amounts. The Danish central bank, on the other hand, could run out of foreign exchange reserves, having spent all it had to buy back krone. In that case, the central bank of the Netherlands would also be committed to making a loan to its Danish colleague, allowing for continuing interventions as long as necessary. Other ERM central banks, even if they were not directly involved, could decide to give a helping hand, by also intervening on the foreign exchange markets, buying krone, or lending directly to the Danish central bank.

### 12.1.3 Joint management of exchange rate realignments

How long should this game be pursued? Clearly, if markets remained unimpressed by the artillery lined up against them, the central banks providing theoretically unlimited support could become concerned. In that case, the solution would be to throw in the towel, acknowledge the market pressure and realign exchange rates. How was that done?

Allowing any central bank to change its exchange rate as it pleases would have made little contribution to the establishment of a level playing field. The founding fathers of the EMS were quite concerned that individual countries might try to achieve unfair trade advantage through recurrent devaluations, the infamous beggar-thy-neighbour practice of the inter-war period perceived to have been a source of economic and political disintegration. This is why the ERM stipulated that any change in any bilateral exchange rate had to be jointly decided by all members. The consensus rule implied that, in effect, each country gave up exclusive control of its own exchange rate. Realignments, as the exercise came to be known, turned out to involve tough but ultimately successful bargaining, usually concluded by multiple changes, as Table 12-1 shows.

| Dates | 24.9.79 | 30.11.79 | 22.3.81 | 5.10.81 | 22.2.82 | 14.6.82 |
|---|---|---|---|---|---|---|
| No. of currencies involved | 2 | 1 | 1 | 2 | 2 | 4 |
| Dates | 21.3.83 | 18.5.83 | 22.7.85 | 7.4.86 | 4.8.86 | 12.1.87 |
| No. of currencies involved | 7 [a] | 7 [a] | 7 [a] | 5 | 1 | 3 |
| Dates | 8.1.90 | 14.9.92 | 23.11.92 | 1.2.93 | 14.5.93 | 6.3.95 |
| No. of currencies involved | 1 | 3 [b] | 2 | 1 | 2 | 2 |

NOTES: (a) All ERM currencies realigned. (b) In addition, two currencies (pounds sterling and lira) leave the ERM.

TABLE 12-1: ERM REALIGNMENTS

### 12.1.4 The ECU

The EMS included the symbolic creation of the European Currency Unit or ECU. The ECU was a basket of all EMS countries, including those of EC countries that did not participate in the ERM. Each currency entered with a weight meant to represent the country's size and importance in intra-European trade. These weights, which were revised every five years, were initially chosen so that 1 ECU was worth 1 US$. The latest weights are shown in Table 12-2.

The ECU became the official unit of account of the European Community, used for all official transactions and accounts. It was explicitly designed not to be a currency: there were no physical ECUs and central banks did not carry out transactions in ECUs. The private markets, however, adopted the ECU and started to issue debt instruments using this unit. Technically and legally,

| | Amount in ECU 1 | Weight (%) |
|---|---|---|
| Belgian franc | 3.43100 | 8.71 |
| Danish krone | 0.19760 | 2.71 |
| Deutschemark | 0.62420 | 32.68 |
| Dutch guilder | 0.21980 | 10.21 |
| French franc | 1.33200 | 20.79 |
| Greek drachma | 1.44000 | 0.49 |
| Italian lira | 151.80000 | 7.21 |
| Irish punt | 0.00855 | 1.08 |
| Portuguese escudo | 1.39300 | 0.71 |
| Spanish peseta | 6.88500 | 4.24 |
| UK pound sterling | 0.08784 | 11.17 |

TABLE 12-2: THE ECU BASKET

these were currency baskets. When the euro was started on 4 January 1999, it was set to be worth exactly 1 ECU at its first quotation on that day, and the ECU ceased to exist.

### 12.1.5 Assessment: a flexible and cohesive arrangement

Overall, the EMS was built as a flexible yet cohesive arrangement. It allowed membership *à la carte*, permitting countries unhappy with fixed exchange rate regimes not to join the ERM. Even within the ERM, the margins of fluctuations, normally set at ±2.25 per cent, could be temporarily set at ±6 per cent, an option exercised by Italy from 1979 to 1990, and by Spain and Portugal following their entry in 1989 and 1992, respectively.

---

BOX 12-1: THE IMPOSSIBLE TRINITY

The impossible trinity principle holds that the three following characteristics cannot be observed together:

1. A fixed exchange rate
2. Monetary policy independence
3. Full capital mobility.

It is possible to have any pair at a given moment, however. During the early EMS period, for example, many countries restricted capital movements; they could award themselves some degree of monetary independence even though they were part of the ERM. The UK dismantled its capital controls in the early 1980s and retained monetary policy independence by staying out of the ERM. The Netherlands, which removed its capital controls early, soon tied the guilder rigidly to the DM, effectively giving up any pretence at monetary policy independence. The trinity proved to be a curse to those countries that were in the ERM and were gradually allowing increased capital mobility, and yet were reluctant to give up the monetary policy instrument. Many of the ERM crises can be directly traced back to failed attempts at breaking this iron law.

---

On the other hand, the arrangement implied a deep commitment from member central banks. As long as the exchange rate peg was being adhered to, there was little policy independence left, as was explained in Chapter 11. The corresponding principle, the impossible trinity, is presented in Box 12-1 and is formally an implication of the theory presented in Section 11.1.3. In addition, changing the exchange rate, the last major remaining degree of monetary policy freedom, was removed from national control through the consensus rule. In return, mutual support, the agreement that interventions ought to be bilateral, automatic and unlimited, represented an unusually strong collective commitment. Although sterilizations were possible, the arrangement reproduced many of the features of the Gold Standard, and aimed to achieve a similar degree of robustness (see Chapter 10).

## 12.2 EMS-1: from divergence to convergence and blow-up

The response to the challenge of the impossible trinity has varied over time. During the first period, which continued until the mid-1980s, ERM members had opted for exchange rate stability and policy independence, with capital controls in place in the devaluation-prone countries. Monetary independence mainly meant the ability for each country to operate with a different inflation rate. Realignments were frequent. In a second stage, the aim was to bring down the inflation rate, in effect gradually converging to the lowest rate. In effect, monetary policy independence was being surrendered. This is when Germany, the perennial low inflation country and now the standard to emulate, established its dominance – an evolution that ultimately prompted the next move to monetary union.

### 12.2.1 The first version of EMS: agreeing to disagree (1979–85)

The EMS was conceived to avoid large fluctuations in intra-European real exchange rates. Building a robust ERM was one thing, but the constraints implied by the impossible trinity was something else. After the first oil shock of 1973, inflation rates started to diverge markedly, and the second oil shock did nothing to improve the situation. Once committed to a system of fixed-but-adjustable exchange rates, the ERM countries faced a choice between two strategies. Plan A was to dedicate monetary policies to the exchange pegs. This required similar inflation rates, for any lasting difference would inexorably hurt the competitiveness of high-inflation countries relative to that of low-inflation countries. Plan B was to accept lasting divergences in inflation and adjust the exchange rates as frequently as needed to avoid competitiveness problems and trade imbalances. As Fig. 12-1 clearly shows, Plan B was chosen in the initial period and Table 12-1 confirms that realignments occurred frequently.

The economic interpretation of this choice is quite straightforward. It is based on the relationship between money and inflation established in Chapter 10. Because, in the long term, inflation depends on money growth, Plan A would have required that all countries adopt similar rates of money growth. However, it was not easy to decide which country's inflation rate should be the target. Low inflation is better than high, of course, but money is not neutral in the short term. Aiming at low rates of money growth and inflation would have led to contractionary policies and rising unemployment in high-inflation countries, and, naturally, low-inflation countries were unwilling to accept higher rates. France, a country traditionally committed to low unemployment, would not agree to adopt contractionary measures while Germany, a country deeply attached to low inflation, would not countenance any monetary policy relaxation. The inability to resolve this conflict, as well as considerations of national prestige, explains why Plan B was chosen by default.

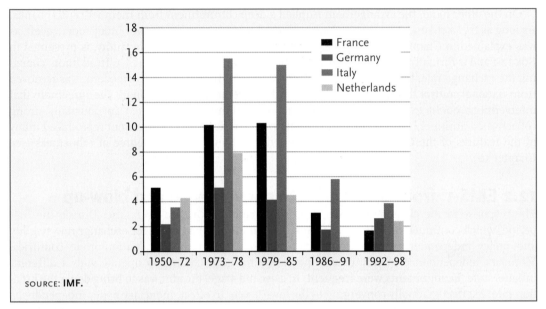

SOURCE: **IMF.**

FIGURE 12-1: INFLATION

## 12.2.2 The second version of EMS: towards a greater DM area (1986–92)

Plan B did not function without problems, and two main difficulties emerged. First, in-between realignments, high-inflation countries would see their trade accounts deteriorate. When it came time to take remedial action, the consensus rule for realignments meant that low-inflation countries, which enjoyed a trade surplus, were quite reluctant to allow deep depreciations. The bargaining usually resulted in a depreciation that corrected for the accumulated difference in inflation, but no more. As a result, high-inflation countries were more or less permanently in external deficit while the low-inflation countries exhibited surpluses. This is illustrated in Fig. 12-2 which shows Italy's current account and real exchange rate *vis-à-vis* Germany (the figure shows the previous year's exchange rate since it takes time to affect the current account). The Italian account's seesaw behaviour closely mirrors the evolution of the real exchange rate: in-between realignments the real exchange rate appreciates and the current account deteriorates, and devaluations are soon followed by an improvement in the current account.

Another serious problem with Plan B was that realignments were easily foreseen. The precise date could be in doubt – although shrewd observers often correctly identified many of them by looking at the timing of elections and other important political events – but the need to ultimately realign was plain to see. Looking at Fig. 12-2, it is quite obvious that the DM could only be revalued and the lira could only be devalued. To make the bet even easier, the gradually deepening external imbalance unambiguously signalled when this would happen. Speculators did not miss these signals and played what came to be called 'one-way bets': they speculated against the currencies of high-inflation countries and accumulated the currencies of low inflation countries. As a result, most realignments took place in the midst of acute speculative crises, hardly the 'island of monetary stability' promised by the founding fathers of the EMS. Plan B quickly exhausted its charms.

A key problem with Plan A had always been the difficulty of agreeing upon a standard in terms of monetary policy. Germany never had any doubt that the Bundesbank had it right but the French

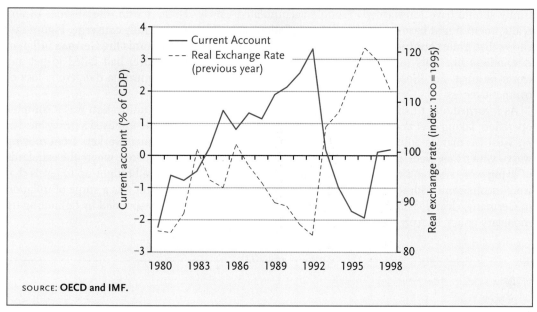

SOURCE: **OECD and IMF.**

FIGURE 12-2: ITALY IN THE EMS

(and the Italians, Belgians, etc.) would not easily share this view. By late 1983, France had gone through three humiliating devaluations in just one year, each of which had been preceded by costly speculative attacks. Recently elected President Mitterrand had tried his leftist medicine[2] and it had clearly failed. His Finance Minister, Jacques Delors, convinced him that France ought to 'play the European card'. The strategy of competitive disinflation was born: from now on France would endeavour to replace devaluations with low inflation, hopefully lower even than in Germany. The perennially weak franc would become the 'franc fort'. Monetary policy was redirected towards that overarching objective, eschewing short-term gains from easy money.

Over the following years, all central banks followed suit and emulated the Bundesbank, effectively using the DM as an anchor. For nearly six years, from early 1987 to September 1992, there was no realignment,[3] as inflation rates gradually declined towards the low German level (Fig. 12-1). During that time, in anticipation of the 1992 Single Act, capital controls were progressively dismantled throughout Europe, and were formally banned as of July 1990. The impossible trinity meant that all central banks had effectively given up their ability to carry out an independent monetary policy. The Bundesbank was the only central bank free to act on its own, which it did with two important consequences: the other countries became eager to move to a monetary union as a way of recovering some influence on their monetary policies, and the EMS exploded.

## 12.2.3 The crises of 1992–93
The long period of complete exchange rate stability that followed the adoption of the DM anchor convinced many that it could last for ever. This proved to be terribly wrong, as the impossible

---

[2] Soon after his election, Mitterrand relaxed monetary and fiscal policies, significantly raised minimum wages, reduced the working week and proceeded to nationalize several banks and large corporations.
[3] The 1990 realignment (Table 12-1) was not really a realignment. As Italy switched to the narrow ±2.25 per cent band of fluctuation, it brought its central parity closer to its weak margin.

trinity should have forewarned. Trouble accumulated slowly. To start with, the absence of any realignment might have looked good, but inflation rates did not quite fully converge. Figure 12-3 shows that while countries like Denmark and France indeed moved towards the German inflation rate, others like Italy (or Portugal and Spain, not shown in the figure) had failed to get any closer by 1991. For these countries, the fixed exchange rate strategy meant a dangerous loss of competitiveness.

As it turned out, this is when the Berlin wall collapsed. Germany's unification was a complex operation: taking over an impoverished country of 16 million inhabitants imposed a heavy burden on West Germany's public finances.[4] In addition, to prevent East German workers from moving west – which they were instantaneously entitled to do as unification occurred, where the standards of living were several times higher than those in the east – wages were brought up to levels that were inconsistent with the productivity of East German firms. The result was a surge of inflation in Germany, clearly visible in Fig. 12-3. Predictably, the Bundesbank responded by tightening up monetary policy, sharply raising the interest rate.

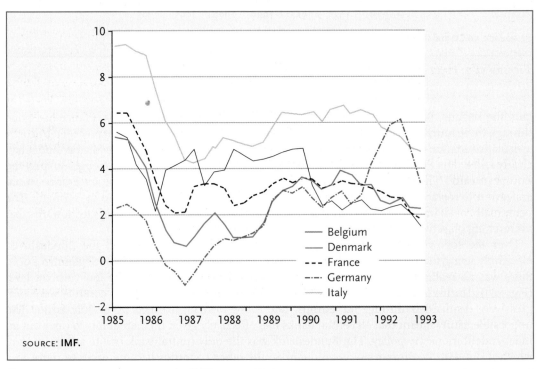

SOURCE: **IMF.**

FIGURE 12-3: INFLATION RATES (1985Q1–1992Q4)

What could the other ERM members do? One solution would have been to let the DM appreciate. Blinded by the stability of ERM exchange rates and recent successes in bringing inflation down, and bent on achieving strong currency status, they rejected what they saw as a humiliating depreciation *vis-à-vis* the DM. This meant that they had to stick with the strategy of blindly

[4] For an account of the economic challenges, see David Begg, Jean-Pierre Danthine, Francesco Giavazzi, and Charles Wyplosz (1990) 'The East, the Deutschemark and EMU', *Monitoring European Integration* 1, CEPR, London, and Gerlinde Sinn and Hans-Werner Sinn (1992), *Jumpstart. The Economic Unification of Germany*, MIT Press, Cambridge, Mass.

following the Bundesbank. But faced with the unification shock, the Bundesbank adopted a tight policy of high interest rates, that was much too tight for the other ERM members. Bad luck played its part, too. Outside Germany, the early 1990s were years of slow growth and the wrong time for tight monetary policies. The ERM started to look suspicious.

The last stroke came from the EMU project itself. The Maastricht Treaty had been signed in December 1991 and was to be ratified by each member country during 1992. The first country to initiate the ratification process was Denmark where law mandates that international treaties be submitted to referenda. For a variety of reasons, the Danes voted down the Treaty by a few thousands votes. The Treaty included one provision which stated that it would be void unless ratified by all European Union countries. Thus, before the other countries even had a chance to ratify it, the Treaty was technically dead by mid-1992. This alarmed the exchange markets who had bought into the authorities' excessive confidence in both the ERM and the monetary union project. Speculative attacks started immediately, initially targeting Italy (the lira was seriously overvalued by then) and the UK. The UK had finally joined the ERM a year earlier, soon after John Major had replaced Margaret Thatcher as Prime Minister (largely because her opposition to ERM membership appeared anachronistic in the midst of a wave of Euro-optimism), yet the central rate chosen for the pound was seen to be overvalued.

In response to the speculative attacks, the strong currency central banks initially intervened in support of the embattled Banca d'Italia and Bank of England. By mid-September 1992, the attacks had become massive; a frightened Bundesbank decided that truly unlimited interventions were not reasonable and stopped its support. Left to themselves, with foreign exchange reserves falling rapidly, the lira and the pound withdrew from the ERM and the markets concluded that the ERM was considerably more fragile than hitherto admitted. Speculation shifted to the currencies of Ireland, Portugal and Spain, which twice had to be devalued. Contagion then spread to Belgium, Denmark and France, even though inflation in these countries had converged to below the German level and their currencies were not overvalued. By the summer of 1993, huge amounts of reserves had been thrown in the foreign exchange markets and speculation was still going strong. In order to uphold the principle of the ERM, and save face at the same time, the monetary authorities adopted new ultra-large (±15 per cent) bands of fluctuations. Figure 12-4 shows the ERM history of the DM/French franc parity. The tight ERM was dead.

It was not only that monetary integration seemed to be a failure, but bad blood had been spilled, which complicated any reconstruction efforts. The Bundesbank's reneging of the principle of unlimited interventions offended Italy and the UK, so much so that the Bundesbank next publicly announced that it would not let the French franc sink. After a decade of hesitation, Britain had finally shed its traditional euro-scepticism and joined the ERM, and its forcible departure left a scar that would not heal easily.

## 12.2.4 The lessons

A number of features of the experience remain controversial. Inflation was successfully reduced among ERM countries, suggesting the usefulness of tying the hands of central banks through an exchange rate peg. However, a comparison with non-ERM countries does not indicate that inflation has declined more quickly or less painfully. At the same time, the sharp turnaround of France in 1983 is often related to a political decision to uphold ERM membership and maintain exchange rate stability. A possible interpretation is that, lacking adequate domestic economic and political institutions, an external arrangement like the ERM has a useful substitution role to play.[5] This is a popular view in Italy, a country with a history of chronically high inflation, which could explain why, despite the 1993 setback, it has made a major effort to be a founding member of the Euro area.

---

[5] A similar argument concerns the Stability and Growth Pact presented in Chapter 15.

On the other hand a number of lessons seem to be generally accepted:

- The impossible trinity requires that domestic monetary policy independence be abandoned if the exchange rate is rigidly fixed. This is a tall order of requirement when economic conditions differ across countries (Germany was too different as it went through unification).
- As long as the weaker currency countries imposed restrictions on capital movements, speculative attacks were manageable. Once full capital mobility was achieved, central banks soon realized that even large stocks of foreign exchange reserves are too small, and that unlimited interventions are practically impossible.
- In particular, once a speculative attack has started, attempting to defend a parity implies offering the market one-way bets: either the peg is abandoned and the speculators win, or it is upheld and they lose nothing.
- Consequently, monetary integration with separate currencies is a very risky endeavour, possibly a hopeless quest. Monetary union is one response.

## 12.3 The EMS re-engineered

### 12.3.1 A softer ERM

The post-crisis ERM agreed upon in 1993 differed little from a floating exchange rate regime. Bilateral parities could move by 30 per cent, a very wide margin. Unsurprisingly, therefore, the (non)system worked well. Figure 12-4 shows that the DM/FRF fluctuated slightly outside of its earlier narrow ±2.25 per cent range for a few years and then gently converged to its ultimate EMU conversion rate.

One precondition set by the Maastricht Treaty for joining EMU is at least two years of ERM membership (the other conditions are presented in Chapter 14). This is why Italy returned to the

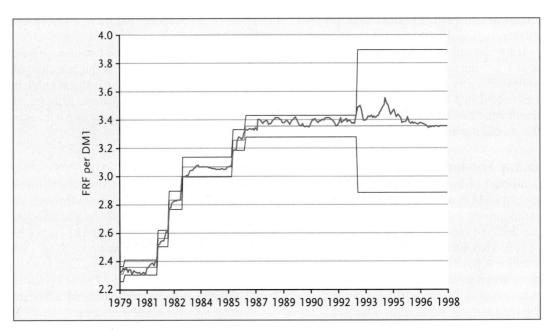

FIGURE 12-4: DM/FRF IN ERM

ERM in 1997, as did two new members of the European Union, Austria and Finland. The UK, not interested in joining EMU, has not returned and argues that this condition should not be interpreted literaly since the wide bands have little practical relevance. This position is supported by Sweden, which has also decided to stay out of EMU after joining the Union at the same time as Austria and Finland.

## 12.3.2 EMS-2

The adoption of the euro in January 1999 has been accompanied by the launch of a new EMS. EMS-2, as it is called, is described in Box 12-2. It incorporates most of the features of its predecessor, yet differs in some key aspects:

- While EMS-1 was a symmetric system based on a grid of bilateral parities, in EMS-2 parities are defined *vis-à-vis* the euro, which is clearly the centre currency. There is no grid, just a table.
- The margin of fluctuation is less precisely defined. *De facto*, the 'standard' band is ±15 per cent as in the latter version of EMS-1, but a narrower band is also possible.
- Interventions are still automatic and unlimited, but there is a clear signal that the ECB may decide to suspend this obligation.

Thus the system is more flexible and less committal, no doubt a consequence of the 1992–93 crisis. In addition, it is *à la carte*, allowing different margins of fluctuation. So far, two countries have joined: Greece, with the standard ±15 per cent band, until it joined the EMU in January 2000, and Denmark, which has adopted the narrow ±2.25 per cent that prevailed in the first version of EMS-1. Sweden and the UK have decided to stay out 'for the time being' and continue to argue that ERM membership is not a prerequisite should they wish to join the EMU.

---

BOX 12-2: THE AMSTERDAM RESOLUTION OF THE EUROPEAN COUNCIL ON THE ESTABLISHMENT OF AN EXCHANGE RATE MECHANISM IN THE THIRD STAGE OF ECONOMIC AND MONETARY UNION (JUNE 1997) – EXCERPTS.[6]

'A central rate against the euro will be defined for the currency of each Member State outside the euro area participating in the exchange-rate mechanism. There will be one standard fluctuation band of plus or minus 15 per cent around the central rate. Intervention at the margins will in principle be automatic and unlimited, with very short-term financing available. However, the ECB and the central banks of the other participants could suspend intervention if this were to conflict with their primary objective.'

'On a case-by-case basis, formally agreed fluctuation bands narrower than the standard one and backed up in principle by automatic intervention and financing may be set at the request of the non-euro area Member States concerned.'

'The details of the very short-term financing mechanism will be determined in the agreement between the ECB and the national central banks, broadly on the basis of the present arrangements.'

---

[6] The full text is available, for example, on the website of the Danish central bank at:
http://www.nationalbanken.dk/nb/nb.nsf/alldocs/Fthe_erm_ii_agreement.

### 12.3.3 The next wave

A further 10 countries[7] are expected to join the European Union on 1 May 2004, as explained in Chapter 1. What will be their position regarding the EMS? The Amsterdam resolution states that:

> Participation in the exchange-rate mechanism will be voluntary for the Member States outside the euro area. Nevertheless, Member States with a derogation can be expected to join the mechanism. A Member State which does not participate from the outset in the exchange-rate mechanism may participate at a later date.

This establishes a presumption that they will be asked to join the ERM, but the British and Swedish examples constitute a precedent that they might use. There are some good reasons not to join too early. Table 12-3 shows that inflation in the CEECs, although declining quickly, is still significantly above the EMU area's rate. If they decide to pursue disinflation, the CEECs undoubtedly can converge, but they may have other policy priorities. This issue may make the accession process even more lengthy and complex. Furthermore, some countries have adopted a currency board, so they are already effectively using the euro by proxy. One of them, Estonia, has clearly indicated that it wishes to go straight into the EMU, without passing through the ERM purgatory.

| | Czech Rep. | Estonia | Hungary | Latvia | Lithuania | Poland | Slovak Rep. | Slovenia | EU |
|---|---|---|---|---|---|---|---|---|---|
| 1996 | 8.1 | 23.1 | 23.4 | 17.6 | 24.6 | 20.0 | 5.2 | 9.9 | 2.7 |
| 1997 | 7.4 | 10.6 | 18.0 | 8.4 | 8.9 | 14.7 | 6.0 | 8.4 | 2.1 |
| 1998 | 9.1 | 8.2 | 13.3 | 4.7 | 5.1 | 11.5 | 6.1 | 7.9 | 1.7 |
| 1999 | 3.8 | 3.3 | 10.7 | 2.4 | 0.8 | 6.9 | 10.2 | 6.2 | 1.2 |
| 2000 | 2.8 | 4.0 | 9.6 | 2.7 | 1.0 | 9.6 | 11.3 | 8.9 | 1.9 |
| 2001 | 4.3 | 5.7 | 9.0 | 2.5 | 1.2 | 5.4 | 7.0 | 8.4 | 2.4 |
| 2002 | 4.0 | 3.6 | 5.5 | 1.3 | 0.3 | 5.0 | 6.0 | 7.5 | 1.8 |
| SOURCE: OECD and EBRD. | | | | | | | | | |

TABLE 12-3: INFLATION IN EASTERN AND CENTRAL EUROPEAN COUNTRIES

## 12.4 Summary

■ The EMS was adopted in 1979 to preserve, as much as possible, exchange rate stability within Europe. All EU members are members of the EMS but the active part of the system, the ERM, was initially optional.

■ The ERM was based on a grid specifying all bilateral parities and the corresponding margins of fluctuations, normally ±2.25 per cent.

■ ERM members were committed to jointly defend their bilateral parities, if necessary through unlimited interventions and loans. Realignments were possible, but required the consent of all members.

■ In practice, the EMS went through three phases. During the first period, inflation differed quite widely from one country to another and realignments were frequent. Then, all countries decided to adopt the Bundesbank's low inflation strategy, in effect adopting the DM as an anchor and avoiding further realignments. The 1992–93 crisis ended with the adoption of wide margins, allowing the ERM to nominally survive until the launch of the euro.

---

[7] Cyprus, the Czech Republic, Estonia, Hungary, Latvia, Lithuania, Malta, Poland, Slovakia and Slovenia.

- The 1992–93 crisis provides an example of the impossible trinity. The liberalization of financial markets and the fixity of exchange rates was incompatible with divergent monetary policies, especially as Germany, the central country, was going through its unification shock.
- With the adoption of a single currency, a new EMS was established. EMS-2 mainly differs from EMS-1 in that the euro is now the reference currency. All EU members are required to take part in this new exchange rate mechanism unless they have a derogation, which is the case of the UK and, *de facto*, of Sweden.
- EMS-2 remains a prerequisite for joining the Euro area. The 10 new members of the EU are to join the mechanism on accession.

## SELF-ASSESSMENT QUESTIONS

1. List the similarities and differences between the ERM and the Gold Standard.
2. How does EMS-2 differ from EMS-1?
3. Find out about the balance sheet of a central bank and show how these interventions are traced.
4. Consider a high-inflation ERM country. Draw the evolution over time of the price level, and the nominal and real exchange rates, allowing for occasional devaluations. Do the same for a low-inflation country that occasionally revalues its nominal exchange rate.
5. Imagine three ERM countries. Compute a fictional parity grid linking their three currencies pairwise.
6. What do we mean by saying the EMS has become a 'Deutschemark area'? How did that happen and could it have been foreseen?
7. How could the ERM countries have reacted to German unification in 1991?

## ESSAY QUESTIONS

1. Why was the Bundesbank concerned about unlimited interventions in EMS-1?
2. Can other groups of countries also form a system like the EMS?
3. In retrospect it is claimed that the 1992–93 crisis of the EMS could have been anticipated. Why and why not? Once the crisis started, could Italy and the UK have stayed in the system, and if so under what conditions?
4. Would the Bretton Woods system have survived had it been patterned after the ERM?
5. Contrast the two periods of the EMS: 1979–85 and 1986–92.
6. What lessons do you draw from the 1992–93 wave of speculative attacks? In particular, why did speculators attack some currencies that were obviously not overvalued (the Belgian and French francs, the Danish kronor) after other currencies were forced to leave the ERM or to devalue?
7. After they join the European Union in 2004, the new members will have to operate for at least two years within EMS-2. What problems can you envision? What alternatives would you suggest?
8. By 1990, the EMS was seen as a major success. Can you provide your own evaluation of the system's performance over the period 1979–90? (You may use any criteria of success that you wish, but be explicit about them.)

## FURTHER READING: THE AFICIONADOS CORNER

### The EMS

A very useful description of the EMS is given in Chapter 1 of:
Kenen, P. (1995) *Economic and Monetary Union in Europe*, Cambridge University Press, New York.

On the history of the EMS and its evolution towards EMU, see:

Gros, D. and N. Thygesen (1998) *European Monetary Integration*, Second Edition, Addison Wesley Longman Ltd, London.

## *Enlargement of the EU*

A study of the exchange rate regime treatment of accessing countries can be found in:

Begg, D., B. Eichengreen, L. Halpern, J. von Hagen, and C. Wyplosz (2003) *Sustainable Regimes of Capital Movements in Accession Countries*, Policy Paper 10, Centre for Economic Policy Research, London.
http://www. cepr.org/pubs/books/PP10.asp

## USEFUL WEBSITES

### *The EMS*

The European Parliament's factsheet, a concise summary:
http://www.europarl.eu.int/factsheets/5_2_0_en.htm

## REFERENCES

Begg, D., B. Eichengreen, L. Halpern, J. von Hagen, and C. Wyplosz (2003) *Sustainable Regimes of Capital Movements in Accession Countries*, Policy Paper 10, Centre for Economic Policy Research, London.
http://www. cepr.org/pubs/books/PP10.asp
Eichengreen, B. (2002) *Lessons of the Euro for the Rest of the World*, December.
http://emlab.berkeley.edu/users/eichengr/policy.html
Sinn, G. and H.W. Sinn (1992) *Jumpstart. The Economic Unification of Germany*, MIT Press Cambridge, Mass.

# PART V The Monetary Union

This part studies the monetary union. It proceeds in two steps, theory and practice. Chapter 13 presents the optimum currency area (OCA) theory. This is where we ask the fundamental question: Which countries stand to benefit from sharing the same currency? The theory does not provide a black-and-white answer, rather it develops a set of criteria to evaluate the costs and the benefits of forming a monetary union. Applying these criteria to Europe, we find that some criteria are fulfilled, but not others. This conclusion illustrates the unending debates on the merits of the European Monetary Union. It also serves as a warning of where problems may surface, and suggests some answers on how to deal with them. Chapter 14 then describes the monetary union, its principles and institutions. It also provides a review of the first few years of the euro.

# 13 Optimum Currency Areas

This chapter presents the optimum currency area theory, a systematic way of trying to decide whether it makes sense for a group of countries to abandon their national currencies. Giving up the exchange rate instrument cannot be innocuous, so the question really is: Under what conditions is such a step relatively painless? The theory develops a battery of economic and political criteria which recognize that the real economic cost of giving up the exchange rate instrument arises in the presence of asymmetric shocks, shocks that do not affect all currency union member countries. The chapter then examines whether Europe passes these tests, and concludes that it is not really an optimum currency area, but nor does it fully fail. It is also observed that national characteristics are not frozen and that, over time, because it has adopted a single currency, Europe may satisfy all or most of the criteria.

## 13.1 The question, the problem, and the answer

For a long time the rule seemed to be: to each country its own currency. National symbols are displayed on coins and banknotes, much as feudal lords had their faces stamped on gold and silver coins. There have been few exceptions to this rule, most of them seemingly exotic. And yet, is this association between nation and currency *economically* sensible? If we forget about nations and focus purely on economic relations, how would we redraw the map of the world? This is the question explored in this chapter.

---

BOX 13-1: THE CASE FOR A CALIFORNIAN DOLLAR

In the late 1980s, something bad happened to the state of California. The cold war ended shortly after the retirement of President Reagan who had championed the building up of the military and, in particular, a investment in high-tech equipment. The result was sharp cuts in defence spending. As many of the big weapon-producing firms were based in California, this state suffered a serious blow, which hit at the time of a cyclical downturn in the USA and else-where in the world. Figure 13-1 documents the impact of these events. The California Gross State Product declined abruptly, and growth remained negative for three years, a performance far worse than elsewhere in the USA. In fact, by 2003, California had still not recovered the relative position as a percentage of US GDP that it held before the crisis. Hundreds of thousands of jobs were lost. In the mid-1990s, California was the great beneficiary of the information communication technology revolution. Firms were desperately looking for manpower as they were trying to seize on the apparently unbounded opportunities lying ahead of them.

Imagine that the state of California had its own currency. A depreciation in the early 1990s would have enhanced the battered state's competitiveness. An appreciation in the late 1990s would have moderated the boom and the accompanying job scarcities. Sharing the same currency as the rest of the USA certainly increased the size and duration of the imbalances brought about by these two shocks. Yet, no one seriously proposed a monetary secession. Somehow, belonging to the US dollar currency area provides benefits that outweigh the costs. The OCA theory's purpose is to explain how and why.

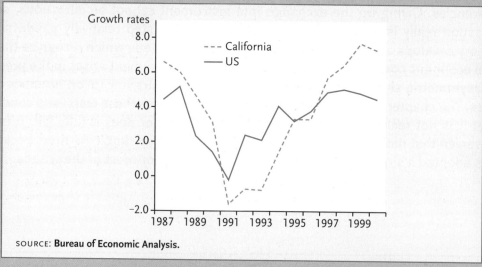

SOURCE: **Bureau of Economic Analysis.**

FIGURE 13-1: GROWTH RATES IN CALIFORNIA AND THE USA (1987–2000)

To start with, does the world need more than one currency? Could Zimbabwe, Peru and China share the same currency? Most likely not. At the other extreme, should each city have its own currency, as was sometimes the case a few centuries ago? No, of course not. These answers seem obvious, but exactly why? Box 13-1 presents an example that is suggestive of the issues involved.

Money is useful because it makes commercial and financial transactions easier than barter and because it is immediately recognized. The more that people accept it, the more useful is a currency. In that sense, the world would benefit from having just one currency that was acceptable everywhere and allowed global trade to proceed unencumbered by costly transactions. This is why small currency areas – geographic zones which share the same currency – are clearly not optimum. That part of the answer is quite straightforward. It means that the usefulness of a currency grows with the size of the area over which it is being used.[1] Figure 13-2 symbolically represents this observation with an upward-sloping marginal usefulness schedule.

However, as a currency area grows larger, it becomes more diverse and, intuitively, diversity brings in costs, which may well grow with the size of the area. This idea is depicted in Fig. 13-2 by the downward-sloping marginal 'practicability' schedule. There are many ways in which diversity matters – some are economic, some are political. The economic aspects are related to the fact that a common currency requires a single central bank that is unable to react to particular local conditions. As long as these conditions are homogeneous, this is not a problem. Asymmetric shocks, those which affect some countries (or regions) and not others, or which produce different effects in different countries, raise the costs of sharing the same currency.

The theory OCA aims at identifying more precisely the trade-off suggested by the figure. The idea is that the best border of a currency area corresponds to the situation when the costs and the benefits from sharing the same currency balance each other, as shown in Fig. 13-2. As will become clear, the figure is highly symbolic and there should be no pretence that we can actually draw these schedules.

This section proceeds in three steps. First, it examines asymmetric shocks and their effects. Second, it studies the problems that arise in the presence of asymmetric shocks in a currency area. Finally, it asks how the effects of asymmetric shocks can be mitigated when national exchange rates are no longer available.

### 13.1.1 How does an adverse shock work?

As emphasized in Chapter 11, the exchange rate regime matters because prices and wages are sticky. Imagine that the world demand for a country's exports decline, because tastes change or because alternative goods are developed elsewhere. This opens up a hole in the balance of trade. To re-establish its external balance, the country needs to make its exports cheaper. This calls for enhancing competitiveness. With a national currency, this is readily done through a depreciation. Without its own money, a country that is part of a wider currency area needs to find other ways to lower prices, which requires lower production costs and, hence, lower wages.

The situation is depicted in Fig. 13-3 which relates demand for, and supply of, domestic goods to the real exchange rate, defined as the relative price of domestic to foreign goods ($\lambda = EP/P^*$).[2] The supply of domestic goods rises as the real exchange rate appreciates because profitability rises at home when some of the production costs are tied to foreign prices (for example, imported machinery and semi-finished goods, oil). Demand declines when the real exchange rate appreciates for the familiar reason that both domestic and foreign customers will shift to cheaper foreign goods.

---

[1] Technically, money is said to generate network externalities. The theory is developed in Dowd, K. and D. Greenaway (1993) 'Currency competition, network externalities and switching costs: towards an alternative view of optimum currency areas', *Economic Journal*, 103 (420), 1180–89. Network externalities are studied in Chapter 16.

[2] Real and nominal exchange rates are defined in Chapter 11.

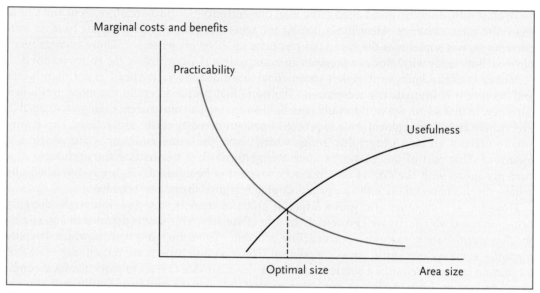

FIGURE 13-2: THE LOGIC OF THE OPTIMUM CURRENCY AREA THEORY

An alternative way of defining the real exchange rate is in terms of production costs ($EW/W^*$, where $W$ and $W^*$ are the production costs at home and abroad, each measured in the local currency). Because production costs quickly feed into prices, it matters little whether we use one definition or the other. It will prove helpful to keep in mind that the real exchange rate also represents the evolution of production costs, because production costs are closely associated with labour costs and, therefore, wages.

The adverse demand shock is represented in Fig. 13-3 as the leftward shift of world (domestic and foreign) demand for domestically produced goods, from $D$ to $D'$. If the nominal exchange rate is allowed to depreciate, or if prices and wages are flexible, the effect will be a shift from point $A$ to point $B$: output declines and the real exchange rate depreciates from $\lambda_0$ to $\lambda_1$. This is a painful move, of course, but an unavoidable one given the adverse shock.

The outcome is more painful if the exchange rate is fixed and prices and wages are rigid. In that case, the outcome is represented by point $C$ where the decline is even deeper. At the unchanged real exchange rate $\lambda_0$, domestic producers continue to supply the output corresponding to point $A$, but point $B$ represents the new, lower, demand. The distance $AC$ represents an accumulation of unsold goods, so the situation will not last for ever. The recession that sets in implies a rise in unemployment, which should generate incentives to gradually cut prices and wages, eventually bringing the economy to point $B$. But this is likely to be the outcome of a painful and protracted process.

The example illustrates why exchange rate fixity, when combined with sticky prices and wages, makes an already bad situation worse. The general point is that a monetary union rules out nominal exchange rate changes within the currency area, and yet the real exchange rate of the affected country must be adjusted. Instead of a simple once-and-for-all change in the nominal exchange rate, the real exchange rate adjustment can only come from changes in prices and wages. If prices and wages are sticky, the adjustment can take time, creating hardship along the way.

## 13.1.2 Asymmetric shocks

So far we have thought of a country in isolation. Now we look at two countries, called A and B, which consider forming a currency area. Note carefully that country A has two (nominal and real)

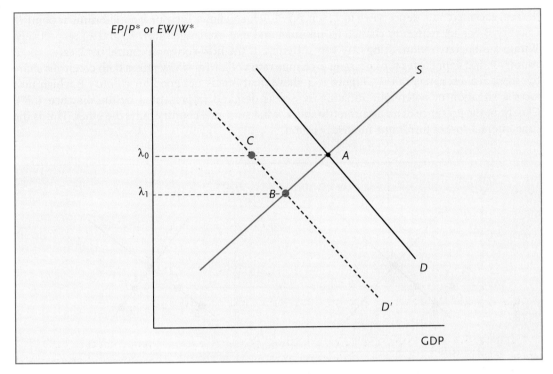

FIGURE 13-3: AN ADVERSE DEMAND SHOCK

exchange rates: one *vis-à-vis* county B and one *vis-à-vis* the rest of the world. The same applies to country B, of course.

If countries A and B are hit by the same adverse shock, they both have to undergo a real depreciation *vis-à-vis* the rest of the world and, to a first approximation, there is no need for their bilateral (nominal and real) exchange rate to change. They are in the same boat facing the same headwinds. The situation is very different, however, if country A is the only one hit by an adverse shock. Country A now must undergo a real depreciation *vis-à-vis* both country B and the rest of the world.

This reasoning shows that the loss of the exchange rate within a currency union is of no consequence as long as all member countries face the same shocks. In the presence of symmetric shocks, the union simply adjusts its common exchange rate *vis-à-vis* the rest of the world and its member countries are as well-off as if they had each independently changed their own exchange rate.

With asymmetric shocks, however, monetary union membership become seriously constraining. What happens then? The question is examined in Fig. 13-4 that pursues the study of a two-country monetary union. The vertical axis measures each country's real exchange rate *vis-à-vis* the rest of the world: $EP_A/P^*$ and $EP_B/P^*$, where $P_A$ and $P_B$ are the prices of domestic goods in country A and country B, respectively, $P^*$ the price level in the rest of the world, and $E$ is the common currency's exchange rate, initially equal to $E_o$. Points A in both panels represent the initially balanced situation, with a real exchange rate $\lambda_o$, assumed to be the same in both countries: $\lambda_o = E_o P_A/P^* = E_o P_B/P^*$. Prices are assumed to be sticky – otherwise, the exchange rate regime does not matter.

Now let an adverse shock affect country A alone. This is represented in the left panel, which describes country A, as the shift of the demand schedule from $D$ to $D'$. If country A is not part of a monetary union and can change its own exchange rate at will, it will let it depreciate to $E_1$ such that the real exchange rate depreciates to $\lambda_1 = E_1 P_A/P^*$, which allows for a new equilibrium at point $B$. Country B has no reason to change its nominal and real exchange rates, $E_0$ and $\lambda_0$ respectively. Within a monetary union, things are very different. If the now-common central bank cares about country A and depreciates the common exchange rate to $E_1$, with sticky prices both countries share the same real exchange rate $\lambda_1$. Figure 13-4 shows that this is not good for country B which now faces a situation of potentially inflationary excess demand (represented by the distance $B'B''$). Clearly, in the presence of an asymmetric shock, what suits one country hurts the other. This is the fundamental cost of forming a monetary union.

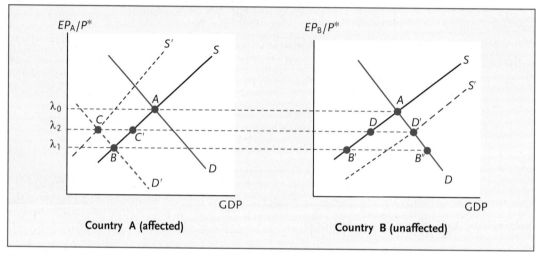

FIGURE 13-4: AN ASYMMETRIC SHOCK IN A CURRENCY UNION

If the union's common external exchange rate floats freely, it will depreciate because of the adverse shock in one part of the area, but not all the way to $E_1$. It will decline to an intermediate level such as $E_2$, to which corresponds a real exchange rate $\lambda_2 = E_2 P_A/P^* = E_2 P_B/P^*$.[3] This new exchange rate level is 'correct' on average, but it is still too strong for country A, which is in recession, and too weak for country B, which is overheating. The outcome is a combination of excess supply in country A (represented by $CC'$) and excess demand in country B (represented by $DD'$). Both countries are in disequilibrium. This is another way to see how the cost of belonging to a monetary union materializes.

Disequilibria cannot last for ever. What further adjustments can we envision? The common exchange rate *vis-à-vis* the rest of the world has no reason to change from $E_2$, it has already done its job of taking into account the average situation in the union. The required adjustment will have to come from prices and wages, in both countries. Country A cannot sell all of its production, so its price must eventually decline until the real exchange rate depreciates to $\lambda_1$, the equilibrium level previously identified. A recession will set in – remember, country A's goods are in excess supply – and unemployment will rise, putting downward pressure on prices and wages. The price of country A's goods will decline until it reaches level $P'_A$ such that $\lambda_1 = E_2 P'_A/P^*$.

Country B is in the opposite situation: facing buoying demand, the price of its goods will rise to $P'_B$ such that its real exchange rate appreciates back to its equilibrium level, which is the original

---

[3] Where exactly $E_2$ lies depends on a host of factors, like the relative size of the two countries and how sensitive is their trade to changes in the real exchange rate.

level $\lambda_o = E_2 P'_B/P^*$. Recession and disinflation in country A, boom and inflation in country B, these are the costs of operating a monetary union when an asymmetric shocks occurs.

The OCA theory starts with the realization that asymmetric shocks are unavoidably painful, but argues that a currency area is not necessarily a bad idea. We need to balance costs and benefits, as in Fig. 13-2, which means that there is no simple, black-and-white answer to the question of whether it is a good idea to adopt a common currency in a particular area. What the OCA theory does is to propose criteria by which to judge the costs and the desirability of sharing the same currency.

The OCA theory takes is for granted that a common currency carries important benifits. Later chapters will further elaborate on these benefits. A useful and succinct summary is provided in the Chancellor of the Exchequer's assessment on UK membership.

> 'EMU membership could significantly raise UK output and lead to a lasting increase in jobs in the long term. As noted above, the assessment shows that intra-euro area trade has increased strongly in recent years as a result of EMU, perhaps by as much as 3 to 20 per cent; that the UK could enjoy a significant boost to trade with the euro area of up to 50 per cent over 30 years; and that UK national could rise over a 30-year period by between 5 and 9 per cent'

*UK Membership and the Single Currency*, HM Treasury, London, June 2003. p. 222.

### 13.1.3 Symmetric shocks with asymmetric effects

The analysis has focused on asymmetric shocks, but it applies also to the case of symmetric shocks that produce asymmetric effects. There are many reasons why no two countries react exactly in the same way to the same shock. This can be due to their different socioeconomic structures, including labour market regulations and traditions, the relative importance of industrial sectors, the role of the financial and banking sectors, the country's external indebtedness, the ability to strike agreements between firms, trade unions and the government, etc. A good example is the case of a sudden increase in the price of oil and gas. This shock hurts oil- and gas-importing countries but benefits exporting countries, such as the Netherlands, Norway and the UK. It is one reason why the two latter countries have not joined the European Monetary Union.

Another asymmetry concerns the way monetary policy operates. When a common central bank reacts to a symmetric shock, it is not a foregone conclusion that the effect of its action will be the same throughout the currency union. Differences in the structure of banking and financial markets or in the size of firms – and their ability to borrow – may result in asymmetric effects. Chapter 16 examines this aspect.

When these various effects are different, the analysis of asymmetric shocks carried out in the previous section fully applies. In particular, the effects can be seen as implying the same situation as the one described in Fig. 13-4. This is why, from here onwards, when reference is made to asymmetric shocks, it also includes the case of symmetric shocks with asymmetric effects.

## 13.2 The optimum currency area criteria

There are three classic economic criteria and an additional three which are political. The first criterion looks at a way of minimizing the costs of an asymmetric shock within a currency area. The two next criteria look at a different question: they aim at identifying which economic areas are unlikely to be hit by asymmetric shocks infrequently or moderately enough to be of limited concern. The last three criteria deal with more political aspects; they ask whether different countries are likely to help each other when faced with asymmetric shocks. This section lists and explains the logic of the OCA criteria, section 13.3 will examine whether they are satisfied in Europe.

### 13.2.1 Labour mobility (Mundell)
The first criterion was proposed by Robert Mundell (Box 13-2) when he first formulated the notion of an OCA. The idea is that the cost of sharing the same currency would be eliminated if the factors of production, capital and labour were fully mobile across borders. Since it is conventionally assumed that capital is mobile, the real hurdle then comes from the lack of labour mobility.

MUNDELL CRITERION
**Optimum currency areas are those within which people move easily.**

BOX 13-2: FOUNDERS OF THE OPTIMUM CURRENCY AREA THEORY

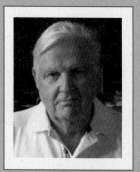

Robert A. Mundell, a Canadian-born economist at Columbia University, won the Nobel prize in part for having created the OCA theory, in part for having started the field of open-economy macro-economics. Most students are familiar with the Mundell–Fleming model.

Source: http://www.columbia.edu/~ram15/portraits.html

Peter Kenen, from Princeton University, is a leading contributor to our understanding of the international monetary system and a keen observer of European monetary integration.

Source: http://www.princeton.edu/3pbkenen/

Ronald McKinnon, from Stanford University, has made major contributions to the international monetary literature. He is known for his critical appraisal of European Monetary Union.

Source: http://www.stanford.edu/~mckinnon/

The reasoning is illustrated in Fig. 13-4 where the adversely affected country A undergoes unemployment while non-affected country B faces inflationary pressure. Both problems could be solved by a shift of the idle production factors in country A to country B where they are in short supply. This reallocation is shown as a shift of both countries' supply schedules to $S'$. At the new equilibrium exchange rate, country A is at point $C$ and country B is at as is point $D'$. What is remarkable is that there is no need for price and wage change in either country. Once the factors of production have moved, the currency area's nominal exchange rate $E_2$ delivers the equilibrium real exchange rate $\lambda_2$.

The factors of production that need to move are capital and labour. Three comments are warranted. First, concerning labour mobility, actual currency areas generally coincide with nation-states. Common culture and language, right and ease of resettling, etc. make labour mobility easier within a country than across borders. Thus a national currency is not just a symbol of state-hood, it is usually justified by labour mobility. Across borders, not only do cultural and linguistic differences restrain migration, but institutional barriers further discourage labour mobility. Changes in legislation may make cross-border labour mobility easier and enlarge the size of optimum currency areas and, indeed, this is part of Europe's quest for closer integration.

Second, the view that capital is mobile needs to be qualified. Financial capital can move freely and quickly, unless impeded by exchange controls. Installed physical capital (means of production such as plants and equipment) is not mobile. It takes time to build plants and shift the location of economic activities. Closing plants in country A can be done quickly – although social-political resistance may create stumbling blocks – but creating new production facilities in country B may take months, if not years. Even if labour were highly mobile, which it is not, shifting the supply curves as described in Fig. 13-4 may take many years.

Finally, goods produced in country A may differ from those produced in country B. It may take quite some time to retrain workers from country A to produce the goods of country B, if at all possible. Thus labour mobility is not a panacea, just a factor that mitigates the costs of an asymmetric shock in a currency union.

### 13.2.2 Production diversification (Kenen)

A natural question to ask is whether the asymmetric demand shocks are likely to occur frequently within a potential currency area. If not, the area is likely to qualify as an OCA. This question can be further broken down. First, what are the most likely sources of substantial shocks? Most of the likely demand shocks can be associated with shifts in spending patterns, which may be a consequence of changing tastes (e.g. German beer consumers find it fashionable to drink wine) or of new technology that brings about new products and makes older ones obsolete (e.g. internet displaces faxes). Such shocks actually occur every day and every year, but most of them are hardly noticed outside the affected industries. To create a problem for a monetary union, a shock must be large and asymmetric.

The most likely victims of severe shocks are countries that have specialized in a narrow range of goods. For example, many of the African countries that are part of the CFA franc zone export a narrow range of agricultural products such as coffee or cacao. A decline in the demand for coffee – which may occur because new producers emerge from elsewhere in the world – affects some countries in the CFA franc zone and not others, thus provoking an asymmetric shock. Conversely, a country that produces a wide range of products will be little affected by changes affecting demand or supply of a particular good because that good weighs relatively little in total production.

This explains the second criterion for an optimum currency area, initially stated by Kenen (Box 13-2): currency area member countries ought to be well diversified and producing similar goods. In that case, good-specific shocks are likely to be of little aggregate consequence and to affect all member countries in a similar way, thus lessening the need for any exchange rate adjustment. Put differently, asymmetric shocks are mostly minor and a common trade structure implies that the demand schedules shown in Fig 13-4 tend to move together.

> ### KENEN CRITERION
> **Countries whose production and exports are widely diversified and of similar structure form an optimum currency area.**

### 13.2.3 Openness (McKinnon)

The next relevant question is whether the exchange rate is a useful tool to deal with an asymmetric shock. If not, little is lost by giving it up. In the analysis of section 13.1, the distinction between 'domestic' and 'foreign' goods refers to where the goods are produced. However, many standard goods, such as paper sheets or electric bulbs, may be produced in different countries but they are virtually identical and their origin is usually undistinguishable. In that case, if trade is flowing freely, their prices will be the same at home and abroad, or nearly so, independent of the exchange rate. Consequently, changing the exchange rate will not affect the relative prices of such domestic and foreign goods. Put differently, when expressed in domestic currency, prices are not sticky anymore and exchange rate changes leave the country's competitiveness unchanged. The more open the economy, the more relevant is this observation. This is the basis of the third criterion formulated by McKinnon (Box 13-2).

> ### McKINNON CRITERION
> **Countries which are very open to trade and trade heavily with each other form an optimum currency area.**

The criterion can be made more precise as follows. When two countries A and B do not share the same currency, they each have their own exchange rate *vis-à-vis* the rest of the world, $E_A$ and $E_B$. If they are very open and trade intensively with each other, the distinction between domestic and foreign goods loses much of its significance as competition will equalize the prices of most goods when expressed in the same currency.[4] For example, if the price of country A's domestic goods in domestic currency is $P_A$, expressed in the rest of the world's currency it is $E_A P_A$, and similarly country B's price is $E_B P_B$. Competition ensures that $E_A P_A = E_B P_B$. Any change of one country's nominal exchange rate, say $E_A$, must be immediately followed by a change in local currency prices $P_A$ such that the world price level $E_A P_A$ remains unchanged. In that case, the real exchange rates of both countries *vis-à-vis* the rest of the world are also equal: $E_A P_A / P^* = E_B P_B / P^*$. In such a situation, with flexible prices, creating a currency union by giving up the exchange rate entails no serious loss of policy independence.[5]

---

[4] This property is known as the law of one price. Despite its name, it is not very well verified in practice. Yet, while deviations from the law of one price are commonplace, the main argument – that exchange rate changes fail to seriously affect their relative prices – remains largely valid.

[5] Because most goods, nowadays, have little national specificity, a useful distinction is between goods that are traded (exported and imported) and those that are 'non-traded'. Among closely integrated and similar countries, traded goods follow the previous description and their prices differ little. Non-traded goods include many services (e.g. car repair, hairdressing or medical advice) and goods that do not travel easily (e.g. cement that is very heavy or flowers that are perishable). Their prices differ sizeably from one country to another. Openness then is better defined as the share of traded goods in total consumption. When this share is high, there are relatively few non-traded goods, and exchange rate changes have relatively small effects.

## 13.2.4 Fiscal transfers

An important aspect of the analysis of section 13.1.2 is that, in a currency area, country B suffers from the adverse shock that hits country A. It is therefore in the interest of country B to help alleviate the impact of the shock. One possibility is for country B to send money to country A. Such a transfer tends to reduce asymmetric shifts in Fig. 13-4. It mitigates both the recession in country A and the boom in country B, giving time for the shock to disappear if it is temporary, or to work its effects through prices if it is longer lasting. As shocks occur randomly, today's provider of help will be tomorrow's beneficiary. In effect, such transfers work like a common insurance against bad shocks.

> **TRANSFER CRITERION**
> Countries that agree to compensate each other for adverse shocks form an optimum currency area.

Transfer schemes of this kind exist across regions in every country. Sometimes they are explicit, most often they are implicit. For example, if a particular region suffers from an asymmetric shock, then, as income declines, so do tax payments while welfare support – chiefly unemployment benefits – rise. In the net, the region receives transfers from the rest of the country. These transfers are often implicit, part and parcel of the redistributive mechanism at work in the country. Some federal countries, such as Germany and Switzerland, operate explicit transfer systems.

## 13.2.5 Homogeneous preferences

Political conditions matter even for symmetric shocks. Section 13.1.2 argues that symmetric shocks do not pose any problem as long as each country reacts in the same way to the shock. But this result assumes that all countries agree on how to deal with each and every possible shock. In practice, however, there rarely exists a 'best way' to deal with a shock. For example, should we be more concerned about inflation or about unemployment? Should we favour the exporters – who wish to have weak exchange rates to buttress competitiveness – or the consumers – who wish to have strong exchange rates to raise their purchasing power?

If the currency area member countries do not share the same preferences over such trade-offs, each of them will want the common central bank to pursue different policies. Whatever the central bank chooses to do will be controversial and will leave some, possibly all, countries unhappy. At best, there will be resentment, at worst the currency union may not survive.

> **HOMOGENEITY OF PREFERENCES CRITERION**
> Currency union member countries must share a wide consensus on the way to deal with shocks.

Why should preferences differ? A shock, and the way to deal with it, typically has redistributive effects: some groups will lose more than others, and some may even benefit. Each group carries some political weight and will naturally mobilize support in its favour. The collective preference, which shapes the policy response, thus intimately depends on domestic politics, and there is no reason for all the countries of a currency area to share the same balance of political forces. The fifth criterion states that these differences should not be too wide.

### 13.2.6 Commonality of destiny vs nationalism

The final criterion goes deeper into political considerations. Since none of the previous criteria is likely to be fully satisfied, no currency area is ever optimum. This is even true for individual countries which casually operate as currency areas. Shocks, therefore, even when symmetric, generate political disagreements – a familiar feature in any country. Such disagreements are usually accepted as the cost of living together, the natural consequence of statehood. The outcome is ultimately seen as acceptable because citizens of the same country readily accept some degree of solidarity with one another.

When separate countries contemplate the formation of a currency area, they need to realize that there will be times when there will be disagreements and that these disagreements may form along national lines, especially if the shocks are asymmetric or produce asymmetric effects. For such disagreements to be tolerated, the people that form the currency union must accept to live together and to extend their sense of solidarity to the whole union. In short, they must have a shared sense of common destiny that outweighs the nationalist tendencies that would otherwise call for intransigent reactions.

> SOLIDARITY CRITERION
>
> **When the common monetary policy gives rise to conflicts of national interests, the countries that form a currency area need to accept the costs in the name of a common destiny.**

## 13.3 Is Europe an optimum currency area?

In principle, the OCA theory should tell us whether it did make sense to establish a monetary union in Europe. As already noted, however, the answer is unlikely to be black and white. The benefits are hard to quantify, as are the six OCA criteria which may be only partly fulfilled. This section distillates that rich and unending debate. Box 13-3 reports on the interesting conclusions reached in May 2003 by the British Chancellor of the Exchequer on the basis of five tests inspired by the OCA theory.

### 13.3.1 Asymmetric shocks

The starting point must be whether asymmetric shocks happen often enough, and are large enough, to be of serious concern. Of course, we do not know what the future keeps in store. The best that can be done is to assume that the past can be a guide to the future – a poor assumption challenged in section 13.4 – and examine the pre-EMU record. This section looks at the frequency of shocks and how often the national exchange rate has been used to cushion them. If there were only a few shocks, or if the European countries had made little use of their exchange rates, giving up national currencies would be of little importance.

In looking at the record, we have to keep in mind that there are two main reasons for changing the exchange rate. The first, which is the subject of the OCA approach, is the occurrence of asymmetric shocks that are best dealt with through currency realignments. The second is to accommodate inflationary policies, which is ruled out in the EMU as explained in Chapter 14 and must now be ignored.

Figure 13-5 presents a synthetic OCA index computed by asking the following question: based on past experience, how much would European countries have adjusted their exchange rates *vis-à-vis* the German Deutschemark (taken, quite reasonably, as the centre currency of Euroland) to deal with asymmetric shocks relevant to the three classic OCA principles of Mundell, Kenen and

> ## Box 13-3: Why Britain is not yet ready for the euro
>
> When he was appointed Chancellor of the Exchequer in 1997, Gordon Brown awarded himself a right of veto on the highly political decision of British Euro area membership. He announced that he would form his verdict on the basis of five economic tests:
>
> 1. *Convergence*: Are business cycles and economic structures compatible so that we and others could live comfortably with euro interest rates on a permanent basis?
> 2. *Flexibility*: If problems emerge is there sufficient flexibility to deal with them?
> 3. *Investment*: Would joining the EMU create better conditions for firms making long-term decisions to invest in Britain?
> 4. *Financial services*: What impact would entry into the EMU have on the competitive position of the UK's financial services industry, particularly the City's wholesale markets?
> 5. *Growth, stability and employment*: In summary, will joining the EMU promote higher growth, stability and a lasting increase in jobs?
>
> In May 2003, the Chancellor finally released his first assessment. He found that the convergence and flexibility tests were not met, that the investment and financial services tests were met, and the fifth test would be met when the first two were met. From this he concluded that Britain was not yet ready, adding: 'We will report on progress in the Budget next year. We can then consider the extent of progress and determine whether on the basis of it we make a further Treasury assessment of the five tests which – if positive next year – would allow us at that time to put the issue before the British people in a referendum.'[6]
>
> Two characteristics of this procedure are striking. First, the heavy and explicit use of OCA economic principles. Test 1 deals with the presence of asymmetric shocks, Test 2 with the ability to cope with asymmetric shocks with heavy emphasis on labour markets while Test 3 looks at capital mobility. Test 5 summarizes the OCA approach. Test 4 is specific to Britain's specialization in financial services. Second, the tests are specified in an obviously intended vague way, leaving the Chancellor free to implicitly weigh the political aspects of the undertaking.

McKinnon? The index is larger the more frequent asymmetric shocks have been and, therefore, the more actively the exchange rate should have been used.[7]

Interestingly, the countries at the top of the list – with the worst OCA index – have decided, initially at least, not to join the EMU, in contrast with those at the bottom. There are a few noteworthy exceptions: Finland, which has undergone unusual disturbances in the early 1990s, and Switzerland, which is not a member of the EU. The next sections go into more detail, examining one by one the three classic criteria.

Another aspect of asymmetry noted in section 13.1.3 is the possibility of asymmetric effects of monetary policy. Figure 13-6 shows estimates of the effect, after two years, on GDP(left panel) and prices (right panel) of a 1 percentage point increase in the interest rate. Quite clearly, there are important differences. Some of these differences are explained by the way credit is distributed in each country, including the relationship between banks and firms, and the relative proportion of small firms which are more easily denied loans during periods of restrictive monetary policy.

---

[6] The various documents are avilable on www.hm-treasury.gov.uk. They include a large number of specially commissioned studies that are well worth reading.

[7] Technically, the index is computed as: $SD(ER) = -0.09 + 1.46\ SD(\Delta y) + 0.022\ DISSIM - 0.054\ TRADE + 0.012\ SIZE$, where SD stands for standard deviation (a statistical measure of variability), ER the exchange rate *vis-à-vis* the mark, $\Delta y$ is the difference between growth in the country and in Germany, a measure of cyclical mismatch meant to capture asymmetric shocks, DISSIM is a measure of the dissimilarity of trade structures meant to capture the Kenen criterion (see section 13.3.3), TRADE is a measure of the intensity of trade with Germany meant to capture the McKinnon criterion, and SIZE is a measure of the country's economic size (its GDP). The particular weights are obtained from a regression analysis. For full details, see Bayoumi and Eichengreen (1997).

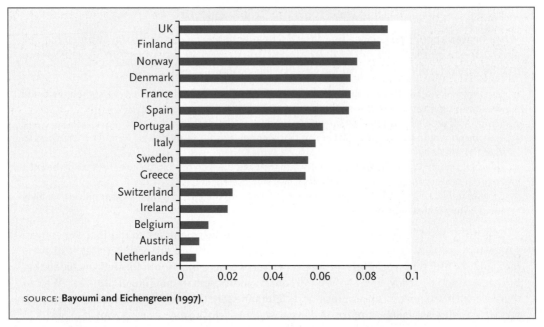

SOURCE: **Bayoumi and Eichengreen (1997).**

FIGURE 13-5: OCA INDEX

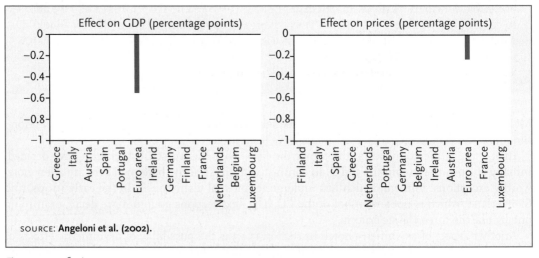

SOURCE: **Angeloni et al. (2002).**

FIGURE 13-6: ASYMMETRIC EFFECTS OF MONETARY POLICY

These features suggest that asymmetry is a concern in the Euro area, even though over time these sharp differences may be erased.

### 13.3.2 Openness

Openness matters in the OCA theory because, in a small open economy, most of the goods produced and consumed are traded on international markets. Accordingly, their prices on the local market are largely independent of local conditions and any change in the value of the currency tends to be promptly passed into domestic prices. When this is the case, exchange rate changes fail to affect the country's competitiveness and are, hence, essentially useless, which is exactly the McKinnon criterion.

Openness is defined as the share of economic activity devoted to international trade. The ratio of exports to GDP measures the proportion of domestic production that is exported. The ratio of imports to GDP measures the proportion of domestic spending that falls on imports. Table 13-1 presents the average of these two ratios, it shows that most European countries are very open, usually the more so the smaller they are, which explains why the smaller countries have been traditionally the most enthusiastic supporters of the monetary union. The USA and Japan appear as largely closed, as is the European Union as a whole.

| | | | |
|---|---|---|---|
| Austria | 53.5 | Spain | 33.6 |
| Belgium | 91.7 | Sweden | 48.8 |
| Denmark | 43.1 | UK | 30.7 |
| Finland | 39.9 | | |
| France | 31.5 | | |
| Germany | 38.4 | EU | 12.3 |
| Greece | 29.9 | USA | 13.5 |
| Ireland | 85.4 | Japan | 10.8 |
| Italy | 29.9 | Australia | 23.0 |
| Netherlands | 65.3 | Canada | 44.1 |
| Portugal | 38.3 | Switzerland | 51.3 |

Source: European Economy 73, (2001)

TABLE 13-1: OPENNESS IN 2002
(AVERAGE OF RATIOS OF EXPORTS AND IMPORTS TO GDP, %)

A second way to look at the question is to directly measure the pass-through effect, i.e. how domestic prices respond to exchange rate changes. If all prices respond one for one to exchange rate changes, the pass-through is complete and the exchange rate only affects inflation, not competitiveness. Figure 13-7 compares openness (as shown in Table 13-1) and estimates of the short-term pass-through, measured as the impact of exchange rate changes on import prices: for instance, a 0.6 pass-through coefficient means that a 10 per cent depreciation is followed within three months by a 6 per cent increase in import prices. By and large – with some 'strange' results likely to be due to the imprecision of the estimates – the more open the economy the larger is the pass-through. Most European countries are characterized by both significant openness and large pass-through coefficients in contrast with the US and Japan.

The available evidence is quite clear. As far as the McKinnon criterion is concerned, most European economies qualify for joining a monetary union. They are very open and domestic prices tend to be dominated by the exchange rate. This observation applies very strongly to the smaller countries, less so to the larger ones but certainly more than to many other advanced countries.

## 13.3.3 Diversification and trade dissimilarity

The Kenen criterion rests on the idea that asymmetric shocks are less likely among countries that share similar production patterns and whose trade is diversified. Figure 13-8 presents an index of dissimilarity of European trade as of end-1995. The index looks at how each country's trade structure differs from the situation in Germany, which serves as benchmark. The index is based

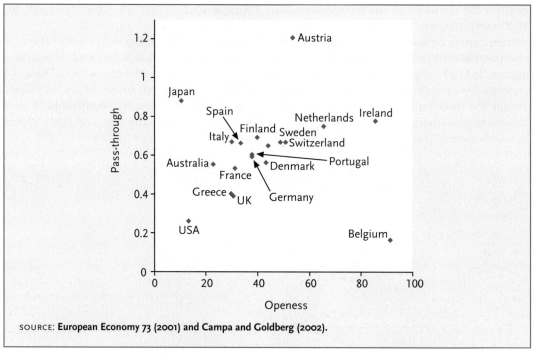

SOURCE: **European Economy 73 (2001) and Campa and Goldberg (2002).**

FIGURE 13-7: PASS-THROUGH AND OPENNESS

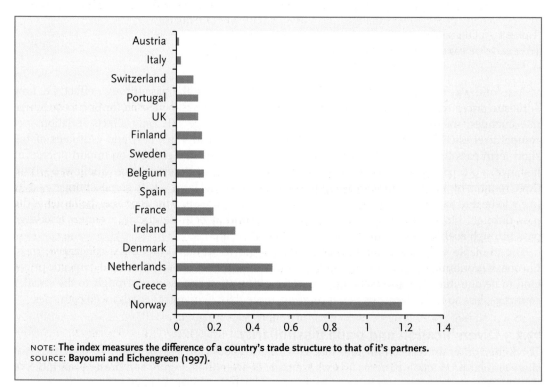

NOTE: **The index measures the difference of a country's trade structure to that of it's partners.**
SOURCE: **Bayoumi and Eichengreen (1997).**

FIGURE 13-8: TRADE DISSIMILARITY INDEX (1995)

on the decomposition of trade into three classes of goods: agriculture, minerals and manufacturing. Dissimilarity with Germany is highest for Norway, an oil-exporting country, Greece where agriculture plays a major role, and the Netherlands, which is a major exporter of gas.

Dissimilarity predicts well that Norway, whose trade is dominated by oil and fish, is not interested in joining the monetary union. It also exposes the case of the Netherlands, quite dependent on natural gas and yet an enthusiastic, and so far happy, member of the EMU. This case is a good illustration that the OCA criteria are not absolute, and that they focus on the costs of EMU membership, ignoring the economic and political benefits. The Dutch authorities believe that their economy is far too integrated with the European economy to afford exchange rate fluctuations and wish to be deeply involved in European integration. This is to be contrasted with the cases of Switzerland and the UK, both of which rank well on the dissimilarity index and yet, so far, have remained outside the EMU largely for the broader political reasons presented in sections 13.2.5 and 13.2.6.

### 13.3.4 Labour mobility

The OCA theory suggests that labour mobility can go a long way towards alleviating the costs of an asymmetric shock when the exchange rate cannot be adjusted. In this case, labour mobility is about how easily people move in response to economic incentives. Here again, the criterion is a matter of degree. People always move, but to some varying degree, and full mobility is never to be seen. Full labour mobility would occur if people would immediately take advantage of any difference in earnings, and move to where they can earn more. Even such a simple definition is fraught with difficulties. A correct appraisal of 'earnings' must include the following:

- The cost of moving, possibly including the selling and buying of dwellings.
- The prospect of becoming unemployed, both in the country of origin and in the country of immigration.
- Career opportunities, which means not only current but also future earnings.
- Family career prospects, including the spouse and children, sometimes even more distant relatives.
- Social benefits including unemployment, health and retirement.
- Taxation of earnings from both labour and savings.

Labour mobility is also subject to non-economic incentives such as:

- Cultural differences (language, religion, traditions, possibly racism and xenophobia) in the country considered for immigration.
- Family and friendship links that can be weakened.
- Commitment to one's country of origin (nationalism).

For these reasons, labour mobility can only be relative and a natural approach is to proceed by comparison with existing, well-functioning currency areas, such as Canada and the USA. We first compare international migration. Figure 13-9 shows the percentage of local population which is foreign-born. Clearly, there is less immigration to European countries than to the USA and Canada, and differences within Europe are wide. The figure also shows, where available, how many of these immigrants come from other EU countries. This is generally a small proportion of the total (Belgium is a noteworthy exception). Europeans seem to take little advantage of the Single Market which allows them to work and settle anywhere in the EU.

In fact, Europeans show little movement across regions within their own countries. Figure 13-10 makes that point: it displays the flow of people, as a percentage of the total population, who migrated internally, when each country is spliced into several regions (e.g. 11 regions for Belgium or 12 regions for the UK). It is simply a fact of life that Europeans move only half as often as US citizens.[8] Over the 1990s, 38 per cent of EU citizens changed residence, most of whom (68 per

---

[8] This section partly draws on the final report of the High Level Task Force On Skills And Mobility sponsored by the de Rodolfo De Benedetti Foundation of Università Bocconi.

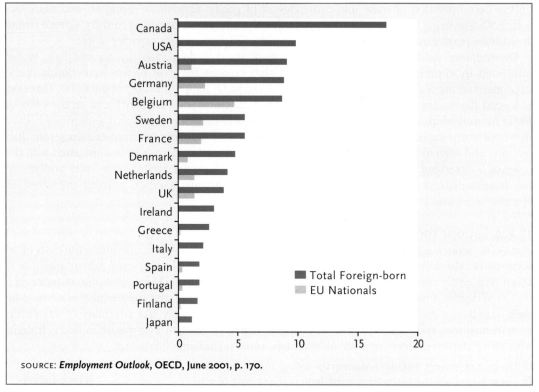

SOURCE: **Employment Outlook, OECD, June 2001, p. 170.**

FIGURE 13-9: FOREIGN-BORN POPULATION (1998) (% OF TOTAL POPULATION)

cent) moved within the same town or village and 36 per cent moved to another town in the same region. In Europe, while 21 per cent moved to another region in the same Member State, only 4.4 per cent moved to another Member State. Even worse for the OCA criterion, Europeans move mainly for personal reasons since professional reasons account for only 5 per cent of moves.

Why do Europeans move so little? One reason is language, another is customs and traditions. Yet another is that housing tends to be more expensive in Europe than in the USA. Furthermore, moving means changing from one welfare system to another, with serious difficulties regarding health and retirement benefits. In the USA, in contrast, no such difficulty arises when moving from one US state to another. Europeans, in any event, move relatively little within their own countries, where none of these barriers apply.

Low migration by European nationals could be compensated by immigration from outside the EU. If immigrant workers were to move to where job offers exceed supply, some of the costs of a monetary union would be reduced. Even viewed this way, immigration – a big political issue in Europe – is smaller in Europe than in the USA. In the early 2000s, immigration flows amounted to some 0.3 per cent of the total population in the EU, and to 0.5 per cent in the USA.

In summary, Europe is far from fulfilling the labour mobility criterion. This characteristic implies that asymmetric shocks are likely to be met by unemployment in countries facing a loss of competitiveness. Box 13-4 reports that, indeed, when asymmetric shocks occur, migration plays a smaller role in Europe than in the USA, with the unfortunate result that employment takes most of the burden.

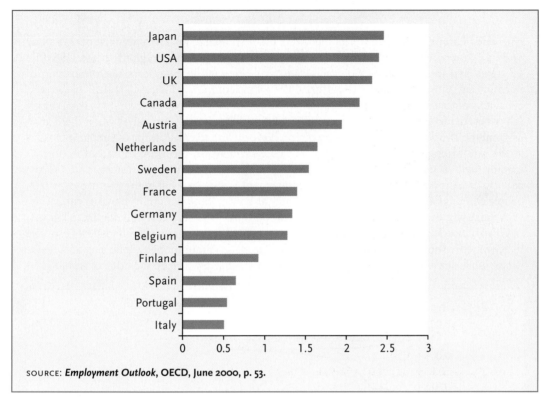

SOURCE: *Employment Outlook*, OECD, June 2000, p. 53.

FIGURE 13-10: INTERNAL MIGRATION ACROSS REGIONS (1995) (% OF TOTAL POPULATION)

### 13.3.5 Fiscal transfers

Countries hit by a temporary adverse shock could receive transfers from better-off countries as compensation for having lost the exchange rate instrument for the common good. Within most countries, seen as currency areas, these transfers are automatic. They are typically the outcome of the combined effect of the tax system and welfare payments (unemployment benefits, subsidies to poor people, etc.). In the USA, for instance, it has been estimated that any shortfall of income in a state is compensated by federal transfers that amount to between 10 and 40 per cent of the loss. There is no such system at work in the European Union. The EU budget is small, less than 2 per cent of GDP, and almost entirely spent on the Common Agricultural Policy and the Structural Funds which support the poorer regions irrespective of whether they are hit by shocks. Any transfer system would need a significant increase in the EU budget, which is not likely in the near future.

On this criterion, Europe is definitely not an optimum monetary union.

### 13.3.6 Homogeneous preferences

Do all countries share similar views about the use of monetary policy? On the basis of past inflation rates (the evidence is reviewed in Chapter 12), this does not seem to be the case. Low-inflation Germany and formerly high-inflation Italy or Greece have very little in common. Similarly, looking at public debts (Chapter 15), there seems a gulf that separates European countries. So, is the verdict negative? It may be too early to tell.

Why has the quality of macroeconomic policies been so diverse in Europe? Is it in the genes? Medical research has not yet turned up any clue, but economic research has a lot to say about

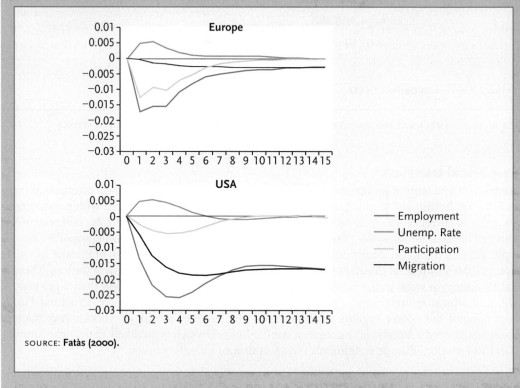

**Box 13-4: The effects of asymmetric shocks in Europe and the USA**
How does Europe's low labour mobility affect the response to an asymmetric shock? A study by Fatás (2000) compares Europe and the USA. Fatás looks at 51 regions in the USA (the 50 states and the District of Columbia) and at 54 regions in Europe (a decomposition of 14 countries, all EU countries with the exception of Luxembourg). Figure 13-11 depicts the joint behaviour of total employment, the employment rate and the participation rate in each region (all compared to the overall situation in the USA and Europe, respectively)[9] when there is an asymmetric shock that affects a single region. Europe and the USA witness similar increases in the rate of employment. The difference lies elsewhere. In the USA, most of the drop in employment is met by regional emigration, people move to more fortunate parts of the country. In Europe, most of the drop in employment is met by a fall in the participation rate, people withdraw from the labour force and stay at home. Interestingly, in the long run, in the USA those who leave do not return, and in Europe those who stop working remain inactive.

This study corroborates partly the OCA theory: labour mobility crucially affects the response to asymmetric shocks. The twist is that with low European labour mobility, following an adverse shock, while some people become unemployed, others simply give up the hope of working.

SOURCE: **Fatàs (2000).**

FIGURE 13-11: LABOUR MARKET RESPONSES

---

[9] This may look arcane. If we call $N$ the total population of working age (15–64), $L$ the labour force (the people of working age who either have a job or actively look for one), $E$ employment, $U$ the number of people unemployed, and $O$ those people of working age who are out of the labour force, we have the following accounting relationships: $N = L + O$ and $L = E + U$. The employment rate is $e = E/L$, the unemployment rate is $u = U/L$ and, obviously $e + u = 1$. The participation rate is $p = L/N$, which measures the proportion of the population of working age involved in the labour market, i.e. leaving aside those who are not working voluntarily ($O$).

incentives. Policy makers seem to respond to the incentives provided by political institutions, and these institutions differ from one country to another.

European integration is accompanied by the adoption of common institutions. In fact, one reason why the inflation-prone countries have been eager to join the monetary union is that it provides for a degree of monetary policy discipline that has been elusive in the past.[10] As Chapter 14 shows, the European Monetary Union has been consciously built to guarantee macro-economic instability: the European Central Bank is strongly independent and constitutionally committed to price stability. National deficits are bound by an excessive deficit procedure. This still does not mean that all countries share the same culture of macroeconomic stability, but they are increasingly operating under common institutions accepted by all Member States.

### 13.3.7 Commonality of destiny vs nationalism

How deep is European sentiment? There is no simple, uncontroversial way to measure the willingness of European citizens to give up parts of their national sovereignties in the pursuit of common interests. A crude indication is given in Fig. 13-12 which reports the degree of trust in national governments and in the EU. The measure shown is the difference between the percentage of citizens who trust and those who do not trust the relevant institution. Important national differences reveal much heterogeneity in citizen sentiments towards politics in general, and Europe in particular. Overall, national governments are trusted by 39 per cent and distrusted by 51 per cent of citizens (a score of −12 in Fig. 13-12), while the EU is trusted by 46 per cent and distrusted by 37 per cent of citizens (a score of 9).[11]

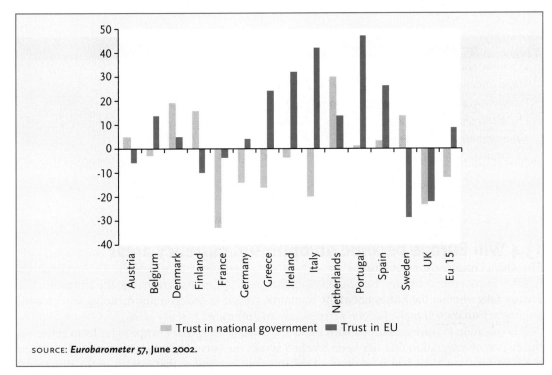

SOURCE: *Eurobarometer 57,* June 2002.

FIGURE 13-12: TRUST IN INSTITUTIONS

---

[10] This aspect is touched upon in Chapter 12.
[11] An interesting study shows that those who are best informed about the EMU tend to be more positively inclined towards it: Hayo, Bernd (1999) 'Knowledge and attitude towards European Monetary Union', *Journal of Policy Modelling,* **21** (5), 641–51.

Looking around the world, there is no other example of countries willing to share so widely some important components of sovereignty. While national sentiment dominates, the first years of the EMU have not provoked the kind of backlash that differing economic situations could have provoked. Europe may not be scoring highly on this criterion, but nor, it seems, is it fully failing,

### 13.3.8 So, is Europe an optimum currency area?

In the end, most European countries do well on openness and diversification, two of the three classic OCA criteria, and fail on the third one, labour mobility. Europe also fails on fiscal transfers, with an unclear verdict of the remaining two political criteria. Table 13-2 summarizes this admittedly debatable appraisal. The mixed performance that it reveals can be interpreted in two ways.

First, it explains why the single currency project has been so controversial. Neither the supporters nor the opponents have been able to produce an irrefutable case. After all, that was only to be expected as the OCA theory mostly focuses on the costs of forming a monetary union, taking the benefits for granted. Neither the benefits nor the costs can be measured, and the OCA criteria are rarely black and white, entirely satisfied or entirely violated. In the end, the economic case is undecided, and the decision to create the monetary union must rest on political considerations.

Second, the partial fulfilment of the OCA criteria implies that, given that the decision to go ahead has been taken, there will be costs. The OCA theory identifies these costs and suggests two main conclusions: the costs will mainly arise in the labour markets and fiscal transfers will have to be rethought.

| Criterion | Satisfied? |
|---|---|
| Labour mobility | No |
| Trade openness | Yes |
| Production diversification | Yes |
| Fiscal transfers | No |
| Homogeneity of preferences | Probably |
| Commonality of destiny | ? |

TABLE 13-2: OCA SCORE CARD

## 13.4 Will Europe become an optimum currency area?

The OCA characteristics of Europe are not frozen. The extent to which the OCA criteria are fulfilled in part reflect history, but the very fact that the EMU exists can change the situation. This section asks whether the fulfilment of the economic criteria is endogenous, meaning that creating a monetary union will make Europe increasingly an optimum currency area.

It is common to contrast Europe with the USA, and conclude that Europe is far from achieving the degree of integration that has been reached across the Atlantic. But one can ask: How would the USA function today had it retained all the different currencies that existed in the nineteenth century? Four main questions arise. First, does a common currency promote further trade integration? Second, does trade integration leads to more diversification and similarity? Third, how do labour market conditions respond to the loss of the exchange rate? Finally, can Europe-wide transfers be envisioned? We consider these questions in turn.

## 13.4.1 Effects of a currency union on trade

European policy makers strongly believe that stable exchange rates promote trade integration. The reasoning is that exchange rate uncertainty deters trade: why try to sell abroad and take the risk of losses on foreign currency deals? Unfortunately, this is not unambiguously confirmed by the facts. Nor is it necessarily the case from a purely logical viewpoint. To start with, exchange rate movements can lead not only to exchange losses, but to gains as well. Next, traders can insure themselves against currency fluctuations at little cost.[12] On the other hand, no such protection exists for long-term exchanges – for example foreign direct investment, an issue taken up in Chapter 16.

Recent evidence points towards a very strong effect of currency unions on trade. It has been found that countries that join a currency area *ceteris paribus* double their trade.[13] This is large – perhaps unbelievably so – but so far the result holds up well to intense scrutiny. Early evidence, presented in Fig. 13-13, seems to detect a significant EMU effect.[14] Over the decade 1993–2003, bilateral trade flows in Europe have grown and ebbed as overall economic growth has risen and declined, but trade among the EMU member countries has risen faster and declined less than trade among non-member countries. If confirmed, the evidence suggests that the trade integration criterion, already largely fulfilled within the EMU, will become even more favourable in time.

## 13.4.2 Effects of trade on specialization

Assuming that adoption of a common currency deepens trade integration, the next question is what effect trade integration may have on diversification, the third criterion. The evidence is open to debate. On one side, it has been argued that trade leads to more specialization as each country or region focuses on its comparative advantage. This would go against the diversification (Kenen) criterion. On the other side, it is argued that each country develops its own brands to compete for the same goods with other countries, which would strengthen fulfilment of both the diversification and openness (McKinnon) criteria.[15] The jury is still out, but the evidence accumulated so far seems to support the view that diversification increases with trade integration. In that case, the performance of the EMU with regards to that criterion stands to improve further.

## 13.4.3 Effects of a currency union on labour markets

European labour mobility is low and few expect it to increase dramatically in the near future. An alternative to mobility is flexibility, and the argument runs as follows. European labour markets are noticeably less flexible than their US counterparts. For example, in the USA, firms are quite free to fire workers when economic conditions worsen, while in Europe firing is costly because of heavy severance compensations and numerous regulations. In addition, US unemployed workers receive less generous welfare support, which encourages them to find and accept another job as soon as possible, sometimes elsewhere in the country, possibly less well paid and in a different activity. Europeans frown on US harshness, but the result is that unemployment is generally higher and longer lasting in Europe.

---

[12] Exporters can sell forward the amounts of money that they expect to receive and importers can buy forward the amount of foreign currency that they will need.

[13] The result from Glick and Rose (2001) has been confirmed by others, see the 'aficionados corner' at the end of this chapter.

[14] Bilateral trade is measured as an index (1997 = 100). For every OECD country, trade is recorded with EMU countries and with non-EMU countries. The EMU–EMU index is the un-weighted average of the EMU country's EMU trade indices. The non-EMU–non-EMU index is the un-weighted average of the non-EMU country's non-EMU trade indices. The EMU–non-EMU index is the average of all 'cross group' indices. Nations in the sample: Australia, Austria, Belgium–Luxembourg, Canada, Denmark, Finland, France, Germany, Greece, Iceland, Ireland, Italy, Japan, New Zealand, the Netherlands, Norway, Portugal, Spain, Sweden, Switzerland, the UK, and the USA.

[15] If trade is mostly of the inter-industry (Hecksher–Ohlin) type, integration means more specialization. If instead it is mostly of the intra-industry type, integration reduces specialization. Intra-European trade is increasingly of the intra-industry type, supporting the view that specialization should decline.

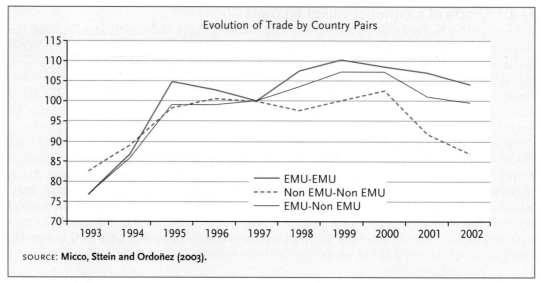

Evolution of Trade by Country Pairs

Legend:
— EMU-EMU
- - - Non EMU-Non EMU
— EMU-Non EMU

SOURCE: **Micco, Sttein and Ordoñez (2003).**

FIGURE 13-13: EMU COUNTRIES' TRADE BEFORE AND AFTER THE EMU

The question is whether the adoption of a common currency will change that. It is too early to tell, and counter arguments have been produced. They all revolve around the reason why European labour markets are rigid. In a nutshell, European workers are attached to the high degree of social protection that they have achieved. They understand that this may have costs, in particular in the form of unemployment and low participation rates, but then they insist on welfare programmes which protect the unemployed and those out of the labour force. This all comes at the cost of lower growth, but they consider that the economic performance is not an end by itself and ought to be related to fairness, solidarity and quality of life. Will monetary union change that? Chapter 17 offers a detailed appraisal of these questions, which can be summarized as follows.

One view is that of a virtuous circle. The idea is that the monetary union will increase the costs of the 'European way' and reduce opposition to measures that aim at flexing the labour markets. When each country had its own currency, workers were advocating using monetary policy and the exchange rate to boost the economy. This is now impossible, at least at the national level, and to date there are no pan-European trade unions. In addition, with prices set in euros across the Union, there is increasing transparency in goods markets, which should benefit countries where labour markets are more flexible. Thus, it is believed, economic competition will indirectly lead to competition among the welfare programmes and this will shift the trade-off between economic performance and labour protection.

The opposite view sees a hardening of labour market rigidities. This view is based on the increasing emphasis on a 'Social Europe'. Advocates of a high degree of labour protection well understand the risk of competition among the welfare programmes and they have successfully called for the adoption of Union-wide minimum standards. A new title on employment has been incorporated in the Amsterdam Treaty and the so-called Lisbon Process, adopted in 1999, provides for an annual set of guidelines that each country must implement under its National Action Plan (NAP). It is not yet clear whether this process will discourage labour market reforms by stifling competition or, on the contrary, lead to benchmarking (observing what works best) and peer pressure towards more flexibility.

## 13.4.4 Fiscal transfers

There is presently no political support for established extensive and automatic intra-European transfers, but proposals regularly surface. It has been suggested that a European tax could be established that could support a European unemployment benefit scheme, for example. Some limited funds are disbursed by the European Commission when a country is hard hit by a natural disaster. It is reasonably certain that, in the not-too-distant future, Europe will have adopted some form of transfer scheme.

## 13.4.5 Beyond the OCA criteria: politics

We have reached two important conclusions. First, Europe is not exactly an optimum currency area; it does well on some, but not all of the criteria. Second, it is not just labour mobility that is insufficient but, more generally, the labour markets display significant rigidity. As a consequence, monetary union may worsen an already painful situation of high unemployment, at least in a number of countries.

It is natural therefore to ask why the European heads of state and governments who gathered in Maastricht in 1991 still decided to take the risk and set up a monetary union. The answer is: politics.[16] A fundamental force driving the European integration process from the late 1940s has been the belief that a thousand (or more) years of war has to come to an end and that the solution is ever deeper economic integration. When Europeans have reached a state where economic interests are deeply intertwined, so goes the argument, there will be no incentive to compete other than on the markets, to the benefit of all. And indeed, at each critical juncture when negotiations become hard, political leaders end up making the concessions needed to produce some sort of agreement, often half-satisfactory, and are prompt to justify it as a step to strengthen peace on the continent. In this important sense, the Europeans share a sense of commonality of destiny.

Interestingly enough, Harvard economist Martin Feldstein, a sharp critic of the EMU, sees it as a source of conflict:

> Political leaders in Europe seem to be prepared to ignore these adverse consequences because they see EMU as way of furthering the political agenda of a federalist European political union ... The adverse economic effects of EMU and the broader political disagreements will nevertheless induce some countries to ask whether they have made a mistake in joining. Although a sovereign country could in principle withdraw from the EMU, the potential trade sanctions and other pressures on such a country are likely to make membership in EMU irreversible unless there is widespread economic dislocation in Europe or, more generally, a collapse of peaceful coexistence within Europe.
>
> Feldstein (1997), pp. 41–2

In his view, the EMU is not only unjustified on economic grounds (it is not an OCA) but its survival will require a major step towards a federal Europe, including common defence and foreign policies as well as a generalized harmonization of taxation and labour market regulations. Much the same view, that the EMU will trigger a bandwagon of pro-federal moves at the expense of the nation-states, was also harboured by former Prime Minister Margaret Thatcher, and underpinned her staunch opposition to the EMU. In every member country of the Union, a large number of people share this view and adamantly want to preserve the nation-state.

---

[16] For a detailed discussion, see the exchange between Feldstein and Wyplosz in the Symposium published in the *Journal of Economic Perspectives*, 11 (4, Fall 1997), 3–42.

## 13.5 **Summary**

■ Money is more useful the more people use it. This would call just one currency for the whole world. But sharing a common currency also carries costs. The optimum currency area theory balances the benefits and the costs of sharing a common currency.

■ Because prices and wages are sticky, exchange rates are useful in dealing with shocks. In a currency union, what matters are asymmetric shocks.

■ The OCA theory asks what characteristics may either reduce the incidence of asymmetric shocks or take the edge off asymmetric shocks. It develops criteria which, if satisfied, would make the loss of the exchange rate instrument painless.

■ The three classic economic OCA criteria are: labour mobility, openness to trade and diversified exports. One additional criterion is the existence of transfers. The two political criteria are: homogeneous preferences regarding the aims of macroeconomic policies and a shared sense of commonality of destiny.

■ Europe does well on three criteria: openness, diversification and homogeneity of preferences. It does not pass the labour mobility and fiscal transfers conditions.

■ There are good reasons to believe that the degree to which the OCA criteria are satisfied are endogenous: being in a currency union makes it more likely that the criteria are satisfied.

■ In the end, forming a monetary union cannot be a black-or-white decision. It involves risks and may require accompanying measures. This is the case in Europe.

### SELF-ASSESSMENT QUESTIONS

**1.** In section 13.1.2, it is asserted that the real exchange rate $\lambda = EP/P^*$ can be depreciated either through a depreciation of the nominal exchange rate $E$ or through a change in the price level $P$. Explain.

**2.** In the presence of an adverse shock, an alternative to devaluation is to cut imports by raising tariffs. Why is this alternative usually unpalatable?

**3.** Provide a list of plausible asymmetric shocks. In particular consider the case of a reduction of the working time length and investigate its effects using the graphical apparatus in Fig. 13-4.

**4.** The labour mobility criterion implicitly assumes that the labour force is homogeneous, which is not the case as workers are most often specialized. How should this criterion be refined?

**5.** Why does a deepening of trade through intra-industry exchanges help with both the diversification (Kenen) and openness (McKinnon) criteria?

**6.** In Fig. 13-4 an adverse asymmetric shock is met by a depreciation. What does the size of the depreciation depend upon?

**7.** Why are European people less mobile than Americans? Note that low mobility is not just observed across national borders but also within each country. What measures could increase labour mobility in Europe?

**8.** Why can commercial integration lead to more national or regional specialization? Why can it lead to less specialization?

**9.** It is sometimes argued that, because the automatic stabilizers are larger in Europe than in the USA, there is less need for automatic transfers. Explain the argument.

### ESSAY QUESTIONS

**1.** Could immigration be a solution to the labour immobility problem?

**2.** Imagine that California is severely hit by a recession in the information technology industry. What would happen if it seceded from the US monetary union and introduced the Californian dollar?

**3.** You are given the task of designing a transfer system to cope with asymmetric shocks. Consider both how to collect and how to spend these resources.

**4.** The African countries that make up the CFA zones do not satisfy the classic OCA economic criteria: labour mobility is low, they trade very little with each other and they are specialized in different commodity exports. And yet, the currency union has lasted for 40 years. What can the explanation(s) be?

**5.** Early evidence is that trade is increasing faster among the EMU countries than among other European non-EMU countries. How can such evidence affect the debate on EMU membership in countries such as Norway, Sweden, Switzerland or the UK?

**6.** Evaluate the 9 May 2003 statement by the British Chancellor of the Exchequer, Gordon Brown, explaining why he recommends that Britain should not join Euroland, at least not yet. (*Source*: http://www.hm-treasury.gov.uk.)

**7.** Write a science-fiction story: a severe asymmetric shock occurs and leads to such economic hardship that the European Monetary Union is dissolved. Carefully explain each step in the process.

**8.** Write a science-fiction story: Northern England adopts its own currency.

## FURTHER READING: THE AFFICONADOS CORNER

### Is Europe an OCA?

When in 1996, it was trying to decide whether to join the monetary union from its start, the Swedish government appointed a special commission to review the question. The Calmfors Commission came out cautiously approving EMU membership, the government decided to wait and see. Its report has been published as a book that provides a detailed and careful analysis of the pros and cons of monetary union in Europe. In May 2003, the British government has released its own study on EMU membership, in fact closely following the OCA criteria. This study represents an excellent way of putting to work the material presented in this chapter. A concise summary of the debates throughout Europe can be found in Wyplosz (1997).

Calmfors, L. et al. (1997) *EMU, A Swedish Perspective*, Kluwer Academic Publishers, Dordrecht.
HM Treasury (2003) *UK Membership of the Single Currency*, HM Stationery Office, Norwich. Also available, with additional detailed studies, on: http://www.hm-treasury.gov.uk
Wyplosz, C. (1997) 'EMU: Why and how it might happen', *Journal of Economic Perspectives*, **11** (4), 3–22.

### The three classic OCA criteria

Mundell, R. (1961) 'A theory of optimum currency area', *American Economic Review*, **51**, 657–65.
McKinnon, R. (1962) 'Optimum currency areas', *American Economic Review*, **53**, 717–25.
Kenen, P. (1969) 'The theory of optimum currency areas', in R. Mundell and A. Swoboda (eds) *Monetary Problems of the International Economy*, Chicago University Press.

### Additional readings

An excellent collection of readings:

De Grauwe, P. (2001) *The Political Economy of Monetary Union*, Edward Elgar Publishing Ltd, Cheltenham.

A detailed review of OCA theory and evidence:
Mongeli, F.P. (2002) 'Ne2' Views on the Optimum Currency Area Theory: What is EMU Telling US?, Working Paper No. 138, ECB, April. http://www.ecb.int
The British analysis of its membership includes a large number of excellent studies:
http://www.hm-treasury.gov.uk

### Integration, trade and specialization

An interesting debate on specialization has been triggered by the following exchanges:
Krugman, P. (1993) 'Lessons of Massachusetts for EMU', in F. Torres and F. Giavazzi (eds) *Adjustment and Growth in the European Monetary Union*, Cambridge University Press, Oxford, New York and Melbourne.
Frankel, J. and A. Rose (1998) 'The endogeneity of the optimum currency area criteria', *Economic Journal*.

Glick, R. and A. Rose (2001) *Does a Currency Union affect Trade? The Time Series Evidence*, NBER Working Paper No. 8396.

A paper using early information from the creation of the EMU, with a review of related studies:
Micco, A., E. Stein and G. Ordoñez (2003) 'Euro's trade effect', *Economic Policy*, **37**.

Another approach, known as the 'border effect', examines prices in different cities in Canada and the USA and finds that, while markets are less well integrated the further apart they are, the border seems to add the equivalent of some 3000 km!

Engel, C. and J. Rogers (1996) 'How wide is the border?', *American Economic Review*, **86** (December), 1112–25.

## Useful websites

Mundell won the Nobel Memorial Prize partly for his work on currency unions. His website is worth a tour: http://www.columbia.edu/~ram15/i.e./ietoc.html

## References

Angeloni, I., A. Kashyap, B. Mojon and D. Terlizzese (2002) *Monetary Transmission in the Euro Area: Where Do We Stand?*, Working Paper No. 114, ECB, Frankfurt.

Bayoumi, T. and B. Eichengreen (1997) 'Ever closer to heaven? An optimum currency area index for European countries', *European Economic Review*, **41**, 761–70.

Campa, J. and L. Godlberg (2002) *Exchange Rate Pass-Through into Import Prices: A Macro or Micro Phenomenon?*, Federal Reserve Bank of New York.

Fatás, A. (2000) 'Intranational migration: business cycles and growth', in E. van Wincoop and G. Hess (eds) *Intranational Macroeconomics*, University Press, Cambridge.

Feldstein, M. (1997) 'The political economy of the European Economic and Monetary Union: political sources of an economic liability', *Journal of Economic Perspectives*, **11** (4), 23–42.

Glick, R. and A. Rose (2001) *Does a Currency Union affect Trade? The Time Series Evidence*, NBER Working Paper, No. 8396.

Micco, A., E. Stein and G. Ordoñez (2003) 'Euro's trade effect', *Economic Policy*, **37**.

Mundell, R. (1973) 'A plan for a european currency', in H. Johnson and A. Swoboda (eds) *The Economics of Common Currencies*, George Allen & Unwin Ltd, London.

" A normal central bank is a monopolist. Today's Eurosystem is, instead, an archipelago "
of monopolists.

**Tommaso Padoa-Schioppa**

# 14 The European Monetary Union

The European monetary union did not come as a surprise. It was carefully mapped out in the Maastricht Treaty, which specified how and when the single currency would be launched and laid down a precise set of institutional arrangements. The Treaty also prescribed the essential elements of the monetary policy doctrine that would prevail. This is the subject matter of this chapter. The main elements of the Maastricht Treaty are presented in section 14.1. Section 14.2 describes the working of the central bank system, a unique combination of a common central bank and national central banks. Section 14.3 explains how monetary policy is conducted: its objectives and its mode of operation. Then we look at the independence of the Eurosystem and its democratic accountability. The last section reviews the first years of the single currency.

## 14.1 The Maastricht Treaty

### 14.1.1 Main components

The Maastricht Treaty marks the end of a long road – three decades of attempts to achieve a monetary union, briefly summarized in Table 14-1. It was agreed upon in the picturesque Dutch town of Maastricht in December 1991 and ratified by all signatories over the next year and half in an eventful process recounted in Box 14-1. The Treaty also represents a new beginning of not only the monetary union but much more. In many ways, the Economic and Monetary Union (EMU) changed the nature of the integration process. At the symbolic level, the official name of the European Community (EC) was changed to European Union (EU) to recognize that the Treaty was not just about economics but also included political considerations. Two new pillars – foreign and defence policies, justice and internal security – were added to the first, economic pillar. The power of the European Parliament was enhanced and it was also agreed to substitute 'qualified majority' for 'unanimity' for Council decisions on a number of issues. Many of these ambitious-looking steps were incomplete, which called for the subsequent treaties of Amsterdam and Nice, and then for the Convention.[1] The monetary union part of the Treaty, however, was fully worked out with the irrevocable decision to adopt a single currency by 1 January 1999. The detailed working of the system was fully described, including the statutes of the ECB and the conditions under which monetary union would start.

| Towards Maastricht | | Between Maastricht and the single currency | | The single currency | |
|---|---|---|---|---|---|
| 1970 | Werner Plan | 1994 | European Monetary Institute (precursor of ECB) | 1999 | Monetary union starts |
| 1979 | EMS starts | 1997 | Stability and Growth Pact | 2001 | Greece joins |
| 1989 | Delors Committee | 1998 | Decision on membership | 2002 | Euro coins and notes introduced |
| 1991 | Maastricht Treaty signed | 1998 | Conversion rates set | | |
| 1993 | Maastricht Treaty ratified | 1998 | Creation of ECB | | |

TABLE 14-1: EMU TIMETABLE

BOX 14-1: RATIFICATION OF THE MAASTRICHT TREATY

Any international treaty must be ratified by the signatories. The ratification procedure varies from one country to another: some countries require a referendum, others must obtain Parliament's approval, yet others can decide between these two alternatives.

The first country to undertake ratification of the Maastricht Treaty was Denmark, and it had to be by referendum. The Danish people chose to reject the Treaty by a small margin. A clause

[1] The various aspects were examined in detail in Part I of this volume.

stipulated that, to enter into existence, the Treaty must be ratified by all the signatories. Th_ the Treaty looked dead before the other countries even had a chance to consider it! Yet, hoping that a legal solution would be found, it was decided to continue with the ratification process.

France offered to be the second country to consider ratification. In the hope of reversing the bad impression created by Denmark's popular rejection, President Mitterrand chose the referendum procedure, with polls indicating strong support. As the campaign started, support started to erode and even to be reversed in some polls. Fearing a collapse of the whole project, the exchange markets became jittery and speculation gained momentum. In the event, Italy and the UK were ejected from the ERM and several currencies had to be devalued, some of them many times, as described in Chapter 12. Meanwhile the French approved the Treaty by a narrow margin.

The Danes were asked to return to the polls, after the Danish government committed itself to invoke the right not to adopt the single currency as had been allowed in a special protocol to the Treaty, as is further explained below. This time, they approved the Treaty. And, finally, the German Constitutional Court was asked by opponents to decide whether the Treaty was unconstitutional. The Court took several months to deliver its opinion, keeping the process hanging. The Court decided that the Treaty did not contradict the German constitution. This allowed Germany to ratify the Treaty in late 1993, the last country to do so.

## 14.1.2 Convergence criteria

When the Treaty was under preparation, the economic situation differed widely from one country to another. Germany, deeply attached to price stability, was concerned that some countries were not quite ready to play by the rules that it had successfully set for itself for several decades. It insisted that admission to the monetary union – all countries are *de facto* EMU members – would be selective. The selection process was designed to certify which countries had adopted a 'culture of price stability', meaning that they had durably achieved German-style low inflation. In order to join the monetary union, a country has to fulfil the following five convergence criteria, which remain applicable to all future candidate countries.

### INFLATION

The first criterion deals directly with inflation. To be eligible for monetary union membership, a country's inflation rate should not exceed the average of the three lowest inflation rates achieved by the European Union Member States by more than 1.5 percentage points. Figure 14-1 shows how the 'Club Med' countries of southern Europe managed to bring their inflation rates to within the tolerance margin by 1998. Greece (not shown) failed (actually it did not even try and decided to join later, which it did in 2001).

### LONG-TERM NOMINAL INTEREST RATE

An inflation-prone country could possibly squeeze down inflation temporarily, on the last year before admission – for example, by freezing regulated prices (electricity, transports) – only to relax the effort afterwards. In order to weed out cheaters, a second criterion requires that the long-term interest rate should not exceed the average rates observed in the three lowest inflation rate countries by more than 2 percentage points. The reasoning is shrewd. Long-term interest rates

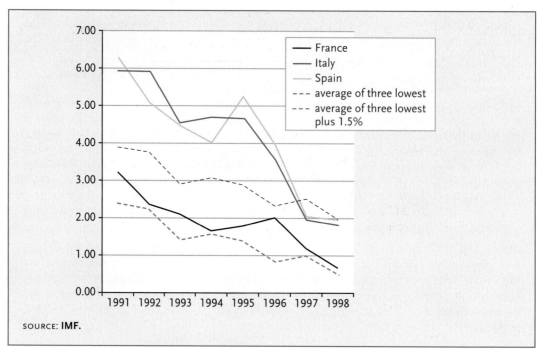

SOURCE: **IMF.**

FIGURE 14-1: INFLATION CONVERGENCE (1991–98)

mostly reflect markets' assessment of long-term inflation.[2] Achieving a low long-term interest rate therefore requires convincing the naturally sceptical financial markets that inflation would remain low 'for ever'.

### EMS MEMBERSHIP

The same concern about a superficial conversion to price stability lies behind the third criterion. Here the idea is that a country must have demonstrated its ability to keep its exchange rate tied to its future monetary union partner currencies. The requirement is therefore that every country must have taken part to the ERM[3] for at least two years without having to devalue its currency.

### BUDGET DEFICIT

In the end, why do countries tolerate inflation? Inflation is not really desirable, so its acceptance must reflect some deeper problem. Indeed, inflation is typically the result of large budget deficits which the government eventually finds hard to finance by borrowing from the financial markets, issuing bonds. The alternative to bond-financing is to ask the central bank to run its printing press. This is how large budget deficits tend to translate into fast money growth which ultimately delivers high inflation.

This is why the fourth convergence criterion sets a limit on acceptable budget deficits. But what limit? Here again German influence prevailed. Germany had long operated a 'golden rule', which

---

[2] This is based on the Fisher principle: nominal interest rate = real interest rate + expected inflation. Since the real interest rate is reasonably constant and set world wide, the main driving force determining the long-term interest rate is the expected long-term inflation rate. See Box 14-4 for an elaboration.
[3] The exchange rate mechanism is presented in detail in Chapter 12.

specifies that budget deficits are only acceptable if they correspond to public investment spending (on roads, telecommunication, other infrastructures). The idea is that public investment is a source of growth which eventually generates the resources needed to pay for the initial borrowing. The German 'golden rule' considers that public investment typically amounts to some 3 per cent of GDP. Hence the requirement that budget deficits should not exceed 3 per cent of GDP.[4]

## PUBLIC DEBT

Much as inflation can be lowered temporarily, deficits can be made to look good on any given year (for example by shifting public spending and taxes from one year to another). Thus it was decided that a more permanent feature of fiscal discipline ought to be added. The fifth and last criterion mandates a maximum level for the public debt. Here again, the question was: which ceiling? Unimaginatively perhaps, the ceiling was set at 60 per cent of GDP because it was the average debt level when the Maastricht Treaty was being negotiated in 1991. An additional reason was that the 60 per cent debt limit can be seen as compatible with a deficit debt ceiling of 3 per cent as explained in Box 14-2.

---

### Box 14-2: THE ARITHMETICS OF DEFICITS AND DEBTS

Debts grow out of deficits, but how does the debt/GDP ratio relate to the deficit/GDP ratio? A little arithmetic helps. If total nominal debt at the end of year $t$ is $B_t$, its increase during the year is $B_t - B_{t-1}$, and this is equal to the annual deficit $D_t$:

$$B_t - B_{t-1} = D_t \qquad (1)$$

The two fiscal convergence criteria refer not to the debt and deficit levels, but to their ratios to nominal GDP $Y$, denoted as $b_t$ and $d_t$, respectively. Divide the previous accounting equality by the current year GDP to get:

$$\frac{B_t - B_{t-1}}{Y_t} = \frac{D_t}{Y_t} \quad \text{or} \quad b_t - \frac{B_{t-1}}{Y_t} = d_t \qquad (2)$$

Then note that $\dfrac{B_{t-1}}{Y_t} = \dfrac{B_{t-1}}{Y_{t-1}} \dfrac{Y_{t-1}}{Y_t} = \dfrac{b_{t-1}}{1+g_t}$ where $g_t = \dfrac{Y_t - Y_{t-1}}{Y_{t-1}} = \dfrac{Y_t}{Y_{t-1}} - 1$ is the growth rate of GDP in year $t$. We can rewrite the debt growth equation (2) as:

$$b_t - b_{t-1} = (1 + g_t) d_t - g_t b_t \qquad (3)$$

If the debt to GDP ratio $b$ is to remain constant, we need to have $b_t = b_{t-1}$, which from (3) implies:

$$d_t = \frac{1 + g_t}{g_t} b_t \qquad (4)$$

---

The fiscal convergence criteria sets $d_t = 3$ per cent and $b_t = 60$ per cent. If nominal GDP grows by 5 per cent, (4) is approximately satisfied. The implicit assumption is therefore that real GDP annual growth is about 3 per cent and inflation is 2 per cent, hence a nominal GDP growth rate of 5 per cent.

  The logic is that if the debt level is constant, the debt/GDP ratio declines as the result of GDP growth, the more so the faster nominal GDP grows. This means that some debt increase, and therefore some deficit, is compatible with a constant debt/GDP ratio, and the tolerable deficit is larger the faster nominal GDP grows.

---

[4] This limit is maintained after entry in EMU. The next chapter studies the Stability and Growth Pact.

However, by definition of an average, some countries had debts in excess of 60 per cent of GDP, and some much larger. Such was the case of Belgium, whose debt stood at some 120 per cent of GDP, and this created a new problem. Debts cannot be reduced overnight, it takes many years to repay them. By 1991, Belgium, had just overhauled its public finances and was adamant that it was now committed to adhere to a strict budgetary discipline. As a founding member of the Common Market in 1957, an enthusiastic European country, and a long advocate of monetary union, Belgium argued that it could not be left out because of past sins now firmly repudiated. At its request, the criterion was couched in prudent terms, calling for a debt to GDP ratio either less than 60 per cent or 'moving in that direction'.

Figure 14-2 shows how deficits and debts looked in 1998, the last year before the launch of the monetary union, which was used to determine which country fulfilled the criteria. All countries managed to bring their deficits below the 3 per cent threshold, sometimes thanks to accounting tricks.[5] Few, however, could report debts below 60 per cent of GDP, but all were saved by the 'Belgian clause'.

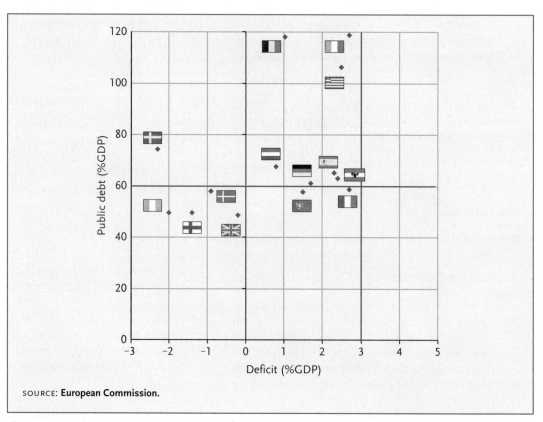

SOURCE: **European Commission.**

FIGURE 14-2: DEFICITS AND DEBTS IN 1998

[5] France privatized part of its state-owned telecommunication corporation, which brought the revenues needed to achieved the target. Italy collected in end 1998 taxes which would have normally been due in early 1999. Even the German government considered selling gold to pay back its debt but backed off as the Bundesbank publicly attacked the idea.

### 14.1.3 Two-speed Europe

An important aspect of the Maastricht Treaty is that it introduced, for the first time, the idea that a major integration move would leave some countries out. Initially, the intention was to protect price stability and not let the inflation wolf enter the den. Then things turned out differently.

Prime Minister Thatcher's Britain was firmly opposed to monetary union. For a while, Thatcher stonewalled the discussions, which went ahead without her. The view in London was that this was a bizarre idea with no future at all, a sort of conventional exercise that no one really intended to bring to fruition. When it realized that the other European countries were in fact serious, Britain found itself cut off from a major negotiation that would powerfully shape Europe's future. Partly because of her unwillingness to engage her partners on the issue, Thatcher was dismissed and replaced by John Major. Unable to scuttle the project, the best he could achieve was to obtain an opt-out clause, which stated that Britain, alone, was not bound to join the monetary union. This further confirmed that Europe could move at different speeds. A similar opt-out clause was given to Denmark, and was invoked after a first rejection of the Treaty by Danish voters (see Box 14-1).

In 1995, Sweden joined the European Union. The Swedish authorities made it clear that they were less than enthusiastic towards the monetary union. They asked for an opt-out clause, which was denied. The diplomatic solution was a gentleman's agreement whereby Sweden did not enter the ERM and was therefore disqualified for monetary union membership. *De facto*, Sweden is treated as Denmark, with the right to decide when to apply for membership to the Euro area.

In the end, the monetary union started on time with 11 members. The 'outs' included Greece, which did not meet the convergence criteria, Britain and Denmark, which invoked the opt-out clause, and Sweden. Greece converged later and joined in January 2001.

The story starts anew when the European Union expands in 2004 with 10 new members: the Czech Republic, Hungary, Poland, the Slovak Republic, Slovenia, Estonia, Latvia, Lithuania, Cyprus and Malta. Some of these countries have long attached their currencies first to the DM, and then to the euro. Others have let their currencies float freely. As members of the EU, they are supposed to enter the ERM and then fulfil the convergence criteria before joining the monetary union (see section 12.3.3).

## 14.2 The Eurosystem

### 14.2.1 *N* countries, *N* + 1 central banks

With a single currency there can be only one interest rate, one exchange rate *vis-à-vis* the rest of the world, and therefore one monetary policy. Normally this implies a single central bank, but this is not quite the way the EMU was set up. Each member still comes equipped with its own central bank, the last remaining vestige of lost monetary sovereignty. No matter how daring the founding fathers of the EMU were, they stopped short of merging the national central banks into a single institution, partly for fear of having to dismiss thousands of employees. In fact, as Table 14-2 shows, national central banks have hardly downsized their staff. Paradoxically perhaps, downsizing has been larger in non-Euro area central banks.

The solution was inspired by federal states like Germany and the USA where regional central banks co-exist with the federal central bank. But the European Union is not a federation, and the word 'federation' is highly politically incorrect in Europe. Inevitably, therefore, the chosen structure is complicated. The newly created European Central Bank (ECB) co-exists with the national central banks, one of which did not even exist prior to 1999 since Luxembourg, long part of a monetary union with Belgium, only established its own central bank to conform to the new arrangement.

| | Staff | % Change 1997–2002 | Staff per million inhabitants | | Staff | % Change 1997–2002 | Staff per million inhabitants |
|---|---|---|---|---|---|---|---|
| Austria | 1 153 | 0.3 | 143 | Ireland | 805 | 29.8 | 210 |
| Belgium | 2 316 | −17.4 | 226 | Italy | 8 482 | −5.3 | 146 |
| Finland | 708 | −8.8 | 136 | Luxembourg | 200 | 51.5 | 455 |
| France | 15 216 | −5.9 | 257 | Netherlands | 1 826 | 6.1 | 114 |
| Germany | 15 834 | −1.3 | 192 | Portugal | 1 814 | 0.2 | 181 |
| Greece | 3 090 | −2.6 | 308 | Spain | 3 050 | −5.5 | 76 |
| | | | | Denmark | 611 | 5.5 | 115 |
| ECB | 1 094 | 98.9[a] | 4 | Sweden | 501 | −24.5 | 57 |
| Eurosystem | 55 588 | −2.7 | 183 | UK | 2 242 | −34.6 | 38 |

SOURCE: Gros and Lannoo (2000), updated by these authors in 2003.

NOTE: (a) Change relative to the ECB's predecessor, the European Monetary Institute.

TABLE 14-2: STAFF IN NATIONAL CENTRAL BANKS AND THE ECB IN 2002

On the other hand, in many respects the euro was meant to be a continuation of Europe's most successful currency, the Deutschemark. The structure of the Bundesbank was used as a blueprint for the monetary union. This inspiration is visible in the new institution but also in the policy objective and framework, and in the location of the ECB in Frankfurt, only a few kilometres from the Bundesbank.

## 14.2.2 The system

The European System of Central Banks (ESCB) is composed of the new, specially created European Central Bank (ECB) and the national central banks (NCBs) of all EU Member States. Since not all EU countries have joined the monetary union, a different term, Eurosystem,[6] has been coined to refer to the ECB and the participating NCBs. The Eurosystem implements the monetary policy of the euro area, as described below. If needed, it also conducts foreign exchange operations, in agreement with the Finance Ministers of the member countries. It holds and manages the official foreign reserves of the EMU Member States. It monitors the payment systems and it is involved in the prudential supervision of credit institutions and the financial system.

As shown in Fig. 14-3, the ECB is run by an Executive Board of six members, appointed by the heads of state or governments of the countries that have joined the monetary union, following consultation of the European Parliament and the Governing Council of the ESCB. It comprises the six members of the Executive Board and the governors of the NCBs of monetary union Member States. The Governing Council is the key authority deciding on monetary policy. Its decisions are, in principle, taken by majority voting with each member holding one vote, although it seems to operate by consensus. A transitory body, the General Council, includes the members of the Governing Council and the governors of the NCBs of the countries that have not joined the monetary union. The General Council is essentially fulfilling a liaison role and has no authority.

[6] For a full and formal description, see the July 1999 issue of the ECB's *Monthly Bulletin*, pp. 55–63.

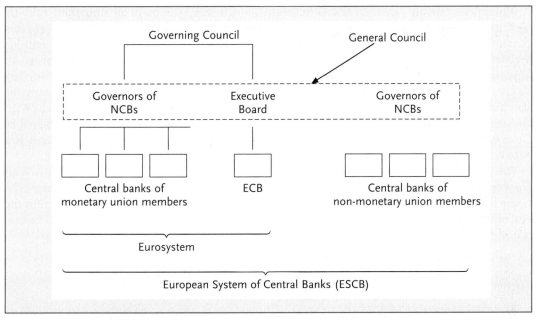

FIGURE 14-3: THE EUROPEAN SYSTEM OF CENTRAL BANKS

WIM DUISENBERG (1998–2003)

Wim Duisenberg, the first president of the ECB, was born in 1932. He holds a PhD in economics, worked at the IMF and was professor of macroeconomics at the University of Amsterdam before entering politics in the Labour Party and serving as Minister of Finance. Later on, he joined De Netherlandsche Bank and became its governor in 1982. In 1997, he was appointed President of the European Monetary Institute, in charge or preparing the introduction of the single currency

www.ecb.int

JEAN-CLAUDE TRICHET (2003–2011)

His successor, Jean-Claude Trichet, was also a central bank governor prior to taking over the ECB. Born in 1942, he studied econmics and civil engineering before attending the elite Ecole Nationale d'Administration. He capped a distinguished career in the French Finance Minstry by becoming head of the Treasury and, in 1993, Governor of the Banque de France. While at the Treasury, he disigned the *franc fort* policy of disinflation.

www.banque-france-fr

While decisions are taken by the Governing Council, the ECB plays an important role. Its Chairman presides over the meetings of the Governing Council and reports its decisions at press conferences. The ECB prepares the meetings of the Governing Council and implements its decisions. It also gives instructions to the NCBs to carry out the common monetary policy. An important characteristic of the ECB is that its Executive Board members are not representing any country: they are appointed as individuals, even though the large countries (France, Germany, Italy and Spain) all had a national sitting in the first Board. The first Chairman was Dutch, Wim Duisenberg, and his successor is French, Jean-Claude Trichet, both having previously served as Governors of their own NCBs. Thus the ECB is of a federal nature while the Eurosystem is a hybrid, partly federal (the ECB) and partly including national institutions (the NCBs).

The size of the Governing Council is seen by external observers as a source of difficulty. With $6 + n$ members, where $n$ is the number of countries that have joined the monetary union, the Council is large. It will become larger as new members, possibly 10 or more, join the union by the end of the decade, although some change will be introduced to ensure that the decision-making committee's size is and remains efficient, see Box 14-3.

---

**Box 14-3: Changing the rules of the Eurosystem[7]**

Monetary policy choices are often delicate, with many pros and cons to be balanced. For this kind of decision, smaller committees are more efficient than larger ones. The expansion of the EU challenges the Eurosystem decision-making process as the size of the Governing Council could eventually grow to 30 or more members, a small parliament! The Nice Treaty of 2000 includes an enabling clause which calls upon the Eurosystem to make a recommendation to the Council on how to prevent an unwieldy situation. After long internal deliberations, the Eurosystem has made its position known in December 2002. It suggests to cap the number of NCB Governors exercising a voting right at 15. While all Council members will be attending the meetings, NCB Governors will exercise a voting right on the basis of a rotation system. The frequency at which every NCB Governor will rotate will depend on the size of the financial market of his/her country, following a complex procedure. This proposition, which will take its effect when the sixteenth member joins the Euro area, must be approved by the EU Council and then ratified by all EU member countries. In the end, the matter is likely to be settled by the Intergovernmental Conference that will deal with the Convention.

---

## 14.3 Objectives, instruments and strategy

### 14.3.1 Objectives

The treaty specifies that the main task of the Eurosystem is to deliver price stability, but the formulation is both vague and ambiguous:

> The primary objective of the ESCB shall be to maintain price stability. Without prejudice to the objective of price stability, the ESCB shall support the general economic policies in the Community with a view to contributing to the achievement of the objectives of the Community as laid down in Article 2.

(Article 105)

---

[7] For a complete description, see the May 2003 issue of the ECB's *Monthly Bulletin*, pp. 73–83.

The Treaty does not give an exact definition of price stability. The Eurosystem has chosen to interpret it first as follows: 'Price stability is defined as a year-on-year increase in the Harmonized Index of Consumer Prices (HICP)[8] for the Euro area of below 2 per cent. Price stability is to be maintained over the medium term.' In 2003, admist years of deflation, 'the Governing Council agreed that in the pursuit of price stability it will aim to maintain inflation rates close to 2 per cent over the medium term.'[9] Thus, while many central banks typically announce an admissible range for inflation, the Eurosystem only indicates an imprecise target. It does not specify the meaning of 'the medium term'.

The Treaty considers price stability as a 'primary objective'. Secondary objectives are described in Delphic terms, referring to Article 2 which states the objectives of the European Union as including 'economic and social progress, and a high level of employment'. Price stability clearly takes precedence over these secondary objectives, but leaves the Eurosystem with quite some leeway to decide its strategy. The Eurosystem has chosen to emphasize price stability and to discount the other aspects.

---

**BOX 14-4: THE EXPECTATIONS THEORY OF INTEREST RATES**

We consider periods of short duration to be one day or one week. The nominal interest over such a short period $t$ is $i_t$. We also look at a very long period $T$, say 5 or 10 years. We can borrow for the entire period $T$, at an interest $I_T$. Alternatively we can borrow for just one period, the coming one $t = 1$, at interest $i_1$, and then borrow again at rate $i_2$, and again and again until the end of the long period $T$. Since we can go either way, the cost should be the same.[10] But, while we know the interest rates $i_1$ and $I_T$ on short- and long-term loans that are currently available, we don't know the interest rates on loans available in the future. In particular, $i_t$ the short-term one-period rate for period $t$ can only be guessed. We denote as $E[i_t]$ our best guess of the expected short-term rate; it is called the expected value of $i_t$.

The cost of the long-term loan is $(1 + I_T)$: we must reimburse the principal and the interest. The expected cost of the series of chained short-term loans is $(1 + i_1)(1 + E[i_2]) \ldots (1 + E[i_T])$. Equality is between the two expected costs:

$$(1 + I_T) = (1 + i_1)(1 + E[i_2]) \ldots (1 + E[i_T])$$

As time passes, the central bank will eventually control all the short-term rates $i_1, i_2, \ldots, i_T$, but it does not control today's expectations $E[i_2], E[i_3], \ldots, E[i_T]$. This is why it cannot control the long-term interest rate $I_T$. Since its actions will determine the future short-term rates $i_2, i_3, \ldots, i_T$, the markets try to guess future monetary policy when they set the long-term rate $I_T$.[11]

In most countries, the very short-term rates are only used by banks and other financial institutions when they deal with each other, and therefore do not affect households and firms. In some countries, such as Portugal and the UK, the long-term rates are indexed on the short-term rate: for example, when the short-term rate increases, so does the longer-term rate, according to a contractual formula. In this way, the central bank controls not only the short-term but also the longer-term interest rates.

---

[8] The Harmonized Index of Consumer Prices is an area-wide consumer price index.

[9] *Monthly Bulletin*, ECB, May 2003, p. 8.

[10] We consider a 'risk-free' rate, i.e. assuming that that no one fears that we will default and that we can freely borrow in each period.

[11] Implicitly, the interest rates are not written in annualized form as they are usually quoted. If the long period $T = 20$ years, the annualized interest rate is $I_T$, such that the total cost of the loan is $(1 + I_T)^{20}$. Similarly, if the short period is one week, the annualized interest rate $i_t$ is such that the cost is $(1 + i_t)^{1/52}$. Then the formula is:

$$(1 + I_T)^{20} = (1 + i_1)^{1/52}(1 + E[i_2])^{1/52} \ldots (1 + E[i_T])^{1/52}$$

This does not affect the reasoning.

### 14.3.2 Instruments

Like most other central banks, the Eurosystem uses the short-term interest rate to conduct monetary policy. The reason is that very short-term assets – 24 hours or less – are very close to cash. As central banks have a monopoly on the supply of cash, they can control very short-term rates. On the other hand, longer-term financial instruments can be supplied by both the public and private sectors, making it nearly impossible for central banks to dominate the market and control the rate. In fact, longer-term rates incorporate market expectations of future inflation and future policy actions (Box 14-4 presents the expectation theory of interest rates). These expectations are beyond the control of the central bank, and therefore long-term interest rates cannot be steered with any degree of precision. By concentrating on short-term rates, central banks can achieve greater precision.

The problem is that central banks control the short maturity while it is the long-term interest rate that affects the economy because households and firms borrow for relatively long periods, typically from 1 to 20 years or more (see Box 14-4 for exceptions). Stock prices and exchange rates, which are the other channels through which monetary policy affects the economy,[12] also incorporate longer-term expectations, similar to those that move the long-term interest rates. Thus central banks act indirectly on the economy. They affect the long-term interest rates through their influence on future short-term rates and inflation. Being clear about longer-run aims and intentions is part of the art of central banking.

The Eurosystem focuses on the overnight rate EONIA (European Over Night Index Average), a weighted average of overnight lending transactions in the Euro area's interbank market). Control over EONIA is achieved in two ways:

- ■ The Eurosystem creates a ceiling and a floor for EONIA by maintaining open lending and deposit facilities at pre-announced interest rates. The marginal lending facility means that banks can always borrow directly from the ECB (more precisely, from the NCBs) at the corresponding rate; they would never pay more on the overnight market, so the marginal lending rate is effectively a ceiling. Similarly, since banks can always deposit cash at the ECB's deposit rate, they would never agree to lend at a lower rate, and this rate is the floor. Figure 14-4 shows that, indeed, EONIA moves within the corridor thus established.
- ■ The Eurosystem conducts, usually weekly, auctions at a rate that it chooses. These auctions, called main refinancing operations, are the means by which the ECB provides liquidity to the banking system and the chosen interest rate serves as a precise guide for EONIA.

How does liquidity flow from the Eurosystem to all the corners of the Euro area banking system? As noted above, on a regular basis the Eurosystem organizes auctions. Each NCB collects bids from its commercial banks and passes the information to the ECB. The ECB then decides which proportion of bids will be accepted and instructs the NCBs accordingly. The commercial banks can then disseminate the liquidity on the interbank market. It does not matter where the initial injection is made: since there is a single interest rate throughout the Euro area, the area-wide interbank market ensures that money is available where needed.

### 14.3.3 Strategy

How does the Eurosystem go about using its instrument (the short-term interest rate) to achieve its objective (inflation close to 2 per cent)? It announced its strategy in October 1998, a few months before starting its operation. In the Spring of 2003, it conducted a strategy review to take stock of the experience accumulated so far.[13] As stated, the strategy relies on three main elements: the

---

[12] The channels of monetary policy are presented in Chapter 16.
[13] The initial strategy is presented in the ECB's *Monthly Bulletin*, January 1999. The strategy review is presented in the ECB's *Monthly Bulletin*, June 2003.

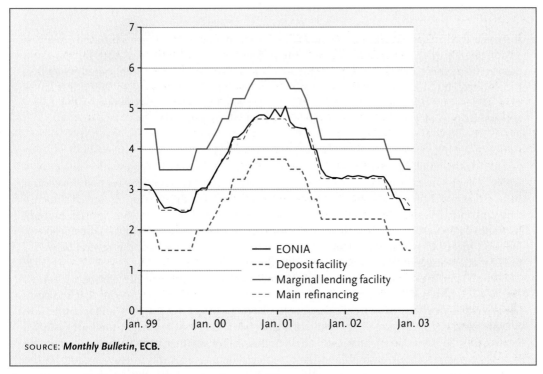

SOURCE: *Monthly Bulletin*, **ECB.**

FIGURE 14-4: ECB INTEREST RATES (JAN. 1999–MAY 2003)

definition of price stability, as presented in section 14.3.1, and two 'pillars' used to identify risks to price stability.

The first pillar is what the Eurosystem calls 'economic analysis'. It consists of a broad review of the recent evolution and likely prospects of economic conditions (including growth, employment, prices, exchange rates, foreign conditions). The second pillar, the 'monetary analysis', studies the evolution of monetary aggregates (M3, in particular) and credit which, in the medium to long term, affect inflation, in line with the neutrality principle developed in Chapter 11. In the Eurosystem's words, 'these two perspectives offer complementary analytical frameworks to support the Governing Council's overall assessment of risks to price stability. In this respect, the monetary analysis mainly serves as a means of cross-checking, from a medium- to long-term perspective, the short- to medium-term indications coming from economic analysis.'[14]

What does this mean in practice? The Governing Council is presented by its Chief Economist with a broad analysis, including forecasts of inflation and growth. Monetary conditions are then used to qualify the forecasts and allow the Council to form a view of where inflation is heading. Then the real debate starts: What should happen to the interest rate? Should it be raised because inflation is perceived as excessive? How much weight should be attached to other considerations, such as growth and employment, or the exchange rate and stock markets? Officially, the Eurosystem is only dealing with inflation, but it has visibly adjusted its actions when it has felt the need to smooth the edges of what it considers to be secondary concerns. Importantly, the Eurosystem does not take any responsibility for the exchange rate, which is freely floating.

---

[14] 'The ECB's monetary policy strategy', Press Release, ECB, 8 May 2003 (http://www.ecb.int).

## Box 14-5: A Taylor rule for the ECB?

A simple way of describing the behaviour of central banks is to assume that they follow a Taylor rule, i.e. that they set the interest rate in reactions to deviations of both inflation and output from their desired levels.[15] Most central banks reject this interpretation as too mechanistic, but it is often amazing how well the rule fits actual behaviour. When this is the case, the Taylor rule reveals a central bank's preferences. In their overview of the ECB's actions, Begg et al. (2002) finds that the following Taylor rule is adequate:

$$i = i^* + a(\pi - \pi^*) + b(y - y^*)$$

where $i^*$ is the equilibrium interest rate, $\pi$ is the inflation rate and $\pi^*$ the inflation objective, $y$ is the GDP growth rate and $y^*$ is the GDP growth trend. This formulation says that the central bank raises the interest rate above its equilibrium level – i.e. tightens up its policy stance – when inflation rises above its objective and/or during cyclical upturns, when growth exceeds its trend. Of special interest are the weights that represent the Eurosystem's relative dislike of inflation (parameter $a$) and cyclical fluctuations (parameter $b$). If $b = 0$, the central bank is a pure inflation-targetter, it pays no attention to the cyclical situation.[16]

Using Fisher's principle (see footnote 2), the equilibrium interest rate can be written as $i^* = r^* + \pi^*$, where $r^*$ is the equilibrium real interest rate. Begg et al. consider that the equilibrium real interest rate $r^* = 2$ per cent, that the inflation target is 2 per cent, and that the GDP growth trend is 1.2 per cent. They find that the weights that best represent the Eurosystem's relative dislike of inflation and cyclical fluctuations are $a = 2.0$ and $b = 0.8$, i.e. that the Eurosystem cares about both inflation and cyclical fluctuations, with a heavy weight on the former. Figure 14-5 provides a reasonable, yet far from perfect, interpretation of the actions of this rule over its short history.

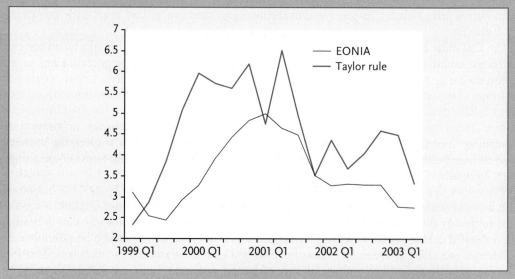

FIGURE 14-5: THE EUROSYSTEM'S TAYLOR RULE

---

[15] The rule is named after the Stanford economist Taylor who first suggested this interpretation. John Taylor (1993) 'Discretion vs. Policy Rules in practice', *Carnegie-Rochester Conference Series on Public Policy*, **39**, 195–214.

[16] Thing are never as simple as they look. The cyclical term $(y - y^*)$ can be used by a pure inflation-targeting central bank as a predictor of future inflation, so that $b > 0$ may indicate forward-looking behaviour.

Is the Eurosystem's strategy special? Over the last decade, many central banks have adopted the inflation-targeting strategy. In Europe, this is the case of most non-monetary union member central banks (including the Czech Republic, Hungary, Norway, Poland, Sweden and the UK). Inflation targeting comprises announcing a target, publishing an inflation forecast at the relevant policy horizon (usually one to two years ahead) and adjusting the interest rate according to the difference between the forecast and the target. For example, if the forecast exceeds the target, the presumption is that monetary policy is tightened, i.e. that the interest rate is raised.

The Eurosystem has clearly resisted this approach, along with the US Federal Reserve and the Bank of Japan. Part of the reason seems that the Eurosystem wants to claim the Bundesbank heritage, and the Bundesbank did not target inflation. On the other hand, the Eurosystem's strategy resembles inflation targeting: there is an implicit target (the 2 per cent definition of price stability) and an inflation forecast is published twice a year. What the Eurosystem seems to reject is giving the appearance that it acts mechanically.

### 14.3.4 One money, one policy

Occasionally, there are complaints that the Eurosystem does not pay attention to economic conditions in this or that country. The fact is that with one money there can only exist one central bank, and therefore one monetary policy. The Eurosystem can only deal with the Euro area as a whole. It would open a Pandora's box should it ever attempt to bend its policy to a particular country. After all, a key implication of the OCA theory, presented in Chapter 13, is that joining the monetary union implies the acceptance that there will occasionally be costs to be borne by member countries.

A more difficult question concerns the impact that the single monetary policy has on member countries. The same change in the interest rate may well have different effects in different countries. This may be due to a host factors, in particular the structure of the financial sector and the economic structure. For example, in countries where firms chose to raise money from stock markets rather than by borrowing from banks, monetary policy may have a more limited impact because stock prices tend to follow less closely the short-term interest rate than bank lending rates. Similarly, small firms are rarely quoted on stock markets and depend therefore entirely on bank loans. Preliminary evidence is that these differences are present. This may indeed complicate the task of the Eurosystem.[17] On the other hand, over time, we may expect that these differences will gradually fade away.

## 14.4 Independence and accountability

A central bank at present is primarily entrusted with the task of delivering price stability. To that effect, it must be free to pursue this task without outside interference. While, in principle, everyone approves of price stability, some important actors occasionally have second thoughts. As noted in section 14.1.2, financially stressed governments may come to see the printing press as the least bad option. Exporters like low exchange rates and are frequently asking their central banks to relax their policies, with the support of trade unions concerned with employment. Debtors like inflation for it erases the value of their (non-indexed) liabilities. Financial institutions often make larger profits when liquidity is plentiful. In any democracy, these are formidable coalitions, and this is why the modern trend of focusing monetary policy on price stability also argues in favour of central bank independence, from all segments of society and, in particular, from the political powers.

---

[17] Some evidence is shown in section 13.3.1. In the language of the OCA theory, this can be characterized as a source of heterogeneity that raises the cost of a monetary union.

On the other hand, monetary policy affects citizens of the monetary union in a number of ways. The interest rate directly impacts on the cost of borrowing and on the returns from saving; the exchange rate affects the competitiveness of firms and the purchasing power of citizens; and both of these factors indirectly influence wealth. In effect, by granting independence to their central bank, the citizens delegate a very important task to a group of individuals who are appointed, not elected, and who cannot be removed unless they commit grave illegal acts. In a democratic society, delegation to unelected officials needs to be counter-balanced by democratic accountability. This section examines how these two goals are dealt with in the EMU.

### 14.4.1 Independence

The Eurosystem is characterized by a great degree of independence; it is probably the world's most independent central bank. Both the ECB and the NCBs are strictly protected from political influence. Before joining the Euro area, each country must adapt the statutes of its NCB to match a number of common requirements. In particular, the EU Treaty explicitly rules out any interference by national or European authorities in the deliberations of the Eurosystem:

> When exercising the powers and carrying out the tasks and duties conferred upon them by this Treaty and the Statute of the ESCB, neither the ECB, nor a national central bank, nor any member of their decision making bodies shall seek or take instructions from Community institutions or bodies, from any government of a Member State or from any other body. The Community institutions and bodies and the governments of the Member States undertake to respect this principle and not to seek to influence the members of the decision-making bodies of the ECB or of the national central banks in the performance of their tasks.
>
> (Article 108)

In addition, to guarantee their personal independence, the members of the Executive Board are appointed for a long period (eight years) and cannot be reappointed, which reduces the opportunity for pressures.[18] Similar conditions apply to the NCB governors, although they differ slightly from one country to another, but their mandates must be for a minimum of five years. No official can be removed from office unless he/she becomes incapacitated or is found guilty of serious misconduct, with the Court of Justice of the European Communities competent to settle disputes.

The independence of the Eurosystem applies to the choice of both policy objectives and instruments. The Treaty sets the objective in terms vague enough to allow the Eurosystem to decide what it tries to achieve, as explained in section 14.3.1. The Treaty further leaves the Eurosystem completely free to decide which instruments it uses, and how. Other central banks sometimes only have instrument independence. This is the case of the Bank of England which is instructed to pursue an inflation target set by the Chancellor of the Exchequer.

Finally the ECB is financially independent. It has its own budget, independent from that of the European Union. Its accounts are not audited by the European Court of Auditors, which monitors the European Commission, but by independent external auditors.

### 14.4.2 Accountability

Democratic accountability is typically exercised in two ways: reporting and transparency. Formally, the Eurosystem operates under the control of the European Parliament. Its statutes require that an annual report be sent to the Parliament, as well as to the Council and the Commission. This report is debated by the Parliament. In addition, the Parliament may request that the President of the

---

[18] In order to ensure a smooth rotation, the first members received mandates of staggered length, from four to eight years. Subsequent appointments are always for eight years.

| | Fed | ESCB | Bank of Japan | Bank of England | Bank of Canada | Swedish Riksbank |
|---|---|---|---|---|---|---|
| Interest-rate decision immediately announced | Yes (after 1994) | Yes | Yes | Yes | Yes | Yes |
| Supporting statement giving some rationale for a change | Yes | Yes | Yes | Sometimes | Yes | Yes |
| Release of minutes | 5–8 weeks[a] | No | 1 month | 13 days | NA | 2–4 weeks |
| Official minutes provide full details of | | | | | | |
| ■ internal debate | Yes | No | Yes | Yes | NA | No |
| ■ individuals' views | No | No | No | No | NA | No |
| Verbatim records of MP meetings are kept | Yes | No | Yes | No | No | No |
| Verbatim records released to the public after: | 5 years | NA | 10 years | NA | NA | NA |

NOTE: [a] The minutes are released after the following FOMC meeting.

SOURCE: Blinder et al. (2001).

TABLE 14-3: PROVISION OF INFORMATION ON MONETARY POLICY MEETINGS

ECB and the other members of the Executive Board testify to the Parliament's Economic and Monetary Affairs Committee. In practice, the President appears before the committee every quarter and the members of the Executive Board also do so quite often. In addition, the President of the EU Council and a member of the European Commission may participate in the meetings of the Governing Council without voting rights.

Transparency contributes powerfully to accountability. By revealing the contents of its deliberations, a central bank conveys to the public (the media, the financial markets, and independent observers) the rationale and difficulties of its decisions. The Eurosystem does not provide detailed reports of the meetings of its Governing Council. Instead the President of the ECB holds a press conference immediately after the monthly policy-setting meeting to present its decisions in highly standardized terms.

In this respect, the Eurosystem is probably less transparent than many other major central banks. Table 14-3 shows how major central banks reveal the work of their decision-making committee meetings. Several of them publish the committee meeting's minutes within a month, but since they can be heavily edited, minutes are not very informative. Very few (the US Federal Reserve and the Bank of Japan) publish extensive records of the discussion, but with very long delays, which makes the publication irrelevant except for historical purposes. Many central banks report on individual votes, which is a clear way of indicating how certain policy makers feel about their collective decisions. The Eurosystem is nearly alone in doing none of that. It considers that revealing individual votes could be interpreted in a nationalistic manner that does not, in fact, correspond to the thinking of members of the Governing Council.

## 14.5 The first years

In its maiden flight, the Eurosystem has faced a number of turbulences. In 2000, oil prices rose three-fold. An oil shock means both more inflation and less growth, a classic dilemma situation that all central banks fear. Then in 2001 stock markets fell world wide, the end of a long-lasting financial bubble fed by unrealistic expectations of the impact of the information technology revolution. Within months, the US economy went into recession, and Europe's economy also slowed down. Then, the terrorist attacks of 11 September 2001 shook the world economy. Finally, during the summer of 2002, stock markets crashed world wide. The result has been a very poor economic performance, extending surprisingly far into 2003.

The result has been an inflation rate above the then-stated objective of keeping inflation below 2 per cent. Energy costs fuelled by the oil shock, and import prices propelled upwards by the declining exchange rate, are the reasons for this resurgence of inflation in the Euro area. Figure 14-6 shows that, from early 2000 onwards, the Eurosystem has been in the embarrassing position of failing to deliver price stability as defined. This may explain why, as part of its strategy review, the Eurosystem announced in May 2003 that it now aims at an inflation of 'close to 2 per cent'.

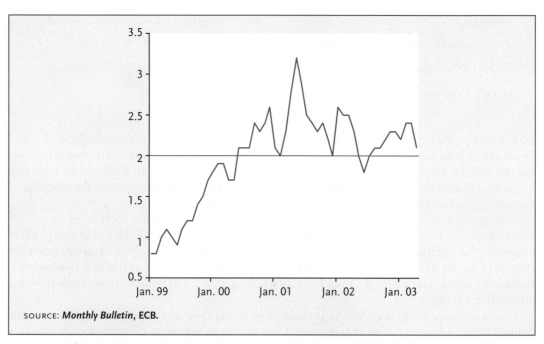

SOURCE: *Monthly Bulletin,* **ECB.**

FIGURE 14-6: INFLATION IN THE EURO AREA (JAN. 1999–APRIL 2003)

To further complicate the issue, in early 1999 the dollar started to rise *vis-à-vis* all major currencies, including the euro and, to a lesser extent, the pound sterling. Given that the US dollar has long been the word's standard, the general interpretation was that the euro was weak *vis-à-vis* the dollar and the pound. The Eurosystem, committed to its price stability objective was unwilling to act openly to prop up the euro, leaving the impression that it was unable to deliver the strong currency that had been predicated upon its rhetoric. Then, from late 2002 onwards, the dollar has started to fall. Instead of praising the Eurosystem for having finally delivered a strong currency, critics have started to complain that the strong euro is hurting European exporters and prolongs the cyclical slowdown. Yet, as Fig. 14-7 shows, the movements of the dollar/euro exchange rate have not been particularly out of step with the past. The Eurosystem has clearly announced that it

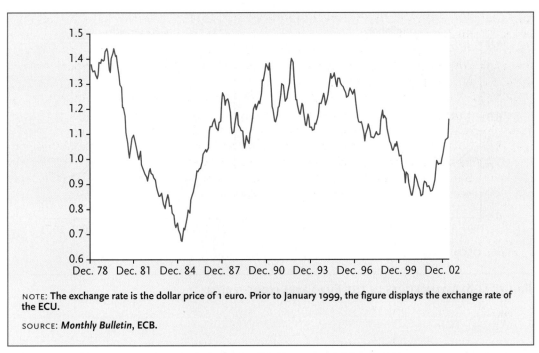

NOTE: **The exchange rate is the dollar price of 1 euro. Prior to January 1999, the figure displays the exchange rate of the ECU.**

SOURCE: *Monthly Bulletin*, ECB.

FIGURE 14-7: THE DOLLAR–EURO EXCHANGE RATE (JAN. 1979–MAY 2003)

takes no responsibility for the exchange rate,[19] but these movements have been weighing on perceptions at a time when the young institution is closely monitored, which probably makes its task more complicated.

It would be wrong to conclude that the ECB has failed in a major, meaningful way. Bad luck has brought a series of adverse shocks, but bad luck is something that policy makers must contend with. In fact, in the circumstances, the Eurosystem has responded well to the challenge. The problem lies elsewhere: by defining price stability in an excessively strict way, the Eurosystem has put itself in a straitjacket and taken the risk of not being able to deliver on its commitment. Yet, over all, the average inflation rate is about 2 per cent, which most people will recognize as suitably low.

How about the much feared asymmetric shocks emphasized by the OCA theory? Fig. 14-8 documents how different economic conditions have occurred throughout the Euro zone, before and after monetary union (the figure displays average inflation and real GDP growth rates across the member countries, along with the highest and lowest national rates each year). Inflation differences have dramatically narrowed down during the Maastricht-mandated convergence years. In the aftermath of the oil shock, there has been a tendency towards some divergence but it has remained subdued. Real growth, too, has tended to narrow down and has stayed that way. So far, at least, there is no evidence of any dramatic asymmetric shocks.

## 14.6 Summary

■ The EMU was decided upon in 1991 and started on target in 1999. Several years were considered to be needed for countries to prepare themselves and to meet five convergence criteria.

---

[19] Chapter 11 examines exchange rate regimes.

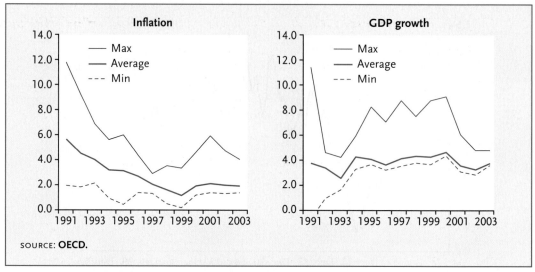

FIGURE 14-8: ASYMMETRIES IN THE EURO AREA (1991–2003)

- The convergence criteria were designed to ensure that inflation is low, and permanently so, and that public budgets are in surplus or that the deficits are small.
- An important innovation implicit in the convergence criteria and the opt-out clauses is 'two-speed Europe', the agreement that not all countries need to agree to further integrative steps.
- The EMU includes all EU member countries, but only those that have joined the Euro area have their national central banks included in the Eurosystem alongside the European Central Bank. The system's main body is the Governing Council, chaired by the president of the ECB.
- The Eurosystem has decided that price stability is achieved when the EMU-wide inflation rate is close to 2 per cent. It aims at achieving this objective 'in the medium term'.
- The Eurosystem sets the euro short-term interest rate through three channels: it sets a ceiling (the marginal refinancing facility), a floor (the deposit facility), and conducts regular auctions at the main refinancing rate to hit the middle.
- The Eurosystem's strategy relies on the price stability objective and on two pillars, economic analysis (the medium impact of current conditions on inflation) and monetary analysis (the longer-term impact of monetary aggregates on inflation).
- In the monetary union, there is one central bank and one monetary policy. The Eurosystem can only care about the whole Euro area, not about individual member countries. It takes no responsibility for the exchange rate that is freely floating.
- The Eurosystem constitutionally enjoys considerable independence, both in defining its objectives and in deciding how to conduct monetary policy.
- The ECB is only accountable to the European Parliament to which it presents an annual report, with additional hearings of the Chairman and members of the Executive Board.
- The first years of the euro have been marked by several shocks, complicating the Eurosystem's task. Fortunately, these shocks have been symmetric.

## SELF-ASSESSMENT QUESTIONS

**1.** What are the five convergence criteria and what is the logic behind each of them?
**2.** 'With one money there can only exist one central bank, and therefore one monetary policy.' What, then, is the role of national central banks in the EMU?

**3.** Why can inflation rates differ across the EMU member countries? What are the consequences?

**4.** Find data and assess how the countries of Central and Eastern Europe perform regarding the five convergence criteria.

**5.** What is the difference between objective and instrument independence?

**6.** What is the process of liquidity dissemination in the Euro area? How do we know that every bank that needs liquidity will get it?

**7.** The Eurosystem sets the money supply in the Euro area, but what drives the money stock in each country? How does this relate to Hume's mechanism and the Gold Standard (Chapter 10)?

**8.** What is the Eurosystem's definition of price stability? What would be your definition?

**9.** Why can't the Eurosystem take responsibility for national inflation rates?

## Essay questions

**1.** The Eurosystem asserts that, in its deliberations, it never pays attention to local (i.e. national) economic conditions. The reason is that there is a single monetary policy and that 'one size fits all'. Discuss this approach and imagine alternative approaches.

**2.** It is sometimes asserted that independence and accountability are substitutes, i.e. that more independence requires less accountability and vice versa. Discuss this assertion.

**3.** In the USA, monetary policy decisions are made by the Federal Open Market Committee which comprises the seven members of the Board – the equivalent of the ECB's Executive Board – the President of the Federal Reserve Bank of New York, who implements the committee's decisions, and by annually rotating four of the remaining 11 regional Reserve Bank Presidents. Can this be a model for the Eurosystem?

**4.** Find on http://www.ecb.int the latest press conference on monetary policy decision and interpret the text in the light of the stated strategy.

**5.** The Maastricht Treaty describes in minute detail the creation of the Euro area but is silent on a possible break-up. Imagine that a country is suffering from a severe adverse shock. Could it leave? How? What could the other countries do to try to keep it in?

**6.** Box 14-3 presents the solution proposed by the Eurosystem to face the enlargement of the Euro area after 2004. Evaluate this proposal and make your own suggestions.

**7.** Why are transparency and accountability so important for the Eurosystem? What kind of difficulties can you envision if the system is perceived as not sufficiently accountable? Not sufficiently transparent?

**8.** The convergence criteria are about nominal conditions (inflation, deficits and debts) but not about real conditions (GDP per capita, growth). This was understandable for the original founders but what does it mean for the upcoming wave of accession by countries from Central and Eastern Europe? Should the same criteria apply? Why or why not? Is the lack of real convergence problematic?

**9.** The British Chancellor of the Exchequer has stated that Britain will join when five economic tests are passed. These five tests are:

■ Are business cycles and economic structures compatible so that we and others could live comfortably with euro interest rates on a permanent basis?

■ If problems emerge is there sufficient flexibility to deal with them?

■ Would joining the EMU create better conditions for firms making long-term decisions to invest in Britain?

■ What impact would entry into the EMU have on the competitive position of the UK's financial services industry, particularly the City's wholesale markets?

■ In summary, will joining the EMU promote higher growth, stability and a lasting increase in jobs?

Evaluate these tests.

## FURTHER READING: THE AFICIONADOS CORNER

The Eurosystem's initial definition of its strategy can be found in Chapters 3 and 4 of European Central Bank *The Monetary Policy of the ECB*, Frankfurt, 2001. The strategy review appears in the June 2003 issue of the ECB's *Monthly Bulletin*.

Presentations of the Eurosystem:
Mottiar, R. (1999) 'Monetary policy in the Euro area: the role of national central banks' *Central Bank of Ireland Quarterly Bulletin*, Winter.
Padoa-Schioppa, T. (a member of the Executive Board of the ECB) *An Institutional Glossary of the Eurosystem*. http://www.ecb.int/key/00/sp000308_1.htm

A debate among central bankers on accountability and transparency:
Buiter, W. (1999) *Alice in Euroland*, CEPR Policy Paper 1, Centre for Economic Policy Research, London.
Issing, O. (1999) *The Eurosystem: Transparent and Accountable or Willem in Euroland*, CEPR Policy Paper 2, Centre for Economic Policy Research, London.

On central bank independence:
Berger, H., J. de Haan and S. Eijffinger (2001) 'Central Bank Independence: an update of theory and evidence', *Journal of Economic Surveys*, **15** (1), 3–40.

## USEFUL WEBSITES

The ECB website:
http://www.ecb.int

The Treaty of Maastricht:
http://europa.eu.int/eur-lex/en/treaties/index.html

Professor Giancarlo Corsetti's euro home page is the No.1 website on the Euro area:
http://www.econ.yale.edu/~corsetti/euro

The President of the ECB reports every quarter to the Committee of Economic and Monetary Affairs of the European Parliament. The transcripts of the meetings, gentlemanly called 'Monetary Dialogue', as well as background reports can be found at:
http://www.europarl.eu.int/comparl/econ/emu/default_en.htm

Public opinion on the euro:
http://europa.eu.int/comm/dg10/epo/euro_en.html

A website dedicated to EONIA and interest rates in the euro area:
http://www.euribor.org/default.htm

Annual reports on the ECB by academic observers: *Monitoring the European Central Bank*, published by the Centre for Economic Policy Research:
http://www.cepr.org

## REFERENCES

Blinder, A., C. Goodhart, P. Hildebrand, D. Lipton and C. Wyplosz (2001) 'How do central banks talk?', *Geneva Reports on the World Economy* **3**, Centre for Economic Policy Research, London.
Gros, D. and K. Lannoo (1999) *The Euro Capital Market*, John Wiley & Sons, Chichester.
Begg, D., F. Canova, P. de Grauwe, A. Fatás and P. Lane (2002) 'Surviving the slowdown', *Monitoring the European Central Bank*, **4**, Centre for Economic Policy Research, London.

# PART VI Beyond Money: Budgets, Financial Markets, Jobs

Building a monetary union is not just about launching a new currency and establishing a common central bank. The Euro area is a considerably more cohesive and complex structure than the community of countries that have joined. New opportunities and new challenges emerge. Chapter 15 looks at fiscal policies, the last remaining national macroeconomic stabilization tool. Can individual countries keep running their fiscal policies as before? The chapter looks at the principles that guide the answer to this question and at the solution that has been adopted, the Stability and Growth Pact. Chapter 16 next focuses on European financial markets. One expected benefit from adopting the single currency is to deepen financial integration. It appears that some markets have integrated almost immediately, while others remain national. The chapter asks why, and also asks what this contrasting landscape implies for the working of the union, particularly its monetary policy and its exchange rate. The last chapter looks at economic integration and the labour markets. Many European countries suffer from high unemployment, so it is natural to ask whether the euro will have a beneficial impact, or whether this chequered situation can make things more difficult.

❝ Economic prosperity and the viability of the monetary union cannot be sustained ❞
without tackling past fiscal policy failures, i.e. a trend towards increasing government
expenditure and taxation levels combined with high structural budget deficits and
government debt accumulation.

**European Commission (2001)**

❝ The Stability and Growth Pact is increasingly held responsible for the inability of the ❞
Euro area economy to sustain demand and maintain growth.

**Olivier Blanchard and Francesco Giavazzi (2002)**

# 15 Fiscal Policy and the Stability Pact

The monetary union implies the loss of monetary policy as a macroeconomic stabilization instrument, which seems to enhance the role of fiscal policy. However, national fiscal policies affect other countries. Do these spillover effects also call for sharing the fiscal policy instrument? This chapter first reviews how fiscal policy operates across national boundaries and presents the principles that can help to decide whether some limits in national decisions are in order. This lays the ground for an understanding of the Stability and Growth Pact. The chapter next examines the pact's impact on policy choices and the controversies that have arisen in the early years of its implementation.

# 15.1 Fiscal policy in the monetary union

### 15.1.1 An ever more important instrument?

When joining a monetary union a country gives up one of its two macroeconomic instruments – monetary policy – but retains full control of the other – fiscal policy. Does this mean that fiscal policy has to do double work? In the simple Keynesian $IS-LM$ world, monetary and fiscal policy are nearly substitute tools to stabilize output and employment fluctuations. It means that, in the Euro area, fiscal policy becomes even more important. In the event of asymmetric shocks – identified by the optimum currency area theory in Chapter 13 as the main source of costs in a monetary union – fiscal policy is the only available macroeconomic instrument. This is a good departure point to keep in mind but, in practice, some important differences imply that the two instruments are not as easily substitutable as suggested by the $IS-LM$ analysis. In particular, fiscal policy is more difficult to activate and less reliable than monetary policy.

A common problem with both instruments is that they affect spending largely through expectations. For monetary policy, as explained in Chapter 14, the central bank can only control very short-term interest rates while private spending is financed through long-term borrowing. For fiscal policy, changes in spending and/or taxes impact on the budget balance, which immediately raises the question of the financing of the public debt. Consider, for instance, a cut in income taxes that creates a budget deficit. The government will have to borrow and increase the public debt, but how will this new debt be reimbursed? If, as is plausible, taxes are eventually raised, the policy action is properly seen as the combination of a tax reduction today and a tax increase later. This is an action unlikely to wildly boost consumption.[1]

Fiscal policy faces a major additional drawback: it is very slow to implement. A central bank can decide to change the interest rate whenever it deems necessary, and can do so in a matter of seconds. Not so for fiscal policy. Establishing the budget is a long and complicated process. The government must first agree on the budget, with lots of heavy-handed negotiations among ministers. The budget must then be approved by the Parliament, a time-consuming and highly political process. Then spending decisions must be enacted through the bureaucracy, and taxes can only be changed gradually as they are never retroactive. For example, income taxes can only affect future incomes, implying long delays. On the other hand, once implemented, fiscal policy actions tend to have a more rapid affect on the economy (6 to 12 months) than monetary policy (12 to 24 months).

As a result, fiscal policy is like a tanker, it changes course very slowly. The delay may even be such that, when fiscal policy finally affects the economy, the problem that it was meant to solve has disappeared. In principle, macroeconomic policies are meant to be counter-cyclical, i.e. to slow down a booming economy or speed up a sagging economy. Fiscal policy has occasionally been found to be pro-cyclical: an expansionary action designed to deal with a recession hits the economy when it has already recovered. If this is the case, it actually speeds up the economy when it is already desirable to slow it down.

### 15.1.2 Borrowing instead of transfers

Another way of looking at fiscal policy is that the government borrows and pays back on behalf of its citizens. During a slowdown, the government opens up a budget deficit that is financed through public borrowing. In an upswing, the government runs a budget surplus which allows it to pay back its debt. In the end, a government that borrows to reduce taxes now and raises taxes

---

[1] The extreme case where consumers save all of the tax reduction to pay for future tax increases is called Ricardian equivalence. It is explained, and its empirical validity assessed, in, for example, Burda and Wyplosz (2001), Chapter 6.

later to pay back its debt is, in effect, lending to its citizens now and making them pay back later. Individual citizens and firms could, in principle, do it on their own, borrowing in bad years and paying back in good years. This would have the same stabilizing effect as fiscal policy. Is fiscal policy a futile exercise or, worse, a bad political trick? Not quite.

To start with, it is true that, in the previous example, the government simply acts as a bank *vis-à-vis* its citizens. The reason why it may make sense is that, when the economy slows down, lending becomes generally riskier and banks become very cautious. Many citizens and firms cannot borrow in bad times, or can only borrow at high cost. Indeed, workers who lose their jobs are considered by their banks as bad risk, and so are firms that face sagging profits or even losses. When governments are considered a good risk, which is generally the case in Europe, they can borrow at all times at reasonably low cost. This is why counter-cyclical fiscal policy can be effective.

An additional reason is related to one of the optimum currency area criteria examined in Chapter 12, the desirability of substantial inter-country transfers. In that dimension, Europe was found to do very poorly. Can this problem be alleviated? Fiscal policy is part of the answer. When a country faces an adverse asymmetric shock, its government can borrow from countries that are not affected by the shock. This is the equivalent of a transfer: instead of receiving a loan or a grant[2] from other EMU governments or from 'Brussels', the adversely affected country's government borrows on international private markets. In this way fiscal policy makes up for the absence of 'federal' transfers in a monetary union. The transfers are inter-temporal instead of being inter-regional.

### 15.1.3 Automatic stabilizers and discretionary policy actions

#### AUTOMATIC STABILIZERS

Fiscal policy has one important advantage: it tends to be spontaneously counter-cyclical. When the economy slows down, individual incomes are disappointingly low, corporate profits decline and spending is rather anaemic. This all means that tax collection declines: income taxes, profit taxes, VAT, etc., are less than they would be in normal conditions. At the same time, spending on unemployment benefits and other subsidies rises. All in all, the budget worsens and fiscal policy is automatically expansionary. These various effects are called the automatic stabilizers of fiscal policy. Table 15-1, which displays estimates of the size of the stabilizers, shows that, on average, a 1 per cent decline in growth leads a deterioration of the budget balance of about 0.5 per cent of GDP. There are some differences from one country to another, which reflect the structure of taxation and of welfare payments.[3]

| Sensitivity of government budget balances to a 1 per cent decline in economic growth | | | | | | | |
|---------|------|---------|------|-------------|------|----------|------|
| Germany | −0.5 | Austria | −0.5 | Greece      | −0.6 | Portugal | −0.4 |
| France  | −0.5 | Belgium | −0.5 | Ireland     | −0.4 | Spain    | −0.5 |
| Italy   | −0.4 | Denmark | −0.7 | Netherlands | −0.6 | Sweden   | −0.5 |
| UK      | −0.6 | Finland | −0.5 |             |      |          |      |

SOURCE: OECD (1997).

TABLE 15-1: AUTOMATIC STABILIZERS

[2] A grant is not to be reimbursed but a collective system of grants implies that any country is supposed to be alternatively giving and receiving, the total averaging zero over the long run. This is no different from long-term borrowing, receiving now, paying back later.
[3] For example, the more progressive are income taxes, the more tax collection declines during a slowdown, hence a more stabilization effect. Similarly, the automatic stabilizers are stronger the larger the unemployment benefits.

The Economics of European Integration: **Part VI**

## DISCRETIONARY FISCAL POLICY

The automatic stabilizers just happen. Discretionary fiscal policy, on the contrary, requires explicit decisions to change taxes or spending. As noted above, such decisions are slow to be made and implemented. This is why, in some countries, the budget law sets aside some funds that can be quickly mobilized by the government if discretionary action is needed. Even then, the amounts are small and their use is often politically controversial.

Figure 15-1 illustrates this point in the case of the Netherlands. The output gap is a measure of the country's cyclical position, the percentage difference between actual and potential GDP; a negative gap indicates that the economy is underperforming, it operates below its potential. The cyclically adjusted budget balance is an estimate of what the balance would be in a given year if the output gap were zero. The actual budget balance is lower than the cyclically adjusted budget balance when output is below potential – i.e. when the output gap is negative – and conversely when the output gap is positive. The figure confirms that this is indeed the case. The difference between the actual and the cyclically adjusted budget balance is the footprint of the automatic stabilizers.

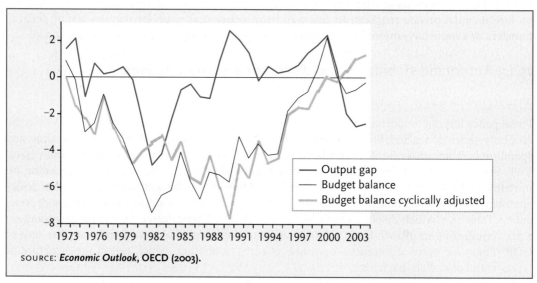

SOURCE: *Economic Outlook*, OECD (2003).

FIGURE 15-1: ACTUAL AND CYCLICALLY ADJUSTED BUDGETS IN THE NETHERLANDS (1973–2004)

On the other hand, if the government would never change its fiscal policy, the cyclically adjusted budget balance would remain constant, at least to a first approximation.[4] Thus, changes in the cyclically adjusted budget balance represent discretionary policy actions. In some years the cyclically adjusted budget balance declines when the output gap worsens, a sign of successful counter-cyclical action, but in other years the cyclically adjusted budget balance improves when the gap declines, a sign of pro-cyclical action.[5] These two questions – the role of the automatic stabilizers and the distinction between the actual and cyclically adjusted budgets – play a crucial role in what follows.

[4] Why to first approximation? Because as the economy grows, more people climb the income ladder and face higher tax rates. Also the structure of the economy changes, possible changing the way taxes are collected.
[5] Note also the continuous improvement of both budget measures over 1993–2002. The Dutch authorities clearly worked hard at meeting first the Maastricht fiscal conditions, and then the Stability Pact requirement.

## 15.2 Fiscal policy externalities

### 15.2.1 Spillovers and co-ordination

So far, the discussion has concerned individual countries, but fiscal policy actions by one country may spill over to other countries through a variety of channels: income and spending, inflation, borrowing costs. Such spillovers, called externalities, mean that one country's fiscal policy actions can help or hurt other countries. In such a situation, when one country decides what to do, it cannot ignore the effect on its partners and, conversely, it also has to take into account policy decisions taken elsewhere. This implies that countries subject to each other's spillovers stand to benefit from co-ordinating their fiscal policies. In principle, all concerned countries could agree on each other's fiscal policy to achieve a situation that befits them all. This is what policy co-ordination is about.

While, formally, fiscal policy remains a national prerogative, it is natural to ask whether the deepening economic integration among EMU countries calls for some degree of co-ordination. On the one hand, the setting up of a monetary union strengthens the case for fiscal policy co-ordination as it promotes economic integration. On the other hand, fiscal policy co-ordination requires binding agreements on who does what and when. Such detailed arrangements would limit each country's sovereignty, precisely at a time when the fiscal policy instrument assumes greater importance. The question is whether sharing the same currency increases the spillovers to the point where some new limits on sovereignty are desirable and justified. To answer this question, we review the channels through which spillovers occur and examine what difference the EMU makes.

### 15.2.2 Cyclical income spillovers

Business cycles are transmitted through exports and imports. When Germany enters an expansion phase, for instance, it imports more from its partner countries. For these partner countries, the German expansion means more exports and more incomes, and the expansion tends to be transmitted across borders. Figure 15-2, which displays output gaps in Germany and its three smaller neighbours, confirms that business cycles are highly synchronized. Quite obviously, the spillover is stronger the more the countries trade with each other, and the larger the country taking action. This is one reason why Germany's fiscal policy is carefully watched everywhere else in Europe.

What does this mean for fiscal policy? Consider, first, the case when two monetary union member countries undergo synchronized cycles, for example both suffer from a recession. Each government will want to adopt an expansionary fiscal policy, but to what extent? If each government ignores the other's action, their combined action may be too strong as each economy pulls the other one from the recession – an effect of the Keynesian multiplier. If, instead, each government relies on the other to do most of the work, too little might be done. Consider next the case when the cycles are asynchronized. An expansionary fiscal policy in the country undergoing a slowdown stands to boost spending in the already booming country. Conversely, a contractionary fiscal policy move in the booming country stands to deepen the recession in the other country. The risk, in this case, is too much policy action.

### 15.2.3 Borrowing cost spillovers

A fiscal expansion increases public borrowing or reduces public saving. As the government is usually the country's biggest borrower, large budget deficits may push interest rates up. Once they share the same currency, EMU member countries share the same interest rate. One country's deficits, especially if the country is large and its deficits sizeable, may impose higher interest rates

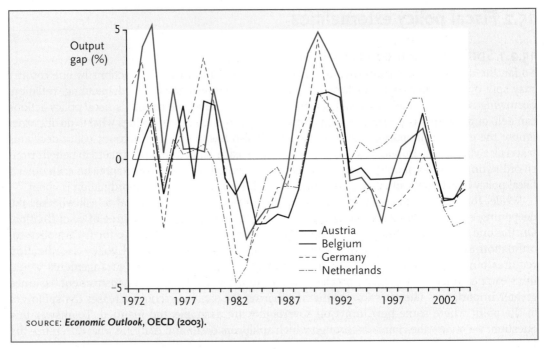

SOURCE: *Economic Outlook*, OECD (2003).

FIGURE 15-2: INCOME SPILLOVERS (1972–2004)

throughout the Euro area.[6] As high interest rates deter investment, they affect long-term growth. This is another spillover channel.

As stated, the argument is weak, however. Europe is fully integrated in the world's financial markets so any one country's borrowing is unlikely to make much of an impression on world and European interest rates. On the other hand, heavy borrowing may elicit capital inflows. This could result in an appreciation of the euro, which would hurt the area's competitiveness and cut into growth. Borrowing costs thus represent another channel for spillovers.

### 15.2.4 Excessive deficits and the no-bailout clause

The question of debt sustainability cannot be taken lightly in Europe in view of the near-tripling of public debts as a share of GDP since 1975, as Fig. 15-3 shows.[7] In the distant past, public debts have occasionally risen but only in difficult situations, and mostly during wars. The recent generalized debt build-up is partly related to the oil shocks of the 1970s and 1980s, but this is not the only reason. The figure illustrates what is sometimes called the 'deficit bias', a disquieting tendency for governments to run budget deficits for no other reason than political expediency. Does it call for a specific collective measure?

In principle, it is in each country's interest to resist the deficit bias, so fiscal discipline does not call for any collective measure unless spillovers can be identified. What happens when a public debt becomes unsustainable? As noted in Chapter 14, financially hard-pressed governments may

---

[6] Jürgen Stark, a high-level German official who was influential in designing the Stability and Growth Pact, writes: 'The state's absorption of resources which would otherwise have found their way into private investments results in higher long-term interest rates.' ('Genesis of a Pact', in A Brunila, M. Buti and D. Franco (eds) *The Stability and Growth Pact*, Palgrave, Basingstoke, 2001, p. 79.

[7] This is the debt for the whole zone, but the situation differs from country to country. Two countries, Belgium and Italy, have a debt in excess of 100 per cent of GDP. These debts are seen as the weak elements of the chain.

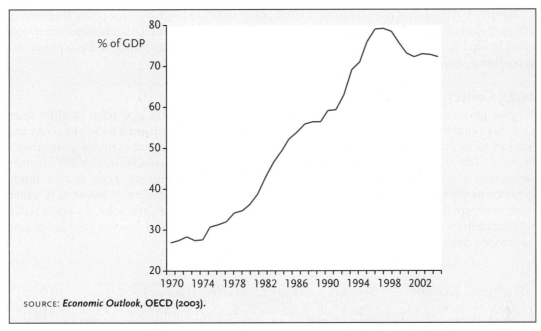

SOURCE: *Economic Outlook*, **OECD (2003).**

FIGURE 15-3: PUBLIC DEBT OF THE EUROAREA (1970–2003)

be tempted to call upon the central bank to finance their deficits, the traditional route to inflation. Should the Eurosystem oblige, inflation would rise throughout the Euro area. This spillover door is explicitly closed by the Maastricht Treaty, which forbids the Eurosystem (the ECB and the NCBs) from providing direct support to governments.

Heavy public borrowing by one country is a sign of fiscal indiscipline that could trouble the international financial markets. If markets believe that one country's public debt is unsustainable, they could view the whole Euro area with suspicion. The result would be sizeable capital outflows and euro weakness. This is a potential source of spillover.

There is another potential spillover. If a government accumulates such a debt that it can no longer service it, it must default. The experience with such defaults is that the immediate reaction is a massive capital outflow, a collapse of the exchange rate and of the stock markets, and a prolonged crisis complete with a deep recession and skyrocketing unemployment. Too bad for the delinquent country, but being part of a monetary union changes things radically. It is now the common exchange rate that is the object of the market reaction. The spillover can further extend to stock markets throughout the whole monetary union.

The further fear is that the mere threat of one member country's default would so concern all other member governments that they would feel obliged to bail out the nearly-bankrupt government. In fact, this risk has been clearly identified in the Maastricht Treaty which includes a no-bailout clause. This clause clearly states that no official credit can be extended to a distressed member government.

In spite of the no-bailout clause, it remains that, in the midst of an emergency, some arrangement could still be found to bail out a bankrupt government. For example, the ECB could be 'informally' pressed to relax its monetary policy to make general credit more abundant at a lower cost, which would result in inflation. More generally, it is feared that a sovereign default would badly affect the Euro area and undermine its credibility with seriously adverse effects on the euro.

These spillovers do not rely on standard fiscal policy income effects but on the risk of excessive, and potentially unsustainable, deficits. It points to a catastrophic event. Defaults, however, do not occur in blue skies – it takes years to accumulate large debts. The implication is that a preventive procedure is required to avoid the need to deal with an emergency.

## 15.2.5 Collective discipline

Why do governments seem to have a deficit bias, and why does this bias seem to differ from country to country, as can be seen in Table 15-2? Deficits allow governments to deliver goods and services today without facing the costs, passing the burden of debt service to future governments or even to future generations. It is tempting to do so, especially when elections near, but adequate democratic accountability should prevent governments from indulging. Even though future generations are not here to weigh in, the current generation may reasonably expect to be called upon to service the debt, and anyway most people care about the next generation. So a debt build-up often reflects a failure of democratic control over governments. Why has this been happening in Europe's democracies?

| Austria | Belgium | Denmark | Finland | France | Germany | Greece | Ireland |
|---------|---------|---------|---------|--------|---------|--------|---------|
| 59.9 | 101.8 | 44.2 | 42.0 | 65.4 | 62.5 | 97.6 | 27.4 |
| Italy | Luxembourg | Netherlands | Portugal | Spain | Sweden | UK | Euro area |
| 105.2 | 3.7 | 50.9 | 51.7 | 69.8 | 52.5 | 50.9 | 71.4 |

SOURCE: *Economic Outlook*, OECD

TABLE 15-2: PUBLIC DEBTS IN EUROPE IN 2002 (PER CENT OF GDP)

Public spending often favours narrow interest groups (civil servants, the military, public road contractors, etc.), while the debt service is diffused and borne by an unstructured majority, and interest groups are well organized and influential with the government. The time of reckoning should come when elections are held, but the electoral process is not always effective at imposing budgetary discipline. Indeed, some political regimes – typically parliamentary regimes which involve large coalitions – seem to be doing less well in keeping deficits and debts in check.

Changing the democratic regime (the form of democracy, how elections are organized) could help, but it is a rather intractable endeavour. This is why some governments find it appealing to seek external restraint and to invoke 'Brussels' as a scapegoat that can be blamed when resisting interest groups and political friends. Collective discipline, even if not necessarily justified by spillovers, can be used as a substitute for adequate domestic institutions.

## 15.3 Principles

The existence of spillovers is one argument for sharing policy responsibilities among independent countries. It is not the only argument, however; and there are powerful counter-arguments. The broader question is: at which level of government – regional, national, supranational – should policies be conducted? The theory of fiscal federalism deals with this question. The principle of subsidiarity is another, different way of approaching the issue. Both approaches have been presented earlier (Chapter 3) and are briefly recalled in this section.

## 15.3.1 The theory of fiscal federalism

The theory of fiscal federalism asks how, in one country, fiscal responsibilities should be assigned between the various levels (national, regional, municipal) governments. It can be transposed to Europe's case, even though Europe is not a federation, by asking which tasks should remain in national – possibly regional in federal states – hands and which ones should be a shared responsibility, i.e. delegated to 'Brussels'. There are two good reasons to transfer responsibility to 'Brussels' and two good reasons to keep it at the national level. An additional concern is the quality of government at the national and supranational level.

### TWO ARGUMENTS FOR SHARING RESPONSIBILITIES: EXTERNALITIES AND INCREASING RETURNS TO SCALE

As noted before, spillovers, also called externalities – when one country's actions affect other countries – lead to inefficient outcomes when each country is free to act as it wishes. Sometimes too much action is taken, sometimes not enough. This is the case of tariffs (see Chapter 4) and fiscal policy. The other argument is that some policies are more efficient when carried out on a large scale. Increasing returns to scale can be found in the use of money,[8] in the design of commercial law or in defence (army, weapons development and production), among others.

One solution is co-ordination, which preserves sovereignty but calls for repeated and often piecemeal negotiations, with no guarantee of success. Another solution is to give up sovereignty, partly or completely, and delegate a task to a supranational institution. In Europe, some important tasks have already been delegated to the European Commission (the internal market and trade negotiations) and to the Eurosystem (monetary policy).

### TWO ARGUMENTS FOR RETAINING SOVEREIGNTY: HETEROGENEITY OF PREFERENCES AND INFORMATION ASYMMETRIES

Consider the example of common law concerning family life (marriages and divorces, raising children, dealing with ageing parents, etc.). Practices and traditions differ across countries, sometimes to a considerable extent. In this domain, preferences are heterogeneous and a supranational arrangement is bound to create much dissatisfaction.

Now consider the decisions of where to build roads, how large to make them, where to set up traffic lights, etc. These require a good understanding of how people move, or wish to move, in a geographical area: it is a case of information asymmetry, since it is likely that the information is more readily available at the local level than at a more global level.

Heterogeneity of preferences and information asymmetries imply that it would be inefficient to share competence at a supranational level. Much of the criticism levelled at 'Brussels' concerns cases where either heterogeneity or information asymmetries are important: deciding on the appropriate size of cheese or the way to brew beer are best left to national governments, or even local authorities, no matter how important the externalities or increasing returns to scale.

### THE QUALITY OF GOVERNMENT

An implicit assumption so far is that governments always act in the best interest of their citizens. While this may generally be the case, there are numerous instances when governments either pursue their own agendas or are captured by interest groups. Indeed, like any institution, governments often wish to extend their domain of action, possibly in order to increase their own power or because they genuinely believe that they can deal with important problems. In addition, there is

---

[8] Chapter 13 argues that this is a key benefit from a large currency area.

no such thing as 'the best interest of citizens': some citizens favour some actions, others do not. Governments exist in part to deal with such conflicts and do so under democratic control but, as noted in section 15.2.5, elections cannot sanction every one of the millions of decisions that favour well-connected interests. In spite of all the good things that can be said about democracy, it is not a perfect system, and it often fails.[9]

Once this fact of life is recognized, the principles from the theory of fiscal federalism need to be amended. There is no general rule here, only the need to always keep in mind that a good solution may turn out to be bad if the government is misbehaving. In particular, the quality of government and of democratic control ought to be brought into the picture. The question here is whether 'Brussels' performs better than the national governments.

### 15.3.2 The principle of subsidiarity[10]

It should be clear by now that in most cases the four arguments for and against centralization at the Union level are unlikely to lead to clear-cut conclusions, and the warning about the quality of government further complicates the issue. In each case, one has to weigh the various arguments and trade off the pros and cons. This is often mission impossible, hence another question: where should the burden of proof lie?

The European Union has taken the view that the burden of proof lies with those who argue in favour of sharing sovereign tasks. This is the principle of subsidiarity and it is enshrined in the European Treaty:

> In areas which do not fall within its exclusive competence, the Community shall take action, in accordance with the principle of subsidiarity, only if and insofar as the objectives of the proposed action cannot be sufficiently achieved by the Member States and can therefore, by reason of the scale or effects of the proposed action, be better achieved by the Community.
>
> (Article 5)

### 15.3.3 Implications for fiscal policy

A KEY DISTINCTION: MICRO VS MACROECONOMIC ASPECTS OF FISCAL POLICY
It is crucial to separate two aspects of fiscal policy. The first aspect is structural; that is, mainly microeconomic. It concerns the size of the budget, what public money is spent on, how are taxes raised, i.e. who pays what, and redistribution designed to reduce inequalities or to provide incentives to particular individuals or groups. The second aspect is macroeconomic. This is the income stabilization role of fiscal policy, the idea that it can be used as a counter-cyclical instrument.

Here, we focus on the macroeconomic stabilization component of fiscal policy, ignoring the structural aspects. To simplify, we look at the budget balance and ignore the size and structure of the budget and the resulting evolution of the public debt. We apply the principles of fiscal federalism to ask whether there is a case for limiting the free exercise of sovereignty on national budget balances and debts.

THE CASE FOR COLLECTIVE RESTRAINT
Section 15.2 identified a number of spillovers: income flows, borrowing costs and the risk of difficulties in financing runaway deficits, possibly leading to debt default. Some of these spillovers can have serious effects across the Euro area. In addition, some countries have not established

---

[9] Churchill is rumoured to have said: 'Democracy is the worst possible system, except for all others.'
[10] Subsidiarity is presented in Chapter 3.

political institutions that are conducive to fiscal discipline so it may be in their own best interest to use 'Brussels' as an external agent of restraint. On the other hand, it is difficult to detect a scale economy.

These externalities call for some limits on national fiscal policies, and such limits can take various forms, ranging from co-ordination and peer pressure to mandatory limits on deficits and debts.

## THE CASE AGAINST COLLECTIVE RESTRAINT

Working in the opposite direction are important heterogeneities and information asymmetries. Macroeconomic heterogeneity occurs in the presence of asymmetric shocks. A common fiscal policy, on top of a common monetary policy, would leave each country without any counter-cyclical macroeconomic tool. Heterogeneity can also be the consequence of differences of opinions regarding the effectiveness of the instrument. Some countries (e.g. France and Italy) have long been active users of fiscal policy while others (e.g. Germany) have a tradition of scepticism towards Keynesian policies. Finally, national political processes are another source of heterogeneity. In some countries, the government has quite some leeway to adapt the budget to changing economic conditions while in others the process is cumbersome and politically difficult.

Information asymmetries chiefly concern the perception of the political implications of fiscal policies. Each government faces elections, and economics is often an important factor shaping voter preferences. Whether, and how to use fiscal policy at a particular juncture is part of a complex political game, which makes national politics highly idiosyncratic. While governments have a lot of understanding for each other's electoral plight, they have a hard time absorbing all the fine details of foreign national politics.

## OVERALL

It is therefore far from clear that the macroeconomic component of fiscal policy should be subject to external limits. Quite clearly, a single common fiscal policy is ruled out, but what about some degree of co-operation? The debate is ongoing and is unlikely to be settled in the near future. The subsidiarity principle implies that, as long as the case is not strong, fiscal policy should remain fully a national prerogative. On the other hand, the spillover that could result from *excessive* deficits is important, as it forms the logical basis for the Stability and Growth Pact.

## 15.3.4 Fiscal policy co-ordination

Traditional macroeconomic arguments also illuminate the issue of fiscal policy co-ordination. The open economy *IS–LM* apparatus – often referred to as the Mundell–Fleming model – leads to the important conclusions summarized in Table 11-3. When the exchange rate is fixed, the monetary policy instrument is lost because it must be dedicated to the exchange rate objective. To recover this instrument, the exchange rate must be allowed to float, but then the fiscal policy instrument becomes lost as its use is frustrated by movements in the exchange rate.

As a country joins the monetary union, it obviously gives up monetary policy, but retains the fiscal policy instrument. For the monetary union as a whole, in contrast, the fact that the euro is floating means that monetary policy is effective, hence the importance of the task attributed to the Eurosystem. On the other hand, the overall fiscal policy stance of the monetary union may matter for the euro's value, but it is likely to be an ineffective instrument. This analysis suggests that fiscal policy should continue to be exerted at the national level (where the exchange rate is irremediably fixed) while there is little to be gained by aiming at a high level of co-ordination, beyond the spillover aspects studied in section 15.2.

### 15.3.5 So, what does it means for fiscal policy?

Applying the principles of fiscal federalism to the macroeconomic fiscal policy instrument leaves us with few uncontroversial conclusions. There are valid reasons for jointly imposing discipline and for policy co-ordination. There are equally valid arguments in the opposite direction. All in all, the case for further transfers of sovereignty is weak. This conclusion is challenged by some who attach much importance to spillovers and think that macroeconomic co-ordination is both promising and relatively easy to implement. It is also challenged from the opposite end of the spectrum by those who see co-ordination as a collusion of self-interested governments. Sceptics tend to conclude that, given the weakness of the case, subsidiarity should be applied and leave fiscal policy entirely in national hands. The debate has been around for a decade and is not likely to disappear for some time.[11] It seems to have been partly settled by the adoption of the Stability and Growth Pact, but the pact itself is highly controversial. It is presented in the next section.

## 15.4 The Stability and Growth Pact

### 15.4.1 From convergence to the permanent regime

As explained in Chapter 14, admission to the monetary union requires a budget deficit of less than 3 per cent of GDP and a public debt of less than 60 per cent of GDP, or declining toward this benchmark. But what about afterwards, in the permanent monetary union regime? Could countries achieve the two fiscal criteria, join the monetary union and then freely relapse in unbridled indiscipline? This would be odd, and it would raise the fears detailed in section 15.2.4. The founding fathers of the Maastricht Treaty were keenly aware of this risk and indeed Article 104 unambiguously states that 'Member States shall avoid excessive government deficits' and goes on to outline a detailed 'excessive deficit procedure'. The Treaty left the practical details of the procedure to be settled later – and this is the task fulfilled by the Stability and Growth Pact.[12]

### 15.4.2 The pact

EXCESSIVE DEFICITS

The pact considers that deficits are excessive when they are above 3 per cent of GDP. In order to leave room for the automatic stabilizers to play their role, the pact also stipulates that participants in the monetary union commit themselves to a medium-term budgetary stance 'close to balance or in surplus'. The medium term is understood to represent about three years.

The pact recognizes that serious recessions, beyond any government control, can quickly lead to deepening deficits. Trying to close down deficits during a recession implies adopting a contractionary policy, which may deepen the recession with potentially disastrous consequences. Consequently, the pact defines exceptional circumstances when its provisions are automatically suspended. A deficit in excess of 3 per cent is considered as exceptional if the country's GDP declines by at least 2 per cent in the year in question. The pact also identifies an intermediate situation, when the real GDP declines by less than 2 per cent but by more than 0.75 per cent. In that case, if the country can demonstrate that its recession is exceptional in terms of its abruptness

[11] Some references are provided in the further reading section at the end of this chapter.
[12] The initiative was taken by Germany in 1995 and the pact decided in June 1997 by the European Council. Informed by its own inter-war history, Germany was always concerned that fiscal indiscipline could lead to inflation. This is why it insisted on a clear and automatic procedure. It wanted to make full use of the provisions of the Maastricht Treaty, which allowed for fines in the case of excessive deficits. The other countries were less enthusiastic but Germany was holding the key of the EMU. France, in particular, was unhappy with the German proposal. It obtained the symbolic addition of the word 'growth' to what Germany had initially called the Stability Pact.

or in relation to past output trends, the situation can also be deemed exceptional. When output declines by less than 0.75 per cent no exceptional circumstance can be claimed.

## WARNINGS AND CORRECTIVE ACTION

When a country is found exceeding the limit, the Commission issues a report which is submitted to the Council of Economic and Finance Ministers. The Council then decides whether the country is indeed in excessive deficit. If the Council finds against the country, it will issue recommendations and a deadline. The Council may decide, or not, to make its decision public.

Countries found exceeding the limit must take corrective action 'as quickly as possible after their emergence'. The timing of fiscal policy decisions and the rhythm at which the Commission, which monitors the process, prepares its reports imply that a country can run deficits in excess of 3 per cent of GDP for two successive years without incurring sanctions.

## SANCTIONS

If a country fails to take corrective action and to bring its deficit below 3 per cent by the deadline set by the Council, it is sanctioned. The sanction takes the form of a non-remunerated deposit. The deposit starts at 0.2 per cent of GDP and rises by 0.1 of the excess deficit up to a maximum of 0.5 per cent of GDP, as shown in Table 15-3. Deposits are imposed each year until the excessive deficit is corrected. If the excess is not corrected within two years, the deposit is converted into a fine, otherwise it is returned.

| Size of deficit (% of GDP) | Amount of fine (% of GDP) |
| --- | --- |
| 3% | 0.2% |
| 4% | 0.3% |
| 5% | 0.4% |
| 6% and above | 0.5% |

TABLE 15-3: SCHEDULE OF FINES

## 15.4.3 The stability programmes and the Broad Economic Policy Guidelines

Several aspects of the Stability and Growth Pact are noteworthy. First, formally, it does not remove fiscal policy sovereignty. Governments are in full control, they only agree to bear the consequences of their actions. Second, the intent is clearly pre-emptive since there is a lengthy procedure between the time a deficit is deemed excessive and the time when a deposit is imposed, with two more years before the deposit is transformed into a fine. Third, while a fine is politically a nuclear bombshell, the declaration that a country is in violation of the pact is a more conventional bombshell, meant to elicit prompt corrective action. Finally, all decisions are in the hands of the Council, a highly political body that can exploit many of the 'ifs' included in the pact. [13]

The best way to avoid reaching a point where sanctions are imposed is to reinforce precautionary measures. The treaty and the pact prescribe a detailed procedure called 'stability programmes'. This procedure, part of the wider peer-monitoring arrangement described in Box 15-1, calls for every country to submit its budgetary positions for the following three years to the Council and the

[13] For example, the pact stipulates that the Council 'is invited always to impose sanctions if a participating Member State fails to take the necessary steps to bring the excessive deficit situation to an end as recommended by the Council'. Notice the firmness of 'always' and the niceness of 'invited'.

Commission, annually. Here the objective is not just to keep deficits below 3 per cent but to aim and achieve a budget 'close to balance or in surplus', which would leave room for policy action in the case of a moderate slowdown.

The national budget plans are examined by the Commission and the Council. The intention is to determine whether fiscal policy is compatible with the Stability and Growth Pact and whether the actual policies conform to previous commitments. The Commission prepares an annual report and the Council draws the conclusions. It can issue a warning, which is made public at its discretion. A warning can be seen as a political hand grenade.

---

### Box 15-1: The Broad Economic Policy Guidelines

Over recent years, the European Council has concluded that enhanced co-operation is not just needed for fiscal policy but also for several other economic aspects such as labour market policies, research and development, goods market competition, financial markets, etc. In each case, we find the same tension between preserving sovereignty and dealing with spillovers or increasing returns to scale. The half-way solution is 'multilateral surveillance', for which the Stability and Growth Pact is a model. It takes the form of the adoption by the Council of Broad Economic Policy Guidelines (BEPG) against which each country's performance can be assessed. In fact, the pact's stability programmes are embedded in the Broad Economic Policy Guidelines. The procedure takes the form of annual reports by each government. These reports are examined by the Commission whose conclusions are then submitted to the ECOFIN Council. The Council approves country-specific assessments and may issue warnings (peer pressure), but fines can only be imposed for violations of the Stability and Growth Pact.

The BEPG – including the Stability and Growth Pact – concern all EMU members, whether they are members of the monetary union or not. However, sanctions can only be imposed on monetary union member countries.

---

## 15.4.4 The pact and counter-cyclical fiscal policies: how much room to manoeuvre?

Early experience with the Stability and Growth Pact has revealed some problems, as Box 15-2 recalls. These early difficulties raise the question of whether the pact leaves enough room for counter-cyclical fiscal policies. The answer requires consideration of the two aspects of fiscal policy mentioned in section 15.1.3: the automatic stabilizers and discretionary policy.

### The automatic stabilizers

The automatic response of budget balances to cyclical fluctuations is a source of difficulty. The pact's strategy is that budgets should be normally balanced to leave enough room for the automatic stabilizers. A simple example illustrates the idea. Table 15-1 above shows that, on average, a 1 per cent decline in GDP growth tends to worsen the budget deficit by 0.5 per cent of GDP. Using this estimate, the left panel of Fig. 15-4 shows how much, depending on the initial budget position, the GDP can decline before the automatic stabilizers bring the budget to a deficit of 3 per cent. Obviously, if the budget is already at the 3 per cent limit, there is no room left and the stabilizers must be prevented – fiscal policy becomes pro-cyclical – for any slowdown. If, instead, the budget is initially balanced, it would take a fall of 6 per cent of GDP to reach a deficit of 6 per cent. In

## Box 15-2: The first warnings

*Ireland*

Ireland is the first country to be formally 'warned' under the Stability and Growth Pact rule. This is an odd case. The official statement is even more surprising:

> In 2000, due to a strongly growing economy the surplus is estimated to have been 4.5 per cent of GDP, 1.2 percentage points higher than originally expected. The 2000 update of the stability programme for the period 2001–03 projects high surpluses of 4.2 per cent of GDP on average and a further decline in the debt ratio to less than one quarter of GDP by 2003. The public finances are sound. (...) However, in its meeting of 12 February the (ECOFIN) Council considered budgetary plans for 2001 inappropriately expansionary and thus inconsistent with the 2000 BEPGs, and issued a recommendation to Ireland to end this inconsistency.
>
> Council Recommendation, 15 June 2001

Explanation: in 2001, the budget ended up with a surplus of 1.7 per cent, against a commitment of 4.3 per cent made in December 2000. The year 2001 was an election year and the outgoing government relaxed its virtuous stance. As Ireland was booming in 2000–01 (while growth in most of Europe was sluggish), the Council concluded that an expansionary fiscal policy was not adequate. The Irish government and citizens were infuriated and saw the heavy hand of 'Brussels' invading their national sovereignty.

*France and Germany*

The years 2002–03 have not been good for most of the European countries. The economy significantly slowed down, not sufficiently to claim exceptional circumstances, but enough to drag down budget balances. The monetary union's two largest countries, France and Germany, have faced deficits in excess of 3 per cent. Part of the problem is that their budgets did not improve enough during the earlier better years, leaving these two countries with too little room to use fiscal policy as a counter-cyclical tool. In the case of Germany, even allowing the automatic stabilizers freedom to operate was too much, while France actually reduced taxes – an election pledge by President Chirac. Both were issued a warning for 2002, and recommendations for 2003. They stand to be fined if their 2004 budget deficits do not reduce to below 3 per cent.

*What to do with the pact?*

This has triggered a lively debate. The French Finance Minister announced that France had other priorities, implying that he would not implement counter-cyclical policy, while his German colleague energetically pledged spending cuts and yet could not improve the deficit, and may have worsened the 2003 recession. In July 2003, Chancellor Schroeder has announced that he would bring forward a tax cut set for the following year, arguing that this would revive the economy and improve the budget. No one believes that this will be the case, quite to the contrary, and yet the Commission has expressed some cautious support. Clearly, fining Germany is not on the agenda.

The wisdom of adopting restrictive fiscal policies in the midst of a cyclical slowdown is openly questioned, as is the use of sanctions. This has prompted the President of the Commission, Romano Prodi, to publicly brand the pact as 'stupid', and *The Economist* has followed by adopting the nickname of 'Stupidity Pact'. The search is on for some adjustments, but those countries that had brought their budgets into balance or in surplus in previous years, defend the integrity of the pact.

comparison, the GDP decline that has led France and Germany to breach the limit in 2003 was about 2 per cent.

## DISCRETIONARY POLICY

This, however, assumes that fiscal policy is not used in a discretionary way to cushion business cycles. Relying solely on the automatic stabilizers when the economic situation worsens may not be enough to stem a recession. This can prove to be politically unacceptable for real-life governments, especially if they face elections. What is needed, therefore, is for governments to gain themselves enough room for discretionary manoeuvre in case of a slowdown. The right panel of Fig. 15-4 shows how the budget can be changed (as a percentage of GDP) over and above the automatic stabilizers in case of a 2 per cent decline of GDP, depending again on the initial budget position. If the budget was initially in a deficit of 2 per cent, there is no room for discretionary fiscal policy, and the only possibility is to let the automatic stabilizers play fully. If the budget was initially balanced, the government can let the stabilizers operate and further increase the deficit by 2 per cent of GDP.

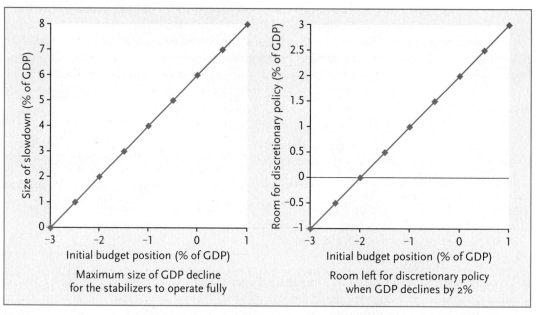

FIGURE 15-4: ROOM FOR MANOEUVRE IN THE STABILITY AND GROWTH PACT

## BRINGING BUDGETS TO THE SAFE ZONE

Thus the Stability and Growth Pact intentionally provides a strong incentive to bring the budget to a position of balance, or even surplus. When this is achieved, monetary union member countries should recover almost all the required room for manoeuvre, since only deep recessions will prevent the counter-cyclical use of fiscal policy, and deep recessions will qualify as exceptional. The main challenge, therefore, lies in the early years, when a number of countries still run deficits. They need to close those deficits but this is not always politically easy. This is precisely the difficulty faced by the pact in 2002–03.

### 15.4.5 Limits of the pact

The Stability and Growth Pact serves two main useful purposes: it counteracts the deficit bias and greatly reduces the odds of a debt default within the monetary union which, as noted in section 15.2.4, could result in highly painful spillover effects. Yet, it does not come without a number of weaknesses.

Imposing fiscal discipline from outside has the obvious advantage of protecting governments from interest groups. On the other hand, using 'Brussels' as a scapegoat may be good politics in the short term but, if invoked too often, can undermine general support for European integration. In particular, the imposition of fines could be met with popular rejection. But, without fines, the pact is unlikely to have enough teeth and could be overlooked when it is politically convenient, which effectively means that there is no pact.

The 3 per cent limit is artificial. In the face of economic and political difficulties, governments may find it hard to justify this particular number. Those who stand to suffer from the imposition of the pact may ask: Why 3 per cent and not 3.5 per cent?

The room for manoeuvre can be quickly eroded by a few consecutive adverse shocks. Leaving member countries without the fiscal policy instrument would accentuate the costs of belonging to the monetary union. As long as Europe remains less than an optimum currency area, this is not desirable – neither economically nor politically.

The pact is asymmetric in two ways. First, it is binding in bad times but not in good times when governments could build a safety margin by running surpluses. Second, it focuses on a lower limit but provides no incentive to limit surpluses or accept deficits when the need arises. The discussion of policy co-ordination in section 15.2.1 shows that it may be desirable that fiscal policy be expansionary over and above what each country would prefer to do in isolation.

Finally, the politicization of Council decisions in the first years raises the question of the quality of governments. Part of the appeal of the pact is to impose discipline onto governments that operate in a political environment that generates a deficit bias. On the other hand, any transfer of authority to the union level must factor in the quality of joint decision making at that level. In contrast to national governments, the union's institutions, including the Council and the Commission, are subject to very limited democratic control and therefore enjoy limited democratic legitimacy. Imposing fines is that much harder.

### 15.4.6 Possible reforms

These limits have not gone unnoticed and various proposals have been put forward. One solution is to set limits for the cyclically adjusted budget, not the actual budget. The Commission has made a proposal in this direction. This idea, while logical, raises other problems. If, as sometimes suggested, the pact would require that the cyclically adjusted budget be balanced every year, fiscal policy would be strictly confined to the automatic stabilizers, a tight straitjacket when asymmetric shocks occur, especially in the absence of national monetary policy. Furthermore, computing cyclically adjusted budgets is more art than science, and involves a great deal of arbitrariness. It would be very hard to impose sanctions on the basis of numbers that can always be objected to.

Another solution would be to target, the public debt, over the medium term – not the budget balance year after year. This would leave governments free to use fiscal policy as they see fit in the short term, while anchoring their actions to the need to pay back previous borrowing. This solution, however, is not devoid of difficulties. Promising to be virtuous in the future is easy, but it is not so easy to make it happen. In addition, what would happen if adverse asymmetric shocks occur when the medium term, however defined, is about to be reached? Any deadline stands to be seen as too arbitrary to warrant sanctions. Finally, as previously noted, official debt figures grossly underestimate actual public commitments, in particular, potentially huge retirement plans.

## 15.5 **Summary**

■ The loss of national monetary policy leaves fiscal policy as the only macroeconomic instrument. Budgets can be seen as a substitute for the absence of intra-EMU transfers.

■ Fiscal policy operates in two ways. The automatic stabilizers come into play without any policy action because deficits increase when the economy slows down, and decline or turn into surpluses when growth is rapid. Discretionary policy results from willing actions taken by the government.

■ One country's fiscal policy affects economic conditions in other EMU countries. The main spillover channels are: income flows via exports and imports; the cost of borrowing as there is a single interest rate; the impact of possible defaults on the common exchange rate; and the effect of fiscal indiscipline of the union's credibility.

■ The theory of fiscal federalism provides arguments for and against the sharing of policy instruments. The presence of spillovers and of increasing returns to scale argue for policy sharing. The existence of national differences in economic conditions and preferences, and of asymmetries of information, argue against policy sharing. Finally the quality of government matters.

■ The weight of the fiscal federalism arguments is that there is no ground for transfers of competence to the union level. The economic argument leads to the same conclusion. On the other hand, the worst case scenario of default supports the view that the monetary union requires some safeguards against fiscal indiscipline.

■ The Stability and Growth Pact reflects the view that excessive deficits are a matter of common concern in a monetary union. It aims at making permanent the fiscal convergence criteria. It is an application of the excessive deficit procedure envisioned in the Maastricht Treaty.

■ The pact defines what excessive deficits are. It calls for annual medium-term projections. It monitors the outcomes and calls for the Council to issue warnings. When the warnings are not heeded, sanctions can be applied, including fines.

■ The pact limits the counter-cyclical use of fiscal policy – including the full working of the automatic stabilizers – when the budget is not initially in the safe zone of balance or surplus. This provides an incentive to achieve such a position as soon as possible.

■ The early implementation of the Stability and Growth Pact has revealed many cracks. Combining budgetary discipline and fiscal policy flexibility is not easy, nor is it easy to find a good compromise between preserving sovereignty and dealing with potentially dangerous spillovers.

### SELF-ASSESSMENT QUESTIONS

1. What is the difference between actual and cyclically adjusted budgets? Why are discretionary actions only visible in changes of the cyclically adjusted budget balance?

2. In Fig. 15-1 identify years when fiscal policy is pro-cyclical, and years when it is counter-cyclical.

3. What are externalities or spillovers? How do they operate in the case of fiscal policy?

4. Explain the no-bailout clause.

5. Why is heterogeneity of preferences an argument against moving policy decisions from a lower to a higher level of government?

6. What is the intended purpose of the Stability and Growth Pact?

7. Why is fiscal policy useful at the country level in the monetary union and not at the overall union level?

8. When is a deficit of 5 per cent automatically seen as exceptional by the Stability and Growth Pact? When can it be non-automatically seen as exceptional?

9. When can the Council impose fines in the framework of the Stability and Growth Pact?

10. If the pact required the cyclically adjusted budget to be balanced every year, explain why fiscal policy would be strictly confined to the automatic stabilizers.

11. Why are fines under the Stability and Growth Pact sometimes described as pro-cyclical fiscal policy?

## ESSAY QUESTIONS

**1.** Apply the principles of fiscal federalism to the European Union in the following areas: education, internal security, migration and foreign affairs.

**2.** How would you reform the Stability and Growth Pact?

**3.** Imagine that an EMU member country is running budget deficits and accumulating a large public debt. What scenario can you envision when financial markets refuse to further finance the deficits? In your story, consider the reaction of domestic citizens as well that of the Commission and the Council.

**4.** How would you rate your own government as a benevolent protector of the interests of its citizens?

**5.** Explain how the Stability and Growth Pact could work if the criterion could be cyclically adjusted rather than actual budget deficits.

**6.** When the Stability and Growth Pact was being negotiated, some countries wanted it to be a fully automatic procedure, others wanted decisions to be interpreted by the Finance Ministers. Why is this distinction important? How does the agreed-upon pact reflect this difference of opinions?

**7.** Some countries have argued that the monetary union needs a common fiscal policy to match the common monetary policy. Evaluate this view.

**8.** With the Stability and Growth Pact and its limits on fiscal policy, what is left for governments to do in the monetary union?

**9.** As part of its decision on whether to join the Euro area, the UK Treasury has studied the Stability and Growth Pact and states:

> Where debt is low and there is a high degree of long-term fiscal sustainability, the case for adopting a tighter fiscal stance to allow room for governments to use fiscal policy more actively is not convincing. Provided that arrangements are put in place to ensure that discretionary policy is conducted symmetrically, then long-term sustainability would not in any way be put at risk.
>
> *Fiscal Stabilization and EMU*, HM Treasury, May 2003

Interpret and comment.

## FURTHER READING: THE AFICIONADOS CORNER

*General*

An excellent collection of readings is Part III in:
De Grauwe, P. (ed.) (2001) *The Political Economy of Monetary Union*, Edward Elgar, Cheltenham.

For a presentation and a defence of the Stability and Growth Pact, see:
Brunila, A., M. Buti and D. Franco (eds) (2001) *The Stability and Growth Pact*, Palgrave, Basingstoke.

For a detailed and critical presentation of the Stability and Growth Pact, see:
Eichengreen, B. and C. Wyplosz (1998) 'The Stability Pact: more than a minor nuisance?', *Economic Policy*, **26**, 65–104.

On the cyclical behaviour of fiscal policy, see:
European Commission (2001) 'Fiscal policy and cyclical stabilization in EMU', *European Economy*, **3**, 57–80.
Melitz, J. (2000) 'Some cross-country evidence about fiscal policy behaviour and consequences for EMU', *European Economy*, **2**, 3–21.
Hallerberg, M. and R. Strauch (2002) 'On the cyclicality of public finances in Europe', *Empirica*, **29**, 183–207.

On the tendency of governments not to always serve their citizens' interests and what it means for the European Union, see:
Persson, T. and G. Tabellini (2000) *Political Economics*, MIT Press, Cambridge, Mass.
Vaubel, R. (1997) 'The constitutional reform of the European Union', *European Economic Review*, **41** (3–5), 443–50.

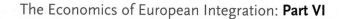
The case for fiscal policy co-ordination is developed in:
Coeuré, B. and J. Pisani-Ferry (2003) 'A sustainability pact for the Eurozone', available on: http://www.pisani-ferry.net.

For analyses on the politico-economic aspects of fiscal policy, see:
Alesina, A. and R. Perotti (1995) 'The political economy of budget deficits', *IMF Staff Papers*, **42** (1), 1–37.
Persson, T., G. Roland and G. Tabellini (2000) 'Comparative politics and public finance', *Journal of Political Economy*, **108** (6), 1121–61.
von Hagen, J. and I.J. Harden (1994) 'National budget processes and fiscal performance', *European Economy Reports and Studies*, **3**, 311–408.

An introduction to the theory of fiscal federalism:
Oates, W. (1999) 'An essay in fiscal federalism', *Journal of Economic Literature*, **37** (3), 1120–49.

## USEFUL WEBSITES

The official texts can be found on the Commission's website:
http://ue.eu.int

The Broad Economic Policy Guidelines, including the Council's annual assessment are on:
http://ue.eu.int/emu/broad/en/indexen.htm

## REFERENCES

Burda, M. and C. Wyplosz (2001) *Macroeconomics*, Oxford University Press, Oxford.
European Commission (2001) *Communication from the Commission to the Council and the European Parliament*, ECFIN/581/02-EN rev.3, 21.11.2001.
Olivier, B. and F. Giavazzi (2002) 'Reforms that can be done: improving the SGP through a proper accounting of public investment.' http://web.mit.edu/blanchar/www/

> "The big payoff on the Euro is, of course, in the capital markets. [...] It will move from the dull bank-based financing structure to big-time debt markets and markets for corporate equities that offer transparency for the mismanaged or sleepy European companies. Capital markets are good at kicking butt."
>
> Rudi Dornbusch (2000), p. 242

# 16 The Financial Markets and the Euro

Banking and finance are part of the service industry. The Single Market was meant to promote competition in that industry too, but so far the results have been somewhat slow to materialize. This chapter starts by outlining what is special about the financial services industry, distinguishing between banks and financial markets. It provides a review of the situation before and after the adoption of the single currency. It then considers the unfinished business of adapting the national regulation and supervision of financial activities to the new challenges of the common currency. Finally comes the question whether the euro will become a currency used world wide alongside the US dollar, why it matters and what has happened so far.

## 16.1 What is special about financial markets and why a single currency might matter

This chapter looks at the very recent evolution of European financial markets. The adoption of a single currency is intended to deeply change the landscape, providing savers and borrowers alike with more and better opportunities. This, in turn, is expected to improve the overall productivity of the European economy and possibly affect the way monetary policy works.

An important aspect of this experiment is that financial institutions and markets have been shaped by centuries of national traditions. The Single Market (presented in Chapter 4) has already deeply modified the financial markets but important differences remain. The single currency might well usher a new era of transformation, exposing many limitations of the Single Market and calling for further actions, which are examined here.

Finally, monetary policy works through the financial markets. Central banks act on very short-term interest rates but, as described in Chapter 14, the effect of monetary policy on the economy mostly comes from longer-term rates and from the exchange rate, as well as from credit availability. Each national central bank had developed its own strategy to deal with local conditions but now the Eurosystem operates simultaneously through different national financial markets, with possibly different effects in different countries. The possible asymmetric effects of monetary policy represent an additional challenge.

Whether these hoped-for benefits are being reaped is another matter. It may be too early to see the effects of the single currency, but some changes are already observable, sometimes, but not always, for the better. The preliminary evidence is scant and therefore highly tentative, but quite exciting.

### 16.1.1 What are financial institutions and markets?

The financial services industry is dedicated to borrowing and lending. What makes this industry special is that lending is inherently risky. A loan implies giving out money against the promise of future repayment. In the meantime, the borrower may face difficulties that make repayment partly or totally impossible, and some borrowers may simply be dishonest. As lenders protect themselves, they may pass some of the risk on to borrowers.

The best-known financial institutions are banks: they receive deposits, in effect borrowing from their customers; they offer loans; and they often provide assistance for managing portfolios. In contrast to these universal banks, investment banks specialize in managing portfolios; they do not even accept deposits and sometimes cater only to wealthy customers. Many fund management firms do not even deal with individuals; they offer 'wholesale' services to banks and insurance companies. Insurance companies are also considered to be financial institutions. Part of their activity is to provide insurance, which, strictly speaking, is not a financial service. Yet, in order to face potentially high payments, they accumulate large reserves, which they obviously want to manage in order to obtain as high returns as possible. In effect, they take 'deposits' – the insurance premia paid by their customers – that they use to 'make loans' as they invest in financial assets. In addition, many insurance companies propose pension schemes and life insurance, which can be seen as deposits with very long maturities. In fact, recent years have seen the emergence of financial conglomerates that combine classic universal banking, investment banking and insurance.

The bond and stock markets represent the other component of the financial system. Like banks, they are designed to collect savings and lend them back to borrowers, with the crucial difference that the end users – lenders and borrowers – 'meet' each other on the markets. Bonds are debts issued by firms and governments for a set maturity at an explicit interest rate, which can be indexed and therefore variable. Stocks (also called shares) are ownership titles to firms: they have no maturity since they last as long as the firm itself, and the returns are determined by the firm's performance. Lenders (also called investors), usually operate though intermediaries – brokers, investment banks – which they instruct to buy or sell assets on their behalf on the markets. Most small investors, and many large ones too, in fact purchase funds, which are ready-made baskets of shares and bonds managed by financial intermediaries. Each fund has particular characteristics: the relative importance of bonds and stocks, the industry or country where they invest, the degree of risk and associated guarantees, as explained in the next section.

Financial institutions come in all shapes and sizes. A few huge international banks coexist with small, strictly local ones. Some financial markets attract lenders and borrowers from all over the world (New York's Wall Street and the City of London are the two largest), while others deal in a very narrow range of local assets. As will be explained below, financial markets are more efficient the larger they are.

## 16.1.2 Functions of the financial markets

### MATCHING LENDING AND BORROWING NEEDS

The function of financial markets is to make savers and borrowers meet and to offer each saver and each borrower the best possible deal. This, of course, includes returns, but also the available menu of size and maturity of assets, as well as the ability to sell or buy any amount at any time.

Imagine an individual who wants to save a given amount over, say, two years. She can always deposit this amount with her bank, but the interest rate offered is quite low. She can do better by buying bonds, which offer a set interest, or stocks, which offer no guarantee and can be highly rewarding or promptly lose value. The saver faces a trade-off between return and risk, both rising in tandem as shown in Fig. 16-1. Depending on her appetite for risk and return, she will chose where on the curve she would like to be. She must then find a borrower that will offer the mix of risk and return that she wishes, for the amount that she has at her disposal and over the two-year

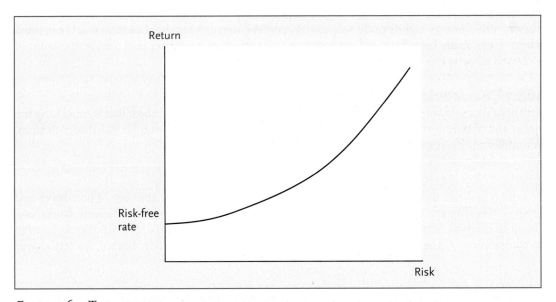

FIGURE 16-I: THE RISK–RETURN TRADE-OFF

period that she has in mind. She may also be interested in having the possibility of cashing in earlier, or of keeping her savings longer. Enter the financial markets. A large market will promptly match the saver's preferences with the needs of one or many borrowers.

This example illustrates how financial markets indirectly connect millions of savers and borrowers. Efficient financial markets are characterized by depth or liquidity–the possibility of quickly selling and reselling the assets; and breadth–the availability of a wide array of needs and offers.

### PRICING RISK
Different savers will pick different points on the risk–return trade-off schedule because they have different degrees of aversion to risk. No one likes risk, at least in financial matters, and this observation carries two implications. First, risk has a price. Those who hate risk are prepared to compensate less risk-averse players who are willing to provide them some protection against risky outcomes.[1] The solution is for a risk-averse saver to hand over to a more adventurous counterpart a very risky asset against a safer one. Naturally, everything else being equal, the less risky asset will be cheaper. The price difference is the price of the risk. There exist many ways, some of them highly sophisticated, to exchange risk. The end result is that the markets put a price tag on risk and that all assets nicely fit on the same risk–return schedule shown in Fig. 16-1.[2] The risk–return schedule reveals the price of risk, and financial markets allow everyone to trade off a higher return for more risk, or the converse, depending on personal preferences.

### REDUCING RISK THROUGH DIVERSIFICATION
The second implication is that reducing risk is desirable, and financial markets also perform this function. The underlying principle is diversification, which can be described with a simple example. Consider two assets, one pays €100 on sunny days and the other one pays €100 on rainy days. Assume further that, on average, the number of sunny days equals the number of rainy days, so that on average each asset pays €50 daily. Taken separately, each asset is risky: for instance, a long string of sunny days will leave the holders of rainy-day assets without cash. However, holding one €50 sunny-day and one €50 rainy-day asset completely eliminates risk. This is exactly how diversification works. By holding a large number of assets that do well under different circumstances, one can very significantly reduce risk.[3] Indeed, most savers hold portfolios of diversified assets. Here again, large financial markets are more effective since they pool a wide spectrum of risks and allow savers to greatly reduce the risk they face.

## 16.1.3 Characteristics of financial markets
Financial markets are shaped to deal with the functions previously described: that is, matching the needs and preferences of borrowers and lenders, pricing risk and allowing for risk diversification. A number of characteristics follow.

### SCALE ECONOMIES
Matching and risk diversification are both easier when there is a large number of borrowers and lenders. The finance industry is subject to massive scale economies, which affects banks and financial markets. Where small banks and markets survive, it is not difficult to find some barriers to competition. The existence of different currencies is one such barrier. Indeed, an Irish saver

[1] This is yet another similarity between financial services and insurance.
[2] How risk is measured is an important issue that is described in finance texts.
[3] In finance jargon, the sunny- and rainy-days assets are perfectly negatively correlated (their correlation coefficient is −1). More generally, risk diversification is higher the more negatively correlated are the assets.

who purchased Portuguese assets faced currency risk in addition to the normal lending risk, and this made Irish assets more attractive to her. The creation of a single currency removes this particular barrier to competition.

## NETWORKS

One response to scale economies is the emergence of large financial institutions and markets. Another response, which goes hand in hand with the first, is the building up of networks. When a financial firm receives funds from a saver, it needs to relend these funds as soon as possible since 'time is money'. With some luck, it will find among its customers a borrower with matching needs and preferences, but more often not. The solution is to relend the saver's money to another financial firm which may have spotted a borrower, or identified another financial firm which may have spotted a borrower, etc. This is why financial markets operate as networks. Indeed, money passes quickly from firm to firm until it finds a house – a suitable borrower – somewhere in the network, and quite possibly in a very different corner of the world.

A financial firm is like a telephone hook-up: if you are the only one having a hook-up, it is of no use. A telephone is more useful, the more people are connected to the network. This effect is called a network externality. A financial firm can offer better deals when it is in contact with a large number of other firms which deal with many, many customers, savers and borrowers alike. Network externalities exploit increasing returns to scale: the larger the network, the better it works. The best network could well be the whole world, hence the tendency towards the globalization of financial services.

## ASYMMETRIC INFORMATION

A fundamental characteristic of financial activities is that the borrower always knows more about his own riskiness than the lender. This information asymmetry carries profound implications. Borrowers may intentionally attempt to conceal some damning information for the sake of obtaining a badly needed loan. As a consequence, lenders are very careful, not to say suspicious. They may simply refuse to lend rather than take unbounded risks. Alternatively, they may set the price of risk very high, i.e. they ask for very large risk premia. This, in turn, may discourage low-risk borrowers who cannot convincingly signal their true riskiness, while desperate borrowers are willing to pay any premium. If this process goes unchecked, only bad risks are present in the market and, knowing that, lenders withdraw.[4] At best, the price of risk is excessive, at worst the financial market dries out.

Asymmetric information is unavoidable and it tends to undermine the development of financial institutions and markets. This phenomenon explains many features of the financial services industry presented below. One general response is regulation, i.e. legislative measures that aim at reducing the overall riskiness.

## 16.1.4 Effects of the single currency on financial markets

The adoption of the euro eliminates the currency risk within the Euro area. In principle, therefore, savers do not have to worry about where the asset is issued as long at it is denominated in euros, and borrowers can tap the whole area by taking on euro-denominated debt. There is no longer any reason for financial markets to be Finnish, Greek or German.

A single financial market first means more competition as national currencies that used to act as non-tariff barriers are eliminated.[5] Rents associated with dominating positions should

---

[4] This phenomenon is called adverse selection. Borrowing in a desperate situation is sometimes called 'gambling for resurrection'.
[5] Chapter 3 presents non-tariff barriers, i.e. restrictions to trade that are designed to protect local firms by such means as specific regulation, standards, administrative authorizations and controls, etc.

## The Economics of European Integration: **Part VI**

disappear and the need to retain and attract new customers should push financial institutions to constantly improve their performance. A unified financial market should also allow a better exploitation of scale economies, with the emergence of large financial institutions and markets. Table 16-1 shows that only three Euro area banks are in the Top 10 league (until recently, US banks were hamstrung by legislation that prevented them from operating in more than one state). Similarly the Euro area stock markets (Frankfurt, Paris, Milan, etc.) are small in comparison to Wall Street and the City of London. Furthermore, the emergence of a single financial market along with the elimination of the exchange risk should allow for more depth and breadth as the market serves more savers and borrowers.

One negative aspect, however, is that the potential for diversification shrinks. Before the advent of the euro, a Belgian saver could diversify her portfolio by acquiring German, Italian and other European assets. Now these assets are less diverse as they all share the same currency and as cyclical conditions become more homogeneous (as discussed in Chapter 14). To achieve a high degree of diversification they may have to move further, to less well-known parts of the world. All in all, however, the positive effects of scale economies in a wider unified market are likely to outweigh the negative effects of reduced diversification.

Thus, more competition and wider opportunities should benefit the end users, the ultimate borrowers and lenders. This, in turn, should promote growth as a consequence of better borrowing opportunities.[6] It should also allow countries with important borrowing needs to better tap savings elsewhere in the Euro area, further adding to the growth effect.

Finally, the fact that the US dollar is a world currency gives US citizens and firms some advantages. The potential emergence of the euro as another world currency, and the expected benefits, is examined in section 16.3.

| Rank | Bank | Country | Rank | Bank | Country |
|---|---|---|---|---|---|
| 1 | Mizuho | Japan | 6 | UBS | Switzerland |
| 2 | Citigroup | USA | 7 | BNP Paribas | France |
| 3 | Sumitomo | Japan | 8 | HSBC | UK |
| 4 | Deutsche Bank | Germany | 9 | JP Morgan Chase | USA |
| 5 | Mitsubishi | Japan | 10 | Hypo Vereinsbank | Germany |

SOURCE: *The Banker*, July 2002.

TABLE 16-1: THE TOP 10 COMMERCIAL BANKS IN 2002

# 16.2 Financial institutions and markets

## 16.2.1 Banking

### WHAT IS SPECIAL ABOUT BANKING?

The banking industry is special in three respects. First, banks are naturally fragile and bank failures can be systemic, as explained in section 16.2.4. As a consequence, banks are highly regulated and supervised. Second, the information asymmetry problem is acute since banks primarily earn profits from their lending activities. This is yet another reason why banking does not conform to the perfect market model.

---

[6] The general growth effects of the Single Market are presented in Chapter 3.

One implication is that some customers cannot borrow at all and are excluded from the loan market. In such a situation, long-term relationships are important as they provide banks with track records of their customers and help to build up confidence, breaking somewhat the information asymmetry. The downside is that well-established customers have little incentive to quit their banks. While this attachment alleviates the information asymmetry problem, it also reduces competition.

That aspect is further reinforced by a third feature of banking: it is plainly painful to change bank. Many payment orders are automated, some payments and receipts are always under way, so it is never practical to shift to another bank. Proximity of the branch also often discourages switching. For these reasons, most banking relationships tend to be longlasting, much longer than in most other service industries, and competition is less severe. Importantly, competition aims less at satisfying customers than at developing wide and well spread out networks – another source of scale economies.

## THE STARTING POINT

These features explain why banks started to develop at the local level, which allowed them to know their customers reasonably well, thus minimizing information asymmetries. Scale economies next led to a process of growth and mergers as banks sought to become ever bigger, but so far this process has generally taken place within national boundaries. As shown below, the number of banks has declined in the Euro area recently, and a large part of this decline is explained by mergers and acquisitions. However, Fig. 16-2 indicates that a vast majority (74 per cent) of these mergers and acquisitions take place within countries. The number of banking institutions in the European Union between 1998 and 2001 was[7]:

| 1998 | 1999 | 2000 | 2001 |
|------|------|------|------|
| 8379 | 7955 | 7521 | 7219 |

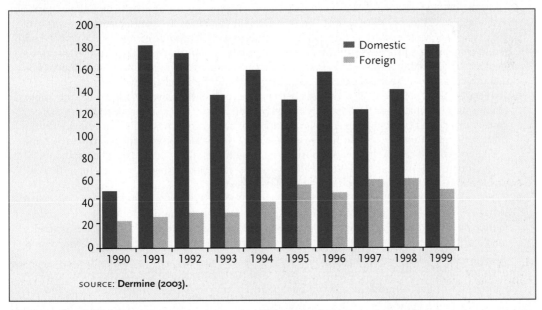

SOURCE: **Dermine (2003).**

FIGURE 16-2: MERGERS AND ACQUISITIONS OF EU BANKS (1995–MID-2000)

[7] See *Structural Analysis of the EU Banking Sector*, ECB, November 2002.

## NATIONAL OR PAN-EUROPEAN CONCENTRATION

The fact that each country had its own currency – in Europe the exception has been the Belgium–Luxembourg currency union – and that many restrictions to capital movements were in place until the late 1980s, explains why the concentration process has taken place within, and not across, countries. The advent of the euro could change all that, but little has happened so far. Several reasons have been advanced to explain the continuing apparent parochialism of banks, in contrast with other industries.

First, local regulations still differ. This has long been recognized and has led to a succession of harmonization efforts, described in Box 16-1. In addition, while in theory a 'single banking market' is now in place, several non-regulatory hurdles remain. They operate like NTBs and are used by national authorities to protect home-grown banks and, in effect, stifle competition.

Second, cultural differences remain prevalent. For several centuries, banks have developed along diverse lines. Traditions in banking differ significantly from one country to another. While acquiring a foreign bank could be the easiest way of adjusting to that country's specific culture, problems with integrating personnel seem to deter mergers and acquisition.

---

### BOX 16-1: HARMONIZATION OF BANKING REGULATION IN EUROPE

Efforts at building a unified banking market in Europe go far back in history. The main steps are as follows:

■ In 1973, a directive on *The Abolition of Restrictions on Freedom of Establishment and Freedom to Provide Services for self-employed Activities of Banks and other Financial Institutions* established the principle of national treatment. All banks operating in one country are subject to the same non-discriminatory regulations and supervision as local banks. Yet, widespread capital controls limited competition and, in the absence of any co-ordination of banking supervision, banks were deterred from operating in different countries.

■ In 1977, the First Banking Directive on *The Co-ordination of Laws, Regulations and Administrative Provisions Relating to the Taking Up and Pursuit of Credit Institutions* established a gradual phasing in of the principle of home country control. Under this principle, it is the home country of the parent bank that is responsible for supervising the bank's activities in other EU countries. The directive left open a number of loopholes, including the need to obtain authorization from the local supervision authorities to establish subsidiaries and continuing restrictions on capital movements.

■ In 1989, the Second Banking Directive was designed to apply to the banking industry the provisions of the Single Act which mandated the elimination of capital controls. The directive stipulates that any bank licensed in a EU country can establish branches or supply cross-border financial services in the other countries of the EU without further authorization. It can also open a subsidiary on the same conditions as nationals of the host state. The parent bank must now consolidate all its accounts for supervision by its own authority. Yet, the host country can impose specific regulations if they are deemed to be 'in the public interest'.

■ Facing a lack of progress, a Financial Services Action Plan (FSAP) was adopted in 1999. The stated aim is to achieve full integration of banking and capital markets by the year 2005. The Plan outlines four objectives: (1) a single EU wholesale market; (2) open and secure retail banking and insurance markets; (3) the development of state-of-the-art prudential rules and supervision; (4) wider conditions (essential fiscal rules) for an optimal single financial market.

The 'single banking market' is not limited to the EU members. When the EFTA countries, with the exception of Switzerland, joined the European Economic Area in 1992, they accepted the European banking legislation.

*Source*: Dermine (2003).

Finally, the tax treatment of savings differs from country to country. Thus the choice of where to bank may be driven by tax purposes rather than by the quality of banking services. Tax evasion may well have become as strong an incentive to scout the European banking scene as the search for better service or risk diversification, thus undermining the very purpose of financial integration.

The evidence so far is that, through mergers and acquisitions, banks have been consolidating at the national level. Their strategy seems to be, first, to reach a size that is large enough to enable them to next engage in foreign purchases. Meanwhile, as banks merge at the national level, concentration increases (Fig. 16-3) which may result in less, not more, competition. Thus, in contrast with the effects expected from the Single Act as laid out in Chapter 3, it could be that the early impact of the monetary union is to reduce competition. This could be the perverse effect of combining partial integrative measures with continuing NTB protectionism. More optimistically, we may just be at the eve of a wave of pan-European mergers and acquisitions that will eventually make the single banking market a reality.

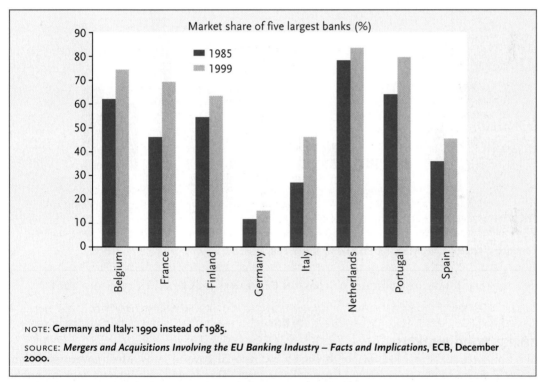

NOTE: **Germany and Italy: 1990 instead of 1985.**

SOURCE: *Mergers and Acquisitions Involving the EU Banking Industry – Facts and Implications*, **ECB, December 2000.**

FIGURE 16-3: CONCENTRATION IN NATIONAL BANKING (1985–1999)

## TRADE IN SERVICES

While banks do not consolidate at the pan-European level, they could still offer services across borders. This form of competition is exactly what the Second Banking Directive was meant to promote, and the elimination of exchange risk should reinforce it. They can open new branches and move close to their customers to circumvent the information asymmetry. Figure 16-4 shows the percentage of local branches of banks from the European Economic Area.[8] With few exceptions, there is not yet sign of a powerful euro effect that would prompt banks to move into other countries. They may expect that it will be very hard to win away customers because of the large fixed costs involved in changing banks. The limited extent of cross-border competition is further confirmed by bank charges for bank transfers from one euro area country to another which have been kept so high (some €17 on average for a €100 transfer in 2000, about 10 times the cost of a domestic transfer) that the Commission stepped in and imposed a new regulation which prohibits banks from charging for within-Euro area transfers a different fee from the one they apply to domestic transfers.

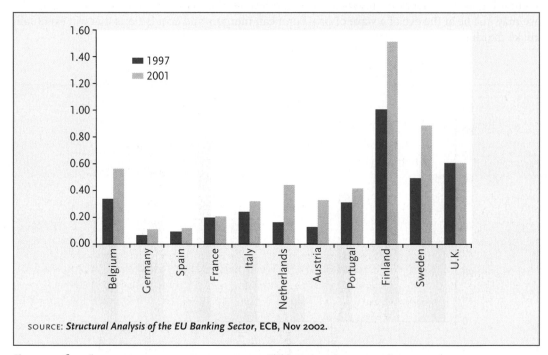

SOURCE: *Structural Analysis of the EU Banking Sector*, ECB, Nov 2002.

FIGURE 16-4: SHARE OF BRANCHES OF FOREIGN EEA BANKS (PER CENT) IN 1997 AND 2001

## 16.2.2 Bond markets

We first look at the market for bonds issued by national governments. Most governments are believed to be highly trustworthy, financially at least. This is why the interest rate on public debts is often considered risk-free and therefore directly comparable, without having to adjust for risk.

Figure 16-5 shows the evolution of interest rates on government long-term bonds. For decades, interest was lowest on German bonds. Since the other currencies were perceived as being weaker than the mark, other governments had to pay higher rates to compensate for currency

---

[8] The EEA includes the 15 EU member countries as well as Iceland, Liechtenstein and Norway which have accepted the European banking legislation.

risk.[9] As the date of launching the single currency drew nearer and more certain, the currency risk declined and gradually became irrelevant. The figure shows an impressive convergence of all yields towards the German level.

Yet a keen eye will detect that convergence is not complete. This may reflect differences in the perceived quality of governments as borrowers,[10] or less than full integration because of remaining institutional differences in this market segment. This second interpretation is confirmed in Fig. 16-6 where we look at the very short-term interest rate segment, interbank rates. These are rates charged among banks, and they are considered as equally riskless. The convergence is total after January 1999, in fact there is now a unified interbank market. Note the difference with Greece, which joined the euro area in January 2001, and the UK which has not yet joined. Most observers conclude that full integration has been achieved on the interbank market, not on the government bond market, and much less on the market for private bonds issued by large corporations.

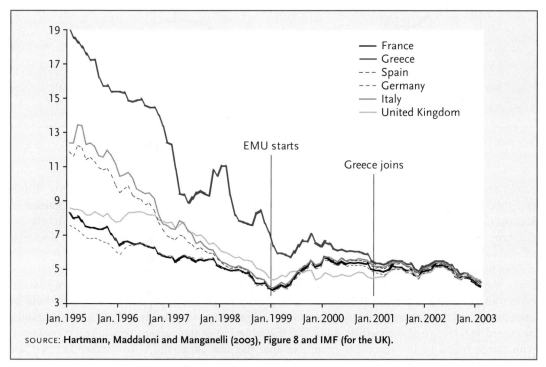

SOURCE: **Hartmann, Maddaloni and Manganelli (2003), Figure 8 and IMF (for the UK).**

FIGURE 16-5: INTEREST RATES ON LONG-TERM GOVERNMENT BONDS (JAN. 1995–FEB. 2003)

## 16.2.3 Stock markets

The stock market is where large – and some medium-sized – firms go to finance capital spending. They issue shares which are held by individuals or by large institutional investors, such as pension

---

[9] This is the interest parity principle which can be stated as:

Interest rate in Italy = Interest rate in Germany + Expected depreciation of the lira

[10] This could reflect different public debt size or varying degrees of compliance with the Stability and Growth Pact (Chapter 15). The fact that interest rates on the German debt remain the lowest while Germany's deficit is excessive suggests that this is not the explanation.

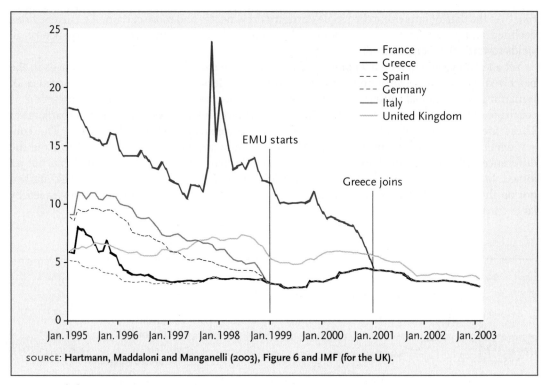

EMU starts

Greece joins

SOURCE: **Hartmann, Maddaloni and Manganelli (2003), Figure 6 and IMF (for the UK).**

FIGURE 16-6: INTERBANK (3 MONTHS) INTEREST RATES (JAN. 1995–FEB. 2003)

funds and insurance companies. Increasingly individuals buy shares from collective funds designed to offer good risk-return trade-offs through extensive diversification, as explained in section 16.1.2. Yet, for all the hype about globalization, it is striking that stock markets are characterized by a strong home bias: borrowers and savers alike tend to deal mostly on domestic markets and to hold domestic assets.

One reason for the home bias is information asymmetry: investors know more about domestic firms. Another reason, currency risk, has been eliminated within the Euro area, so we would expect less of a home bias. Is it happening? Fig. 16-7 looks at the proportion of assets held by investing funds that report pursuing a European-wide strategy. Clearly, these funds have markedly increased their share of the market following the adoption of the euro in 1999. The comparison with funds based in the three EU countries that did not adopt the euro further support the plausibility of a strong euro effect.

Another bit of evidence is provided by the evolution of stock exchanges, the market place where shares are traded. Every European country has at least one stock exchange, which was natural when currency risk was segmenting the various national markets. As Table 16-2 shows, with the exception of London (and Euronext, see Box 16-2), which along with New York is a worldwide financial centre, European exchanges remain small, and therefore likely to suffer from limited scale economies.

The adoption of a common currency should lead to fewer exchanges. After all, there are only four stock exchanges in the USA, so why should there be more in Europe? Indeed, as described in Box 16-2, three exchanges (Amsterdam, Brussels and Paris) merged to form Euronext in

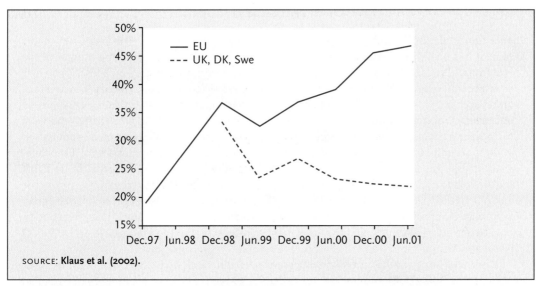

SOURCE: **Klaus et al. (2002).**

FIGURE 16-7: ASSET SHARE OF EUROPEAN-WIDE FUNDS

|  | € bn | % GDP |  | € bn | % GDP |
|---|---|---|---|---|---|
| Athens | 72 | 47.9 | New York | 8435 | 89.5 |
| Copenhagen | 84 | 43.0 | Tokyo | 1826 | 51.1 |
| Frankfurt | 714 | 32.9 | London | 1738 | 101.8 |
| Euronext | 1466 | 63.7 | Zurich | 507 | 181.2 |
| Helsinki | 124 | 83.8 | Stockholm | 188 | 72.7 |
| Rome | 481 | 37.1 |  |  |  |
| Vienna | 35 | 15.9 |  |  |  |

SOURCES: European centres: The Federation of European Securities Exchanges; New York and Tokyo: NYSE; GDP estimates from *Economic Outlook*, OECD.

NOTE: Euronext is Paris, Brussels and Amsterdam.

TABLE 16-2: SIZE OF STOCK MARKETS (JUNE 2003)
(TOTAL CAPITALIZATION)

September 2000 after failed negotiations between Frankfurt and the London Stock Exchange. This is unlikely to be the end since Euronext is still smaller than London and one-seventh the size of New York.

## 16.2.4 Regulation and supervision

### THE RATIONALE

Section 16.1 has identified a number of characteristics specific to financial markets: these markets display important scale economies, they operate as networks, and they suffer from information asymmetries. These characteristics imply that financial markets suffer from 'market failures', i.e.

> ### BOX 16-2: CONSOLIDATION OF STOCK MARKETS
>
> Some consolidation is taking place among traditional stock markets. The most noticeable example has been the creation of Euronext in September 2000, the result of a merger of the Amsterdam, Brussels and Paris stock exchanges. Euronext is subject to Dutch legislation and has a subsidiary in each of the participating countries. Each subsidiary holds a local stock market licence that gives access to trading in all the participating countries. Euronext achieved consistency in some, but not all, of the institutional characteristics of its predecessor markets. Single quotation and a common order book are guaranteed as well as price dissemination systems, a unified trading platform and one clearing and settlement system, Euroclear. Nevertheless, the local markets are not legally merged, which implies, for example, that the regulatory body in each of the participating countries retains its prerogatives. From the beginning, Euronext was not intended to be a closed structure and was eager to finalize agreements with other stock exchanges. In 2001, this resulted in the acquisition of Liffe, the London derivatives trading platform, and the agreement to integrate also the Portuguese exchanges of Lisbon and Porto.
>
> Before Euronext, another even larger merger between stock exchanges was tried. In 1998, the Deutsche Börse (DB) and the London Stock Exchange (LSE) were planning to merge in an attempt to gain the leadership position in Europe. The creation of iX ('international Exchange') was officially announced on May 2000. The DB and the LSE planned to participate in equal measure as shareholders of the new exchange, which would be subject to British legislation. It was envisaged to quote the 'blue chips' of both exchanges in London and the technology stocks in Frankfurt. The trading system would have been the German one (Xetra), considered to be more modern and more reliable. While the negotiations between the two stock exchanges were still in process, the OM Gruppen, owner of the Stockholm stock exchange, made an unexpected public offer and tried to take over the LSE. This event critically affected the projected merger between DB and LSE, which was subsequently rejected by the LSE Board. Several reasons led to the failure of the merger. In general, there were some doubts that the merger would create value added and would consistently exploit economies of scale. First, contrary to Euronext, where companies belonging to the same sector retained the freedom to chose the location of their listing, iX required the 'blue chips' to be traded in London and the technology stocks in Frankfurt. This solution would have implied costs for both exchanges. Second, some of the companies would have had to move from one exchange to the other and deal with the change in regulations and supervisory authorities. Finally, the new entity did not include the creation of a common clearing and settlement system, hence it would have failed to provide lower settlement costs.
>
> Adapted from Hartmann, Maddaloni and Manganelli (2003)

deviations from the textbook description of perfect markets. In the presence of failures, markets may malfunction, which justifies interventions by the authorities. Indeed, in every country, financial markets are regulated and the financial institutions are closely supervised.

The presence of scale economies implies that a few large firms eventually dominate the market. The tendency for competition to become monopolistic challenges the perfect competition assumption.[11] It also means that financial markets are vulnerable to difficulties suffered by one or two of

---

[11] As explained in Chapter 6, monopolistic competition describes the situation where a small number of large firms dominate the market.

these important players. This vulnerability is sharpened by the two other characteristics. The network feature means that all large financial institutions are continuously dealing with each other, and routinely borrowing and lending huge amounts from and to each other. If one of these institutions fails, all the others may be pulled down. Failures tend to be systemic.

The third characteristic, the presence of information asymmetries, means that all financial firms routinely take risks. Every asset represents the right to receive payments in the future, be it 24 hours or 15 years. It is trivial to observe that the future is unknown, but this feature has deep implications for financial markets. Today's value of an asset represents the best collective judgement by financial market participants of the likely payments that the asset holder may expect to receive upon maturity. But one thing is sure: the future will differ from today's expectations. The asset can turn out to yield better returns than expected, but can also be revealed as catastrophic and its value can deeply deteriorate. When this happens, asset holders see their wealth decline, and the decline is typically sudden. This is why financial systems are inherently fragile and prone to panics and crises.

As the financial institutions are central to modern economies, systemic failures immediately provoke severe disruptions that leave no firm or citizen unharmed. When declines in asset values are widespread, those who hold large amounts of assets can become insolvent. Many financial institutions (banks, pension funds, insurance companies) that hold large amounts of assets may then fail, spreading the hardship to the whole economy as countless examples – from the Wall Street crash of 1929 to Korea in 1998 or Argentina in 2002 – remind us.

## REGULATION AND SUPERVISION

To reduce the incidence of such catastrophic events, and possibly even eliminate them, financial institutions are regulated. Over the years, regulation has changed and become more sophisticated. The general thrust is to ensure that financial institutions adopt prudent strategies. This is done by requiring them to hold enough high-quality assets, for example bonds issued by respectable governments or by solid corporations.

Regulation, in turn, requires supervision. It is not enough to edict good rules, it is essential to make sure that they are respected. Since financial conditions can quickly deteriorate, supervision must be continuous. Given the complexity of modern finance, and the possibility of hiding emerging problems, supervisors must be as sophisticated as the financiers themselves, and they need to exercise their duties with great diligence and firmness.

## THE CURRENT SITUATION

Regulation – the establishment of rules – is largely designed at the EU level[12] while supervision – the implementation and enforcement of regulation – continues to be carried out at the national level. This assignment of tasks is understandable. The EU's central aim is often described as 'the four freedoms': free mobility of goods, services, assets and people. For financial services to move freely, financial institutions need to be allowed to operate throughout the EU if they so wish. If national regulations differed, financial institutions would have to register in each and every country where they wished to operate. This would greatly hamper the mobility of financial services. Savers, unsure about the quality of foreign regulations, would prefer to keep their money at home.

---

[12] More precisely, EU-level regulation sets minimum standards, leaving individual countries free to establish more stringent – but not more lenient – rules. Within this principle, national-level rules are subject to the principle of mutual recognition, i.e. foreign rules are recognized as substitutes for domestic ones.

What about supervision? One argument for keeping it at the national level is the existence of another kind of information asymmetry, this time between supervisor and supervisee. Obviously each financial firm knows more about its business, and the risks that it is taking, than its supervisor. Quite likely, most firms wish to hide their difficulties, especially if their disclosure would lead to fines or outright closure. It is argued that these information asymmetries are lower at the national than at the union level. National supervisors know their financial institutions well and over the years have developed a relationship that allows for a smooth process. Another argument is subsidiarity: unless proved impossible or inefficient, supervision should remain at the national level. So far, in the absence of any major shake-up, it is impossible to prove that national-level supervision is inadequate. Yet most observers believe that this is the case and that the true reason for retaining national-level supervisions is a lack of interest. After all, this is also about jobs in Amsterdam, Helsinki and Madrid, and old, possibly cosy links between supervisors and supervisees.

## ADAPTING REGULATION AND SUPERVISION TO THE SINGLE CURRENCY

National supervisors differ in important ways. Their legal briefs vary and their level of expertise is not uniform. This can be problematic if and when financial crises suddenly occur, because, at that stage, in an effort to stunt systemic effects, prompt reaction is of the essence. The authorities must decide whether to bail out – at taxpayer's expense – failing institutions or let them fail. Given the networking among financial institutions, the bailout decision is unlikely to concern a single country.[13] A proper reaction therefore calls for instantaneous and extensive sharing of information, based on an intimate knowledge of the institutions and their managers.

The current solution relies on co-operation among national supervisors but there is no presumption that all can be told quickly enough. More ominously, national supervisors may be sensitive to the interests of their national financial institutions and wish to protect them. Proximity may reduce information asymmetries but it can also nurture nationalistic sentiments. If that is the case, co-operation is unlikely to develop into a fully trusted partnership. Finally, the national agencies in charge of supervision have an obvious interest in not being closed down. Some of them are actually part of the national central banks which have already lost their monetary policy-making role and are highly reluctant to be deprived of their last important function, supervision.

Even if an agreement to establish Europe-wide supervision could be reached, should it be carried out by the ECB or by a separate agency? Currently, as Table 16-3 shows, the responsibility for supervising financial institutions rests with central banks in some countries, and with specialized agencies in others. Recently Sweden and the UK have opted for a single independent supervisor. Technical discussions are under way, but 'turf' considerations are present.

## 16.2.5 Channels of monetary policy

The link between a financial system and monetary policy is tight. Monetary conditions deeply affect the daily functioning of financial markets. Financial systems cannot blossom unless the currency is reasonably stable and monetary policy cannot operate without a well-functioning financial market. Because most of what we call money is in the form of bank deposits, the good functioning of the banking and financial systems is crucial to the trust that underwrites any money. This is one reason why central banks have a direct interest in the quality of the financial system.

Another reason is that monetary policy decisions are transmitted via financial markets through the availability and cost of credit. The financial system is the channel through which monetary

---

[13] Small banks are typically not operating internationally, so the problem concerns larger banks, precisely those that are important for systemic contagion.

| Country | Number of public institutions responsible for supervision | Form of central bank involvement in banking supervision | | | | |
|---|---|---|---|---|---|---|
| | | | Central bank is not the banking supervisor | | | |
| | | Central bank is involved in banking supervision [a] | Central bank is the banking supervisor | Central bank is involved in the management of the banking supervisor [b] | Central bank specific tasks in banking supervision [c] | Central bank and banking supervisor share resources |
| Belgium | 2 [d] | Yes | No | Yes | No | No [e] |
| Denmark | 1 | No | No | No | No | No |
| Germany | 1 | Yes | No | No | Yes | Yes |
| Greece | 3 | Yes | Yes | | | |
| Spain | 3 | Yes | Yes | | | |
| France | 6 [f] | Yes | No | Yes | No | Yes |
| Ireland | 1 [g] | Yes | No | No | No | Yes |
| Italy | 3 | Yes | Yes | | | |
| Luxembourg | 2 | No | No | No | No | No |
| Netherlands | 3 [h] | Yes | Yes | | | |
| Austria | 1 | Yes | No | Yes | Yes | No |
| Portugal | 3 | Yes | Yes | | | |
| Finland | 2 | Yes | No | Yes | No | Yes |
| Sweden | 1 | Yes | No | Yes | No | No [i] |
| United Kingdom | 1 | Yes | No | Yes | No | No [j] |

NOTES:
[a] The central bank is involved in banking supervision when it is the banking supervisor itself or, where this is not the case, involved in the management/oversight of the banking supervisor, contributes to supervisory policy-shaping, carries out tasks in line supervision, processes supervisory reporting or shares resources with the supervisory agency.
[b] The central bank is involved in the management of the banking supervisor if the former is represented in the management (e.g. management committee, secretary-general and chairman) or in the supervisory or oversight board of the latter.
[c] The central bank carries out off- and on-site monitoring in specific areas.
[d] The two existing supervisors will merge on 1 January 2004 into one institution.
[e] The law foresees a pooling of resources between the *Commission Bancaire et Financière/Commissie voor het Bank- en Financiewezen* (Banking and Finance Commission – CBF), the *Office de Contrôle des Assurances/Centrale dienst voor verzekeringen* (Insurance Control Office – OCA/CDV) and the central bank, the Banque Nationale de Belgique/Nationale Bank van België (BNB/NBB).
[f] A variety of institutions and bodies are involved in the supervisory framework. The number given (six) includes the *Commission Bancaire* (Banking Commission), the *Comité de la Réglementation Bancaire et Financière* (Committee on Banking and Financial Regulation – CRBF), the *Comité des Etablissements de Crédit et des Entreprises d'Investissement* (Committee for the Establishment of Credit Institutions and Investment Companies – CECEI), the *Autorité des Marchés Financiers* (Financial Market Authority – FMA), the *Commission de Contrôle des Assurances* (Insurance Supervision Commission – CCA) and the Ministry of Economic Affairs and Finance. The *Conseil Nationale du Crédit et des Titres* (National Credit and Securities Council – CNCT), the *Collège des Autorités de Contrôle des Entreprises du Secteur Financier* (Board of Financial Sector Authorities – CACESF) and the new committees envisaged in the future, i.e. the *Comité Consultatif du Secteur Financier* (Advisory Committee on the Financial Sector – CCSF) and the *Comité Consultatif de la Législation et de la Réglementation Financière* (Advisory Committee on Financial Legislation and Regulation – CCLRF) are not included.
[g] The single supervisory authority (IFSRA) is a constituent but autonomous part of the central bank and is responsible for the day-to-day supervision of all areas of financial services. The Governor of the central bank retains the right to appoint officers to inspect financial institutions if he so wishes. Information technology and other resources are shared between the constituent parts of the CBFSAI.
[h] There will be only two institutions in January 2005 (at the latest), as a result of the planned integration of the De Nederlandsche Bank and the *Pensioen- en Verzekeringskamer* (Pensions and Insurance Supervisory Authority).
[i] The Swedish Finansinspektionen (SFSA) and Sveriges Riksbank have concluded a Memorandum of Understanding, which includes similar features as that between the UK authorities (see next footnote to this table), apart from explicit arrangements for the secondment of staff.
[j] The Bank of England (BoE) and the Financial Services Authority (FSA) are obliged to share information. Under a specific Memorandum of Understanding, the avoidance of duplication of labour is stated, while an agreement on the collecting institution and on data communication is foreseen to be reached in cases where the FSA and the BoE need the same information. The BoE and the FSA occasionally second staff to each other, which might be viewed as a form of sharing resources.

SOURCE: ECB.

TABLE 16-3: FINANCIAL SUPERVISION IN THE EU MEMBER STATES (AS OF JULY 2003)

policy affects the economy, its growth and its inflation rates. The fact that the euro is the currency of different countries, each with its own financial system, creates a novel situation.

The main question is whether a given policy decision can have different and unwanted effects in different countries. There are many reasons why this can be the case:

- The ECB sets the short-term interest rate (EONIA) as described in Chapter 14. In most countries, loans depend on longer-term interest rates which typically move less than short-term rates and whose movements depend on the reaction of the financial market. In these countries, the effect of central bank actions is both muted and somewhat uncertain. In some countries, however, the interest rate that applies to loans is indexed on the short-term rate and central bank actions have a stronger impact.
- The effect of the interest rate largely depends on the importance of bank credit. In some countries, bank credit is the main source of financing for most firms and households, but in other countries firms make more important use of stock markets. Monetary policy will have a more direct effect in the first group of countries than in the latter, where the evolution of share prices will become an important, yet uncertain, channel.
- Monetary policy also operates through the exchange rate. With a common exchange rate, those countries that have a higher share of external trade with the non-euro area stand to be more strongly affected.

EMU countries differ on all these dimensions, which raises the possibility that monetary policy could be a source of asymmetric shocks, precisely what the OCA theory suggests is the main drawback of a monetary union (see Chapter 12). Whether all these differences add up to a serious problem, however, is another question, so far with no clear answer. A further issue is whether, over time, the existing structural differences will fade away. Early indications are that it is the case.[14]

## 16.3 The international role of the euro

The classic attributes of money apply to its international role. Externally, a currency can be a medium of exchange used for international trade, a unit of account used to price other currencies or widely traded commodities, and a store of value used by foreign individuals and authorities. Domestically these attributes are underpinned by the legal status of money, internationally they have to be earned.

In the nineteenth century, sterling was the undisputed international currency. It was displaced by the dollar in the twentieth century. These precedents indicate that only large economies can expect their currency to achieve an international status, a condition that the Euro area fulfils. Currently, some 305 million people live in the Euro area, and new membership could eventually bring this number to 470 million, to be compared with 280 million people living in the USA. The EU's GDP is 75 per cent of that the USA. Another condition is that the currency must be stable. The Eurosystem's commitment to price stability further suggests that, eventually, the euro can aspire to having a large international role.

### 16.3.1 Trade invoicing

There is some evidence that European firms are increasingly able to invoice trade in euros – for example, trade with Japan, as shown in Fig. 16-8. Yet, the bulk of primary commodities (oil, gas, raw materials) are priced in dollars in specialized markets, and this is unlikely to change in the foreseeable future. Even if European firms can now more often avoid exposure to currency risk by using the euro, the dollar is and will remain the currency of choice among countries which are in

---

[14] The ECB and the NCBs have conducted a detailed investigation of the channels of monetary policy. A summary of the results is in the ECB's *Monthly Bulletin*, October 2002.

neither the USA nor the Euro currency areas. The exception seems to be countries in the periphery of the EU, mostly those in Europe that will join the EU in the coming years.

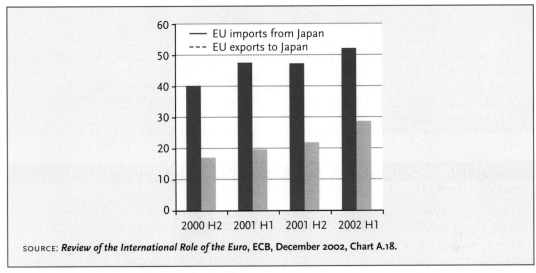

SOURCE: *Review of the International Role of the Euro*, ECB, December 2002, Chart A.18.

FIGURE 16-8: SHARE OF EURO INVOICING IN TRADE BETWEEN THE EU AND JAPAN

## 16.3.2 Vehicle currencies on foreign exchange markets

The foreign exchange market is a network of financial institutions that trade currencies among themselves. This is a huge market where, on any average day, some $1000 billion worth of exchanges take place (this amounts to more than one month of activity in the whole of the US economy). Each transaction must involve two currencies. Since there exist more than 180 currencies in the world, there are about 16 000 bilateral exchange rates.[15] If all these bilateral rates were traded, most of them (think of the exchange rate between the Samoan tala and the Honduran lempira) would involve very few trades, resulting in a host of shallow, hence inefficient and volatile, markets. This is why foreign exchange markets use the property of triangular arbitrage to considerably reduce the number of currency pairs that are traded.

The idea is simple and illustrated in Fig. 16-9. Consider two currencies A and B and their bilateral exchange rate $e_{AB}$. Currency A has an exchange rate *vis à vis* the dollar, $e_{A\$}$, and so does currency B, $e_{B\$}$. Once these two rates are known, the bilateral rate can be found as $e_{AB} = e_{A\$}/e_{B\$}$. In this example, the dollar is used as a currency vehicle and the implied bilateral rate $e_{AB}$ is called a cross-rate.

In practice, cross-rates are very rarely traded, the bulk of transactions involve a vehicle currency. Table 16-4 reports the percentage of trades that involve, on one side or another, the three main world currencies (the sum for all currencies would be 200 per cent since each transaction involves a pair of currencies). The share of the euro before 1999 is computed as the sum of the shares of all the currencies that were merged into the single currency, the last column displaying the particular share of the Deutschemark. The drop of the euro's share in 2001 corresponds to the elimination of exchange rate transactions among the currencies that joined the Euro area. Overall, the table reveals considerable stability. The pre-eminence of the dollar remains unchallenged.

---

[15] For $n$ currencies, there exist $n(n-1)/2$ bilateral exchange rates. Here 16 110 = $(180 \times 179)/2$

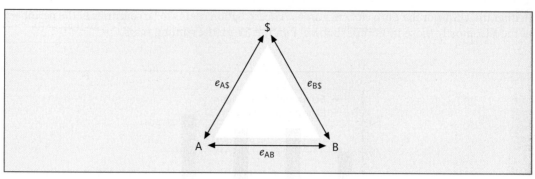

FIGURE 16-9: TRIANGULAR ARBITRAGE

|  | US dollar | Euro | Yen | Deutschemark |
|---|---|---|---|---|
| 1992 | 86.7 | 47.3 | 24.2 | 39.0 |
| 1995 | 90.0 | 48.5 | 26.0 | 36.1 |
| 1998 | 90.8 | 46.4 | 21.6 | 29.8 |
| 2001 | 90.4 | 37.6 | 22.7 | |

NOTE: If all currencies were listed, the sum would be 200 per cent since each exchange involves two currencies. Prior to 1999, the euro column reports the sum of its constituent currencies.

SOURCE: Bank for International Settlements Annual Report (2002).

TABLE 16-4: CURRENCY COMPOSITION OF EXCHANGE TRADING VOLUME (PER CENT)

### 16.3.3 Bond markets

Large firms and governments borrow on the international markets by issuing long-term debt, bonds. This is an enormous market. Figure 16-10 shows that the share of bonds issued in euros has taken off following the launch of the euro. This is not very surprising when we look at Fig. 16-5. The national bond markets have been promptly unified into a single euro market whose depth does not differ markedly from that of the dollar bond market. As a result, Europe can now claim its fair share of the market, and is increasingly doing so. Interestingly, the City of London has become the leading marketplace for this instrument while New York seems disinterested.

### 16.3.4 International reserves

All national central banks hold foreign exchange reserves to underpin trust in their currencies and, if need be, to intervene on foreign exchange markets. Currencies appropriate for this role as a store of value must be widely traded and be perceived as having long-term stability. As of 2001, the dollar made up 64.6 per cent of official reserves; the euro followed far behind with a share of 14.2 per cent, but ahead of the pound sterling (5.3 per cent), the yen (4.7 per cent), and the Swiss franc (1.1 per cent).

The launch of the euro has not yet altered the currency composition of reserves, but there are indications that it might. European countries at the periphery of the Euro area (including the UK) are gradually replacing dollars with euros. A number of developing countries have also announced their intention to do so, largely for political reasons.

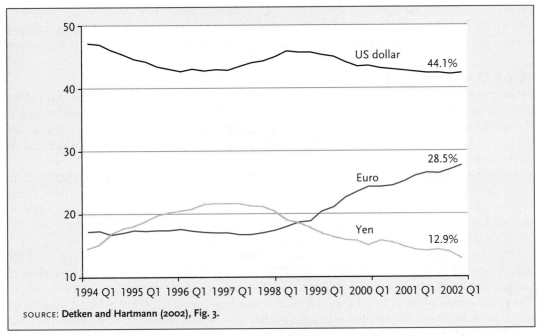

SOURCE: **Detken and Hartmann (2002), Fig. 3.**

FIGURE 16-10: CURRENCY SHARES OF INTERNATIONAL BONDS

## 16.3.5 The euro as an anchor

When a country does not let its exchange rate float freely, it must adopt an anchor, a foreign currency to which its own currency is more or less rigidly tied. The anchor, which works as a unit of account, can be a single currency or a basket of currencies. The link can be deliberately vague – known as a managed float – or quite explicit, ranging from wide crawling bands to the wholesale adoption of a foreign currency (for details, see Chapter 11).

By the end of 2001, out of some 150 currencies not classified as freely floating, 54 used the euro as an anchor in one way or another. For 35 of these cases, the euro is the only anchor, elsewhere it is part of a basket. Most of the countries that use the euro as an anchor are geographically close to the Euro area (Central and Eastern Europe, northern Africa) or have historical ties to one of its constituent legacy currencies (e.g. French-speaking Africa). Two former members of the Yugoslav Federation, Kosovo and Montenegro, have 'euroized', i.e. they have adopted unilaterally the euro as their own currency but are not part of the Eurosystem. Three countries operate a currency board tied to the euro: Bulgaria, Estonia and Lithuania.

## 16.3.6 Parallel currencies

Foreign currencies are also sometimes used alongside the domestic currency, fulfilling all three functions of means of payment, unit of account and store of value. Parallel currencies, as the phenomenon is called, emerge in troubled countries where the value of domestic currency is eroded by very rapid inflation or political instability. In most cases, the parallel currency circulates in cash form, but a number of countries also allow bank deposits.

The dollar is the universal parallel currency of choice but the Deutschemark has also been used in Central and Eastern Europe and in Turkey, and the French franc used to circulate widely in northern Africa and parts of Sub-Saharan Africa. In all these countries the euro has replaced the

Deutschemark and the franc. In Russia, its role remains modest but seems to be spreading. During the first six months following the introduction of euro notes in 2002, the ECB has shipped about 8 per cent of the total euros in circulation outside the Euro area. No doubt, more has leaked.

### 16.3.7 Does it matter?

In the minds of some Europeans, launching the euro also means challenging the supremacy of the dollar. Indeed, the dollar reigns supreme: it is the currency of choice for international trade; it is the first foreign currency that is held by individuals, corporations and central banks; and it is also the currency most widely used to denominate financial assets. The wish to displace the dollar is no doubt driven by political sentiment, but what about the economic advantages?

When international trade is invoiced in a foreign currency, importers and exporters face an exchange risk. Between the time a commercial contract is undertaken and payment is made, many months can elapse. In the intervening period, the exchange rate may change, imposing a risk on traders. They can purchase insurance (in the form of forward exchange contracts) but at cost. US firms, which mostly carry international transactions in dollars, thus enjoy some advantage.

In addition, 'greenbacks' are conspicuous all over the world. It is estimated that half of the dollars printed by the USA circulate outside its borders. Paper money is virtually costless to produce but, of course, it is not freely provided, being exchanged against goods, services or assets. The profit earned by the central bank, known as seigniorage, is a form of tax. When it is levied on residents, it is just one form of domestic taxation, but when levied on foreigners it represents a real transfer of resources. The value of expatriate dollars is about 3 per cent of the US GDP – a nice sum. However, once we realize that it has been accumulated over several decades, it is not really a significant source of revenue.

All in all, the economic benefits of having a world currency are quite modest. This explains why the ECB considers that a possible international role for the euro is something that it should neither encourage nor discourage. Beyond some legitimate pride, it does not really care.

## 16.4 Summary

- ■ Financial markets play a crucial role: they allow savers and borrowers to 'meet' to their mutual benefit. They also set a price on risk and offer ways to reduce exposure to risk via diversification.
- ■ Financial markets are also special. They are subject to economies of scale, they operate as networks, and they face important information asymmetries. As a consequence, they do not conform to the perfect market assumption. In particular, they are prone to systemic instability.
- ■ This instability, as well as other market failures, explains why financial systems are regulated and supervised. For the most part, regulation has been fully harmonized throughout the EU but supervision remains at the national level. This is unlikely to be a lasting solution, but further centralization faces stiff opposition.
- ■ Banks share these characteristics, which explains why competition does not take the form implied by perfect markets. In particular, large switching costs and information asymmetries explain why the adoption of the euro has not been followed by a deep restructuring of this industry. So far bank mergers and acquisitions have occurred mostly at the national level and few banks have tried to expand across borders. Differences in national regulations and some degree of protectionism on the part of supervisors also seem to limit changes. Plans have been drawn up to break this logjam.
- ■ For much of the post-1945 period, European financial markets were small and largely disconnected with each other. The reasons were limits to capital mobility and exchange risk.
- ■ Soon after the launch of the euro, bond markets have been unified. Stock markets, on the other hand, remain small. Some consolidation is taking place but the largest European exchange, London, remains undersized relative to New York or Tokyo.

■ The euro has the potential for challenging the dollar as an international currency, but old habits die hard and, despite some changes, the dollar's supremacy has not been seriously dented. Some progress has been achieved in trade invoicing, bond issuance and, in the periphery of the Euro area, the role as anchor for currencies and a parallel currency. Little change is reported regarding the function of a vehicle currency or foreign exchange reserves holdings.

## SELF-ASSESSMENT QUESTIONS

**1.** What is depth in financial markets? What is breadth? What are network externalities?
**2.** What is the phenomenon of inflation asymmetry? How can it explain why banks refuse credit to some customers? How can it contribute to systemic risk in financial markets?
**3.** List the reasons why banks are subject to increasing returns to scale. Why do fixed switching costs matter for competition among banks?
**4.** How do we know that bond markets have been unified in the Euro area upon the launch of the euro? Why has this not happened for stock markets?
**5.** Explain the home bias in equity holdings.
**6.** Explain how the three functions of money apply at the international level.
**7.** What is the phenomenon of gambling for resurrection? Why can it be lethal to financial markets?
**8.** Why is the ECB concerned with financial market integration?
**9.** How are banks responding to the introduction of the euro?
**10.** What is the difference between regulation and supervision? What are the dangers of decentralized supervision in the Euro area? Why is centralization resisted?
**11.** What is the difference between a parallel and a vehicle currency?
**12.** Where is the euro used as a parallel currency?

## ESSAY QUESTIONS

**1.** Banks can expand through either organic growth (winning new customers) or mergers and acquisitions. How does this distinction matter for the Single European Banking Market?
**2.** Imagine how financial markets could operate in the Euro area if regulation had not been harmonized.
**3.** Write the cases for and against bank regulation and supervision to be carried out inside the central bank. (Recently the UK has set up an independent agency, the Financial Services Authority, to regulate and supervise *all* financial institutions. Its website, http://www.fsa.gov.uk/, provides a justification for this set up.)
**4.** In which ways can the existence of different national financial system complicate monetary policy in the Euro area? What kind of measures could help the ECB?
**5.** The largest dollar banknote denomination is $100, the largest euro denomination is €500. This has led some to suspect that Europe wants to capture the market of currencies used for illegal transactions. What is your view of this motive?
**6.** How do you foresee the European banking system 20 years from now? Describe the number of major banks, their ownership structure and the way they compete.
**7.** What, in your view, can reduce the home bias in equity holdings across Europe?
**8.** As several countries from Central and Eastern Europe join the EU and then the Euro area, what can be the effects on their financial markets and on the financial markets in the rest of the Euro area?
**9.** Comment on the quote at the head of this chapter.
**10.** Finance is a major industry in the UK, accounting for some 5 per cent of its GDP. Does this characteristic makes membership to the Euro area rather more or rather less appealing?

## FURTHER READING: THE AFICIONADOS CORNER

General texts on financial markets and the euro:

Ingo, W. and R.C. Smith (2000) *High Finance in the Euro-Zone*, Financial Times/Prentice Hall, London.

Dermine, J. and P. Hillion (eds) (1999) *European Capital Markets with a Single Currency*, Oxford University Press, Oxford.

Gros, D. and K. Lannoo (1999) *The Euro Capital Market*, Wiley, Chichester.

Gaspar, V., P. Hartmann and O. Sleijpen (eds) (2003) *The Transformation of the European Financial System*, European Central Bank, Frankfurt.

On the structure of the European banking system:

*Structural Analysis of the EU Banking Sector*, ECB, November 2002 (available on http://www.ecb.int)

On financial integration:

Cabral, I., F. Dierick and J. Vesala (2002) *Banking Integration in the Euro Area*, Occasional Paper No.6, European Central Bank, Frankfurt.

On bank mergers and acquisition:

*Mergers and Acquisitions Involving the EU Banking Industry – Facts and Implications*, ECB, December 2000 (available on http://www.ecb.int)

Dermine, J. (2003) 'European banking, past, present, and future', in V. Gaspar, P. Hartmann and O. Sleijpen (eds) *The Transformation of the European Financial System*, European Central Bank, Frankfurt.

Bush, C. and G. DeLong (2003) 'Determinants of cross-border bank mergers: is Europe different', in H. Herrmann and R.E. Lipsey (eds) *Foreign Direct Investment in the Real and Financial Sector of Industrial Countries*, Springer Verlag.

On integration of European financial markets:

Adjaouté, K. and J.-P. Danthine (2003) 'European financial integration and equity returns: a theory-based assessment', in V. Gaspar, P. Hartmann and O. Sleijpen (eds) *The Transformation of the European Financial System*, European Central Bank, Frankfurt.

De Bondt, G. (2002) *Euro Area Corporate Debt Securities Market: First Evidence*, ECB Working Paper No. 164 (available on http://www.ecb.int)

Hartmann, P., A. Maddaloni and S. Manganelli (2003) 'The Euro area financial system: structure, integration and policy initiatives', *Oxford Review of Economic Policy*, **19** (1), 180–213.

Klaus, A., T. Jappelli, A. Menichini, M. Padula and M. Pagano (January 2002) *Analyse, Compare and Apply Alternative Indicators and Monitoring Methodologies to Measure the Evolution of Capital Market Integration in the European Union*, Report for the European Commission.

*The Lamfalussy Report* (a 2001 report on measures to take to support further integration of European financial markets): http://europa.eu.int/comm/internal_market/en/finances/general/lamfalussyen.pdf

On the international role of the euro:

Hartmann, P. (1998) *Currency Competition and Foreign Exchange Markets: The Dollar, the Yen, and the Euro*, Cambridge University Press, Cambridge.

ECB (December, 2002) *Review of the International Role of the Euro* (available on http://www.ecb.int).

Detken, C. and P. Hartmann (2002) 'Features of the Euro's role in international financial markets', *Economic Policy*, **35** (October), 555–69.

On stock markets in the accessing countries:

Claessens, S., R. Lee and J. Zechner (2003) *The Future of Stock Exchanges in European Union Accession Countries*, Centre for Economic Policy Research, London (available on http.//www.cepr.org).

## USEFUL WEBSITES
### Regulation and supervision:

The Basel Committee on Banking Supervision:
http://www.bis.org/bcbs/aboutbcbs.htm

Financial Stability Institute (FSI)
http://www.bis.org/fsi/index.htm

The ECB–CFS research network:
http://www.eu-financial-system.org

The Euro Homepage on the website of Giancarlo Corsetti:
http://www.econ.yale.edu/~corsetti/euro/

The Financial Services Action Plan website, full or reports and legal texts:
http://europa.eu.int/comm/internal_market/en/finances/actionplan/

## REFERENCES

Dermine, J. (2003) 'European banking, past, present, and future', in V. Gaspar, P. Hartmann and O. Sleijpen (eds) *The Transformation of the European Financial System*, European Central Bank, Frankfurt.

Detken, C. and P. Hartmann (2002) 'Features of the Euro's role in international financial markets', *Economic Policy*, **35** (October), 555–69.

Dornbusch, R. (2000) *Keys to Prosperity, Free Markets, Sound Money and a Bit of Luck*, MIT Press, Cambridge, MA.

ECB (November 2002) *Structural Analysis of the EU Banking Sector* (available on http://www.ecb.int).

ECB (December 2002) *Mergers and Acquisitions Involving the EU Banking Industry – Facts and Implications* (available on http://www.ecb.int).

ECB (December 2002) *Review of the International Role of the Euro* (available on http://www.ecb.int).

Hartmann, P., A. Maddaloni and S. Manganelli (2003) 'The Euro area financial system: structure, integration and policy initiatives', *Oxford Review of Economic Policy*, **19** (1), 180–213.

Klaus, A. T. Jappelli, A. Menichini, M. Padula and M. Pagano (2002) *Analyse, Compare and Apply Alternative Indicators and Monitoring Methodologies to Measure the Evolution of Capital Market Integration in the European Union*, Report for the European Commission.

" As the extent of economic integration approaches that of the United States, labour market institutions and labour market outcomes may also begin to resemble their American counterparts [...]. Full and irreversible economic integration may call for harmonization of social and market-market institutions within the European Union. "

**Giuseppe Bertola (2000)**

# 17 Economic Integration and Labour Market Institutions

17.1   National labour markets and economic integration
17.2   Labour market institutions
17.3   A European model: what's on the menu?
17.4   Summary

By fostering more integration and competition among its Member States, in particular by removing the exchange rate option, the EMU is challenging existing labour market practices. A running theme of this chapter is that labour market institutions aim at social objectives that often conflict with economic efficiency. The result is sharp controversies with many open questions and few generally accepted results. The chapter starts by recalling that the optimum currency area theory emphasizes the need for labour market flexibility. It then presents some of Europe's key labour market institutions, examining how they may be affected by the adoption of a single currency. At each step, the controversies resurface, as does the conflict between social and economic logics. The chapter concludes by reviewing a few stylized 'models', national attempts to find a balance between social cohesion and economic efficiency.

## 17.1 National labour markets and economic integration

A key message from the optimum currency area (OCA) theory, presented in Chapter 12, is that forming a monetary union among regions with limited labour mobility can be costly when an adverse asymmetric shock occurs. On that dimension, Europe does not score well. Yet, limited labour mobility may be at least partly compensated by flexibility in the labour market.

Indeed, in order to re-establish national competitiveness in the presence of adverse asymmetric shocks, domestic production costs must be reduced. Production costs include three main components: labour costs, the price of equipment and the price of imported materials. The latter two cannot be influenced since they are largely determined abroad. Labour costs, which typically amount to over 50 per cent of total production costs, then move to centre stage.

Despite important differences from one country to another, the European labour markets are among the most rigid in the world. The combination of low mobility and high labour market rigidity stands in sharp contrast with the situation in the USA, where high mobility and flexibility are understood to play an important role in the smooth working of the 'dollar area'.[1] At the heart of this question lies the fact that, compared to economic efficiency, European labour market-institutions have long attached considerably more weight to social justice and cohesion than in the US tradition.

The central question examined in this chapter is whether deepening economic (the Single Act, the adoption of the euro, financial market unification, enlargement) and political (the Convention and the ensuing Intergovernmental Conference) integration will lead to changes in European labour market institutions and, if so, how.

### 17.1.1 The landscape

Labour market institutions have already changed in many countries, partly in response to the massive rise in unemployment that occurred in the 1970s and 1980s. Figure 17-1 shows that, in the USA, the rate of unemployment has increased – a little – and then moved back down. The

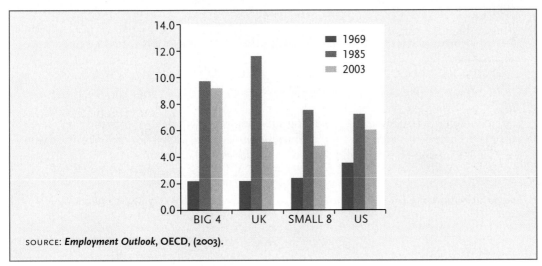

SOURCE: *Employment Outlook*, OECD, (2003).

FIGURE 17-1: UNEMPLOYMENT RATES (1969–2003)

---

[1] Chapter 13, especially section 13.3.4, provides the relevant evidence.

VI
PART

situation is similar in the UK and in many of the smaller EMU member countries. The four large European countries stand apart: unemployment there has gone up and up, never to fall again.[2]

Another worrisome indication is that, when they lose jobs, Europeans spend considerably more time finding new employment. Table 17-1 shows that in the Big Four countries nearly half of the unemployed workers have been out of work for at least one year. This proportion is significantly higher than in the other European countries, and an order of magnitude greater than the US rate. For some reason, European job markets do not allow for people to find jobs as easily as they can in the USA.

| France | Germany | Italy | Japan | Netherlands |
|---|---|---|---|---|
| 42.5 | 51.5 | 60.8 | 25.5 | 32.7 |

| Spain | Sweden | Switzerland | UK | USA |
|---|---|---|---|---|
| 47.6 | 26.4 | 29.1 | 28.0 | 6.0 |

NOTE: (a) Share of people unemployed for one year or more.

SOURCE: OECD.

TABLE 17-1: PROPORTION OF LONG-TERM [a] UNEMPLOYMENT – 2002 (PER CENT)

BOX 17-1: LABOUR MARKET CONCEPTS[3]

The unemployment rate ($u$) is the ratio between the number ($U$) of people who declare themselves unemployed (they have no job and are actively looking for one) and the labour force ($L$), the sum of the employed ($E$) and the unemployed ($U$):

$$u = \frac{U}{L}, \quad \text{where } L = E + U$$

The employment rate ($e$) is the remaining proportion of the labour force, composed of those who hold jobs:

$$e = \frac{E}{L} = 1 - u$$

The labour force is distinct from the working age population ($N$), defined conventionally as all valid people between 15 and 65 years old. Thus the working age population includes those who are employed and unemployed and those who are out of the labour force ($O$):

$$N = L + O = E + U + O$$

The participation rate ($p$) is the ratio of the labour force to the working age population:

$$p = \frac{L}{N} = 1 - \frac{O}{N}$$

[2] The Big Four are France, Germany, Italy and Spain. The Small Eight are: Austria, Belgium, Denmark, Ireland, Luxembourg, the Netherlands, Portugal and Sweden. Finland, which underwent a massive shock in the early 1990s is kept apart, as is Greece which resembles the big four.
[3] These concepts are further defined and explained in International Labour Organization (ILO) publications. See: http://www.ilo.org.

Unemployment is but one symptom of a malfunctioning labour market. Another gauge is the participation rate, the proportion of the working age population which either works or is actively looking for a job (Box 17-1 provides precise definitions of frequently used concepts). Figure 17-2 displays both indicators. It shows that where the rate of unemployment is high, participation tends to be low. In these countries, large segments of the population of working age do not work, sometimes because they are unemployed, but more often because they are simply not trying to find work. This concerns, for example, 38 per cent of working age Italians. So, what do they do?

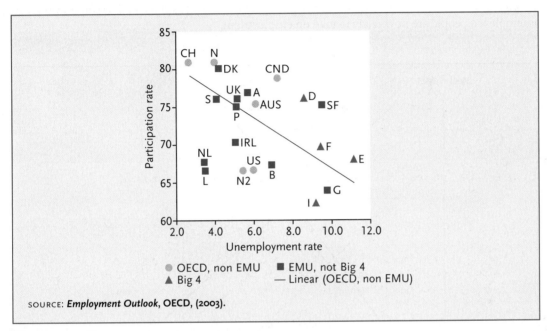

FIGURE 17-2: UNEMPLOYMENT AND PARTICIPATION IN 2003

Some of them may work in the black market or are involved in criminal activities, but the majority simply stay home, perhaps taking care of the family, but also because they are discouraged or not even interested in finding a job. The younger ones pursue studies for lack of better alternatives; the older ones have been asked to take early retirement. Others prefer to cash in welfare payments, unemployment benefits or, in some cases, permanent disability benefits – in the Netherlands, for instance, 2 per cent of the healthy looking working age population is unemployed while nearly 9 per cent qualify for permanent disability. In the end, most European countries devote considerable efforts towards educating their children and preparing them for a successful adult life, but they fail to provide them with rewarding job opportunities. This massive waste of resources reveals severe rigidities in the labour markets.

A broad-brush interpretation, to be explained and refined in the following sections, goes as follows. The flexible US labour markets have been able to recover easily from the bad shocks that hit the world in the 1970s and 1980s. Labour markets in the smaller EMU countries and the UK were quite inflexible, so the shocks led to a strong rise in unemployment, but successful reforms in the 1990s resulted in sharp improvements. The Big Four started with inflexible labour markets, implemented few reforms, and still face very high unemployment.

### 17.1.2 Labour market rigidities: a simple interpretation

If labour markets were operating just like any other market, there would be little concern. Faced with an adverse shock, say a decline in world demand for domestic goods and, indirectly, for domestic labour services, wages would decline. This is illustrated in Fig. 17-3 where employment is measured as total hours worked – the product of the number of people employed and the number of hours that they work. The demand for labour is downward-sloping since an increase in real wages leads firms to shift to more capital-intensive production processes or to relocate in cheaper countries. The supply of labour is upward-sloping to describe the tendency of workers to be willing to work for more hours when the pay is better, as well as the fact that some voluntarily unemployed people are now ready to take up employment.

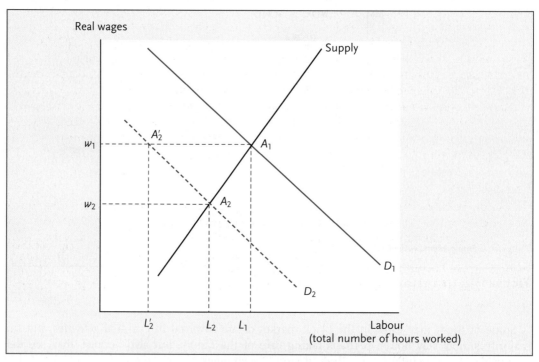

FIGURE 17-3: LABOUR MARKET ADJUSTMENT TO AN ADVERSE SHOCK

An adverse shock is represented by the leftward shift of the labour demand schedule. Employment – measured in total hours worked, an issue to which we return below – declines from $L_1$ to $L_2$ while real wages (nominal wages $W$ adjusted for the cost of living $P$, i.e. $w = W/P$) decline from $w_1$ to $w_2$. This is rather unpleasant, of course, but since we remain on the labour supply curve the drop in employment is voluntary.[4]

However, this is not the way real-life labour markets behave. The good that is bought and sold on this market is people's time, talent and effort. Quite obviously, this is a very special good, and indeed labour markets are highly organized and regulated. The price of labour, the real wage, is not set like the price of oil or corn, through bidding. It is negotiated, normally through collective

---

[4] The distinction between voluntary and involuntary unemployment, and the special characteristics of labour markets, are presented in standard textbooks. See, for example, Chapter 4 of Burda and Wyplosz (2001).

negotiations that bring together unions of employers and employees, and set for periods that extend usually to one year or more. In most countries, it is illegal for an employer to cut nominal wages. In addition, there often exists legislation that sets limits to dismissals and mandates compensatory payments. As a result, when the demand for labour declines, firms do not simply discard labour. Labour relations involve complex, sometimes adversarial, considerations: skills acquired on the job, the reputation of the employers as fair providers of jobs, possibly collective opposition including strikes.

To see how these things play out, and simplifying somewhat, consider that, for legal, social or fairness reasons, it is impossible to cut the real wage, which remains at the pre-shock level $w_1$. In that case, if firms are free to adjust the number of hours they hire (either by firing some workers or by reducing the number of hours worked by each worker), the situation is now described by point $A_2'$. Employment falls to $L_2'$, a larger reduction than when wages are flexible. More importantly, perhaps, point $A_2'$ is no longer on the labour supply curve. This means that some workers are frustrated and, indeed, the distance $A_1 A_2'$ represents involuntary unemployment, either people laid off but willing to work, or a forced reduction of hours worked and, therefore, labour income. If real wages are inflexible and tight restrictions exist on firing and hours worked, we could stay at point $A_1$ with no decline in employment but off the new labour demand curve. When firms are forced to keep more workers than they wish on their payrolls, their profits decline and may even turn negative. If the shock is mild, firms will react by cutting other expenses, chiefly investment in productive capacity, hurting future growth and employment. If the shock is severe and lasting, a number of firms will face bankruptcy, which involves collective labour dismissals, bringing us to point $A_2'$ through an indirect but dangerous route.

## 17.1.3 Economic and social reasons of rigidities

Behind the symbolic description of labour market rigidity in the previous section lies the fundamental observation that labour markets are somewhat special, but how and why? A number of observers complain that social and political norms severely reduce the economic effectiveness of labour markets by making them more rigid. They seem to long for a world in which labour markets would be 'normal'. This misses the crucial fact that, for a number of purely economic reasons, labour markets cannot be 'normal', and this section briefly explains why labour markets are special.[5]

### ECONOMIC MARKET FAILURES

Even in the dubious rejection of any social consideration, labour markets are characterized by a number of features that prevent them from operating as the textbook's perfect market paradigm. The main reasons, and their implications, can be summarized as follows:

- ■ *The possibility for one side of the market to exercise excessive power.* Dominant employers will set wages too low (as was widely the case a century ago), dominant trade unions will set the wages too high (as in closed shop firms where trade unions control hiring and working conditions). Rules and legislations are required to prevent dominance of either side. This includes instituting and regulating a negotiation process.
- ■ *A serious information asymmetry.* Employers cannot monitor work effort and skills, while employees cannot determine their own contributions to productivity, hence what their wages should be. As a consequence, wages cannot be set individually, hence the need for industry and national norms that further curtail free competition on the labour market.

[5] A good overview of the vast literature, with special emphasis on European labour markets, is Chapter 4 of the IMF's *World Economic Outlook*, April 2003.

- *Individual workers are highly vulnerable to uncertainty.* Losing a job, a normal occurrence in a market economy, leaves workers with no viable options. This calls for the adoption and funding of mandatory insurance (unemployment, health, retirement) and for limits on the ability to fire redundant workers.
- *Human capital.* Many individual skills are acquired on the job. Firms have an incentive to train their workers but such training involves spillovers that benefit society as a whole. A large pool of qualified workers allow all firms to efficiently respond to their market needs. Thus individual firms may not sufficiently invest in their workers' human capital. In addition, the human capital of unemployed workers not only depreciates their own loss but also society's loss. Compulsory training and re-training schemes, employment protection, hiring subsidies are some of the responses.

These specific features, sometimes called market failures, call for measures that inevitably reduce the economic effectiveness of labour markets. A key issue is how best to compensate for market failures, i.e. which solutions both limit the failures and preserve overall economic effectiveness.

### SOCIAL IMPERATIVES

To further complicate matters, economic effectiveness is not the only consideration that drives labour markets. Social considerations also matter a great deal, and apparently more so in Europe than elsewhere, such as the USA. A shortlist includes the following:

- *Fairness.* People are born different, with varying skills and fortunes. Education opportunities will further aggravate differences in the ability to perform on the labour markets. To a varying degree, our societies see these inherited and acquired disparities as unfair. Free and open education is one response, but other measures are required to protect the weaker during their professional lives. This includes minimum wages, social minima, established working conditions (hours, vacations, wage increases, etc.).
- *Income stability.* Uncertainty and aversion to risk, identified above as sources of economic failure, also include a social concern. Losing a job or becoming too ill to work does not only affect the worker, it also affects his family and the education opportunities of his children. This explains why welfare systems often go beyond the minimum insurance that economic effectiveness would justify.
- *Job security.* Beyond the economic aspects, having a 'good job' is contributing to people's sense of belonging to, and contributing to, society. Where unemployment is high, as in some suburban areas, significant segments of the population feel estranged from society, which leads to the deterioration of the quality of life, not to mention crime and insecurity. Bringing people, especially those less qualified, into professional life, may call for special programmes and subsidies.

### 17.1.4 The challenge of economic integration

There is no obvious 'first best' solution to the often conflicting economic and social logics. Throughout their political and social histories, different countries have established different labour market institutions which imply various degrees and forms of rigidity.

This is as it should be, but deep economic integration – including but not limited to monetary union – implies that labour market institutions become a strategic characteristic. The ability of firms to compete across borders on the single market depends on the ability of employers and employees to react adequately to adverse shocks which, as seen above, may require reductions in production costs and in the number of hours worked. In brief, the more inflexible is the labour market, the higher are the costs of dealing with an asymmetric shock.

Europe presents the unique combination of a high and increasing degree of economic integration and mostly inflexible labour markets. The adoption of a single currency further removes the possibility of devaluing the exchange rate to boost competitiveness and create jobs, closing a politically convenient door. Even the countries that have not joined the Euro area understand that · they cannot freely use the exchange rate to boost competitiveness. A crucially important question, therefore, is are our labour markets responding to this increasing challenge.

Given the special nature of labour relations – the outcome of specific historical and social traditions – these problems must first and foremost be dealt with at the national level.[6] The 'Lisbon strategy', adopted in 1999 and integrated in the Broad Economic Policy Guidelines,[7] pledges that Europe must 'become the most competitive and dynamic knowledge-based economy in the world capable of sustainable economic growth with more and better jobs and greater social cohesion'. A less enthusiastic reading of the Lisbon strategy is that the Heads of State have recognized that the benefits from economic integration require urgent treatment of the European labour markets. What type of treatment is the issue explored in the following sections.

## 17.2 Labour market institutions

Labour market institutions take various forms. They include specific legislation, the practice of collective negotiations, and a welfare state that provides resources to those who face hardships because of unemployment, health concerns and old age. We shall now review the economic implications of these institutions and note how they are affected by the deepening of economic integration. Two kinds of rigidities can be distinguished: those that prevent real wages from adjusting to market conditions and those that prevent employment from being adjusted. We refer to them as wage and employment rigidities. It is important to keep in mind that these institutions create rigidities as a by-product of their social aims.

### 17.2.1 Collective negotiations

A key feature that distinguishes labour markets from other markets is that job characteristics – wages, contract lengths, working conditions, hiring and firing practices – are not set freely between employers and employees. They are negotiated, usually within the framework of complex regulations, between powerful employer associations and trade unions. Collective negotiations have been introduced long ago to protect individual workers and counter-balance the power of employers, some of whom mistreated or underpaid their employees.

#### ECONOMIC ANALYSIS

Point $A$ in Fig. 17-4 shows the outcome of the free interplay of demand and supply in the labour market: employment is $E$ and the real wage is $w$. If wage negotiations succeed in raising the real wage to $w'$, the outcome is represented by point $B$: as labour is now more expensive, firms respond by aiming at production processes that are less labour-intensive and employment declines to $E'$. Yet, at the new, higher wage level $w'$, the amount of labour that workers wish to supply increases to $E''$, corresponding to point $C$. The result is involuntary unemployment represented by the distance $BC$. As described, collective negotiations are a source of wage rigidity, but they also affect the employment level and introduce employment rigidities.

While unemployed individuals are frustrated, those who retain jobs are satisfied with the pay rise and they support their union's action. Since the overwhelming majority of workers are employed, this outcome is democratically justified. In fact, the next step of the employees or their trade unions will be to ask for subsidies for the unemployed. Unemployment benefits are usually financed, partly at least, through taxes paid for by the employed who then feel that they are acting in full solidarity with their unlucky colleagues. Of course, the net after-tax wage is less than $w'$, but as long as it exceeds the after-tax wage corresponding to $w$,[8] the employed workers perceive the situation as beneficial to them and fair to the unemployed.

[6] Using the principles developed in Chapters 3 and 15, labour market policy exhibits limited spillovers and no returns to scale, while differing social norms imply significant heterogeneity and information asymmetries.

[7] The Broad Economic Policy Guidelines are presented in Box 15-1.

[8] This is the case when the taxes levied to serve unemployment benefits are not entirely borne by the workers. In most countries, the employers contribute to the unemployment benefit system.

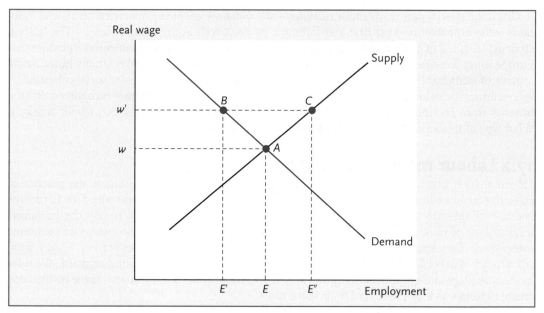

FIGURE 17-4: THE ROLE OF COLLECTIVE NEGOTIATIONS: AN ILLUSTRATION

## CENTRALIZATION OF NEGOTIATIONS

Labour market negotiations may take place at three different levels:

- at the plant level
- at the industry level, e.g. for all steel or retail trade workers
- at the national level, setting base wages for all workers, with particular firms or industries possibly topping up.

When they negotiate at the plant level, workers and their unions are keenly aware that high wage settlements could endanger their firm's competitiveness and result in job losses or, worse, in the firm's bankruptcy. This realization should exert a moderating influence on wage claims. Similarly, when trade unions conduct negotiations at the national level, they can see that the whole economy's competitiveness is at stake, which presumably leads them to be careful about the employment implications of high wages. At the industry level, in contrast, unions feel responsible for neither the entire economy nor any particular firm. They have little incentive to restrain their wage claims.

This reasoning suggests that we can expect that the adverse employment effects of trade union pressure for higher wages is more likely to be felt when negotiations are partially co-ordinated (e.g. occur at the industry level) than when they are either fully unco-ordinated or fully co-ordinated. This conjecture receives some support from Fig. 17-5 which displays the degree of co-ordination in wage bargaining on the horizontal axis (0 meaning no co-ordination and 1 full co-ordination at the national level), and the average employment ratio on the vertical axis. The curve is statistically fitted to represent as best as possible the link between co-ordination and employment.[9] Of course, it misses most points because of other effects to be examined further below, but it suggests indeed that the soft-belly in the middle is less employment-friendly than either extremes, with the fully unco-ordinated case the most conducive to low wages and high employment.

[9] Formally, this is a third-order polynomial trend.

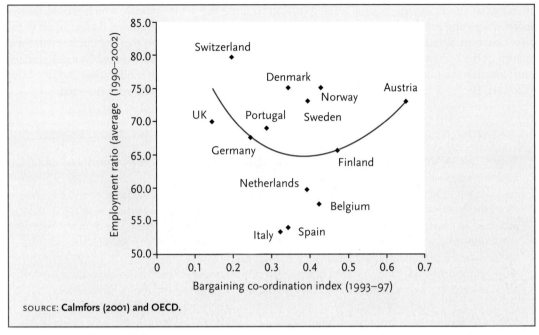

FIGURE 17-5: WAGE BARGAINING CO-ORDINATION AND EMPLOYMENT

## THE MONETARY UNION IMPACT

What effect, if any, will the monetary union have on wage negotiations? This is a hotly debated question. Some claim that we should now look at the Euro area as a single economic area, each country being a 'regional' unit. In that view national-level negotiations become 'regional-level', and industry-level negotiations only concern firms in a 'region'. *De facto*, all negotiations are then less co-ordinated than before as if all countries were moving to the left in Fig. 17-5, except of course those already in the far left. This implies more wage moderation and more employment for those countries currently in the middle range, which may be good news for some, but bad news for those initially to the right and moving towards the centre.

Another idea is that the removal of the 'exchange rate option' will lead to more wage restraint. When each country had its own currency, trade unions could aim at high wages and expect that any loss in national competitiveness would be compensated for through an exchange rate depreciation. This encouraged them to be quite hawkish during negotiations. With this option now gone, trade unions are expected to feel more pressure to moderate wage claims, especially at the co-ordinated end the spectrum. This would offset the bad news part in the previous reasoning. All in all, then, the adoption of a single currency should lead to more wage moderation and flexibility.

A different line of reasoning describes central banks and trade unions as engaged in a power play. Concerned that rising unemployment could lead to calls for easy money, central banks feel the need to tame wage claims and may adopt a more restrictive stance than otherwise warranted. When trade unions, on the other hand, push wages higher, they understand that the result may hurt employment, but they are ready to blame the central bank for being the true culprit with an excessively restrictive stance. In this game, each side tries to gain the upper hand. The Eurosystem has been vested with considerable powers; after all, it is the only true 'federal institution' in Europe. One possible conclusion, then, is that the Eurosystem, being more powerful than any of its national predecessors, is in a better position to tame the trade unions, which would deliver lower wages and more employment. This assumes, however, that trade unions do not adapt to the new situation. What if, facing this challenge, national trade unions form pan-European coalitions, mainly at the industry level? In Fig. 17-5, such an evolution would be represented by a generalized shift towards the middle of the centralization axis, precisely where wage moderation and flexibility is lowest. Box 17-2 looks at one important reason why such a shift has not yet happened.

### Box 17-2: The national base of trade unions

In contrast to almost any other institution in Europe, including football teams and central banks, trade unions remain organized exclusively along national lines. This stands in sharp contrast with their counterparts (i.e. firms) that are increasingly consolidating across borders. As a result, employers are able to play workers against each other, threatening to move their activities to other countries in order to extract concessions. It would be in the clear interest of employees to match the strategy of employers, so what is holding them? Most likely, the likelihood that trade unions would lose much of their existing power.

In many countries, trade unions effectively control labour negotiations even though they have few active members, as can be seen in Table 17-2. The table's first column displays the proportion of employees whose working conditions are set in collective negotiations where unions represent the employees. By and large, nearly all EU employees are covered by

| | Collective bargaining coverage (%) 1994 | Union density 1996–98 | Extension laws |
|---|---|---|---|
| Austria | 99 | 39 | Yes |
| Belgium | 90 | n.a. | Yes |
| Denmark | 69 | 76 | No |
| Finland | 95 | 80 | Yes |
| France | 95 | 10 | Yes |
| Germany | 92 | 27 | Yes |
| Ireland | n.a. | 43 | No |
| Italy | 82 | 37 | Yes |
| Netherlands | 85 | 24 | Yes |
| Norway | 70 | 55 | No |
| Portugal | 71 | 25 | Yes |
| Spain | 78 | 18 | Yes |
| Sweden | 89 | 87 | No |
| Switzerland | 53 | 23 | Yes |
| UK | 40 | 35 | No |
| USA | 17 | 14 | No |

SOURCE: Nickell (2002).

TABLE 17-2: TRADE UNIONS IN EUROPE

collective negotiations, the exception being Ireland and the UK. This is the case independently of the unions' representativity, as measured by union density – that is, the percentage of employees who are union members, reported in the second column. The most spectacular case is France, where only 10 per cent of employees are union members while nearly all of them are covered by negotiations conducted between employers and trade unions. How can that be? The answer is provided in the last column, which indicates the existence of legislation that automatically applies the outcome of collective negotiations to all firms in the same industry. The odd man out here are the Nordic countries where there is no such legislation but where a huge proportion of employees are union members. The reason for the apparent popularity of unions in the Nordic countries lies in another piece of legislation that arranges for unions to distribute unemployment benefits.[10]

The table illustrates a key feature of European labour market institutions: the influence of trade unions rests on legal arrangements. This feature can be contrasted with the Anglo-Saxon countries (Ireland, the UK and the USA) where no such laws exist and where, accordingly, unions are considerably less influential. Given that their power depends on national legislation, it is understandable that trade unions are highly reluctant to reorganize themselves at the EU level. To do so, they would have to be reassured that they would benefit from similar EU-wide legislation. Since social issues can only be decided at the EU level by majority voting, the unions have good reasons to fear that they would not enjoy a similar privilege, if only because the UK is likely to veto any such move in view of its own evolution, described in section 17.3.3 below.

## 17.2.2 Labour market institutions: the controversies

The obviously controversial[11] description of the effect of collective negotiations presented in the previous section is one example of the general observation that, relative to the free market outcome (point *A* in Fig. 17-5), collective labour market behaviour is a source of economically inefficient distortions which usually result in lower employment (point *B*), and therefore less production and less income. Employees and their trade unions call upon governments and lawmakers to provide broad public insurance against the many misfortunes of economic life, especially unemployment and illnesses, and to limit wage inequalities. This is how labour market institutions have been gradually built up as part of the welfare system.

Welfare systems have been designed to protect the weaker people, those that are unemployed or who have not acquired the skills that allow them to deal with changing economic conditions. Welfare systems also care for the sick and the elderly. At the same time, they interfere with economic efficiency and may be the source of widespread costs that can hurt everyone, even those that they intend to protect. Controversies abound, both in reaching a diagnosis and in contemplating reforms.

Continental Europe has developed extensive welfare safety nets, in contrast with the USA which relies more heavily on individual responsibilities. The unfavourable employment record of Europe is often seen as proof that too much welfare hurts more than it helps. Yet, some European countries (e.g. Sweden and Denmark) have established some of the most developed welfare systems and display low unemployment rates.

---

[10] Section 17.3 describes the Nordic and Anglo-Saxon models.
[11] A critique is presented in Dolado et al. (2000) who argue that the point of reference should not be the free market outcome but a situation where the employers dominate (technically, they are natural monopsonists in their labour market relations).

Growing economic integration – spurred by the monetary union – puts economic efficiency at a premium. In particular, the adoption of a single currency prevents the use of national monetary policies, inflation and the exchange rate, leading some to predict – with delight or awe – that Europe has no alternative to following the US way. Such a conclusion, too, is disputed. This section reviews some of the controversies and the equally controversial evidence produced so far.

## Minimum wages

Minimum wages exist in nearly every advanced economy. They aim at two main social objectives. First, minimum wage legislation is meant to protect the less well educated and more vulnerable people from having to accept meagre compensation, no matter how low it is, simply because they need to earn a living. Indeed, below-poverty line wages can be found in countries where minimum wage legislation does not exist. Second, minimum wage legislation intends to reduce inequality by compressing the wage scales. Even though there exist more economically efficient ways of dealing with inequality – taxes and transfers – minimum wages have historically been seen as a crucial tool and remain a powerful symbol.

Minimum legislation may carry economic costs, as can be understood by reinterpreting Fig. 17-5. In the absence of minimum wages, poorly trained workers would earn $w$ as indicated by the free-market equilibrium point $A$. If the minimum wage is $w'$, these workers will find less jobs. Thus minimum wage legislation is a source of wage rigidity that both protects and hurts the less-qualified workers. It protects those who have a job and hurts those that cannot find one because they are perceived as too expensive given their productivity.[12]

A particularly disquieting implication is that the less-qualified workers, especially the younger ones, are the first to be fired during economic downturns, as illustrated by the case of France in Fig. 17-6. Thus, protecting the less-skilled and weaker workers increases their vulnerability to

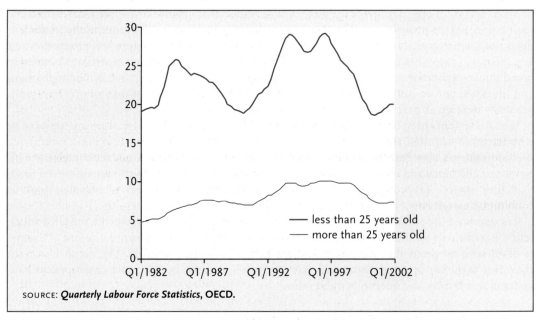

FIGURE 17-6: UNEMPLOYMENT IN FRANCE BY AGE GROUP (PERCENTAGE OF GROUP LABOUR FORCE)

[12] Here again, the conclusion can be challenged following the argument presented in footnote 11.

economic uncertainties. This is likely to occur in the Euro area when a country faces an adverse asymmetric shock.

A key question, therefore, is whether the minimum wage legislations in existence throughout Europe will be rethought to take into account the new conditions created by the adoption of a single currency. Trade unions are opposed to any reduction in minimum wages. Instead, they call for the harmonization of national legislations, usually taking as benchmark those countries where minimum wages are highest. Their view is that competition across the Euro area risks triggering a race to the bottom whereby each country attempts to boost its competitiveness by reducing minimum wages – and the whole social protection system as well. They foresee a cycle whereby each country will respond to others' lower standards in a vain effort at becoming more competitive, in effect leading to a dismantling of minimum wage legislations throughout Europe and leading to more inequalities.

Trade unions further consider that if unemployment remains high in Europe it is because firms transfer production facilities to countries where labour is cheap and poorly protected. Box 17-3

---

### Box 17-3: Social dumping when rebuilding East Germany[13]

On 1 March 1996, a minimum wage of DM18 per hour was introduced for all construction work performed in Germany; this minimum wage applied irrespective of both the worker's nationality and the country where his or her employment contract was drafted and signed. The relevant piece of legislation was passed almost simultaneously with another that substantially reduced the unemployment benefits payable in the construction sector. The two laws were quite transparently related, and motivated by the peculiar situation that saw increasing unemployment among German construction workers at the same time as East German reconstruction proceeded at the hands of a veritable army of workers operating under contracts won by British, Portuguese and Italian construction firms (under Single Market rules that require public procurement contracts to be open to competitive tendering).

Out of about 1.3 million German construction workers, roughly 400 000 were unemployed in early 1997, and about the same number of foreign workers were legally or illegally employed on German construction sites. In Berlin alone, alongside 40 000 German workers, there were 30 000 workers from other EU countries, some 8000 legal East Europeans, and an estimated 25 000 illegal workers; but there were also about 17 000 unemployed German construction workers. The hourly wage of foreign workers, in the neighbourhood of DM14 before the minimum wage law became binding, was lower even than the generous, and essentially open-ended, unemployment benefits of German unemployed construction workers.

German construction businesses, but not employers at large, were in favour of the minimum wage law. Not surprisingly, a heated debate ensued in Brussels and Strasbourg as foreign construction firms and governments contested the validity of the legislation. Eventually, the European Commission issued the Posted Workers Directive (96/71/EC) which, while restating the principle of free labour mobility in the Single Market, admitted that this and similar national legislation was legal. The Directive is very carefully phrased and purports to support freedom of service provision and fair competition; to justify the imposition of minimum compensation standards, the Directive invokes 'Social Clause' arguments, purporting to prevent 'exploitation' of guest workers.

---

[13] This box is adapted from Bean et al. (1998), pp. 49–50.

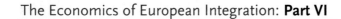

provides a vivid example of this process. Their conclusion is that such transfers ought to be discouraged by appropriate legislation, including protection against unfair competition seen as 'social dumping'. This view is opposed by free-trade advocates who see economic benefits accruing when trade deepens between high- and low-wage countries: income levels grow in poor countries and rich countries specialize in high value added production. Furthermore, the accession to the European Union of countries in Central and Eastern Europe means free trade with low-wage economies that cannot be hindered by protectionist measures.

### UNEMPLOYMENT INSURANCE

Becoming unemployed is a major risk faced by every worker. In principle, whenever possible, any risk ought to be covered by some form of insurance. Furthermore, because people often underestimate the risk of becoming unemployed, insurance must be compulsory, a logic that applies to many other major risks like health, home fire or car accidents. A special feature found in most countries, however, is that the compulsory insurance premium is levied on wages and that the insurance is provided publicly, not by private companies. Here again, the social rationale is clear: unemployment insurance is perceived as solidarity between those who have jobs and those who have lost theirs.

The economic side of unemployment insurance is worrisome, however, for two main reasons. First, since the insurance is financed out of wages, it acts as a payroll tax, which may hurt employment as explained below. This may lead to a vicious circle: as more people become unemployed, the payroll taxes must be raised, which then increases unemployment, which further calls for higher payroll taxes, and so on. Second, when unemployment benefits are generous, the unemployed can afford to be more choosy when they look for a new job. When the benefits are a significant proportion of the wage rate (this proportion is called the benefit ratio) and are served over a long period of time, the incentives to accept a job that does not fit perfectly the skills and geographical preferences of the unemployed are low. The result is an 'unemployment trap', whereby the unemployed in effect cannot afford to accept job offers once they compare the wages that they would get with the unemployment benefits they receive. The comparison is even less favourable when considering transport and other costs – including child and house care – involved when working. Overall, unemployment benefits are a source of employment rigidity.

Figure 17-7 displays the proportion of people who have been unemployed for more than 12 months (unemployment duration) and an index of generosity of the unemployment benefit system. This index is computed as the product of the replacement ratio and the legal maximum duration of unemployment benefits; it measures the maximum amount of insurance that can be drawn upon becoming unemployed. The figure suggests, and more detailed studies confirm, that the unemployment benefit system reduces the intensity of job search by the unemployed. In the end, unemployment insurance serves a crucial social purpose but becomes an additional source of unemployment.

If, as predicted by the OCA theory, EMU membership – and more generally, deepening integration – results in wider GDP and employment fluctuations, it is important that unemployed workers be well protected, but also that they quickly find jobs when the adverse asymmetric shock has gone. Generous unemployment benefits stand in the way of this process and may therefore amplify the costs of monetary union membership. Restructuring the unemployment insurance systems to minimize their disincentive effects could help, but the economic logic is strongly opposed by the trade unions as they emphasize the social needs of workers subject to more employment volatility.

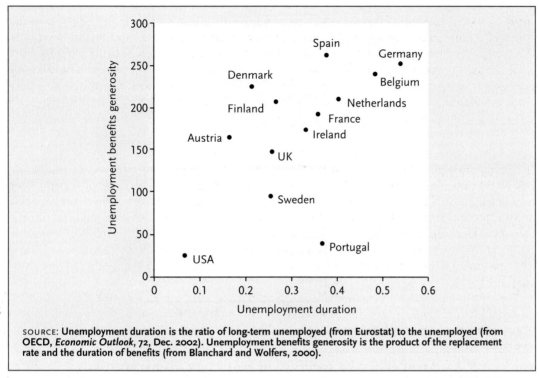

SOURCE: **Unemployment duration is the ratio of long-term unemployed (from Eurostat) to the unemployed (from OECD,** *Economic Outlook***, 72, Dec. 2002). Unemployment benefits generosity is the product of the replacement rate and the duration of benefits (from Blanchard and Wolfers, 2000).**

FIGURE 17-7: LONG-TERM UNEMPLOYMENT AND UNEMPLOYMENT BENEFITS (2001)

## EMPLOYMENT PROTECTION LEGISLATION

One response advocated by those who emphasize the social aspects of unemployment is to further restrict firing by firms. Nowadays firms face a number of legislative barriers when they want to dismiss employees. These restrictions include procedures that can be lengthy and cumbersome, advanced notice, mandatory severance pay, the possibility of appeal against unfair dismissal, regulations on fixed-term contracts, etc. Figure 17-8 presents an index designed to measure the level of restrictions on dismissals. This index, which corresponds to the situation in the late 1990s, ranges from 0 (no restriction) to 6 (highest level of restrictions).

The social justification is clear, but what are the economic effects? The evidence is that strict legislation indeed limits dismissals during economic downturns. As firms face higher costs of dismissal, they tend to retain a larger workforce than they would otherwise require. However, during better times firms anticipate that they may not be able to adjust their workforce in future bad times, and they limit hiring. Overall, there is no evidence that employment protection legislation raises or lowers employment, but it is an important source of employment rigidity.

## PAYROLL TAXES

Payroll taxes introduce a wedge between labour costs borne by the employer and the income received by the employees. At unchanged employer's revenue, payroll taxes raise labour costs and discourage the demand for labour. Conversely, at unchanged cost to the employer, the taxes reduce earned incomes and discourage the supply of labour. Either way, the higher the taxes, the lower the level of employment.[14] Like any other tax, payroll taxes are distortionary. In this case, the distortion

---

[14] The effect on unemployment is less clear-cut.

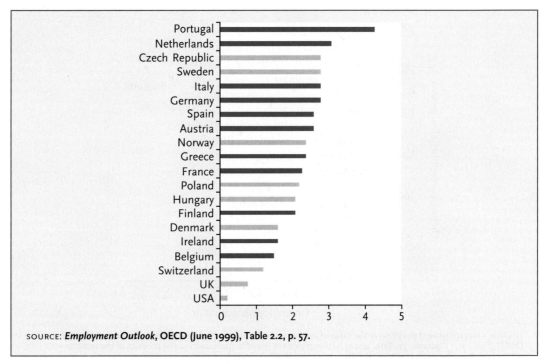

SOURCE: *Employment Outlook*, OECD (June 1999), Table 2.2, p. 57.

FIGURE 17-8: A MEASURE OF OVERALL STRICTNESS OF PROTECTION AGAINST DISMISSALS

is especially large because workers have no substitute to working for earning a living, unless they move to the black market, which many do.

Figure 17-9 shows the average size of payroll taxes as a percentage of gross wages, i.e. wages including taxes paid by employers and employees. The differences are large. As economic integration deepens, a number of countries have called for tax harmonization, including in the labour markets, as they fear that different taxes distort competition. They fear a race-to-the-bottom in a tit-for-tat game where countries attempt to make labour cheaper by cutting payroll taxes. Other countries strongly reject the idea of harmonization. They point out that countries with large tax wedges could significantly increase employment by reducing them. Cutting payroll taxes, however, is not politically easy because these taxes are used to finance the welfare state, unemployment and health insurances and retirement pensions. Either these welfare payments must be reduced, which would face strenuous opposition, or other taxes must be raised, which is unlikely to be popular.

## 17.2.3 The integration impact

### CONFLICTING ECONOMIC AND SOCIAL GOALS

Summing up and simplifying somewhat, labour market institutions are designed to protect employees but at cost in terms of economic efficiency, the most visible of which is low employment and, quite possibly, constrained growth. Economic integration is challenging these institutions by sharpening the conflicting needs for social protection and economic efficiency. On the one hand, with a reduced ability to conduct macroeconomic stabilization, each country may find the general economic environment more volatile. This raises the value of insurance and should, if

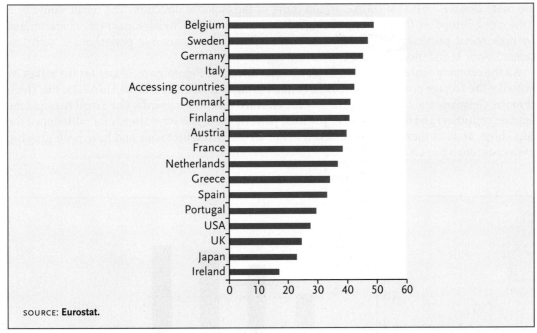

FIGURE 17-9: PAYROLL TAXES (2001)

SOURCE: **Eurostat.**

anything, call for a strengthening of the welfare state. On the other hand, economic integration means more competition within Europe, favouring countries with flexible labour markets. The contrast between the unemployment and growth performances in the Small Eight and the Big Four well illustrates the stakes.

The current equilibrium between social concerns and economic efficiency is, in each country, the result of its history, which has often witnessed deep conflicts that remain vivid in the national conscience. Most European countries currently put a high weight on social concerns relative to economic efficiency, while the USA and the UK tilt the other way. The question is whether deeper integration will shake existing equilibria and, if so, in which direction.

In the USA, wage flexibility is high and restraints on hiring and firing are limited. The European countries have often used inflation and exchange rate changes to re-establish competitiveness. This instrument is now lost at the national level. Deeper integration means less asymmetric national and more symmetric shocks.[15] Increasingly, the Euro area will resemble the USA. Does this mean that European labour markets too will evolve towards the US model? Section 17.3 deals with the socio-political aspects of this crucial question; here we confine ourselves to the economic issues.

## TWO SCENARIOS: STATUS QUO VS 'TWO-SPEED EUROPE'

As the degree of competition within the Euro area increases, can labour market institutions continue to deeply differ from one country to another? Higher competition raises the economic costs of the social safety nets. Labour market inflexibility will exact higher costs in terms of unemployment and reduced growth potential. The ability of workers to move across borders may result in migration of unemployment-prone workers to those countries that offer the best protection, while the most enterprising and better educated move to countries where labour markets

[15] See section 12.4.

are more flexible. Firms, of course, would move in the opposite direction. The result would be a 'two-speed Europe', with one group of laggard countries acting as 'welfare magnets', characterized by high social protection and heavy tax burdens, alongside economic powerhouses with low unemployment and more moderate taxes and regulations.

All the economic incentives seem to play in this direction. Figure 17-10 illustrates the stakes by showing the average growth rates in three country groupings, the UK and the USA. The Big Three (France, Germany and Italy) are the largely unreformed potential laggards. The Small Nine (all the smaller countries) and the UK are the potential powerhouses, and have already far outstripped the Big Three. Most of them have undertaken major labour market reforms and have been growing even faster than the USA.[16]

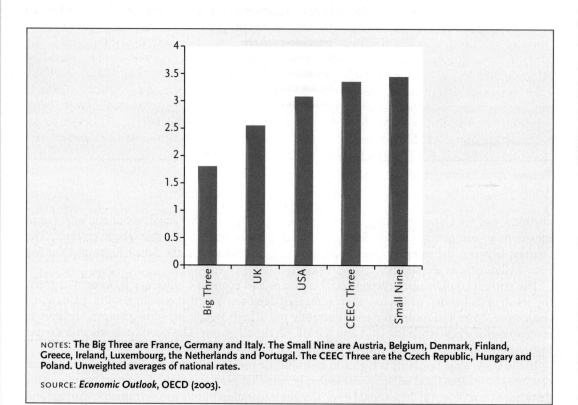

NOTES: **The Big Three are France, Germany and Italy. The Small Nine are Austria, Belgium, Denmark, Finland, Greece, Ireland, Luxembourg, the Netherlands and Portugal. The CEEC Three are the Czech Republic, Hungary and Poland. Unweighted averages of national rates.**

SOURCE: *Economic Outlook*, OECD (2003).

FIGURE 17-10: AVERAGE GDP GROWTH RATES (1995–2003)

What could prevent the 'two-speed Europe' scenario? One possibility is that labour mobility will remain low in Europe.[17] The attachment of Europeans to their land is rooted in both tradition and language/cultural differences. But the incentives to migrate are also stifled by the social safety nets. Unemployment insurance makes it highly unappealing to face the substantial economic and emotional costs of migration while wage compression reduces the expected benefits, assuming that employment opportunities are plentiful. Thus, in a way, the status quo is quite stable.

---

[16] Greece is the exception.
[17] Chapter 13 presents some evidence on labour mobility.

What would be the effect of the 'two-speed Europe' scenario? As a number of countries go their own way and significantly reduce the generosity of their welfare systems and boost labour flexibility, competition in the good markets turns into a competition among welfare systems, with a race to the bottom towards the US model. Alternatively, the 'two-speed Europe' scenario could generate its own antidote, the harmonization of welfare systems designed to suppress a competition often seen as 'social dumping'.

It is difficult to guess which scenario, if any, will prevail. Understandably, the Big Three governments are concerned. They have argued in favour of minimum social norms, a way of imposing their own rigidities on leaner competitors, which is resisted by many of the smaller, but less powerful countries. The outcome has been the Lisbon Strategy, a grand declaration by the Heads of State and Governments. As explained in section 17.1.4, the strategy calls for annual Social Summits that review national experiments and reform progress and could be used for anything from shaming countries that do not reform their labour markets to setting social minima. The likely agreement, following the Convention, that decisions on social matters require unanimity, suggests that the Social Summits will not make any decision.[18] It reflects deep divisions among EU Member States. Of interest, too, is the position that the newly accessing countries will take. Figure 17-10 shows that they have a strong growth potential and may feel close to the powerhouse countries, yet they have inherited from their past a deep taste for social protection. Overall, so far, the Social Summits oscillate between harmonization and the search for economic efficiency. One thing is sure: the US model is not popular with European voters.

# 17.3 A European model: what's on the menu?

The general distaste for the US approach is deeply rooted. The Europeans largely reject what they see as unfettered individualism which creates harsh conditions for those who are unable to fight for themselves, being unemployed, poorly educated, sick or simply elderly. A sense of solidarity and egalitarianism prevails, even if it hurts economic performance. Yet, there is no single European model. Different countries have built up different welfare systems and seem generally attached to them. Thus the debate seems to be more in favour of adopting one of the European models rather than the economically better performing US system. The Lisbon Strategy rests on benchmarking national experiences and evolving towards a common model that takes the best of each. This is one possibility, but the risk is to build a multi-headed monster that has desirable features but does not add up to a coherent lot.

## 17.3.1 The continental model

The continental model[19] rests on a general refusal to leave the labour markets to economic forces. It best describes the situation in Austria, Belgium, France and Germany. Trade unions are given, often by law, an important role on all labour issues and even sometimes in general management, even if membership is low. Labour market legislation is detailed and concerns all aspects of employment. In many countries, negotiations take place at the industry level, the soft mid-point in Fig. 17-5. It usually combines strict restrictions on dismissals, fairly high minimum wages and generous unemployment benefits. As a result, the employment rate is relatively low and unemployment spells tend be longlasting. In addition, as seen in Fig. 17-11, the number of hours worked by the average worker tends to be low and inflexible, so that required changes in demand for labour fall more on the number of people employed than on adjusting the use of those employed.

---

[18] See Chapter 3 for an analysis of decision making rules.
[19] As with the other 'models' described in the following sections, generalizing comes at the expense of ignoring some important details. This should be kept in mind. This section borrows from Bertola et al. (2001).

In a way, the citizens are pampered by a highly developed welfare system that follows every citizen 'from cradle to grave', including free high-quality education, early and generous retirement and all-encompassing health insurance. They enjoy short working days and long vacations. Unemployment is generally high – with some exceptions[20] – and longlasting, but benefits protect those who do not have jobs. No surprise, therefore, that the welfare system and the continental way of life is staunchly defended by most citizens, who are willing to pay high taxes in exchange for the sense of security and the more leisured lifestyle that they receive in return.

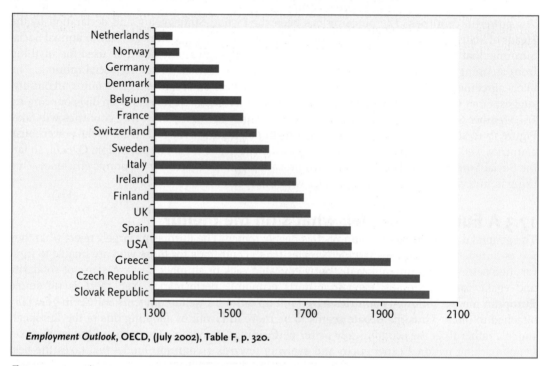

*Employment Outlook*, OECD, (July 2002), Table F, p. 320.

FIGURE 17-11: AVERAGE ANNUAL HOURS WORKED IN 2001

This model is directly threatened by economic integration which rewards economic efficiency and triggers a competition among welfare states. Paradoxically, the continental countries of Europe, which have been at the forefront on integration moves, now face serious threats to their social model. Unsurprisingly, their reaction is to call for the harmonization of social arrangements, hoping that their model will become the benchmark.

## 17.3.2 The Nordic model

The Nordic countries – the Netherlands can also be associated with this model – offer the most extensive welfare systems in the world. These are also countries in which some of the highest taxes prevail, the proceeds of which finance extensive and high-quality public services. At the same time, the approach to labour markets combines generosity with strictness. In Sweden, for example, the unemployment benefit rate is one of the highest but it is served for a short period of time with no

---

[20] The Netherlands stands out for one of the lowest unemployment rates in Europe but a surprisingly large number of workers are on permanent health disability and receive benefits similar to those served to the unemployed.

exceptions, thus encouraging workers to actively search for and accept jobs (Fig. 17-7). Sweden has pioneered active labour market policies that, in contrast with passive benefits, promptly encourage those who become unemployed into training and orientation schemes designed to limit the duration of unemployment spells – in effect, reducing the temptation to draw on welfare payments.

The Nordic countries are also deeply attached to income equality. A high degree of equality is achieved by the combination of wage compression and heavy, progressive taxation. Figure 17-12 displays the ratio between the average earnings of the 10 per cent best-paid population to those of the 10 per cent at the bottom of the scale. It confirms that the Nordic countries are world leaders on this dimension. Such a degree of wage compression is frowned upon by many economists who believe that there is little reward left for hard work and risk taking, and therefore may hurt growth. On the other hand, a high degree of equality underpins social cohesion and reduces crime, both of which may help to achieve economic efficiency and support growth.

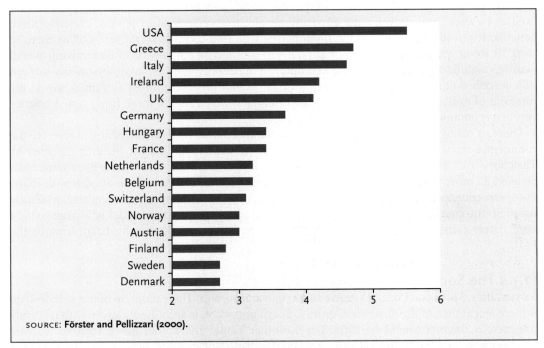

SOURCE: **Förster and Pellizzari (2000).**

FIGURE 17-12: EARNINGS INEQUALITY IN 1999

From a socio-political viewpoint, the Nordic model combines a unique degree of social cohesion and solidarity with relative harshness in dealing with unemployment. High taxes, extreme income equality, and an all-encompassing welfare state that may stifle individual initiatives are often identified as the price to pay. All in all, by most measures, the Nordic countries display an economic performance (growth, employment) on a level with the other European economies. Their populations do not show any willingness to shake their time-honoured welfare state.

In the benchmarking exercise associated with the Lisbon Strategy, the Nordic model tends to receive high marks for the fight against unemployment, but its large welfare state is often seen as excessive, at least regarding the rate of taxation that it requires. On the other hand, the Scandinavians are adamantly opposed to the continental model which they regard as socially and economically inefficient.

### 17.3.3 The Anglo-Saxon model

Ireland and the UK are usually associated with this model. The UK had long been sharing the continental Europe model, with powerful trade unions influential beyond the confines of the labour markets. Margaret Thatcher changed all that in the 1980s whom she purposely decided to weaken trade unions and then proceeded to dismantle many of the labour market measures that protect the weakest on the grounds that they also impeded competition and reduced economic growth. She imposed decentralized labour negotiations (Fig. 17-5) and in many ways took Britain away from the continental model towards the US model.

The results, once highly controversial, are now undisputed, even by Thatcher's former political adversaries.[21] The rate of unemployment is one of the lowest in Europe, the rate of employment is one of the highest and Britain, long one of the slowest-growing economies in Europe, is now in the leading pack. At the same time, inequalities are high and public services rank among the worst in Europe.

More recently, Britain has started to experiment with new active unemployment policies. The 'welfare to work' programme aims at paying people to work instead of serving unemployment benefits. It provides subsidies to the unemployed who find jobs; these subsidies allow them to work for lower wages, and hence to be attractive to prospective employers, while receiving overall earnings significantly higher than the unemployment benefits, thus escaping the unemployment trap described in section 17.2.2. Together with the Scandinavian countries, Britain is now at the forefront of exploring new labour market institutions which aim at a more finely tuned balance between economic efficiency and social cohesion.

Unless a major reversal occurs, the British population shows no sign of wishing to revert to the continental model. They support many of the US model labour market features installed by Thatcher – and reinforced by her successors from both parties – but would like to limit some of its excesses in other areas such as health and public services. This puts Britain at odds with many European countries. The UK will not support any move towards harmonization that would be based on the continental model, nor does it wish to adopt the Swedish model of a large welfare state. These considerations play an important role in Britain's lack of enthusiasm towards the EMU.

### 17.3.4 The Southern European model

Greece, Italy, Spain and Portugal form a rather disparate group. Their adoption of the welfare state is more recent than in the previous countries. Social protection is accordingly lower, with relatively ungenerous unemployment benefits. On the other hand, this model has a tradition of very strict employment protection. Spain, for example, has only recently started to dismantle the paternalistic approach that characterized the Franco dictatorship, when temporary work was illegal.

This model puts relatively limited emphasis on wage equality, relying instead on a still lively tradition of sharing incomes within the extended family, especially between parents and children. Minimum wages, where they exist, are sufficiently low not to be binding. This model, therefore, tends to generate more employment than wage rigidities.

### 17.3.5 The new accessing countries: another model?

The accession to the European Union of half a dozen former Soviet bloc countries may bring in yet a new model. Their citizens recognize that the Soviet model has failed but they are not willing to

---

[21] Prime Minister Tony Blair is rumoured to having said 'we are all Thatcherites now'. He has explicitly stated the view that Margaret Thatcher was right about the economy but that he disagreed with her social policies.

give it up wholesale. Half a century of communism has developed a taste for wage equality, public subsidies and cradle-to-grave social services. Indeed, in many countries, the citizens have elected politicians associated with the former communists.

Their early experience with markets has been one of deep and longlasting recessions, usually coupled with a surge in unemployment. They have thus discovered that capitalism can be harsh. As they are preparing themselves to face new disruptions in the wake of their accession to the European Union, they seem to feel closer to the continental model. In many respects, they are already there, but not firmly.

It may well be that these new EU members will find themselves in the position of arbitrating the debates on the Luxembourg Process. Their attachment to social cohesion makes them true Continental Europeans. They have no model to propose, which allows them to judge with some detachment what works and what does not.

## 17.4 **Summary**

- The employment effects of an adverse shock are reduced when the real costs of labour can be reduced. One solution is to depreciate the exchange rate, but this option is ruled out in the Euro area and frowned upon inside the Single Market. Asymmetric shocks, therefore, are best dealt with when the labour market is flexible.
- European labour markets, however, are known for being rather inflexible. The existing labour market institutions have been created to deliver social cohesion more than economic efficiency. Deepening economic integration challenges these institutions.
- A number of economic reasons explain why labour markets do not operate as in the perfect competition paradigm. Power (of employers as well as of workers' unions) plays an important role. Serious information asymmetries render individual wage-setting impossible. Individual workers are highly vulnerable to job losses and need appropriate insurance. Finally, investment in human capital generates significant spillovers. For all these reason, labour markets require specific institutions that are likely to interfere with economic effectiveness.
- Social concerns further explain specific features of labour market institutions. There is limited tolerance for the kind of income inequality that the unfettered market delivers. Income stability matters not just for the individual workers, but for their families. Likewise, the lack of job security has widespread consequences for society as a whole.
- There is no best way of trading-off social aims and economic efficiency. As a result, each arrangement is highly controversial, as is any reform proposal.
- Trade unions, for instance, have an important role to play in protecting workers from the harshness inherent in economic efficiency and in promoting some degree of equality across wage-earners. At the same time, trade unions have become powerful institutions that protect the interests of their members – the employed – occasionally at the expense of the unemployed.
- In general, labour market institutions – minimum wages, unemployment benefits, employment protection legislation – all have a useful role to play, but they do not come without economic costs, and many of these costs are likely to rise as economic integration deepens.
- There is general agreement that the high level of unemployment in Europe must be rolled back. The governments have agreed to review the situation at their annual Social Summits and to learn from each other's experience – the so-called benchmarking exercise.
- While Europeans generally reject the US model of individualism, they profoundly differ on how best to combine social cohesion and economic efficiency. At one end, the continental model clearly favours social cohesion, sharing some aspects of the Southern European model. At the other end, the British model represents a sharp move towards the US model. The Nordic model is yet another way of combining an all-encompassing welfare state and strict limits to inefficient social expenditures. The newly accessing countries, which have come a long way from their days in the Soviet bloc, have still to decide on the model that best suits each of them.

## The Economics of European Integration: **Part VI**

SELF-ASSESSMENT QUESTIONS

**1.** Figure 17-13 depicts the evolution of the unemployment rate in France and in the UK, distinguishing between a trend and deviations from the trend. In the UK, the rate tends to deviate more from its trend than in France. Can you explain this pattern?

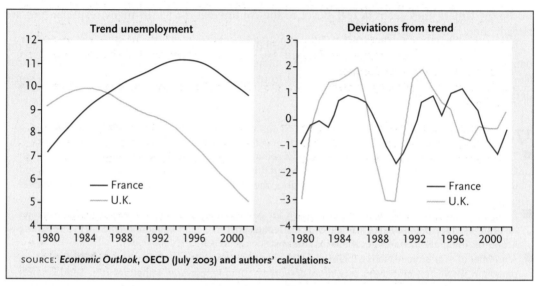

SOURCE: *Economic Outlook*, OECD (July 2003) and authors' calculations.

FIGURE 17-13: UNEMPLOYMENT IN FRANCE AND THE UK

**2.** List the sources of wage rigidities and of employment rigidities.

**3.** Why can deeper integration make existing labour market institutions ill-suited?

**4.** Why is it the case that we observe less people moving from job to job in those countries where employment protection legislation is strictest?

**5.** What is a welfare magnet?

**6.** What are the different models of labour market institutions?

**7.** What would be the effect of eliminating labour taxes and replacing them with higher VAT rates?

**8.** In Spain, the rules regarding eligibility to unemployment benefits has recently changed. Unemployed workers are not allowed to turn down job offers more than twice. What is the rationale and what could be the effects of this change?

**9.** Before the EMU, inflation was used to change relative labour costs across industries. How could that work?

ESSAY QUESTIONS

**1.** Why don't unemployed workers underbid wages to get jobs?

**2.** Some economists predict that the EMU will eventually make labour markets more efficient; others predict the opposite. What is your view, and why?

**3.** European trade unions seem to be unable to work together. Can you imagine why?

**4.** Which is your preferred model of labour institutions, and why?

**5.** Assume that some EMU member countries adopt the Anglo-Saxon model while others retain the continental model. Describe the likely effects.

**6.** Assume that European trade unions agree to merge. What would be the effect if wage negotiations were conducted at the European level? At the industry level? At the plant level?

**7.** If we move to similar labour institutions, will governments lose any role in social policies?

**8.** It is argued – and it is the case in some countries – that the minimum wage should be set at different levels for the young, for the older, for the unskilled or for particular industries. Evaluate this argument.

**9.** Italy exhibits a 'Mezzogiorno problem'. For decades now, Italy's south has benefited from generous subsidies initially designed to compensate for being less developed than the north. Yet, unemployment in the south is high and growth is slow, while northern Italy is one of the most vibrant economic regions in Europe. How can you interpret this situation and what lessons can you draw for Europe?

**10.** Evaluate the following statement in the UK Treasury's assessement of Euro area membership:

'It is important to make more progress at the European level, in particular on employment flexibility, trade and the Single Market in financial services. The less progress on flexibility is achieved in the EU, the greater the premium on a high level of flexibility in the UK economy.'

## FURTHER READING: THE AFICIONADOS CORNER

General overviews:

Bean, C., S. Bentolila, G. Bertola and J. Dolado (1998) 'Social Europe: one for all?', *Monitoring European Integration* 8, Centre for Economic Policy Research, London.

Bertola, G. (2000) 'Labour markets in the European Union', *Ifo-Studien*, **46** (1), 99–122.

Bertola, G., F.D. Blau and L.M. Kahn (2002) 'Comparative analysis of labour market outcomes: lessons for the US from international long-run evidence', in A. Krueger and R. Solow (eds) *The Roaring Nineties: Can Full Employment be Sustained?*, Russell Sage and Century Foundations, pp. 159–218.

Nickell, S. (2002) *Unemployment in Europe: Reasons and Remedies* (available on http://www.cesifo.de)

Saint-Paul, G. (2000) *The Political Economy of Labour Market Institutions*, Oxford University Press, Oxford.

On different European models:

Atkinson, A. (1999) *The Economic Consequences on Rolling Back the Welfare State*, MIT Press, Cambridge, MA.

Bertola, G., J.F. Jimeno, R. Marimon and C. Pissarides (2001) 'Welfare systems and labour markets in Europe: what convergence before and after EMU?', in G. Bertola, T. Boeri and G. Nicoletti (eds) *Welfare and Employment in a United Europe*, MIT Press, Cambridge, MA.

On trade unions:

Checci, D. and C. Lucifora (2002) 'Unions and Labour market institutions in Europe', *Economic Policy*, **35**, 361–408.

Calmfors, L., A. Booth, M. Burda, D. Checchi, R. Naylor, and J. Visser (2001) 'What do unions do in Europe? Prospects and challenges for union presence and union influence', in T. Boeri, A. Brugiavini and L. Calmfors (eds) *The Role of Unions in the Twenty-first Century*, Oxford University Press, Oxford.

On the economic effects of minimum wages:

Delado, J.J., F. Felgueroso and J.F. Jimeno-Serrano (2000) 'The role of the minimum wage in the welfare state: an appraisal', *Swiss Journal of Economics and Statistics*, **136** (3), 223–45.

On employment protection legislation:

Chapter 2 of *Employment Outlook*, OECD, (June 1999).

*Employment Outlook*, OECD

Bertola, G., T. Boeri and S. Cazes (2000) 'Employment protection in industrialized countries: the case for new indicators', *International Labour Review*, **139** (1), 57–72.

On labour taxes:

Pissarides, C. (1998) 'The impact of employment tax cuts on unemployment and wages; the role of unemployment benefits and tax structure', *European Economic Review*, **42** (1), 155–83.

Daveri, F. and G. Tabellini (2000) 'Unemployment, growth and taxation in industrial countries', *Economic Policy*, **30**, 47–104.

## USEFUL WEBSITES
Official sites relevant to the Lisbon Process:
http://ue.eu.int/Newsroom/LoadDoc.asp?BID=76&DID=43659&from=&LANG=1
http://ue.eu.int/emu/en/index.htm

The website of the Rodolfo de Benedetti Foundation, dedicated to European labour market issues:
http://www.frdb.org

## REFERENCES

Bean, C., S. Bentolila, G. Bertola and J. Dolado (1998) 'Social Europe: one for all?', *Monitoring European Integration* 8, Centre for Economic Policy Research, London.

Bertola, G. (2000) 'Labour markets in the European Union', *Ifo-Studien* , **46** (1), 99–122.

Bertola, G., J.F. Jimeno, R. Marimon and C. Pissarides (2001) 'Welfare systems and labour markets in europe: what convergence before and after EMU?', in G. Bertola, T. Boeri, G. Nicoletti (eds) *Welfare and Employment in a United Europe*, MIT Press, Cambridge, MA.

Blanchard, O.J. and J. Wolfers (2000) 'The role of shocks and institutions in the rise of european unemployment: the aggregate evidence', *Economic Journal*, 110, (462), 1–33.

Burda, M. and C. Wyplosz (2001) *Macroeconomics*, Oxford University Press, Oxford.

Calmfors, L. (2001) 'Wages and wage-bargaining institutions in the EMU – A survey of the issues', *Empirica*, **28** (4), 325–51.

Delado, J.J., F. Felgueroso and J.F. Jimeno-Serrano (2000) 'The role of the minimum wage in the welfare state: an appraisal', *Swiss Journal of Economics and Statistics*, **136** (3), 223–45.

Förster, M.F. assisted by M. Pellizzari (2000) *Trends and Driving Factors in Income Distribution and Poverty in the OECD Area*, Labour Market And Social Policy, Occasional Papers No. 42, OECD, Paris.

Nickell, S. (2002) *Unemployment in Europe: Reasons and Remedies* (available on http://www.cesifo.de).

# Index